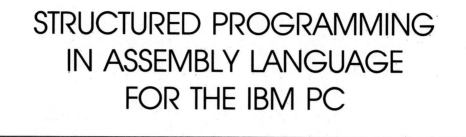

STRUCTURED PROGRAMMING
IN ASSEMBLY LANGUAGE
FOR THE IBM PC

THE PWS-KENT SERIES IN COMPUTER SCIENCE

Advanced Structured BASIC: File Processing with the IBM PC, Payne

Assembly Language for the PDP-11: RT-RSX-UNIX, Second Edition, Kapps and Stafford

Data Structures, Algorithms, and Program Style, Korsh

Data Structures, Algorithms, and Program Style Using C, Korsh and Garrett

FORTRAN 77 for Engineers, Borse

FORTRAN 77 and Numerical Methods for Engineers, Borse

Logic and Structured Design for Computer Programmers, Rood

Microprocessor Systems Design: 68000 Hardware, Software, and Interfacing, Clements

Modula-2, Beidler and Jackowitz

Problem Solving with Pascal, Brand

Problem Solving Using Pascal: Algorithm Development and Programming Concepts, Skvarcius

Programming Using Turbo Pascal, Riley

Structured BASIC for the IBM PC with Business Applications, Payne

Structured Programming in Assembly Language for the IBM PC, Runnion

Turbo Pascal for the IBM PC, Radford and Haigh

Using BASIC: An Introduction to Computer Programming, Third Edition, Hennefeld

Using Microsoft and IBM BASIC: An Introduction to Computer Programming, Hennefeld

VAX Assembly Language and Architecture, Kapps and Stafford

STRUCTURED PROGRAMMING IN ASSEMBLY LANGUAGE FOR THE IBM PC

William C. Runnion
Embry-Riddle Aeronautical University

PWS-KENT PUBLISHING COMPANY
Boston

PWS–KENT
Publishing Company

20 Park Plaza
Boston, Massachusetts 02116

PWS-KENT Publishing Company is a division of Wadsworth, Inc.

"IBM" is a registered trademark of International Business Machines Corporation.
"Intel" is a registered trademark of Intel Corporation.
"Microsoft" and "MS" are registered trademarks of Microsoft Corporation.

The programs appearing in this book and the software included with it are for educational purposes only. Although they have been carefully tested, they are not guaranteed for any purpose other than instruction. The publisher and the author offer no warranties or representations and accept no liabilities with respect to the software.

Library of Congress Cataloging-in-Publication Data

Runnion, William C.
    Structured programming in assembly language for the IBM PC
William C. Runnion.
        p.   cm.
    Includes index.
    ISBN 0-534-91480-2
    1. IBM Personal Computer—Programming. 2. Assembler language
(Computer program language) 3. Structured programming. I. Title.
QA76.8.I2594R86 1988
005.265—dc19   87-30886
                                                    CIP

Sponsoring Editor: Robert Prior
Production Coordinator: Robine Andrau
Production: Bookman Productions/Robin Lockwood
Interior Design: Julie Gecha
Cover Design: Robine Andrau
Cover Photo: The Picture Cube/Leonard A. Sroka
Interior Illustration: The Universities Press Ltd/Keyword Publishing Services
Typesetting: The Alden Press Ltd
Cover Printing: Phoenix Color Corp.
Printing and Binding: The Alpine Press, Inc.

Printed in the United States of America

88 89 90 91 92 — 10 9 8 7 6 5 4 3 2 1

To my wife, Ann; my son, Paul; and my daughter, KC

PREFACE

The purpose of *Structured Programming in Assembly Language for the IBM PC* is to teach structured Assembly language programming to computer science students while introducing them to computer organization. The intended audience is students at the sophomore or junior level who are taking a concentration in computer science. Students are expected to have successfully completed one high-level language programming course. They will be at an advantage if that high-level language course emphasized structured programming.

A course in Assembly language is still an essential part of the computer science curriculum. The demand for Assembly language programmers has increased in recent years due largely to the need for high-performance software for microcomputers. However, the justification for an Assembly language course should never be based on the need for Assembly language programmers. The development of good Assembly language programmers is obviously not accomplished through one course in Assembly language, but rather through years of experience. Instead, the justification for an Assembly language course stems from its value in bridging the gap between computer programming and computer science. The computer programmer needs to know how things work in the virtual machine provided by the operating system and the high-level programming language being used. The computer scientist needs to know how things work at the real-machine level. A course in Assembly language provides an introduction to how things work at the machine level.

This text is based on the CS 3 course in *ACM Curriculum '78*. The main emphasis is on structured programming in Assembly language, which keeps students on familiar ground—that of solving problems with computer programs—and enables them to relate constructs appearing in high-level languages to implementations of those constructs at the machine level. Computer organization is woven throughout the text to give students a clearer understanding of how things work at the machine level.

The stand-alone environment of a microcomputer enhances the CS 3 course and allows the student to experiment with capabilities, such as direct input/output, that are hidden by the operating system in a time-shared environment. Where possible, the advantages of the stand-alone environment have been exploited in this book.

The basic approach of this book is to teach by example in an incremental fashion. Most chapters concentrate on a particular subset of the IBM PC Assembly language instructions. The capabilities provided by a particular subset of instructions are presented in detail. Short instruction sequences are used to illustrate the instructions of the subset, and example programs or procedures are used to illustrate the use of the instructions in the solution of a problem. The example programs are designed to emphasize the use of the subset of instructions just presented while reinforcing the use of instructions from subsets covered in previous chapters.

Several unique features set this book apart from other books on the subject of IBM PC Assembly language:

Input/Output Subprocedure Package

The object code for a comprehensive set of input/output subprocedures is included on the diskette enclosed in this book. These subprocedures enable the student to write meaningful Assembly language programs without first having to encounter the difficult-to-master concept of input/output at the machine level. These subprocedures are used in the example programs of the book for all input/output operations. The source code for one of these procedures is gradually revealed in the book, and the source code for another is revealed in Chapter 9, the chapter on interrupts and input/output. These I/O subprocedures have been class-tested since the fall of 1984. The I/O subprocedures and their interface specifications are described in Appendix D.

Example Programs

Each chapter contains one or more programs or subprocedures to illustrate the major topics of that chapter. The example programs illustrate topics from the current chapter and reinforce the topics covered in previous chapters. These are not just program fragments but complete programs or subprocedures that provide a solution to an interesting problem. The source code for each of these example programs is included on the enclosed diskette.

Pseudocode Comments

All the programs used in this text are documented using a high-level pseudocode, which appears as in-line comments in the Assembly language code. Each pseudocode statement appears as the comment on the first of the sequence of Assembly language instructions that implement the statement. A control structure, such as REPEAT-UNTIL, brackets the sequence of instructions that implement the structure. Indentation is used in the pseudocode comments to emphasize the nesting of control structures. The pseudocode comments provide the following advantages:

1. They facilitate the reading and understanding of the example programs. Students can first read the pseudocode to gain an understanding of the algorithm being implemented by the program; they can then con-

centrate on the Assembly language code corresponding to each control structure in the pseudocode to see how that control structure is actually implemented.

2. They enable students to relate high-level constructs to machine-level implementations of those constructs.

3. They provide a general description of the algorithm being implemented by the program. This description is an algorithm design that can be implemented in any programming language. The student could readily implement the algorithm in another language for comparison.

4. They encourage good programming style and demonstrate the value of structured programming, even at the machine level.

The pseudocode used in the example programs is described in detail in Appendix C.

Reference Appendixes

The six appendixes at the end of this book eliminate the need for a separate reference manual to support programming in the IBM PC Assembly language.

This book contains more than enough material for a one-semester course in Assembly language. Several paths could be taken through the material, depending on the inclination of the instructor. The following graph shows the dependencies of the chapters:

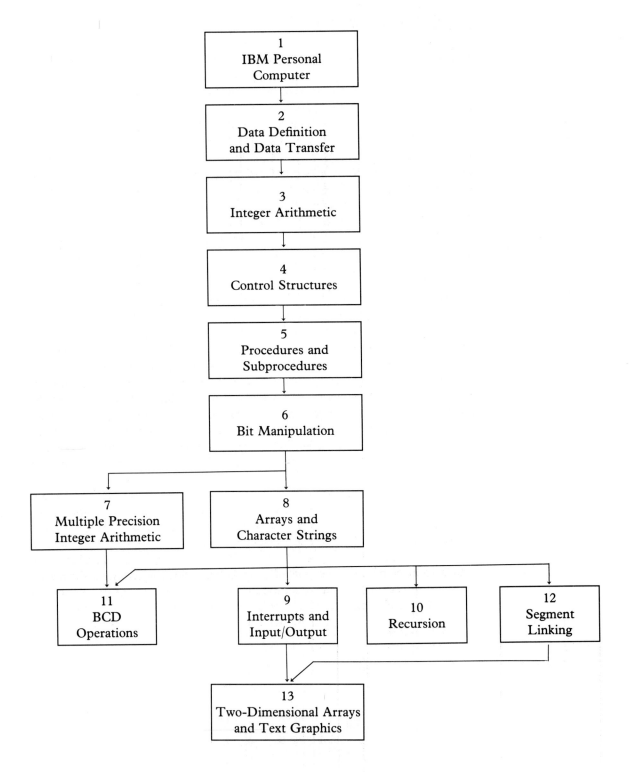

ACKNOWLEDGMENTS

I would like to express my gratitude to Beth Siglin for helping to get the whole project started. Beth wrote the original version of the I/O subprocedure package. The excellence of her work has been well proven through three years of heavy use. To the many students that have taken my Assembly language course since the fall of 1984, thanks for helping me class-test the material. Your intelligent questions have helped me in fine-tuning the book. To Ray Draper and Glenn Phillips, who took my Assembly language course before its immigration to the IBM PC, thanks for your help in the immigration process. To my wife, Ann, who took my Assembly language course and its prerequisite, thanks for the honesty and the understanding. I am grateful for the many casual conversations with Thomas Hilburn, Andrzej Kornecki, Roger Goldberg, and Peter Bauert on topics related to the subject matter of this book. Thanks to Karen Kinnaird and Debbie Lombard for their efficient and timely typing of the manuscript.

The following people were involved in reviewing all or part of the manuscript: Gerald Caton, Rockford College; William H. Dodge, Rensselaer Polytechnic Institute; Donald L. Gustafson, Texas Tech University; Mary Howard, Kirkwood Community College; Farrell Ostler, Computer System Architects; James Payne, Kellogg Community College; Maria Petrie, Florida Atlantic University. The comments of the reviewers helped me more than I ever thought possible. Their enthusiasm for this project has been greatly appreciated.

PWS-KENT editor, Bob Prior, has done much to make this an enjoyable and enlightening experience. I look forward to working with him again in the future. To all who were involved in the production phase of the project, I have gained a real appreciation for your skills. In particular, I am grateful to Robine Andrau of PWS-KENT Publishing Company, Robin Lockwood of Bookman Productions, and Cici Teter for their guidance and availability during the production of this text.

There are four people who deserve a special word of appreciation: my aunt, Wilma Abrams, who encouraged my writing when I was a child; my uncle, Edward Runnion, who taught me the value of a positive self-image; my father, Charles Runnion, who taught me, when I was taking geometry in high school, always to question why things work the way they do; and my brother, Ed Runnion, who introduced me to the field of computer science, thereby giving me the reason I needed to pursue a college education. Without the influence of these four, I would likely never have been in a position to even attempt such a project.

CONTENTS

1 | Microcomputers and the IBM Personal Computer   1

    1.1   IBM Personal Computers   2
    1.2   Microcomputer Architecture   3
    1.3   Positional Number Systems   20
    1.4   IBM PC Architecture   33
    1.5   Anatomy of an IBM PC Assembly Language Program   42
           Program Listing 1.1   **46**
    1.6   Support Software   51
    Numeric Exercise   57
    Programming Exercises   57
           Program Listing 1.2   57

2 | Data Definition and Data Transfer   59

    2.1   Computer Representations of Data   59
    2.2   Data Defining Pseudo-Operations   68
    2.3   Memory Addressing   75
    2.4   Data Transfer Instructions   78
    2.5   Example Program—Demonstrate Data Definition and Data
           Transfer   **88**
           Program Listing 2.1   **88**
           Debug Listing 2.2   **96**
    2.6   Additional Capabilities in the IBM PC-AT Assembly Language   106
    Numeric Exercises   107
    Programming Exercises   108
           Program Listing 2.3   **109**
           Program Listing 2.4   **110**

3 | Integer Arithmetic   111

    3.1   Binary Arithmetic   **111**
    3.2   Integer Arithmetic Instructions   **115**

3.3   Programming Examples   **130**
          Program Listing 3.1   **130**
          Program Listing 3.2   **134**
          Assembler Listing 3.3   **139**
          Debug Listing 3.4   **141**
3.4   Overflow Detection   **143**
Numeric Exercises   **146**
Programming Exercises   **147**
          Debug Listing 3.5   **148**

4   **Control Structures   149**

4.1   JUMP Instructions   **149**
4.2   Decision Structures   **156**
          Program Listing 4.1   **163**
          Program Listing 4.2   **168**
4.3   Loop Structures   **172**
          Program Listing 4.3   **178**
          Program Listing 4.4   **183**
4.4   Nested Control Structures   **185**
          Program Listing 4.5   **187**
Programming Exercises   **192**

5   **Procedures, Subprocedures, and Macros   195**

5.1   Terminology   **195**
5.2   Subprocedures   **196**
5.3   Subprocedure Interface   **199**
5.4   IBM PC Assembly Language Subprocedures   **203**
          Program Listing 5.1   **204**
          Program Listing 5.2   **211**
          Program Listing 5.3   **212**
5.5   Local Data Segments   **214**
          Program Listing 5.4   **216**
5.6   Additional Capabilities in the IBM PC-AT Assembly Language   **219**
5.7   Assembler Macros   **220**
          Program Listing 5.5   **223**
          Assembler Listing 5.6   **228**
          Program Listing 5.7   **230**
          Program Listing 5.8   **236**
          Program Listing 5.9   **237**
          Program Listing 5.10   **239**
          Assembler Listing 5.11   **240**
5.8   Macro versus Subprocedure   **242**
Programming Exercises   **243**

6   **Bit Manipulation   247**

   6.1   Shift Operations   247
         Program Listing 6.1   255
   6.2   Logical Operations   258
         Program Listing 6.2   266
   6.3   Flag Bit Operations   268
   6.4   Programming Example—Display Binary Integer (PUTBIN
         Version 2)   269
         Program Listing 6.3   270
         Programming Exercises   272

7   **Multiple Precision Integer Arithmetic Using the Carry Flag   275**

   7.1   Addition and Subtraction Using Carry/Borrow Flag   275
   7.2   Multiple Register Shifts   281
   7.3   Programming Examples   286
         Program Listing 7.1   290
         Program Listing 7.2   296
         Program Listing 7.3   297
         Programming Exercises   305
         Program Listing 7.4   307
         Program Listing 7.5   310

8   **Arrays and Character Strings   313**

   8.1   One-Dimensional Array   313
   8.2   Defining and Initializing Arrays   314
   8.3   Accessing Array Elements   315
         Program Listing 8.1   339
   8.4   Addressing Modes   341
         Program Listing 8.2   349
   8.5   Programming Examples   350
         Program Listing 8.3   351
         Program Listing 8.4   357
         Output Listing 8.5   363
         Program Listing 8.6   364
         Programming Exercises   370

9   **Interrupts and Input/Output   374**

   9.1   Interrupts   374
         Program Listing 9.1   383
   9.2   Single-Step Mode   386
         Program Listing 9.2   388
   9.3   Input/Output   392

Program Listing 9.3   **396**
Program Listing 9.4   **402**
Program Listing 9.5   **411**
9.4 Additional Capabilities in the IBM PC-AT Assembly Language   **412**
Programming Exercises   **413**
Program Listing 9.6   **415**

10 | Recursion   **416**

10.1 Recursive Definitions   **416**
10.2 Recursive Algorithms   **417**
10.3 Implementation of Recursive Algorithms   **419**
Program Listing 10.1   **425**
Program Listing 10.2   **441**
Programming Exercises   **443**

11 | BCD Operations   **447**

11.1 Decimal Encoding   **448**
11.2 BCD Number System   **449**
11.3 Internal BCD Representations   **456**
Program Listing 11.1   **462**
Program Listing 11.2   **464**
11.4 BCD Arithmetic Instructions   **468**
Program Listing 11.3   **479**
Program Listing 11.4   **483**
11.5 BCD Input/Output   **486**
Program Listing 11.5   **489**
Program Listing 11.6   **495**
Numeric Exercises   **501**
Programming Exercises   **501**

12 | Segment Linking   **505**

12.1 Segment Pseudo-Operation   **505**
12.2 Combining Segments   **507**
Program Listing 12.1   **509**
Program Listing 12.2   **510**
Load Map Listing 12.3   **511**
Program Listing 12.4   **512**
Program Listing 12.5   **513**
Load Map Listing 12.6   **514**
12.3 Stack Segments   **516**
12.4 Overlay Segments   **518**
Program Listing 12.7   **522**
Program Listing 12.8   **524**
12.5 Combining Code Segments with Data Segments   **526**

              Program Listing 12.9   **527**

              Program Listing 12.10   **528**

              Load Map Listing 12.11   **529**

              Debug Listing 12.12   **530**

    Programming Exercises   **532**

13   Two-Dimensional Arrays and Text Graphics   534

    13.1   One-Dimensional Array Revisited   **534**

            Program Listing 13.1   **538**

    13.2   Two-Dimensional Arrays   **540**

            Program Listing 13.2   **546**

    13.3   Text Graphics (a Two-Dimensional Array Application)   **548**

            Program Listing 13.3   **554**

            Program Listing 13.4   **556**

    13.4   Programming Examples   **557**

            Program Listing 13.5   **560**

            Program Listing 13.6   **565**

    13.5   Changing Position of Video Buffer   **568**

            Program Listing 13.7   **569**

    Programming Exercises   **573**

    Appendix A   Instruction Summary   **A–1**

    Appendix B   Pseudo-Operations   **A–56**

    Appendix C   Pseudocode   **A–72**

    Appendix D   Input/Output Procedures   **A–77**

    Appendix E   ASCII Character Set   **A–83**

    Appendix F   Support Software   **A–88**

                Index   **I–1**

1 MICROCOMPUTERS AND THE IBM PERSONAL COMPUTER

This book combines structured Assembly language programming with an introduction to computer organization. Microcomputers provide a single-user environment that makes them an excellent vehicle for the study of Assembly language and computer organization. With a microcomputer, you have access to instructions that are hidden by the operating system in a time-shared environment (e.g., direct input/output instructions). This book presents the architecture and Assembly language for the IBM PC, PC-XT, and other microcomputers that are based on the Intel 8088 and Intel 8086 microprocessors. Specific sections discuss some of the additional capabilities available in the Assembly language for the IBM PC-AT, which are applicable to microcomputers that are based on the Intel 80286 microprocessor.

This chapter provides background material and establishes a foundation for the study of the IBM PC and its architecture. It begins with a brief discussion of the IBM family of personal computers and the microprocessors on which they are based. The notion of a microprocessor's machine language and its symbolic form (i.e., Assembly language) are introduced. The architecture of microcomputers in general and the architecture of the IBM PC and the Intel 8088 microprocessor are discussed. This chapter also includes a section on number systems in general and the binary and hexadecimal number systems in particular. The binary number system is used by most digital computers. The hexadecimal number system is used as an abbreviation for the binary number system. The basic components of an IBM PC Assembly language program are presented. The chapter concludes with a brief discussion of some system software packages that are available to support IBM PC Assembly language programmers.

1.1 | IBM Personal Computers

The IBM Corporation has developed a family of microcomputers called Personal Computers (PCs). This family includes: the IBM PCjr, the IBM PC, the IBM PC-XT, the IBM Portable PC, the IBM PC Convertible, and the IBM PC-AT. The first five members of the PC family are designed around the Intel 8088 microprocessor; the last member, the IBM PC-AT, is designed around the Intel 80286 microprocessor. The **microprocessor** interprets and executes the **machine language**, which is a set of general-purpose instructions. Machine language is a numeric language, which means that all machine language instructions and the data on which those instructions operate are in a numeric form. Each microprocessor has its own machine language. A family of microprocessors may have a common machine language or compatible machine languages. For example, the machine language of the Intel 8088 microprocessor is a subset of the machine language for the Intel 80286 microprocessor. This compatibility allows any program that executes on the IBM PC and PC-XT to execute on the IBM PC-AT. However, some programs that execute on the IBM PC-AT cannot execute on the IBM PC and PC-XT. Even though the machine language for the Intel 8088 is a subset of the machine language for the Intel 80286, the two microprocessors interpret a few common instructions in a slightly different manner. Most of the example programs used in this book execute the same on the IBM PC, PC-XT, and PC-AT. In the cases in which instructions interpret differently between the two microprocessors, this difference is explained.

A machine language program is a sequence of numbers that represents instructions and data. Since both instructions and data are represented by numbers, the microprocessor cannot tell the difference between instructions and data simply by appearance. By the way a program is written and by specifying where in the program execution is to begin, the programmer tells the processor how to interpret the contents of each memory location (i.e., as an instruction or as a data item). Since the microprocessor gets its instructions and data from the memory component of the computer, a machine language program must be loaded into memory before it can be executed. Therefore, to program in machine language, a programmer must specify the contents of memory locations both for instructions and data.

Assembly language is just a symbolic form of machine language. Numeric operation codes are replaced by mnemonics; numeric memory addresses are replaced by symbolic names; data values may be specified in a number system other than the computer's number system; and numeric codes are replaced by symbolic codes. To program in Assembly language, the programmer must specify the contents of memory locations, both for instructions and data, in a symbolic form. There is a one-to-one correspondence between Assembly language entities and machine language entities: Each Assembly language instruction translates to one machine language instruction. Each Assembly language data value translates to one machine language data value. The **Assembler** program performs the translation from Assembly language to machine language.

Microcomputer Architecture

A microcomputer consists of three components: the *central processing unit* (*CPU*), the *memory*, and the *I/O subsystem*. They are connected by a bus system. A **bus** is a set of parallel wires over which digital data is transmitted. Figure 1.1 shows a simple block diagram of the microcomputer components. The bus system in the figure includes an address bus, a data bus, and a control bus.

Microprocessors

The **CPU** of a microcomputer is called a microprocessor. The microprocessor includes three major components: the *control unit* (*CU*), the *arithmetic logic unit* (*ALU*), and a set of *registers*. Figure 1.2 shows a simple block diagram of the CPU components. The **control unit** of a microprocessor interprets machine language instructions and transmits signals that control the various components of the computer system as they perform the operations necessary to execute the instructions. The **ALU** performs arithmetic computations (e.g., addition and subtraction) and logical operations (e.g., logical conjunction and disjunction). These operations are performed under the control of the CU. The **register set** provides the capability for temporary storage of numeric data within the CPU itself. The registers act like a "scratch pad" for the microprocessor; they keep track of the instructions, data, memory addresses, and status indicators the microprocessor is working with. The following types of registers are typically found in microprocessors:

Instruction register holds the instruction that the microprocessor is currently decoding and executing.

Program counter holds the memory address of the next instruction to be executed.

FIGURE 1.1
Microcomputer
block diagram

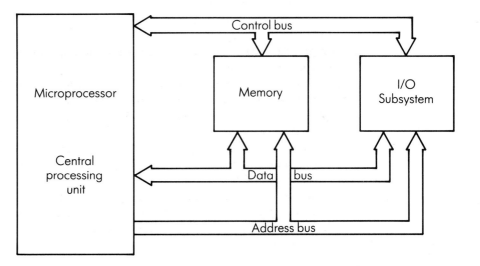

FIGURE 1.2
Microprocessor
block diagram

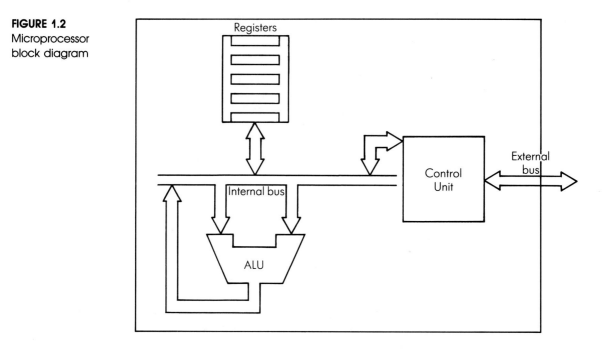

Accumulator registers are used to hold operands for ALU operations and to hold the result of ALU operations.

Index registers are used as counters (to perform operations such as loop control) and as subscripts (to access elements of data structures like arrays and strings).

Processor status word contains information regarding the current state of the CPU. Among other things, the processor status word contains information that describes the result of the ALU's latest arithmetic or logic operation (e.g., whether the result was negative, zero, or positive or whether the result was too large to be stored in an accumulator register).

A microprocessor performs a cyclic process, as shown in Figure 1.3. It fetches an instruction from memory, updates the program counter, decodes the instruction, and sends the appropriate control signals to the affected components of the computer system to direct execution of the instruction. The microprocessor then repeats the process over and over until it receives a special halt instruction or a specific external event occurs (i.e., the operator presses a halt button or the power is removed). Execution of an instruction may involve operations that can be performed entirely within the microprocessor—for example, addition of two operands that are already in processor registers. However, instruction execution may involve operations that require the services of other components of the computer system—for example, an operand may have to be fetched from memory, or the result of a computation may have to be stored in memory.

FIGURE 1.3
Cyclic process performed by a microprocessor

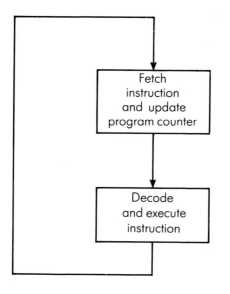

The kinds of instructions that can be interpreted and executed by a typical microprocessor include:

Arithmetic operations, for example:
   Add two numbers.
   Subtract two numbers.
Logical operations, for example:
   AND two truth values.
   Invert a truth value.
Data transfer operations, for example:
   Move a value from memory to a CPU register.
   Exchange the values of two CPU registers.
Transfer of control operations, for example:
   Fetch the next instruction from a specified memory location.
   Fetch the next instruction from a specified memory location only if a certain condition holds True. Otherwise, continue with sequential instruction execution.

Memory

The instructions that the microprocessor interprets and executes and the data required for execution of those instructions are obtained from memory. The **memory** of a microcomputer can be viewed as a linear array of storage cells in which each cell is capable of holding a fixed size number (i.e., a fixed number of digits), the size being the same for all storage cells in a given computer's memory. Each storage cell is identified by a unique number, called its **address**. For a memory with n storage cells, the addresses generally range from 0 to $n - 1$, as shown in Figure 1.4.

FIGURE 1.4

n-cell by *m*-digit memory

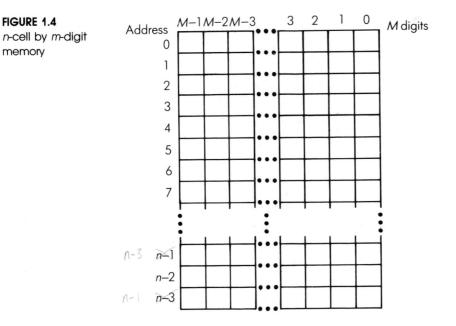

A microcomputer's memory is somewhat analogous to a set of post office boxes in a post office. Each box has a unique number (the box number) by which it is identified (addressed). The analogy fails, however, when the notion of contents is considered. A post office box may be empty, it may contain a single letter, or it may contain many letters, and the letters in a post office box may be of different sizes. The contents of a memory cell, on the other hand, are always exactly one *m*-digit number, in which *m* digits is the fixed size of each storage cell. A memory cell can never be empty; it always contains a value. However, the value of a given storage cell may not have meaning to the program that is executing. Whenever a new *m*-digit number is stored in a given storage cell, it replaces the *m*-digit number previously stored in that cell. When the contents are fetched from a storage cell, the contents are not removed. Only a copy of the contents of that cell is obtained. The value in the storage cell remains unchanged. The *m*-digit number in a storage cell may be interpreted in many ways: It may be interpreted as an instruction or as part of an instruction; it may be interpreted as an integer, as part of an integer, or as several integers; and it may be interpreted as one or more characters in a character string.

The CPU can perform two operations with respect to memory. The CPU may fetch the contents of a memory cell, or it may replace the contents of (store a new value in) a memory cell. To fetch a copy of a memory cell's contents, the CPU places the address of the memory cell on the address bus (see Figure 1.1) and sends a control signal on the control bus to memory, instructing the memory to perform a fetch operation. The memory reads the address from the address bus, extracts a copy of the contents of the specified memory cell, and places that value on the data bus. The CPU then reads the copy of the memory cell's contents from the data bus.

To store a new value in a memory cell, the CPU places the address of the memory cell on the address bus, places the data to be stored at that address on the data bus, and sends a control signal to memory instructing it to perform a store operation. The memory reads the address from the address bus and replaces the value of the specified memory cell with a copy of the value read from the data bus.

I/O Subsystem

The **I/O subsystem** provides the communications link between the microprocessor/memory and the input/output devices (e.g., keyboard, display monitor, and printer). The I/O subsystem in its simplest form consists of a set of **I/O ports**, which is similar to a set of memory locations. The main difference between a memory location and an I/O port is that a port has an electrical connection to some external device. As in the case of memory, the set of I/O ports is connected to the bus system. To select a specific I/O port, its address is placed on the address bus. Data can be transmitted to or received from the selected port via the data bus. A signal on the control bus is used to indicate whether the bus system is being used to communicate with memory or to communicate with an I/O port. An I/O port temporarily holds numeric data that are being transmitted between the microprocessor and an external device. A port may be used for transmitting data to or receiving data from a device, transmitting control information to a device, or receiving status information from a device.

Hypothetical Computer

Consider the hypothetical machine whose architecture is shown in Figure 1.5. The characteristics of this hypothetical machine are described as follows:

Main Memory   The main memory of the machine contains 1000 storage locations addressed by the consecutive integers 000 to 999. Each memory location holds a five-digit decimal integer (i.e., the word size of the machine is five decimal digits). The value stored in a memory location can represent either a single machine language instruction or a nonnegative integer.

Central Processing Unit   The CPU of the machine contains a control unit (not shown in Figure 1.5), an arithmetic logic unit, and the following registers:

> *Arithmetic registers*—These two registers supply operands to the ALU for arithmetic operations and receive results from the ALU. Each of the arithmetic registers is capable of holding a five-digit decimal integer. The A-register is the main arithmetic register. The B-register is used as an extension of the A-register for multiply and divide operations. That is, the combined A- and B-register can hold a 10-digit decimal integer.

FIGURE 1.5
Hypothetical
machine

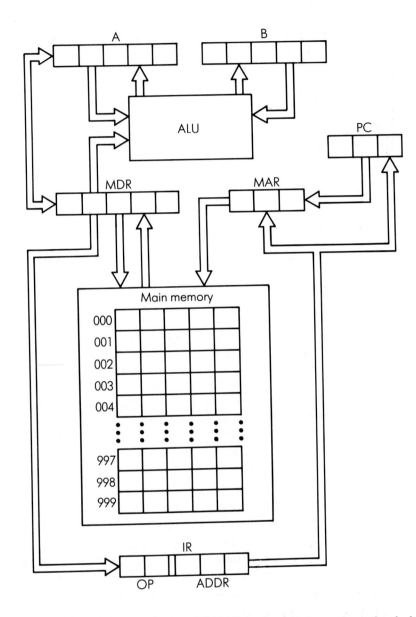

Program counter (PC)—The PC-register is the register that holds the main memory address of the next instruction to be executed. The size of the PC-register is dependent on the size of the main memory. It must be capable of holding a value at least as large as the highest memory address (999). The PC-register in Figure 1.5 can hold a three-digit decimal integer.

Instruction register (IR)—The instruction register holds the machine instruction currently being executed. Its size is dependent on the machine langauge. The instruction register in Figure 1.5 can hold a five-digit decimal integer.

Memory address register (MAR)—The memory address register holds the address of the memory location where an instruction or data value is to be fetched or stored. Its size is dependent on the size of the main memory. It must be capable of holding a value at least as large as the highest memory address. The memory address register in Figure 1.5 can hold a three-digit decimal integer.

Memory data register (MDR)—The memory data register holds the instruction or data value just fetched from memory or about to be stored in memory. Its size is dependent on the word size of the machine. The memory data register in Figure 1.5 can hold a five-digit decimal integer.

Everything outside the main memory in Figure 1.5 is part of the CPU. The connection between the MAR and the main memory represents the address bus, and the connections between the MDR and the main memory represent the bidirectional data bus. All other connections are part of the CPU's internal bus.

A machine language instruction for the hypothetical machine is represented by a five-digit decimal integer. Figure 1.6 shows the format for this machine language instruction. The **operation code** (op code) field is made up of the first two digits and identifies the operation to be performed. The address field is made up of the last three digits and identifies the memory location that contains the operand. Not all machine language instructions require an operand from memory; for example, the address field may have another meaning for an instruction, which means it may have another meaning in some instructions. Table 1.1 describes the operations performed for a selected subset of machine language op codes for this hypothetical machine.

The instruction execution cycle for the hypothetical machine includes the operations shown in Figure 1.3. The process labeled "Fetch instruction and update program counter" consists of the following steps in the hypothetical machine:

1. Move PC value to the MAR.

2. Activate memory to perform a fetch operation. To perform the fetch operation, memory receives the address from the MAR via the address bus, extracts a copy of the contents of the specified memory location, and transmits the extracted value to the MDR via the data bus.

3. Update the value of the PC-register. The PC-register value is incremented by 1, so that it addresses the next instruction in sequence.

4. Move the fetched instruction from the MDR to the IR.

The steps of the process labeled "Decode and execute instruction" in Figure 1.3 depend on the operation code of the instruction itself. The steps of this process are shown by tracing an example program fragment. Suppose the

FIGURE 1.6

Instruction format for the hypothetical machine

TABLE 1.1
Machine language
operations for the
hypothetical
machine

Op Code	Operation Performed
01	Load the A-register with a copy of the contents of the memory location specified by the address in the instruction's address field.
02	Store a copy of the value of the A-register in the memory location specified by the address in the instruction's address field.
03	Exchange the contents of the A-register with the contents of the B-register. The address field of the instruction is ignored.
04	Load the A-register with the value zero. The address field of the instruction is ignored.
20	Add the contents of the memory location specified by the address in the address field to the contents of the A-register, leaving the result in the A-register.
21	Subtract the contents of the memory location specified by the address in the address field from the contents of the A-register, leaving the result in the A-register.
22	Multiply the contents of the memory location specified by the address in the address field by the contents of the A-register, leaving the result in the combined A- and B-register.
23	Divide the contents of the combined A- and B-register by the contents of the memory location specified by the address in the address field, leaving the quotient in the A-register and the remainder in the B-register.
30	Set the program counter (PC-register) to the value in the address field of the instruction—that is, jump to the instruction in the memory location specified by the address in the address field.
99	Halt instruction execution.

state of the machine at the beginning of the instruction cycle is as shown in Figure 1.7. The PC-register indicates that memory location 000 contains the next instruction to be executed. Figures 1.8 through 1.14 trace the execution of three instructions in this machine.

The first iteration of the instruction execution cycle begins with an instruction fetch. The PC-register identifies the location in memory of the next instruction to be fetched. The PC-register value (000) is copied into the memory address register, and a memory fetch operation is initiated. While the memory fetch operation is being performed, the processor increments the value in the PC-register (from 000 to 001). The memory fetch operation includes the following steps:

1. The contents of the MAR (000) are placed on the address bus.

2. The contents (01999) of the memory location specified by the address on the address bus (000) are copied onto the data bus.

3. The value on the data bus (01999) is copied into the MDR.

The value fetched from memory (01999) is copied from the MDR into the instruction register, completing the instruction fetch portion of the execution

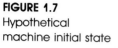

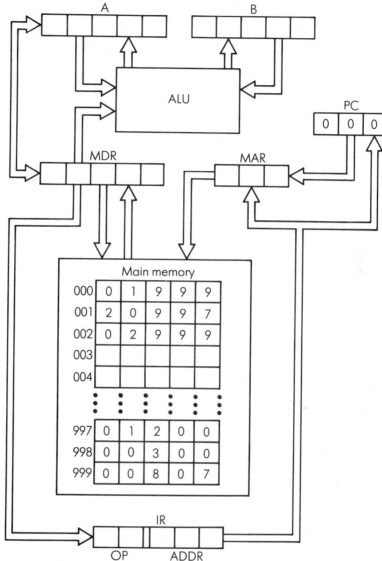

FIGURE 1.7
Hypothetical
machine initial state

cycle. After completing the instruction fetch, the state of the machine is as shown in Figure 1.8.

The first iteration of the instruction execution cycle continues with the instruction decode phase. During this phase, the control unit determines the operations to be performed in executing the instruction in the instruction register. The operation code in the first two digits of the instruction register value (01) indicates that a "load A-register from memory" operation is to be performed.

The execution phase for this instruction begins with a data fetch. The last three digits of the value in the instruction register identify the memory location

FIGURE 1.8

Hypothetical
machine after first
instruction fetch

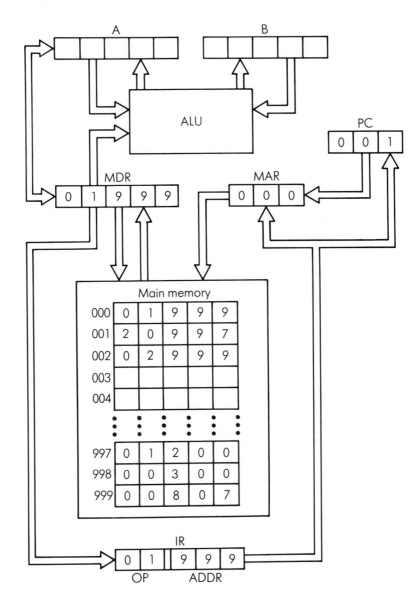

of the data to be fetched. The address field of the instruction register (999) is
copied from the instruction register into the memory address register, and a
memory fetch operation is initiated. The steps for this data fetch operation are
similar to those for the instruction fetch operation discussed previously. The
value fetched from memory (00807) is copied from the MDR into the A-register,
completing the execution phase for the instruction. After completing the first
iteration of the execution cycle—that is, after completing the execution of the
first instruction—the state of the machine is as shown in Figure 1.9.

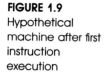

FIGURE 1.9
Hypothetical
machine after first
instruction
execution

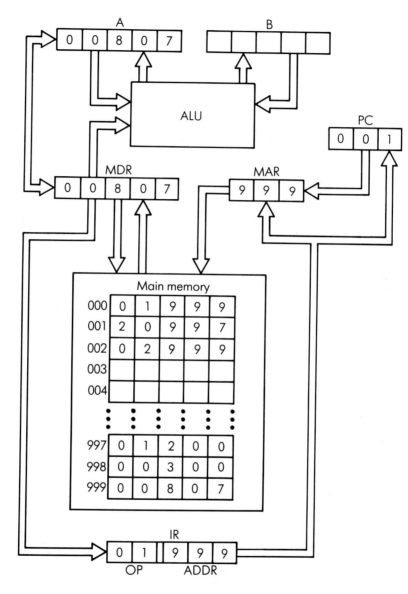

The second iteration of the instruction execution cycle also begins with an instruction fetch. The PC-register again identifies the location in memory (001) of the next instruction to be fetched. The steps of the instruction fetch are similar to those for the first instruction fetch. After completing the second instruction fetch, the state of the machine is as shown in Figure 1.10.

The second iteration of the instruction execution cycle continues with the instruction decode phase. During this phase, the control unit determines the operations to be performed in executing the instruction in the instruction register.

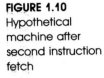

FIGURE 1.10
Hypothetical
machine after
second instruction
fetch

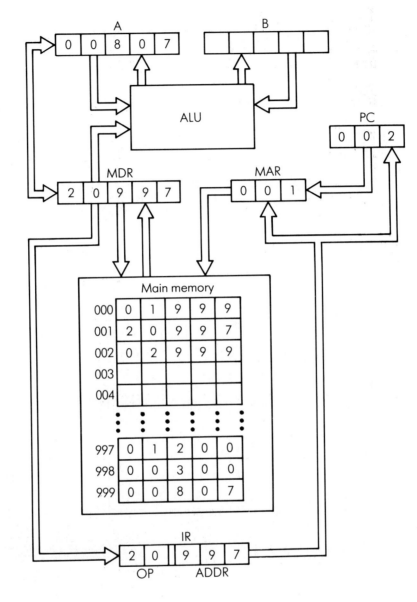

The op code in the first two digits of the instruction register value (20) indicates that an "add to A-register from memory" operation is to be performed.

The execution phase for this instruction begins with a data fetch. The last three digits of the value in the instruction register (997) identify the memory location of the data to be fetched. After completing the data fetch operation, the state of the machine is as shown in Figure 1.11. The next step in the execution phase is the addition operation. This operation is performed by the ALU. The ALU receives its operands from the A-register (00807) and the memory data register (01200). The result of the addition operation (02007) is returned to the

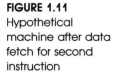

FIGURE 1.11
Hypothetical
machine after data
fetch for second
instruction

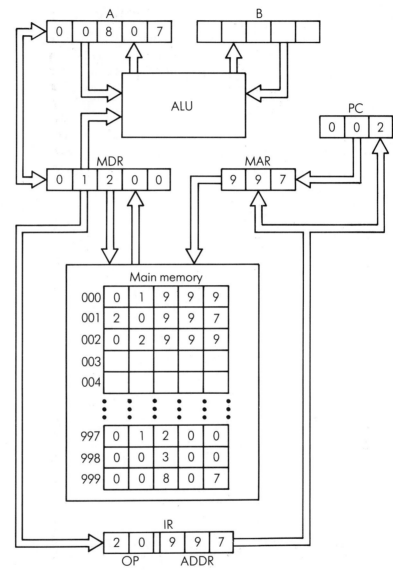

A-register. After completing the second iteration of the instruction execution cycle—that is, after completing the execution of the addition instruction—the state of the machine is as shown in Figure 1.12.

The third iteration of the instruction execution cycle also begins with an instruction fetch. The PC-register again identifies the memory location (002) of the next instruction to be fetched. After completing the third instruction fetch, the state of the machine is as shown in Figure 1.13.

The third iteration of the cycle continues with the instruction decode phase. During this phase, the control unit determines the operations to be

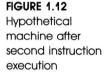

FIGURE 1.12
Hypothetical
machine after
second instruction
execution

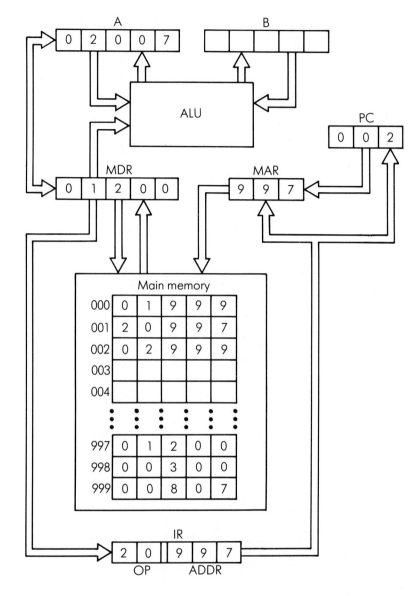

performed in executing the instruction in the instruction register. The operation code in the first two digits of the instruction register value (02) indicates that a "store from A-register into memory" operation is to be performed.

The execution phase for this instruction involves a data store operation. The last three digits of the value in the instruction register (999) identify the memory location where the data is to be stored. The value of the A-register (02007) is the value that is to be stored in that memory location. The contents of the address field of the instruction register (999) are copied into the memory address register, the A-register value (02007) is copied into the memory data

FIGURE 1.13
Hypothetical
machine after third
instruction fetch

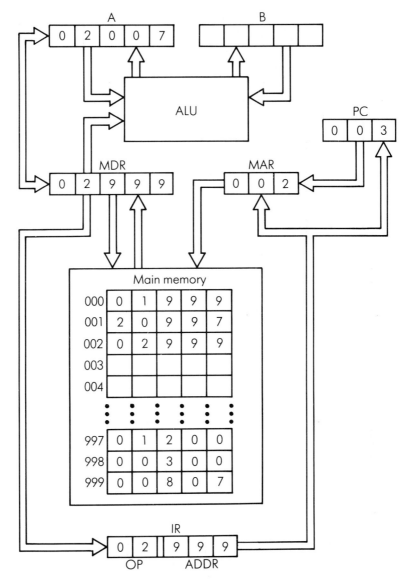

FIGURE 1.13
Hypothetical
machine after third
instruction fetch

register, and a memory store operation is initiated. The memory store operation includes the following steps:

1. The contents of the MAR (999) are placed on the address bus.

2. The contents of the MDR (02007) are placed on the data bus.

3. The contents of the memory location specified by the address on the address bus (999) are replaced by the value on the data bus (02007).

After completing the third iteration of the instruction execution cycle—that is, after completing the execution of the store operation—the state of the

FIGURE 1.14
Hypothetical
machine after third
instruction
execution

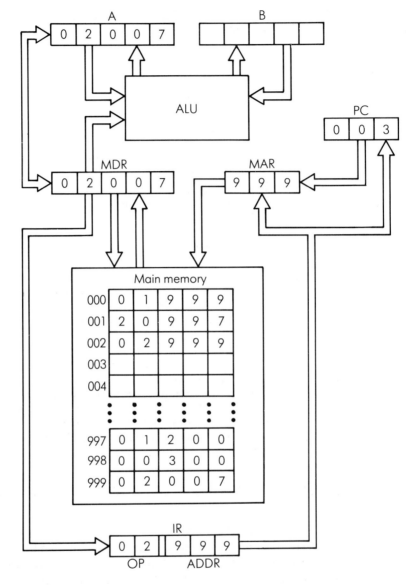

machine is as shown in Figure 1.14. The instruction execution cycle continues in this manner, as the microprocessor steps its way through the instructions of a machine language program.

The machine language program fragment shown in the memory of the hypothetical machine is in a numeric form, the form understood by the machine; but, machine language is not a convenient form for humans to use for writing programs. Assembly language provides a more convenient form for writing programs, because it is a symbolic representation of the machine language. Table 1.2 shows the Assembly language version of the machine language given in Table

TABLE 1.2

Symbolic form of
machine language
operations

Machine Code	Assembler Format	Operation Performed
01	LDA *addr*	Load the A-register with a copy of the contents of the memory location specified by the symbolic name in the *addr* field of the instruction.
02	STA *addr*	Store a copy of the value of the A-register in the memory location specified by the symbolic name in the *addr* field of the instruction.
03	XAB	Exchange the contents of the A-register with the contents of the B-register.
04	CLA	Load the A-register with the value zero.
20	ADD *addr*	Add the contents of the memory location specified by the symbolic name in the *addr* field to the contents of the A-register, leaving the result in the A-register.
21	SUB *addr*	Subtract the contents of the memory location specified by the symbolic name in the *addr* field from the contents of the A-register, leaving the result in the A-register.
22	MUL *addr*	Multiply the contents of the memory location specified by the symbolic name in the *addr* field by the contents of the A-register, leaving the result in the combined A- and B-register.
23	DIV *addr*	Divide the contents of the combined A- and B-register by the contents of the memory location specified by the symbolic name in the *addr* field, leaving the quotient in the A-register and the remainder in the B-register.
30	JMP *addr*	Set the program counter (PC-register) to the value specified by the symbolic name in the *addr* field of the instruction. That is, jump to the instruction in the memory location specified by the symbolic name in the *addr* field.
99	HLT	Halt instruction execution.

1.1. The decimal operation codes are replaced by three-character mnemonics, and the decimal memory addresses are replaced by symbolic names that are used to represent memory addresses. The machine language program fragment shown in the memory of the hypothetical machine could be translated into the following Assembly language code:

```
        LDA    Z
        ADD    X
        STA    Z

           .
           .
           .

X       DEC    01200
Y       DEC    00300
Z       DEC    00807
```

The operation code DEC is referred to as a **pseudo-operation**. It does not represent a machine language operation code but is a directive to the Assembler. The directive

```
X    DEC    01200
```

tells the assembler to allocate a storage cell in memory to be associated with the symbolic name X and to give that storage cell an initial value of 1200. Thus, whenever X is used in the program, it is a reference to this storage cell. In Assembly language, the programmer does not need to determine or even to know the storage cell associated with a symbolic name. The assembler, in conjunction with other support software, determines the storage cell to be associated with any specific symbolic name. Any time the symbolic name is referenced, it refers to the same storage cell.

1.3   Positional Number Systems

Most people are familiar with the decimal number system, which is a **positional number system**. Each positional number system has a base (or **radix**) that defines the number of symbols used to represent numbers in that system. With a positional number system, the value given to each digit is determined by its position relative to a reference point, called the **radix point**. The position values of digits to the left of the radix point are based on the right-to-left progression of the nonnegative powers of the base. The position values of digits to the right of the radix point are based on the left-to-right progression of the negative powers of the base.

The decimal number system is a positional number system in which the base is 10, and the radix point is referred to as the **decimal point**. The decimal number system uses 10 symbols, the digits 0, 1, 2, 3, 4, 5, 6, 7, 8, and 9. The position values of digits to the left of the decimal point are based on the right-to-left progression of the nonnegative powers of 10. The position values of digits to the right of the decimal point are based on the left-to-right progression of the negative powers of 10.

EXAMPLE

The number 1427.73 in the base 10 number system represents

$$1 \times 10^3 + 4 \times 10^2 + 2 \times 10^1 + 7 \times 10^0 + 7 \times 10^{-1} + 3 \times 10^{-2}$$

$$1000 + \quad 400 + \quad 20 + \quad 7 + \quad .7 + \quad .03$$

Consider the notion of counting in the decimal number system. We begin with 0, the lowest-valued digit, and count through the digits, in order, by value (0, 1, 2, 3, 4, 5, 6, 7, 8, and 9). When we reach the highest-valued digit, we place a 0 in that position and increment the next higher position by 1, producing 10 in this case. We then count through the digits again (10, 11, 12, 13, 14, 15, 16, 17, 18, and 19). Having reached the highest-valued digit, we place a 0 in that position and increment the next higher position by 1, producing 20 in this case. We then count through the digits again (20, 21, 22, 23, 24, 25, 26, 27, 28, and 29). The process continues until we reach 90, 91, 92, 93, 94, 95, 96, 97, 98, and 99. Having reached the highest-valued digit, we place a 0 in that position and increment the next higher position by 1. However, we also have reached the highest-valued digit in that position. Therefore, we place a 0 in that position too and increment the next higher position by 1, producing 100.

This procedure for counting can be stated in algorithm form. When counting from the n-digit decimal integer

$$d_{n-1} d_{n-2} \ldots d_2 d_1 d_0$$

to its successor, we perform the following steps:

```
I = 0
WHILE d_I = 9
        d_I = 0
        I = I + 1
ENDWHILE
d_I = successor of d_I
```

The preceding algorithm instructs you to start with the rightmost digit of the number and work left. When the highest-valued digit (9 in the case of decimal) is encountered, set that digit to 0 and carry a 1 into the next digit position. When a digit that is less than the highest-valued digit is reached, set it to its successor (i.e., add 1 to it) and stop the process.

EXAMPLE

The successor of 13499 is 13499
13500.

Binary Number System

The components of a computer system are two-state devices—that is, they can be in only one of two possible states at any given time.

EXAMPLES

Magnetic materials such as the tiny magnetic cores used in the main memory of some computers are magnetized either in one direction or in the opposite direction.
Transistors are either conducting or nonconducting.
Switches are either open or closed.
Electrical pulses are either present or absent.

This two-state property gives rise to the base 2 number system, called the **binary number system**. The binary number system is a positional number system with a base of 2 and uses two symbols to represent numbers: 0 and 1. The radix point is referred to as the **binary point**, and a single **binary digit** is called a **bit**.

Counting in Binary

Counting in binary can be described using a slight modification to the decimal counting algorithm already given. When counting from the n-bit binary integer

$$b_{n-1} b_{n-2} \ldots b_2 b_1 b_0$$

to its successor, we perform the following steps:

```
I = 0
WHILE b_I = 1
        b_I = 0
        I = I + 1
ENDWHILE
b_I = successor of b_I
```

The preceding algorithm instructs you to start with the rightmost digit of the number and work left. When the highest-valued digit (1 in the case of binary) is encountered, set that digit to 0 and carry a 1 into the next digit position. When a digit that is less than the highest-valued digit is reached, set it to its successor (i.e., add 1 to it) and stop the process. Table 1.3 compares counting in binary to counting in decimal.

TABLE 1.3
Counting in binary and decimal

Binary	Decimal	Binary	Decimal	Binary	Decimal
0	0	1000	8	10000	16
1	1	1001	9	10001	17
10	2	1010	10	10010	18
11	3	1011	11	10011	19
100	4	1100	12	10100	20
101	5	1101	13	10101	21
110	6	1110	14	10110	22
111	7	1111	15	10111	23

Binary-to-Decimal Conversion

Since the binary number system is a positional number system, the value given to each digit in a binary number is determined by its position relative to the binary point. The position values of digits to the left of the binary point are based on the right-to-left progression of the nonnegative powers of two (10 in binary). The position values of digits to the right of the binary point are based on the left-to-right progression of the negative powers of two. The number 10110.101 in the binary number system represents

$$1 \times 10^{100} + 0 \times 10^{11} + 1 \times 10^{10} + 1 \times 10^{1} + 0 \times 10^{0} + 1 \times 10^{-1}$$
$$+ 0 \times 10^{-10} + 1 \times 10^{-11}$$

Note that this expression is written entirely in binary.

To convert a number from binary to decimal, first express that number in terms of powers of the base. Then convert that expression to decimal and carry out the arithmetic in the decimal number system. The binary number 10110.101, previously expressed in terms of powers of the base, converts to the following decimal expression:

$$1 \times 2^{4} + 0 \times 2^{3} + 1 \times 2^{2} + 1 \times 2^{1} + 0 \times 2^{0} + 1 \times 2^{-1} + 0 \times 2^{-2}$$
$$+ 1 \times 2^{-3}$$

Carrying out the arithmetic in the decimal number system yields

$$16 + 0 + 4 + 2 + 0 + 0.5 + 0.0 + 0.125 \ = \ 22.625$$

Therefore, 22.625 is the decimal equivalent of the binary number 10110.101.

Consider another example: The binary number 110101011.011 is expressed as

$$1 \times 10^{1000} + 1 \times 10^{111} + 0 \times 10^{110} + 1 \times 10^{101} + 0 \times 10^{100} + 1 \times 10^{11}$$
$$+ 0 \times 10^{10} + 1 \times 10^{1} + 1 \times 10^{0} + 0 \times 10^{-1} + 1 \times 10^{-10}$$
$$+ 1 \times 10^{-11}$$

Converting this expression to decimal yields

$$1 \times 2^{8} + 1 \times 2^{7} + 0 \times 2^{6} + 1 \times 2^{5} + 0 \times 2^{4} + 1 \times 2^{3} + 0 \times 2^{2} + 1 \times 2^{1}$$
$$+ 1 \times 2^{0} + 0 \times 2^{-1} + 1 \times 2^{-2} + 1 \times 2^{-3}$$

Carrying out the arithmetic in decimal yields

$$256 + 128 + 0 + 32 + 0 + 8 + 0 + 2 + 1 + 0.0 + 0.25 + 0.125$$
$$= 427.375$$

Note that as you move left in a binary number, the value associated with each digit position is twice the value of the previous digit position, and as you move right in a binary number, the value associated with each digit position is one-half the value of the previous digit position.

EXAMPLE

101101011.1011

1	0	1	1	0	1	0	1	1	1	0	1	1
×	×	×	×	×	×	×	×	×	×	×	×	×
256	128	64	32	16	8	4	2	1	.5	.25	.125	.0625

$$256 + 0 + 64 + 32 + 0 + 8 + 0 + 2 + 1 + .5 + 0 + .125 + .0625$$

$$363.6875$$

The decimal equivalent of the binary integer 101101011.1011 is 363.6875.

Decimal-to-Binary Conversion

To convert decimal numbers to binary, first separate the integer and fractional portions of the decimal number, convert the two portions separately, and then rejoin the two converted parts to get the equivalent binary number.

To convert the integer portion of the decimal number to binary, perform the following algorithm, in which NUMBER represents the decimal integer to be converted and is an input to the algorithm:

```
I = 0
REPEAT
      I = I + 1
      DIGIT(I) = NUMBER mod 2
      NUMBER   = NUMBER / 2 (truncated to an integer)
UNTIL NUMBER = 0
WHILE I ≠ 0
      OUTPUT DIGIT(I)
      I = I - 1
ENDWHILE
```

TABLE 1.4
Conversion of 327 from decimal to binary

Number / 2	=	Quotient	Remainder
327 / 2		163	1
163 / 2		81	1
81 / 2		40	1
40 / 2		20	0
20 / 2		10	0
10 / 2		5	0
5 / 2		2	1
2 / 2		1	0
1 / 2		0	1
0			

This algorithm can be summarized as follows: Repeatedly divide NUMBER by 2 and replace NUMBER with the quotient of the division each time. Continue this division process until NUMBER becomes zero. Writing down the remainders of these divisions in the reverse order from which they were produced provides the equivalent binary integer. Table 1.4 traces this process for the decimal integer 327. Writing down the remainders in the reverse order from which they were produced provides 101000111, which is the binary number equivalent to the decimal integer 327.

To convert the fractional portion of the decimal number to binary, perform the following algorithm, in which FRACTION represents the decimal fraction to be converted and COUNT represents the number of fractional digits to be produced. FRACTION and COUNT are the inputs to the algorithm:

```
OUTPUT binary point
REPEAT
        NUMBER = FRACTION * 2
        OUTPUT integer portion of NUMBER
        FRACTION = fractional portion of NUMBER
        COUNT = COUNT - 1
UNTIL COUNT = 0 or FRACTION = 0
```

The algorithm can be summarized as follows: Repeatedly multiply FRACTION by 2 and replace FRACTION with the fractional portion of the product each time. The integer portion of the product becomes the next digit to the right of the binary point. Repeat the process until FRACTION becomes zero or until the desired number of fractional digits has been produced. Table 1.5 traces this process for the decimal fraction .3125. The binary fraction that is equivalent to the decimal fraction .3125 is .0101. Joining the integer and fractional portions from the previous two examples gives

$$327.3125 \text{ decimal} = 101000111.0101 \text{ binary}$$

Table 1.6 traces the fractional conversion process for the decimal FRACTION .1, using a digit COUNT of 10. The binary fraction that is equivalent to the decimal fraction .1 is .00011001100110011 . . . Note that the binary fraction is a repeating fraction—that is, the decimal fraction .1 cannot be represented in binary with a finite number of digits. When representing decimal fractions in a computer, you can only store a finite number of digits. Thus, the fraction stored in the machine may only be an approximation to the decimal fraction that it represents. This representational error can be significant in certain computations.

TABLE 1.5
Conversion of .3125 from decimal to binary

Fraction * 2	=	Number	Binary Digit	Next Fraction
.3125 * 2		0.625	0	.625
.625 * 2		1.250	1	.25
.25 * 2		0.500	0	.5
.5 * 2		1.0	1	.0

TABLE 1.6
Conversion of .1
from decimal to
binary

Fraction * 2	=	Number	Binary Digit	Next Fraction
.1 * 2		0.2	0	.2
.2 * 2		0.4	0	.4
.4 * 2		0.8	0	.8
.8 * 2		1.6	1	.6
.6 * 2		1.2	1	.2
.2 * 2		0.4	0	.4
.4 * 2		0.8	0	.8
.8 * 2		1.6	1	.6
.6 * 2		1.2	1	.2
.2 * 2		0.4	0	.4

Octal Number System

Two number systems are widely used for abbreviations of binary numbers: the octal and hexadecimal number systems. The octal number system is a positional number system with base 8. The octal number system uses eight symbols (0, 1, 2, 3, 4, 5, 6, and 7) to represent numbers. The radix point is referred to as the **octal point**. Counting works the same in the octal number system as it does in any other positional number system. Table 1.7 compares counting in octal with counting in decimal.

Since the octal number system is a positional number system, the value given to each digit in an octal number is determined by its position relative to the octal point. The position values of digits to the left of the octal point are based on the right-to-left progression of the nonnegative powers of eight (10 in octal). The position values of digits to the right of the octal point are based on the left-to-right progression of the negative powers of eight. The octal number 217.43, may be expressed as

$$2 \times 10^2 + 1 \times 10^1 + 7 \times 10^0 + 4 \times 10^{-1} + 3 \times 10^{-2}$$

Note that this expression is written entirely in octal.

TABLE 1.7
Counting in octal
and decimal

Octal	Decimal	Octal	Decimal	Octal	Decimal
0	0	10	8	20	16
1	1	11	9	21	17
2	2	12	10	22	18
3	3	13	11	23	19
4	4	14	12	24	20
5	5	15	13	25	21
6	6	16	14	26	22
7	7	17	15	27	23

Octal-to-Decimal Conversion

To convert a number from octal to decimal, express the number in terms of powers of the base, convert that expression to decimal, and carry out the arithmetic in the decimal number system. The octal number 217.43, previously expressed in terms of powers of the base, converts to the following decimal expression:

$$2 \times 8^2 + 1 \times 8^1 + 7 \times 8^0 + 4 \times 8^{-1} + 3 \times 8^{-2}$$

Carrying out the arithmetic in the decimal number system produces

$$(2 \times 64) + (1 \times 8) + (7 \times 1) + (4 \times .125) + (3 \times .015625)$$

$$128 \quad + \quad 8 \quad + \quad 7 \quad + \quad .5 \quad + \quad .046875 = 143.546875$$

Therefore, 143.546875 is the decimal equivalent of the octal number 217.43.

Decimal-to-Octal Conversion

Decimal-to-octal conversion can be performed using an algorithm similar to the one that was used for decimal-to-binary conversion. The difference is that the division in the integer conversion and the multiplication in the fractional conversion are by eight rather than by two. Tables 1.8 and 1.9 show the steps in converting 143.546875 from decimal to octal. Copying the remainders from Table 1.8 in the reverse order from which they were produced provides 217, the octal equivalent of the decimal integer 143. Copying the integer portion of each of the products from Table 1.9 provides .43, the octal equivalent of the decimal fraction .546875. That is,

$$143.546875 \text{ decimal } = 217.43 \text{ octal}$$

TABLE 1.8
Conversion of 143 from decimal to octal

Number / 8	=	Quotient	Remainder
143 / 8		17	7
17 / 8		2	1
2 / 8		0	2
0			

TABLE 1.9
Conversion of .546875 from decimal to octal

Fraction * 8	=	Number	Octal Digit	Next Fraction
.546875 * 8		4.375	4	.375
.375 * 8		3.0	3	.0

TABLE 1.10
Binary equivalents
of octal digits

Octal	Binary
0	000
1	001
2	010
3	011
4	100
5	101
6	110
7	111

Binary-to-Octal Conversion

The octal number system is useful in dealing with binary numbers, because there is a direct translation between the two systems. Table 1.10 shows each octal digit along with its three-digit binary equivalent. Note that all possible combinations of three binary digits are consumed in representing the eight octal digits. This situation occurs because the base of the octal number system (8) is a power of the base of the binary number system (2): $2^3 = 8$.

To convert a binary number to octal, start at the binary point and work in both directions, collecting the bits into groups of threes. Leading zeros can be added to the integer to complete a group of three, and trailing zeros can be added to the fraction to complete a group of three. Then use Table 1.10 to convert each three-bit group to the corresponding octal digit.

EXAMPLE

10101110.10001

Grouping the bits by threes about the binary point and converting each group to its octal equivalent produces

$$010\ 101\ 110.100\ 010$$
$$2\quad 5\quad 6\ .\ 4\quad 2$$

Therefore, the octal equivalent of the binary number 10101110.10001 is 256.42.

Octal-to-Binary Conversion

To convert an octal number to binary, simply translate each octal digit to its three-bit binary equivalent. Then eliminate any leading zeros in the integer and any trailing zeros in the fraction.

EXAMPLE

713.34

Converting each octal digit to its binary equivalent produces 111 001 011.011 100. Therefore, the binary equivalent is 111001011.0111.

TABLE 1.11
Decimal equivalents
of hexadecimal
digits

Hexadecimal	Decimal	Hexadecimal	Decimal
0	0	8	8
1	1	9	9
2	2	A	10
3	3	B	11
4	4	C	12
5	5	D	13
6	6	E	14
7	7	F	15

Hexadecimal Number System

The hexadecimal number system is a positional number system with base 16. The hexadecimal number system uses 10 digits (0, 1, 2, 3, 4, 5, 6, 7, 8, and 9) and six letters (A, B, C, D, E, and F). Table 1.11 shows the decimal equivalents of the hexadecimal digits. The radix point is referred to as the **hex point**. Counting works the same in the hexadecimal number system as it does in any other positional number system. Table 1.12 compares counting in hexadecimal with counting in decimal.

Since the hexadecimal number system is a positional number system, the value given to each digit in a hexadecimal number is determined by its position relative to the hex point. The position values of digits to the left of the hex point are based on a right-to-left progression of the nonnegative powers of 16 (10 in hexadecimal). The position values of digits to the right of the hex point are based on a left-to-right progression of the negative powers of 16. The hexadecimal number 4AF.9 may be expressed as

$$4 \times 10^2 + A \times 10^1 + F \times 10^0 + 9 \times 10^{-1}$$

Note that this expression is written entirely in hexadecimal.

TABLE 1.12
Counting in
hexadecimal and
decimal

Hex	Decimal	Hex	Decimal	Hex	Decimal
0	0	C	12	18	24
1	1	D	13	19	25
2	2	E	14	1A	26
3	3	F	15	1B	27
4	4	10	16	1C	28
5	5	11	17	1D	29
6	6	12	18	1E	30
7	7	13	19	1F	31
8	8	14	20	20	32
9	9	15	21	21	33
A	10	16	22	22	34
B	11	17	23	23	35

Hexadecimal-to-Decimal Conversion

To convert a number from hexadecimal to decimal, express the number in terms of powers of the base, convert that expression to decimal, and carry out the arithmetic in the decimal number system. The hexadecimal number 4AF.9, previously expressed in terms of powers of the base, converts to the following decimal expression:

$$4 \times 16^2 + 10 \times 16^1 + 15 \times 16^0 + 9 \times 16^{-1}$$

Carrying out the arithemetic in the decimal number system produces

$$(4 \times 256) + (10 \times 16) + (15 \times 1) + (9 \times .0625)$$

$$1024 \quad + \quad 160 \quad + \quad 15 \quad + \quad .5625 \quad = \quad 1199.5625$$

Therefore, 1199.5625 is the decimal equivalent of the hexadecimal number 4AF.9.

Decimal-to-Hexadecimal Conversion

Decimal-to-hexadecimal conversion can be performed using an algorithm similar to the one that was used for decimal-to-binary conversion. The difference is that the division in the integer conversion and the multiplication in the fractional conversion are by 16 rather than by 2. The remainders produced by division and the integer portions of the products produced by multiplication will be integers in the range 0–15. These integers must be converted to the corresponding hexadecimal digits (see Table 1.11). Table 1.13 and Table 1.14 show the steps in converting 1004.546875 from decimal to hexadecimal. Copying the hexadecimal digits that correspond to the remainders from Table 1.13 in the reverse order from which they were produced provides 3EC, the hexadecimal equivalent of the

TABLE 1.13
Conversion of 1004 from decimal to hex

Number / 16	=	Quotient	Remainder	Hex Digit
1004 / 16		62	12	C
62 / 16		3	14	E
3 / 16		0	3	3
0				

TABLE 1.14
Conversion of .546875 from decimal to hex

Fraction * 16	=	Number	Hex Digit	Next Fraction
.546875 * 16		8.75	8	.75
.75 * 16		12.0	C	.0

decimal integer 1004. Copying the hexadecimal equivalents of the integer portion of each of the products from Table 1.14 produces .8C, the hexadecimal equivalent of the decimal fraction .546875—that is, 1004.546875 decimal = 3EC.8C hexadecimal.

Binary-to-Hexadecimal Conversion

The hexadecimal number system also is useful in dealing with binary numbers, because there is a direct translation between the two systems. Table 1.15 shows each hexadecimal digit along with its 4-bit binary equivalent. Note that all possible combinations of four binary digits are consumed in representing the 16 hexadecimal digits. This situation occurs because the base of the hexadecimal number system (16) is a power of the base of the binary number system (2): $2^4 = 16$.

To convert a binary number to hexadecimal, start at the binary point and work in both directions, collecting the bits into groups of four. You can add leading zeros to the integer to complete a group of four, and you can add trailing zeros to the fraction to complete a group of four. You can use Table 1.15 to convert each four-bit group to the corresponding hexadecimal digit.

EXAMPLE

1101011100.10111

Grouping the bits by four about the binary point and converting each 4-bit group to its hexadecimal equivalent produces

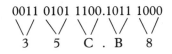

0011 0101 1100.1011 1000
3   5   C . B   8

Therefore, the hexadecimal equivalent of the binary number 1101011100.10111 is 35C.B8.

TABLE 1.15
Binary equivalents of hexadecimal digits

Hexadecimal	Binary	Hexadecimal	Binary
0	0000	8	1000
1	0001	9	1001
2	0010	A	1010
3	0011	B	1011
4	0100	C	1100
5	0101	D	1101
6	0110	E	1110
7	0111	F	1111

Hexadecimal-to-Binary Conversion

To convert a hexadecimal number to binary, simply translate each hexadecimal digit to its 4-bit binary equivalent. Then eliminate any leading zeros in the integer and any trailing zeros in the fraction.

EXAMPLE

2A7.C4

Converting each hexadecimal digit to its 4-bit binary equivalent produces 0010 1010 0111.1100 0100. Therefore, the binary equivalent is 1010100111.110001.

In converting numbers between the octal and decimal number systems or between the decimal and hexadecimal number systems, you will find it somewhat easier to convert to binary first. Such a conversion avoids having to deal with the powers of 8 or 16 and avoids multiplication and division by 8 or 16.

EXAMPLE

Convert the hexadecimal number 5F.C8 to decimal, as follows:

Hexadecimal to Binary

$$5 \quad F \; . \; C \quad 8$$

0101 1111.1100 1000

Binary to Decimal

$$1\;0\;1\quad 1\quad 1\quad 1\quad 1\quad 1\quad 1\;0\quad 0\quad 1$$

$$64 + 16 + 8 + 4 + 2 + 1 + .5 + .25 \quad + \quad .03125 \; = \; 95.78125$$

An Assembly language program describes the contents of memory locations including both instructions and data. The Assembler program translates a program from Assembly language into machine language. The output of the assembler can include a binary object program (machine language) and a listing of each line of the Assembly language program with its machine language equivalent. To save space in the listing, most assemblers display the machine language in either octal or hexadecimal, rather than binary. The IBM PC assembler displays the machine language in hexadecimal.

The MS-DOS operating system on the IBM PC includes a utility program called DEBUG, which provides for the execution of a program one instruction at a time with user intervention allowed between instruction executions. Between instruction executions, the user can inspect and/or change the contents of registers and memory locations. This capability allows the user to trace program execution instruction by instruction. If an error is detected during the trace, the user can repair instructions and damaged data before continuing with the execution. The memory addresses and the contents of registers and memory locations are displayed in hexadecimal. The values entered by the user also must be entered in hexadecimal.

An IBM PC Assembly language programmer needs to be proficient in the use of the hexadecimal number system and in performing conversions between the binary, decimal, and hexadecimal systems.

1.4 | IBM PC Architecture

The IBM PC was designed around the Intel 8088 microprocessor, which is a 16-bit microprocessor internally and an 8-bit microprocessor externally. It can perform 16-bit arithmetic; its registers are 16-bit registers; and its internal bus system is a 16-bit bus system. The external data bus is an 8-bit bus—that is, data is transmitted between the microprocessor and memory or between the microprocessor and the I/O ports, 8 bits at a time.

IBM PC Memory Organization

The IBM PC can address up to 1,048,576 storage cells (1024 K, where 1K = 1024). These storage cells are addressed by the integers in the range 0–1048575 decimal (00000–FFFFF hexadecimal). Each storage cell in memory holds an 8-bit binary number called a **byte**, which is the unit of data transmission between the microprocessor, the memory, and the I/O devices—that is, each memory fetch operation fetches a single byte, and each memory store operation stores a single byte.

In the IBM PC, two consecutive bytes can be treated as a single, 16-bit binary number called a **word**. When a word is stored in memory, it must be stored as two consecutive byte values. The low-order byte is stored first followed by the high-order byte (see Figure 1.15). To fetch a word operand from memory, two memory fetch operations are required: one to fetch the low-order byte and one to fetch the high-order byte. To store a word value into memory, two memory store operations are required: one to store the low-order byte and one to store the high-order byte.

Figure 1.16 shows a memory map for the IBM PC. In the minimum configuration, there is 256K of read/write memory with physical addresses 00000–3FFFF; 4K or 16K of read/write memory for video display buffers; and 40K of read-only memory (ROM) that contains a BASIC interpreter and the Basic Input/Output System (BIOS). For the IBM PC-XT, there is an additional 8K of ROM that contains the fixed disk control program. Note that in the minimum configuration, the physical memory space is not all contiguous; however, the 256K of read/write memory is contiguous and begins at location 00000. The first 1K of this memory space is an interrupt vector table and is not actually available for general use. Interrupt vectors are discussed in Chapter 9. Portions

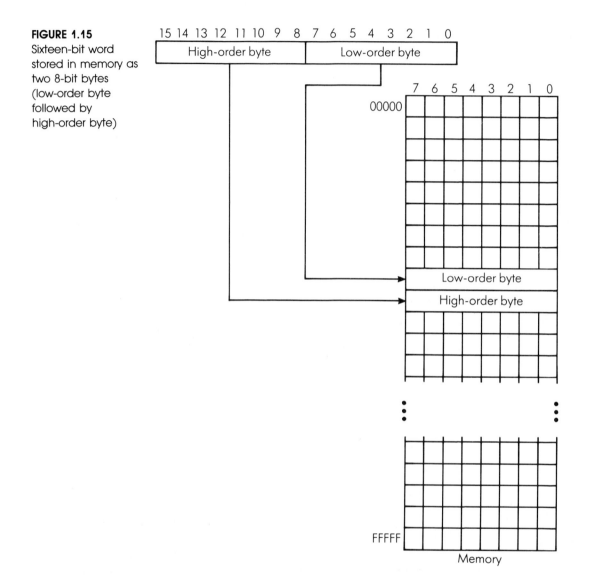

FIGURE 1.15
Sixteen-bit word stored in memory as two 8-bit bytes (low-order byte followed by high-order byte)

of the memory map shown in Figure 1.16 are discussed in more detail in later chapters.

Intel 8088 Microprocessor

The Intel 8088 microprocessor is the CPU in the IBM PC. Figure 1.17 (see page 36) is a block diagram of this microprocessor. The microprocessor consists of two separate processing units: the *execution unit (EU)* and the *bus interface unit (BIU)*. The EU interprets and executes instructions, and the BIU performs bus operations—for example, instruction fetch, operand fetch, data store, and communication with I/O devices.

FIGURE 1.16
IBM PC memory
map

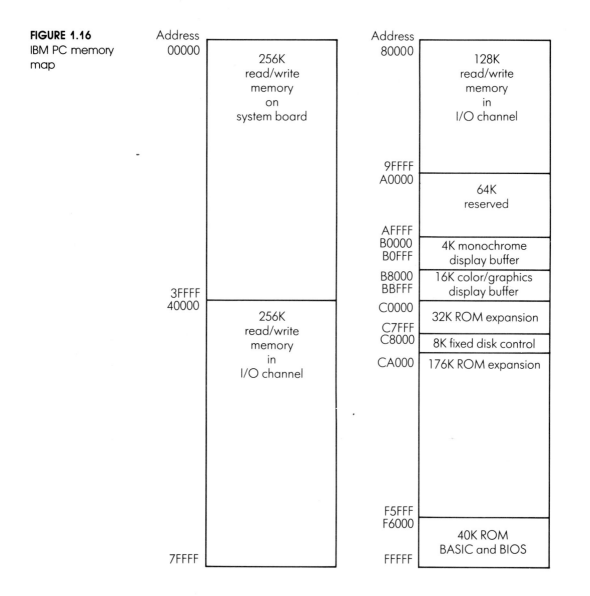

Execution Unit

The **EU** contains control logic for decoding and executing instructions, an ALU for performing arithmetic and logical operations, a set of general-purpose registers, and a control register called the *flags register*. The control logic within the EU interprets machine language instructions and controls the operations necessary for carrying out those instructions. The EU receives instruction bytes from the instruction queue in the order in which they were inserted into the instruction queue by the BIU. When the EU needs an operand from memory or needs to store a result in memory, it directs the BIU to perform the required operation.

The EU provides the components needed by the BIU to compute the physical memory address for the fetch or store operation. The ALU receives its operands via the internal bus from the general registers, from instruction bytes, or from the BIU (i.e., operands fetched from memory). The ALU is capable of performing both 8-bit computations (byte computations) and 16-bit computations (word computations).

Bus Interface Unit

The **BIU** contains bus control logic that controls all external bus operations; an instruction queue for holding instruction bytes for the EU; an adder for generating physical memory addresses; and a set of registers that includes four segment registers, an instruction pointer, and some internal communications registers. The BIU is responsible for controlling all external bus operations, including communications with both memory and I/O ports. The external address bus is used to select a specific memory location or I/O port.

The BIU fetches instruction bytes and places them into the instruction queue for the EU (see Figure 1.17). The BIU can prefetch up to four bytes of instruction code. While the EU is processing one instruction byte, the BIU can be prefetching another instruction byte. As long as the EU is not requesting that the BIU perform a data fetch or data store, the BIU is free to prefetch instruction bytes. Data fetch and data store operations take priority over the instruction prefetch operation. Instruction prefetch allows the BIU and the EU to work in parallel, thus increasing the performance of the microprocessor. This form of computer architecture is known as a **pipeline architecture**, in which instruction bytes are said to be queued up in a pipeline fashion.

Intel 8088 Register Set

An Assembly language programmer's primary interface with the hardware components of the computer is through the microprocessor's register set. The Intel 8088 microprocessor contains fourteen 16-bit registers that can be directly or indirectly manipulated by Assembly language programs. The BIU contains four segment registers and an instruction pointer register. The EU contains eight general-purpose registers and the flags register. These registers are illustrated in Figure 1.18 and are discussed in the following sections.

Segment Registers

An Assembly language program is divided into segments. Each segment can be as large as 64K bytes. A program can have many segments, but only four segments can be active at any one time during program execution. The **start address** (origin address) of each active segment is specified by the contents of one of the four segment registers.

In an IBM PC machine language program, all memory addresses are specified by a **segment origin** (the contents of a segment register) and an offset relative to the segment origin. The BIU **adder** is used to add the offset to the segment origin to generate the physical memory address, which is 20 bits wide. Each of the four segment registers is 16 bits wide. How can a 20-bit segment origin address be specified by the contents of a 16-bit segment register? This specification is accomplished by the requirement that all segments begin on a **paragraph boundary**, a memory address that is divisible by 16. Being divisible by 16 means that the low-order 4 bits of the base address are 0000, which means that only the high-order 16 bits of the segment origin address must be stored in the segment register. In other words, the segment register contains the high-order, 16-bit address of the segment origin and the low-order 4 bits are assumed to be 0000.

FIGURE 1.17 Intel 8088 microprocessor

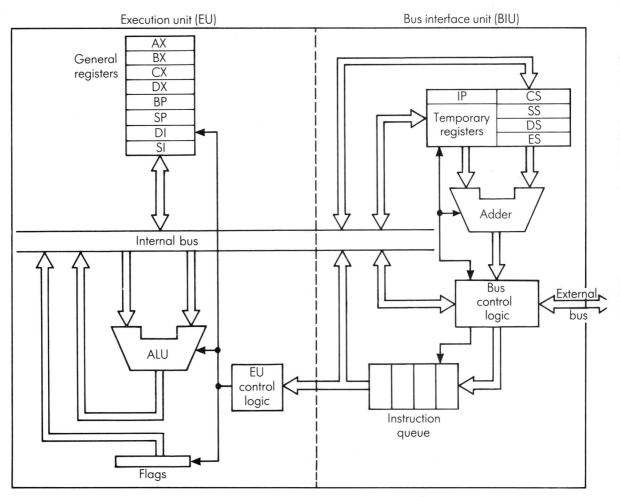

FIGURE 1.18

Intel 8088 registers

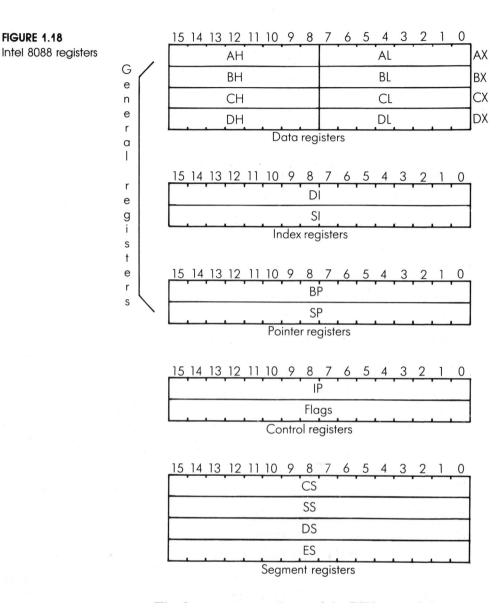

The four segment registers of the BIU are as follows:

CS-Register   The CS-register specifies the address of the origin of the currently active code segment. A *code segment* contains executable instructions.

SS-Register   The SS-register specifies the address of the origin of the currently active stack segment. A *stack segment* contains dynamic data whose storage is allocated and deallocated on demand during execution.

DS-Register   The DS-register specifies the address of the origin of the currently active data segment. A *data segment* usually contains static data whose storage is allocated prior to execution and is deallocated at program termination. Static data storage remains fixed throughout program execution.

ES-Register   The ES-register specifies the address of the origin of the currently active extra segment. An *extra segment*, like a data segment, usually contains static data.

Each of these types of segments is discussed in more detail in Section 1.5.

Instruction Pointer Register

The instruction pointer register (IP-register) always contains the 16-bit offset, within the currently active code segment, of the next instruction byte to be fetched from memory. The CS:IP register pair always specifies the 20-bit memory address of the next instruction byte to be fetched from memory: The CS-register contents specify the segment origin address of the code segment, and the IP-register contains the offset from this origin address to (i.e., the difference between this origin address and) the address of the instruction byte to be fetched. The CS:IP register pair is said to point to the next instruction byte to be fetched from memory and is like the program counter in the hypothetical machine.

General Registers

There are eight, 16-bit general registers in the EU. These registers are divided into three groups in Figure 1.18. There are four **data registers** (AX, BX, CX, and DX), two **index registers** (DI and SI), and two **pointer registers** (BP and SP). Each of these registers can be used to supply a 16-bit operand to and receive the 16-bit result from an arithmetic or logical operation performed by the ALU. The four data registers can each be divided into two 8-bit registers: The high-order half of the AX-register is referred to as the AH-register, and the low-order half is referred to as the AL-register. Similarly, BH and BL are the designators for the two halves of the BX-register, CH and CL for the CX-register, and DH and DL for the DX-register. Each of these eight, 8-bit data registers can be used to supply an 8-bit operand to and receive an 8-bit result from an arithmetic or logical operation performed by the ALU. In addition to supplying operands to and receiving results from the ALU, each register has a specific purpose, as follows:

AX-Register   The AX-register is the accumulator register. It can be used as a single, 16-bit word register or as two, 8-bit byte registers. Where possible, the AX-register should be used to accumulate the result of 16-bit arithmetic and logical operations. The AL-register should be used to accumulate the result of 8-bit arithmetic and logical operations. Even though any of the other general registers can be used as the accumulator in most arithmetic and logical operations, use of the AX and AL registers produces more efficient machine code. They also are used implicitly in multiply and divide operations. (Arithmetic operations are discussed in Chapter 3.) In addition, the AX and AL registers are used in input/output operations.

BX-Register   The BX-register is called the **base register** and is used to access an item in a data structure, for example, an element of an array.

CX-Register   The CX-register is the **count register** and is used as a counter in loop operations. It also is used as a shift counter in multibit shift operations. (Loop operations are discussd in Chapter 4, and a special type of loop operation is presented in Chapter 8. Shift operations and use of the CL-register as a shift counter are discussed in Chapter 6.)

DX-Register   The DX-register is called the **data register**. It is used as an extension to the AX-register for multiplication and division operations and for 32-bit arithmetic.

DI-Register   The DI-register is the **destination index register**. It is used with a special set of instructions called **string instructions**. The string instructions are used for manipulating the elements of character strings and arrays.

SI-Register   The SI-register is the **source index register**. It, like the DI-register, is used with the string instructions. (The string instructions and their use of the SI and DI index registers are discussed in Chapter 8.)

SP-Register   The SP-register is the **stack pointer**. It always contains the offset within the stack segment of the current top-of-stack item. The SS:SP register pair always specifies the 20-bit memory address of the 16-bit word that is the current top-of-stack item. The SS-register contents specify the segment origin address of the stack segment, and the SP-register contains the offset from this origin to the address of the current top-of-stack item. That is, the SS:SP register pair points to the item at the top of the stack. (The concept of a stack and its push and pop operations are discussed further in Section 1.5 and in Chapter 2.)

BP-Register   The BP-register is the **base pointer register**. It is useful as an auxiliary stack segment pointer when arguments are passed to subprocedures via the stack. (Passing arguments via the stack and the use of the BP-register are discussed in the addressing modes section of Chapter 8 and in Chapter 10.)

Flags Register

The **flags register** is a 16-bit register contained in the EU. Only 9 of the 16 bits are implemented, as shown in Figure 1.19. Each of these 9 bits has a distinct

FIGURE 1.19
Flags register

15	14	13	12	11	10	9	8	7	6	5	4	3	2	1	0
				OF	DF	IF	TF	SF	ZF		AF		PF		CF

Overflow flag	(OF)
Direction flag	(DF)
Interrupt flag	(IF)
Trap flag	(TF)
Sign flag	(SF)
Zero flag	(ZF)
Auxiliary carry flag	(AF)
Parity flag	(PF)
Carry flag	(CF)

purpose and indicates something about the current state of the microprocessor. Three of the bits are control flags: the **direction flag** (**DF**), the **interrupt flag** (**IF**), and the **trap flag** (**TF**). The other 6 bits are status flags. The 9 flag bits indicate the following:

Overflow Flag (OF)   When the operands of an addition or subtraction operation are interpreted as signed integer values, the OF bit in the flags register indicates whether or not the result of the operation is too large to be stored in the register or memory location that is designated to receive the result. Producing a result that is too large to be stored is a condition known as an **arithmetic overflow**. The OF bit is also used to indicate whether or not the most-significant bit changes on a shift operation. (The interpretation of binary numbers is discussed in Chapter 2. The concept of arithmetic overflow is discussed in Chapters 3, 6, and 7.)

Direction Flag (DF)   String instructions automatically update the SI and/or DI index registers to point to the next (or previous) character in a string or element in an array. The DF bit in the flags register is used to control whether this automatic update is an increment (DF = 0) to the next character or array element or a decrement (DF = 1) to the previous character or array element. (Manipulation of the DF bit is discussed in Chapters 6 and 8.)

Interrupt Flag (IF)   An external interrupt is a request for service from some external device, for example, a keyboard, printer, or display screen. The IF bit in the flags register controls whether the microprocessor processes external interrupts (IF = 1) or ignores external interrupts (IF = 0). (Interrupts and input/output operations are discussed in Chapter 9.)

Trap Flag (TF)   The microprocessor has a single-step mode that allows for program intervention after each instruction execution of another program—that is, the single-step mode allows one program to trace the execution of another program. The DEBUG utility program helps programmers trace the execution of their programs. It uses the single-step mode to provide this service. The TF bit in the flags register controls whether the microprocessor is in the single-step mode (TF = 1) or is not in the single-step mode (TF = 0). (The DEBUG program is discussed at various points in this book. The single-step mode is discussed in Chapter 9.)

Sign Flag (SF)   The SF bit is used to hold a copy of the most-significant bit of the result of arithmetic and logical operations. If the result is being interpreted as a signed integer, then the SF bit reflects the sign of that result (SF = 0 implies nonnegative; SF = 1 implies negative). The sign flag is used when binary numbers are compared. In conjunction with the zero flag, the sign flag is used to determine which of two unequal binary numbers is the larger.

Zero Flag (ZF)   The ZF bit is used to indicate whether or not the result of an arithmetic or logical operation is zero (ZF = 1 implies the result is zero; ZF = 0 implies the result is nonzero). The zero flag is used when binary numbers are compared. It reflects whether or not two binary numbers are equal.

(The comparison of binary numbers, for the purpose of making decisions in Assembly language programs, is discussed in Chapter 4.)

Auxiliary Carry Flag (AF)   The AF bit of the flags register is used to reflect the carry out of or borrow into bit position 3 on an addition or subtraction operation. It is used in computations involving binary coded decimal (BCD) numbers. (Carry and borrow are discussed in Chapters 3 and 7. The use of the AF bit is discussed in Chapter 11.)

Parity Flag (PF)   A technique that detects single-bit errors in the transmission of binary data is to add a parity bit to each bit pattern transmitted. The parity bit is chosen in such a way that the number of 1 bits in the bit pattern being transmitted is always odd (odd parity code) or always even (even parity code). If the receiving device receives a bit pattern that has the wrong parity, then it knows that an error has occurred in transmission. The PF bit of the flags register reflects the parity of the low-order 8 bits of the result of an arithmetic or logical operation (PF = 0 implies odd parity; PF = 1 implies even parity).

Carry Flag (CF)   The CF bit is used to reflect the carry out of or borrow into the most-significant bit (MSB) in an addition or subtraction operation. The CF bit also is used to record the last bit shifted out of a register or memory operand in a binary shift operation. The CF bit of the flags register reflects overflow of an addition or subtraction operation when the operands and the result are interpreted as unsigned integers. (Carry and borrow are discussed in Chapters 3 and 7. Shift operations are discussed in Chapter 6.)

A bit is said to be **set** if it is a 1. It is said to be **reset** or **cleared** if it is a 0. The bits in the flags register are set and cleared by the execution of machine language instructions. The flag bits indicate conditions that involve some of the operations being performed by the microprocessor. A set of Assembly language instructions called **jump instructions** allows the program to make decisions based on these conditions. (Jump instructions and their use in implementing decision structures are discussed in Chapter 4.)

To describe the execution of an Assembly language instruction completely, its effect on the flags register must be described. As each Assembly language instruction is discussed in this text, its effect on the bits of the flags register is presented.

1.5 Anatomy of an IBM PC Assembly Language Program

An IBM PC Assembly language program is divided into units called **segments**. The various segments that make up a program can be defined in one or more assembly modules. An **assembly module** contains the definition of one or more segments and the links required for names that are used in the assembly module but are defined in other assembly modules. A **segment definition** consists of

Assembly language instructions, data, and directives to the Assembler program that direct the assembler in performing the translation to machine language. Assembler directives are also called *pseudo-operations*.

An assembly module is one complete input to the Assembler program. The assembler translates an assembly module into an object module. An **object module** contains machine language instructions, data, and a list of external references (names used in the assembly module that produced the object module that are defined in other assembly modules).

The *Linkage Editor program (LINK)* combines object modules produced by the assembler into a complete executable program. The Assembler and LINK programs are discussed in more detail later in this chapter.

There are three distinct types of segments in IBM PC Assembly language programs: the stack segment, the data segment, and the code segment. An IBM PC Assembly language program must contain exactly one stack segment, one or more code segments, and zero or more data segments.

Stack Segment

The **stack segment** contains dynamic data. Storage for dynamic data is allocated and deallocated on demand as the program executes. In the abstract, a stack is a data structure of unlimited capacity. It is a list of data items in which all insertions and deletions are made at one end, called the **top of the stack**. Inserting a new data item in a stack is called **pushing** the data item on top of the stack. Removing a data item from the stack is called **popping** the data item from the top of the stack. When a data item is pushed on the stack, it becomes the new top-of-stack data item. All data items previously in the stack are pushed down one position relative to the top of the stack. When the top-of-stack data item is popped from the stack, the data items remaining in the stack pop up one position relative to the top of the stack. The new top-of-stack data item is the one that was at the top of the stack after the popped item was pushed. At any point in time, the only item that can be popped from the stack is the item at the top of the stack, the last item that was pushed on the stack. A stack is also called a **LIFO (LAST-IN-FIRST-OUT)** data structure.

Theoretically, there is no limit to the number of items that can be pushed onto a stack. However, when implemented on a computer, there must be some upper limit to the number of items that the stack can contain. The stack segment definition in an IBM PC Assembly language program defines the size of the program's stack—that is, the maximum number of data items that the stack can hold at any point in time. The address of the origin of the stack segment is contained in the SS segment register. The offset from this origin to the current top-of-stack data item is contained in the SP-register. The SS and SP registers are automatically maintained by the microprocessor as it executes push and pop operations. Normally, these registers are not directly manipulated by the program. The stack segment of a program is used primarily for the temporary storage of data. (It is discussed in more detail in Chapter 2.)

Data Segment

A **data segment** contains static data. Storage for static data is allocated prior to execution of the program and is deallocated at program termination. In other words, storage for static data exists throughout the entire execution of the program. Data in the data segment are referenced by name. The name is translated, by the assembler, to an offset from the beginning of the data segment. The address of the origin of the data segment is contained in either the DS segment register, the ES segment register, or both. The DS and/or ES register must be initialized and maintained by the program. (Data segment definitions are discussed in detail in Chapter 2.)

Code Segment

A **code segment** contains machine language instructions and consists of one or more procedure definitions. A procedure is a block of machine language instructions that has a name by which it can be called into execution. It is either the main procedure or a subprocedure: The main procedure is the one that receives control when the executable program is placed into execution by the operating system; a subprocedure receives execution control when it is called into execution by another procedure in the program. When a subprocedure terminates, it returns execution control to the procedure that called it into execution. When the main procedure terminates, it returns control to the operating system, thus terminating the executable program.

The address of the origin of the code segment that contains the currently executing procedure is maintained in the CS segment register. The offset from this origin to the next instruction byte to be fetched from memory is contained in the IP-register—that is, the CS:IP register pair always specifies the address of the next instruction byte to be fetched from memory. The CS and IP registers are automatically maintained by the microprocessor as it executes instructions. Normally, these registers are not directly manipulated by the program.

Assembly Language Coding Formats

A line of code in an assembly module is categorized as a comment line, a mnemonic representation of a machine language instruction, or a pseudo-operation (a directive to the assembler program):

Comment Line   Any line in an IBM PC Assembly language program whose first nonblank character is a semicolon (;) is a **comment line**. A comment line is essentially ignored by the assembler. It enables the programmer to embed documentation in the program, but it has no effect on the translation to machine language.

Mnemonic Representation of a Machine Language Instruction   A **mnemonic representation of a machine language instruction** is a machine language instruction that is written in symbolic form. It specifies an operation to be performed during program execution.

Pseudo-Operation   A *pseudo-operation* looks like a mnemonic representation of a machine language instruction, but it is a directive to the Assembler program. It specifies an operation to be performed during the translation from Assembly language to machine language.

When discussing the various machine operations and pseudo-operations of the IBM PC Assembly language, this text provides the general form for that operation. The following conventions are used for such general forms:

1. Items shown in capital letters must be coded exactly as shown.
2. Items enclosed in pointed brackets (⟨ ⟩) must be supplied by the programmer.
3. Items enclosed in square brackets ([ ]) are optional.

A line that specifies a machine operation or a pseudo-operation is divided into four fields:

⟨*name*⟩   ⟨*operation code*⟩   ⟨*operand list*⟩   [⟨*comment*⟩]

The fields must be coded in the order shown and must be separated by one or more spaces and/or TAB characters.

The ⟨*name*⟩ field specifies a symbolic name that is to be associated with a memory location. It can contain as many characters as desired, but the assembler only recognizes the first 31 characters. A symbolic name may include any of the following characters:

Alphabetic: A–Z (lowercase letters are converted to uppercase letters on input)

Numeric: 0–9

Special: ?, ., @, _, and $

The first character of a symbolic name must be alphabetic or a special character. If a period (.) is used in a symbolic name, then it must be the first character. The ⟨*name*⟩ field does not have to begin in the first character position of a line, but in the example programs that appear in this book, that convention is followed. (The use of labels, or symbolic names, is discussed in more detail in Chapter 4.)

The ⟨*operation code*⟩ field contains a mnemonic operation code that represents a machine instruction or a pseudo-operation. The ⟨*operand list*⟩ field contains expressions that specify the operands required by the operation specified by the entry in the ⟨*operation code*⟩ field.

The ⟨*comment*⟩ field is used for documentation purposes. It is essentially ignored by the assembler. It also is echoed in the listing generated by the assembler. A semicolon (;) denotes that the remainder of the line is the ⟨*comment*⟩ field.

The only required field in a noncomment line is the ⟨*operation code*⟩ field. For some operation codes, the ⟨*name*⟩ field is required; for others, it is optional; and for still others, it must be omitted. Some operation codes require operands; others do not. If the ⟨*operand list*⟩ field contains more than one operand, then the operands are separated by the delimiter comma (,). Any line may end with a ⟨*comment*⟩ field.

Example Assembly Module

Program Listing 1.1 is an example of an IBM PC assembly module. It contains the definitions of three segments of a twelve segment program and the links for the names that are used in these three segments but are defined in one of the other segments. The nine segments not defined in this assembly module listing are a data segment and eight code segments that are included in the input/output subprocedure library available on diskette to accompany this book. Each of the eight code segments contains a single input/output subprocedure that is referenced directly or indirectly by the program in Program Listing 1.1. The I/O subprocedures available on this library are described in Appendix D. The

```
 1: ;
 2: ;
 3: ;                    PROGRAM LISTING 1.1
 4: ;
 5: ; PROGRAM TO PRINT NUMBER SYSTEM TRANSLATION TABLES
 6: ;
 7:                                        ;PROCEDURES TO
 8:            EXTRN     PUTDEC:FAR         ;DISPLAY 16-BIT DECIMAL INTEGER
 9:            EXTRN     PUTBIN:FAR         ;DISPLAY BYTE OR WORD IN BINARY
10:            EXTRN     PUTOCT:FAR         ;DISPLAY BYTE OR WORD IN OCTAL
11:            EXTRN     PUTHEX:FAR         ;DISPLAY BYTE OR WORD IN HEX
12:            EXTRN     PUTSTRNG:FAR       ;DISPLAY CHARACTER STRING
13:            EXTRN     NEWLINE:FAR        ;DISPLAY NEWLINE CHARACTER
14:            EXTRN     CLEAR:FAR          ;CLEAR SCREEN
15: ;
16: ;S T A C K   S E G M E N T   D E F I N I T I O N
17: ;
18: STACK      SEGMENT STACK
19:            DB        256 DUP(?)
20: STACK      ENDS
21: ;
22: ;D A T A   S E G M E N T   D E F I N I T I O N
23: ;
24: DATA       SEGMENT
25: ;
26: HEADERS    DB        'DECIMAL          '
27:            DB        'BINARY             '
28:            DB        'OCTAL        '
29:            DB        'HEXADECIMAL '
30: SPACES     DB        '        '
31: ;
32: DATA       ENDS
33: ;
34: ;C O D E   S E G M E N T   D E F I N I T I O N
35: ;
36: CODE       SEGMENT
37:            ASSUME    CS:CODE,DS:NOTHING,ES:DATA,SS:STACK
38: EX_1_1     PROC      FAR
39:            PUSH      DS                 ;PUSH RETURN SEG ADDR ON STACK
40:            SUB       AX,AX              ;PUSH RETURN OFFSET OF ZERO
41:            PUSH      AX                 ;ON STACK
42:            MOV       AX,SEG DATA        ;SET ES-REG TO POINT TO
43:            MOV       ES,AX              ;DATA SEGMENT
44:*;
```

```
45: ;
46:             MOV     AX,-128              ;NUMBER = -128
47: NUM_LOOP:                                ;REPEAT
48:             CALL    CLEAR                ;    CLEAR SCREEN
49:             LEA     DI,HEADERS           ;    PRINT HEADERS
50:             MOV     CX,61
51:             CALL    PUTSTRNG
52:             MOV     CX,24                ;    LOOP_COUNT = 24
53: PAGE_LOOP:                               ;    REPEAT
54:             CALL    NEWLINE              ;        SKIP TO NEXT LINE
55:             PUSH    CX                   ;        SAVE LOOP_COUNT
56:             MOV     BH,+1                ;        DISPLAY NUMBER IN DECIMAL
57:             CALL    PUTDEC               ;        RIGHT JUST IN 6 CHAR FIELD
58:             LEA     DI,SPACES            ;        DISPLAY 3 SPACES
59:             MOV     CX,3
60:             CALL    PUTSTRNG
61:             MOV     BL,0                 ;        8-BIT DISPLAY
62:             CALL    PUTBIN               ;        DISPLAY NUMBER IN BINARY
63:             MOV     CX,1                 ;        DISPLAY 1 SPACE
64:             CALL    PUTSTRNG
65:             MOV     BL,1                 ;        16-BIT DISPLAY
66:             CALL    PUTBIN               ;        DISPLAY NUMBER IN BINARY
67:             MOV     CX,3                 ;        DISPLAY 3 SPACES
68:             CALL    PUTSTRNG
69:             MOV     BL,0                 ;        8-BIT DISPLAY
70:             CALL    PUTOCT               ;        DISPLAY NUMBER IN OCTAL
71:             MOV     CX,1                 ;        DISPLAY 1 SPACE
72:             CALL    PUTSTRNG
73:             MOV     BL,1                 ;        16-BIT DISPLAY
74:             CALL    PUTOCT               ;        DISPLAY NUMBER IN OCTAL
75:             MOV     CX,5                 ;        DISPLAY 5 SPACES
76:             CALL    PUTSTRNG
77:             MOV     BL,0                 ;        8-BIT DISPLAY
78:             CALL    PUTHEX               ;        DISPLAY NUMBER IN HEX
79:             MOV     CX,1                 ;        DISPLAY 1 SPACE
80:             CALL    PUTSTRNG
81:             MOV     BL,1                 ;        16-BIT DISPLAY
82:             CALL    PUTHEX               ;        DISPLAY NUMBER IN HEX
83:             POP     CX                   ;        RESTORE LOOP_COUNT
84:             INC     AX                   ;        NUMBER = NUMBER + 1
85:             LOOP    PAGE_LOOP            ;        DECREMENT LOOP_COUNT
86:                                          ;    UNTIL LOOP_COUNT = 0
87:             PUSH    AX                   ;    SAVE NUMBER
88:             MOV     AH,7                 ;    PAUSE AND WAIT FOR
89:             INT     21H                  ;    KEY STROKE
90:             CALL    NEWLINE              ;    SKIP TO NEXT LINE
91:             POP     AX                   ;    RESTORE NUMBER
92:             CMP     AX,256
93:             JGE     RETURN               ;UNTIL NUMBER = 256
94:             JMP     NUM_LOOP
95: RETURN:
96:             RET                          ;RETURN TO OS
97: EX_1_1      ENDP
98: CODE        ENDS
99:*            END     EX_1_1
```

method of linking a program (such as the one in Listing 1.1) with library procedures is discussed later in this chapter.

Lines 1–6 in Program Listing 1.1 are comment lines that act as a prologue to explain the function performed by the program. All example programs used in this book contain a prologue for each main procedure and subprocedure. The prologues explain the purpose of each procedure or subprocedure (not how it does it, but what it does). In addition, the prologue for a subprocedure contains a description of its input/output interface.

Lines 7–14 identify symbolic names that are used in this assembly module but are defined in other assembly modules. External names are declared to the assembler by using the EXTRN psueod-operation, which has the following general form:

EXTRN ⟨ext-name-list⟩   [⟨comment⟩]

in which ⟨ext-name-list⟩ is a list of external name specifications of the form ⟨name⟩:⟨type⟩, in which ⟨name⟩ is a symbolic name and ⟨type⟩ is one of the following type attributes: BYTE, NEAR, WORD, or FAR.

The EXTRN pseudo-operation identifies to the assembler the symbolic names that are referenced in this assembly module but are defined in other assembly modules. The EXTRN pseudo-operation also identifies the type attribute for each of these external names, so that the assembler can determine whether or not the names are being used properly. Line 12, for example, defines PUTSTRNG as the external (EXTRN) name of a subprocedure that is defined in another code segment (FAR). The comment at the end of line 12 explains that this procedure will display a character string. The function of this subprocedure and its interface requirements are described in Appendix D.

Lines 15–17 are comment lines that indicate that a stack segment definition follows. The stack segment definition itself appears in lines 18–20. Every segment definition begins with a SEGMENT pseudo-operation and terminates with an ENDS pseudo-operation. The SEGMENT pseudo-operation has the following general form:

⟨seg-name⟩ SEGMENT [⟨align⟩] [⟨combine⟩] [⟨class⟩]   [⟨comment⟩]

in which ⟨seg-name⟩ is the symbolic name to be associated with the memory location where the segment is to begin, ⟨align⟩ identifies the type of boundary for the beginning of the segment, ⟨combine⟩ indicates the way in which the segment is to be combined with other segments at program link time, and ⟨class⟩ is a symbolic name used to group segments at link time. (All segments with the same class name are to be contiguous in memory.) The ⟨seg-name⟩ field is required. Every segment defined in an assembly module must be given a name.

Most of the optional operands can be omitted at this point. The ⟨align⟩ type is required to be PARA (paragraph) for all segments that are not to be combined with other segments, which simply means that at program load time, the segment is to be aligned so as to begin on a paragraph boundary (an address that is divisible by 16). Since the default for ⟨align⟩ type is PARA, the operand can be omitted.

A ⟨*combine*⟩ type of STACK indicates that the segment is to be part of the run-time stack segment for the program. All segments with a ⟨*combine*⟩ type of STACK are combined into a single stack segment at link time. If the ⟨*combine*⟩ type operand is omitted, then the segment is to be logically separate from other segments in the program, regardless of its placement relative to other segments. For the example programs in most of the chapters of this book, the ⟨*combine*⟩ type STACK is used for stack segments, and the ⟨*combine*⟩ type operand is omitted for code and static data segments. Chapter 12 discusses the SEGMENT pseudo-operation operands in more detail.

The ENDS pseudo-operation has the following general form:

⟨*seg-name*⟩ ENDS   [⟨*comment*⟩]

in which ⟨*seg-name*⟩ is the symbolic name to be associated with the segment and must match the ⟨*seg-name*⟩ used on the SEGMENT pseudo-operation that marked the beginning of the segment definition. The ENDS pseudo-operation marks the physical end of a segment definition.

The SEGMENT and ENDS pseudo-operations in lines 18 and 20 respectively delimit the stack segment definition for the example program. The DB pseudo-operation in line 19 defines the size of the stack segment: 256 decimal (100 hex) bytes. The DB pseudo-operation is discussed further in the next chapter.

Lines 21–23 are comment lines that are used to indicate that a static data segment definition follows. The data segment definition itself appears in lines 24–32. The segment definition begins with the SEGMENT pseudo-operation and ends with the ENDS pseudo-operation. Both of these pseudo-operations specify the name of the segment being defined. The data-defining pseudo-operations appearing in lines 26–30 are discussed in the next chapter.

Lines 33–35 are comment lines that indicate that a code segment definition follows. The code segment definition itself begins with the SEGMENT pseudo-operation in line 36 and ends with the ENDS pseudo-operation in line 98.

Line 37 in the code segment definition is an ASSUME pseudo-operation. The ASSUME pseudo-operation has the following general form:

ASSUME ⟨*seg-reg-assign-list*⟩ [⟨*comment*⟩]

in which ⟨*seg-reg-assign-list*⟩ is a list of segment register assignments of the form ⟨*seg-reg*⟩:⟨*seg-name*⟩ or ⟨*seg-reg*⟩:NOTHING, in which ⟨*seg-reg*⟩ is one of the segment register designators CS, SS, DS, or ES, and ⟨*seg-name*⟩ is the symbolic name of a segment defined by a SEGMENT pseudo-operation in the same assembly module.

The ASSUME pseudo-operation tells the assembler how the segment registers will be associated with the program segments at execution time. The assignment of the DS-register to NOTHING signifies to the assembler that the DS-register will not be used by the program. The operand DS:NOTHING could be omitted, and the effect would be the same. The CS and SS segment registers are initialized by the operating system as part of program invocation. The CS-register is automatically updated by the microprocessor when control is transferred to or from a subprocedure. The DS and ES segment registers must be initialized and maintained by the program itself. The ASSUME pseudo-operation does not perform this initialization; it simply tells the assembler what initialization is to be performed at execution time.

A code segment definition consists of one or more procedure definitions. The code segment definition in Program Listing 1.1 contains the definition of one procedure. This procedure definition appears in lines 38–97. A procedure definition begins with a PROC pseudo-operation and terminates with an ENDP pseudo-operation. The PROC operation has the following general form:

⟨proc-name⟩ PROC ⟨type-attr⟩ [⟨comment⟩]

in which ⟨proc-name⟩ is the symbolic name by which the procedure is invoked, and ⟨type-attr⟩ specifies the scope of the procedure name. The PROC pseudo-operation marks the physical start of a procedure definition and specifies the type attribute of the procedure name. The type attribute can be either NEAR or FAR: NEAR means that the procedure is local to the code segment that contains it and can be invoked only by procedures defined in the same code segment; FAR means that the procedure can be made available to be invoked by procedures in any code segment of the executable program. The main procedure of a program must be a FAR procedure.

The ENDP pseudo-operation has the following general form:

⟨proc-name⟩ ENDP   [⟨comment⟩]

in which ⟨proc-name⟩ is the symbolic name to be associated with the procedure and must match the ⟨proc-name⟩ used on the PROC pseudo-operation that marked the beginning of the procedure definition. The ENDP pseudo-operation marks the physical end of a procedure definition.

The PROC and ENDP pseudo-operations in lines 38 and 97, respectively, delimit the procedure definition for the main procedure of the program. Procedure definitions are discussed in more detail in Chapter 5.

Lines 39–96 are machine language instructions written in symbolic form. Each of the future chapters in this book is devoted to a specific class of Assembly language instructions.

The assembly module in Program Listing 1.1 terminates with an END pseudo-operation in line 99. The END pseudo-operation has the following general form:

END [⟨label⟩] [⟨comment⟩]

in which ⟨label⟩ is the symbolic name that specifies the entry point for the executable program (i.e., the label of the instruction where execution is to begin). The END pseudo-operation defines the physical end of an IBM PC assembly module. It must be the last line of every Assembly language source module. The optional ⟨label⟩ is required on the END pseudo-operation in the assembly module that contains the main procedure definition and must be the label of an instruction in the main procedure. The procedure name is also a name that is associated with the first executable instruction of the procedure. The optional ⟨*label*⟩ must be omitted from the END pseudo-operation in any assembly module that contains only subprocedure definitions.

The algorithm implemented by the program in Program Listing 1.1 is not discussed here. It requires information from a number of future chapters. The purpose of this example is to show the form of an IBM PC Assembly language program. It demonstrates the use of a number of subprocedures in the I/O library. You may wish to refer back to this program for examples of the use of these subprocedures.

1.6 Support Software

There are several software packages available for support of Assembly language programming on the IBM PC. Among the more popular are those developed by the Microsoft Corporation, which include the *DOS operating system*, the *MASM macro assembler*, and their utility programs. These software packages were used in developing the example programs in this textbook. The programs are discussed briefly in this section, and a more detailed discussion can be found in Appendix F.

This section also contains a brief discussion of the I/O subprocedure library referenced in the example programs of this book. A description of each of the subprocedures in this library appears in Appendix D.

Disk Operating System

The **Disk Operating System (DOS)** is a set of programs that aids in operation of the IBM PC. The memory-resident portion of DOS is usually loaded when the machine is turned on and remains in memory while the machine is in use. DOS provides the interface between the user and the resources of the IBM PC. These resources include both hardware and software. DOS provides the interface via a command language. The user enters a command from the keyboard in response to a DOS prompt. A command is, in effect, a request for DOS to execute some program, either a utility program or a user program. DOS interprets the command and invokes the program that provides the service requested.

If the program that provides a requested service is not part of the memory-resident portion of DOS, then DOS loads the program from diskette into memory and begins program execution. While a requested program is executing, it is in control and may prompt the user for input. In most cases, when the requested program terminates, it returns control to DOS. DOS then prompts the user for another command.

If DOS cannot interpret the command as entered or the requested program is not available to be loaded, then DOS displays an appropriate diagnostic message and prompts the user for another command. Consult the DOS manual for a list of the diagnostic messages displayed.

The commands recognized by DOS can be divided into the following categories:

Commands that provide the capability to batch DOS commands, that is, to collect DOS commands into a group that can be invoked by name

Commands that facilitate the creation, maintenance, and deletion of files on the fixed disk (IBM PC-XT and IBM PC-AT) and on diskettes

Commands that set and display the system date and time

Commands that request and control output to the display screen

Commands that request and control output to the printer

Appendix F describes some of the more commonly used DOS commands, although the discussion is by no means exhaustive. The DOS manual can provide further information. Also, tutorials on DOS are available at many colleges and universities. The user should learn to do at least the following with DOS before proceeding to the next chapter:

Bootstrap load the DOS program

Enter the date and time

Format a diskette

Display a directory of the files on a diskette

Copy a file from one diskette to the same or another diskette

Erase a file from a diskette

Display the contents of a text file on the display screen

Print the contents of a text file on the printer

Print a copy of the display screen on the printer

Set the default disk drive

The finer points of DOS can be picked up as needed.

Line Editor

The input to the Assembler program is a text file that contains a complete assembly module in text form. This text file is called a **source code file**. The **line editor** (**EDLIN**) is used to create and maintain this text file. EDLIN provides the following capabilities:

To enter text data via the keyboard into the memory of the computer

To edit text data that is in memory using commands entered from the keyboard

To save text data that is in memory in a file on a diskette

To read text data from a file on diskette into memory

EDLIN is a utility program provided by DOS, and the DOS manual contains a chapter that is devoted to its use. Appendix F discusses some of the more commonly used EDLIN features. In addition, tutorials on EDLIN are available at some colleges and universities. There are text editors other than EDLIN, and other word processors can be used to create and edit Assembly language source code files. EDLIN is discussed here because it is available with DOS and because of its simplicity. The user should learn to enter and save an Assembly language program using an available editor before proceeding to the next chapter.

Macro Assembler

The **Macro Assembler** (**MASM**) program translates a program (or part of a program) from Assembly language to machine language. The input to the MASM is a disk file that contains a complete assembly module. This input file is called the source code file. The output produced by the MASM is a disk file that contains the machine language translation of the source code file. This output file is called the **object code file**.

Under DOS, the name of a disk file can be from one to eight characters in length, optionally followed by a filename extension, which is a period (.), followed by from one to three characters. The following characters are allowed in filenames and extensions: A–Z, 0–9, and $, &, #, @, !, %, ', ', (,), −, {, }, and _.

EXAMPLES

DATE_CNV.ASM
EX01.OBJ
A.B
XYZ.$$$

An **explicit file specification** is a filename that is preceded by a **disk drive identifier**, which is the letter designator for the disk drive (e.g., A or B) followed by a colon (:). If the disk drive identifier is omitted, then the default drive identifier specified in the DOS prompt is assumed.

By convention, the suffix .ASM is used as the file extension for a source code file, and the suffix .OBJ is used as the file extension for an object code file. As long as these conventions are used, the file extension can be omitted from filenames appearing in commands that invoke the assembler. It is a good idea to use the suffix .ASM for the file extension on all source code files.

In its simplest form, the command used to invoke the assembler has the following general form:

```
MASM          ⟨source⟩ [, ⟨object⟩];
```

in which ⟨source⟩ identifies the input source code file, and ⟨object⟩ identifies the output object code file. The ⟨source⟩ entry must be present and is an explicit file specification that identifies the disk drive and filename. If the file extension is omitted, then the suffix .ASM is assumed. The ⟨*object*⟩ entry may be specified in any of the following ways:

The entry can be an explicit file specification that identifies the disk drive and filename. If the file extension is omitted, then the suffix .OBJ is assumed.

The entry can be omitted or left blank, which specifies that the object file is to be placed on the diskette in the default drive using the same name as the source file but with the suffix .OBJ as the file extension.

The entry can be the mnemonic NUL, which specifies that the object file is not to be generated.

The entry can be a disk drive identifier (e.g., B:), which specifies that the object file is to be placed on the diskette in the indicated drive using the same name as the source file but with the suffix .OBJ as the file extension.

In its complete form, the MASM command contains two additional entries: one to specify an output listing file and one to specify an output cross-reference file. The semicolon (;), shown in the general form, indicates that these two entries are being omitted and that the assembler is not to generate the corresponding output files.

Consider the assembly module in Program Listing 1.1. Suppose this assembly module has already been entered using EDLIN and has been saved on a diskette with EX_1_1.ASM as the filename. Suppose further that the diskette containing the MASM program is in drive A, the diskette containing the source code file EX_1_1.ASM is in drive B, and the default disk drive is drive A. To assemble this assembly module, the following command can be entered in response to the A⟩(prompt) from DOS:

```
MASM          B: EX_1_1, B: ;
```

This command instructs MASM to translate the assembly module in file EX_1_1.ASM on the diskette in drive B to machine language. MASM places the object code file on the diskette in drive B with EX_1_1.OBJ as the filename.

When the MASM program encounters an error in the assembly module it is translating, it displays the line of code that contains the error and an error number. The Macro Assembler program manual contains a list of these error numbers with a brief description of the probable cause.

The complete form of the MASM command is described in Appendix F and in the Macro Assembler manual. The abbreviated form given here will suffice for now.

Linkage Editor

Assembly language programs are often divided into several assembly modules. The individual assembly modules that make up a program are each assembled separately by the assembler, producing separate object code files. In such a form, the object code files cannot be loaded and executed. They first must be combined into one executable machine language program.

For example, the assembly module in Program Listing 1.1 is only part of a program. The procedure defined in that assembly module references seven external procedures, each of which appears in a separate assembly module. In fact, one of the seven external procedures references an eighth external procedure that appears in yet another assembly module. Therefore, the program, of which Program Listing 1.1 is a part, consists of nine assembly modules, each of which is assembled separately, producing nine object code files. Eight of these object code files already exist in the I/O subprocedure library. The object code file produced from the assembly module in Program Listing 1.1 must be combined with the other eight modules to produce a complete and executable program.

The program that combines object code files into a complete executable machine language program is the **Linkage Editor** (**LINK**) program. The input to LINK is a sequence of object code files. The output is a relocatable object code module called a **run file**, or **executable file**, which contains a complete program that can be loaded and executed.

By convention, the suffix .OBJ is used as the file extension for object code files, the suffix .EXE is used as the file extension for the executable code file, and the suffix .LIB is used for libraries of object files. As long as these conventions are used, the file extension may be omitted from filenames appearing in commands that invoke LINK.

The command used to invoke LINK has the following general form:

LINK ⟨*obj-list*⟩,⟨*runfile*⟩,⟨*loadmap*⟩,⟨*lib-list*⟩

in which ⟨*obj-list*⟩ is a list of object file specifications separated by spaces or plus (+) signs, ⟨*runfile*⟩ identifies the file that is to receive the relocatable object module (i.e., the executable file), ⟨*loadmap*⟩ identifies the file that is to receive the load map listing, and ⟨*lib-list*⟩ is a list of library specifications separated by spaces or plus (+) signs.

The ⟨*obj-list*⟩ entry identifies object files that are to be linked to create an executable program. There must be at least one item in this list, and each item in the list must be an explicit file specification that identifies the disk drive and the filename. If the file extension is omitted from a filename, then the suffix .OBJ is assumed. The need for more than one entry in the ⟨*obj-list*⟩ will not exist until Chapter 5.

The ⟨*runfile*⟩ entry may be specified in any of the following ways:

The entry can be an explicit file specification that identifies the disk drive and the filename. If the file extension is omitted from the filename, then the suffix .EXE is assumed.

The entry can be omitted or left blank, which specifies that the executable file is to be placed on the diskette in the default drive using the same name as the first file in the ⟨*obj-list*⟩ but with the suffix .EXE as the file extension.

The entry can be a disk drive identifier (e.g., B:), which specifies that the executable file is to be placed on the diskette in the indicated drive using the same name as the first file in the ⟨*obj-list*⟩ but with the suffix .EXE as the file extension.

Another option for the ⟨*runfile*⟩ entry is given in Appendix F. The ones given here more than suffice for now.

The LINK program can be directed to generate and output a load map. This load map shows where each segment will be loaded in memory relative to the other segments in the executable file. The map also shows the size in bytes for each segment in the executable program. The ⟨*loadmap*⟩ entry in the command line that invokes the LINK program specifies whether this load map is to be generated and where it is to be output. The ⟨*loadmap*⟩ may be specified in one of the following ways:

The entry can be the mnemonic NUL, which specifies that the load map is not to be generated.

The entry can be the mnemonic CON, which specifies that the load map is to be generated and displayed on the video screen.

Other options for the ⟨*loadmap*⟩ entry are given in Appendix F. The NUL entry is probably the most often used by beginning IBM PC Assembly language programmers.

The ⟨*lib-list*⟩ entry identifies library files that are to be searched for other object files needed to complete the executable program. Each item in the list must be an explicit file specification that identifies the disk drive and the filename. If the file extension is omitted, then the suffix .LIB is assumed.

Consider again the assembly module in Program Listing 1.1. Suppose this assembly module has already been assembled, that the object code is on the diskette in drive B, and that EX_1_1.OBJ is the name of the object code file. Suppose further that the diskette containing the LINK program and the I/O subprocedure library IO.LIB is in drive A. To link file EX_1_1.OBJ with the appropriate object code files from IO.LIB, the following command can be entered in response to the DOS A⟩(prompt):

```
LINK B:EX_1_1,B:,NUL,IO
```

This command instructs the LINK program to combine file EX_1_1.OBJ from the diskette in drive B with the appropriate object files from the library IO.LIB on the diskette in drive A and to place the executable code file on the diskette in drive B using EX_1_1.EXE as the filename. The load map listing is not generated.

The complete form of the LINK command is described in Appendix F and in the LINK chapter of the Macro Assembler manual. The abbreviated form given here suffices for most of this book.

DEBUG

The **DEBUG** program provides the capability for tracing the execution of a machine language program by executing one instruction or a selected group of instructions at a time. Between instruction group executions, DEBUG provides the user with the opportunity to inspect and/or change the contents of registers and memory locations.

A description of a DEBUG session is included at the end of the next chapter. Appendix F has a section devoted to DEBUG, and the Macro Assembler manual has a chapter devoted to DEBUG.

Input/Output Subprocedure Library

A set of input/output subprocedures has been developed by the author so that beginning IBM PC Assembly language students can start writing programs without first having to master the difficult concepts of input and output at the machine level. These I/O subprocedures and their interface requirements are described in Appendix D. An object file library containing the object code files for these subprocedures is available. The name of the library is IO.LIB.

NUMERIC EXERCISE

1.1 Fill in the blanks in the following table.

Decimal	Binary	Octal	Hexadecimal
237.4375			
	11010111.10101		
		237.4375	
			C4.B4

PROGRAMMING EXERCISES

1.1 Using EDLIN, enter the program in Program Listing 1.1 and save it on diskette using PR_1_1.ASM as the filename. Assemble the program and link it with the I/O subprocedures from IO.LIB. Execute the program. The program will display a table on the video screen and then pause, waiting for you to press a key at the keyboard. When you press any key, the program will display another page and pause again. Continue this process until 16 pages of output have been displayed. Can you print each screenful at the printer? Try it.

1.2 Using EDLIN, enter the program in Program Listing 1.2 and save it on diskette using PR_1_2.ASM as the filename. Assemble the program and link it with the I/O subprocedures from IO.LIB. Execute the program.

```
;
;               PROGRAM LISTING 1.2
;
; PROGRAM TO ACCEPT AN INTEGER IN SIGNED DECIMAL FORM, AND TO
; DISPLAY THE RESULTING BIT PATTERN ALONG WITH  ITS   UNSIGNED
; DECIMAL INTERPRETATION.
;
;                              ;PROCEDURES TO
```

```
            EXTRN    GETDEC:FAR              ;INPUT SIGNED DECIMAL INTEGER
            EXTRN    NEWLINE:FAR             ;DISPLAY NEWLINE CHARACTER
            EXTRN    PUTBIN:FAR              ;DISPLAY BINARY INTEGER
            EXTRN    PUTDEC:FAR              ;DISPLAY SIGNED DECIMAL INT.
            EXTRN    PUTDEC$:FAR             ;DISPLAY UNSIGNED DECIMAL INT
            EXTRN    PUTSTRNG:FAR            ;DISPLAY CHARACTER STRING
;
; S T A C K    S E G M E N T    D E F I N I T I O N
;
STACK       SEGMENT STACK
            DB       256 DUP(?)
STACK       ENDS
;
; D A T A    S E G M E N T    D E F I N I T I O N
;
DATA        SEGMENT
;
PROMPT      DB       'ENTER AN INTEGER IN THE RANGE -32768 TO +32767'
BIN_MSG     DB       'THE INTERNAL BIT PATTERN FOR THE INPUT NUMBER IS: '
DEC_MSG     DB       'THE UNSIGNED INTEGER INTERPRETATION OF THIS '
            DB       'BIT PATTERN IS:'
;
DATA        ENDS
;
; C O D E    S E G M E N T    D E F I N I T I O N
;
CODE        SEGMENT
            ASSUME   CS:CODE,SS:STACK,ES:DATA,DS:NOTHING
PR_1_2      PROC     FAR
            PUSH     DS                      ;PUSH RETURN SEG ADDR ON STACK
            MOV      AX,0                    ;PUSH RETURN OFFSET OF ZERO
            PUSH     AX                      ;ON STACK
            MOV      AX,SEG DATA             ;SET ES-REGISTER TO POINT TO
            MOV      ES,AX                   ;DATA SEGMENT
            LEA      DI,PROMPT               ;PROMPT FOR INTEGER
            MOV      CX,46
            CALL     PUTSTRNG
            CALL     NEWLINE
            CALL     GETDEC                  ;GET INTEGER (SIGNED DECIMAL)
            CALL     NEWLINE
            LEA      DI,BIN_MSG              ;DISPLAY INTEGER IN BINARY
            MOV      CX,50
            CALL     PUTSTRNG
            MOV      BL,1
            CALL     PUTBIN
            CALL     NEWLINE
            LEA      DI,DEC_MSG              ;DISPLAY INTEGER AS AN
            MOV      CX,59                   ;UNSIGNED DECIMAL INTEGER
            CALL     PUTSTRNG
            MOV      BH,1
            CALL     PUTDEC$
            CALL     NEWLINE
            RET                              ;RETURN
PR_1_2      ENDP
CODE        ENDS
            END      PR_1_2

A>
```

2 DATA DEFINITION AND DATA TRANSFER

The previous chapter identified the basic components of an IBM PC Assembly language program. As discussed, the major component is the segment definition, which consists of symbolic representations of machine language instructions and directives to the assembler. This chapter is concerned with the definition of data and the movement of data within the computer. It first presents some traditional methods for representing data in a computer, and then it discusses the pseudo-operations used in the definition of stack and data segments in an IBM PC Assembly language program. With these pseudo-operations, the user can define 8-bit or 16-bit variables in memory, assign initial values to those variables, and assign names to constants used in the program. The Assembly language instructions for the movement of data between the memory and the microprocessor registers of the IBM PC also are discussed.

2.1 Computer Representations of Data

Data are represented in the computer by groups of two-state components. A lamp is an example of a two-state device: Assuming that a lamp has a two-way switch and no dimming device, then the lamp is either on or off. Figure 2.1(a) shows the two possible states of a single lamp, and Figure 2.1(b) shows the possible states of a group of two lamps. By adding a second lamp, the number of possible states has been doubled from two to four. Figure 2.1(c) shows the possible states of a group of three lamps. By adding a third lamp, the number of possible states has been doubled again from four to eight. Note that the first four states in Figure 2.1(c) contain all possible states of lamps 2 and 3 with lamp 1 off, and the last four states contain all possible states of lamps 2 and 3 with lamp 1 on. In this manner, the number of possible states is doubled each time

FIGURE 2.1
The possible states
of groups of lamps:
(a) a single lamp,
(b) two lamps, (c)
three lamps

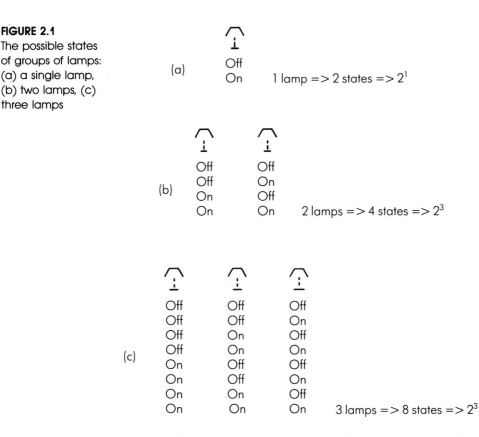

(a)   Off
           On   1 lamp => 2 states => 2^1

(b)

Off	Off
Off	On
On	Off
On	On

2 lamps => 4 states => 2^3

(c)

Off	Off	Off
Off	Off	On
Off	On	Off
Off	On	On
On	Off	Off
On	Off	On
On	On	Off
On	On	On

3 lamps => 8 states => 2^3

a new lamp is added to the group. Each of the possible states can be used to represent some information: With a single lamp, two pieces of information can be represented; with a group of two lamps, four pieces of information can be represented; with a group of three lamps, eight pieces of information can be represented; and so on. In general, with a group of n lamps, 2^n pieces of information can be represented.

A single, two-state component can store one binary digit (i.e., one of the two states represents a binary 0, and the other state represents a binary 1). The bits in the computer's main memory are organized into fixed size units called **memory cells**. That is, each memory cell is a fixed size group of two-state components. Each memory cell has associated with it a unique number, called its **address,** by which it is referenced. If a memory has n cells, then the addresses generally range from 0 to $n - 1$. This addressable memory cell is the unit of data transmission in the computer. That is, whenever data is stored in memory or retrieved from memory, it is done one memory cell at a time by address. In the IBM PC, this addressable unit of storage is called a **byte**, and its size is 8 bits. The IBM PC also provides the capability to combine two contiguous 8-bit bytes into a 16-bit **word**. If the size of a memory cell is n bits, then the binary bit pattern contained in that cell will be one of 2^n possible bit patterns. These bit patterns can be used to represent integers, either nonnegative integers only or both negative and nonnegative integers. These bit patterns also can be used to represent textual data. The following subsections discuss one number system for representing nonnegative integers, four number systems for representing both negative and nonnegative integers, and a code for representing text characters.

Modulo 2^n (Unsigned)

Suppose the size of a memory cell is 8 bits and that the bit pattern contained in a memory cell represents the corresponding nonnegative binary integer. Table 2.1 shows the range of nonnegative decimal integers that can be represented by

TABLE 2.1

Range of integer values for the 8-bit modulo 2^8 number system

Bit Pattern	Modulo 2^8 Integer
00000000	0
00000001	1
00000010	2
00000011	3
00000100	4
00000101	5
00000110	6
00000111	7
.	.
.	.
.	.
01111100	124
01111101	125
01111110	126
01111111	127
10000000	128
10000001	129
10000010	130
10000011	131
.	.
.	.
.	.
11111000	248
11111001	249
11111010	250
11111011	251
11111100	252
11111101	253
11111110	254
11111111	255

the 256 possible values of an 8-bit binary number. This number system is referred to as the **modulo 2^8 (modulo 256) number system**.

With 8-bit binary numbers, the integers in the modulo 2^8 number system can be represented; that is, integers in the range 0 to $2^8 - 1$ or 0 to 255 can be represented. In general, with n-bit binary numbers, the integers in the modulo 2^n number system (i.e., integers in the range 0 to $2^n - 1$) can be represented. The IBM PC uses the modulo 2^n number system to represent unsigned integers.

Sign Magnitude

The **sign magnitude number system** provides for both negative and non-negative integers. With the sign magnitude number system, the leftmost bit in a bit pattern is used to represent the sign of the integer (0 for positive and 1 for negative), and the remaining bits in the bit pattern represent the magnitude of the integer.

EXAMPLES

The 8-bit binary number 00010101 represents the decimal integer $+21$. The leftmost bit represents the sign (0 implies $+$), and the remaining bits are the binary representation for the decimal integer 21.

The 8-bit binary number 10010101 represents the decimal integer -21. The leftmost bit represents the sign (1 implies $-$), and the remaining bits are the binary representation for the decimal integer 21.

Table 2.2 shows the range of integers that can be represented in the sign magnitude number system using 8-bit binary bit patterns. This range is from $-(2^7 - 1)$ to $+(2^7 - 1)$, which is -127 to $+127$. In general, the range of integers that can be represented by n-bit binary integers in sign magnitude form is from $-(2^{n-1} - 1)$ to $+(2^{n-1} - 1)$. To negate a number in the sign magnitude number system, simply invert the leftmost bit, the **sign bit**. The magnitude bits remain the same.

The sign magnitude number system takes the available bit patterns and chooses half of them to represent positive integers and the other half to represent negative integers. Note that in sign magnitude form there are two representations for zero: positive zero and negative zero. This method runs contrary to standard mathematics where zero is neither positive nor negative.

One's Complement

The **one's complement number system** provides for both negative and nonnegative integers. Table 2.3 (see page 64) shows the range of integers that can be represented by the 8-bit one's complement number system. This range is from $-(2^7 - 1)$ to $+(2^7 - 1)$, which is -127 to $+127$. In general, the range of

TABLE 2.2
Range of integer values for the 8-bit sign magnitude number system

Bit Pattern	Sign Magnitude Integer
00000000	0
00000001	1
00000010	2
00000011	3
00000100	4
00000101	5
00000110	6
00000111	7
.	.
.	.
.	.
01111100	124
01111101	125
01111110	126
01111111	127
10000000	-0
10000001	-1
10000010	-2
10000011	-3
.	.
.	.
.	.
11111000	-120
11111001	-121
11111010	-122
11111011	-123
11111100	-124
11111101	-125
11111110	-126
11111111	-127

integers that can be represented by n-bit binary integers in one's complement form is from $-(2^{n-1} - 1)$ to $+(2^{n-1} - 1)$.

Note that in the one's complement number system, all negative integers have a 1 in the leftmost bit position, and all positive integers have a 0 in the leftmost bit position. The leftmost bit is, therefore, the sign bit. To negate an integer in the one's complement number system, simply invert every bit of the integer (i.e., change each 0 to a 1, and change each 1 to a 0).

EXAMPLES

The bit pattern 00010101 represents the integer $+21$ in the 8-bit one's complement number system. Inverting each bit of this bit pattern gives the bit pattern 11101010, which represents the integer -21 in the 8-bit one's complement number system.

TABLE 2.3
Range of integer
values for the 8-bit
one's complement
number system

Bit Pattern	One's Complement Integer
00000000	0
00000001	1
00000010	2
00000011	3
00000100	4
00000101	5
00000110	6
00000111	7
.	.
.	.
.	.
01111100	124
01111101	125
01111110	126
01111111	127
10000000	-127
10000001	-126
10000010	-125
10000011	-124
.	.
.	.
.	.
11111000	-7
11111001	-6
11111010	-5
11111011	-4
11111100	-3
11111101	-2
11111110	-1
11111111	-0

The bit pattern 00000000 represents the integer 0 in the 8-bit one's complement number system. Inverting each bit of this bit pattern gives the bit pattern 11111111, which represents the integer -0 in the 8-bit one's complement number system.

The one's complement number system takes the available bit patterns and chooses half of them to represent positive integers and the other half to represent negative integers. Note that in one's complement form there are two representations for zero: positive zero and negative zero. This method runs contrary to standard mathematics where zero is neither positive nor negative.

Two's Complement

The **two's complement number system** provides for both negative and nonnegative integers. The IBM PC uses the two's complement number system to represent signed integers. Table 2.4 shows the range of integers that can be represented by the 8-bit two's complement number system. This range is from -2^7 to $+2^7 - 1$, which is -128 to $+127$. In general, with n-bit binary numbers in the two's complement number system, the integers in the range -2^{n-1} to $+2^{n-1} - 1$ can be represented.

In the two's complement number system, all negative integers have a 1 in the leftmost bit position, and all nonnegative integers have a 0 in the leftmost bit position. The leftmost bit is, therefore, the sign bit.

TABLE 2.4

Range of integer values for the 8-bit two's complement number system

Bit Pattern	Two's Complement Integer
00000000	0
00000001	1
00000010	2
00000011	3
00000100	4
00000101	5
00000110	6
00000111	7
.	.
.	.
.	.
01111100	124
01111101	125
01111110	126
01111111	127
10000000	-128
10000001	-127
10000010	-126
10000011	-125
.	.
.	.
.	.
11111000	-8
11111001	-7
11111010	-6
11111011	-5
11111100	-4
11111101	-3
11111110	-2
11111111	-1

In the two's complement number system, negating an integer is a two-step process:

1. Invert each bit in the binary number (i.e., change each 1 to a 0, and each 0 to a 1). The result of this step is called the **one's complement** of the original binary number.
2. Then add 1 to the result of step 1 using modulo 2^n addition, in which n is the number of bits in the binary number being negated.

An alternate method for negating an integer in the two's complement number system is as follows:

1. Copy all bits up to and including the first bit that is a 1 (start with the rightmost bit of the binary number and work left).
2. Invert all of the remaining bits to the left.

EXAMPLES

Method 1	*Method 2*
00001100	0 0 0 0 1 1 0 0
11110011	I I I I I C C C
+ 1	
11110100	1 1 1 1 0 1 0 0

Method 1	*Method 2*
11101000	1 1 1 0 1 0 0 0
00010111	I I I I C C C C
+ 1	
00011000	0 0 0 1 1 0 0 0

$$I \Rightarrow \text{Invert}$$
$$C \Rightarrow \text{Copy}$$

Negating a number in the two's complement number system is called "taking the two's complement" of the number. The negative of a number is called the **two's complement** of that number.

The two's complement number system takes the available bit patterns and chooses half of them to represent negative integers and the other half to represent nonnegative integers. Note that in two's complement form there is only one representation for zero. As well, there is one negative integer that has no corresponding positive integer: -128 (i.e., -2^7). In the n-bit two's complement number system, this extra negative integer is -2^{n-1}, which is represented by the n-bit pattern having a 1 in the leftmost bit and a 0 in all other bit positions.

Excess 2^{n-1}

The **excess 2^{n-1} number system** provides for both negative and nonnegative integers. Table 2.5 shows the range of integers that can be represented by the 8-bit excess 2^7 (excess 128) number system. This range is from -2^7 to $+2^7 - 1$, which is -128 to $+127$. In general, with n-bit binary numbers in the excess 2^{n-1} number system, integers in the range -2^{n-1} to $+2^{n-1} - 1$ can be represented.

In the excess 2^{n-1} number system, the n-bit binary number used to represent an integer is 2^{n-1} larger than the integer that it represents; that is, the binary bit pattern is in excess by 2^{n-1} of the integer that it represents. In this number system all negative integers have a 0 in the leftmost bit position, and all nonnegative integers have a 1 in the leftmost bit position. The leftmost bit is, again, an indication of the sign.

TABLE 2.5

Range of integer values for the 8-bit excess 2^7 number system

Bit Pattern	Two's Complement Integer
00000000	-128
00000001	-127
00000010	-126
00000011	-125
00000100	-124
00000101	-123
00000110	-122
00000111	-121
.	.
.	.
.	.
01111100	-4
01111101	-3
01111110	-2
01111111	-1
10000000	0
10000001	1
10000010	2
10000011	3
.	.
.	.
.	.
11111000	120
11111001	121
11111010	122
11111011	123
11111100	124
11111101	125
11111110	126
11111111	127

It is interesting to note that in the excess 2^{n-1} number system the bit pattern used to represent a given integer is the same as the bit pattern used to represent that integer in the two's complement number system with the sign bit inverted. To negate an integer in the excess 2^{n-1} number system, simply take the two's complement of that integer.

The excess 2^{n-1} number system takes the available bit patterns and chooses half of them to represent negative integers and the other half to represent nonnegative integers. Note that in excess 2^{n-1} form there is only one representation for zero. As well, there is one negative integer that has no corresponding positive integer: -128 (i.e., -2^7). In the n-bit excess 2^{n-1} number system, this extra negative integer is -2^{n-1}, which is represented by the bit pattern that contains all zeros. An excess 2^{n-1} number system often is used to represent the exponent of a floating point number.

ASCII Code

The **American Standard Code for Information Interchange (ASCII)** is a 7-bit code adopted by the American National Standards Institute (ANSI). ASCII code is used to represent characters such as A, $, b, 7, ?, and] using binary bit patterns. With a 7-bit code, a total of 128 characters can be represented. The first 32 binary codes in the ASCII character set (0000000 to 0011111, which is 00 HEX to 1F HEX) are used to represent control characters, such as form feed and line feed for the printer. The remaining binary codes (0100000 to 1111111, which is 20 HEX to 7F HEX) are used to represent the printable characters, including the uppercase and lowercase letters, the decimal digits, and special characters such as $, ?, SPACEBAR,], and /.

For the IBM PC, the ASCII character code has been extended to an 8-bit code, in which the first 128 codes in the extended ASCII character set (00000000 to 01111111, which is 00 HEX to 7F HEX) are used to represent the standard ASCII character set. The remaining 128 binary codes in the extended ASCII character set (10000000 to 11111111 which is 80 HEX to FF HEX) are used to represent a variety of symbols that include graphics symbols, math symbols, and Greek letters. The IBM PC also provides for an additional 32 graphics symbols (00000000 to 00011111, which is 00 HEX to 1F HEX) that can be interpreted as special graphics symbols rather than control characters when the codes are output to the display. The tables in Appendix E show both the standard ASCII character set and the IBM PC extended ASCII character set.

2.2 | Data Defining Pseudo-Operations

A data segment definition includes a series of pseudo-operations that describes to the assembler how the static data is to be organized. These pseudo-operations provide the following information:

1. The size of (i.e., number of bytes in) the static data segment
2. The symbolic names that are to be associated with specific locations in the static data segment
3. The initial values to be placed in specific locations in the static data segment
4. The symbolic names that are to be associated with a constant value

Variable Definitions

Variables are defined in a static data segment using the DB and DW pseudo-operations. The **DB pseudo-operation** has the following general form:

[⟨*name*⟩] DB ⟨*byte-constant-list*⟩ [⟨*comment*⟩]

in which ⟨*name*⟩ is the symbolic name to be associated with the memory location in which the sequence of data bytes is to begin and ⟨*byte-constant-list*⟩ is a list of byte constants separated by commas.

A ⟨*byte-constant*⟩ is one of the following:

1. A **binary byte constant** is a signed or unsigned string of up to eight significant binary digits followed by the letter B (upper case or lower case).

2. An **octal byte constant** is a signed or unsigned string of octal digits followed by either the letter O or the letter Q (upper case or lower case). The octal value must lie in the range 0–377.

3. A **hexadecimal byte constant** is a signed or unsigned string of up to two significant hexadecimal digits followed by the letter H (upper case or lower case). The first character in the string must be a digit 0–9; for example, the hexadecimal constant F8 would have to be written as 0F8H. This rule allows the assembler to distinguish between the hexadecimal constant F8H and the symbolic name F8H.

4. A **decimal byte constant** is a signed or unsigned string of decimal digits optionally followed by the letter D (upper case or lower case). The decimal string must be in the range 0–255.

5. A string of characters enclosed in apostrophes (') or double quotation marks ("), in which each character in the string defines one byte constant.

6. A question mark (?), which indicates that a byte of storage is to be allocated but that an initial value is not being specified. The initial value for the allocated byte is unknown.

Each ⟨*byte-constant*⟩ with the exception of a string constant specifies the allocation of one byte of storage. The value of the constant specifies the initial value of that byte. The order of the constants in the list specifies the order in which the storage bytes are to appear in the static data segment. The symbolic ⟨name⟩ is associated with the first byte in the list.

Note that a binary, octal, hexadecimal, or decimal constant may be signed or unsigned. A minus sign (−) in front of a byte constant simply instructs the assembler to perform the two's complement of the binary representation of the constant.

EXAMPLES

The octal constant 377Q is translated by the assembler to the binary bit pattern 11111111. The octal constant − 377Q is translated to the two's complement of this bit pattern, producing the bit pattern 00000001.

The decimal constant 144 is translated by the assembler to the binary bit pattern 10010000. The decimal constant − 144 is translated to the two's complement of this bit pattern, producing the bit pattern 01110000. Note that the decimal integer 144 is within the range for 8-bit unsigned integers. However, the decimal integer − 144 is *not* within the range for 8-bit signed two's complement integers. Unfortunately, the assembler does not flag this occurrence as an error. It translates − 144 to the binary representation for 112 decimal.

EXAMPLE

The following data segment definition instructs the assembler to generate a 12-byte static data segment with the symbolic names and initial values as shown in Table 2.6:

```
DATA        SEGMENT
NUMBER      DB      8CH
COUNT       DB      ?
TWELVE      DB      12
NEG_ONE     DB      -1
ALL_ONES    DB      11111111B
ONE         DB      -377Q
STRING      DB      'A1 (2)'
DATA        ENDS
```

The **DW pseudo-operation** has the following general form:

[⟨name⟩] DW ⟨word-constant-list⟩   [⟨comment⟩]

in which ⟨name⟩ is the symbolic name to be associated with the memory location in which the sequence of data words is to begin and ⟨word-constant-list⟩ is a list of 16-bit constants separated by commas.

A ⟨word-constant⟩ is one of the following:

1. **A binary word constant** is a signed or unsigned string of up to 16 significant binary digits followed by the letter B (upper case or lower case).

TABLE 2.6
Twelve-byte data segment

Symbolic Name	Byte Offset	Hex Contents
NUMBER	0000	8C
COUNT	0001	?
TWELVE	0002	0C
NEG_ONE	0003	FF
ALL_ONES	0004	FF
ONE	0005	01
STRING	0006	41
	0007	31
	0008	20
	0009	28
	000A	32
	000B	29

(? means initial value unknown)

2. An **octal word constant** is a signed or unsigned string of octal digits followed by either the letter O or the letter Q (upper case or lower case). The octal value must lie in the range 0–177777.

3. A **hexadecimal word constant** is a signed or unsigned string of up to four significant hexadecimal digits followed by the letter H (upper case or lower case). The first character in the string must be a digit 0–9.

4. A **decimal word constant** is a signed or unsigned string of decimal digits optionally followed by the letter D (upper case or lower case). The decimal string must be in the range 0–65535.

5. A label, which represents a 16-bit offset within a segment.

6. A question mark (?), which indicates that two bytes (one word) of storage are to be allocated but that an initial value is not being specified. The initial value for the allocated word is unknown.

Each ⟨*word-constant*⟩ specifies the allocation of two consecutive bytes (one word) of storage, with the value of the constant being the initial value of that word. The low-order byte of the 16-bit initial value is stored in the first byte, and the value's high-order byte is stored in the second byte. The order of the constants in the list specifies the order in which the words are to appear in the static data segment. The symbolic ⟨*name*⟩ is associated with the first word in the list.

Note that a binary, octal, hexadecimal, and decimal word constant may be signed or unsigned. A minus sign (−) in front of a word constant simply instructs the assembler to perform the two's complement of the binary representation of the constant.

The following data segment definition instructs the assembler to generate a 6-word (12-byte) static data segment with the symbolic names and initial values as shown in Table 2.7:

```
DATA          SEGMENT
X             DW          ?
Y             DW          -377Q
ORDER         DW          12ABH
ADDR          DW          ORDER
HUNDRED       DW          100
MINUS_ONE     DW          -1
DATA          ENDS
```

The entry

```
ADDR          DW              ORDER
```

allocates a word of storage and assigns as the initial value the offset associated with the symbolic name ORDER (0004). ADDR is said to be a **pointer** to the variable ORDER.

A constant list that contains repetition can be abbreviated somewhat by the use of a duplicate clause. A **duplicate clause** has the following general form:

⟨*repeat-count*⟩ DUP (⟨*constant list*⟩)

This clause specifies that the ⟨*constant-list*⟩ is to be duplicated ⟨*repeat-count*⟩ times in succession. The ⟨*constant-list*⟩ itself may contain a duplicate clause. That is, duplicate clauses may be nested.

TABLE 2.7
Six-word data segment

Symbolic Name	Byte Offset	Hex Contents
X	0000	?
	0001	?
Y	0002	01
	0003	FF
ORDER	0004	AB
	0005	12
ADDR	0006	04
	0007	00
HUNDRED	0008	64
	0009	00
MINUS_ONE	000A	FF
	000B	FF

(? means initial value unknown)

EXAMPLES

The duplicate clause

```
12 DUP(0)
```

is an abbreviation for the constant list

```
0, 0, 0, 0, 0, 0, 0, 0, 0, 0, 0, 0
```

The duplicate clause

```
3 DUP (3 DUP(0),1)
```

is an abbreviation for the constant list

```
0, 0, 0, 1, 0, 0, 0, 1, 0, 0, 0, 1
```

DB and DW pseudo-operations can be used in the same data segment definition.

EXAMPLE

The following data segment definition instructs the assembler to generate a 24-byte static data segment with the symbolic names and initial values as shown in Table 2.8:

```
DATA      SEGMENT
PROMPT    DB        'ENTER N',ØDH,ØAH
N         DW        ?
HUNDRED   DW        1ØØ
ARRAY     DW        5 DUP(?)
FLAG      DB        Ø
DATA      ENDS
```

The entry

```
ARRAY     DW        5 DUP(?)
```

allocates five consecutive words (10 bytes) of storage. The name ARRAY is the symbolic name to be associated with the first of these five words. The question mark (?) means that an initial value is not being specified for any of the five words. The entry, in effect, defines a 5-word array named ARRAY. (The definition and use of arrays is discussed in detail in Chapter 8.)

Constant Definitions

A constant can be given a symbolic name in an IBM PC Assembly Language Program. This symbolic name can then be used anywhere in the program that a constant can be used—it is simply another name for that constant. A symbolic name is assigned to a constant by means of the EQU (equate) pseudo-operation.

TABLE 2.8
Twenty-four-byte
data segment

Symbolic Name	Byte Offset	Hex Contents
PROMPT	0000	45
	0001	4E
	0002	54
	0003	45
	0004	52
	0005	20
	0006	4E
	0007	0D
	0008	0A
N	0009	?
	000A	?
HUNDRED	000B	64
	000C	00
ARRAY	000D	?
	000E	?
	000F	?
	0010	?
	0011	?
	0012	?
	0013	?
	0014	?
	0015	?
	0016	?
FLAG	0017	00

(? means initial value unknown)

The **EQU pseudo-operation** has the following general form:

⟨*name*⟩ EQU ⟨*constant-expression*⟩

in which ⟨*name*⟩ is the symbolic name to be associated with the value of the ⟨*constant-expression*⟩, and ⟨*constant-expression*⟩ can be, among other things, a word constant or a byte constant.

EXAMPLE

```
FALSE  EQU  0
TRUE   EQU  1
```

The symbolic name FALSE can be used anywhere in the program that the constant 0 can be used. The values of FALSE and TRUE cannot be changed during execution.

2.3   Memory Addressing

The Intel 8088 microprocessor can address 1,048,576 bytes (1 megabyte) of memory. To address this amount of memory, a 20-bit address is required. All memory addresses in an IBM PC machine language program are in the form of a segment origin and an offset within the segment. This setup is used whether the address is for an instruction fetch, a data fetch, or a data store. The segment origin is specified by the contents of one of the four segment registers in the BIU of the microprocessor. The offset within the segment can be specified in the machine language instruction itself: by the contents of a pointer register (SP, BP, or IP), by the contents of an index register (DI or SI), or by some combination of these three.

EXAMPLES

The memory address of the next instruction byte to be fetched is specified by the contents of the CS : IP register pair: That is, the contents of the CS-register specifies the start address of the current code segment, and the contents of the IP-register is the offset within that code segment of the instruction byte to be fetched.

The memory address of the top-of-stack item for a push or pop operation is specified by the contents of the SS : SP register pair: That is, the contents of the SS-register specifies the start address of the stack segment, and the contents of the SP-register is the offset within the stack segment of the top-of-stack item.

Address Computation

The generation of a 20-bit physical memory address from a segment origin and an offset within the segment is performed by the BIU, which contains an adder (see Figure 1.17) that converts a memory address from a 16-bit segment origin and a 16-bit offset to a 20-bit physical memory address. Figure 2.2 describes the operation performed by this adder. First the contents of the specified segment register are expanded from 16 bits to 20 bits by concatenating 0000 (binary) onto the lower end of the segment register value. Recall that all segments must begin on a paragraph boundary (i.e., a memory cell whose address is divisible by 16), which means that the 20-bit start address of a segment always ends with 0000, and the 0000 is not stored in the segment register. Only the high-order 16 bit of the start address are stored in the segment register. The 0000 is concatenated to the contents of the segment register before adding an offset. Next the 16-bit offset is added to the expanded 20-bit segment origin address to produce the 20-bit physical memory address.

FIGURE 2.2
IBM PC memory
address generation

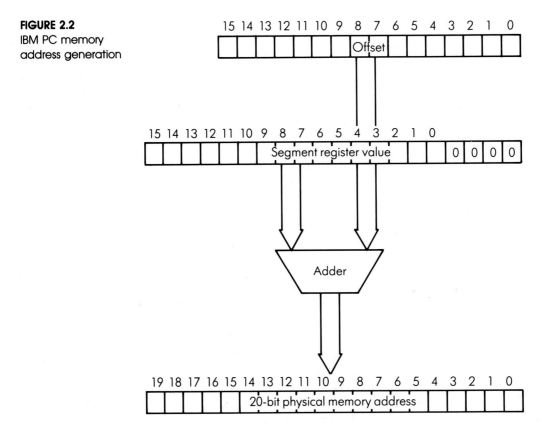

EXAMPLE

Suppose the BIU is about to fetch the next instruction byte and the contents of the CS and IP registers are as follows:

$$CS = 0928 \text{ hex}$$
$$IP = 0022 \text{ hex}$$

The 16-bit contents of the CS-register specifies the 20-bit base address as 09280 hex. Therefore, the adder performs the following operation:

$$\begin{array}{r} 09280 \\ \underline{0022} \\ 092A2 \end{array}$$

The physical memory address of the next instruction byte to be fetched is thus 092A2 hex.

Addressing Modes

Some of the instructions in the machine language of the Intel 8088 microprocessor specify the location of one or more operands to be used in execution of the instruction. For example, an addition instruction specifies the locations of two 8-bit operands or two 16-bit operands to be added together. An operand of such an instruction may be the contents of a general register, a value contained in the instruction itself (an immediate value), or the contents of a memory location. The example programs presented in the early chapters of this book deal primarily with scalar (single-valued) data items and use three Assembly language addressing modes to specify operands.

Register Addressing

With **register addressing**, the operand is the contents of one of the 8-bit or 16-bit registers. A specific register is addressed by coding its two-character symbolic name in the operand field of the instruction. The two-character register designators recognized by the MACRO assembler (MASM) are given in Table 2.9.

Immediate Addressing

With **immediate addressing**, the operand is an 8-bit or 16-bit constant contained in the machine language representation of the instruction. A specific immediate value is referenced by coding a constant representation for the value in the operand field of the instruction. The various constant forms allowed in the IBM PC Assembly language were discussed in Section 2.2.

Direct Addressing

With direct addressing, the operand is the 8-bit contents of a memory location or the 16-bit contents of two consecutive memory locations. A specific memory location is addressed directly by coding its symbolic name into the operand field of the instruction.

TABLE 2.9
Register designators used in register addressing

General Registers		Segment Registers
8-Bit	16-Bit	
AL	AX	CS
BL	BX	SS
CL	CX	DS
DL	DX	ES
AH	BP	
BH	SP	
CH	DI	
DH	SI	

With a direct address, the symbolic name identifies both a segment and an offset within the segment; thus, it identifies a unique memory location. In most cases, the symbolic name used in a direct address is completely defined in the same assembly module. The assembler knows the segment in which the symbolic name is defined, and through the ASSUME pseudo-operation, it knows which segment register is to contain the address of that segment's origin during program execution. The segment register is specified (implicitly or explicitly) in the machine language representation of the instruction. The offset associated with the symbolic name is dependent on the order in which items are defined in the segment that contains the symbolic name. Therefore, the assembler has the information to determine the offset within the segment. The offset is also part of the machine language representation of the instruction. (Several additional methods for specifying operands from memory are discussed in Chapter 8.)

2.4   Data Transfer Instructions

There are three types of data transfer instructions in the IBM PC Assembly language:

1. Instructions for moving data among CPU registers and between memory and CPU registers (MOV and XCHG instructions)
2. Instructions for moving data on and off the stack (PUSH, POP, PUSHF, and POPF instructions)
3. Instructions for moving the address of a memory location to a CPU register (LEA instruction)

Figure 2.3 shows the data transfer capabilities provided by the MOV, XCHG, PUSH, POP, PUSHF, and POPF instructions. The LEA instruction does not appear in Figure 2.3, because it transfers the address of the memory cell and the ones shown transfer the contents of a register or memory cell. Each of these instructions is discussed in the following subsections.

MOV and XCHG Instructions

The two instructions for moving data among CPU registers and between CPU registers and memory are MOV and XCHG. The **MOV instruction** has the following general form:

[⟨*label*⟩] MOV ⟨*destination*⟩, ⟨*source*⟩   [⟨*comment*⟩]

in which ⟨*label*⟩ is the symbolic name to be associated with the memory location in which the instruction is to begin, ⟨*source*⟩ identifies the location of the data that is to be copied, and ⟨*destination*⟩ identifies where the data is to be moved.

The MOV instruction causes a copy of the value of the source operand to replace the value of the destination operand. The value of the source operand is not modified by execution of the MOV instruction. The type attribute of the source and destination operands must match (i.e., both must be byte or both

FIGURE 2.3
Data transfer
instructions

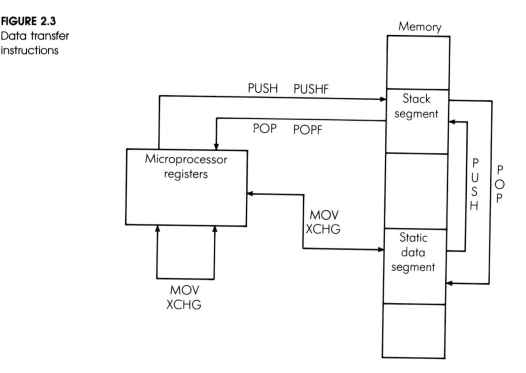

must be word). For technical reasons, not all combinations of destination and source operands are allowed. Figure 2.4 shows the permissible combinations of destination and source operands. Each arrow in the figure indicates a permissible combination of operands for the MOV instruction, that is, an arrow originates at the source operand and points to a destination operand: For example, a MOV instruction can copy the contents of a general register into a segment register (i.e., an arrow leads from general register to segment register). However, the figure also illustrates that a MOV instruction cannot copy the contents of one memory location into another memory location (i.e., no arrow leads from main memory to main memory). None of the bits in the flags register are affected by the execution of a MOV instruction.

EXAMPLES

```
MOV     BH, AL
```

copies the 8-bit value of the AL-register into the BH-register.

```
MOV     AX, COUNT
```

copies the 16-bit value that begins at the memory location specified by COUNT into the AX-register.

```
MOV     CX, 40
```

copies the 16-bit constant 40 from the instruction into the CX-register.

FIGURE 2.4
Allowable operands
for the MOV
instruction

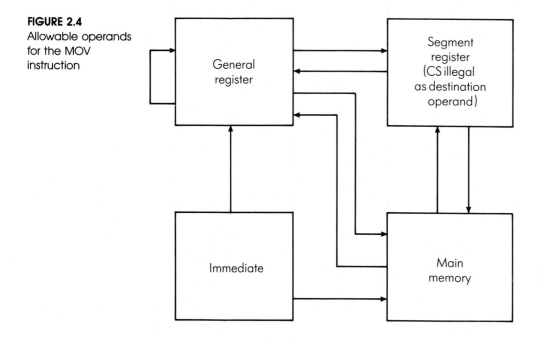

The **XCHG instruction** has the following general form:

[⟨*label*⟩] XCHG ⟨*destination*⟩, ⟨*source*⟩   [⟨*comment*⟩]

in which ⟨*source*⟩ and ⟨*destination*⟩ identify the locations of the values to be exchanged. This instruction causes the value of the source operand to replace the value of the destination operand, and at the same time, causes the value of the destination operand to replace the value of the source operand; that is, the values of the two operands are interchanged. Figure 2.5 shows the possible combinations of operands. Both source and destination operands can be general registers, or one operand can be a general register and the other a memory location. None of

FIGURE 2.5
Allowable operands
for the XCHG
instruction

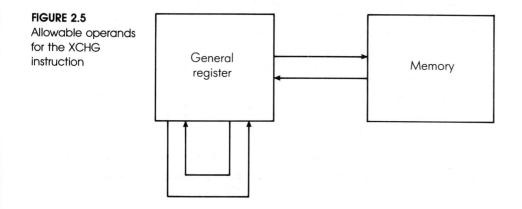

the bits in the flags register are affected by execution of an XCHG instruction. For example,

```
XCHG      AX,DX
```

interchanges the values of the AX and DX registers.

Stack Operations

The stack segment is a list of data words (*not bytes*) in which all insertions and deletions are made at one end of the stack, which is called the **top of the stack**. Inserting a new word in the stack segment is referred to as **pushing** the word onto the top of the stack. Removing a word from the stack is referred to as **popping** the word off the top of the stack. When a word is pushed onto the stack, it becomes the new top-of-stack data item. All data items previously in the stack are pushed down one position relative to the top of the stack. When the word at the top of the stack is popped from the stack, the data items remaining in the stack pop up one position relative to the top of the stack. The new top-of-stack data item is the word that was at the top of the stack when the popped item was pushed. The only item that can be popped from the stack is the word at the top of the stack, which is also the last word that was pushed onto the stack.

During execution of an IBM PC Assembly language program, the SS : SP register pair always addresses the top-of-stack data item. The SS-register contains the address of the origin of the stack segment, and the SP-register contains the offset within the stack segment of the current top-of-stack data item. The bottom of the stack is fixed at the highest offset, and the top of the stack changes dynamically as push and pop operations are performed. The SS and SP registers are automatically maintained by the microprocessor and are not directly manipulated by the program.

The instructions for moving data on and off the stack are PUSH, POP, PUSHF, and POPF.

The **PUSH instruction** has the following general form:

[⟨*label*⟩] PUSH ⟨*source*⟩   [⟨*comment*⟩]

in which ⟨*source*⟩ identifies the location of a 16-bit value to be pushed onto the stack. This instruction causes the value of the SP-register to be decremented by 2 and the 16-bit value of the source operand to be stored in the stack segment at the location pointed to by the SS : SP register pair (the new top of the stack). The source operand can be either a general register, a segment register, or a memory location. The type attribute of the source operand must be word. None of the bits in the flags register are affected by execution of a PUSH instruction.

The **POP instruction** has the following general form:

[⟨*label*⟩] POP ⟨*destination*⟩   [⟨*comment*⟩]

in which ⟨*destination*⟩ identifies the location in which the data popped from the top of the stack is to be placed. This instruction causes a copy of the 16-bit stack segment value pointed to by the SS : SP register pair (i.e., the top-of-stack value) to replace the 16-bit value of the destination operand and the SP-register to be incremented by 2. The increment of the SP-register logically pops up all subsequent stack segment values one position relative to the top of the stack. The new top-of-stack value is the one that was at the top of the stack when the value just copied was pushed onto the stack. The destination operand can be either a general register, a segment register other than the CS-register, or a memory location. The type attribute of the destination operand must be word. None of the bits in the flags register are affected by execution of a POP instruction.

The **PUSHF instruction** has the following general form:

[⟨*label*⟩] PUSHF   [⟨*comment*⟩]

This instruction causes the value of the SP-register to be decremented by 2 and the 16-bit value of the flags register to be stored in the stack segment at the location pointed to by the SS : SP register pair (i.e., the new top of the stack). None of the bits in the flags register are modified by execution of a PUSHF instruction.

The **POPF instruction** has the following general form:

[⟨*label*⟩] POPF   [⟨*comment*⟩]

This instruction causes a copy of the 16-bit stack segment value pointed to by the SS : SP register pair (that is, the top-of-stack value) to replace the 16-bit value of the flags register and the SP-register to be incremented by 2. All of the bits in the flags register are potentially modified by execution of a POPF instruction. Note that the POPF instruction provides the only way for a program to modify explicitly certain bits of the flags register. (Explicit modification of flags register bits is discussed in Chapter 6.)

EXAMPLES

PUSH AX

pushes the 16-bit value of the AX-register onto the stack.

POP BX

pops the 16-bit value from the top of the stack and places it in the BX-register.

PUSHF

pushes the 16-bit value of the flags register onto the stack.

POPF

pops the 16-bit value from the top of the stack and places it in the flags register.

Figures 2.6–2.10 show the mechanics of stack operations in an IBM PC Assembly language program. The stack segment shown is an 8-word (16-byte) stack segment. Figure 2.6 shows how the stack is initialized to empty. In the figure, the SS-register contains the address of the origin of the stack segment, and the SP-register contains the offset of the memory location immediately following the stack segment.

Data is pushed onto the stack and popped from the stack in units of 16 bits (1 word). A push operation first decrements the offset in the SP-register by 2 (i.e., 2 bytes or 1 word) and then stores a 16-bit word at memory locations SS:SP (low-order byte) and SS:SP + 1 (high-order byte). A pop operation copies the word at memory locations SS:SP (low-order byte) and SS:SP + 1 (high-order byte) and then increments the contents of the SP-register by 2. The SS:SP register pair always specifies the memory address of the top-of-stack data item.

Figure 2.7 shows the result of pushing the hexadecimal value 4A9F onto the empty stack. The SP-register has been decremented to 000E, the offset of the top-of-stack item 4A9F. Note that the two bytes of the 16-bit value 4A9F are stored in reverse order beginning at offset 000E; that is, the low-order byte (9F) is stored at offset 000E, and the high-order byte (4A) is stored at offset 000F.

Figure 2.8 shows the result of pushing the hexadecimal value 373F onto the stack. The SP-register has been decremented to 000C, the offset of the new top-of-stack item 373F. Again, the two bytes of the value are stored in reverse order.

A pop operation would copy the hexadecimal value 373F to the destination operand and leave the stack segment as shown in Figure 2.9. The SP-register has been incremented to 000E, the offset of the new top-of-stack item 4A9F. This item is the item that was at the top of the stack at the time that 373F, the value just popped, was pushed onto the stack. Note that the value 373F is still in the stack segment, but it is not included in the logical stack. The logical stack begins with the word pointed to by the top-of-stack pointer (i.e., the SS:SP register pair) and goes through the end of the stack segment, which is the bottom of the logical stack. The storage cells from the origin of the stack segment up to but not including the word pointed to by the SS:SP register pair currently are not part of the logical stack.

Figure 2.10 shows the result of pushing the hexadecimal value 60C2 onto the stack. The SP-register has been decremented to 000C, the offset of the new top-of-stack item 60C2. Note that the value 60C2 replaces the value 373F that had previously been stored in these locations.

The SS and SP registers are automatically maintained by the microprocessor as it executes push and pop operations. These registers are not normally manipulated directly by the program.

Address Accessing Operators and Instructions

It is often necessary in an Assembly language program to obtain the memory address of a data value rather than the value itself. Several of the I/O sub-

FIGURE 2.6
Stack segment—
empty stack

Hexadecimal memory address	Stack segment	Offset	SS : SP
09170		0000	0917 | 0010
09171		0001	
09172		0002	09170
09173		0003	0010
09174		0004	‾‾‾‾‾
09175		0005	09180
09176		0006	
09177		0007	
09178		0008	
09179		0009	
0917A		000A	
0917B		000B	
0917C		000C	
0917D		000D	
0917E		000E	
0917F		000F	

FIGURE 2.7
Stack segment—
after push of 4A9F

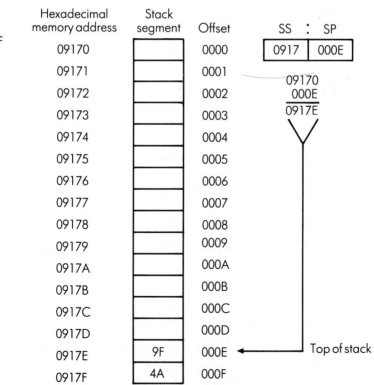

Hexadecimal memory address	Stack segment	Offset	SS : SP
09170		0000	0917 | 000E
09171		0001	
09172		0002	09170
09173		0003	000E
09174		0004	‾‾‾‾‾
09175		0005	0917E
09176		0006	
09177		0007	
09178		0008	
09179		0009	
0917A		000A	
0917B		000B	
0917C		000C	
0917D		000D	
0917E	9F	000E	← Top of stack
0917F	4A	000F	

FIGURE 2.8
Stack segment—
after push of 4A9F
and 373F

Hexadecimal memory address	Stack segment	Offset
09170		0000
09171		0001
09172		0002
09173		0003
09174		0004
09175		0005
09176		0006
09177		0007
09178		0008
09179		0009
0917A		000A
0917B		000B
0917C	3F	000C
0917D	37	000D
0917E	9F	000E
0917F	4A	000F

SS : SP

0917	000C

$$\begin{array}{r} 09170 \\ 000C \\ \hline 0917C \end{array}$$

Top of stack

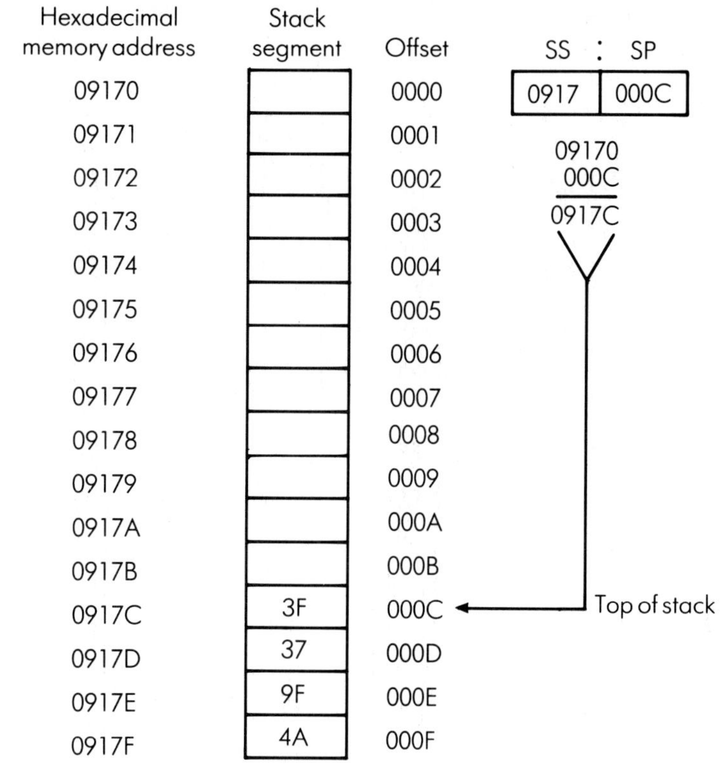

FIGURE 2.9
Stack segment—
after push of 4A9F
and 373F and pop
of 373F

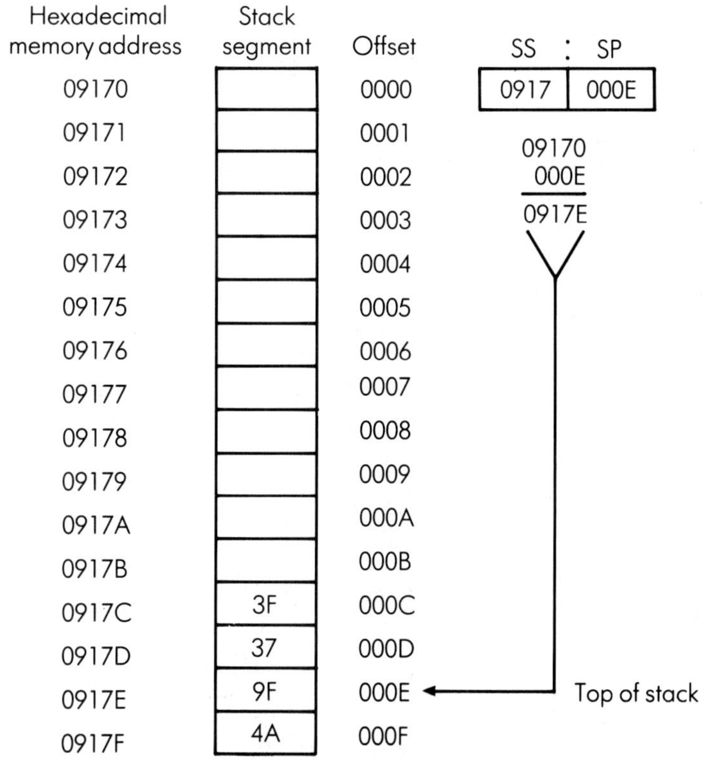

Hexadecimal memory address	Stack segment	Offset
09170		0000
09171		0001
09172		0002
09173		0003
09174		0004
09175		0005
09176		0006
09177		0007
09178		0008
09179		0009
0917A		000A
0917B		000B
0917C	3F	000C
0917D	37	000D
0917E	9F	000E
0917F	4A	000F

SS : SP

0917	000E

$$\begin{array}{r} 09170 \\ 000E \\ \hline 0917E \end{array}$$

Top of stack

85

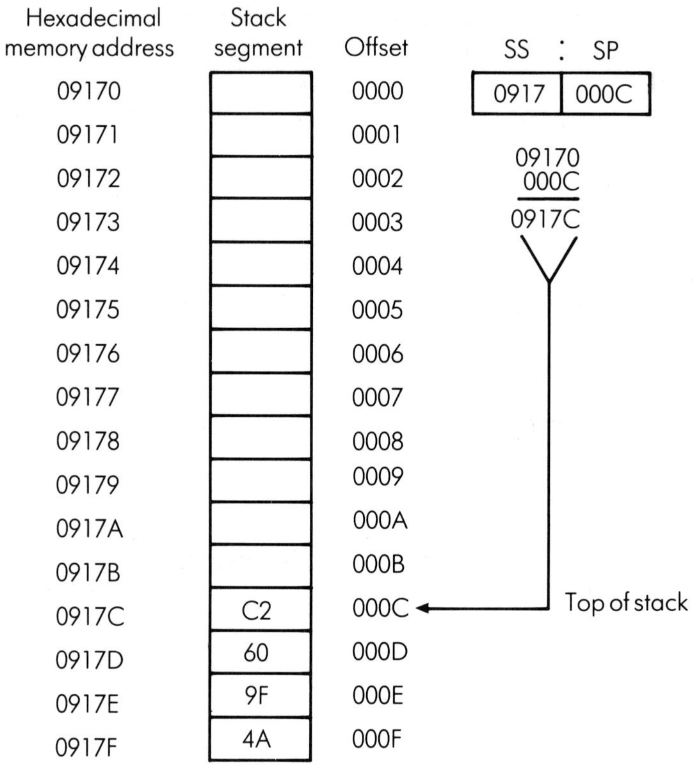

FIGURE 2.10
Stack segment—
after push of 4A9F
and 373F, pop of
373F, and push of
60C2

Hexadecimal memory address	Stack segment	Offset
09170		0000
09171		0001
09172		0002
09173		0003
09174		0004
09175		0005
09176		0006
09177		0007
09178		0008
09179		0009
0917A		000A
0917B		000B
0917C	C2	000C
0917D	60	000D
0917E	9F	000E
0917F	4A	000F

SS : SP

0917	000C

$$\begin{array}{r} 09170 \\ \underline{000C} \\ 0917C \end{array}$$

Top of stack (at offset 000C)

procedures referenced in this book require as an input the beginning address of a memory area in the caller's environment. This address identifies either memory locations that contain the data to be output or memory locations in which the input data are to be stored. Recall that all memory addresses in the IBM PC machine language are in the form of a segment origin (value of a segment register) and an offset within the segment. The two operators SEG and OFFSET and the load effective address (LEA) instruction are used to obtain either the segment or offset portion of the address of a memory location.

The **SEG operator** is a value-returning operator that appears as follows:

SEG ⟨*symbolic-name*⟩

in which ⟨*symbolic-name*⟩ is either a variable name or the label of an instruction. This operator when used with a ⟨*symbolic-name*⟩ is an immediate operand whose 16-bit value is the high-order 16 bits of the segment portion of the memory address associated with the ⟨*symbolic-name*⟩. This operator can be used in any instruction that allows an immediate operand.

The **OFFSET operator** is a value-returning operator that appears as follows:

OFFSET ⟨*symbolic-name*⟩

in which ⟨*symbolic-name*⟩ is either a variable name or the label of an instruction. This operator when used with a ⟨*symbolic-name*⟩ is an immediate operand whose 16-bit value is the offset portion of memory address associated with the ⟨*symbolic-name*⟩. It can be used in any instruction that allows an immediate operand.

EXAMPLES

```
MOV AX,SEG DATA
```

moves to the AX-register the high-order 16 bits of the segment portion of the address of the variable DATA.

```
MOV DI,OFFSET MSG
```

moves to the DI-register the offset portion of the address of the variable MSG.

The **load effective address (LEA) instruction** generates the offset portion of a memory address as an operand. The LEA instruction has the following general form:

[⟨*label*⟩] LEA ⟨*destination*⟩, ⟨*source*⟩   [⟨*comment*⟩]

in which ⟨*destination*⟩ is the designation of the 16-bit general register whose value is to be replaced by the offset and ⟨*source*⟩ is the address expression from which the offset is to be computed. This instruction causes the value of the 16-bit general register specified as the destination operand to be replaced by the computed offset of the memory location specified by the source operand. None of the bits of the flags register are affected by execution of an LEA instruction.

EXAMPLE

```
LEA DI,PROMPT
```

compute the offset portion of the address of the memory location associated with the name PROMPT and place that value in the DI-register.

The two instructions

```
LEA DI,PROMPT
```

and

```
MOV DI,OFFSET PROMPT
```

have the same effect as each other. Both load the DI-register with the offset portion of the address of the variable PROMPT. The OFFSET operator actually directs the assembler to compute the offset of variable PROMPT and to embed that value in the machine language instruction as an immediate operand, which means that the operand of the OFFSET operator must be a symbolic name whose offset is known at assembly time. The LEA instruction, on the other hand, causes the offset of PROMPT to be computed when the LEA instruction is executed, which means that the source operand of an LEA instruction can be any address expression. (The various forms of memory addresses that can appear in memory referencing instructions are discussed in Section 8.4.)

2.5 Example Program—Demonstrate Data Definition and Data Transfer

Explanation of Program

Program Listing 2.1 illustrates a program that demonstrates the data definition pseudo-operations and data transfer instructions presented in earlier sections of this chapter. It shows a complete IBM PC Assembly language program that consists of three segments, a stack segment, a data segment, and a code segment.

```
 1: ;                    PROGRAM LISTING 2.1
 2: ; PROGRAM TO DEMONSTRATE
 3: ;           1. DATA DEFINITION PSEUDO-OPERATIONS
 4: ;           2. DATA TRANSFER INSTRUCTIONS
 5: ;
 6: ; S T A C K   S E G M E N T   D E F I N I T I O N
 7: ;
 8: STACK         SEGMENT STACK
 9:               DB      16 DUP (?)
10: STACK         ENDS
11: ZERO_ONE      EQU     55H                   ;55 HEX
12: ;
13: ; D A T A   S E G M E N T   D E F I N I T I O N
14: ;
15: DATA          SEGMENT
16: ;                                           ;BYTE        WORD
17: BYTE1         DB      0                     ;00 HEX
18: BYTE2         DB      ZERO_ONE              ;55 HEX
19: BYTE3         DB      0AAH                  ;AA HEX
20: BYTE4         DB      377Q                  ;FF HEX
21: WORD3         DW      1010101011111111B     ;FF HEX      AAFF HEX
22:                                             ;AA HEX
23: WORD4         DW      000125Q               ;55 HEX      0055 HEX
24:                                             ;00 HEX
25: WORD1         EQU     WORD PTR BYTE1        ;BYTE2:BYTE1 = 5500 HEX
26: WORD2         EQU     WORD PTR BYTE3        ;BYTE4:BYTE3 = FFAA HEX
27: DATA          ENDS
28: ;
29: ; C O D E   S E G M E N T   D E F I N I T I O N
30: ;
31: CODE          SEGMENT
32:               ASSUME  CS:CODE,SS:STACK,DS:DATA
33: EX_2_1        PROC    FAR
34:               PUSH    DS                    ;PUSH RETURN SEG ADDR ON STACK
```

```
35:                  SUB      AX,AX           ;PUSH RETURN OFFSET OF ZERO
36:                  PUSH     AX              ;ON STACK
37:                  MOV      AX,SEG DATA     ;SET DS REGISTER TO
38:                  MOV      DS,AX           ;POINT TO DATA SEGMENT
39:                  NOP
40:                                           ;AH AL BH BL CH CL DH DL
41:                  MOV      AL,BYTE1        ;   00
42:                  MOV      AH,AL           ;00 00
43:                  MOV      AL,ZERO_ONE     ;00 55
44:                  MOV      BX,WORD3        ;00 55 AA FF
45:                  MOV      CX,WORD2        ;00 55 AA FF FF AA
46:                  MOV      DX,WORD4        ;00 55 AA FF FF AA 00 55
47:                  XCHG     DH,DL           ;00 55 AA FF FF AA 55 00
48:                  PUSH     AX              ;00 55 AA FF FF AA 55 00
49:                  PUSH     CX              ;00 55 AA FF FF AA 55 00
50:                  POP      AX              ;FF AA AA FF FF AA 55 00
51:                  POP      CX              ;FF AA AA FF 00 55 55 00
52:                  XCHG     CX,DX           ;FF AA AA FF 55 00 00 55
53:  ;
54:                  MOV      WORD1,BX        ;WORD1 BYTE1    FF HEX
55:                                           ;      BYTE2    AA HEX
56:                  MOV      BYTE3,DL        ;WORD2 BYTE3    55 HEX
57:                  MOV      BYTE4,CL        ;      BYTE4    00 HEX
58:                  MOV      WORD3,CX        ;WORD3          00 HEX
59:                                           ;               55 HEX
60:                  MOV      WORD4,AX        ;WORD4          AA HEX
61:                                           ;               FF HEX
62:                  RET                      ;RETURN TO OS
63:  EX_2_1         ENDP
64:  CODE           ENDS
65:*                END      EX_2_1
```

*

The program begins with a prologue (lines 1–4) that explains the function of the program. This program does not implement an algorithm for solving a specific problem. It simply demonstrates the pseudo-operations and instructions covered in this chapter.

The definition of the program's stack segment appears in lines 5–10: Lines 5–7 are comment lines used to indicate that a stack segment definition follows; the actual definition of the stack segment appears in lines 8–10. Recall that a segment definition begins with a SEGMENT pseudo-operation (line 8) and terminates with an ENDS pseudo-operation (line 10). The DB pseudo-operation in line 9 defines the size of the stack segment as being 16 bytes (8 words) and specifies that no initial values are to be assigned to the stack segment locations. Note that no label is to be associated with the stack locations.

The EQU pseudo-operation in line 11 equates the symbolic name ZERO_ONE with the 8-bit constant 55 hex (01010101 binary). Anywhere that the symbolic name ZERO_ONE appears, the assembler substitutes the constant 55 hex. The symbolic name ZERO_ONE is simply another way of saying 55H in this program. ZERO_ONE is not a variable name and the value associated with the symbolic name ZERO_ONE cannot be changed during program execution.

The comments in lines 12–14 indicate that a static data segment definition follows. The data segment definition begins with the SEGMENT pseudo-operation in line 15 and terminates with the ENDS pseudo-operation in line 27. The organization of the data segment generated by this definition is described in Table 2.10.

The size of the data segment is 8 bytes as defined by the DB and DW pseudo-operations in lines 17–23. The first byte in the data segment, the byte at offset 0000 from the beginning of the data segment, is defined by the DB pseudo-operation in line 17. This byte can be referenced by the symbolic name BYTE1 and is assigned an initial value of zero. The second byte in the data segment (offset 0001) is defined by the DB pseudo-operation in line 18. It can be referenced by the symbolic name BYTE2 and has the initial value 55 hex (01010101 binary). The constant that appears in the operand field of line 18 is the named constant ZERO_ONE, whose definition appears in line 11. The third byte in the data segment (offset 0002) is defined by the DB pseudo-operation in line 19. It can be referenced by the symbolic name BYTE3 and has the initial value AA hex (10101010 binary). The fourth byte in the data segment (offset 0003) is defined by the DB pseudo-operation in line 20. It can be referenced by the symbolic name BYTE4 and has the initial value 377 octal (FF hex or 11111111 binary).

The fifth and sixth bytes in the data segment (offsets 0004 and 0005) are defined by the DW pseudo-operation in line 21. These two bytes can be referenced collectively as a 16-bit word by the symbolic name WORD3. The initial value of this 16-bit word is 1010101011111111 binary (AAFF hex). In an IBM PC's memory, a 16-bit word is stored as two consecutive 8-bit bytes. The low-order byte is stored first, followed by the high-order byte. This sequencing means that the fifth byte of the data segment has the initial value 11111111 binary (FF hex), and the sixth byte has the initial value 10101010 binary (AA hex).

The seventh and eighth bytes in the data segment (offsets 0006 and 0007) are defined by the DW pseudo-operation in line 23. These two bytes can be referenced collectively as a 16-bit word by the symbolic name WORD4. The initial value of this 16-bit word is 000125 octal (0055 hex or 0000000001010101

TABLE 2.10

Organization of the static data segment defined in Program Listing 2.1

Symbolic Name(s)	Offset from Beginning of Segment	Initial Value (Hexadecimal)
BYTE1/WORD1	0000	00
BYTE2	0001	55
BYTE3/WORD2	0002	AA
BYTE4	0003	FF
WORD3	0004	FF
	0005	AA
WORD4	0006	55
	0007	00

binary). Since the low-order byte is stored first followed by the high-order byte, the initial value of the seventh byte is 01010101 binary (55 hex), and the initial value of the eighth byte is zero.

The initial value of a variable is the value of that variable at the time program execution begins. A variable's value can be changed during program execution. The initial value of a variable remains until replaced by a new value during program execution.

The symbolic names BYTE1, BYTE2, BYTE3, and BYTE4 each has a type attribute of BYTE and is a reference to an 8-bit operand in the data segment. The symbolic names WORD3 and WORD4 each has a type attribute of WORD and is a reference to a 16-bit operand in the data segment.

Lines 25 and 26 demonstrate an additional capability provided by the EQU pseudo-operation. In line 25, this pseudo-operation equates the symbolic name WORD1 to the same offset that is referenced by the symbolic name BYTE1, offset 0000. The operator PTR with the WORD type prefix overrides the type attribute of the symbolic name BYTE1 with the type attribute WORD; that is, the symbolic name WORD1 has a type attribute of WORD. A reference to the symbolic name WORD1 is a reference to the 16-bit value beginning at offset 0000 within the data segment. Since the low byte is stored first followed by the high byte, the 16-bit initial value of WORD1 is 5500 hex. The EQU pseudo-operation in line 26 equates the symbolic name WORD2 to the same offset that is referenced by the symbolic name BYTE3, offset 0002. The symbolic name WORD2 has type attribute WORD, whereas the symbolic name BYTE3 has type attribute BYTE. A reference to the symbolic name WORD2 is a reference to the 16-bit value beginning at offset 0002 within the data segment. The initial value of WORD2 is FFAA hex.

The comments in lines 28–30 indicate that a code segment definition follows. The code segment definition begins with the SEGMENT pseudo-operation in line 31 and terminates with the ENDS pseudo-operation in line 64. The ASSUME pseudo-operation in line 32 tells the assembler to assume that, at execution time, the CS-register will specify the origin of the code segment, the SS-register will specify the origin of the stack segment, and the DS-register will specify the origin of the data segment. All machine language addresses generated by the assembler specify a segment register and an offset from the segment origin specified by that segment register. Each symbolic name referenced in the program has associated with it an offset within the segment in which it is defined. For example, the symbolic name BYTE4 references the byte at offset 0003 from the beginning of the data segment. The ASSUME pseudo-operation in line 32 tells the assembler to assume that the origin of the data segment will be in the DS-register at execution time. So the address of BYTE4 is offset 0003 relative to the origin specified by the contents of the DS-register (DS:0003). The code segment and stack segment origins in the CS and SS segment registers are initialized automatically by DOS when the program is placed into execution. However, it is the program's responsibility to initialize the DS-register with the origin of the data segment, and this initialization must be done prior to the first reference to an item in the data segment.

The code segment definition in Program Listing 2.1 contains one procedure definition. The procedure definition begins with the PROC pseudo-operation in line 33 and terminates with the ENDP pseudo-operation in line 63. The procedure can be referenced by the symbolic name EX_2_1 and has a type attribute FAR. (The type attributes NEAR and FAR are discussed in Chapter 5.).

Before DOS loads an executable program and places the main procedure of that program into execution, it sets up a 256-byte memory block called the **program segment prefix (PSP)**. The PSP is set up at the lowest available paragraph boundary in memory, and the program is loaded immediately following the PSP. The PSP is the communication link between DOS and the executable program. Among other things, the PSP contains an instruction that, when executed, returns control to DOS. This instruction is located at offset 0000 in the PSP. When the user program terminates, it can return to DOS by jumping to the instruction at offset 0 of the PSP. The return to DOS can be accomplished by execution of an RET instruction if the segment origin and offset of the first location of the PSP are at the top of the stack. The three instructions in lines 34–36 place the segment origin and offset of the first location of the PSP at the top of the stack. When DOS passes control to the main procedure of an executable program, both the DS and ES segment registers specify the segment origin of the PSP. The PUSH instruction in line 34 pushes this segment origin onto the stack. The SUB (subtract) instruction in line 35 puts a zero into the AX-register. (The SUB instruction is discussed in detail in Chapter 3.) The PUSH instruction in line 36 pushes the zero in the AX-register onto the stack. Zero is the offset from the segment origin of the first location of the PSP, the location of the instruction that returns control to DOS. Both lines 35 and 36 are required to push zero onto the stack, since the PUSH instruction cannot have an immediate value as its operand.

The instruction

```
MOV AX, 0
```

accomplishes the same task as the instruction

```
SUB AX, AX
```

However, the MOV instruction is a 3-byte instruction, whereas the SUB instruction is a 2-byte instruction. At this point, such considerations are not so important, but in large programs efficiency considerations may become quite important.

The two instructions in lines 37 and 38 initialize the DS-register to contain the origin of the data segment defined in lines 15–27. The MOV instruction in line 37 moves to the AX-register the high-order 16 bits of the segment portion of the memory address associated with the symbolic name DATA. This instruction loads the AX-register with the origin of the data segment. The MOV instruction in line 38 moves this segment origin from the AX-register to the DS-register. Two instructions are required here because the instruction

```
MOV DS, SEG DATA
```

is syntactically illegal. The operand SEG DATA is an immediate operand, and a MOV instruction whose destination operand is a segment register cannot have an immediate value as its source operand (see Figure 2.4).

The instruction in line 39 has an op code NOP that stands for *No OPeration* and performs no operation. That is, this instruction has no effect on the program. Its purpose is discussed later in this section.

The instructions in lines 41–61 demonstrate various forms of the MOV, XCHG, PUSH, and POP instructions using the data defined in the data segment. The comments on the instructions in lines 41–52 show the resulting value in the AX (AH and AL), BX (BH and BL), CX (CH and CL), and DX (DH and DL) registers. A blank indicates that the value of that register is unknown.

The MOV instruction in line 41 moves the value of the variable BYTE1, which in this case is zero, to the AL-register. This instruction performs a copy operation, so the value of variable BYTE1 is not modified. In this MOV instruction, the destination operand is an 8-bit general register (AL-register), and the source operand is the 8-bit contents of the memory location specified by BYTE1.

The MOV instruction in line 42 moves to the AH-register a copy of the value of the AL-register (zero). The AL-register is not modified by execution of this instruction. In this MOV instruction, the destination operand is an 8-bit general register (AH-register), and the source operand is another 8-bit general register (AL-register).

The MOV instruction in line 43 moves to the AL-register a constant byte value of 55 hex, which is contained in memory immediately following the first byte of the MOV instruction. In this MOV instruction, the destination operand is an 8-bit general register (AL-register), and the source operand is an immediate value (a constant value that is part of the machine language representation of the MOV instruction). Recall that the symbolic name ZERO_ONE is a name for the constant 55 hexadecimal. It was defined by the EQU pseudo-operation in line 11.

The MOV instruction in line 44 moves to the BX-register a copy of the 16-bit value of the variable WORD3 (AAFF hexadecimal). The MOV instruction in line 45 moves to the CX-register a copy of the 16-bit value of the variable WORD2 (FFAA hexadecimal). The MOV instruction in line 46 moves to the DX-register a copy of the 16-bit value of the variable WORD4 (0055 hexadecimal). In each of these MOV instructions, the destination operand is a 16-bit general register, and the source operand is the 16-bit contents of two consecutive memory locations. In each case, the source operand (the memory operand) is not modified by execution of the instruction.

The XCHG instruction in line 47 interchanges the values of two 8-bit general registers (DH and DL registers). Prior to execution of this XCHG instruction, the DH-register had the value 00 hex, and the DL-register had the value 55 hex. After execution of this XCHG instruction, the DH-register has the value 55 hex, and the DL-register has the value 00 hex.

The PUSH and POP instructions in lines 48–51 interchange the values of the 16-bit AX and CX registers. The PUSH instruction in line 48 pushes the 16-bit value of the AX-register onto the top of the stack. The PUSH instruction in line 49 pushes the 16-bit value of the CX-register onto the top of the stack, which pushes the AX-register value down one position relative to the top of the stack. The POP instruction in line 50 pops the top-of-stack value (a copy of the CX-register value) into the AX-register, which returns the previous AX-register value to the top of the stack. The POP instruction in line 51 pops the top-of-stack value (the previous AX-register value) into the CX-register. Prior to execution of these PUSH and POP instructions, the AX-register had the value 0055 hex, and the CX-register had the value FFAA hex. After execution, the AX-register has the value FFAA hex, and the CX-register has the value 0055 hex.

The XCHG instruction in line 52 interchanges the values of two 16-bit general registers (CX and DX registers). Prior to this execution, the CX-register had the value 0055 hex, and the DX-register had the value 5500 hex. After execution, the CX-register has the value 5500 hex, and the DX-register has the value 0055 hex.

At this point, the variables defined in the data segment still have their initial values as shown in Table 2.10, and the general registers have the values shown in Table 2.11.

The MOV instruction in line 54 replaces the 16-bit value of the two memory locations specified by the symbolic name WORD1 with a copy of the value of the BX-register (AAFF hex). Since a 16-bit value is stored in memory with low byte followed by high byte, BYTE1 receives the value FF hex, and BYTE2 receives the value AA hex. The value of the BX-register is not modified by execution of this MOV instruction. In this instruction, the destination operand is a 16-bit memory location (the one specified by the symbolic name WORD1), and the source operand is a 16-bit general register (BX-register).

The MOV instruction in line 56 replaces the 8-bit value of the memory location specified by the symbolic name BYTE3 with a copy of the value in the DL-register (55 hex). The MOV instruction in line 57 replaces the 8-bit value of the memory location specified by the symbolic name BYTE4 with a copy of the value in the CL-register (00 hex). In each of these MOV instructions, the destination operand is an 8-bit byte in memory, and the source operand is an 8-bit general register. In each case, the source operand (the 8-bit general register) is not modified by execution of the instruction.

The MOV instruction in line 58 replaces the 16-bit value of the two memory locations specified by the symbolic name WORD3 with a copy of the value in the CX-register (5500 hex). The MOV instruction in line 60 replaces the 16-bit value of the two memory locations specified by the symbolic name WORD4 with a copy of the value in the AX-register (FFAA hex). In each of these MOV instructions, the destination operand is a 16-bit word in memory,

TABLE 2.11

General register values at line 53 of Program Listing 2.1

Register	AX		BX		CX		DX	
	AH	AL	BH	BL	CH	CL	DH	DL
Hex Value	FF	AA	AA	FF	55	00	00	55

TABLE 2.12

Data segment
values at line 61 of
Program Listing 2.1

Symbolic Name(s)	Offset from Beginning of Segment	Value (Hexadecimal)
BYTE1/WORD1	0000	FF
BYTE2	0001	AA
BYTE3/WORD2	0002	55
BYTE4	0003	00
WORD3	0004	00
	0005	55
WORD4	0006	AA
	0007	FF

and the source operand is a 16-bit general register. In each case, the source operand (the 16-bit general register) is not modified by execution of the instruction.

At this point, the general registers still have the values shown in Table 2.11, and the variables defined in the data segment have the values shown in Table 2.12.

The RET instruction in line 62 pops the offset and segment origin of the first location of the PSP from the top of the stack and transfers control to that location. The instruction at that location returns control to DOS.

The END pseudo-operation (line 65) follows the code segment definition and marks the physical end of the assembly module. This operation tells the assembler that program execution is to begin at the first instruction in the procedure whose symbolic name is EX_2_1.

Debug Trace of Program

DEBUG Listing 2.2 shows a trace of Program Listing 2.1 using the DEBUG utility program. This listing is a hard copy of the inputs and outputs that appeared on the display during the debug session. To get a printout of a debug session, press CTRL PRTSC at the keyboard before invoking debug. The command

```
debug ex_2_1.exe
```

loads the debug program, begins execution of the debug program, and has the debug program load the executable module ex_2_1.exe for tracing (see DEBUG Listing 2.2). The hyphen (-) prompt in DEBUG Listing 2.2 is the prompt output by debug to indicate that it is ready to accept commands.

The first command in DEBUG Listing 2.2, r, is a request to display the current value of each of the processor registers. DEBUG responds by displaying three lines (see DEBUG Listing 2.2). Note that all values in this display are in hexadecimal.

```
                            DEBUG LISTING 2.2
debug ex_2_1.exe
-r
AX=0000  BX=0000  CX=0059  DX=0000  SP=0010  BP=0000  SI=0000  DI=0000
DS=0916  ES=0916  SS=0926  CS=0928  IP=0000   NV UP DI PL NZ NA PO NC
0928:0000 1E            PUSH     DS
-t

AX=0000  BX=0000  CX=0059  DX=0000  SP=000E  BP=0000  SI=0000  DI=0000
DS=0916  ES=0916  SS=0926  CS=0928  IP=0001   NV UP DI PL NZ NA PO NC
0928:0001 2BC0          SUB      AX,AX
-t

AX=0000  BX=0000  CX=0059  DX=0000  SP=000E  BP=0000  SI=0000  DI=0000
DS=0916  ES=0916  SS=0926  CS=0928  IP=0003   NV UP DI PL ZR NA PE NC
0928:0003 50            PUSH     AX
-t

AX=0000  BX=0000  CX=0059  DX=0000  SP=000C  BP=0000  SI=0000  DI=0000
DS=0916  ES=0916  SS=0926  CS=0928  IP=0004   NV UP DI PL ZR NA PE NC
0928:0004 B82709        MOV      AX,0927
-d ss:0,f
0926:0000   00 00 00 00 00 00 04 00-28 09 10 06 00 00 16 09    ........(.......
-t

AX=0927  BX=0000  CX=0059  DX=0000  SP=000C  BP=0000  SI=0000  DI=0000
DS=0916  ES=0916  SS=0926  CS=0928  IP=0007   NV UP DI PL ZR NA PE NC
0928:0007 8ED8          MOV      DS,AX
-t

AX=0927  BX=0000  CX=0059  DX=0000  SP=000C  BP=0000  SI=0000  DI=0000
DS=0927  ES=0916  SS=0926  CS=0928  IP=000A   NV UP DI PL ZR NA PE NC
0928:000A A00000        MOV      AL,[0000]                        DS:0000=00
-d ds:0,f
0927:0000   00 55 AA FF FF AA 55 00-00 00 00 00 00 00 00 00    .U*..*U.........
-t

AX=0900  BX=0000  CX=0059  DX=0000  SP=000C  BP=0000  SI=0000  DI=0000
DS=0927  ES=0916  SS=0926  CS=0928  IP=000D   NV UP DI PL ZR NA PE NC
0928:000D 8AE0          MOV      AH,AL
-t

AX=0000  BX=0000  CX=0059  DX=0000  SP=000C  BP=0000  SI=0000  DI=0000
DS=0927  ES=0916  SS=0926  CS=0928  IP=000F   NV UP DI PL ZR NA PE NC
0928:000F B055          MOV      AL,55
-t

AX=0055  BX=0000  CX=0059  DX=0000  SP=000C  BP=0000  SI=0000  DI=0000
DS=0927  ES=0916  SS=0926  CS=0928  IP=0011   NV UP DI PL ZR NA PE NC
0928:0011 8B1E0400      MOV      BX,[0004]                        DS:0004=AAFF
-t

AX=0055  BX=AAFF  CX=0059  DX=0000  SP=000C  BP=0000  SI=0000  DI=0000
DS=0927  ES=0916  SS=0926  CS=0928  IP=0015   NV UP DI PL ZR NA PE NC
0928:0015 8B0E0200      MOV      CX,[0002]                        DS:0002=FFAA
-t

AX=0055  BX=AAFF  CX=FFAA  DX=0000  SP=000C  BP=0000  SI=0000  DI=0000
DS=0927  ES=0916  SS=0926  CS=0928  IP=0019   NV UP DI PL ZR NA PE NC
0928:0019 8B160600      MOV      DX,[0006]                        DS:0006=0055
-t
```

```
AX=0055  BX=AAFF  CX=FFAA  DX=0055  SP=000C  BP=0000  SI=0000  DI=0000
DS=0927  ES=0916  SS=0926  CS=0928  IP=001D     NV UP DI PL ZR NA PE NC
0928:001D 86F2          XCHG     DL,DH
-t

AX=0055  BX=AAFF  CX=FFAA  DX=5500  SP=000C  BP=0000  SI=0000  DI=0000
DS=0927  ES=0916  SS=0926  CS=0928  IP=001F     NV UP DI PL ZR NA PE NC
0928:001F 50            PUSH     AX
-t

AX=0055  BX=AAFF  CX=FFAA  DX=5500  SP=000A  BP=0000  SI=0000  DI=0000
DS=0927  ES=0916  SS=0926  CS=0928  IP=0020     NV UP DI PL ZR NA PE NC
0928:0020 51            PUSH     CX
-t

AX=0055  BX=AAFF  CX=FFAA  DX=5500  SP=0008  BP=0000  SI=0000  DI=0000
DS=0927  ES=0916  SS=0926  CS=0928  IP=0021     NV UP DI PL ZR NA PE NC
0928:0021 58            POP      AX
-d ss:0,f
0926:0000  00 00 21 00 28 09 10 06-AA FF 55 00 00 00 16 09    ..!.(...*.U.....
-t

AX=FFAA  BX=AAFF  CX=FFAA  DX=5500  SP=000A  BP=0000  SI=0000  DI=0000
DS=0927  ES=0916  SS=0926  CS=0928  IP=0022     NV UP DI PL ZR NA PE NC
0928:0022 59            POP      CX
-t

AX=FFAA  BX=AAFF  CX=0055  DX=5500  SP=000C  BP=0000  SI=0000  DI=0000
DS=0927  ES=0916  SS=0926  CS=0928  IP=0023     NV UP DI PL ZR NA PE NC
0928:0023 87CA          XCHG     DX,CX
-d ss:0,f
0926:0000  00 00 21 00 22 00 23 00-28 09 10 06 00 00 16 09    ..!.".#.(.......
-t

AX=FFAA  BX=AAFF  CX=5500  DX=0055  SP=000C  BP=0000  SI=0000  DI=0000
DS=0927  ES=0916  SS=0926  CS=0928  IP=0025     NV UP DI PL ZR NA PE NC
0928:0025 891E0000      MOV      [0000],BX                    DS:0000=5500
-t

AX=FFAA  BX=AAFF  CX=5500  DX=0055  SP=000C  BP=0000  SI=0000  DI=0000
DS=0927  ES=0916  SS=0926  CS=0928  IP=0029     NV UP DI PL ZR NA PE NC
0928:0029 88160200      MOV      [0002],DL                    DS:0002=AA
-t

AX=FFAA  BX=AAFF  CX=5500  DX=0055  SP=000C  BP=0000  SI=0000  DI=0000
DS=0927  ES=0916  SS=0926  CS=0928  IP=002D     NV UP DI PL ZR NA PE NC
0928:002D 880E0300      MOV      [0003],CL                    DS:0003=FF
-t

AX=FFAA  BX=AAFF  CX=5500  DX=0055  SP=000C  BP=0000  SI=0000  DI=0000
DS=0927  ES=0916  SS=0926  CS=0928  IP=0031     NV UP DI PL ZR NA PE NC
0928:0031 890E0400      MOV      [0004],CX                    DS:0004=AAFF
-t

AX=FFAA  BX=AAFF  CX=5500  DX=0055  SP=000C  BP=0000  SI=0000  DI=0000
DS=0927  ES=0916  SS=0926  CS=0928  IP=0035     NV UP DI PL ZR NA PE NC
0928:0035 A30600        MOV      [0006],AX                    DS:0006=0055
-t

AX=FFAA  BX=AAFF  CX=5500  DX=0055  SP=000C  BP=0000  SI=0000  DI=0000
DS=0927  ES=0916  SS=0926  CS=0928  IP=0038     NV UP DI PL ZR NA PE NC
```

```
0928:0038 CB                RETF
-d ds:0,f
0927:0000    FF  AA  55  00  00  55  AA  FF-00  00  00  00  00  00  00  00    .*U..U*.........
-q

A>
```

The first line of the DEBUG response shows the values of the eight general registers just prior to execution of the first instruction of the program. The AX, BX, DX, BP, SI, and DI registers have been initialized to zero by the DEBUG program. DOS will *not* perform such initializations. Therefore, a program *must never* depend on registers being initialized to zero automatically. The CX-register is initialized by the DEBUG program to contain the length, in bytes, of the executable program. DOS does *not* perform this initialization either. The SP-register is initialized to the offset from the origin of the stack segment of the memory location immediately following the end of the stack segment. This initialization denotes an empty stack.

The second line of the DEBUG response shows the values of the four segment registers, the IP register, and the flags register prior to execution of the first instruction of the program. Recall that the value in a segment register is the high-order 16 bits of a 20-bit address and that the low-order 4 bits are always zero. The initial value of the DS-register and the ES-register is the origin of the program segment prefix (hexadecimal location 09160 in this case). The initial value of the SS-register is the origin of the stack segment (hexadecimal location 09260 in this case). The SS:SP register pair always points to the memory location within the stack segment that contains the current top-of-stack data word. The stack segment for this program was defined to have a size of 16 bytes (see line 9 of Program Listing 2.1). Since the stack's origin is location 09260, the stack segment ends at location 0926F. The SS:SP register pair currently points to location 09270 (09260 + 0010). This location is one location beyond the end of the stack segment, thus denoting an empty stack.

The initial value of the CS-register is the origin of the code segment (hexadecimal location 09280 in this case). The initial value of the IP-register is zero, the offset of the first location in the code segment. The CS:IP register pair always points to the memory location that contains the next instruction byte to be fetched. Initially, the CS:IP register pair points to the location of the first byte of the first instruction in the program.

The flag bits in the flags register are all cleared (i.e., set to 0) initially. Table 2.13 shows the abbreviations used for the flags register display.

The third line of the response in DEBUG Listing 2.2 shows the next instruction to be executed, which, in this case, is the first instruction in the program. The hexadecimal pair 0928:0000 is the segment origin and offset of the memory location that contains the first byte of the instruction. The segment value 0928 is the contents of the CS-register, and the offset value 0000 is the contents of the IP-register. The 1-byte hexadecimal value 1E is the machine language representation of the instruction. The string PUSH   DS is an Assembly language interpretation of the machine language instruction 1E.

TABLE 2.13

Abbreviations used
by debug in the
flags register display

Flat Bit	Abbreviation for 0 (Clear)	Abbreviation for 1 (Set)
OF	NV	OV
DF	UP	DN
IF	DI	EI
SF	PL	NG
ZF	NZ	ZR
AF	NA	AC
PF	PO	PE
CF	NC	CY

Following the three-line DEBUG response, the hyphen (-) prompt is displayed to indicate that DEBUG is ready to accept the next command. The trace command t is a request for DEBUG to trace execution of one instruction. The instruction that is to be executed is the one that appeared at the end of the three-line DEBUG response, the PUSH   DS instruction. DEBUG executes the instruction and displays the three-line register display again. A comparison of the two register displays shows part of the effect of executing the PUSH   DS instruction. Only two registers have changed. The SP-register has been decremented by 2. A copy of the value of the DS-register (0916 hex) was pushed onto the stack, and the SS : SP register pair (0926 : 000E) now points to the location of that top-of-stack item. The IP-register has been incremented by 1, the size in bytes of the machine language instruction just executed. The CS : IP register pair (0928 : 0001) now points to the location of the first byte of the next instruction to be executed. The last line of the three-line register display shows the next instruction to be executed. This instruction begins at the memory location whose address is the hexadecimal number 09281. The machine language representation of the instruction is the 2-byte hexadecimal number 2BC0. The Assembly language interpretation of the machine language instruction is

```
SUB AX,AX
```

Again, the hyphen (-) prompt is displayed in DEBUG Listing 2.2 to indicate that DEBUG is ready to accept another command. The next trace command t causes the

```
SUB AX,AX
```

instruction to be executed and the three-line register display to be displayed once again. The SUB instruction subtracted the AX-register value from itself, leaving the result (zero) in the AX-register. The AX-register value did not change, since it was already zero. (If the program had been executed directly from DOS, this situation might not have been the case.) Note that several bits in the flags register changed to reflect the result of the SUB instruction execution. The ZF and PF bits of the flags register now are set to reflect the fact that the result of the subtract operation is zero and that the result has even parity. The effect of the subtract instruction on the flags register is discussed in detail in Chapter 3.

The IP-register has been incremented by 2, the size in bytes of the machine language instruction just executed. The CS : IP register pair (0928 : 0003) now points to the location of the first byte of the next instruction to be executed. The last line of the three-line register display shows the next instruction to be executed. The address of the first byte of the instruction is 09283. The machine language representation of the instruction is 50 hexadecimal. The Assembly language interpretation of the instruction is

```
PUSH AX
```

Again, the hyphen (-) prompt is displayed to indicate that DEBUG is ready to accept another command. The next trace command causes this PUSH instruction to be executed and the three-line register display to be displayed once again. The SP-register has been decremented by 2. A copy of the value of the AX-register (zero) was pushed onto the stack, and the SS : SP register pair (0926 : 000C) points to the location of the new top-of-stack item. The current status of the stack segment is shown in Figure 2.11.

FIGURE 2.11
Status of the stack segment after execution of the instruction in line 36 of Program Listing 2.1

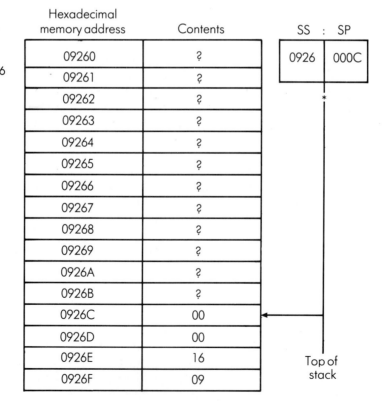

Hexadecimal memory address	Contents
09260	?
09261	?
09262	?
09263	?
09264	?
09265	?
09266	?
09267	?
09268	?
09269	?
0926A	?
0926B	?
0926C	00
0926D	00
0926E	16
0926F	09

SS	:	SP
0926		000C

Top of stack

(? means value unknown)

The next instruction to be executed is the 3-byte machine instruction B82709, which is contained in memory locations 09284–09286. The interpretation of this machine language instruction is

```
MOV AX,0927
```

This interpretation corresponds to the instruction

```
MOV AX,SEG DATA
```

that appears in line 37 of Program Listing 2.1. The operand SEG DATA represents an immediate operand that is inserted into the executable module by the DOS loader program. The decision of where in memory to place various segments of the executable program is made by DOS at load time. The DEBUG program traces the execution of machine language instructions that it obtains from the executable module file (ex_2_1.exe). It knows that the machine language instruction B82709 is an instruction to move the immediate value 0927 to the AX-register. However, DEBUG does not know that the immediate value 0927 is the high-order 16 bits of the origin of the data segment. Therefore, an Assembly language instruction displayed by DEBUG is its interpretation of a machine language instruction.

The next command issued to DEBUG after the hyphen (-) prompt in DEBUG Listing 2.2 is the command

```
d ss:0,f
```

The d stands for dump. It is a request to DEBUG to display the contents of the memory locations specified by the remainder of the command line. This command line specifies that stack segment locations 0000–000F are to be displayed. The last 4 bytes of the display are 00 00 16 09, which are the two words that were pushed onto the stack by the two previous PUSH instructions. The first PUSH pushed the DS-register value (0916) onto the stack. Recall that a 16-bit word always is stored in memory as two consecutive 8-bit bytes, low-byte (16 in this case) followed by high-byte (09 in this case). The second PUSH pushed the AX-register value (0000) onto the stack. The other values in the stack segment, the values from offset 0000–000B, are unknown to the program; that is, they are not part of the current stack. Compare this line of the stack segment in DEBUG Listing 2.2 to the predicted values shown in Figure 2.11.

Again, the hyphen (-) prompt is displayed to indicate that DEBUG is ready to accept another command. The next trace command causes the instruction

```
MOV AX,0927
```

to be executed. The next three-line register display shows that the AX-register now has the value 0927 hexadecimal. The IP-register has been incremented by 3, the size in bytes of the machine language instruction just executed. The CS:IP register pair now points to the first byte of the next instruction to be executed.

The next trace command causes two instructions to be executed:

```
MOV DS,AX
NOP
```

are executed (see lines 38 and 39 of Program Listing 2.1). The DEBUG program uses the single-step mode of the microprocessor to implement the trace command. When in the single-step mode, the processor generates a single-step interrupt following most instruction executions. The DEBUG program is the interrupt service procedure that is invoked to service the single-step interrupt. The processor will not generate a single-step interrupt following a MOV or POP instruction whose destination operand is a segment register. Therefore, no single-step interrupt is generated following execution of the

```
MOV DS, AX
```

instruction. The processor will execute the NOP instruction before generating the single-step interrupt and returning control to DEBUG. The NOP instruction was used so that only one significant instruction would be executed in response to the trace command. (The single-step interrupt is discussed in detail in Chapter 9.)

The three-line register display shows that the DS-register now has the value 0927. The IP-register has been incremented by 3, the size in bytes of the two machine language instructions just executed. The CS : IP register pair now points to the first byte of the next instruction to be executed.

The next command issued to the DEBUG program is another d (dump) command that specifies that data segment locations 0000–000F are to be displayed. The first value displayed in DEBUG Listing 2.2 is 0927 : 0000, which is the segment and offset of the first memory location to be dumped. The remainder of the display shows the hexadecimal contents of consecutive memory locations beginning with the specified location. The next eight values (00 55 AA FF FF AA 55 00) are the initial values of the 8 bytes defined in the data segment. Compare this dump to Table 2.10. The last eight values (all zeros) are the values of memory locations 09278–0927F, which are not used by the program. They lie between the data and code segments of the program. Recall that each program segment must begin on a paragraph boundary. The difference between the origins of two segments must be a multiple of 16. Since the size of the data segment is only 8 bytes, there must be 8 unused bytes prior to the beginning of the next segment so that it may begin on a paragraph boundary.

The remainder of the display (.U*..*U.........) is the ASCII interpretation of the 16-byte values that appeared previously on the line. A period (.) indicates that the corresponding ASCII code is a nonprintable character. In this dump, 55 is the ASCII code for U, AA is the ASCII code for *, and 00 and FF are ASCII codes for nonprintable control characters. This part of the display is quite useful when the locations being dumped contain ASCII codes for characters in character strings, because it precludes the need for human translation from hexadecimal to character.

If the preceding dump command had been issued earlier in the DEBUG session, then the first 16 bytes of the program segment prefix (PSP) would have been displayed instead of the data segment. At the beginning of the DEBUG session, the DS-register contained the origin of the PSP. It was not until the last instruction trace that the DS-register was set to contain the origin of the data segment.

The following six trace commands execute the six MOV instructions in lines 41–46 of Program Listing 2.1. An inspection of the register displays shows the effects of execution of the corresponding instructions. Note that the flag bits in the flags register do not change during execution of the six MOV instructions —because none of the bits in the flags register are affected by execution of a MOV instruction. Note also the display form of the last of these six MOV instructions, which looks like the following:

```
0928:0019 8B160600 MOV DX,[0006]  DS:0006=0055
```

The machine language instruction begins at location 09299 hexadecimal and is 4 bytes in length. The machine language instruction is 8B160600 and has the following Assembly language interpretation:

```
MOV DX,[0006]
```

The square brackets indicate that the value 0006 is the offset within the data segment of the memory location that contains the operand. The rightmost part of the display (DS:0006 = 0055) indicates that the word that begins at offset 0006 within the data segment currently has the hexadecimal value 0055. That is, the value 0055 is the value that is moved into the DX-register when the instruction is executed. The register display that follows indicates that this is the case.

The next trace command causes the instruction

```
XCHG DL,DH
```

to be executed. The register display that contains this instruction shows a DX-register value of 0055 hexadecimal; that is, the DH-register contains 00, and the DL-register contains 55 hex just prior to execution of the instruction. The following register display shows a DX-register value of 5500 hexadecimal; that is, the DH-register contains 55 hex, and the DL-register contains 00 just after execution of the instruction.

The next two trace commands cause the PUSH instructions in lines 48 and 49 of Program Listing 2.1 to be executed. The first of these two instructions pushes a copy of the value in the AX-register (0055 hex) onto the stack. The second one pushes a copy of the value in the CX-register (FFAA hex) onto the stack. With each of these instructions, the SP-register is decremented by 2 so that the SS:SP register pair points to the new top-of-stack item. The current status of the stack segment is shown in Figure 2.12.

The next command issued to DEBUG in DEBUG Listing 2.2 is a request to display the contents of the stack segment. Compare this display of the stack segment to the predicted values shown in Figure 2.12.

The next two trace commands cause the two POP instructions in lines 50 and 51 of Program Listing 2.1 to be executed. Execution of the first POP causes the value at the top of the stack, FFAA hex (the previous CX-register value), to be copied into the AX-register and the SP-register to be incremented by 2. After execution, the SS:SP register pair points to the new top-of-stack value, 0055 hex (the previous AX-register value). Execution of the second POP causes the new top-of-stack value to be copied into the CX-register and the SP-register to be incremented by 2. After execution, the SS:SP register pair points to the new

FIGURE 2.12
Status of the stack
segment after
execution of the
instruction in line 49
of Program Listing
2.1

Hexadecimal memory address	Contents	SS	SP
09260	?	0926	0008
09261	?		
09262	?		
09263	?		
09264	?		
09265	?		
09266	?		
09267	?		
09268	AA		
09269	FF		
0926A	55		
0926B	00		
0926C	00		
0926D	00		
0926E	16	Top of	
0926F	09	stack	

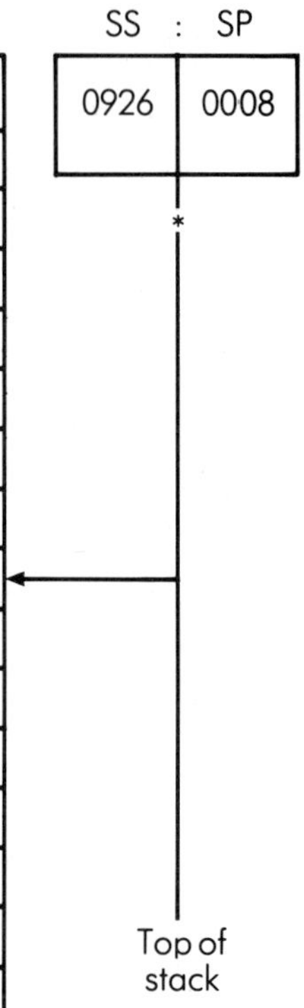

(? means value unknown)

top-of-stack value, 0000, which was pushed onto the stack by execution of the PUSH instruction in line 36 of Program Listing 2.1. The current status of the stack segment is shown in Figure 2.13. Note that the values 0055 and FFAA still exist in the physical stack segment. However, the SP-register has been updated so that these values are not part of the logical stack.

The next command issued to DEBUG in DEBUG Listing 2.2 is a request to display the contents of the stack segment. A comparison of this display with the predicted values shown in Figure 2.13 shows that the values 0055 and FFAA are no longer in the stack segment. They have been replaced by the values 0610 and 0928, respectively. How did these values get into the stack segment? It appears that no other PUSH operations have been performed. But the reason that these values have changed is that during the transition between the user program and the single-step interrupt service procedure (part of DEBUG), the address of the next instruction to be executed in the user program is saved on the user program's stack. The three items above the user program's top of stack are 0610, 0928, and 0023, the last two of which are the CS and IP register values for the next instruction to be executed in the user program. (The mechanism by which these values are pushed onto the stack is discussed in Chapter 9.) These

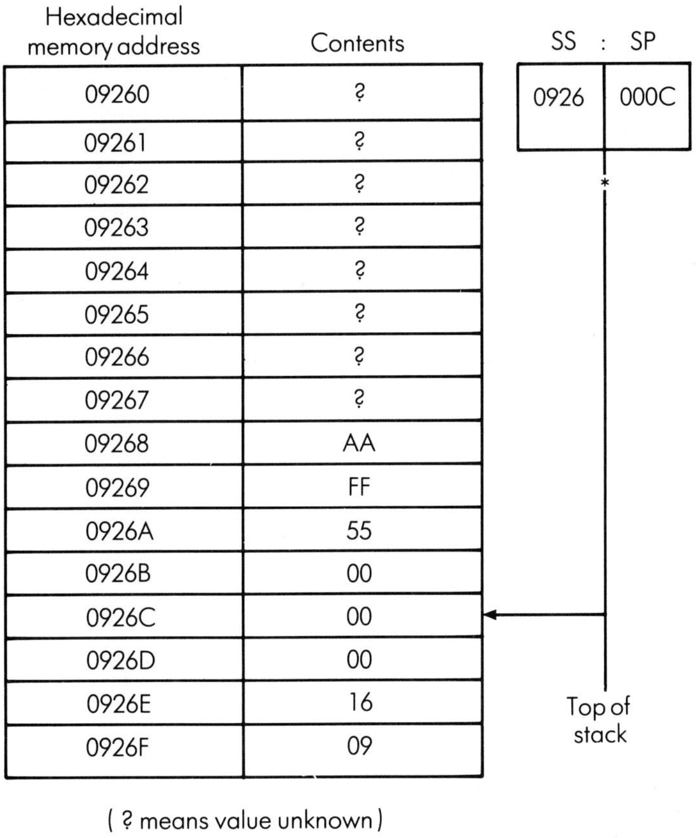

FIGURE 2.13
Status of the stack
segment after
execution of the
instruction in line 51
of Program Listing
2.1

Hexadecimal memory address	Contents	SS	:	SP
09260	?	0926		000C
09261	?			
09262	?			
09263	?			
09264	?			
09265	?			
09266	?			
09267	?			
09268	AA			
09269	FF			
0926A	55			
0926B	00			
0926C	00			
0926D	00			
0926E	16			
0926F	09			

Top of
stack

(? means value unknown)

values are popped from the stack as part of returning control from the interrupt
service procedure to the user program.

The next trace command causes the instruction

```
XCHG DX, CX
```

to be executed. The register display that contains this instruction shows
a DX-register value of 5500 hexadecimal and a CX-register value of 0055
hexadecimal. The following register display shows a DX-register value of 0055
hexadecimal and a CX-register value of 5500 hexadecimal.

The last five trace commands in DEBUG Listing 2.2 cause the five MOV
instructions in lines 54–60 of Program Listing 2.1 to be executed. The destination operand in each of these MOV instructions is the location of a byte or
word in the data segment. These five instructions modify the data segment
values. The next command to the DEBUG program is a request to dump the
contents of the data segment. Compare the current values of the data segment
shown in this display with the initial values of the data segment shown in
Table 2.10 and the predicted final values of the data segment shown in
Table 2.12.

The last command issued to DEBUG in DEBUG Listing 2.2 is the q (quit) command. This command terminates DEBUG and causes control to be returned to DOS. The last register display shows the instruction RETF as the next instruction to be executed (see line 62 of Program Listing 2.1). The F indicates that this is a return from a FAR procedure (the type attribute FAR was introduced in Section 1.5 and is discussed further in Chapter 5). Continuing to issue trace commands at this point would cause single-step execution to proceed into DOS. Tracing the execution of DOS is beyond the scope of an Assembly language text.

2.6   Additional Capabilities in the IBM PC-AT Assembly Language

The IBM PC-AT Assembly language provides several additional capabilities for stack operations in data transfer instructions. The PUSH instruction can have an immediate operand, which means that the two instructions in lines 35 and 36 of Program Listing 2.1 could be replaced by the single instruction

PUSH 0

As well, two stack manipulation instructions are provided: PUSHA (PUSH ALL) and POPA (POP ALL). The **PUSHA instruction** has the following general form:

[⟨label⟩] PUSHA   [⟨comment⟩]

The PUSHA instruction causes the values of all eight 16-bit general registers to be pushed onto the stack. The order in which the general registers are pushed onto the stack is AX, CX, DX, BX, SP, BP, SI, and DI. The value that is pushed onto the stack for the SP-register is the value that the SP-register had before the first register (AX) was pushed onto the stack.

The **POPA instruction** has the following general form:

[⟨label⟩] POPA   [⟨comment⟩]

The POPA instruction causes the top eight words on the stack to be popped into the eight general registers. The order in which the registers are popped from the stack is DI, SI, BP, SP, BX, DX, CX, and AX. The fourth value popped is actually discarded rather than being popped into the SP-register. The SP-register is automatically incremented by 2 as each word is popped from the stack.

The PUSHA and POPA instructions are convenient for saving and restoring the general registers in a subprocedure, and they are discussed further in Chapter 5.

There is one difference in execution of PUSH between the Intel 8088 (the microprocessor used in the IBM PC and the IBM PC-XT) and the Intel 80286 (the microprocessor used in the IBM PC-AT). This difference occurs in the case where the PUSH operand is the SP-register. The

PUSH SP

instruction in the Intel 80286 pushes the value that existed in the SP-register just prior to execution of the instruction. In the Intel 8088, the SP-register is first decremented by 2 and the resulting value then is pushed onto the stack.

The instruction

```
POP SP
```

executes the same in both microprocessors. The value in the SP-register after execution is the value that was at the top of the stack just prior to the execution, and there is no additional increment of the SP-register by 2, as one might logically expect.

EXAMPLE

Suppose the SP-register contains the value 0100 hexadecimal when the instructions

```
PUSH SP
POP  SP
```

are executed. With the Intel 8088 microprocessor, the resulting SP-register value is 00FE hex. With the Intel 80286 microprocessor, the resulting SP-register value is 0100 hex.

NUMERIC EXERCISES

2.1 Fill in the blanks in the following table:

Eight-Bit Binary Bit Pattern	Modulo 2^7 Interpretation	Two's Complement Interpretation
10110111		
	145	
		− 115

2.2 Fill in the blanks in the following table:

Eight-bit Binary Bit Pattern	Sign Magnitude Interpretation	One's Complement Interpretation	Excess 128 Interpretation
10110111			
	125		
		− 115	

2.3 State the range of integers that can be represented with 12-bit binary numbers using (a) the modulo 2^{12} number system, (b) the two's complement number system, (c) the one's complement number system, (d) the sign magnitude number system, and (e) the excess 2^{11} number system.

2.4 Translate the character string

```
IBM PC
```

to six 8-bit binary codes (one per character) using the extended ASCII character code table in Appendix E. State the codes in both binary and hexadecimal.

PROGRAMMING EXERCISES

2.1 The program in Program Listing 2.3 contains four checkpoints indicated by comments in lines 36, 44, 50, and 55. Fill in the blanks in the following table to show the hexadecimal values of the AX, BX, CX, DX, SP, and flags registers at each of these points during program execution. Fill in the blanks in the second table to show the hexadecimal values in the stack segment at each of these points during program execution. Use the question mark character (?) for values that are unknown. Verify your answers by tracing the program with DEBUG.

2.2 The program shown in Program Listing 2.4 contains three checkpoints indicated by comments in lines 37, 45, and 50. Place the symbolic names ALPHA, BETA, GAMMA, LAMDA, and OMEGA in the appropriate positions in the first column of the table. Fill in the blanks in the third, fourth, and fifth columns with the hexadecimal values that would appear in the data segment at the indicated points during program execution. Verify your answers by tracing the program with DEBUG.

Register Values at Each Checkpoint

Checkpoint	AX	BX	CX	DX	SP	Flags
A						
B						
C						
D						

Stack Segment Values at Each Checkpoint

Stack Segment Offset	Stack Segment Value at Checkpoint A	B	C	D
0000				
0001				
0002				
0003				
0004				
0005				
0006				
0007				
0008				
0009				
000A				
000B				
000C				
000D				
000E				
000F				

Data Segment Values at Each Checkpoint

Symbolic Name	Data Segment Offset	Value at Checkpoint A	B	C
	0000			
	0001			
	0002			
	0003			
	0004			
	0005			
	0006			
	0007			

```
 1: ;
 2: ;
 3: ;                         PROGRAM LISTING 2.3
 4: ;
 5: ;                         PROGRAM FOR EXERCISE 2.1
 6: ;
 7: ; S T A C K    S E G M E N T    D E F I N I T I O N
 8: ;
 9: STACK          SEGMENT STACK
10:                DB       16 DUP(?)
11: STACK          ENDS
12: ;
13: ; D A T A    S E G M E N T    D E F I N I T I O N
14: ;
15: DATA_SEG       SEGMENT
16: ;
17: FLAGS          DW       0000110011010101B
18: ;
19: DATA_SEG       ENDS
20: ;
21: ; C O D E    S E G M E N T    D E F I N I T I O N
22: ;
23: CODE           SEGMENT
24:                ASSUME   CS:CODE,SS:STACK,DS:DATA_SEG
25: PR_2_1         PROC     FAR
26:                PUSH     DS                 ;PUSH RETURN SEG ADDR ON STACK
27:                SUB      AX,AX              ;PUSH RETURN OFFSET OF ZERO
28:                PUSH     AX                 ;ON STACK
29:                MOV      AX,SEG DATA_SEG    ;SET DS-REGISTER TO POINT
30:                MOV      DS,AX              ;TO DATA SEGMENT
31:                NOP
32:                MOV      AX,0123H
33:                MOV      BX,4567H
34:                MOV      CX,89ABH
35:                MOV      DX,0CDEFH
36: ;*** CHECKPOINT A ***
37:                PUSH     FLAGS
38:                POPF
39:                PUSH     AX
40:                PUSH     BX
41:                PUSHF
42:                PUSH     CX
43:                PUSH     DX
44: ;*** CHECKPOINT B ***
45:                POP      AX
46:                POP      BX
47:                POPF
48:                PUSH     AX
49:                PUSH     BX
50: ;*** CHECKPOINT C ***
51:                POP      DX
52:                POP      CX
53:                POP      BX
54:                POP      AX
55: ;*** CHECKPOINT D ***
56:                RET                          ;RETURN
57: PR_2_1         ENDP
58: CODE           ENDS
59:*               END      PR_2_1
*
```

```
 1: ;
 2: ;
 3: ;                      PROGRAM LISTING 2.4
 4: ;
 5: ;                      PROGRAM FOR EXERCISE 2.2
 6: ;
 7: ; S T A C K    S E G M E N T    D E F I N I T I O N
 8: ;
 9: STACK         SEGMENT STACK
10:               DB       16 DUP(?)
11: STACK         ENDS
12: ;
13: ; D A T A    S E G M E N T    D E F I N I T I O N
14: ;
15: DATA_SEG      SEGMENT
16: ;
17: ALPHA         DB       35
18: BETA          DW       01ABH
19: GAMMA         DW       45EFH
20: LAMDA         DB       CONSTANT
21: OMEGA         DW       67CDH
22: CONSTANT      EQU      10001001B
23: ;
24: DATA_SEG      ENDS
25: ;
26: ; C O D E    S E G M E N T    D E F I N I T I O N
27: ;
28: CODE          SEGMENT
29:               ASSUME   CS:CODE,SS:STACK,DS:DATA_SEG
30: PR_2_2        PROC     FAR
31:               PUSH     DS                  ;PUSH RETURN SEG ADDR ON STACK
32:               SUB      AX,AX               ;PUSH RETURN OFFSET OF ZERO
33:               PUSH     AX                  ;ON STACK
34:               MOV      AX,SEG DATA_SEG     ;SET DS-REGISTER TO POINT
35:               MOV      DS,AX               ;TO DATA SEGMENT
36:               NOP
37: ;*** CHECKPOINT A ***
38:               MOV      AH,CONSTANT
39:               MOV      AL,ALPHA
40:               MOV      BX,GAMMA
41:               XCHG     AH,BH
42:               XCHG     AX,BETA
43:               MOV      ALPHA,AH
44:               MOV      LAMDA,AL
45: ;*** CHECKPOINT B ***
46:               MOV      CX,OMEGA
47:               XCHG     BL,CH
48:               MOV      GAMMA,BX
49:               MOV      OMEGA,CX
50: ;*** CHECKPOINT C ***
51:               RET                          ;RETURN
52: PR_2_2        ENDP
53: CODE          ENDS
54:*              END      PR_2_2
*
```

3

INTEGER ARITHMETIC

.The previous chapter presented various ways of representing data inside a computer. The pseudo-operations for defining and initializing data in an IBM PC Assembly language program and the instructions for data transfer were discussed. To solve some simple, meaningful problems with Assembly language programs, instructions for performing arithmetic computations are needed. Integer arithmetic operations are the subject of this chapter. Integer addition and subtraction in the binary number system are discussed first. Then the instructions for performing integer arithmetic operations in an IBM PC Assembly language program are presented. As well, the notion of arithmetic overflow is discussed in detail.

3.1 Binary Arithmetic

This section is devoted to arithmetic in binary number systems with finite bounds, the type of number systems used in computers. The discussion is limited to addition and subtraction in the modulo 2^n and two's complement number systems (the number systems of the IBM PC). Table 3.1 shows the range of integer values that can be represented by 8-bit binary numbers in both the unsigned and the signed two's complement number systems.

Addition

To add the n-bit binary integer

$$A_{n-1}A_{n-2} \ldots A_2A_1A_0$$

TABLE 3.1
Range of integer values for 8-bit unsigned and signed two's complement number systems

Bit Pattern	Unsigned	Signed Two's Complement
00000000	0	0
00000001	1	1
00000010	2	2
00000011	3	3
00000100	4	4
00000101	5	5
00000110	6	6
00000111	7	7
.	.	.
.	.	.
.	.	.
01111100	124	124
01111101	125	125
01111110	126	126
01111111	127	127
10000000	128	-128
10000001	129	-127
10000010	130	-126
10000011	131	-125
.	.	.
.	.	.
.	.	.
11111000	248	-8
11111001	249	-7
11111010	250	-6
11111011	251	-5
11111100	252	-4
11111101	253	-3
11111110	254	-2
11111111	255	-1

to the n-bit binary integer

$$B_{n-1} B_{n-2} \ldots B_2 B_1 B_0$$

the following algorithm can be used:

```
CARRY = 0
I = 0
WHILE I < n
     SUM = A_I + B_I + CARRY
     S_I = rightmost bit of SUM
     CARRY = SUM with rightmost bit removed
     I = I + 1
ENDWHILE
```

TABLE 3.2
Addition of two
corresponding bits
and a carry (in)
producing a sum
bit and a carry
(out)

A_I	B_I	Carry (In)	Carry (Out)	S_I
0	0	0	0	0
0	0	1	0	1
0	1	0	0	1
0	1	1	1	0
1	0	0	0	1
1	0	1	1	0
1	1	0	1	0
1	1	1	1	1

The output of this algorithm is the n-bit binary sum

$$S_{n-1} S_{n-2} \ldots S_2 S_1 S_0$$

and the carry out of the most-significant bit position, **CARRY**. There are only eight possibilities for the addition

A_I + B_I + CARRY

which produces a sum bit, S_I, and a carry into the next-highest bit position. These possibilities are summarized in Table 3.2. Due to similarities, only four possibilities are significant:

1. All three bits are zero:

    $0 + 0 + 0 = 00$ $S_I = 0$ Carry $= 0$

2. Exactly one of the three bits is a 1:

    $0 + 0 + 1 = 01$ $S_I = 1$ Carry $= 0$

3. Exactly two of the three bits are 1:

    $0 + 1 + 1 = 10$ $S_I = 0$ Carry $= 1$

4. All three bits are 1:

    $1 + 1 + 1 = 11$ $S_I = 1$ Carry $= 1$

EXAMPLES

```
  0110110   ◄── Carry values
  00110110
+ 00110110
0   01101100  ◄── Sum
    └──► Carry out of the most-significant bit
```

```
  1 1 1 1 0 0 0   ◄── Carry values
    1 1 1 0 1 1 0 0
+   0 0 1 1 1 0 0 0
1     0 0 1 0 0 1 0 0   ◄── Sum
```
└──► Carry out of the most-significant bit

As far as the computer is concerned, binary addition can be handled in the same manner for both the modulo 2^n and the two's complement number systems. The difference is the way in which the operands and the sum are interpreted. Table 3.3 shows some examples of 8-bit binary addition in both the modulo 2^8 and the two's complement number systems.

Subtraction

Most computers perform subtraction by adding the two's complement of the subtrahend to the minuend. That is, the subtraction operation is replaced by a two's complement operation followed by an addition operation. As far as the computer is concerned, binary subtraction can be handled in this manner for both the modulo 2^n and the two's complement number systems. The difference is, again, the way in which the operands and the result are interpreted. Table 3.4 shows some examples of 8-bit binary subtractions and their interpretations in both the modulo 2^n and the two's complement number systems.

TABLE 3.3
Binary addition with both modulo 2^8 and two's complement number systems

Addition Operation	Modulo 2^8 Interpretation	Two's Complement Interpretation
11111000	248	-8
00000101	5	5
0 11111101	253	-3
00110110	54	54
00110110	54	54
0 01101100	108	108
11011100	220	-36
00001100	12	12
0 11101000	232	-24
↑		
Carry		

TABLE 3.4
Binary subtraction with both modulo 2^n and two's complement interpretations

Subtraction Operation	Modulo 2^n Interpretation	Two's Complement Interpretation
01101011 Minuend	107	107
− 00110100 Subtrahend	− 52	− 52
01101011 Minuend		107
+ 11001100 Two's complement		+ (− 52)
00110111	55	55
11100111 Minuend	231	− 25
− 10111100 Subtrahend	− 188	− (− 68)
11100111 Minuend		− 25
+ 01000100 Two's complement		+ 68
00101011	43	43
11011011 Minuend	219	− 37
− 00011001 Subtrahend	− 25	− 25
11011011 Minuend		− 37
+ 11100111 Two's Complement		+ (− 25)
11000010	194	− 62

Arithmetic Overflow

The range of integers that can be represented with n-bit binary numbers is 0 to $2^n - 1$ in the modulo 2^n number system and -2^{n-1} to $+2^{n-1} - 1$ in the two's complement number system. For $n = 8$, the ranges are 0 to 255 and − 128 to + 127, respectively. If an arithmetic operation produces a result that is outside the range of integers for the number system being used, then a condition called arithmetic overflow occurs (which is discussed in Section 3.4). Table 3.5 shows some examples of 8-bit binary additions that result in an arithmetic overflow in at least one of the two number systems. Note that in each of the examples in Table 3.5, if the sum is extended by one bit, the carry bit, then the sum is correct. Thus, on overflow, the sum produced is actually the lower n bits (8 bits in Table 3.5) of the correct sum.

3.2 | Integer Arithmetic Instructions

The Intel 8088 provides a set of instructions for performing integer arithmetic operations. These instructions can operate on either 8-bit or 16-bit operands, which can be interpreted as either unsigned integer values (modulo 2^8 and modulo 2^{16} number systems) or signed integer values (two's complement number system). Table 3.1 shows the range of integer values that can be represented by

TABLE 3.5
Binary addition with both modulo 2^n and two's complement interpretations

Addition Operation	Modulo 2^n Interpretation	Two's Complement Interpretation
01111110	126	126
01111100	124	124
0 11111010	250	-6
		(Overflow)
11111100	252	-4
00001100	12	12
1 00001000	8	8
	(Overflow)	
10000001	129	-127
10011001	153	-103
1 00011010	26	26
↑	(Overflow)	(Overflow)
Carry		

8-bit binary numbers in both unsigned form and signed two's complement form. For 16-bit operands, the ranges are 0 to 65,535 for the unsigned integer form, and $-32,768$ to $32,767$ for the signed two's complement form.

For addition and subtraction operations, the microprocessor is unaware of the interpretation being applied to the operands, and the same instructions are used for both types of operands. For multiplication and division operations, the microprocessor must know the interpretation being applied to the operands, and it provides two sets of instructions, one set for unsigned operands and the other for signed two's complement operands. Programs must be written in such a way that consistent interpretations are applied.

The interpretation of a binary integer is applied when a value is input for the integer or when the value of the integer is being output. The I/O sub-procedures used in the example programs of this book include two procedures for 16-bit decimal input (GETDEC and GETDEC$) and two procedures for 16-bit decimal output (PUTDEC and PUTDEC$).

GETDEC   This procedure accepts a 16-bit integer from the keyboard in signed decimal form and returns it to the caller. The range of integers allowed is $-32,768$ to $+32,767$. The procedure does not prompt for the input—that responsibility belongs to the caller. Error messages are output to the video display in response to input errors, and then another input is accepted. The procedure expects no inputs from the caller. The input value is returned to the caller in the AX-register.

GETDEC$ This procedure accepts a 16-bit integer from the keyboard in unsigned decimal form and returns it to the caller. The range of integers allowed is 0 to 65,535. The procedure does not prompt for the input—that responsibility belongs to the caller. Error messages are output to the video display in response to input errors, and then another input is accepted. The procedure expects no inputs from the caller. The input value is returned to the caller in the AX-register.

PUTDEC   This procedure displays a 16-bit integer in signed decimal form, beginning at the current cursor position on the video screen. The procedure expects the value to be displayed in the AX-register and a display code in the BH-register. The display code is interpreted as follows:

$$BH < 0 \rightarrow \text{left-justify output in a six-character field}$$

$$BH = 0 \rightarrow \text{display with no leading or trailing blanks}$$

$$BH > 0 \rightarrow \text{right-justify output in a six-character field}$$

PUTDEC$ This procedure displays a 16-bit integer in unsigned decimal form, beginning at the current cursor position on the video screen. The procedure expects the value to be displayed in the AX-register and a display code in the BH-register. The display code is interpreted as follows:

$$BH < 0 \rightarrow \text{left-justify output in a six-character field}$$

$$BH = 0 \rightarrow \text{display with no leading or trailing blanks}$$

$$BH > 0 \rightarrow \text{right-justify output in a six-character field}$$

Addition and Subtraction

The general-purpose binary addition instruction is the ADD instruction, and the general-purpose subtraction instruction is the SUB instruction. The **ADD instruction** has the following general form:

[⟨*label*⟩ ADD ⟨*destination*⟩, ⟨*source*⟩   [⟨*comment*⟩]

in which ⟨*source*⟩ identifies the location of the addend and ⟨*destination*⟩ identifies the location of the augend that is to be replaced by the sum. This instruction causes the source operand to be added to the destination operand, and the destination operand is to be replaced by the sum.

The **SUB instruction** has the following general form:

[⟨*label*⟩] SUB ⟨*destination*⟩, ⟨*source*⟩   [⟨*comment*⟩]

in which ⟨*source*⟩ identifies the location of the subtrahend, and ⟨*destination*⟩ identifies the location of the minuend that is to be replaced by the difference. This instruction causes the source operand to be subtracted from the destination operand, and the destination operand to be replaced by the difference. The subtraction is actually performed by adding the minuend (destination operand), the one's complement of the subtrahend (source operand), and 1. This operation, in effect, adds the two's complement of the subtrahend to the minuend.

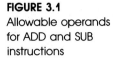

FIGURE 3.1
Allowable operands
for ADD and SUB
instructions

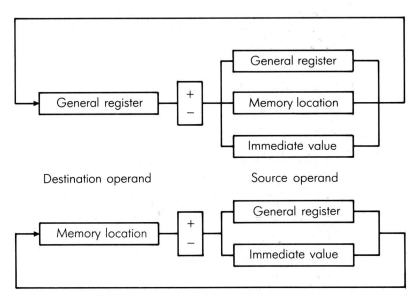

The type attribute of the two operands must match for both the ADD and SUB instructions (i.e., both byte or both word). Figure 3.1 shows the possible combinations of destination and source operands. If the destination operand is a general register, then the source operand can be either a general register, a memory location, or an immediate value. If the destination operand is a memory location, then the source operand can be either a general register or an immediate value.

EXAMPLES

The instruction

```
ADD BH,DL
```

adds the 8-bit value in the DL-register to the 8-bit value in the BH-register, leaving the sum in the BH-register.

The instruction

```
ADD DX,17
```

adds the constant 17 to the 16-bit value in the DX-register, leaving the sum in the DX-register.

Suppose the data segment definition for a program contains the following definitions

```
X DW ?
Y DW ?
Z DW ?
```

and that the GETDEC procedure has been used to input signed integer values for X and Y. The following instructions implement the assignment:

```
Z = 2X - 2Y

MOV AX, X
ADD AX, X
SUB AX, Y
SUB AX, Y
MOV Z, AX
```

The first instruction places a copy of the value of variable X into the AX-register. The second instruction adds the value of variable X to the value of the AX-register, leaving the result in the AX-register. The AX-register now contains the value X + X = 2X. The third instruction subtracts the value of variable Y from the value of the AX-register, leaving the result in the AX-register. The AX-register now contains the value 2X − Y. The fourth instruction again subtracts the value of variable Y from the value of the AX-register, leaving the result in the AX-register. The AX-register now contains the value 2X − 2Y. The last instruction replaces the value of variable Z with a copy of the result (the value in the AX-register).

The ADD and SUB instructions perform straight binary addition and subtraction. The same instructions are used for both unsigned and signed integer operations. It is the programmer's responsibility to make sure that interpretation of the operands is consistent (i.e., both operands are interpreted as unsigned integers, or both operands are interpreted as signed two's complement integers). Table 3.3 and Table 3.5 show some examples of 8-bit binary additions and their interpretations for both unsigned and signed integer forms. Table 3.4 shows some examples of 8-bit binary subtractions and their interpretations for both unsigned and signed integer forms.

The OF, SF, ZF, PF, CF, and AF bits of the flags register are all affected by execution of ADD and SUB instructions.

OF   In an addition operation, if the carry into the most-significant bit differs from the carry out of the most-significant bit, then the OF bit is set. Otherwise, the OF bit is cleared. (Recall that subtraction is performed by complement and addition.) If the two operands represent signed two's complement integers, then the OF bit reflects whether or not execution of the ADD or SUB instruction resulted in an overflow.

SF   The SF bit is a copy of the most-significant bit of the result of the addition or subtraction operation. If the two operands represent signed two's complement numbers, then the SF bit reflects the sign of the result.

ZF   If the result of the addition or subtraction operation is zero, then the ZF bit is set. Otherwise, the ZF bit is cleared.

PF   The PF bit is set to reflect the parity of the low-order eight bits of the result. (See the discussion of the flags register in Chapter 1.)

CF   If an addition operation produces a carry of 1 out of the most-significant bit (bit 7 for byte addition, bit 15 for word addition), or if a subtraction operation requires a borrow into the most-significant bit, then the CF bit is set. Otherwise, the CF bit is cleared. If the two operands represent unsigned integer values, then the CF bit reflects whether or not execution of the ADD or SUB instruction resulted in an overflow. (Arithmetic overflow is discussed in detail in Section 3.4.) The CF bit also is useful in performing addition and subtraction operations on operands that are longer than 16 bits (see Chapter 7 for more details on this subject).

AF   The AF bit is handled in a manner similar to the CF bit. However, the AF bit reflects the carry out of or the borrow into bit 3. The AF bit is used in addition and subtraction operations involving **binary coded decimal (BCD)** numbers. (The AF bit is discussed further in Chapter 11.)

Incrementing and Decrementing

The IBM PC Assembly language includes two instructions expressly for the frequently used operations of adding 1 to a value and subtracting 1 from a value: the INC and DEC instructions. The **INC instruction** has the following general form:

[⟨*label*⟩] INC ⟨*destination*⟩   [⟨*comment*⟩]

in which ⟨*destination*⟩ identifies the location of the value to be incremented. This instruction causes the value in the register or memory location specified by the ⟨*destination*⟩ operand to be incremented by 1.

The **DEC instruction** has the following general form:

[⟨*label*⟩] DEC ⟨*destination*⟩   [⟨*comment*⟩]

in which ⟨*destination*⟩ identifies the location of the value to be decremented. This instruction causes the value in the register or memory location specified by the ⟨*destination*⟩ operand to be decremented by 1.

For both the INC and DEC instructions, the ⟨*destination*⟩ operand can be a general register (byte or word) or a memory location (byte or word).

Both the INC and DEC instructions affect the OF, SF, ZF, AF, and PF bits in the flags register.

OF   In an addition operation, if the carry into the most-significant bit differs from the carry out of the most-significant bit, then the OF bit is set. Otherwise, the OF bit is cleared. If the operand represents a signed two's complement integer, then the OF bit reflects whether or not the increment or decrement resulted in an overflow.

SF   The SF bit is a copy of the most-significant bit of the result of the increment or decrement operation. If the operand represents a signed two's complement number, then the SF bit reflects the sign of the result.

ZF   If the result of the increment or decrement operation is zero, then the ZF bit is set. Otherwise, the ZF bit is cleared.

AF   If an increment operation produces a carry of 1 from bit 3 or a decrement operation produces a borrow into bit 3, then the AF bit is set. Otherwise, the AF bit is cleared.

PF   The PF bit is set to reflect the parity of the low-order 8 bits of the result.

Note that the CF bit is not affected by execution of an INC or DEC instruction, which is important to remember when using the INC instruction or the DEC instruction with unsigned integer values. This pitfall is illustrated in Program Listing 4.1.

Negation

The IBM PC Assembly language provides an instruction to perform the unary minus operation (negation): the NEG instruction. The **NEG instruction** has the following general form:

[⟨*label*⟩]   NEG   ⟨*destination*⟩   [⟨*comment*⟩]

in which ⟨*destination*⟩ identifies the location of the value to be negated. This instruction performs the two's complement of the value in the general register or memory location specified by the ⟨*destination*⟩ operand. The two's complement operation is actually performed by subtracting the destination operand from zero. Recall that subtraction is performed by adding the minuend (zero in this case), the one's complement of the subtrahend (the value to be negated in this case), and 1. The ⟨*destination*⟩ operand can be a general register (byte or word) or a memory location (byte or word). The destination operand must be interpreted as a signed two's complement integer value for the NEG operation to have meaning.

Execution of a NEG instruction affects the OF, SF, ZF, AF, PF, and CF bits in the flags register.

OF   In an addition operation, if the carry into the most-significant bit differs from the carry out of the most-significant bit, then the OF bit is set. Otherwise, the OF bit is cleared. The IBM PC represents signed integers in two's complement form, and as mentioned, the NEG operation has meaning only for signed integers. With the two's complement representation, the range of integers that can be represented is -128 to $+127$ for byte operands, and $-32,768$ to $+32,767$ for word operands. In each case, one value cannot be successfully negated: For byte operands, this value is -128 (i.e., there is no representation for $+128$ in 8-bit two's complement); for word operands, this value is $-32,768$ (i.e., there is no representation for $+32,768$ in 16-bit two's complement). Taking the two's complement of the byte value -128 or the word value $-32,768$ results in an arithmetic overflow, and setting of the OF bit. In all other cases, the OF bit is cleared.

SF   The SF bit is a copy of the most-significant bit (sign bit) of the result of the negation operation. That is, the SF bit reflects the sign of the result.

ZF   If the result of the negation operation is zero, then the ZF bit is set. Otherwise, the ZF bit is cleared.

AF   If the NEG operation requires a borrow into bit 3, then the AF bit is set. Otherwise, the AF bit is cleared.

PF   The PF bit is set to reflect the parity of the low-order 8 bits of the result.

CF   If the result of the negation operation is nonzero, then the CF bit is set. Otherwise, the CF bit is cleared. This situation occurs because of the way in which the 8088 microprocessor performs the two's complement operation. The destination operand value is subtracted from zero. A subtraction is performed by adding the minuend, the one's complement of the subtrahend, and 1. Since this is a subtraction, the carry out of the sign bit is inverted to reflect a borrow. That is, any nonzero value that is subtracted from zero requires a borrow into the most-significant bit. However, zero can be subtracted from zero without borrowing. Table 3.6 lists some examples of the negation operation on byte values and the resulting value of the CF bit.

TABLE 3.6

Setting of the carry flag by execution of a NEG instruction

Destination Operand	Operation Performed
00000000	00000000
	11111111
	1
	1 00000000
	0 → CF
00000001	00000000
	11111110
	1
	0 11111111
	1 → CF
01111111	00000000
	10000000
	1
	0 10000001
	1 → CF
11111111	00000000
	00000000
	1
	0 00000001
	1 → CF

Multiplication

The IBM PC Assembly language provides two integer multiply instructions: one for unsigned integer values (MUL) and one for signed two's complement integer values (IMUL). The **MUL instruction** has the following general form:

[⟨*label*⟩] MUL ⟨*source*⟩ [⟨*comment*⟩]

in which ⟨*source*⟩ identifies the location of the multiplier. The ⟨*source*⟩ operand can be either a general register (byte or word) or a memory location (byte or word). If the source operand has a type attribute of byte, then the MUL instruction causes the 8-bit unsigned integer value in the AL-register to be multiplied by the 8-bit unsigned integer value of the source operand. This multiplication produces a 16-bit unsigned integer product that replaces the value in the AX-register. If the source operand has a type attribute of word, then the MUL instruction causes the 16-bit unsigned integer value in the AX-register to be multiplied by the 16-bit unsigned integer value of the source operand. This multiplication produces a 32-bit unsigned integer product that replaces the value in the DX : AX register pair.

Execution of a MUL instruction affects the SF, ZF, AF, PF, OF, and CF bits in the flags register:

1.   The SF, ZF, AF, and PF bits are undefined following execution of a MUL instruction.

2.   If the upper half of the product (AH-register for byte multiplication, DX-register for word multiplication) is nonzero, then the OF and CF bits are set. Otherwise, the OF and CF bits are cleared. These bits indicate whether or not the product overflows 8 bits for byte multiplication or 16 bits for word multiplication.

EXAMPLES

The instruction

```
MUL BL
```

multiplies the 8-bit unsigned integer value in the AL-register by the 8-bit unsigned integer value in the BL-register, leaving the 16-bit unsigned integer product in the AX-register. If the AH-register is nonzero (i.e., the product does not fit in the 8-bit AL-register), then the OF and CF bits of the flags register are set.

Suppose the data segment definition for a program contains the variable definition

```
TWO DW   2
```

The instruction

```
MUL TWO
```

multiplies the 16-bit unsigned integer value in the AX-register by the 16-bit unsigned integer value of variable TWO, leaving the 32-bit unsigned integer product in the DX:AX register pair. If the DX-register is nonzero (i.e., the product does not fit in the 16-bit AX-register), then the OF and CF bits of the flags register are set. Note that the instruction

```
MUL TWO
```

could not be replaced by

```
MUL 2 ;SYNTACTICALLY ILLEGAL
```

because the MUL instruction cannot have an immediate operand.

The **IMUL instruction** has the following general form:

[⟨*label*⟩] IMUL ⟨*source*⟩ [⟨*comment*⟩]

in which ⟨*source*⟩ identifies the location of the multiplier. The source operand can be either a general register (byte or word) or a memory location (byte or word). If the source operand has a type attribute of byte, then the IMUL instruction causes the 8-bit signed integer value in the AL-register to be multiplied by the 8-bit signed integer value of the source operand. This multiplication produces a 16-bit signed integer product that replaces the value in the AX-register. If the source operand has a type attribute of word, then the IMUL instruction causes the 16-bit signed integer value in the AX-register to be multiplied by the 16-bit signed integer value of the source operand. This multiplication produces a 32-bit signed integer product that replaces the value in the DX:AX register pair.

Execution of an IMUL instruction affects the SF, ZF, AF, PF, OF, and CF bits of the flags register:

1. The SF, ZF, AF, and PF bits are undefined following execution of an IMUL instruction.

2. If the upper half of the product (AH-register for byte multiplication, DX-register for word multiplication) is the sign extension of the lower half, then the OF and CF bits are cleared. Otherwise, the OF and CF bits are set. These bits indicate whether or not the product overflows 8 bits for byte multiplication or 16 bits for word multiplication.

EXAMPLES

The instruction

```
IMUL BL
```

multiplies the 8-bit signed integer value in the AL-register by the 8-bit signed integer value in the BL-register, leaving the 16-bit product in the AX-register. If the AH-register is not the sign extension of the AL-register (that is, if the product does not fit in the 8-bit AL-register), then the OF and CF bits of the flags register are set.

Suppose the data segment definition for a program contains the variable definition

```
MINUSTWO DW    -2
```

The instruction

```
IMUL MINUSTWO
```

multiplies the 16-bit signed integer value in the AX-register by the 16-bit signed integer value of variable MINUSTWO, leaving the 32-bit signed integer product in the DX:AX register pair. If the DX-register is not the sign extension of the AX-register (i.e., the product does not fit in the 16-bit AX-register), then the OF and CF bits of the flags register are set. Note that the instruction

```
IMUL MINUSTWO
```

could not be replaced by

```
IMUL -2   ; SYNTACTICALLY ILLEGAL
```

because the IMUL instruction cannot have an immediate operand.

Note that for both the MUL and the IMUL instructions, the ⟨source⟩ operand cannot be an immediate value. Also, the destination operand is implicit. The multiplicand always must be in the AL-register for byte multiplication and in the AX-register for word multiplication. The double-length product is always left in the AX-register for byte multiplication and in the DX:AX register pair for word multiplication.

Table 3.7 lists some examples of byte multiplications for both signed and unsigned integer interpretations. The effect of the multiplication on the carry

TABLE 3.7
Signed and unsigned integer multiplication showing the influence of carry and overflow flags

AL and BL Registers	MUL BL				IMUL BL			
	AH	AL	OF	CF	AH	AL	OF	CF
00011000 00000101	00000000	01111000	0	0	00000000	01111000	0	0
00111100 00000011	00000000	10110100	0	0	00000000	10110100	1	1
11101000 00000101	00000100	10001000	1	1	11111111	10001000	0	0
11111111 00000001	00000000	11111111	0	0	11111111	11111111	0	0
10000000 11111110	01111111	00000000	1	1	00000001	00000000	1	1

and overflow flags is also shown. Note that in the third row of the table, the AL and BL register values are specified as 11101000 and 00000101:

1. For the unsigned integer interpretation, these bit patterns represent 232 and 5. When multiplied using the MUL instruction, the product is 0000010010001000 (1160 decimal). The upper half of the product is nonzero, which means the product is greater than 255. Therefore, the OF and CF flag bits are set.

2. For the signed integer interpretation, these bit patterns represent -24 and 5. When multiplied using the IMUL instruction, the product is 1111111110001000 (-120 decimal). The upper half of the product is the sign extension of the lower half, which means the product is in the range -128 to $+127$. Therefore, the OF and CF flag bits are cleared.

Division

The IBM PC Assembly language provides two integer division instructions: one for unsigned integer values (DIV) and one for signed two's complement integer values (IDIV). The **DIV instruction** has the following general form:

[⟨*label*⟩] DIV ⟨*source*⟩   [⟨*comment*⟩]

in which ⟨*source*⟩ identifies the location of the divisor. The ⟨*source*⟩ operand can be either a general register (byte or word) or a memory location (byte or word). If the source operand has a type attribute of byte, then the DIV instruction causes the 16-bit unsigned integer value in the AX-register to be divided by the 8-bit unsigned integer value of the source operand. This division produces an 8-bit unsigned integer quotient and an 8-bit unsigned integer remainder. The quotient replaces the value in the AL-register, and the remainder replaces the value in the AH-register. If the source operand has a type attribute of word, then the DIV instruction causes the 32-bit unsigned integer value in the DX:AX register pair to be divided by the 16-bit unsigned integer value of the source operand. This division produces a 16-bit unsigned integer quotient and a 16-bit unsigned integer remainder. The quotient replaces the value in the AX-register, and the remainder replaces the value in the DX-register.

The OF, SF, ZF, AF, PF, and CF bits of the flags register are undefined following execution of a DIV instruction. If the division results in a quotient that is too large for the destination (AL-register for byte division, AX-register for word division), then the quotient and remainder are undefined, and the processor generates a Type 0 interrupt. This condition occurs if the divisor is not greater than the high-order half of the dividend. Note that a divisor of zero is one such case. DOS services the Type 0 interrupt by displaying the message

```
Divide overflow
```

on the screen and then aborting program execution. (Interrupts are discussed in Chapter 9.)

EXAMPLES

The instruction

```
DIV BL
```

divides the 16-bit unsigned integer value in the AX-register by the 8-bit unsigned integer value in the BL-register, leaving the 8-bit unsigned integer quotient in the AL-register and the 8-bit unsigned integer remainder in the AH-register.

Suppose the data segment definition for a program contains the variable definition

```
THREE DW   3
```

The instruction

```
DIV THREE
```

divides the 32-bit unsigned integer value in the DX:AX register pair by the 16-bit unsigned integer value of variable THREE, leaving the 16-bit unsigned integer quotient in the AX-register and the 16-bit unsigned integer remainder in the DX-register. Note that the instruction

```
DIV THREE
```

could not be replaced by

```
DIV 3     ; SYNTACTICALLY ILLEGAL
```

because the DIV instruction cannot have an immediate operand.

The **IDIV instruction** has the following general form:

[⟨*label*⟩] IDIV ⟨*source*⟩   [⟨*comment*⟩]

in which ⟨*source*⟩ identifies the location of the divisor. The ⟨*source*⟩ operand can be either a general register (byte or word) or a memory location (byte or word). If the source operand has a type attribute of byte, then the IDIV instruction causes the 16-bit signed integer value in the AX-register to be divided by the 8-bit signed integer value of the source operand. This division produces an 8-bit signed integer quotient and an 8-bit signed integer remainder. The quotient replaces the value in the AL-register, and the remainder replaces the value in the AH-register. If the source operand has a type attribute of word, then the IDIV instruction causes the 32-bit signed integer value in the DX:AX register pair to be divided by the 16-bit signed integer value of the source operand. This division produces a 16-bit signed integer quotient and a 16-bit signed integer remainder. The quotient replaces the value in the AX-register, and the remainder replaces the value in the DX-register.

The OF, SF, ZF, AF, PF, and CF bits in the flags register are undefined following execution of an IDIV instruction. If the division results in a quotient that is too large for the destination (AL-register for byte division, AX-register for word division), then the quotient and remainder are undefined, and the processor generates a Type 0 interrupt. This condition occurs if the divisor is not greater in magnitude than the high-order 9 bits of the dividend for byte division or the high-order 17 bits of the dividend for word division.

The instruction

```
IDIV BL
```

divides the 16-bit signed integer value in the AX-register by the 8-bit signed integer value in the BL-register, leaving the 8-bit signed integer quotient in the AL-register and the 8-bit signed integer remainder in the AH-register.

Suppose the data segment definition for a program contains the variable definition

```
MINUS3 DW    -3
```

The instruction

```
IDIV MINUS3
```

divides the 32-bit signed integer value in the DX:AX register pair by the 16-bit signed integer value of variable MINUS3, leaving the 16-bit signed integer quotient in the AX-register and the 16-bit signed integer remainder in the DX-register. Note that the instruction

```
IDIV MINUS3
```

could not be replaced by

```
IDIV -3    ; SYNTACTICALLY ILLEGAL
```

because the IDIV instruction cannot have an immediate operand.

Note that for both the DIV and IDIV instructions, the ⟨source⟩ operand cannot be an immediate value. Also, the destination operand is implicit. The dividend must always be in the AX-register for byte division and the DX:AX register pair for word division. The quotient is always left in the AL-register for byte division and in the AX-register for word division. The remainder is always left in the AH-register for byte division and in the DX-register for word division.

When performing a byte division, it often is necessary to expand the dividend from 8 bits to 16 bits prior to the division operation. As well, when performing a word division, it is often necessary to expand the dividend from 16 bits to 32 bits prior to the division operation. For unsigned integer division, this expansion is simply a matter of moving zero into the upper half of the double length dividend. That is, to expand the 8-bit unsigned integer value in the AL-register to a 16-bit integer value in the AX-register, use the instruction

```
MOV AH,0
```

As well, to expand the 16-bit unsigned integer value in the AX-register to a 32-bit value in the DX:AX register pair, use the instruction

```
MOV DX,0
```

For signed two's complement integer values, this expansion requires extending the sign of the lower half throughout the upper half. The IBM PC Assembly language provides two instructions for expanding an 8-bit or a 16-bit signed integer value to double length: change byte to word (CBW) and change word to double word (CWD).

The **CBW instruction** has the following general form:

```
[⟨label⟩]  CBW        [⟨comment⟩]
```

Execution of a CBW instruction causes the signed integer value in the AL-register to be expanded into a word that replaces the value in the AX-register. This expansion is accomplished by extending the sign bit (bit 7 of the AL-register) through the entire AH-register.

The **CWD instruction** has the following general form:

```
[⟨label⟩]  CWD        [⟨comment⟩]
```

Execution of a CWD instruction causes the signed integer value in the AX-register to be expanded to 32 bits, replacing the value in the DX:AX register pair. This expansion is accomplished by extending the sign bit (bit 15 of the AX-register) through the entire DX-register.

None of the bits in the flags register are affected by the execution of a CBW or a CWD instruction.

EXAMPLES

Suppose the data segment definition for a program contains the following variable definitions

```
COUNT DB ?
X     DW ?
```

Suppose further that the variable COUNT has been given an unsigned integer value, and the variable X has been given a signed integer value.

The following instructions load the CL-register with the value of CEILING(X/2), the smallest integer that is greater than or equal to X/2:

```
MOV AL,COUNT
MOV AH,0
MOV DL,2
DIV DL
ADD AL,AH
MOV CL,AL
```

The first instruction loads the AL-register with the unsigned integer value of the variable COUNT. The second instruction expands this value to a 16-bit unsigned integer value in the AX-register. The third instruction loads the

DL-register with the 8-bit divisor. The fourth instruction divides the 16-bit expansion of the value of the variable COUNT by 2, leaving the quotient in the AL-register and the remainder in the AH-register. The remainder of the division is either 0 or 1. If the remainder is zero, then the quotient is the ceiling of X/2. If the remainder is 1, then 1 must be added to the quotient to produce the ceiling of X/2. That is, adding the remainder to the quotient produces the ceiling of X/2, which is the job of the fifth instruction. The last instruction moves the ceiling of X/2 to the CL-register.

The following instructions divide the signed integer value of variable X by 3, replacing the value of variable X with the quotient:

```
MOV   AX, X
CWD
MOV   BX, 3
IDIV  BX
MOV   X, AX
```

Since the value of X is being interpreted as a signed integer value, the CWD instruction must be used to expand the dividend from 16 bits (in the AX-register) to 32 bits (in the DX:AX register pair). The CWD instruction copies the sign of the AX-register throughout the DX-register.

3.3   Programming Examples

This section presents two example programs: The first involves signed two's complement integers; the second involves unsigned integers.

Fahrenheit-to-Centigrade Conversion

Consider the problem of converting a temperature from degrees Fahrenheit to degrees centigrade. The formula to be used is as follows:

$$C = 5 * (F - 32)/9$$

in which F is temperature in degrees Fahrenheit and C is temperature in degrees centigrade. The resulting centigrade temperature is to be rounded to the nearest integer.

Program Listing 3.1 shows an IBM PC Assembly language program that performs this conversion. Lines 1–7 are the prologue that explains the program's

```
1: ;                    PROGRAM LISTING 3.1
2: ;
3: ; PROGRAM  TO  CONVERT  A  TEMPERATURE  FROM
4: ; FAHRENHEIT TO CENTIGRADE USING THE FORMULA
```

```
 5: ;
 6: ; C = 5*(F-32)/9  ROUNDED TO NEAREST INTEGER
 7: ;
 8:                                         ;PROCEDURES TO
 9:             EXTRN   GETDEC:FAR          ;GET 16-BIT DECIMAL INTEGER
10:             EXTRN   NEWLINE:FAR         ;DISPLAY NEWLINE CHARACTER
11:             EXTRN   PUTDEC:FAR          ;DISPLAY 16-BIT DECIMAL INTEGER
12:             EXTRN   PUTSTRNG:FAR        ;DISPLAY CHARACTER STRING
13: ;
14: ; S T A C K   S E G M E N T   D E F I N I T I O N
15: ;
16: STACK       SEGMENT STACK
17:             DB      256 DUP(?)
18: STACK       ENDS
19: ;
20: ; D A T A   S E G M E N T   D E F I N I T I O N
21: ;
22: DATA        SEGMENT
23: ;
24: PROMPT      DB      'ENTER TEMPERATURE IN DEGREES FAHRENHEIT  '
25: ANNOTATION  DB      '        TEMPERATURE IN DEGREES CENTIGRADE  '
26: ;
27: DATA        ENDS
28: ;
29: ; C O D E   S E G M E N T   D E F I N I T I O N
30: ;
31: CODE        SEGMENT
32:             ASSUME  CS:CODE,SS:STACK,ES:DATA
33: EX_3_1      PROC    FAR
34:             PUSH    DS                  ;PUSH RETURN SEG ADDR ON STACK
35:             SUB     AX,AX               ;PUSH RETURN OFFSET OF ZERO
36:             PUSH    AX                  ;ON STACK
37:             MOV     AX,SEG DATA         ;SET ES-REGISTER TO POINT
38:             MOV     ES,AX               ;TO DATA SEGMENT
39: ;
40:             LEA     DI,PROMPT           ;PROMPT FOR F_TEMP
41:             MOV     CX,42
42:             CALL    PUTSTRNG
43:             CALL    GETDEC              ;GET F_TEMP
44:             SUB     AX,32               ;C_TEMP = (F_TEMP -32) * 5 / 9
45:             MOV     BX,5
46:             IMUL    BX
47:             MOV     BX,9
48:             IDIV    BX
49:             XCHG    AX,DX               ;REMAIN = (F_TEMP-32)*5 mod 9
50:             MOV     BL,5                ;ROUND  = REMAIN / 5
51:             IDIV    BL
52:             CBW
53:             ADD     AX,DX               ;C_TEMP = C_TEMP + ROUND
54: ;
55:             LEA     DI,ANNOTATION       ;DISPLAY C_TEMP
56: ;           MOV     CX,42
57:             CALL    PUTSTRNG
58:             MOV     BH,0
59:             CALL    PUTDEC
60:             CALL    NEWLINE
61:             RET                         ;RETURN
62: EX_3_1      ENDP
63: CODE        ENDS
64:*            END     EX_3_1
```

function. Lines 9–12 identify the external procedures that are called by this program. The GETDEC procedure is used to input the temperature in degrees Fahrenheit. The PUTDEC procedure is used to output the temperature in degrees centigrade. The PUTSTRNG procedure is used to display a prompt message to the user and to annotate the output. Lines 13–18 define the stack segment in the standard way.

Lines 19–27 define the data segment for the program. Two entries appear in the data segment definition. Line 24 defines a 42-character prompt message to ask the user to 'ENTER TEMPERATURE IN DEGREES FAHRENHEIT.' Line 25 defines a 42-character annotation message that describes the output as 'TEMPERATURE IN DEGREES CENTIGRADE.'

Lines 28–63 define the code segment for the program. The code segment contains only one procedure, the main procedure labeled EX_3_1. The procedure begins in the standard way by pushing the return address onto the stack (lines 34–36) and initializing the segment register (lines 37–38). The ES-register is being used to point to the data segment, because both data segment entries are going to be inputs to the PUTSTRNG procedure, and the PUTSTRNG procedure expects the string address to be input in the ES:DI register pair.

Lines 40–42 display the prompt message on the screen using the PUTSTRNG subroutine. The call to GETDEC in line 43 is used to accept a signed integer value from the keyboard. GETDEC returns the input value in the AX-register. This discussion assumes that the input value is 11—that is, the value in the AX-register is now 11.

The SUB instruction in line 44 subtracts 32 from the AX-register, leaving a value of -21 in the AX-register. Lines 45 and 46 are used to multiply the value in the AX-register by 5. Note that it is *not* possible to replace these two instructions with the single instruction

```
IMUL 5
```

because the IMUL instruction cannot have an immediate value as its operand. The constant 5 is moved into the BX-register, and then the value in the AX-register is multiplied by the value in the BX-register. The IMUL instruction is used because temperature values can be positive or negative. The product (-105 in this example) is in the combined DX:AX register pair.

The next step is to divide this product by 9. If 16-bit division is used, then the 32-bit dividend must be in the combined DX:AX register pair. The product is already in the DX:AX register pair. Therefore, there is no need to worry about expanding the dividend before the divide. This situation is often the case when a division operation follows a multiplication operation. The division by 9 is performed by the two instuctions in lines 47 and 48. Again these two instructions could *not* be replaced by the single instruction

```
IDIV 5
```

because the IDIV instruction cannot have an immediate value as its operand. The IDIV instruction is used because the computation involves signed two's complement integer values. The quotient of the division (-11 in this example) is in the AX-register, and the remainder (-6 in this example) is in the DX-register.

The next step is to round the quotient to the nearest integer. The remainder of a division by 9 is in the range 0 to 8 if the dividend is positive and is in the range 0 to -8 if the dividend is negative. A remainder of n represents a fraction of $n/9$. If n is greater than or equal to 5, then 1 must be added to the quotient. If n is less than or equal to -5, then -1 must be added to the quotient. Otherwise, the quotient is left as is. This rounding can be accomplished by dividing the remainder by 5 and then adding the quotient of that division (either 0, 1, or -1) to the quotient of the division by 9, which is accomplished in lines 49–53 of the Program Listing 3.1. In line 49, the remainder (-6) is moved into the AX-register, and the quotient (-11) is moved into the DX-register. Since the AX-register already contains the dividend in 16-bit form, and since the value in the DX-register must be protected, a byte division is performed. The constant 5 is moved into the BL-register (line 50), and the byte division is performed by the IDIV instruction in line 51. The quotient (-1) is in the AL-register, and the remainder (-1) is in the AH-register. The next step is to add the quotient of this division (-1 in the AL-register) to the quotient of the division by 9 (-11 in the DX-register). However, one of these quotients is a byte operand, and the other is a word operand. The two operands must be of the same type before the addition operation can be performed. The CBW instruction in line 52 expands the byte operand in the AL-register into a word operand in the AX-register by extending the sign of the AL-register through the entire AH-register. With the ADD instruction in line 53, the operand in the DX-register (-11) is added to the operand in the AX-register (-1), leaving the sum (-12) in the AX-register. This quantity in the AX-register is the centigrade temperature.

The instructions in lines 55–57 display the annotation message on the screen. Note that line 56 is a comment line—it is not an instruction to move 42 to the CX-register. Such an instruction would be redundant. The value 42 was moved to the CX-register by the MOV instruction in line 41, and none of the instructions between line 41 and line 56 modify the value of the CX-register. Therefore, the value 42 remains in the CX-register. The comment line in line 56 serves documentation purposes. It indicates that the string being displayed is 42 characters in length. The MOV instruction in line 58 sets the alignment code for the PUTDEC procedure in the BH-register (0 implies that the value is to be displayed with no leading or trailing blanks). The call to PUTDEC in line 59 displays the centigrade temperature in the AX-register according to the alignment code in the BH-register. There is no need to worry that the call to PUTSTRNG in line 57 would destroy the centigrade temperature in the AX-register, because all I/O procedures save and restore the registers that they use.

The RET instruction in line 61 returns control to DOS.

The following are the results from some executions of Program Listing 3.1:

```
ENTER TEMPERATURE IN DEGREES FAHRENHEIT -20
   TEMPERATURE IN DEGREES CENTIGRADE -29
```

```
ENTER TEMPERATURE IN DEGREES FAHRENHEIT 32
      TEMPERATURE IN DEGREES CENTIGRADE 0

ENTER TEMPERATURE IN DEGREES FAHRENHEIT 100
      TEMPERATURE IN DEGREES CENTIGRADE 38

ENTER TEMPERATURE IN DEGREES FAHRENHEIT 212
      TEMPERATURE IN DEGREES CENTIGRADE 100
```

Sum of Cubes of First *n* Positive Integers

Consider the problem of computing the sum of the cubes of the first n positive integers using the following formula:

$$1^3 + 2^3 + 3^3 + \ldots + n^3 = [n(n + 1)/2]^2$$

The value of n will be supplied as an input. Since n is a positive integer, and the computation deals with only positive integers, unsigned integer arithmetic is used in performing this computation.

Program Listing 3.2 shows an IMB PC Assembly language program that performs this computation. Lines 1–7 contain the prologue, which explains the program's function. Lines 8–12 identify the external procedures that are called by the program. The GETDEC$ procedure inputs the unsigned integer value of n. The PUTDEC$ procedure outputs the value of n and the sum of the cubes of the first n positive integers. The PUTSTRNG procedure displays a prompt message to the user and annotates the output. Lines 13–17 define the stack segment in the standard way.

```
 1: ;                     PROGRAM LISTING 3.2
 2: ;
 3: ; GIVEN AN INTEGER VALUE FOR n, THIS PROGRAM COMPUTES THE SUM OF
 4: ; THE CUBES  OF THE FIRST n POSITIVE INTEGERS USING THE FORMULA:
 5: ;
 6: ;  3    3    3           3            2
 7: ; 1  + 2  + 3  + ... + n  = [n(n + 1)/2]
 8:                              ;PROCEDURES TO
 9:           EXTRN   GETDEC$:FAR    ;GET 16-BIT UNSIGNED DEC INTEGER
10:           EXTRN   NEWLINE:FAR    ;DISPLAY NEWLINE CHARACTER
11:           EXTRN   PUTDEC$:FAR    ;DISPLAY 16-BIT UNSIGNED DEC INT
12:           EXTRN   PUTSTRNG:FAR   ;DISPLAY CHARACTER STRING
13: ;
14: ; <***** S T A C K    S E G M E N T    D E F I N I T I O N *****>
15: STACK     SEGMENT STACK
16:           DB      256 DUP(?)
17: STACK     ENDS
18: ;
19: ; <*****    D A T A    S E G M E N T    D E F I N I T I O N *****>
20: DATA      SEGMENT
21: PROMPT    DB      'ENTER A POSITIVE INTEGER VALUE    '
22: MESSAGE_1 DB      'THE SUM OF THE FIRST '
23: MESSAGE_2 DB      ' CUBE(S) IS '
24: TWO       DW      2                  ;CONSTANT 2
25: N         DW      ?                  ;NUMBER OF CUBES TO SUM
26: SUM       DW      ?                  ;SUM OF FIRST N CUBES
```

```
27: DATA        ENDS
28: ;
29: ; <*****  C O D E   S E G M E N T   D E F I N I T I O N *****>
30: CODE        SEGMENT
31:             ASSUME    CS:CODE,SS:STACK,DS:DATA,ES:DATA
32: EX_3_2      PROC      FAR
33:             PUSH      DS                    ;PUSH RETURN SEG ADDR ON STACK
34:             SUB       AX,AX                 ;PUSH RETURN OFFSET OF ZERO
35:             PUSH      AX                    ;ON STACK
36:             MOV       AX,SEG DATA           ;SET DS AND ES REGISTERS TO
37:             MOV       DS,AX                 ;POINT TO DATA SEGMENT
38:             MOV       ES,AX
39:             LEA       DI,PROMPT             ;PROMPT FOR N
40:             MOV       CX,33
41:             CALL      PUTSTRNG
42:             CALL      GETDEC$               ;GET N
43:             MOV       N,AX
44:             INC       AX                    ;SUM = [N(N + 1)/2] ** 2
45:             MUL       N
46:             DIV       TWO
47:             MUL       AX
48:             MOV       SUM,AX
49:             CALL      NEWLINE               ;SKIP TO NEXT LINE ON DISPLAY
50:             LEA       DI,MESSAGE_1          ;DISPLAY 'THE SUM OF THE FIRST '
51:             MOV       CX,21
52:             CALL      PUTSTRNG
53:             MOV       AX,N                  ;DISPLAY N
54:             MOV       BH,0
55:             CALL      PUTDEC$
56:             LEA       DI,MESSAGE_2          ;DISPLAY ' CUBE(S) IS '
57:             MOV       CX,12
58:             CALL      PUTSTRNG
59:             MOV       AX,SUM                ;DISPLAY SUM
60:             CALL      PUTDEC$
61:             RET                             ;RETURN
62: EX_3_2      ENDP
63: CODE        ENDS
64:*            END       EX_3_2
```

Lines 18–27 define the data segment for the program. Six entries appear in the data segment definition. Line 21 defines a 33-character prompt message that asks the user to 'ENTER A POSITIVE INTEGER VALUE'. Lines 22 and 23 define two messages used for annotation of the output. By displaying the value of n after the first message and the value of the sum after the second message, the output line will look like the following:

```
THE SUM OF THE FIRST 5 CUBE(S) IS 225
```

Line 24 defines a word variable TWO and initializes its value to 2. This variable is used as a constant in the program. Line 25 defines a word variable N, which holds the input value. The N variable is not given an initial value. Line 26 defines a word variable SUM, which holds the sum of the cubes of the first n positive integers. The SUM variable is not given an initial value.

Lines 28–63 define the code segment for the program. The code segment contains a single procedure, the main procedure labeled EX_3_2. The procedure begins in the standard way by pushing the return address onto the stack (lines

33–35) and initializing the segment registers (lines 36–38). Both the DS-register and the ES-register are used to point to the data segment. The ES-register addresses the data segment because several entries in the data segment definition (lines 21–23) are strings to be displayed by the PUTSTRNG procedure, which expects the string's address to be in the ES:DI register pair. The DS-register addresses the data segment because its use leads to more efficient machine language representations of memory referencing instructions. Several of the entries in the data segment definition (lines 24–26) are used in memory referencing instructions (e.g., lines 43, 45, and 48). The default segment register for a memory referencing instruction is the DS-register. If a register other than the DS-register is required in a memory referencing instruction, then a 1-byte segment prefix, which identifies that segment register, must be appended to the beginning of that instruction's machine language representation. If the ES-register alone is used to address the data segment, then the additional instruction byte is required. However, if the DS-register also addresses the data segment, then the assembler can use the more efficient machine language representation.

Lines 39–41 display the prompt message to the user. The call to GETDEC$ in line 42 is used to accept a 16-bit unsigned integer value from the keyboard. GETDEC$ returns the input value in the AX-register. This discussion assumes that the input value is 5—thus the AX-register now contains 5. The MOV instruction in line 43 copies the value in the AX-register into the memory location identified by the symbolic name N. The input value of 5 is now the value of variable N as well as the value in the AX-register.

The INC instruction in line 44 increments the value in the AX-register, which now contains 6, the value $(N + 1)$. Line 45 causes the value in the AX-register to be multiplied by the value of variable N, $N(N + 1)$ (30 in this example). The product is in the DX:AX register pair. The MUL instruction is used rather than the IMUL instruction because unsigned integer arithmetic is being used.

The next step is to divide the product by 2. As in Program Listing 3.1, a multiply precedes a divide. Therefore, the dividend is already expanded to 32 bits. The DIV instruction in line 46 divides the 32-bit value in the DX:AX register pair (30) by the 16-bit value of variable TWO (2), leaving the quotient (15) in the AX-register and the remainder (0) in the DX-register.

The value in the AX-register represents $[N(N + 1)/2]$. The MUL instruction in line 47 multiplies the value in the AX-register (15) by the value in the AX-register (15), leaving the result (225) in the DX:AX register pair. This 32-bit unsigned integer value is the sum of the cubes of the first $N = 5$ positive integers. This program assumes that the value can fit into 16 bits. The MOV instruction in line 48 moves the lower 16 bits of the 32-bit result into the variable SUM.

The instructions in lines 50–52 display the first part of the output annotation:

THE SUM OF THE FIRST

The instructions in lines 53–55 display the value of N. The MOV instruction in line 53 places the value of variable N in the AX-register. The MOV instruction in line 54 sets the alignment code in the BH-register (0 implies that the number is to be displayed with no leading or trailing blanks). In line 55, the PUTDEC$ procedure is called to display the value in the AX-register, according to the code in the BH-register. The instructions in lines 56–58 display the last part of the output annotation:

```
CUBE(S) IS
```

The instructions in lines 59 and 60 display the value of the variable SUM. The alignment code now does not have to be set in the BH-register, because the value of the BH-register has not changed since the last call to PUTDEC$.

The RET instruction in line 61 returns control to the DOS.

The following are the results from some executions of this program:

```
ENTER A POSITIVE INTEGER VALUE 3
THE SUM OF THE FIRST 3 CUBE(S) IS 36

ENTER A POSITIVE INTEGER VALUE 8
THE SUM OF THE FIRST 8 CUBE(S) IS 1296

ENTER A POSITIVE INTEGER VALUE 22
THE SUM OF THE FIRST 22 CUBE(S) IS 64009

ENTER A POSITIVE INTEGER VALUE 23
THE SUM OF THE FIRST 23 CUBE(S) IS 10640
```

Note that the sum of the cubes of the first 23 positive integers is less than the sum of the cubes of the first 22 positive integers, which obviously is *not* correct. The sum has to increase as *n* increases. By hand calculation, it is easy to see that 64009 is the correct output for an input of 22 but that 10640 is not the correct output for an input of 23. To locate the problem, a DEBUG trace is used.

To facilitate the trace, an assembler-generated listing of the program can be obtained. The listing requires more than 80 characters per line. However, the default line length used by the assembler is 80 characters. To instruct the assembler to expand the line length to 132 characters (the number of characters per line for the IBM PC graphics printer operating in the compressed mode), the PAGE pseudo-operation is used. The **PAGE pseudo-operation** has the following general form:

```
PAGE ⟨lines/page⟩, ⟨char/line⟩
```

in which ⟨*lines/page*⟩ is an integer constant in the range 10–255 that specifies the maximum number of lines per page of the listing and ⟨*char/line*⟩ is an integer constant in the range 60–132 that specifies the maximum number of characters per line of the listing.

The IBM PC graphics printer can print 6 lines per inch (66 lines per page) or 8 lines per inch (88 lines per page). It can print 80 characters per line (normal mode) or 132 characters per line (compressed mode). The pseudo-operation

```
PAGE 80,132
```

inserted as the first line of the assembly module in Program Listing 3.2 instructs the assembler to generate the listing for 80 lines per page and 132 characters per line. The 80-line page is specified rather than the 88-line page to allow for one inch of margin.

In the MASM command line, the third argument identifies the listing file. The rules for expressing this argument are summarized in Appendix F. The command

```
MASM B:EX_3_2,B:,B:;
```

instructs the assembler to translate the assembly module in file EX_3_2.ASM on the diskette in drive B. MASM places the object code file on the diskette in drive B with EX_3_2.OBJ as the filename, and it places the listing file on the diskette in drive B with EX_3_2.LST as the filename. Assembler Listing 3.3 is a copy of the listing file generated for the assembly module in Program Listing 3.2. Before assembling the module, the first two comment lines in Program Listing 3.2 were replaced by the PAGE and TITLE pseudo-operations that appear prior to the prologue in Assembler Listing 3.3. The text in the operand field of the TITLE pseudo-operation is placed on the second line of every page of the program listing.

To place the IBM PC graphics printer in the compressed mode, use the following command:

```
MODE LPT1:132,8
```

To return the printer to its normal print mode, use the command

```
MODE LPT1:80,6
```

See the **DOS Reference Manual** for a detailed description of the MODE command.

The right-hand portion of the assembler-generated program listing is the Assembly language source code as entered via the EDLIN editor. The left-hand portion of the listing is the machine language translation of the source code, which is given in hexadecimal. The first column of the machine code listing gives offset relative to the beginning of the segment, and the subsequent columns give the contents of consecutive memory locations beginning with that offset. For example, the lines

```
0036 20 43 55 42 45 28        MESSAGE_2 DB        ' CUBE(S) IS '
     53 29 20 49 53 20
```

indicate that the character string MESSAGE_2 begins at offset 0036 hex within the data segment and that the initial values to be stored in the data segment from offset 0036 through offset 0041 are the hex values 20 43 55 42 45 28 53 29 20 49 53 20, which are the ASCII representations of the characters of the string ' CUBE(S) IS '. As another example, the line

```
0007 8E D8         MOV DS,AX         ;POINT TO DATA SEGMENT
```

indicates that the instruction

```
MOV DS,AX
```

```
The Microsoft MACRO Assembler , Version 1.27            Page    1-1
ASSEMBLER LISTING 3.3                                           10-11-87


                              TITLE   ASSEMBLER LISTING 3.3
                              PAGE    80,132
                         ; GIVEN AN INTEGER VALUE FOR n, THIS PROGRAM COMPUTES THE SUM OF
                         ; THE CUBES  OF THE FIRST n POSITIVE INTEGERS USING THE FORMULA:
                         ;    3    3    3         3              2
                         ; 1  + 2  + 3  + ... + n  = [n(n + 1)/2]
                                                             ;PROCEDURES TO
                              EXTRN   GETDEC$:FAR            ;GET 16-BIT UNSIGNED DEC INTEGER
                              EXTRN   NEWLINE:FAR            ;DISPLAY NEWLINE CHARACTER
                              EXTRN   PUTDEC$:FAR            ;DISPLAY 16-BIT UNSIGNED DEC INT
                              EXTRN   PUTSTRNG:FAR           ;DISPLAY CHARACTER STRING
                         ;
                         ; <***** S T A C K   S E G M E N T   D E F I N I T I O N *****>
0000                     STACK   SEGMENT STACK
0000  0100 [                    DB      256 DUP(?)
                 ??
              ]


0100                     STACK   ENDS
                         ;
                         ; <***** D A T A   S E G M E N T   D E F I N I T I O N *****>
0000                     DATA    SEGMENT
0000  45 4E 54 45 52 20  PROMPT  DB      'ENTER A POSITIVE INTEGER VALUE   '
      41 20 50 4F 53 49
      54 49 56 45 20 49
      4E 54 45 47 45 52
      20 56 41 4C 55 45
      20 20 20
0021  54 48 45 20 53 55  MESSAGE_1 DB    'THE SUM OF THE FIRST '
      4D 20 4F 46 20 54
      48 45 20 46 49 52
      53 54 20
0036  20 43 55 42 45 28  MESSAGE_2 DB    ' CUBE(S) IS '
      53 29 20 49 53 20
0042  0002               TWO     DW      2                  ;CONSTANT 2
0044  ????               N       DW      ?                  ;NUMBER OF CUBES TO SUM
0046  ????               SUM     DW      ?                  ;SUM OF FIRST N CUBES
0048                     DATA    ENDS
                         ;
                         ; <***** C O D E   S E G M E N T   D E F I N I T I O N *****>
0000                     CODE    SEGMENT
                                 ASSUME  CS:CODE,SS:STACK,DS:DATA,ES:DATA
0000                     EX_3_2  PROC    FAR
0000  1E                         PUSH    DS                 ;PUSH RETURN SEG ADDR ON STACK
0001  2B C0                      SUB     AX,AX              ;PUSH RETURN OFFSET OF ZERO
0003  50                         PUSH    AX                 ;ON STACK
0004  B8 ---- R                  MOV     AX,SEG DATA        ;SET DS AND ES REGISTERS TO
0007  8E D8                      MOV     DS,AX              ;POINT TO DATA SEGMENT
0009  8E C0                      MOV     ES,AX
000B  8D 3E 0000 R               LEA     DI,PROMPT          ;PROMPT FOR N
000F  B9 0021                    MOV     CX,33
0012  9A 0000 ---- E             CALL    PUTSTRNG
0017  9A 0000 ---- E             CALL    GETDEC$            ;GET N
001C  A3 0044 R                  MOV     N,AX
001F  40                         INC     AX                 ;SUM = [N(N + 1)/2] ** 2
0020  F7 26 0044 R               MUL     N
0024  F7 36 0042 R               DIV     TWO
0028  F7 E0                      MUL     AX
```

```
002A  A3 0046 R                MOV     SUM,AX
002D  9A 0000 ---- E           CALL    NEWLINE          ;SKIP TO NEXT LINE ON DISPLAY
0032  8D 3E 0021 R             LEA     DI,MESSAGE_1     ;DISPLAY 'THE SUM OF THE FIRST '
0036  B9 0015                  MOV     CX,21
0039  9A 0000 ---- E           CALL    PUTSTRNG
003E  A1 0044 R                MOV     AX,N             ;DISPLAY N
0041  B7 00                    MOV     BH,0
0043  9A 0000 ---- E           CALL    PUTDEC$
0048  8D 3E 0036 R             LEA     DI,MESSAGE_2     ;DISPLAY ' CUBE(S) IS '
004C  B9 000C                  MOV     CX,12
004F  9A 0000 ---- E           CALL    PUTSTRNG
0054  A1 0046 R                MOV     AX,SUM           ;DISPLAY SUM
0057  9A 0000 ---- E           CALL    PUTDEC$
005C  CB                       RET                      ;RETURN
005D                 EX_3_2    ENDP
005D                 CODE      ENDS
                               END     EX_3_2
```

The Microsoft MACRO Assembler , Version 1.27   Page   Symbols-1
ASSEMBLER LISTING 3.3   10-11-87

Segments and groups:

N a m e	Size	align	combine	class
CODE	005D	PARA	NONE	
DATA	0048	PARA	NONE	
STACK.	0100	PARA	STACK	

Symbols:

N a m e	Type	Value	Attr	
EX_3_2	F PROC	0000	CODE	Length =005D
GETDEC$.	L FAR	0000		External
MESSAGE_1.	L BYTE	0021	DATA	
MESSAGE_2.	L BYTE	0036	DATA	
N.	L WORD	0044	DATA	
NEWLINE.	L FAR	0000		External
PROMPT	L BYTE	0000	DATA	
PUTDEC$.	L FAR	0000		External
PUTSTRNG	L FAR	0000		External
SUM.	L WORD	0046	DATA	
TWO.	L WORD	0042	DATA	

Warning Severe
Errors   Errors
0   0

A>

begins at offset 0007 within the code segment and is a two-byte instruction whose machine language representation is 8ED8 hexadecimal.

The execution problem encountered in Program Listing 3.2 appears to be in the computation. Tracing the execution of the initialization instructions at the beginning of the program is of no value, as is tracing the execution of the PUTSTRNG and GETDEC$ procedures. It would be nice to begin the trace after return from the GETDEC$ procedure (i.e., just prior to execution of the MOV N,AX instruction). Assembler Listing 3.3 indicates that the instruction

```
MOV N,AX
```

begins at offset 001C within the code segment. DEBUG Listing 3.4 shows a DEBUG session that begins the trace at this instruction. The second command issued to DEBUG was the G(go) command. The command

```
G 1C
```

directed the DEBUG program to begin execution with the instruction addressed by the CS:IP register pair (the instruction at location 092D0 in the example) and to continue executing instructions until the instruction at offset 001C within the code segment was reached. The instructions executed in response to this command included the PUTSTRNG and GETDEC$ procedures. The DEBUG

```
                        DEBUG LISTING 3.4
DEBUG B:EX_3_2.EXE
-R
AX=0000  BX=0000  CX=03F3  DX=0000  SP=0100  BP=0000  SI=0000  DI=0000
DS=0908  ES=0908  SS=0918  CS=092D  IP=0000   NV UP DI PL NZ NA PO NC
092D:0000 1E            PUSH    DS
-G 1C
ENTER A POSITIVE INTEGER VALUE    23

AX=0017  BX=0000  CX=0021  DX=0000  SP=00FC  BP=00A0  SI=0000  DI=0000
DS=0928  ES=0928  SS=0918  CS=092D  IP=001C   NV UP DI PL ZR NA PE NC
092D:001C A34400        MOV     [0044],AX                      DS:0044=0000
-T

AX=0017  BX=0000  CX=0021  DX=0000  SP=00FC  BP=00A0  SI=0000  DI=0000
DS=0928  ES=0928  SS=0918  CS=092D  IP=001F   NV UP DI PL ZR NA PE NC
092D:001F 40            INC     AX
-T

AX=0018  BX=0000  CX=0021  DX=0000  SP=00FC  BP=00A0  SI=0000  DI=0000
DS=0928  ES=0928  SS=0918  CS=092D  IP=0020   NV UP DI PL NZ NA PE NC
092D:0020 F7264400      MUL     WORD PTR [0044]                DS:0044=0017
-T

AX=0228  BX=0000  CX=0021  DX=0000  SP=00FC  BP=00A0  SI=0000  DI=0000
DS=0928  ES=0928  SS=0918  CS=092D  IP=0024   NV UP DI PL ZR NA PE NC
092D:0024 F7364200      DIV     WORD PTR [0042]                DS:0042=0002
-T

AX=0114  BX=0000  CX=0021  DX=0000  SP=00FC  BP=00A0  SI=0000  DI=0000
DS=0928  ES=0928  SS=0918  CS=092D  IP=0028   NV UP DI NG NZ AC PO CY
092D:0028 F7E0          MUL     AX
-T

AX=2990  BX=0000  CX=0021  DX=0001  SP=00FC  BP=00A0  SI=0000  DI=0000
DS=0928  ES=0928  SS=0918  CS=092D  IP=002A   OV UP DI PL NZ NA PO CY
092D:002A A34600        MOV     [0046],AX                      DS:0046=0000
-Q

A>
```

display shows that immediately following the G 1C command, the prompt message was displayed by the PUTSTRNG procedure, the value 23 was entered by the user, and DEBUG regained control with the CS:IP register pairs addressing the

```
MOV N,AX
```

instruction at offset 001C. The value in the AX-register at this point (0017 hex) is the input value (23 decimal) returned by the GETDEC$ procedure.

The remainder of the DEBUG session is the single-step trace of the computation. The first trace command caused the instruction

```
MOV N,AX
```

to be executed. The second trace command caused the instruction

```
INC AX
```

to be executed. The value in the AX-register was incremented from 17 hex to 18 hex (23 decimal to 24 decimal), which is the value $N + 1$. The third trace command caused the instruction

```
MUL N
```

to be executed, which performed the computation

```
(N+1)*N = 24(23)
```

which produced the product 552 decimal (228 hex) in the DX:AX register pair. The fourth trace command caused the instruction

```
DIV TWO
```

to be executed, which performed the computation

```
(N+1)*N/2 = 552/2
```

which produced the quotient 276 decimal (114 hex) in the AX-register. The fifth trace command caused the instruction

```
MUL AX
```

to be executed, which performed the computation

```
((N+1)*N/2)² = (276)²
```

which produced the product 76,176 decimal (12990 hex) in the DX:AX register pair. Note that the OF and CF bits of the flags register were set by execution of this MUL instruction; thus, the product cannot be reduced to 16 bits. However, the program assumes that the product can be reduced to 16 bits, and the next instruction to be executed

```
MOV SUM,AX
```

stores the lower 16 bits of the product. In the example traced in DEBUG Listing 3.4, the value 2990 hex (10,640 decimal) would be stored for the SUM, which is the value that was displayed when the program was executed with an input of 23.

Arithmetic overflow occurred in the computation but was not detected by the program. (Chapter 4 discusses the making of a decision in a program based on a condition such as arithmetic overflow.)

3.4 Overflow Detection

Overflow detection depends on the integer interpretation being used. With the two's complement interpretation, overflow can be detected in addition and subtraction operations by comparing the signs of the operands with the sign of the result. The rules for detecting overflow on an addition operation with the two's complement interpretation are as follows:

1. If the operands have different signs, then overflow is impossible.
2. If the operands have the same sign, then the sign of the sum must be the same as the sign of the operands. If the sign of the sum is *not* the same as that of the two operands, then an arithmetic overflow has occurred.

There is also an alternate method for detecting overflow on an addition operation with the two's complement interpretation:

1. If the carry into the sign bit differs from the carry out of the sign bit, then arithmetic overflow has occurred. If the carry into the sign bit is the same as the carry out of the sign bit, then arithmetic overflow has *not* occurred.

The first method is probably the more convenient method for humans. The second method is easier to implement in the circuitry of a digital computer.

Subtraction in the IBM PC is performed by adding the minuend, the one's complement of the subtrahend, and 1. All of the preceding rules for detection of overflow in addition also apply to detection of overflow in subtraction.

EXAMPLES

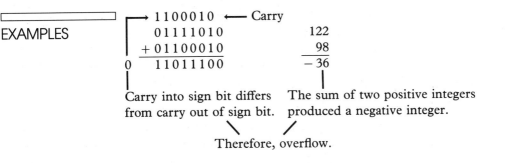

```
      10000110              − 122
    − 01100010            − (+98)

   ┌─→ 0011111   ←── Carry
   │    10000110              − 122
   │  + 10011101            + (− 98)
   │  +         1
   │1   00100100              + 36
   │
```

Carry into sign bit differs   The sum of two negative integers
from carry out of sign bit.   produced a positive integer.

Therefore, overflow.

Recall that with the two's complement interpretation, the range of integers that can be represented with n-bit binary numbers is -2^{n-1} to $+2^{n-1} - 1$. Note that there is always one negative integer for which there is no corresponding positive integer: -2^{n-1}. For $n = 8$, the negative integer that has no corresponding positive integer is -128, which cannot be negated successfully. An attempt to take the two's complement of this integer automatically results in an arithmetic overflow. In the IBM PC, the two's complement operation is implemented by a subtraction operation. To take the two's complement of an integer, the IBM PC simply subtracts the integer from zero. Therefore, the overflow generated by negating the largest-magnitude negative number is detected in the same way that overflow on subtraction is detected.

EXAMPLE

To negate 10000000:

```
   ┌─→ 1111111   ←── Carry
   │    00000000                    0
   │    01111111           − (− 128)
   │           1
   │0   10000000              − 128
   └─→                       Overflow
```

Carry into sign bit differs from carry out of sign bit. Therefore, overflow.

With the unsigned integer interpetation, overflow occurs whenever there is a carry out of the most-significant bit in addition or a borrow into the most-significant bit in subtraction. When subtraction is performed by adding the minuend, the one's complement of the subtrahend, and 1, the carry out of the most-significant bit in the addition is the inverse of the borrow into the most-significant bit for the subtraction. That is:

1. If the carry out of the most-significant bit in the addition portion of the operation is 0, then the borrow into the most-significant bit for the subtraction is a 1.
2. If the carry out of the most-significant bit in the addition portion of the operation is 1, then the borrow into the most-significant bit for the subtraction is a 0.

EXAMPLES

```
  1 1 1 1 1 0 0  ←— Carry
    1 1 1 1 1 0 0              252
  + 0 0 0 0 1 1 0 0          + 12
1   0 0 0 0 1 0 0 0             8
```

└─→ Carry of 1 from the most-significant bit. Therefore, overflow.

```
    0 0 0 0 1 1 0 0           12
  − 0 0 0 0 1 1 1 0         − 14
```

```
    0 0 0 0 0 0 1  ←— Carry
    0 0 0 0 1 1 0 0
  + 1 1 1 1 0 0 0 1
              1
0   1 1 1 1 1 1 1 0          254
```

└─→ Carry of 0 from the most-significant bit means a borrow of 1 into the most-significant bit. Therefore, overflow.

The Intel 8088 microprocessor in the IBM PC detects overflow in addition, subtraction, and negation operations and sets the OF and/or CF bits in the flags register to indicate the overflow condition. In an addition operation or the addition portion of a subtraction or negation operation, if the carry into the most-significant bit differs from the carry out of the most-significant bit, then the OF bit is set in the flags register. Otherwise, the OF bit is cleared following these operations. In an addition operation, the carry out of the most-significant bit is recorded in the CF bit of the flags register. In a subtraction or negation operation, the inverse of the carry out of the most-significant bit (i.e., the borrow into the most-significant bit) is recorded in the CF bit of the flags register. Therefore, the CF bit in the flags register is actually a carry/borrow flag.

In a multiplication operation, arithmetic overflow is impossible. When multiplying two n-bit binary numbers, a $2n$ bit product is produced. Regardless of the magnitude of the two operands, the product will fit in $2n$ bits. The Intel 8088 microprocessor in the IBM PC does, however, provide an overflow check on multiplication. It is an indication of whether or not the product can be reduced to n bits without loss of significant digits. For an unsigned integer multiplication operation, if the upper half of the product is nonzero, then the CF and OF bits in the flags register are set. Otherwise, both the CF and OF bits in the flags register are cleared following execution of an unsigned integer multiply instruction. For a signed two's complement integer multiplication operation, if the upper half of the product is *not* the sign extension of the lower half, then the CF and OF bits in the flags register are set. Otherwise, the CF and OF bits in the flags register are cleared following execution of a signed integer multiply instruction.

In a division operation, overflow is possible. For an unsigned integer division operation, overflow occurs if the divisor is not greater than the high-order half of the dividend. For an n-bit signed integer division operation, overflow occurs if the divisor is not greater than the high-order $n + 1$ bits of the dividend. The Intel 8088 microprocessor detects overflow on a division operation and responds to the condition by generating a Type 0 interrupt.

Note that for addition, subtraction, negation, and multiplication operations, the microprocessor detects arithmetic overflow but does nothing about it, except for setting the CF and/or OF bits in the flags register. These flag bits can be tested by the Assembly language program, and a decision can be made based on their values. Chapter 4 is devoted to decisions and loops (i.e., control structures) in Assembly language programs and discusses an example of how a program can react to an arithmetic overflow condition. Program Listing 3.2 is modified to include an overflow check.

NUMERIC EXERCISES

3.1 Perform the following additions involving 8-bit binary integers in the modulo 2^8 number system. In each case, state whether or not overflow occurs.

   a. 00111011   b. 10110101
       01011001   00110011

   c. 10110011   d. 11101011
       01011011   11110010

3.2 Perform the following additions involving 8-bit binary integers in the two's complement number system. In each case, state whether or not overflow occurs.

   a. 00111011   b. 10110101
       01011001   00110011

   c. 10110011   d. 11101011
       01011011   11110010

3.3 Perform the following subtractions involving 8-bit binary integers in the modulo 2^8 number system by adding the two's complement of the subtrahend to the minuend. In each case, state whether or not overflow occurs.

   a. 00111011   b. 10110101
       01011001   00110011

   c. 10110011   d. 11101011
       01011011   11110010

3.4 Perform the following subtractions involving 8-bit binary integers in the two's complement number system by adding the two's complement of the subtrahend to the minuend. In each case, state whether or not overflow occurs.

   a. 00111011   b. 10110101
       01011001   00110011

   c. 10110011   d. 11101011
       01011011   11110010

PROGRAMMING EXERCISES

3.1 Design an algorithm to convert a temperature from degrees centigrade to degrees Fahrenheit using the formula

$$F = (9/5)C + 32$$

in which C is temperature in degrees centigrade and F is temperature in degrees Fahrenheit. Round the Fahrenheit temperature to the nearest integer. Implement your algorithm with an IBM PC Assembly language program. Your input should be the centigrade temperature entered via the keyboard. Your output should be the Fahrenheit temperature with appropriate annotation. Be sure to prompt the user for the input.

3.2 Design an algorithm to convert a time from seconds to hours, minutes, and seconds. Implement your algorithm with an IBM PC Assembly language program. Your input should be the time in seconds entered via the keyboard. The input value will be in the range 0 to 65,535. Your output should be the equivalent time in the form HH·MM:SS. For example, for an input of 7272 seconds, the program should output 2:1:12. Demonstrate your program with each of the following input values: 0, 59, 60, 3599, 3600, 7272, 32,000, 32,072, and 65,535.

3.3 Design an algorithm to accept as input an integer value for x and to compute and output the corresponding value for y using the function

$$y = x^3 - 11x^2 + 98x - 24$$

Implement your algorithm with an IBM PC Assembly language program. Your input should be a signed integer value for x entered via the keyboard. Your output should be the corresponding value for y with appropriate annotation. Use 16-bit arithmetic in your program. Demonstrate your program with the following set of input values: -30, -29, -28, -27, -12, 0, 12, 30, 31, and 32.

3.4 DEBUG Listing 3.5 shows a useful feature of DEBUG. This DEBUG session verifies row 3 of Table 3.7. The first command issued to DEBUG in this session is the A (assemble) command, which provides the capability for entering Assembly language instructions. DEBUG assembles the instructions as they are entered and loads the machine language representation directly into memory. All numeric values appearing in the instructions entered must be specified in hexadecimal. An address may be included with the A command to specify where in memory the instruction sequence is to begin. If no address is specified, DEBUG chooses the start address of an available block of memory. The machine language representations of the instructions entered are stored in successive memory locations.

In DEBUG Listing 3.5, DEBUG responds to the A command by displaying the address 08F2:0100 on the screen. The instruction

```
MOV AL, E8
```

is entered via the keyboard to be assembled into memory beginning at that location. DEBUG assembles the instruction into memory and then displays the address of the next available memory location, 08F2:0102, on the screen. The procedure continues until all desired instructions have been entered. Pressing only RETURN in response to an address terminates the assemble command. The last instruction (the NOP instruction) acts as a marker for the end of the instruction sequence.

A register display shows that DEBUG is ready to execute the first instruction of the sequence. The remainder of the DEBUG session is a single-step trace of this instruction sequence. Compare the results to row 3 of Table 3.7.

Use the assemble feature to determine the quotient and remainder for each of the following divisions involving signed decimal integers:

$$\frac{17}{3} \qquad \frac{-17}{3}$$

$$\frac{17}{-3} \qquad \frac{-17}{-3}$$

```
                    DEBUG LISTING 3.5
DEBUG
-A
08F2:0100 MOV AL,E8
08F2:0102 MOV BL,5
08F2:0104 MUL BL
08F2:0106 MOV AL,E8
08F2:0108 IMUL BL
08F2:010A NOP
08F2:010B
-R
AX=0000  BX=0000  CX=0000  DX=0000  SP=FFEE  BP=0000  SI=0000  DI=0000
DS=08F2  ES=08F2  SS=08F2  CS=08F2  IP=0100    NV UP DI PL NZ NA PO NC
08F2:0100 B0E8           MOV     AL,E8
-T

AX=00E8  BX=0000  CX=0000  DX=0000  SP=FFEE  BP=0000  SI=0000  DI=0000
DS=08F2  ES=08F2  SS=08F2  CS=08F2  IP=0102    NV UP DI PL NZ NA PO NC
08F2:0102 B305           MOV     BL,05
-T

AX=00E8  BX=0005  CX=0000  DX=0000  SP=FFEE  BP=0000  SI=0000  DI=0000
DS=08F2  ES=08F2  SS=08F2  CS=08F2  IP=0104    NV UP DI PL NZ NA PO NC
08F2:0104 F6E3           MUL     BL
-T

AX=0488  BX=0005  CX=0000  DX=0000  SP=FFEE  BP=0000  SI=0000  DI=0000
DS=08F2  ES=08F2  SS=08F2  CS=08F2  IP=0106    OV UP DI PL NZ NA PO CY
08F2:0106 B0E8           MOV     AL,E8
-T

AX=04E8  BX=0005  CX=0000  DX=0000  SP=FFEE  BP=0000  SI=0000  DI=0000
DS=08F2  ES=08F2  SS=08F2  CS=08F2  IP=0108    OV UP DI PL NZ NA PO CY
08F2:0108 F6EB           IMUL    BL
-T

AX=FF88  BX=0005  CX=0000  DX=0000  SP=FFEE  BP=0000  SI=0000  DI=0000
DS=08F2  ES=08F2  SS=08F2  CS=08F2  IP=010A    NV UP DI PL ZR AC PE NC
08F2:010A 90             NOP
-Q

A>
```

4

CONTROL STRUCTURES

The program of Program Listing 3.1 converts temperature from degrees Fahrenheit to degrees centigrade. That program would be more useful if it produced a table of Fahrenheit temperatures and the corresponding centigrade temperatures for some specified range. This task could be accomplished by adding a loop structure to the program. The program of Program Listing 3.2 computes the sum of the cubes of the first n positive integers. That program could display an incorrect result due to the undetected condition of arithmetic overflow. To produce a more meaningful output, the program needs a decision structure that is based on whether or not overflow occurs during the computation.

This chapter presents two types of control structures: the decision structure and the loop structure. To implement control structures in Assembly language programs, a class of instructions called **transfer of control instructions** is needed. In IBM PC terminology, this class of instructions is called JUMP instructions. The IBM PC Assembly language also contains some additional transfer of control instructions that are called LOOP instructions. These instructions are used for implementing certain types of loop structures. This chapter discusses the use of JUMP and LOOP instructions to implement control structures in IBM PC Assembly language programs.

4.1 JUMP Instructions

Figure 4.1 presents a loose description of the instruction execution cycle for the Intel 8088 microprocessor. The INSTRUCTION FETCH step is the memory fetch for the first byte of an instruction. That first byte indicates the operation that is to be performed and the size of the instruction (i.e., the number of

FIGURE 4.1
Instruction
execution cycle

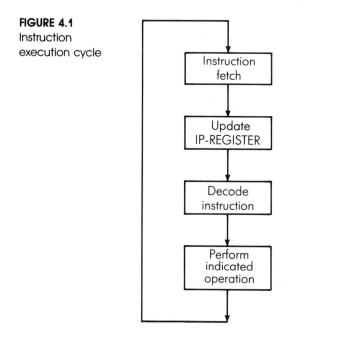

additional bytes to be fetched for the instruction). The UPDATE IP-REGIS-TER step increments the IP-register by 1 so that the CS:IP register pair points to the memory location that contains the next instruction byte to be fetched (i.e., the next byte of this instruction or the first byte of the next instruction). The DECODE INSTRUCTION step decodes the first byte of the instruction to determine the specific steps for the operation that is to be performed. The PERFORM INDICATED OPERATION box includes different steps for different instructions. For the instruction

```
MOV AL, COUNT
```

the detail of the PERFORM INDICATED OPERATION box would include the following steps:

1. Fetch next two bytes of the instruction that contains the offset of the operand COUNT.
2. Update the IP-register.
3. Add the offset to the appropriate segment register value to obtain the effective address of the data.
4. Fetch the data from the memory location specified by the effective address.
5. Move the fetched data to the AL-register.

Following execution of an instruction, the CS:IP register pair points to the first byte of the next instruction to be executed. For the instructions that have been considered thus far, this instruction is the one that immediately follows the instruction just executed. JUMP instructions provide a mechanism for altering the sequence of instruction executions, which is accomplished by altering the CS:IP register pair as part of the PERFORM INDICATED OPERATION step of the instruction execution cycle. There are two types of JUMP instructions: conditional JUMP instructions and unconditional JUMP instructions. A **conditional JUMP instruction** may cause the CS:IP register pair to be altered depending on the current state of the flags register. An **unconditional JUMP instruction** always causes the CS:IP register pair to be altered.

Conditional JUMP Instructions

The PERFORM INDICATED OPERATION step in the instruction execution cycle for a conditional JUMP instruction includes a decision. Depending on the outcome of this decision:

1. No operation is performed, meaning that instruction execution continues with the next instruction in sequence
2. Or, the CS:IP register pair is altered so that instruction execution continues with the instruction at the address specified by the operand of the JUMP instruction.

In the IBM PC Assembly language, the conditional JUMP instructions are divided into three groups:

1. Group 1—provides the capability to make decisions based on the current values of unsigned integers. The instructions in this group are described in Table 4.1. The first column of this table gives the operation code. In each case, a choice of two operation codes is given for the

TABLE 4.1

Conditional JUMP instructions for unsigned numbers

Operation Code	Description	Will Jump If
JA/JNBE	Jump if above Jump if not below nor equal	CF = 0 and ZF = 0
JAE/JNB	Jump if above or equal Jump if not below	CF = 0
JB/JNAE	Jump if below Jump if not above nor equal	CF = 1
JBE/JNA	Jump if below or equal Jump if not above	CF = 1 or ZF = 1
JE/JZ	Jump if equal to zero	ZF = 1
JNE/JNZ	Jump if not equal to zero	ZF = 0

operation. The second column gives an interpretation for the operation codes. The third column gives the flag settings that cause the CS:IP register pair to be altered for the given instruction. In the table, the term "above" for unsigned integers is analogous to the term "greater than" for signed integers, and the term "below" for unsigned integers is analogous to the term "less than" for signed integers.

2. Group 2—provides the capability to make decisions based on the current values of signed integers. The instructions in this group are described in Table 4.2. This table has the same form as that of Table 4.1.

3. Group 3—provides the capability to make decisions based on the current state of a specific flag in the flags register. The instructions in this group are described in Table 4.3, which also has the same form as that of Table 4.1.

The **conditional JUMP instructions** have the following general form:

[⟨*label*⟩] ⟨*op-code*⟩ ⟨*short label*⟩ [⟨*comment*⟩]

in which ⟨*op-code*⟩ is one of the operation codes listed in Table 4.1, Table 4.2, or Table 4.3, and ⟨*short label*⟩ is the label of an instruction elsewhere in the procedure. This label must be the label of a memory location that is in the range −128 to +127 from the memory location immediately following the JUMP instruction. The operand value contained in the machine language representation of this instruction is an 8-bit two's complement integer. If the specific condition is met, then this value (extended to 16 bits) is added to the IP-register. None of the bits in the flags register are affected by execution of conditional JUMP instructions.

TABLE 4.2
Conditional JUMP instructions for signed numbers

Operation Code	Description	Will Jump If
JG/JNLE	Jump if greater than Jump if not less nor equal	ZF = 0 and SF = OF
JGE/JNL	Jump if greater than or equal Jump if not less than	(SF xor OF) = 0 (i.e., SF = OF)
JL/JNGE	Jump if less than Jump if not greater nor equal	(SF xor OF) = 1 (i.e., SF ≠ OF)
JLE/JNG	Jump if less than or equal Jump if not greater than	ZF = 1 or SF ≠ OF
JE/JZ	Jump if equal to zero	ZF = 1
JNE/JNZ	Jump if not equal to zero	ZF = 0

TABLE 4.3

Conditional JUMP instructions for the flags register

Operation Code	Description	Will Jump If
JC	Jump if carry	CF = 1
JNC	Jump if no carry	CF = 0
JO	Jump if overflow	OF = 1
JNO	Jump if no overflow	OF = 0
JS	Jump if sign negative	SF = 1
JNS	Jump if nonnegative sign	SF = 0
JZ	Jump if zero	ZF = 1
JNZ	Jump if not zero	ZF = 0
JP/JPE	Jump if parity even	PF = 1
JNP/JPO	Jump if parity odd	PF = 0

Consider the instruction

```
JE ALPHA
```

The assembler computes the difference between the offset of the memory location specified by ALPHA and the offset of the memory location immediately following the JE instruction. If this offset difference is not in the range − 128 to + 127, then the assembler generates the message

```
Error --- 53:Relative jump out of range
```

Otherwise, the 1-byte offset difference is the operand in the machine language representation of the JE instruction.

EXAMPLES

Suppose that in the current code segment the offset of the JE instruction is 0055 hex, the offset of the instruction that follows the JE instruction is 0057 hex, and the offset of the instruction that contains the label ALPHA is 0033 hex. The offset difference is computed as follows:

$$
\begin{array}{rl}
0033 \text{ hex} & 0000000000110011 \text{ binary} \\
- 0057 \text{ hex} & - 0000000001010111 \text{ binary}
\end{array}
$$

$$
\begin{array}{rl}
0033 \text{ hex} & 0000000000110011 \text{ binary} \\
+ \underline{\text{FFA9 hex}} & + \underline{1111111110101001 \text{ binary}} \\
\text{FFDC hex} & 1111111111011100 \text{ binary}
\end{array}
$$

Since the offset difference is in the range − 128 to + 127, it is reduced to 1 byte (DC hex or 11011100 binary) and stored as the operand in the machine language representation of the JE instruction.

Suppose that in the current code segment the offset of the JE instruction is 0018 hex, the offset of the instruction that follows the JE instruction is 001A hex, and the offset of the instruction that contains the label ALPHA is 0024 hex. The offset difference is computed as follows:

$$
\begin{array}{rl}
0024 \text{ hex} & 0000000000100100 \text{ binary} \\
- \, 001A \text{ hex} & - \, 0000000000011010 \text{ binary}
\end{array}
$$

$$
\begin{array}{rl}
0024 \text{ hex} & 0000000000100100 \text{ binary} \\
+ \, \underline{FFE6} \text{ hex} & + \, \underline{1111111111100110} \text{ binary} \\
000A \text{ hex} & 0000000000001010 \text{ binary}
\end{array}
$$

Since the offset difference is in the range -128 to $+127$, it is reduced to 1 byte (OA hex or 00001010 binary) and stored as the operand in the machine language representation of the JE instruction.

The PERFORM INDICATED OPERATION step in the instruction cycle for execution of the JE ALPHA instruction would include the following steps:

1. FETCH the next byte of the instruction that contains the offset difference between the offset of ALPHA and the offset of the next instruction in sequence.
2. Update the IP-register, which forces the CS:IP register pair to point to the next instruction in sequence:

```
IF    ZF = 1
THEN
          Expand offset difference to 16 bits.
          Add expanded offset difference to IP-register.
ENDIF
```

The resulting CS:IP register value identifies the next instruction to be executed. Note that the CS:IP register pair does not change if the condition (ZF = 1) is not True; that is, the CS:IP register pair continues to point to the instruction following the JE instruction.

Unconditional JUMP Instruction

In the IBM PC Assembly language, the **unconditional JUMP instruction** is the JMP instruction. The **JMP instruction** has the following general form:

[⟨*label*⟩] JMP ⟨*target*⟩ [⟨*comment*⟩]

in which ⟨*target*⟩ is one of the following: a label with type attribute NEAR, a label with type attribute FAR, a variable with type attribute WORD, a variable with type attribute DOUBLE WORD, a 16-bit general register. Execution of a JMP instruction causes an unconditional transfer of control to the instruction that begins at the memory location specified by ⟨target⟩. Sequential execution continues from that point until another transfer of control instruction is encountered.

None of the bits in the flags register are affected by execution of an unconditional JUMP instruction.

If the target operand is a label with type attribute NEAR, then the assembler computes the difference between the offset of the memory location specified by the target label and the offset of the memory location immediately following the JMP instruction. This difference is the operand in the machine language representation of the JMP instruction. This machine language operand can be either byte or word. The SHORT operator can be placed prior to the label in a JMP instruction to force the assembler to use a byte offset difference in the machine language representation of the instruction. For example:

```
JMP SHORT ALPHA
```

In this case, the offset difference must be in the range − 128 to + 127. If it is not, then the asembler generates the following message:

```
Error --- 53:Relative jump out of range
```

If the SHORT operator is omitted, then the target label can be anywhere within the current code segment. The SHORT operator is used to conserve memory space.

Other possibilities for a target operand in a JMP instruction are beyond the scope of this book. The JUMP instructions used in the example programs in this text involve labels that are defined in the same procedure as the jump itself.

The JMP instruction does not have a range restriction as do the conditional JUMP instructions. In fact, the JMP instruction can be used to get around the range restriction of a conditional JUMP instruction. Consider the following code fragment:

```
REPEAT:
        MOV   AX,BX
          .
          .
          .
        DEC   BX
        JNE   REPEAT
        LEA   DI,STRING
```

Following execution of the DEC instruction, the flags are set to reflect the value in the BX-register. If the BX-register value is nonzero, then the JNE instruction transfers control to the MOV instruction with label REPEAT. If the BX-register value is zero, then execution continues with the next instruction in sequence, the LEA instruction.

Suppose the JNE instruction causes a "relative jump out of range" error. The code fragment can be modified as follows to eliminate this error:

```
REPEAT:
        MOV   AX,BX
              .
              .
              .

        DEC   BX
        JE    CONTINUE
        JMP   REPEAT
CONTINUE:
        LEA   DI,STRING
```

Following execution of the DEC instruction, the flags are set to reflect the value in the BX-register. If the BX-register value is nonzero, then the JE instruction passes control to the next instruction in sequence (the JMP instruction), and the JMP instruction transfers control to the MOV instruction with label REPEAT. If the BX-register value is zero, then the JE instruction transfers control to the LEA instruction with label CONTINUE.

Both of the preceding code fragments are equivalent logically. The second one corrects an out-of-range error in the first one at the expense of one JMP instruction.

4.2   Decision Structures

Decision structures in programs are based on conditions. Conditions are logical expressions that have a **truth value**. That is, a **logical expression** is one that evaluates to either True or False. The program decision then is based on the truth value of the condition. Most high-level languages provide relational expressions as one form for expressing conditions. The **relational expression** has the following general form:

⟨*arith expr*⟩ ⟨*relational op*⟩ ⟨*arith expr*⟩

in which ⟨*arith expr*⟩ is an arithmetic expression and ⟨*relational op*⟩ is one of the following relational operators: < (is less than), ≤ (is less than or equal to), = (is equal to), ≠ (is not equal to), > (is greater than), or ≥ (is greater than or equal to). To evaluate a relational expression, the two arithmetic expressions must be evaluated first. The value of the relational expression is True if the value of the first arithmetic expression has the specified relationship to the value of the second arithmetic expression. Otherwise, the value of the relational expression is False.

$$X**2 + Y**2 < Z**2$$

The value of the preceding relational expression is True if the value of the expression $X**2 + Y**2$ is less than the value of the expression $Z**2$. Otherwise, the value of the preceding relational expression is False.

In Assembly language, one method of evaluating a relational expression is first to write the instructions to evaluate the two arithmetic expressions and then subtract the value of the second arithmetic expression from the value of the first arithmetic expression. The resulting value will have the same relationship to zero as the value of the first arithmetic expression has to the value of the second arithmetic expression. The bits in the flags register will reflect this relationship.

Consider the relational expression

$$SIDE3 < (SIDE1 + SIDE2)$$

This relational expression is equivalent to the relational expression

$$(SIDE3 - (SIDE1 + SIDE2)) < 0$$

which was obtained by subtracting

$$(SIDE1 + SIDE2)$$

from both sides of the inequality. To set the flags register to reflect this relationship, the following instructions can be used.

```
MOV AX,SIDE3
SUB AX,SIDE1
SUB AX,SIDE2
```

Once the bits in the flags register have been set to reflect the desired relationship, the appropriate conditional JUMP instruction is used to make the decision.

Single-Alternative Decision

Two types of decision structures are introduced at this point: the single-alternative decision and the double-alternative decision.

A **single-alternative decision** structure either performs a sequence of instructions or skips that sequence of instructions depending on the value of a condition. If the condition evaluates as True, then the sequence of instructions is performed. If the condition evaluates as False, then the sequence of instructions is skipped. The flowchart in Figure 4.2 represents a single-alternative decision structure.

FIGURE 4.2
Flowchart of a
single-alternative
decision structure

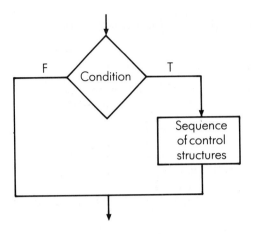

The pseudocode used in this book for a single-alternative decision structure is as follows:

```
IF    ⟨condition⟩
THEN
        ⟨sequence of control structures⟩
ENDIF
```

EXAMPLE

Suppose the data segment definition for a program contains the following variable definitions for three unsigned integer variables:

```
X    DW  ?
Y    DW  ?
SUM DW  ?
```

The following instructions implement the single-alternative decision structure:

```
STRUCTURE:
        IF    X/Y ≠ Y
        THEN
                SUM = SUM + Y
        ENDIF

IMPLEMENTATION:
                MOV AX, X
                MOV DX, 0
                DIV Y
                SUB Y
                JE  ENDIF
                MOV AX, Y
                ADD SUM, AX
        ENDIF:
```

The first two MOV instructions load the AX-register with the unsigned integer value of variable X and expand it to 32 bits in the DX:AX register pair. The DIV instruction computes the value of the left-hand arithmetic expression X/Y. The value of the right-hand arithmetic expression is the value of variable Y. The SUB instruction computes the difference between the two arithmetic expressions, $(X/Y) - Y$. The difference has the same relationship to zero as the value of the left-hand arithmetic expression has to the value of the right-hand arithmetic expression. The SUB instruction sets the flags to reflect this relationship. The JE instruction makes the decision based on this relationship. If the difference is nonzero, then the MOV and ADD instructions are executed (i.e., the jump to ENDIF is not taken). If the difference is zero, then the MOV and ADD instructions are skipped (i.e., the jump to ENDIF is taken). The MOV and ADD instructions implement the assignment

$$SUM = SUM + Y$$

The assignment is the single alternative that is either selected or skipped based on the value of the relational expression.

Double-Alternative Decision

A **double-alternative decision** structure selects one of two sequences of instructions to perform depending on the value of a condition. If the condition evaluates as True, then the first sequence of instructions is selected. If the condition evaluates as False, then the second sequence of instructions is selected. The flowchart in Figure 4.3 represents a double-alternative decision structure.

The pseudocode used in this book for a double-alternative decision structure is as follows:

```
IF      ⟨condition⟩
THEN
        ⟨first sequence of control structures⟩
ELSE
        ⟨second sequence of control structures⟩
ENDIF
```

FIGURE 4.3
Flowchart of a
double-alternative
decision structure

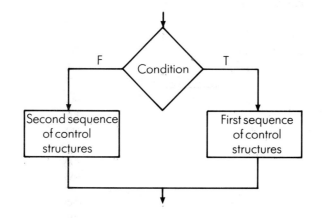

Suppose the data segment definition for a program contains the following variable definitions for two signed integers:

```
X DW ?
Y DW ?
```

The following instructions implement the double-alternative decision structure:

```
STRUCTURE:
     IF   X ≤ 3
     THEN
          Y = 2X - 1
     ELSE
          Y = 5
     ENDIF
```

IMPLEMENTATION:

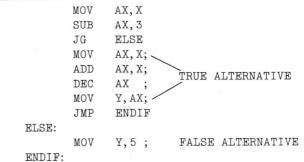

```
                    MOV   AX,X
                    SUB   AX,3
                    JG    ELSE
                    MOV   AX,X;
                    ADD   AX,X;
                    DEC   AX  ;      TRUE ALTERNATIVE
                    MOV   Y,AX;
                    JMP   ENDIF
            ELSE:
                    MOV   Y,5 ;     FALSE ALTERNATIVE
            ENDIF:
```

The first two instructions compute the value X − 3, which has the same relationship to zero as X has to 3. The SUB instruction sets the flags to reflect this relationship. The JG instruction makes the decision based on this relationship. The decision selects one of the two alternatives to be executed: If X − 3 is less than or equal to zero, then the jump to ELSE is not taken, the four instructions of the TRUE ALTERNATIVE are executed, and the JMP instruction causes the FALSE ALTERNATIVE to be skipped; if X − 3 is greater than zero, then the jump to ELSE is taken, the TRUE ALTERNATIVE is skipped, and the one instruction of the FALSE ALTERNATIVE is executed. No matter which alternative is selected, after the alternative instructions have been executed, sequential execution continues with the instruction at label ENDIF.

Compare Instruction

Suppose a decision in a program is to be based on the relationship between the value in the AX-register and the immediate value 15. The instruction

```
SUB AX,15
```

sets the bits in the flags register to reflect this relationship. However, the value in the AX-register now is modified, and that value may be needed in one or both of the alternatives of the decision that is based on this relationship.

The IBM PC Assembly language provides a compare instruction, the CMP instruction, that behaves like the SUB instruction except that the destination operand is not modified (i.e., the difference is not saved). The **CMP instruction** has the following general form:

[⟨*label*⟩] CMP ⟨*destination*⟩,⟨*source*⟩ [⟨*comment*⟩]

in which ⟨*destination*⟩ and ⟨*source*⟩ identify the locations of the two values being compared. This instruction causes the destination operand to be compared to the source operand and the flags to be set to reflect the relationship of the destination operand to the source operand. This task is accomplished by subtracting the source operand from the destination operand and setting the flags to reflect this difference. Neither the source operand nor the destination operand are modified.

For the CMP instruction, the type attribute of the two operands must match (i.e., both byte or both word). Figure 4.4 illustrates the possible combinations of the destination and source operands. If the destination operand is a general register, then the source operand can be a general register, a memory location, or an immediate value. If the destination operand is a memory location, then the source operand can be either a general register or an immediate value.

Note that the mnemonics of the conditional JUMP instructions were designed to have meaning when used in conjunction with the CMP instruction. For a conditional JUMP instruction that immediately follows a CMP instruction, the jump is taken when the destination operand is related to the source operand in the specified way.

FIGURE 4.4
Allowable operands
for CMP instruction

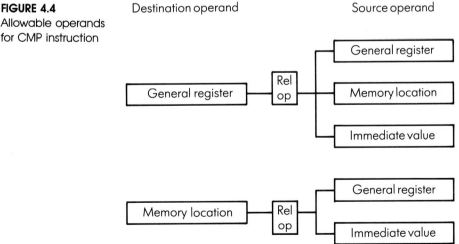

rel op stands for relational operator

With the instructions

```
CMP AX,BX
JG  ENDIF
```

the jump to ENDIF is taken if the signed integer value in the AX-register is greater than the signed integer value in the BX-register.

Execution of a CMP instruction affects the flags in exactly the same way as they would be affected by execution of a SUB instruction with the same operands. See Section 3.2 for an explanation of the flag settings for execution of a SUB instruction.

In the double-alternative decision example, the instruction

```
MOV AX,X
```

appeared twice, because the SUB instruction modified the value in the AX-register, and the original value was needed in the TRUE ALTERNATIVE. Use of the CMP instruction rather than the SUB instruction allows for the elimination of one of the two MOV instructions. Either of the following instruction sequences can be substituted for the sequence in the previous example:

Sequence A:

```
        MOV AX,X
        CMP AX,3
        JG  ELSE
        ADD AX,X
        DEC AX
        MOV Y,AX
        JMP ENDIF
ELSE:
        MOV Y,5
ENDIF:
```

Sequence B:

```
        CMP X,3
        JG  ELSE
        MOV AX,X
        ADD AX,X
        DEC AX
        MOV Y,AX
        JMP ENDIF

ELSE:
        MOV Y,5
ENDIF:
```

Programming Examples

In this section, two problems are considered. The first problem, computing the sum of the cubes of the first *n* positive integers, was introduced in Chapter 3. The program to perform that computation here is modified to include an overflow check. The second problem is that of evaluating a particular step function.

Sum of Cubes of First *n* Positive Integers

Program Listing 3.2 implements an algorithm to compute the sum of the cubes of the first *n* positive integers. It does not check for arithmetic overflow in the computation. Therefore, for any input value of *n* that is greater than 22, the program displays an incorrect result. A better way to handle such inputs would be to display a message to the user that indicates that the input is beyond the program's capability. Program Listing 4.1 shows a modified version of Program

```
 1: ;                    PROGRAM LISTING 4.1
 2: ;
 3: ; GIVEN AN INTEGER VALUE FOR n, THIS PROGRAM COMPUTES THE SUM OF
 4: ; THE CUBES OF THE FIRST n POSITIVE INTEGERS USING THE FORMULA:
 5: ;
 6: ;   3    3    3          3              2
 7: ; 1  + 2  + 3  + ... + n  = [n(n + 1)/2]
 8: ;
 9: ; AN OVERFLOW CHECK IS PROVIDED
10: ;
11:                                       ;PROCEDURES TO
12:           EXTRN    GETDEC$:FAR        ;GET 16-BIT UNSIGNED DEC INTEGER
13:           EXTRN    NEWLINE:FAR        ;DISPLAY NEWLINE CHARACTER
14:           EXTRN    PUTDEC$:FAR        ;DISPLAY 16-BIT UNSIGNED DEC INT
15:           EXTRN    PUTSTRNG:FAR       ;DISPLAY CHARACTER STRING
16: ;
17: ; <***** S T A C K   S E G M E N T   D E F I N I T I O N *****>
18: ;
19: STACK     SEGMENT STACK
20:           DB       256 DUP(?)
21: STACK     ENDS
22: ;
23: ; <***** D A T A   S E G M E N T   D E F I N I T I O N *****>
24: ;
25: DATA      SEGMENT
26: ;
27: PROMPT      DB     'ENTER A POSITIVE INTEGER VALUE  '
28: MESSAGE_1   DB     'THE SUM OF THE FIRST '
29: MESSAGE_2   DB     ' CUBE(S) IS '
30: OVRFLO_MSG  DB     'ARITHMETIC OVERFLOW OCCURRED'
31: TWO         DW     2                  ;CONSTANT 2
32: N           DW     ?                  ;NUMBER OF CUBES TO SUM
33: SUM         DW     ?                  ;SUM OF FIRST N CUBES
34: ;
35: DATA      ENDS
36:*;
```

```
37: ;
38: ; <*****    C O D E    S E G M E N T    D E F I N I T I O N *****>
39: CODE       SEGMENT
40:            ASSUME   CS:CODE,SS:STACK,ES:DATA,DS:DATA
41: EX_4_1     PROC     FAR
42:            PUSH     DS                      ;PUSH RETURN SEG ADDR ON STACK
43:            SUB      AX,AX                   ;PUSH RETURN OFFSET OF ZERO
44:            PUSH     AX                      ;ON STACK
45:            MOV      AX,SEG DATA             ;SET DS AND ES REGISTERS TO
46:            MOV      DS,AX                   ;POINT TO DATA SEGMENT
47:            MOV      ES,AX
48:            LEA      DI,PROMPT               ;PROMPT FOR N
49:            MOV      CX,33
50:            CALL     PUTSTRNG
51:            CALL     GETDEC$                 ;GET N
52:            MOV      N,AX
53:            ADD      AX,1                    ;SUM = [N(N + 1)/2] ** 2
54:            JC       OVRFLO                  ;IF   NO OVERFLOW
55:            MUL      N
56:            JC       OVRFLO
57:            DIV      TWO
58:            MUL      AX
59:            JC       OVRFLO
60:            MOV      SUM,AX                  ;THEN
61:            CALL     NEWLINE                 ;      SKIP TO NEXT LINE ON DISP.
62:            LEA      DI,MESSAGE_1            ;      DISPLAY
63:            MOV      CX,21                   ;      'THE SUM OF THE FIRST '
64:            CALL     PUTSTRNG
65:            MOV      AX,N                    ;      DISPLAY N
66:            MOV      BH,0
67:            CALL     PUTDEC$
68:            LEA      DI,MESSAGE_2            ;      DISPLAY ' CUBE(S) IS '
69:            MOV      CX,12
70:            CALL     PUTSTRNG
71:            MOV      AX,SUM                  ;      DISPLAY SUM
72:            CALL     PUTDEC$
73:            JMP      RETURN
74: OVRFLO:                                    ;ELSE
75:            LEA      DI,OVRFLO_MSG           ;      DISPLAY OVERFLOW MESSAGE
76:            MOV      CX,28
77:            CALL     PUTSTRNG
78: RETURN:                                    ;ENDIF
79:            RET                              ;RETURN
80: EX_4_1     ENDP
81: CODE       ENDS
82:*           END      EX_4_1
```

Listing 3.2. In the modified version, if an overflow occurs in the computation, then the program displays the message

```
ARITHMETIC OVERFLOW OCCURRED
```

This discussion concentrates on the differences between Program Listing 4.1 and Program Listing 3.2. One line (line 9) has been added to the prologue to explain that an overflow check is provided by the program. As well, one line (line 30) has been added in the data segment that defines the message to be displayed to the user in the event that the program detects an overflow in the computation.

The computation being performed by the program is

$$[n(n + 1)/2]^2$$

where n is the input value. Arithmetic overflow could occur at one of three places in this computation. If the input value for n is 65,535, then overflow occurs when $(n + 1)$ is performed. If the input value for n is 1000, then overflow occurs when $n(n + 1)$ is performed. If the input value for n is 23, then overflow occurs when $[n(n + 1)]^2$ is performed.

One common misconception of beginning Assembly language programmers is that once the overflow or carry flag is set it stays set until it is cleared by an explicit instruction that clears the flags. This situation is *not* the case with the IBM PC. Each integer arithmetic instruction in the computation sets or clears the OF and CF bits in the flags register depending on whether or not execution of that instruction resulted in an overflow condition. Therefore, an overflow check has to be made after each part of the computation that could potentially cause an overflow condition. In Program Listing 4.1, the computation involves unsigned integer values. Recall that with unsigned integer values, the CF bit in the flags register is the overflow indicator.

The instructions in lines 52–60 perform the computation and provide the overflow checks. The ADD instruction in line 53 performs the computation $n + 1$. Note that this is done with an ADD instruction rather than the INC instruction used in Program Listing 3.2. ADD is used here because the INC instruction does not affect the CF bit in the flags register, and the ADD instruction does. Execution of the ADD instruction sets the condition. That is, ADD sets or clears the CF bit in the flags register depending on whether or not an overflow occurred in the addition operation. The JC instruction in line 54 makes a decision based on the condition: to continue with the computation if the CF bit in the flags register is 0; or to skip the remainder of the computation and transfer control to the instruction labeled OVRFLO, if the CF bit in the flags register is 1. That is,

```
JC OVRFLO
```

is a conditional JUMP instruction that causes the program to jump to the instruction labeled OVRFLO if the CF bit in the flags register is set; otherwise, the instruction causes the program to continue to the next instruction in sequence.

The MUL instruction in line 55 performs the computation $n(n + 1)$. Execution of the MUL instruction sets the condition. It sets or clears the CF bit in the flags register depending on whether or not an overflow occurred in the multiplication operation. The JC instruction in line 56 again makes a decision based on the condition. Either it makes the decision to continue the computation (CF = 0), or it makes the decision to skip the remainder of the computation (CF = 1). Recall that with integer multiplication instructions, both the CF and OF bits are set, or they are both cleared, depending on whether or not overflow occurred; thus, the JC instruction in line 56 could be changed to a JO instruction without affecting the correctness of the program. The JC instruction is used for consistency when dealing with unsigned integer values.

The DIV instruction in line 57 performs the computation $[n(n + 1)/2]$. For all positive integer values for n, where $n(n + 1)$ does not cause overflow, the value of $n(n + 1)$ is greater than or equal to 2 and is even. Therefore, this division cannot cause an overflow. (Division overflow is handled via interrupts and is discussed further in Chapter 9.)

The MUL instruction in line 58 performs $[n(n + 1)/2]^2$. Execution of the MUL instruction sets the condition. It sets or clears the CF bit in the flags register depending on whether or not an overflow occurred on the multiplication operation. The JC instruction in line 59 again makes a decision based on the condition. Either it makes the decision to save and display the results of the computation (lines 60–72), or it makes the decision to skip the instructions that display the result and to execute the instructions (lines 74–77) to display the message

```
ARITHMETIC OVERFLOW OCCURRED
```

From a high-level, pseudocode standpoint, the program includes a computation followed by a double-alternative decision (see the pseudocode in Program Listing 4.1). The double-alternative decision says that if no overflow occurred during the computation, then display the results of the computation; otherwise, display the overflow message.

The following are the results from some executions of this program:

```
ENTER A POSITIVE INTEGER VALUE        18
THE SUM OF THE FIRST 18 CUBE(S) IS 29241

ENTER A POSITIVE INTEGER VALUE        23
ARITHMETIC OVERFLOW OCCURRED

ENTER A POSITIVE INTEGER VALUE      1000
ARITHMETIC OVERFLOW OCCURRED

ENTER A POSITIVE INTEGER VALUE     65535
ARITHMETIC OVERFLOW OCCURRED
```

Step Function Evaluation

Consider the problem of computing the value of y for the following step function, given an integer value for x:

$$y = -5 \qquad \text{for } x \leq -2$$

$$y = 2x - 1 \qquad \text{for } -2 \leq x \leq 3$$

$$y = 5 \qquad \text{for } x \geq 3$$

Figure 4.5 graphs this step function.

FIGURE 4.5
Graph of a step
function

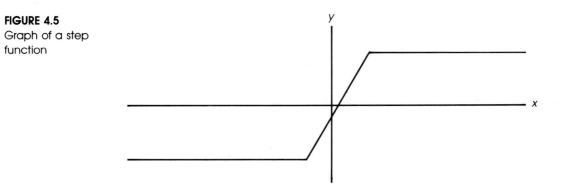

The following is the pseudocode description of an algorithm for solving the preceding step function:

```
GET X
IF   X < -2
THEN
      Y = -5
ELSE
      IF   X ≤ 3
      THEN
            Y = 2X - 1
      ELSE
            Y = 5
      ENDIF
ENDIF
DISPLAY Y
```

This algorithm contains two double-alternative decision structures. The second alternative of one of the double-alternative decision structures is the other double-alternative decision structure. This algorithm illustrates **nested decision structures**. Nested control structures are considered in detail in Section 4.4.

Program Listing 4.2 shows an implementation of the preceding algorithm. The prologue in lines 1–7 explains the program's function, the external definitions in lines 9–12 identify the input/output procedures that are referenced by the program, and the stack segment definition in lines 13–18 is the standard one used in the example programs of this book.

The data segment is defined in lines 19–27. Two variables are defined in the data segment: one to hold the input value for X (line 24) and one to hold the computed value for Y (line 25). Both variables have type attribute WORD. An extra data segment is defined in lines 28–36. Two items are defined in the extra segment: a message to prompt the user to enter an integer value for X (line 33) and an annotation message for the output (line 34). In the previous program listings, the variables and the prompt and annotation messages have been defined in a single data segment. Here there is no specific reason for using two separate segments for static data other than for purposes of illustration.

```
 1: ;                       PROGRAM LISTING 4.2
 2: ;
 3: ; COMPUTE Y GIVEN INTEGER X WHERE
 4: ;       Y = -5            FOR X <= -2
 5: ;       Y = 2X-1          FOR -2 <= X <= 3
 6: ;       Y = 5             FOR X >= 3
 7: ;
 8:                                          ;PROCEDURES TO
 9:             EXTRN    PUTSTRNG:FAR        ;DISPLAY CHARACTER STRING
10:             EXTRN    GETDEC:FAR          ;GET DECIMAL INTEGER
11:             EXTRN    PUTDEC:FAR          ;DISPLAY DECIMAL INTEGER
12:             EXTRN    NEWLINE:FAR         ;DISPLAY NEWLINE CHARACTER
13: ;
14: ; S T A C K    S E G M E N T    D E F I N I T I O N
15: ;
16: STACK       SEGMENT STACK
17:             DB       256 DUP(?)
18: STACK       ENDS
19: ;
20: ; D A T A    S E G M E N T    D E F I N I T I O N
21: ;
22: DATA        SEGMENT
23: ;
24: X           DW       0
25: Y           DW       0
26: ;
27: DATA        ENDS
28: ;
29: ; E X T R A    S E G M E N T    D E F I N I T I O N
30: ;
31: EXTRA       SEGMENT
32: ;
33: PROMPT      DB       'ENTER INTEGER VALUE FOR X',0DH,0AH
34: ANNOTATION DB        0DH,0AH,'Y = '
35: ;
36: EXTRA       ENDS
37:*;
38: ;
39: ; C O D E    S E G M E N T    D E F I N I T I O N
40: ;
41: CODE        SEGMENT
42:             ASSUME   CS:CODE,SS:STACK,DS:DATA,ES:EXTRA
43: EX_4_2      PROC     FAR
44:             PUSH     DS                  ;PUSH RETURN SEG ADDR ON STACK
45:             MOV      AX,0                ;PUSH RETURN OFFSET OF ZERO
46:             PUSH     AX                  ;ON STACK
47:             MOV      AX,SEG DATA         ;SET DS TO POINT TO
48:             MOV      DS,AX               ;DATA SEGMENT
49:             MOV      AX,SEG EXTRA        ;SET ES TO POINT TO
50:             MOV      ES,AX               ;EXTRA SEGMENT
51:             LEA      DI,PROMPT
52:             MOV      CX,27
53:             CALL     PUTSTRNG            ;PROMPT FOR X
54:             CALL     GETDEC              ;GET X
55:             MOV      X,AX
56: IF:                                      ;IF   X < -2
57:             CMP      AX,-2
58:             JGE      ELSE
59:             MOV      Y,-5                ;THEN Y = -5
60:             JMP      ENDIF
```

```
61: ELSE:                                            ;ELSE
62: ____IF:
63:                 CMP     AX,3                      ;    IF   X <= 3
64:                 JG      ____ELSE
65:                 ADD     AX,X                      ;        THEN Y = 2X-1
66:                 SUB     AX,1
67:                 MOV     Y,AX
68:                 JMP     ____ENDIF
69: ____ELSE:                                         ;    ELSE Y = 5
70:                 MOV     Y,5
71: ____ENDIF:                                        ;    ENDIF
72: ENDIF:                                            ;ENDIF
73:                 LEA     DI,ANNOTATION
74:                 MOV     CX,6
75:                 CALL    PUTSTRNG                  ;DISPLAY ANNOTATION
76:                 MOV     AX,Y
77:                 MOV     BH,0
78:                 CALL    PUTDEC                    ;DISPLAY Y
79:                 CALL    NEWLINE
80:                 RET                               ;RETURN
81: EX_4_2          ENDP
82: CODE            ENDS
83:*                END     EX_4_2
```

The code segment is defined in lines 37–82 and contains the single main procedure, EX_4_2. The procedure begins in the standard way by pushing the return address onto the stack (lines 44–46) and initializing the segment registers (lines 47–50). The DS-register points to the data segment, and the ES-register points to the extra segment.

The instructions in lines 51–53 display the prompt message to the user, and the call to GETDEC in line 54 accepts a signed integer value for X from the keyboard. The MOV instruction in line 55 saves the input value of variable X in the data segment.

The outer double-alternative decision structure is implemented in lines 56–72. The labels IF, ELSE, and ENDIF have been used to emphasize the parts of this structure. The test of the condition is performed by the CMP instruction in line 57. This instruction subtracts -2 from the value of X in the AX-register and sets the flags to reflect the result. The value in the AX-register is not modified by execution of this CMP instruction. The conditional JUMP instruction in line 58 makes the decision based on this condition. If the value of X is less than -2, then the jump is *not* taken and execution continues with the MOV instruction in line 59 (the beginning of the True alternative or the then portion of the double-alternative decision). However, if the value of X is greater than or equal to -2, then the jump is taken to the instruction in lines 61–63 (the beginning of the False alternative or the else portion of the double-alternative decision). Note that ELSE and ____IF are both labels for the instruction in line 63. They are not both necessary; they are there for emphasis.

If the value of X is less than -2, the MOV instruction in line 59 stores -5 as the value of Y, and the unconditional JUMP instruction in line 60 transfers control to the end of the double-alternative decision structure (lines 72 and 73, labeled ENDIF).

If the value of X is greater than or equal to − 2, the inner double-alternative decision structure is entered, which is implemented in lines 62–71. The labels ____IF, ____ELSE, and ____ENDIF have been used to emphasize the parts of this structure. The underscore character is legal in a label and can be the first character of a label, as this program illustrates. The test of the condition is performed by the CMP instruction in line 63. This instruction subtracts 3 from the value of X in the AX-register and sets the flags to reflect the result. Again, the value in the AX-register is not modified by execution of this CMP instruction. The conditional JUMP instruction in line 64 makes the decision based on this condition. If the value of X is less than or equal to 3, then the jump is not taken, and execution continues with the ADD instruction in line 65 (the beginning of the True alternative or the then portion of the double-alternative decision). However, if the value of X is greater than 3, then the jump is taken to the instruction in lines 69 and 70 (the beginning of the False alternative or the else portion of the double-alternative decision).

If the value of X is less than or equal to 3, the instructions in lines 65–68 are executed. The instructions in lines 65 and 66 compute the value $(2X − 1)$ in the AX-register, and the MOV instruction in line 67 saves that value as the value of variable Y. The unconditional JUMP instruction in line 68 transfers control to the end of the inner double-alternative decision structure (lines 71–73, labeled ____ENDIF), which is also the end of the outer double-alternative decision structure.

If the value of X is greater than 3, the MOV instruction in line 70 is executed. This instruction stores 5 as the value of variable Y. The next instruction to be executed is the instruction in line 73. That is, the end of the two double-alternative decision structures has been reached.

The instructions in lines 73–79 display the value of Y along with the annotation message. The RET instruction in line 80 returns control to DOS.

The following results are from some executions of this program:

```
ENTER INTEGER VALUE FOR X
-3

Y = -5


ENTER INTEGER VALUE FOR X
-1

Y = -3


ENTER INTEGER VALUE FOR X
0

Y = -1


ENTER INTEGER VALUE FOR X
2

Y = 3
```

```
ENTER INTEGER VALUE FOR X
4

Y = 5
```

Labels

At this point, a discussion of labels is in order. The label for an instruction can be on the same line as the instruction or on a separate line between the instruction and the one that immediately precedes it. That is, a label is associated with the first instruction that follows it in the code. In Program Listing 4.2, the labels ELSE and ____IF are both labels for the CMP instruction in line 63. The advantage of placing the label on a separate line is for ease in program editing. Suppose a program that contains the instruction

```
ALPHA:    ADD   AX, Y
```

needs to be modified to the instructions

```
ALPHA:    MOV   AX, X
          ADD   AX, Y
```

This modification requires that an instruction be added and that the label be moved to the instruction that was added. However, if the original version had been

```
ALPHA:
          ADD   AX, Y
```

then the modification to

```
ALPHA:

          MOV   AX, X
          ADD   AX, Y
```

could be accomplished by addition of a single instruction. The label is moved automatically.

Labels have type attributes associated with them. The value of this type attribute is either NEAR or FAR. A label with type attribute NEAR has as its value a 2-byte offset. This is the offset within the segment of the memory location that is identified by that label. A label with type attribute NEAR can be referenced only from instructions within the same code segment. A label with type attribute FAR has as its value a 2-byte segment address and a 2-byte offset within the segment. This segment address and offset is the address of the actual memory location identified by that label. A label with type attribute FAR can be referenced from instructions in any code segment of the program. The colon (:) appended to a label gives a label the type attribute NEAR. The ⟨short label⟩ operand in a conditional JUMP instruction must be a label with type attribute NEAR. The target operand in an unconditional JUMP instruction may be a label with a type attribute of either NEAR or FAR. Most of the labels appearing in the program listings in this book have colons (:) appended (i.e., they have type attribute NEAR).

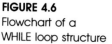

4.3   Loop Structures

A **loop structure** provides a mechanism for repeating a set of instructions based on the value of a condition. A loop structure consists of two parts: the loop test and the loop body. The **loop body** is the sequence of instructions to be repeated. The **loop test** is the evaluation of the condition on which the decision to execute the loop body is based. Two condition-controlled loop structures are discussed in this section: the WHILE loop and the REPEAT-UNTIL loop.

WHILE Loop

With a **WHILE loop structure**, the loop test is at the top of the loop. While the value of the condition is True, the loop body is executed. When the value of the condition is False, the loop is terminated. Since the test is at the top of the loop, it is possible that the loop body will not be executed at all.

The flowchart in Figure 4.6 represents a WHILE loop structure. The pseudocode used in this book for a WHILE loop structure is as follows:

```
WHILE ⟨condition⟩
     ⟨sequence of control structures⟩
ENDWHILE
```

FIGURE 4.6
Flowchart of a
WHILE loop structure

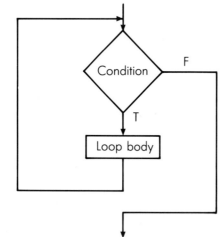

EXAMPLE

To find the smallest value of n for which

$$1^2 + 2^2 + 3^2 + \ldots + n^2 > 1000$$

the following WHILE loop could be used:

```
SUM = 1
N = 1
WHILE SUM ≤ 1000
    N = N + 1
    SUM = SUM + N*N
ENDWHILE
```

The following instructions implement the pseudocode in IBM PC Assembly language. The BX-register is used to maintain the value of SUM, and the CX-register is used to maintain the value of N:

```
            MOV    BX,1
            MOV    CX,1
WHILE:
            CMP    BX,1000
            JA     ENDWHILE
            INC    CX
            MOV    AX,CX
            MUL    CX
            ADD    BX,AX
            JMP    WHILE
ENDWHILE:
```

The first two MOV instructions initialize the values of SUM and N, respectively. The label WHILE marks the top of the loop. It is the label of the instruction that begins the loop test. The CMP and JA instructions perform the loop test. If the SUM (BX-register value) is greater than 1000, then the jump to ENDWHILE is taken, exiting the loop with the desired value of N in the CX-register. If the SUM is less than or equal to 1000, then the loop body

```
INC    CX
MOV    AX,CX
MUL    CX
ADD    BX,AX
```

is executed. After each execution of the loop body, the JMP instruction transfers control to the loop test at the top of the loop.

REPEAT-UNTIL Loop

With a REPEAT-UNTIL loop structure, the loop test is at the bottom of the loop. The loop body is executed, and as long as the condition evaluates as False, the loop body is repeated. When the condition evaluates as True, the loop is terminated. Since the test is at the bottom of the loop, the loop body always is executed at least once.

The flowchart in Figure 4.7 represents a REPEAT-UNTIL loop structure. The pseudocode used in this book for a REPEAT-UNTIL loop structure is as follows:

```
REPEAT
     〈sequence of control structures〉
UNTIL 〈condition〉
```

FIGURE 4.7
Flowchart of a
REPEAT-UNTIL loop
structure

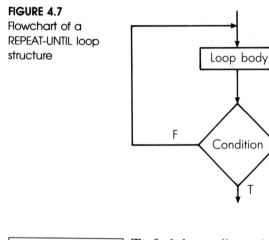

EXAMPLE

To find the smallest value of n for which

$$1^2 + 2^2 + 3^2 + \ldots + n^2 > 1000$$

the following REPEAT-UNTIL loop could be used:

```
SUM = 1
N = 1
REPEAT
     N = N + 1
     SUM = SUM + N*N
UNTIL SUM > 1000
```

The following instructions implement this pseudocode in IBM PC Assembly language. The BX-register is used to maintain the value of SUM, and the CX-register is used to maintain the value of N:

```
        MOV   BX,1
        MOV   CX,1
REPEAT:
        INC   CX
        MOV   AX,CX
        MUL   CX
        ADD   BX,AX
        CMP   BX,1000
        JBE   REPEAT
```

The first two MOV instructions initialize the values of SUM and N, respectively. The label REPEAT marks the top of the loop. It is the label of the first instruction of the loop body. The last two instructions (the CMP and JBE instructions) perform the loop test. If the SUM (BX-register value) is less than or equal to 1000, then the jump is taken to REPEAT, causing the loop body to execute again. If the SUM is greater than 1000, then the loop is exited (i.e., execution continues with the instruction that follows the JBE instruction).

With a condition-controlled loop, there must be something in the loop body that potentially can alter the value of the condition. Otherwise, an endless loop is created.

Loop Instructions

The condition that controls a loop may be based on a count. That is, the count specifies the exact number of times that the loop body is to be executed. When implementing such count-controlled loops in the IBM PC Assembly language, the LOOP instruction may be of use. The **LOOP instruction** uses the CX-register as a counter and has the following general form:

[⟨*label*⟩] LOOP ⟨*short-label*⟩ [⟨*comment*⟩]

in which ⟨*short-label*⟩ is the label of an instruction whose memory location is within −128 to +127 bytes from the memory location immediately following the LOOP instruction. This instruction causes the value in the CX-register to be decremented by 1. If the resulting value in the CX-register is nonzero, then control is transferred to the instruction that begins at the memory location specified by the ⟨*short-label*⟩. Otherwise, execution continues with the next instruction in sequence. None of the bits in the flags register are affected by excution of the LOOP instruction.

Consider the loop skeleton described in the flowchart and pseudocode of Figure 4.8.

The code that implements this loop structure is as follows:

```
          MOV    CX, N      ; COUNT = N
LOOPTOP:                    ; REPEAT
          ⟨loop body⟩       ;    ⟨loop body⟩
          LOOP   LOOPTOP    ;    COUNT = COUNT - 1
                            ; UNTIL COUNT = 0
```

The LOOP instruction performs both the decrement of the COUNT and the test of the COUNT.

A condition-controlled loop can be based on a multiple condition. The loop instructions loop on equal, LOOPE (loop on zero, LOOPZ), and loop on not equal, LOOPNE (loop on nonzero, LOOPNZ), provide a capability of this type.

FIGURE 4.8

Loop skeleton: flowchart and pseudocode

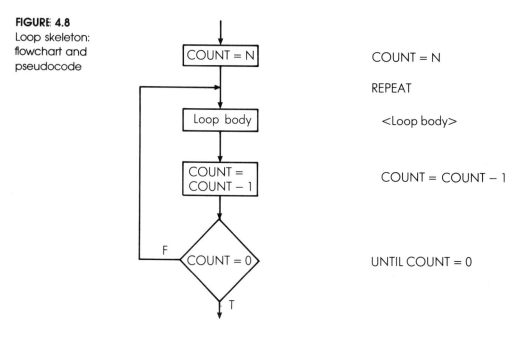

COUNT = N

REPEAT

    \<Loop body>

    COUNT = COUNT − 1

UNTIL COUNT = 0

The **LOOPE (LOOPZ) instruction** has one of the following general forms:

```
[⟨label⟩]   LOOPE   ⟨short-label⟩   [⟨comment⟩]
[⟨label⟩]   LOOPZ   ⟨short-label⟩   [⟨comment⟩]
```

in which ⟨*short-label*⟩ is the label of an instruction whose memory location is within − 128 to + 127 bytes from the memory location following the LOOPE (LOOPZ) instruction. This instruction causes the value in the CX-register to be decremented by 1. If the resulting value in the CX-register is nonzero and the ZF bit in the flags register is set to 1, then control is transferred to the instruction that begins at the memory location specified by the operand. Otherwise, execution continues with the next instruction in sequence. None of the bits in the flags register are affected by execution of this instruction.

The **LOOPNE (LOOPNZ) instruction** has one of the following general forms:

```
[⟨label⟩]   LOOPNE   ⟨short-label⟩   [⟨comment⟩]
[⟨label⟩]   LOOPNZ   ⟨short-label⟩   [⟨comment⟩]
```

in which ⟨*short-label*⟩ is the label of an instruction whose memory location is within − 128 to + 127 bytes from the memory location following the LOOPNE (LOOPNZ) instruction. This instruction causes the value in the CX-register to be decremented by 1. If the resulting value in the CX-register is nonzero and the ZF bit in the flags register is cleared to 0, then control is transferred to the instruction that begins at the memory location specified by the operand. Otherwise, execution continues with the next instruction in sequence. None of the bits in the flags register are affected by execution of this instruction.

The LOOPE (LOOPZ) and LOOPNE (LOOPNZ) instructions are useful in searching arrays and character strings. The count in the CX-register defines a maximum for the number of times to execute the loop body. The loop is terminated when the desired element is found or when the entire array has been searched. (Arrays and character strings are discussed in Chapter 8.)

Programming Examples

In this section, the implementations of two algorithms designed to solve the same problem are discussed. The problem is defined as follows:

The square of an integer n is equal to the sum of the first $|n|$ odd, positive integers:

$$3^2 = 1 + 3 + 5$$

$$7^2 = 1 + 3 + 5 + 7 + 9 + 11 + 13$$

Design an algorithm to accept as input an integer n and to compute n^2 by summing the first $|n|$ odd, positive integers. Implement the algorithm with an IBM PC Assembly language program.

REPEAT-UNTIL Loop Solution

The following pseudocode describes an algorithm using a REPEAT-UNTIL loop structure for solving the problem discussed previously.

```
SQUARE = 0
ODDINT = 1
GET NUMBER
LOOP_COUNT = |NUMBER|
REPEAT
    SQUARE = SQUARE + ODDINT
    ODDINT = ODDINT + 2
    LOOP_COUNT = LOOP_COUNT - 1
UNTIL LOOP_COUNT = 0
DISPLAY NUMBER
DISPLAY SQUARE
```

The absolute value of the input NUMBER is used for the LOOP_COUNT, so that the algorithm can compute the square for both positive and negative integers. Each time through the loop, the next odd, positive integer (ODDINT) is added to the sum (SQUARE), and the value of ODDINT is incremented by 2 to the next odd, positive integer. With loop termination, NUMBER and its SQUARE are displayed.

Program Listing 4.3 shows an implementation of this algorithm. The prologue in lines 1–6 explains the program's function, the external definitions in lines 8–12 identify the input/output procedures that are referenced by the program, and the stack segment definition in lines 13–18 is the standard one used in the program listings in this book.

```
 1: ;                      PROGRAM LISTING 4.3
 2: ;
 3: ;PROGRAM TO COMPUTE THE SQUARE OF AN
 4: ;INTEGER, N, BY  SUMMING  THE  FIRST
 5: ;|N| ODD POSITIVE INTEGERS.
 6: ;
 7:                                             ;PROCEDURES TO
 8:           EXTRN    GETDEC:FAR               ;INPUT DECIMAL INTEGER
 9:           EXTRN    PUTDEC:FAR               ;DISPLAY SIGNED DECIMAL INT.
10:           EXTRN    PUTDEC$:FAR              ;DISPLAY UNSIGNED DECIMAL INT.
11:           EXTRN    PUTSTRNG:FAR             ;DISPLAY CHARACTER STRING
12:           EXTRN    NEWLINE:FAR              ;DISPLAY NEWLINE CHARACTER
13: ;
14: ; S T A C K    S E G M E N T    D E F I N I T I O N
15: ;
16: STACK      SEGMENT STACK
17:           DB       256 DUP(?)
18: STACK      ENDS
19: ;
20: ; D A T A    S E G M E N T    D E F I N I T I O N
21: ;
22: DATA       SEGMENT
23: ;
24: NUMBER     DW       ?                       ;INPUT NUMBER
25: ODDINT     DW       1                       ;ODD POSITIVE INTEGER
26: SQUARE     DW       0                       ;SQUARE OF INPUT NUMBER
27: ;
28: PROMPT     DB       'ENTER INTEGER VALUE',0DH,0AH
29: MSGOUT1    DB       'THE SQUARE OF '
30: MSGOUT2    DB       ' IS '
31: OFLMSG     DB       'OVERFLOW OCCURRED',0DH,0AH
32: ;
33: DATA       ENDS
34:*;

35: ;
36: ; C O D E    S E G M E N T    D E F I N I T I O N
37: ;
38: CODE       SEGMENT
39: EX_4_3     PROC     FAR
40:           ASSUME   CS:CODE,SS:STACK,DS:DATA,ES:DATA
41:           PUSH     DS                       ;PUSH RETURN SEG ADDR ON STACK
42:           SUB      AX,AX                    ;PUSH RETURN OFFSET OF ZERO
43:           PUSH     AX                       ;ON STACK
44:           MOV      AX,SEG DATA              ;SET DS AND ES REGISTERS TO
45:           MOV      DS,AX                    ;ADDRESS DATA SEGMENT
46:           MOV      ES,AX
47:           LEA      DI,PROMPT                ;PROMPT USER TO ENTER AN INTEGER
48:           MOV      CX,21
49:           CALL     PUTSTRNG
50:           CALL     GETDEC                   ;GET NUMBER
51:           MOV      NUMBER,AX                ;
52:           CMP      AX,0                     ;IF    NUMBER < 0
53:           JGE      ENDABS
54:           NEG      AX                       ;THEN NUMBER = -NUMBER
55: ENDABS:                                     ;ENDIF
56:           MOV      CX,AX                    ;LOOP_COUNT = NUMBER
57: LOOPTOP:                                    ;REPEAT
58:           MOV      AX,ODDINT                ;  SQUARE = SQUARE + ODDINT
59:           ADD      SQUARE,AX
```

```
60:               JC        OVRFLO              ;    EXIT ON OVERFLOW
61:               ADD       ODDINT,2            ;    ODDINT = ODDINT + 2
62:               LOOP      LOOPTOP             ;    LOOP_COUNT = LOOP_COUNT - 1
63:                                             ;UNTIL LOOP_COUNT = 0
64:               CALL      NEWLINE
65:               LEA       DI,MSGOUT1
66:               MOV       CX,14
67:               CALL      PUTSTRNG
68:               MOV       AX,NUMBER           ;DISPLAY NUMBER
69:               MOV       BH,0
70:               CALL      PUTDEC
71:               LEA       DI,MSGOUT2
72:               MOV       CX,4
73:               CALL      PUTSTRNG
74:               MOV       AX,SQUARE           ;DISPLAY SQUARE OF NUMBER
75:               CALL      PUTDEC$
76:               CALL      NEWLINE
77:               RET                           ;RETURN
78: ;_____
79: ; O V E R F L O W    H A N D L I N G
80: ;
81: OVRFLO:
82:               LEA       DI,OFLMSG           ;DISPLAY OVERFLOW MESSAGE
83:               MOV       CX,19
84:               CALL      PUTSTRNG
85:               CALL      NEWLINE
86:               RET                           ;RETURN
87: ;_____
88: EX_4_3        ENDP
89: CODE          ENDS
90:*              END       EX_4_3
*
```

The data segment is defined in lines 19–33. Three variables are defined in the data segment: one to hold the input value (NUMBER defined in line 24), one to hold an odd, positive integer (ODDINT defined in line 25), and one to hold the sum (SQUARE defined in line 26). NUMBER is left uninitialized. ODDINT is initialized to 1, the first odd, positive integer. SQUARE is initialized to 0, the sum before any odd, positive integers are added. The value of variable NUMBER is interpreted as a signed two's complement integer value, because the input value can be either positive or negative. The values of variables ODDINT and SQUARE are interpreted as unsigned integer values, which gives SQUARE an upper limit of 65,535.

Four additional items are defined in the data segment: a message to prompt the user to enter an integer value (line 28), two messages used for annotation of the output (lines 29 and 30), and a message to display if an overflow occurs during the computation (line 31).

The code segment is defined in lines 35–89 and contains the single main procedure, EX_4_3. The procedure begins in the standard way by pushing the return address onto the stack (lines 41–43) and initializing the segment registers (lines 44–46).

The instructions in lines 47–49 display the prompt message to the user, and the call to GETDEC in line 50 accepts a signed integer value into the AX-register. The MOV instruction in line 51 stores the input value as the value of the variable NUMBER.

The three instructions in lines 52–55 compute the absolute value of the signed two's complement integer in the AX-register. The CMP instruction in line 52 sets the bits in the flags register to reflect the relationship of the input value to zero. The conditional JUMP instruction in line 53 causes the NEG instruction in line 54 to be skipped if the input value is already greater than or equal to zero. However, if the input value is less than zero, then the jump is *not* taken, and the NEG instruction in line 54 is executed. In either event, when control reaches the instruction in lines 55 and 56, the AX-register contains the absolute value of the input integer. The value in variable NUMBER is still the original input number, and the value in the AX-register is the absolute value of that number.

The instructions in lines 52–55 implement a single-alternative decision. The conditional JUMP instruction in line 53 makes the decision either to execute the NEG instruction in line 54 or skip that instruction depending on the value of the condition tested by the CMP instruction in line 52.

The instruction in line 56 moves the absolute value of the input number into the CX-register, which is being used to hold the loop count. This step is the initialization for the REPEAT-UNTIL loop.

The REPEAT-UNTIL loop is implemented in lines 57–63. The loop body appears in lines 58–61, and the loop test is the LOOP instruction in line 62. The two instructions in lines 58 and 59 add the value of variable ODDINT to the value of variable SQUARE, leaving the sum as the new value of variable SQUARE. The ADD instruction in line 59 sets or clears the CF bit in the flags register depending on whether or not the addition of the two unsigned integer values resulted in an arithmetic overflow condition. The JC instruction in line 60 makes a decision based on this condition. Either it makes the decision to continue with execution of the loop body (CF = 0), or it makes the decision to exit the loop abruptly (CF = 1) and display an error message.

Normally such an abrupt exit from the middle of a REPEAT-UNTIL loop is frowned on in structured programming. However, when a catastrophic event occurs, such as an arithmetic overflow, it is often acceptable to abandon the current sequence of instruction executions and jump to a sequence of instructions provided specifically for handling the current condition. In the pseudocode, such exiting is shown by the statement

```
EXIT ON ⟨condition⟩
```

in the loop body. The catastrophic condition handler appears at the end of the procedure and is bracketed by horizontal lines.

If the ADD instruction in line 59 does not cause an overflow condition, then execution of the loop body continues with the ADD instruction in line 61. This instruction increments the value of variable ODDINT by 2 to the next odd, positive integer.

Execution of the LOOP instruction in line 62 causes the following sequence of events:

1. The value in the CX-register, the loop count, is decremented by 1.
2. If the value in the CX-register is nonzero, then the loop body is repeated. That is, a jump is made to the instruction with label LOOP-TOP. If the value in the CX-register is zero, then execution continues with the next instruction in sequence. That is, the loop is terminated.

With normal loop exit (i.e., the LOOP instruction decrements the CX-register value to zero), the instructions in lines 64–76 are executed. These instructions display NUMBER and its SQUARE. The RET instruction in line 77 then returns control to DOS.

The overflow handler (lines 78–87) is executed only if an overflow condition is detected in the accumulation of the sum (SQUARE) in the REPEAT-UNTIL loop body. The overflow handler simply displays an overflow message to the user (lines 82–85) and then returns control to DOS (line 86).

The following are the results from some executions of this program:

```
ENTER INTEGER VALUE
16

THE SQUARE OF 16 IS 256

ENTER INTEGER VALUE
-16

THE SQUARE OF -16 IS 256

ENTER INTEGER VALUE
255

THE SQUARE OF 255 is 65025

ENTER INTEGER VALUE
-255

THE SQUARE OF -255 is 65025

ENTER INTEGER VALUE
256
OVERFLOW OCCURRED

ENTER INTEGER VALUE
0
OVERFLOW OCCURRED
```

Note that for an input of 0, the program displays the message

```
OVERFLOW OCCURRED
```

This output obviously is *not* correct. The square of 0 is 0, and the program should be able to handle this trivial case. The sum of the first 0 odd, positive integers is 0. To see why this case fails, trace program execution for an input of 0. The value stored in the CX-register in line 56 is the absolute value of 0, or 0; that is, the loop count is 0. Thus, the loop body should be executed zero times, leaving the value of SQUARE at its initial value, 0. However, the loop body of a REPEAT-UNTIL loop always is executed at least once. When the LOOP instruction in line 62 is executed the first time, it decrements the value in the CX-register from 0 to -1. This value is nonzero, so the jump to LOOPTOP is taken, and the loop body is repeated. The CX-register cycles through the following values: $-1, -2, -3, \ldots, -32{,}767, -32{,}768, 32{,}767, 32{,}766, \ldots,$ 3, 2, 1, and 0 before the loop terminates, which means the loop body would be executed 65,536 times. That is, the sum of the first 65,536 odd, positive integers (the square of 65,536) would be computed. Obviously, there would be an overflow along the way—the wrong type of loop was chosen for this solution. This problem can be avoided by using a WHILE loop structure rather than a REPEAT-UNTIL loop structure.

WHILE Loop Solution

The following pseudocode describes an algorithm using a WHILE loop structure for solving the problem defined previously:

```
SQUARE = 0
ODDINT = 1
GET NUMBER
LOOP_COUNT = |NUMBER|
WHILE LOOP_COUNT ≠ 0
    SQUARE = SQUARE + ODDINT
    ODDINT = ODDINT + 2
    LOOP_COUNT = LOOP_COUNT - 1
ENDWHILE
DISPLAY NUMBER
DISPLAY SQUARE
```

The only difference between this algorithm and the previous algorithm is that the REPEAT-UNTIL loop has been changed to a WHILE loop. In this algorithm, if the LOOP_COUNT is zero at time of loop entry the loop terminates without the loop body being executed. Since the value of SQUARE is initialized to zero, the program output will be correct for an input of zero.

Implementation of this algorithm uses the **jump if CX-register equals zero (JCXZ) instruction**, which has the following general form:

[⟨*label*⟩]   JCXZ   ⟨*short-label*⟩   [⟨*comment*⟩]

in which ⟨*short-label*⟩ is the label of an instruction whose memory location is within -128 to $+127$ bytes from the memory location immediately following the JCXZ instruction. If the value in the CX-register is zero, then this instruction causes a transfer of control to the instruction that begins at the memory location specified by the operand. If the value in the CX-register is nonzero, then this instruction causes no operation to be performed (i.e., execution continues with the next instruction in sequence). None of the bits in the flags register are affected by execution of a JCXZ instruction.

Program Listing 4.4 is the same as Program Listing 4.3, except for the loop structure. The WHILE loop structure is implemented in lines 57–65. The loop begins with the loop test in line 58, which is followed by the loop body in lines 59–63. The last instruction in the loop is an unconditional JUMP instruction in line 64 that returns control to the test at the top of the loop.

```
 1: ;                    PROGRAM LISTING 4.4
 2: ;
 3: ;PROGRAM TO COMPUTE THE SQUARE OF AN
 4: ;INTEGER, N, BY  SUMMING  THE  FIRST
 5: ;!N! ODD POSITIVE INTEGERS.
 6: ;
 7:                                         ;PROCEDURES TO
 8:           EXTRN    GETDEC:FAR           ;INPUT DECIMAL INTEGER
 9:           EXTRN    PUTDEC:FAR           ;DISPLAY SIGNED DECIMAL INT.
10:           EXTRN    PUTDEC$:FAR          ;DISPLAY UNSIGNED DECIMAL INT.
11:           EXTRN    PUTSTRNG:FAR         ;DISPLAY CHARACTER STRING
12:           EXTRN    NEWLINE:FAR          ;DISPLAY NEWLINE CHARACTER
13: ;
14: ; S T A C K    S E G M E N T    D E F I N I T I O N
15: ;
16: STACK     SEGMENT STACK
17:           DB       256 DUP(?)
18: STACK     ENDS
19: ;
20: ; D A T A    S E G M E N T    D E F I N I T I O N
21: ;
22: DATA      SEGMENT
23: ;
24: NUMBER    DW       ?                    ;INPUT NUMBER
25: ODDINT    DW       1                    ;ODD POSITIVE INTEGER
26: SQUARE    DW       0                    ;SQUARE OF INPUT NUMBER
27: ;
28: PROMPT    DB       'ENTER INTEGER VALUE',ODH,OAH
29: MSGOUT1   DB       'THE SQUARE OF '
30: MSGOUT2   DB       ' IS '
31: OFLMSG    DB       'OVERFLOW OCCURRED',ODH,OAH
32: ;
33: DATA      ENDS
34:*;


35: ;
36: ; C O D E    S E G M E N T    D E F I N I T I O N
37: ;
38: CODE      SEGMENT
39: EX_4_4    PROC     FAR
40:           ASSUME   CS:CODE,SS:STACK,DS:DATA,ES:DATA
41:           PUSH     DS                   ;PUSH RETURN SEG ADDR ON STACK
42:           SUB      AX,AX                ;PUSH RETURN OFFSET OF ZERO
43:           PUSH     AX                   ;ON STACK
```

```
44:              MOV      AX,SEG DATA         ;SET DS AND ES REGISTERS TO
45:              MOV      DS,AX               ;ADDRESS DATA SEGMENT
46:              MOV      ES,AX
47:              LEA      DI,PROMPT           ;PROMPT USER TO ENTER AN INTEGER
48:              MOV      CX,21
49:              CALL     PUTSTRNG
50:              CALL     GETDEC              ;GET NUMBER
51:              MOV      NUMBER,AX           ;
52:              CMP      AX,0                ;IF   NUMBER < 0
53:              JGE      ENDABS
54:              NEG      AX                  ;THEN NUMBER = -NUMBER
55: ENDABS:                                  ;ENDIF
56:              MOV      CX,AX               ;LOOP_COUNT = NUMBER
57: LOOPTOP:                                 ;WHILE LOOP_COUNT <> 0
58:              JCXZ     LOOPEND
59:              MOV      AX,ODDINT           ;   SQUARE = SQUARE + ODDINT
60:              ADD      SQUARE,AX
61:              JC       OVRFLO              ;   EXIT ON OVERFLOW
62:              ADD      ODDINT,2            ;   ODDINT = ODDINT + 2
63:              DEC      CX                  ;   LOOP_COUNT = LOOP_COUNT - 1
64:              JMP      LOOPTOP             ;ENDWHILE
65: LOOPEND:                                 ;
66:              CALL     NEWLINE
67:              LEA      DI,MSGOUT1
68:              MOV      CX,14
69:              CALL     PUTSTRNG
70:              MOV      AX,NUMBER           ;DISPLAY NUMBER
71:              MOV      BH,0
72:              CALL     PUTDEC
73:              LEA      DI,MSGOUT2
74:              MOV      CX,4
75:              CALL     PUTSTRNG
76:              MOV      AX,SQUARE           ;DISPLAY SQUARE OF NUMBER
77:              CALL     PUTDEC$
78:              CALL     NEWLINE
79:              RET                          ;RETURN
80: ;_____
81: ; O V E R F L O W    H A N D L I N G
82: ;
83: OVRFLO:
84:              LEA      DI,OFLMSG           ;DISPLAY OVERFLOW MESSAGE
85:              MOV      CX,19
86:              CALL     PUTSTRNG
87:              CALL     NEWLINE
88:              RET                          ;RETURN
89: ;_____
90: EX_4_4      ENDP
91: CODE        ENDS
92:*           END       EX_4_4
*
```

The JCXZ instruction in line 58 tests the value in the CX-register and then makes a decision based on that value. If the value in the CX-register is zero, then control is transferred to the instruction with label LOOPEND, the first instruction in the sequence of instructions that displays the result. That is, if the value in the CX-register is zero, then the loop is terminated. If the value in the CX-register is nonzero, then execution continues with the next instruction in sequence. That is, if the value in the CX-register is nonzero, then the loop body is executed again.

The first four instructions of the loop body (lines 59–62) are identical to the loop body in the REPEAT-UNTIL loop in Program Listing 4.3. The DEC instruction in line 63 has been added to the loop body to decrement the loop count each time through the loop. (This decrement was handled by the LOOP instruction in the REPEAT-UNTIL loop version.)

The following are the results from some executions of this program:

```
ENTER INTEGER VALUE
16

THE SQUARE OF 16 IS 256

ENTER INTEGER VALUE
-16

THE SQUARE OF -16 IS 256

ENTER INTEGER VALUE
-255

THE SQUARE OF -255 IS 65025

ENTER INTEGER VALUE
256
OVERFLOW OCCURRED

ENTER INTEGER VALUE
0

THE SQUARE OF 0 IS 0
```

4.4   Nested Control Structures

As noted in Program Listing 4.2, control structures may be nested. **Nesting of control structures** is allowed, in structured programming, as long as one control structure is contained completely within another. If a control structure is nested in a decision structure, then it must be contained completely within one of the alternatives of the decision structure. If a control structure is nested in a loop structure, then it must be completely contained within the loop body of the loop structure. Control structures may be nested to any level required by the algorithm.

To illustrate nested control structures, design an algorithm to classify each of the integers in the range 2–100 as perfect, abundant, or deficient. Implement the algorithm with an IBM PC Assembly language program.

The proper divisors of an integer n are those integers less than n that divide n evenly.

Integer	Proper Divisors
6	1, 2, 3
9	1, 3
12	1, 2, 3, 4, 6
18	1, 2, 3, 6, 9

An integer is said to be a **perfect number** if it is equal to the sum of its proper divisors. The number 6 is the first perfect number:

$$6 = 1 + 2 + 3$$

An integer is said to be an **abundant number** if it is less than the sum of its proper divisors. The number 12 is an abundant number:

$$12 < 1 + 2 + 3 + 4 + 6$$

An integer is said to be a **deficient number** if it is greater than the sum of its proper divisors. The number 9 is a deficient number:

$$9 > 1 + 3$$

The following is the pseudocode of an algorithm to classify each of the positive integers in the range 2–100 as deficient, abundant, or perfect:

```
LOOP_COUNT = 99
NUMBER = 2
REPEAT
    DIVISOR_SUM = 1
    DIVISOR = 2
    UPPER_LIMIT = NUMBER / 2
    WHILE DIVISOR ≤ UPPER_LIMIT
        QUOTIENT = NUMBER / DIVISOR
        REMAINDER = NUMBER mod DIVISOR
        IF   REMAINDER = 0
        THEN
                DIVISOR_SUM = DIVISOR_SUM + DIVISOR
                IF   DIVISOR ⟨ ⟩ QUOTIENT
                THEN
                        DIVISOR_SUM = DIVISOR_SUM + QUOTIENT
                ENDIF
                UPPER_LIMIT = QUOTIENT - 1
        ENDIF
        DIVISOR = DIVISOR + 1
    ENDWHILE
    IF   DIVISOR_SUM = NUMBER
    THEN
            DISPLAY 'PERFECT'
```

```
    ELSE
        IF    DIVISOR_SUM < NUMBER
    THEN
        DISPLAY 'DEFICIENT'
    ELSE
        DISPLAY 'ABUNDANT'
    ENDIF
    ENDIF
    DISPLAY NUMBER
    NUMBER = NUMBER + 1
    LOOP_COUNT = LOOP_COUNT - 1
UNTIL LOOP_COUNT = 0
```

The algorithm contains a REPEAT-UNTIL loop structure. Nested within the REPEAT-UNTIL loop is a WHILE loop structure, which is followed by a double-alternative decision structure. Nested within the WHILE loop is a single-alternative decision structure that itself contains a single-alternative decision structure. Nested within the second alternative of the double-alternative decision structure is another double-alternative decision structure.

Program Listing 4.5 shows an implementation of the preceding algorithm. The program is arranged in the standard way: A prologue (lines 1–5) is followed by the external procedure definitions (lines 6–9), is followed by the standard stack segment definition (lines 10–15), is followed by the data segment definition (lines 16–30), is followed by the code segment definition (lines 31–98), and is concluded with an END pseudo-operation in line 99.

```
 1: ;                    PROGRAM LISTING 4.5
 2: ;
 3: ;PROGRAM TO CLASSIFY EACH OF THE POSITIVE INTEGERS
 4: ;2 - 100  AS DEFICIENT, ABUNDANT, OR PERFECT.
 5: ;
 6:                                     ;PROCEDURES TO
 7:             EXTRN    PUTDEC:FAR      ;DISPLAY DECIMAL INTEGER
 8:             EXTRN    NEWLINE:FAR     ;DISPLAY NEWLINE CHARACTER
 9:             EXTRN    PUTSTRNG:FAR    ;DISPLAY CHARACTER STRING
10: ;
11: ; S T A C K   S E G M E N T   D E F I N I T I O N
12: ;
13: STACK       SEGMENT STACK
14:             DB       256 DUP(?)
15: STACK       ENDS
16: ;
17: ; D A T A   S E G M E N T   D E F I N I T I O N
18: ;
19: DATA        SEGMENT
20: ;
21: NUMBER      DW       ?              ;CURRENT NUMBER BEING CLASSIFIED
22: SUM         DW       ?              ;SUM OF DIVISORS OF NUMBER
23: LIMIT       DW       ?              ;UPPER LIMIT FOR DIVISORS
24: ;
25: ;
26: DEFICIENT   DB       'DEFICIENT   '
```

```
27: ABUNDANT     DB         'ABUNDANT    '
28: PERFECT      DB         'PERFECT     '
29: ;
30: DATA         ENDS
31: ;
32: ; C O D E    S E G M E N T    D E F I N I T I O N
33: ;
34: CODE         SEGMENT
35: EX_4_5       PROC       FAR
36:              ASSUME     CS:CODE,SS:STACK,DS:DATA,ES:DATA
37:              PUSH       DS                 ;PUSH SEGMENT OF RETURN ON STACK
38:              MOV        AX,0               ;PUSH OFFSET  OF RETURN ON STACK
39:              PUSH       AX
40:              MOV        AX,SEG DATA        ;SET DS AND ES REGISTERS TO
41:              MOV        DS,AX              ;DATA SEGMENT
42:*             MOV        ES,AX
*  43: ;
44:              MOV        CX,99              ;LOOP_COUNT = 99
45:              MOV        NUMBER,2           ;NUMBER = 2
46: NUMLOOP:                                  ;REPEAT
47:              MOV        SUM,1              ;   SUM = 1
48:              MOV        BX,2               ;   DIVISOR = 2
49:              MOV        AX,NUMBER          ;   UPPER_LIMIT = NUMBER/2
50:              MOV        DX,0
51:              DIV        BX
52:              MOV        LIMIT,AX
53: DIVLOOP:                                  ;   WHILE DIVISOR <= UPPER_LIMIT
54:              CMP        BX,LIMIT
55:              JG         DLOOPEND
56:              MOV        AX,NUMBER          ;      QUO. = NUMBER/DIVISOR
57:              MOV        DX,0
58:              DIV        BX
59:              CMP        DX,0               ;      IF   DIVISOR DIVIDES
60:              JNE        INC_DIV            ;           NUMBER EVENLY
61:              ADD        SUM,BX             ;      THEN SUM = SUM + DIVISOR
62:              CMP        BX,AX              ;         IF    DIVISOR<>QUO.
63:              JE         CHG_LIMIT          ;         THEN SUM = SUM+QUO.
64:              ADD        SUM,AX
65: CHG_LIMIT:                                ;         ENDIF
66:              SUB        AX,1               ;         UPPER_LIMIT = QUO.-1
67:              MOV        LIMIT,AX
68: INC_DIV:                                  ;      ENDIF
69:              INC        BX                 ;      DIVISOR = DIVISOR + 1
70:              JMP        DIVLOOP
71: DLOOPEND:                                 ;   ENDWHILE
72:              PUSH       CX                 ;   SAVE LOOP_COUNT
73:              MOV        CX,12              ;   CX = CHAR COUNT OF CLASS STR
74:              MOV        AX,NUMBER          ;   IF   SUM = NUMBER
75:              CMP        AX,SUM
76:              JG         DEF_NUM
77:              JL         ABUN_NUM
78:              LEA        DI,PERFECT         ;   THEN DISPLAY 'PERFECT'
79:              JMP        PRT_NUM
80: DEF_NUM:                                  ;   ELSE IF   SUM < NUMBER
81:              LEA        DI,DEFICIENT       ;        THEN DISPLAY 'DEFICIENT'
82:              JMP        PRT_NUM
83: ABUN_NUM:                                 ;        ELSE DISPLAY 'ABUNDANT'
84:              LEA        DI,ABUNDANT
85: PRT_NUM:                                  ;        ENDIF
86:                                           ;   ENDIF
```

```
87:                 CALL    PUTSTRNG
88:                 MOV     AX,NUMBER
89:                 MOV     BH,0
90:                 CALL    PUTDEC          ;    DISPLAY NUMBER
91:                 CALL    NEWLINE
92:                 POP     CX              ;    RESTORE LOOP_COUNT
93:                 INC     NUMBER          ;    NUMBER = NUMBER + 1
94:                 LOOP    NUMLOOP         ;    LOOP_COUNT = LOOP_COUNT - 1
95:                                         ;UNTIL LOOP_COUNT = 0
96:                 RET                     ;RETURN
97: EX_4_5          ENDP
98: CODE            ENDS
99:*                END     EX_4_5
```

Three variables are defined in the data segment. All three have type attribute WORD, and all three are uninitialized. The variable NUMBER, defined in line 21, holds the integer currently being classified. The variable SUM, defined in line 22, accumulates the sum of the proper divisors of the integer currently being classified. The variable LIMIT, defined in line 23, keeps track of an upper limit on the proper divisors of the integer currently being classified. The three classification messages are defined in the data segment (lines 26–28): DEFICIENT, ABUNDANT, and PERFECT.

The code segment contains a single main procedure, EX_4_5. The procedure begins in the standard way by pushing the return address onto the stack (lines 37–39) and initializing the segment registers (lines 40–42).

The classification loop, the REPEAT-UNTIL loop implemented in lines 46–95, executes 99 times, once for each value of NUMBER from 2–100. The MOV instruction in line 44 initializes the loop count in the CX-register to 99, and the MOV instruction in line 45 initializes the value of variable NUMBER to 2. Each iteration of the REPEAT-UNTIL loop (lines 46–95) computes and displays the classification for a single integer. The loop body of this REPEAT-UNTIL loop (lines 47–93) performs the following sequence of steps:

1. The MOV instruction in line 47 initializes the SUM of the proper divisors to 1. Since 1 is a proper divisor of all positive integers, there is no need to test it. It can be added to the SUM initially.

2. The MOV instruction in line 48 initializes the trial divisor to 2. The trial divisor is maintained in the BX-register.

3. The instructions in lines 49–52 initialize the upper limit for trial divisors of the current NUMBER to one-half the current NUMBER. There can be no proper divisor of n that is greater than $n/2$. Thus, there is no need to test values greater than $n/2$.

4. The WHILE loop, implemented in lines 53–71, computes the SUM of the proper divisors of the current NUMBER. This nested loop structure is discussed in detail in the following paragraphs.

5. The PUSH instruction in line 72 saves the value in the CX-register, the REPEAT-UNTIL loop's loop count, because the CX-register is needed to hold a parameter for the PUTSTRNG procedure, which is used to display the classification.

6. The MOV instruction in line 73 stores the length of the classification strings in the CX-register, which is one of the parameters for the PUTSTRNG procedure.

7. The double alternative-decision structure, implemented in lines 74–86, determines the classification to be displayed based on the relationship between the current NUMBER and the SUM of its proper divisors. This decision structure is discussed in detail in the following paragraphs.

8. The call to the PUTSTRNG procedure in line 87 displays the classification.

9. The instructions in lines 88–91 display the current NUMBER followed by a NEWLINE character.

10. The POP instruction in line 92 restores the CX-register with the REPEAT-UNTIL loop's count that was saved by the PUSH instruction in line 72.

11. The INC instruction in line 93 increments the value of variable NUMBER to the integer to be classified on the next iteration of the REPEAT-UNTIL loop body.

The loop instruction in line 94 is the loop count decrement and test for the REPEAT-UNTIL loop. The loop count in the CX-register is decremented by 1. If the resulting value is nonzero, then a jump is made to the instruction labeled NUMLOOP (lines 46 and 47), and the loop body is executed again. If the resulting value is zero, then the REPEAT-UNTIL loop is terminated, and the RET instruction in line 96 returns control to DOS.

The nested WHILE loop implemented in lines 53–71 computes the SUM of the proper divisors of the current NUMBER. The initialization for this loop is performed by the instructions in lines 47–52, which were discussed previously. The WHILE loop test is the sequence of instructions in lines 54 and 55. The CMP instruction in line 54 compares the current trial divisor in the BX-register to the upper LIMIT and sets the flags to reflect the relationship. The JG instruction in line 55 makes a decision based on this relationship. If the trial divisor is greater than the upper LIMIT, then a jump is made to the instruction labeled DLOOPEND (lines 71 and 72). That is, the WHILE loop is terminated when the trial divisor becomes greater than the upper LIMIT. However, if the trial divisor is less than or equal to the upper LIMIT, then the loop body is executed.

The WHILE loop body is implemented in lines 56–69 and performs the following sequence of steps:

1. The instructions in lines 56–58 divide the current NUMBER by the current trial divisor.

2. The single alternative-decision structure in lines 59–68 performs the following sequence of steps if the remainder of the preceding division is zero (i.e., if the trial divisor divides the NUMBER evenly):

   a. The ADD instruction in line 61 adds the trial divisor to the SUM.

   b. The single alternative-decision structure in lines 62–65 adds the quotient of the preceding division to the SUM if the quotient is not equal to the trial divisor. That is, if the remainder of the division is zero, then both the divisor and the quotient are proper divisors of the NUMBER, and therefore, they can both be added to the SUM. However, if the divisor and the quotient are equal, then only one of them should be added to the SUM. To add both of them, in the case that they are equal, would include one of the proper divisors twice.

   c. The instructions in lines 66 and 67 set the upper LIMIT to 1 less than the quotient of the preceding division. As the divisor increases, the quotient of the division decreases. Since the quotient is added to the SUM whenever the divisor is added to the sum (unless they are equal), the quotient minus 1 becomes the new upper LIMIT on divisors that must be tested.

   d. The instruction in line 69 increments the trial divisor by 1.

The unconditional JUMP instruction in line 70 returns control to the loop test at the top of the loop (lines 53 and 54).

The nested double-alternative decision structure in lines 74–86 determines the classification. The instructions in lines 74 and 75 compare the current NUMBER to the SUM of its proper divisors and sets the flags to reflect this relationship. If the NUMBER is greater than the SUM of its proper divisors, then the conditional JUMP in line 76 is used, and the DI-register is loaded with the offset of the message DEFICIENT (line 81). If the NUMBER is less than the SUM of its proper divisors, then the conditional JUMP in line 77 is used, and the DI-register is loaded with the offset of the message ABUNDANT (line 84). Otherwise, the instruction in line 78 is executed, which loads the DI-register with the offset of the message PERFECT. The DI-register is used as one of the inputs to the PUTSTRNG procedure. In all three cases, after loading the DI-register, control is transferred to the instruction in lines 85–87 (i.e., the instruction immediately following the decision structure).

When executed, this program displays 99 lines of output, which is certainly more than one screenful. In Programming Exercise 4.11 at the end of this chapter, a technique is presented for stopping the display, under program control, after each screenful.

PROGRAMMING EXERCISES

4.1 Given a positive integer, $n1$, a sequence of positive integers $n1, n2, n3, \ldots, 1$ can be generated using the following rules:

1. If ni is odd, then $n(i + 1)$ is computed by

$$n(i + 1) = 3 * ni + 1$$

2. If ni is even, then $n(i + 1)$ is computed by

$$n(i + 1) = ni/2$$

3. The sequence is terminated at the first occurrence of the integer 1.

It has been conjectured (but to the author's knowledge never proven) that the length of a sequence is always finite. That is, for any positive integer value of $n1$, the sequence eventually reaches the integer 1 and terminates. The length of a sequence is the number of integers in the sequence.

EXAMPLE

For $n1 = 22$, the sequence is

```
22  11  34  17  52  26  13  40
20  10   5  16   8   4   2   1
```

The length of the sequence is 16.

Design an algorithm to accept as input a positive integer, $n1$, and to compute and output the sequence $n1, n2, n3, \ldots, 1$ and its length. The sequence is to be generated according to the preceding rules. Implement your algorithm with an IBM PC Assembly language program. Your input should be the first integer in the sequence entered via the keyboard. Your output should be the sequence and length displayed on the screen. The sequence should be displayed 10 integers per line, and the length should be displayed on a separate line following the sequence. Your program should detect any overflow in the sequence generation. If overflow occurs, then terminate the sequence and display an appropriate diagnostic message in place of the length output. Demon-

strate your program using the following input values: 1, 22, 38834, 38836, 38838, 93, 97, 9995, and 9997.

In the book, *Using Basic: An Introduction to Computer Programming*, Third Edition, by Julian Hennefeld (Prindle, Weber, and Schmidt), this phenomenon is referred to as Ulam's conjecture. Such a sequence is referred to as an Ulam sequence, and the length of the sequence is referred to as the Ulam length.

4.2 Modify your program from Programming Exercise 3.3 to include an overflow check. If overflow is detected, then display an appropriate diagnostic message. Demonstrate your program with the set of inputs specified in the problem statement.

4.3 Design an algorithm to find and output the count of the number of ways to make change for a dollar using half-dollars, quarters, dimes, nickels, and pennies. Implement your algorithm with an IBM PC Assembly language program. There is no input to your program. Your output should be the count of the number of ways to make change for a dollar displayed on the screen.

4.4 Design an algorithm to find and output all three-digit integers that are equal to the sum of the cubes of their digits. The integer 371 is an example of such an integer:

$$371 = 3^3 + 7^3 + 1^3 = 27 + 343 + 1$$

Implement your algorithm with an IBM PC Assembly language program. There is no input to your program. Your output should be the sequence of three-digit integers that have the given property.

4.5 The four-digit integer 3025 has the property that the square of the sum of the integer formed by its first two digits and the integer formed by its last two digits is equal to the integer itself. That is:

$$3025 = (30 + 25)^2 = (55)^2$$

Design an algorithm to find and output all four-digit integers that have this property. Implement your algorithm with an IBM PC Assembly language program. There is no input to your program. Your output should be the sequence of four-digit integers that have the given property.

4.6 Euclid's algorithm for finding the greatest common divisor (GCD) of two positive integers is given. Implement this algorithm with an IBM PC Assembly language program. Your input should be two positive integers entered via the keyboard. Your output should be the GCD of the two input integers. The output is to be displayed on the screen.

EUCLID'S ALGORITHM:

```
GET X and Y
WHILE Y ≠ 0
    X = X mod Y
        INTERCHANGE X and Y
ENDWHILE
DISPLAY X
```

Recall that X mod Y is the remainder of X divided by Y.

4.7 Design an algorithm to accept as input two 16-bit integers that represent a departure time and an arrival time based on a 24-hour clock (0000–2359) and to compute and output the flight duration in hours and minutes.

EXAMPLES

Departure Time	Arrival Time	Flight Duration
1048	1324	2 hr 36 min
2135	0212	4 hr 37 min

You may assume that no flight lasts longer than 24 hours. Implement your algorithm with an IBM PC Assembly language program. Your input should be two 16-bit integers in the range 0000–2359 entered via the keyboard. Your output should be the hours and minutes of flight duration

displayed on the screen. Demonstrate your program using the following inputs:

Departure Time	Arrival Time
1054	1323
2145	0252
0842	0842
1843	1124

4.8 Given a positive integer, $n1$, a sequence of positive integers $n1, n2, n3, \ldots$ can be generated using the following rule:

$$n(i + 1) = \text{sum of squares of digits of } ni$$

Either one of two events will happen in the sequence:

1. The integer 1 is produced, and therefore, all subsequent integers in the sequence are 1.

2. The integer 4 is produced, and the subsequent integers in the sequence are 16, 37, 58, 89, 145, 42, 20, 4, . . . That is, the sequence contains a cycle, and the integer 1 is never produced in the sequence.

Any positive integer whose sequence eventually produces 1 is said to be an **insipid** integer.

EXAMPLES

8 64 52 29 85 89 145 42 20 4 16
37 58 89 . . .

The number 8 is not an insipid integer.

23 13 10 1 . . .

The number 23 is an insipid integer.

Design an algorithm to accept a positive integer as input and to output the sequence generated by the preceding rule until either the integer 1 or the integer 4 is produced. Implement your algorithm with an IBM PC Assembly language program. Your input should be a positive integer. Your output should be the sequence of integers produced and the word 'INSIPID' if the integer 1 is produced in the sequence.

4.9. A Pythagorean triple is a sequence of three positive integers (x, y, z) that satisfy the equation

$$z^2 = x^2 + y^2$$

For example, the sequence $(3, 4, 5)$ is a Pythagorean triple:

$$5^2 = 3^2 + 4^2$$

$$25 = 9 + 16$$

Design an algorithm to find and output all Pythagorean triples whose integers are in the range 1–50. Be sure that your algorithm does not produce any duplicates, such as $(3, 4, 5)$ and $(4, 3, 5)$. Implement your algorithm with an IBM PC Assembly language program. There is no input to your program. Your output should be a list of the Pythagorean triples displayed on the screen, one triple per line.

4.10 Design an algorithm to compute and print a table of Fahrenheit temperatures and the corresponding centigrade temperatures for Fahrenheit temperatures in the range -60 degrees to 150 degrees in increments of 10 degrees. Implement your algorithm with an IBM PC Assembly language program. There is no input to your program. Your output should be the table of temperature values displayed on the screen.

4.11 The PAUSE procedure, in the I/O subprocedure library, displays a message on the screen, clears the keyboard input buffer, and waits for a keystroke from the keyboard. When the keystroke is received, control is returned to the caller. The message to be displayed is supplied by the caller.

The PAUSE procedure provides the capability for a program to pause during execution and then to continue when the user presses a key on the keyboard. The inputs to the PAUSE procedure are the same as the inputs for the PUTSTRNG procedure. Modify Program Listing 4.5 to pause and wait for a keystroke after each 20 lines of output.

5
PROCEDURES, SUBPROCEDURES, AND MACROS

The program listings in Chapters 1–4 show a single code segment containing a single procedure, the main procedure for the program. Most of these listings also show external references (i.e., EXTRN pseudo-operations) that identify subprocedures to be combined with the main procedure by the linkage editor. The object code for these subprocedures already exists in the I/O subprocedure library.

The subprocedure is an important tool for the Assembly language programmer. Programming in Assembly language becomes much more efficient once a comprehensive library of subprocedures has been developed. The I/O subprocedure library on the diskette that accompanies this book is only a start in this direction. It enables users to develop meaningful programs without having to encounter machine-level input/output operations. Up to this point, the user has made use of already existing subprocedures. This chapter shows how to develop subprocedures and how to link procedures together to form a complete and executable program. This chapter also introduces the assembler's macro feature, which allows a programmer to define new operations in terms of existing machine-level instructions.

5.1 | Terminology

An **executable program** in the IBM PC consists of one or more code segments, a stack segment, and zero or more static data segments. The code segments consist of exactly one main procedure and zero or more subprocedures. The **main procedure** receives execution control of the processor when the executable program initially is placed into execution by the operating system. A **subprocedure** receives execution control of the processor by being referenced or called from another procedure (possibly itself). The procedure that invokes a subprocedure is referred to as the **caller** of the subprocedure. The term **procedure** is used to refer to either a main procedure or a subprocedure.

An **assembly module** is one complete input to the assembler program, and it consists of one or more segment definitions. An assembly module does not have to be a complete program. Object modules produced by assembling various assembly modules are combined into a complete executable program by the Linkage Editor program (LINK).

5.2 | Subprocedures

A subprocedure is similar in many ways to a main procedure. It can perform the same actions as a main procedure. That is, a subprocedure can accept input data, perform computations, and return results (output). However, many differences exist between a main procedure and a subprocedure. One such difference, the way in which they are invoked, was discussed in Section 5.1. A main procedure receives its inputs from a source external to the computer and sends its outputs to a destination external to the computer. Even though subprocedures can communicate with external devices, they generally receive their inputs from the caller and return results back to the caller. Termination of a main procedure terminates execution of the entire executable program. Termination of a sub-procedure returns execution control of the processor to the caller of the sub-procedure. A subprocedure may be called from more than one place in a procedure. Each time the subprocedure terminates, control is returned to the instruction in the calling procedure that immediately follows the instruction that called the subprocedure into execution. This sequence is shown in Figure 5.1.

Uses of Subprocedures

Subprocedures are used in two basic ways:

1. Subprocedures provide a set of instructions that appear only once in an executable program but can be executed more than once to manipulate different sets of input data.

EXAMPLE

Given the coordinates of three vertices of a triangle, $(x1, y1)$, $(x2, y2)$, and $(x3, y3)$, the area of the triangle can be computed as follows:

a. Compute the lengths of the three sides of the triangle:

$$A = \sqrt{(y2 - y1)^2 + (x2 - x1)^2}$$

$$B = \sqrt{(y3 - y2)^2 + (x3 - x2)^2}$$

$$C = \sqrt{(y1 - y3)^2 + (x1 - x3)^2}$$

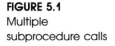

FIGURE 5.1
Multiple
subprocedure calls

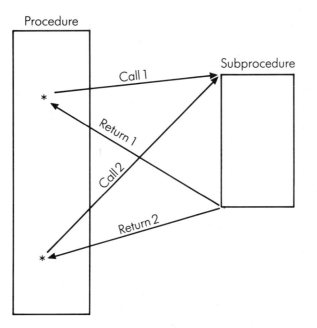

b. Compute the semiperimeter:

$$S \ = \ 1/2(A \ + \ B \ + \ C)$$

c. Compute the area:

$$\text{AREA} \ = \ \sqrt{S(S \ - \ A)(S \ - \ B)(S \ - \ C)}$$

The instructions to compute the square root of a positive real number are needed four times in this computation. Rather than writing the instructions in four places in the program with only slight modifications to accommodate data, the instructions can be written once as a subprocedure that accepts a positive real number as input and returns the square root of that number as its output.

2. Subprocedures facilitate the dividing of a problem into smaller independent subproblems, each of which can be solved separately. The solution to each subproblem is implemented as a subprocedure, and the subprocedures eventually are integrated into a unit using a main procedure that calls the subprocedures in the proper sequence. This modularity feature allows the work of a large programming project to be divided among several programmers, with the programmers able to do much of the work independently of each other.

EXAMPLE

Consider the problem of writing a program that detects palindromes. A palindrome is a word, phrase, or sentence that is spelled the same backward as forward. The following are examples of palindromes:

> No radar on.
> Madam I'm Adam.
> Able was I ere I saw Elba.
> Rats live on no evil star.

Note that there are several considerations to this problem. Characters other than letters must be ignored. The type case of a letter must be ignored; that is, "A" and "a" must be treated the same, for example. The problem could be divided into subproblems as follows:

a. Design an algorithm to accept as input a character string and to produce as output the input string with all nonletters removed.

b. Design an algorithm to accept as input a character string and to produce as output the input string with each lowercase letter changed to the corresponding uppercase letter.

c. Design an algorithm to accept as input a character string and to produce as output the reverse of the input string.

d. Design an algorithm to accept as input two equal-length character strings and to return as output an indication of whether or not the two strings are the same.

e. Design a main program to accept as input a character string, use the subprocedures from (a) and (b) to convert the input string into an uppercase letter string, use the subprocedure from (c) to reverse the uppercase letter string, and use the subprocedure from (d) to compare the uppercase letter string to its reverse to determine if the original input string is a palindrome.

The problem of designing an algorithm to detect palindromes seems to be a rather complex task. However, designing an algorithm to solve any of the subproblems listed is a rather simple task. The original problem has been simplified by modularization.

Types of Subprocedures

Two classes of subprocedures are available in most high-level programming languages: value-returning procedures (functions) and nonvalue-returning procedures (subroutines). A **function** returns an explicit result and is invoked by a reference to the function that appears as an operand in an expression. During evaluation of the expression, when it is time for that operand to be evaluated, the function is invoked. The function is applied to its arguments (inputs). The value returned by the function is used as the value of the function reference in the evaluation of the expression.

EXAMPLE

The Pascal programming language provides the predefined function sqrt that accepts a positive real number as input and returns the square root of that real number as output. The sqrt function can be referenced in an assignment statement like the following:

```
R1 := (-B + sqrt(B*B - 4*A*C))/(2*A)
```

The subexpression

```
sqrt(B*B - 4*A*C)
```

is an operand in the arithmetic expression on the right-hand side of the assignment operator. When the value of that operand is needed in the evaluation of the arithmetic expression, the subexpression

```
B*B - 4*A*C
```

is evaluated, and then the sqrt function is invoked with the value of this subexpression as its input argument. The value returned by the sqrt function takes the place of the operand

```
sqrt(B*B - 4*A*C)
```

in the evaluation of the arithmetic expression.

A **subroutine** does not return an explicit value. It is invoked at time of execution by a special subprocedure invocation statement that references the subroutine.

EXAMPLE

The Pascal programming language provides the predefined procedure write to specify output to the standard output file. The statement

```
write (X)
```

indicates that the write procedure is to be invoked with the value of variable X as its input argument. The procedure outputs the value of variable X to the standard output file.

5.3 | Subprocedure Interface

The interface between a subprocedure and its caller can be described by the occurrence of the following four events:

1. The transfer of control from the caller to the subprocedure (calling the subprocedure)
2. The return of control from the subprocedure to the caller (returning from the subprocedure)

3. The saving and restoring of the state of the processor for the caller
4. The passing of inputs from the caller to the subprocedure and the returning of outputs from the subprocedure to the caller (parameter passing)

Calling a Subprocedure

The **calling of a subprocedure** requires the following:

1. Altering the program count (the CS:IP register pair in the IBM PC) from its current sequence to the memory location where execution is to begin in the subprocedure
2. Saving the address of the instruction that is to be executed when the subprocedure returns control to the caller (the caller's return address).

In the IBM PC Assembly language, a subprocedure is invoked by a **CALL instruction**, which has the following general form:

[⟨label⟩]　CALL　⟨target⟩　[⟨comment⟩]

in which ⟨target⟩ is the name of the procedure that is being invoked (direct CALL) or an address expression that specifies the memory location that contains the address of the procedure being invoked (indirect CALL). The CALL instruction causes the address of the instruction immediately following the CALL instruction (i.e., the return address) to be pushed onto the top of the stack. The CS:IP register pair then is modified to point to the memory location where the first instruction of the called procedure begins.

Returning from a Subprocedure

Returning from a subprocedure requires returning the program count (the CS:IP register pair in the IBM PC) to the instruction in the calling procedure that immediately follows the instruction that invoked the subprocedure. In the IBM PC Assembly language, the **RET instruction** is used to return from a subprocedure to its caller, and it has the following general form:

[⟨label⟩]　RET　[⟨pop-value⟩]　[⟨comment⟩]

in which ⟨pop-value⟩ is an immediate value that specifies the number of argument bytes to be popped from the stack and discarded. The RET instruction causes the return address to be popped from the top of the stack and placed in the CS:IP register pair. The value of the immediate operand is added to the SP-register to pop arguments from the stack. The use of the stack for passing arguments is discussed in detail in Chapter 10; for now, arguments are passed in other ways.

Saving and Restoring Registers

The state of the processor at any point in time is described by the values in the registers, including the flags register. To save the state of the processor, the desired register values are pushed onto the stack using the PUSH and PUSHF instructions. To restore the state of the processor, these values are popped from the stack into the registers from which they came using the POP and POPF instructions. There are two approaches to **saving and restoring the state of the processor**:

1. The burden of saving and restoring the state of the processor can be placed on the caller. Prior to calling the subprocedure, the caller saves the registers it needs, and on return from the subprocedure, the caller restores these registers. With this approach, only the registers that need to be protected are saved and restored, although this method places a sometimes aggravating burden on the subprocedure user.

2. The burden of saving and restoring the state of the processor is placed on the subprocedure. At the beginning of the subprocedure, all registers used by the subprocedure including the flags register are saved. Just prior to return to the caller, these registers are restored. This approach centralizes the saving and restoring of the processor state to one place rather than requiring that it appear around each call. However, the subprocedure must save and restore all of the registers that it uses, whether or not a caller needs them saved.

The author's preference is to use the second approach. The I/O procedure package and the program listings in this book were designed using this philosophy.

Parameter Passing

In high-level languages, subprocedures receive their inputs through parameters defined in the subprocedure definition. The actual inputs for a specific invocation of a subprocedure are specified by arguments that appear in the subprocedure reference and that are bound to the corresponding parameters as part of the subprocedure invocation. Two **parameter passing** mechanisms are popular in high-level programming languages: call-by-value and call-by-location. With **call-by-value**, the value of the argument is bound to the parameter. The argument simply provides an initial value for the parameter on invocation of that subprocedure. The subprocedure's assignment of a new value to the parameter has no effect on the caller's environment. With **call-by-location**, the address of the argument is bound to the parameter. The parameter is just another name for the memory location that contains the argument. The subprocedure's assignment of a new value to the parameter is an assignment of a new value to the corresponding argument in the caller's environment, which is one way for a subprocedure to return values to the caller.

FIGURE 5.2

Subprocedure as a
black box

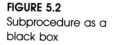

Inputs ⟶ Subprocedure ⟶ Outputs

An important feature of subprocedures is this ability to parameterize their behaviors. The parameters allow the net effect of the subprocedure to be characterized. That is, a subprocedure takes certain inputs and produces certain outputs. The subprocedure can be viewed as a black box of the form shown in Figure 5.2.

From the user's point of view, the parameters characterize the entire effect of the named subprocedure. The way in which the outputs are produced from the inputs is of no concern to the user. The user needs to know only what the procedure does and what the interface is, not how the subprocedure performs its function. The subprocedures in the I/O library of this book have been used in this way; Appendix D describes the function and interface requirements for each of these subprocedures, but it does not describe how the subprocedures perform their functions. The information contained in Appendix D is sufficient for users of these procedures.

In the IBM PC Assembly language, there are three typical ways to pass inputs to a subprocedure and receive outputs from a subprocedure:

1. The input values can be placed in processor registers by the caller, and the subprocedure can pick them up from there. The subprocedure can leave the output values in processor registers, and the caller can pick them up from there. The I/O procedure PUTDEC receives its inputs in this way. For a function subprocedure that returns a single value to be used in further computation, the following conventions typically are used:
   a. If the value being returned is a byte value, then it is returned in the AL-register.
   b. If the value being returned is a word value, then it is returned in the AX-register.
   c. If the value being returned is a double-word value (32 bits), then it is returned in the DX:AX register pair.
   The I/O procedure GETDEC is a function procedure that returns its output in the AX-register.

2. The addresses of arguments can be placed in processor registers by the caller. The subprocedure then has access to a part of the caller's environment. By changing the values at these addresses, the subprocedure can return outputs to the caller. The I/O procedure PUTSTRNG obtains the address of the string to be displayed in this way. The I/O procedure GETSTRNG places the input string at the address specified by the caller.

3. The input values (or their addresses) can be placed in the stack by the caller, and the subprocedure can pick them up from there. The sub-

procedure can leave the output values in the stack, and the caller can pick them up from there. This method, used by some high-level language compilers, can be used in implementing recursive algorithms and is discussed in Chapter 10.

5.4   IBM PC Assembly Language Subprocedures

In the IBM PC Assembly language, a code segment definition contains the definition of one or more procedures. A procedure definition begins with a PROC pseudo-operation and terminates with an ENDP pseudo-operation. The PROC pseudo-operation that marks the beginning of a procedure definition also declares the type of procedure being defined. The type attribute of a procedure is either NEAR or FAR. The Assembly language CALL instruction is translated to one of two different machine language call instructions, depending on whether the procedure being called is type NEAR or type FAR. A RET instruction appearing in a procedure definition is translated to one of two different machine language return instructions, depending on whether the procedure containing the RET instruction is defined as type NEAR or type FAR.

NEAR Procedures

A NEAR subprocedure is one that is defined in the same code segment as the procedure(s) that reference it. It is known by and only can be invoked by procedures in the code segment in which it is defined. The names of variables, labels, and procedures defined within a given assembly module are available to all procedures within that assembly module. A **NEAR procedure** is declared by using the operand NEAR in the PROC pseudo-operation that identifies the beginning of the procedure definition:

⟨ *proc-name* ⟩   PROC   NEAR   [⟨*comment*⟩]

The machine language instruction that calls a NEAR procedure causes only the value of the IP-register to be pushed onto the stack. The IP-register then is set to the offset within the code segment of the subprocedure name. That is, the IP-register is set to the offset of the first instruction in the called procedure. The value of the CS-register does not have to be saved or modified, since the procedure is in the same code segment as its caller.

The machine language instruction that returns from a NEAR procedure pops a single value from the stack and places that value in the IP-register. A NEAR procedure must be written in such a way that the offset pushed onto the stack by the call instruction that invoked the procedure is again at the top of the stack when any RET instruction in the procedure is executed. Then the value popped into the IP-register becomes the offset of the first byte of the instruction that immediately follows the CALL instruction that invoked the procedure.

Programming Example—Display Binary Integer (PUTBIN Version 1)

The assembly module in Program Listing 5.1 has a code segment definition (lines 17–111) that contains two procedure definitions. One is a NEAR subprocedure that displays an 8-bit or 16-bit integer in binary form, and the other is a main procedure that was designed to demonstrate the subprocedure. The subprocedure is called PUTBIN, because, from a functional standpoint, it behaves exactly like the PUTBIN procedure in the I/O procedure package that accompanies this book. However, this subprocedure is not the version of PUTBIN that is included in that package.

```
 1: ;                        PROGRAM LISTING 5.1
 2: ;
 3: ;PROGRAM TO DEMONSTRATE SUBROUTINE INTERFACE
 4: ;
 5:                                            ;PROCEDURES TO
 6:                EXTRN    PUTDEC:FAR          ;DISPLAY DECIMAL INTEGER
 7:                EXTRN    NEWLINE:FAR         ;DISPLAY NEWLINE CHARACTER
 8: ;
 9: ; S T A C K    S E G M E N T    D E F I N I T I O N
10: ;
11: STACK          SEGMENT STACK
12:                DB       256 DUP(?)
13: STACK          ENDS
14: ;
15: ; C O D E    S E G M E N T    D E F I N I T I O N
16: ;
17: CODE           SEGMENT
18: EX_5_1         PROC     FAR
19:                ASSUME   CS:CODE,SS:STACK
20:                PUSH     DS                 ;PUSH RETURN SEG ADDR ON STACK
21:                SUB      AX,AX              ;PUSH RETURN OFFSET OF ZERO
22:                PUSH     AX                 ;ON STACK
23:                MOV      BL,1               ;SET CODE FOR WORD DISPLAY
24:                MOV      AX,0001H           ;LOAD AX WITH
25:                                            ;
26:                                            ;0000000000000001
27:                                            ;
28:                CALL     PUTBIN             ;DISPLAY CONTENTS OF AX
29:                CALL     NEWLINE            ;SKIP TO NEXT LINE ON DISPLAY
30:                MOV      AX,5555H           ;LOAD AX WITH
31:                                            ;
32:                                            ;0101010101010101
33:                                            ;
34:                CALL     PUTBIN             ;DISPLAY CONTENTS OF AX
35:                CALL     NEWLINE            ;SKIP TO NEXT LINE ON DISPLAY
36:                MOV      AX,0AAAAH          ;LOAD AX WITH
37:                                            ;
38:                                            ;1010101010101010
39:                                            ;
40:                CALL     PUTBIN             ;DISPLAY CONTENTS OF AX
41:                CALL     NEWLINE            ;SKIP TO NEXT LINE ON DISPLAY
42:                MOV      AX,0FFFFH          ;LOAD AX WITH
43:                                            ;
44:                                            ;1111111111111111
45:                                            ;
```

```
46:              CALL     PUTBIN                 ;DISPLAY CONTENTS OF AX
47:              CALL     NEWLINE                ;SKIP TO NEXT LINE ON DISPLAY
48:              MOV      BL,0                   ;SET CODE FOR BYTE DISPLAY
49:              MOV      AX,55AAH               ;LOAD AH  AND   AL WITH
50:                                              ;
51:                                              ;01010101 AND 10101010
52:                                              ;-
53:              CALL     PUTBIN                 ;DISPLAY CONTENTS OF AL
54:              CALL     NEWLINE                ;SKIP TO NEXT LINE ON DISPLAY
55:              XCHG     AL,AH                  ;EXCHANGE AL AND AH REGISTERS
56:              CALL     PUTBIN                 ;DISPLAY CONTENTS OF AL
57:              CALL     NEWLINE                ;SKIP TO NEXT LINE ON DISPLAY
58:              RET                             ;RETURN
59: EX_5_1       ENDP
60:*;
```
*
```
61: ;
62: ; PROCEDURE TO DISPLAY AN 8- OR 16-BIT VALUE IN BINARY FORM
63: ;
64: ; INPUT:   AL-REG  8-BIT  VALUE TO BE DISPLAYED
65: ;          BL=0       CODE FOR  8-BIT DISPLAY
66: ;                OR
67: ;          AX-REG  16-BIT VALUE TO BE DISPLAYED
68: ;          BL<>0      CODE FOR 16-BIT DISPLAY
69: ;
70: ; OUTPUT: INPUT VALUE DISPLAYED IN BINARY FORM ON THE
71: ;          SCREEN BEGINNING AT CURRENT CURSOR POSITION
72: ;
73: PUTBIN       PROC     NEAR                   ;PROCEDURE PUTBIN(NUMBER,CODE)
74:              PUSH     AX                          ;SAVE REGISTERS
75:              PUSH     DX
76:              PUSH     DI
77:              PUSH     BX
78:              PUSH     CX
79:              PUSHF                           ;SAVE FLAGS
80:              CMP      BL,0                   ;IF   CODE = BYTE (BL=0)
81:              JNZ      ELSE
82:              MOV      AH,0                   ;THEN EXPAND NUMBER TO 16 BITS
83:              MOV      CX,8                   ;     BIT_COUNT = 8
84:              JMP      ENDIF
85: ELSE:                                        ;ELSE
86:              MOV      CX,16                  ;     BIT_COUNT = 16
87: ENDIF:                                       ;ENDIF
88:              MOV      BX,2
89:              MOV      DI,CX                  ;SAVE BIT_COUNT
90: LOOPTOP:                                     ;REPEAT
91:              MOV      DX,0                   ;   BIT = NUMBER mod 2
92:              DIV      BX                     ;   NUMBER = NUMBER / 2
93:              PUSH     DX                     ;   PUSH BIT
94:              LOOP     LOOPTOP                ;   DECREMENT BIT_COUNT
95:                                              ;UNTIL BIT_COUNT = 0
96:              MOV      CX,DI                  ;RESTORE BIT_COUNT
97:              MOV      BH,0                   ;<DISPLAY CODE>
98: REPEAT:                                      ;REPEAT
99:              POP      AX                     ;   POP BIT
100:             CALL     PUTDEC                 ;   DISPLAY BIT
101:             LOOP     REPEAT                 ;   DECREMENT BIT_COUNT
102:                                             ;UNTIL BIT_COUNT = 0
103:             POPF                            ;RESTORE FLAGS
104:             POP      CX                     ;RESTORE REGISTERS
```

```
105:              POP    BX
106:              POP    DI
107:              POP    DX
108:              POP    AX
109:              RET                          ;RETURN
110: PUTBIN       ENDP                        ;END PUTBIN
111: CODE         ENDS
112:*             END    EX_5_1
*
```

The subprocedure PUTBIN appears in lines 60–110. This subprocedure begins with a prologue in lines 61–72 that describes the subprocedure's function, the inputs expected by the subprocedure, and the outputs produced by the subprocedure. From a user standpoint, the subprocedure is characterized by the way in which the input arguments are passed to the procedure and the way in which outputs are returned to the caller. The PUTBIN subprocedure expects two inputs:

1. A display code is expected in the BL-register. A code of zero implies that an 8-bit value is to be displayed, and a nonzero code implies that a 16-bit value is to be displayed.
2. The value to be displayed is expected in the AL-register for byte output, and it is expected in the AX-register for word output.

PUTBIN returns nothing to the caller. Its output goes to the display screen.

The prologue should contain all of the information required by a user. A user should have no need to look at the code. The prologue should explain what the subprocedure does and how a calling procedure is to interface with the subprocedure. The prologue does not need to give the details of how the subprocedure's function is implemented. This information is provided in the pseudocode comments and in the code itself.

The subprocedure definition begins with the PROC pseudo-operation in line 73 and terminates with the ENDP pseudo-operation in line 110. Both of these pseudo-operations have the name of the subprocedure (PUTBIN) in their label field. The PROC pseudo-operation specifies that the subprocedure is of type NEAR. That is, the subprocedure can only be called from procedures that are defined in the same code segment in which this subprocedure is defined.

The subprocedure begins by saving the values currently in the registers that it will be using. The PUSH instructions in lines 74–78 save the AX, DX, DI, BX, and CX register values on the stack, and the PUSHF instruction in line 79 saves the flags register value on the stack. The subprocedure terminates by restoring the values of the registers that it used and returning to the caller. The POPF instruction in line 103 restores the value of the flags register, and the POP instructions in lines 104–108 restore the values of the CX, BX, DI, DX, and AX registers. Note that the POP operations are in the reverse order from the corresponding PUSH operations in lines 74–79. This situation occurs because the stack is a **last-in-first-out** data structure. These PUSH and POP operations ensure that the state of the processor is the same on return to the caller as it was at the point of call to the subprocedure. The RET instruction in line 109 returns execution control to the caller by popping the return address offset from the stack into the IP-register.

The instructions in lines 80–102 implement the subprocedure's function. The double alternative-decision structure in lines 80–87 tests the input code in the BL-register to determine whether 8-bit or 16-bit output is required and stores the appropriate bit count (8 or 16) in the CX-register. The MOV instruction in line 89 saves a copy of the bit count in the DI-register, which is used to control the number of iterations of the REPEAT-UNTIL loop in lines 90–95 and the REPEAT-UNTIL loop in lines 98–102.

The REPEAT-UNTIL loop in lines 90–95 repeatedly divides the number by 2, pushing the remainder onto the stack and saving the quotient as the number to be divided on the next iteration of the loop. The sequence of remainders is the sequence of bits in the binary representation of the input number. This sequence is produced in right-to-left order and must be displayed in left-to-right order, which is why each bit produced is pushed onto the stack. Since the stack is a last-in-first-out data structure, the bits are popped off in the reverse order from which they were produced (i.e., left-to-right order). Note that the input value is treated as an unsigned integer value and that unsigned integer division is used. As an exercise, try to explain what happens if the division is changed to signed integer division.

The MOV instruction in line 96 restores the CX-register with the bit count, so that it can be used to control the second REPEAT-UNTIL loop. The MOV instruction in line 97 sets the display code for the external procedure PUTDEC. The PUTDEC procedure is used to display the individual bits of the binary number. A display code of zero causes each bit to be displayed with no leading or trailing blanks. (In Chapter 9, a version of PUTBIN is presented that uses the Basic I/O System (BIOS) interrupt procedures to output the individual bits.)

The REPEAT-UNTIL loop in lines 98–102 pops the bits from the stack and displays them using the PUTDEC procedure. On each iteration of the loop, one bit is popped and displayed.

The main procedure, EX_5_1, appears in lines 18–59 of Program Listing 5.1. It begins in the standard way by pushing the return address onto the stack (lines 20–22).

The instructions in lines 23 and 24 set up the inputs for a call to the NEAR subprocedure PUTBIN. The MOV instruction in line 23 sets the display code (BL = 1) to indicate that the 16-bit value in the AX-register is to be displayed. The MOV instruction in line 24 places the value to be displayed (hexadecimal 1) in the AX-register. The call to the PUTBIN procedure in line 28 causes the value 0000000000000001 to be displayed on the screen beginning at the current cursor position. The call to the NEWLINE procedure in line 29 then moves the cursor to the beginning of the next line of the display.

The MOV instruction in line 30 puts the hexadecimal value 5555 in the AX-register in preparation for another call to the PUTBIN procedure. The display code does not have to be set in the BL-register again; nothing has changed its value since it was last set in line 23. Both the PUTBIN and the

NEWLINE procedures preserve registers for their callers. The call to the PUTBIN procedure in line 34 causes the value 0101010101010101 to be displayed on the screen beginning at the current cursor position. The call to the NEW-LINE procedure in line 35 then moves the cursor to the beginning of the next line of the display.

Similarly, the instructions in lines 36, 40, and 41 cause the value 1010101010101010 to be displayed, and the instructions in lines 42, 46, and 47 cause the value 1111111111111111 to be displayed. Each value is displayed on a separate line.

The MOV instruction in line 48 sets the display code for PUTBIN (BL = 0) to indicate that the 8-bit value in the AL-register is to be displayed. The MOV instruction in line 49 places the value 01010101 in the AH-register and the value 10101010 in the AL-register. The call to PUTBIN in line 53 causes the AL-register value 10101010 to be displayed. The XCHG instruction in line 55 places the value 10101010 in the AH-register and the value 01010101 in the AL-register. The call to PUTBIN in line 56 causes the AL-register value 01010101 to be displayed. The complete output for this program is as follows:

```
0000000000000001
0101010101010101
1010101010101010
1111111111111111
10101010
01010101
```

Note that both the main procedure and the PUTBIN subprocedure are part of the same code segment, which begins with the SEGMENT pseudo-operation in line 17 and ends with the ENDS pseudo-operation in line 111. A NEAR procedure *must* be defined in the same code segment as the procedures that reference it.

Note also that the external procedure declarations (lines 6 and 7) include only PUTDEC (called by PUTBIN) and NEWLINE (called by the main procedure). PUTBIN does not appear in the external procedure declarations, because it is defined internal to this assembly module. That is, this program references the internal procedure PUTBIN defined in this program, not the external procedure PUTBIN defined in the I/O library.

FAR Procedures

A FAR subprocedure is one that can be invoked by procedures in other code segments. It can be defined in a code segment that is physically separate from other code segments of the executable program. It can be developed and main-tained in a separate assembly module. The assembly module that contains a FAR subprocedure can also contain stack segments and data segments, in addition to the code segment. At link time, the stack segments are concatenated with other stack segments of the executable program to produce a single stack segment. An executable program contains exactly one stack segment. The data segments can be concatenated with, overlayed on, or separate from other data segments in the executable program. These options are specified in the operand field of the segment pseudo-operation that marks the beginning of the segment definition. (Segmentation features are discussed in detail in Chapter 12.)

A **FAR procedure** is declared by using the operand FAR in the PROC pseudo-operation that identifies the beginning of the procedure definition:

⟨*proc-name*⟩   PROC   FAR   [⟨*comment*⟩]

The machine language instruction that calls a FAR procedure causes the value in the CS-register and then the value in the IP-register to be pushed onto the stack. The CS:IP register pair then is set to the segment and offset associated with the FAR procedure name. That is, the CS:IP register pair is set to the segment and offset of the first instruction in the called procedure.

The machine language instruction that returns from a FAR procedure pops a value from the stack and places that value in the IP-register, and then it pops a second value from the stack and places that value in the CS-register. A FAR procedure must be written in such a way that the segment and offset pushed onto the stack by the call instruction that invoked the procedure are again at the top of the stack when any RET instruction in the procedure is executed. Then, the values popped by the return instruction are the segment and offset of the first byte of the instruction that immediately follows the CALL instruction that invoked the subprocedure.

In addition to the call and return mechanisms, two additional mechanisms are needed for a FAR procedure that is defined in an assembly module separate from the procedure that references it.

A Mechanism to Resolve External References   A call to an external subprocedure cannot be translated fully by the assembler, because it does not know the relative load address for the subprocedure. The best that the assembler can do is to set aside memory space for the address (segment and offset) of the subprocedure and have that memory space filled in with the address at some later point.

A Mechanism to Declare External Names   If a procedure in one assembly module is to invoke a subprocedure in another assembly module, then the assembler must be informed that the subprocedure being referenced is external to this assembly module and will be supplied at a later point. Otherwise, the assembler expects the referenced procedure to be defined in the assembly module.

If a procedure in one assembly module is to be invoked by procedures in other assembly modules, then its name must be made available to the procedures in other assembly modules. However, the names of some procedures in the assembly module may need to be hidden from the procedures in other assembly modules. There must be a way to identify the procedures that are to be known to procedures in other assembly modules.

In the IBM PC, the mechanism to resolve external references is the utility program LINK. The **LINK program** combines object modules into a single executable program. It checks to see that all external references in the object modules are resolved, and if not, it displays appropriate error messages.

In the IBM PC Assembly language, the mechanism to declare external names is a pair of pseudo-operations: EXTRN and PUBLIC. The **EXTRN pseudo-operation** is used in an assembly module to identify symbolic names that are referenced in the assembly module but that are defined in another assembly module, and it has the following general form:

EXTRN   ⟨*ext-spec-list*⟩   [⟨*comment*⟩]

in which ⟨*ext-spec-list*⟩ is a list of external specifications of the form ⟨*name*⟩:⟨*type*⟩ (items in the list are separated by commas), ⟨*name*⟩ is the symbolic name of a label, variable, or procedure that is defined in another assembly module, and ⟨*type*⟩ is the type attribute of the symbolic name and may be one of the following: NEAR, BYTE, ABS, FAR, WORD, or DWORD.

At this point, only external procedures of the FAR type are of interest. An EXTRN pseudo-operation may be placed anywhere in an asembly module as long as it appears before the first reference to the names that it defines. In the program listings used in this book, EXTRN pseudo-operations are placed at the beginning of the assembly module immediately after the prologue.

The **PUBLIC pseudo-operation** is used in an assembly module to identify symbolic names defined in the assembly module that are to be available to procedures in other assembly modules, and it has the following general form:

PUBLIC   ⟨*name-list*⟩   [⟨*comment*⟩]

in which ⟨*name-list*⟩ is a list of symbolic names of the variables, labels, and procedures that are to be known outside of this assembly module. PUBLIC pseudo-operations may be placed anywhere in an assembly module. In the program listings used in this book, the PUBLIC pseudo-operation for a given name is placed next to the definition for that name.

The LINK program matches external names in one object module (defined by EXTRN pseudo-operations in the corresponding assembly module) with the PUBLIC names in other object modules (defined by PUBLIC pseudo-operations in the corresponding assembly modules). The LINK program fills in addresses (segment and offset) in the machine code to resolve external references.

Programming Example—Display Binary Integer (PUTBIN Version 1)

The assembly module in Program Listing 5.3 contains the definition of a FAR subprocedure that displays an 8-bit or 16-bit integer in binary form, and the assembly module in Program Listing 5.2 contains the definition of a main procedure that was designed to demonstrate the subprocedure. The object modules produced by assembling these two modules are to be linked to produce a single, executable program. Program Listings 5.2 and 5.3 are basically the same as Program Listing 5.1 with the subprocedure converted from an internal NEAR

```
 1: ;                        PROGRAM LISTING 5.2
 2: ;
 3: ;PROGRAM TO DEMONSTRATE SUBROUTINE INTERFACE
 4: ;
 5:                                         ;PROCEDURES TO
 6:             EXTRN    NEWLINE:FAR         ;DISPLAY NEWLINE CHARACTER
 7:             EXTRN    PUT_BIN:FAR         ;DISPLAY BINARY INTEGER
 8: ;
 9: ; S T A C K   S E G M E N T   D E F I N I T I O N
10: ;
11: STACK       SEGMENT STACK
12:             DB       256 DUP(?)
13: STACK       ENDS
14: ;
15: ; C O D E   S E G M E N T   D E F I N I T I O N
16: ;
17: CODE        SEGMENT
18: EX_5_2      PROC     FAR
19:             ASSUME   CS:CODE,SS:STACK
20:             PUSH     DS                 ;PUSH RETURN SEG ADDR ON STACK
21:             SUB      AX,AX              ;PUSH RETURN OFFSET OF ZERO
22:             PUSH     AX                 ;ON STACK
23:             MOV      BL,1               ;SET CODE FOR WORD DISPLAY
24:             MOV      AX,0001H           ;LOAD AX WITH
25:                                         ;
26:                                         ;0000000000000001
27:                                         ;
28:             CALL     PUT_BIN            ;DISPLAY CONTENTS OF AX
29:             CALL     NEWLINE            ;SKIP TO NEXT LINE ON DISPLAY
30:             MOV      AX,5555H           ;LOAD AX WITH
31:                                         ;
32:                                         ;0101010101010101
33:                                         ;
34:             CALL     PUT_BIN            ;DISPLAY CONTENTS OF AX
35:             CALL     NEWLINE            ;SKIP TO NEXT LINE ON DISPLAY
36:             MOV      AX,0AAAAH          ;LOAD AX WITH
37:                                         ;
38:                                         ;1010101010101010
39:                                         ;
40:             CALL     PUT_BIN            ;DISPLAY CONTENTS OF AX
41:             CALL     NEWLINE            ;SKIP TO NEXT LINE ON DISPLAY
42:             MOV      AX,0FFFFH          ;LOAD AX WITH
43:                                         ;
44:                                         ;1111111111111111
45:                                         ;
46:             CALL     PUT_BIN            ;DISPLAY CONTENTS OF AX
47:             CALL     NEWLINE            ;SKIP TO NEXT LINE ON DISPLAY
48:             MOV      BL,0               ;SET CODE FOR BYTE DISPLAY
49:             MOV      AX,55AAH           ;LOAD AH  AND  AL WITH
50:                                         ;
51:                                         ;01010101 AND 10101010
52:                                         ;
53:             CALL     PUT_BIN            ;DISPLAY CONTENTS OF AL
54:             CALL     NEWLINE            ;SKIP TO NEXT LINE ON DISPLAY
55:             XCHG     AL,AH              ;EXCHANGE AL AND AH REGISTERS
56:             CALL     PUT_BIN            ;DISPLAY CONTENTS OF AL
57:             CALL     NEWLINE            ;SKIP TO NEXT LINE ON DISPLAY
58:             RET                         ;RETURN
59: EX_5_2      ENDP
60: CODE        ENDS
61:*            END      EX_5_2
```

*

```
 1: ;                      PROGRAM LISTING 5.3
 2: ;
 3: ; PROCEDURE TO DISPLAY AN 8- OR 16-BIT VALUE IN BINARY FORM
 4: ;
 5: ; INPUT:   AL-REG  8-BIT  VALUE TO BE DISPLAYED
 6: ;          BL=0    CODE FOR  8-BIT DISPLAY
 7: ;             OR
 8: ;          AX-REG  16-BIT VALUE TO BE DISPLAYED
 9: ;          BL<>0   CODE FOR 16-BIT DISPLAY
10: ;
11: ; OUTPUT: INPUT VALUE DISPLAYED IN BINARY FORM ON THE
12: ;         SCREEN BEGINNING AT CURRENT CURSOR POSITION
13: ;
14:                                            ;PROCEDURE TO
15:          EXTRN    PUTDEC:FAR               ;DISPLAY DECIMAL INTEGER
16: ;
17: CODE     SEGMENT
18:          ASSUME   CS:CODE
19:          PUBLIC   PUT_BIN
20: PUT_BIN  PROC     FAR             ;PROCEDURE PUT_BIN(NUMBER,CODE)
21:          PUSH     AX                 ;SAVE REGISTERS
22:          PUSH     DX
23:          PUSH     DI
24:          PUSH     BX
25:          PUSH     CX
26:          PUSHF                       ;SAVE FLAGS
27:          CMP      BL,0               ;IF   CODE = BYTE (BL=0)
28:          JNZ      ELSE
29:          MOV      AH,0               ;THEN EXPAND NUMBER TO 16 BITS
30:          MOV      CX,8               ;     BIT_COUNT = 8
31:          JMP      ENDIF
32: ELSE:                               ;ELSE
33:          MOV      CX,16              ;     BIT_COUNT = 16
34: ENDIF:                              ;ENDIF
35:          MOV      BX,2
36:          MOV      DI,CX              ;SAVE BIT_COUNT
37: LOOPTOP:                            ;REPEAT
38:          MOV      DX,0               ;   BIT = NUMBER mod 2
39:          DIV      BX                 ;   NUMBER = NUMBER / 2
40:          PUSH     DX                 ;   PUSH BIT
41:          LOOP     LOOPTOP            ;   DECREMENT BIT_COUNT
42:                                      ;UNTIL BIT_COUNT = 0
43:          MOV      CX,DI              ;RESTORE BIT_COUNT
44:          MOV      BH,0               ;<DISPLAY CODE>
45: REPEAT:                             ;REPEAT
46:          POP      AX                 ;   POP BIT
47:          CALL     PUTDEC             ;   DISPLAY BIT
48:          LOOP     REPEAT             ;   DECREMENT BIT_COUNT
49:                                      ;UNTIL BIT_COUNT = 0
50:          POPF                        ;RESTORE FLAGS
51:          POP      CX                 ;RESTORE REGISTERS
52:          POP      BX
53:          POP      DI
54:          POP      DX
55:          POP      AX
56:          RET                         ;RETURN
57: PUT_BIN  ENDP                   ;END PUT_BIN
58: CODE     ENDS
59:*         END
```

procedure to an external FAR procedure. This discussion concentrates on the differences between the programs.

The assembly module in Program Listing 5.2 contains the definition of the stack segment for the program and the definition for the main procedure. The reference to PUTDEC has been removed from the external procedure declarations. PUTDEC is referenced by PUT_BIN, and procedure PUT_BIN now is defined in a separate assembly module. Since PUT_BIN is defined separately, a declaration for the PUT_BIN procedure has been added to the external procedure declarations (line 7). The name of the subprocedure has been changed from PUTBIN to PUT_BIN so that it is obvious that the subprocedure being used is not the external PUTBIN procedure in the I/O library.

The code segment of this assembly module, defined in lines 17–60 contains only the main procedure, EX_5_2, which is the same as the EX_5_1 procedure in Program Listing 5.1 except that the CALL instructions in lines 28, 34, 40, 46, 53, and 56 have been modified to reflect the new name of the subprocedure.

The assembly module in Program Listing 5.3 contains the definition of the PUT_BIN subprocedure. A number of items were added to the subprocedure when it was extracted and placed in a separate assembly module. The external declaration for the referenced PUTDEC procedure also was extracted and embedded in this assembly module, just after the prologue (line 15). Since an assembly module consists of one or more segment definitions, the definition of the PUT_BIN procedure (lines 20–57) had to be embedded in a code segment; the code segment definition begins with the SEGMENT pseudo-operation in line 17 and ends with the ENDS pseudo-operation in line 58. The code segment contains the definition for a single procedure, the PUT_BIN subprocedure.

The ASSUME pseudo-operation in line 18 tells the assembler that the CS-register will point to this segment when the subprocedure is active. The CS-register will automatically be set to point to this segment as part of the execution of the CALL instruction that invokes the PUT_BIN procedure. The CS-register will automatically be restored (i.e., set to point to the caller's code segment) on execution of a RET instruction in the subprocedure.

The PUBLIC pseudo-operation in line 19 declares that the name PUT_BIN is to be available for reference by procedures in other assembly modules. The LINK program links procedures by replacing external procedure names in one object module with the addresses associated with the corresponding PUBLIC names in other object modules.

The definition of the PUT_BIN procedure begins with the PROC pseudo-operation in line 20 and ends with the ENDP pseudo-operation in line 57. The PROC pseudo-operation specifies that the PUT_BIN procedure is of type FAR, which means that the PUT_BIN procedure can be called from procedures defined in the same or different code segments. Because Listing 5.3 is the code for a complete assembly module, it must terminate with the END pseudo-operation (line 59).

The object modules that correspond to the two assembly modules in Program Listings 5.2 and 5.3 must be linked along with the library routines that they reference to form an executable program. This task is accomplished via

LINK. Suppose the assembly module in Program Listing 5.2 is in a file on diskette in drive B under the name EX_5_2.ASM, and suppose the assembly module in Program Listing 5.3 is in a file on the same diskette under the name EX_5_3.ASM. The DOS commands

```
MASM B:EX_5_2,B:;
MASM B:EX_5_3,B:;
```

assemble these two modules, creating the two object modules

```
B:EX_5_2.OBJ
B:EX_5_3.OBJ
```

To link these two object modules into a complete executable program, the following DOS command can be used:

```
LINK B:EX_5_2 B:EX_5_3,B:,NUL,IO
```

Note the separator between the file specifications for the two object modules. It is a *space* (or a plus sign [+]) not a comma (,). A comma marks the end of the list of object modules, which may contain any number of object module specifications, and the object module specifications may be in any order. The preceding LINK command links the two object modules and any referenced library procedures from IO.LIB, creating an executable program module named B:EX_5_2.EXE. When no name is specified in the LINK command for the executable program module, the name that is used is the same as the name of the first object module in the object module list, with the suffix replaced by EXE.

The output of this program is exactly the same as that for Program Listing 5.1. The subprocedures in Program Listings 5.1 and 5.3 are examples of subroutines (nonvalue-returning procedures).

5.5   Local Data Segments

It is often the case that an external subprocedure requires its own local data. The assembly module that contains the subprocedure also may contain one or more data segments. The data in these segments is available to any procedure defined in the code segment of the same assembly module. If a subprocedure defined in the code segment of one assembly module is to be invoked by procedures defined in other assembly modules, then the subprocedure should assume that the caller is using both the DS and ES segment registers. To use one of these segment registers to point to a local data segment, the subprocedure is responsible for performing the following operations:

1. On entry, the subprocedure must save the value of the segment register for the caller and then set the segment register to point to the local data segment.

2. Just prior to return to the caller, the subprocedure must restore the value of the segment register for the caller.

This protocol allows the caller and the callee to use their own, private data segments. It is possible for procedures defined in separate assembly modules to share data segments. (Data segment sharing is discussed in Chapter 12.)

The data contained in a local data segment for a subprocedure is static in nature. That is, the storage for the data exists prior to the first invocation of the subprocedure and persists through the last invocation of the subprocedure, which means that the values of the variables in the local data segment persist from one invocation of the subprocedure to the next invocation.

Programming Example—Random Number Generator

Applications involving simulation often require a sequence of random numbers. A random number generator is a procedure that provides the capability of producing a sequence of pseudo-random numbers in some specified range. Program Listing 5.4 is such a procedure. This random number generator is a function procedure that returns an integer in the range 0–9999. The integer is produced by evaluating an expression. One of the variables in the expression changes on each invocation of the procedure, which means that the expression evaluation potentially produces different values on successive invocations of the procedure. A sequence of n calls to the procedure produces n pseudo-random integers in the range 0–9999.

The algorithm used to produce the pseudo-random integers is an application of the technique known as the **linear congruential method**. The following two formulas are evaluated to produce a single integer:

$$\text{SEED} = ((\text{SEED} * 3621) + 1) \bmod 65536$$

$$\text{RANDOM} = \text{SEED}/256*10000/256$$

The value of RANDOM, which is an integer in the range 0–9999, is the pseudo-random integer returned by the function procedure. The value of SEED, an integer in the range 0–65535, is saved for the next call to the procedure. On each call to the procedure, the previous SEED value is used to compute a new value for SEED, and the new SEED value is used to compute the pseudo-random integer (RANDOM) to be returned to the caller. The SEED value must persist from one invocation of the procedure to the next. A local data segment is used to maintain the value of SEED.

The assembly module in Program Listing 5.4 is an implementation of this random number generator as an IBM PC Assembly language external FAR procedure with its own local data segment. The assembly module begins with a prologue (lines 1–9) that explains the procedure's function, inputs, and outputs. There are no inputs for the procedure. The SEED for the random number generator is maintained in a local data segment. The only output is the function value (the pseudo-random integer), and it is returned in the AX-register.

There are two named constants defined in the assembly module, the Boolean constants True and False. The label FALSE is equated to the constant

```
 1: ;                     PROGRAM LISTING 5.4
 2: ;
 3: ; r a n d o m   n u m b e r   g e n e r a t o r
 4: ;
 5: ; GENERATES PSEUDO-RANDOM INTEGERS IN THE RANGE
 6: ;                   0 TO 9999
 7: ; INPUT:  NONE
 8: ; OUTPUT: AX-REG CONTAINS RANDOM INTEGER
 9: ;
10: FALSE       EQU     0                  ;CONSTANT FALSE
11: TRUE        EQU     1                  ;CONSTANT TRUE
12: ;
13: ; D A T A   S E G M E N T
14: ;
15: RAND_DATA   SEGMENT
16: ;
17: SEED        DW      ?                  ;SEED FOR RANDOM NUMBER GEN.
18: MULTIPLIER  DW      3621               ;MULTIPLIER FOR LINEAR
19: ;                                      ;CONGRUENTIAL METHOD
20: FIRST_CALL  DB      TRUE               ;FIRST CALL FLAG
21: TWO_56      DW      256                ;CONSTANT 256
22: TEN_THOU    DW      10000              ;CONSTANT 10000
23: ;
24: RAND_DATA   ENDS
25: ;
26: ; C O D E   S E G M E N T
27: ;
28: CODE        SEGMENT
29:             ASSUME  CS:CODE,DS:RAND_DATA
30:             PUBLIC  RANDOM
31: RANDOM      PROC    FAR                ;FUNCTION RANDOM()
32:             PUSHF                      ;SAVE FLAGS
33:             PUSH    CX                 ;SAVE REGISTERS
34:             PUSH    DX
35:             PUSH    DS
36:             MOV     AX,SEG RAND_DATA   ;SET DS-REGISTER TO POINT
37:             MOV     DS,AX              ;TO LOCAL DATA SEGMENT
38: ;
39:             CMP     FIRST_CALL,TRUE    ;IF   FIRST_CALL
40:             JNE     ENDIF
41:             MOV     FIRST_CALL,FALSE   ;THEN FIRST_CALL = FALSE
42:             MOV     AH,0               ;     SEED = LOWER HALF OF
43:             INT     1AH                ;             TIME OF DAY CLOCK
44:             MOV     SEED,DX
45: ENDIF:                                 ;ENDIF
46:             MOV     AX,SEED            ;X = SEED * MULTIPLIER
47:             MUL     MULTIPLIER
48:             INC     AX                 ;SEED = (X + 1) mod 65536
49:             MOV     SEED,AX
50:             MOV     DX,0
51:             DIV     TWO_56             ;RANDOM = SEED/256*10000/256
52:             MUL     TEN_THOU
53:             DIV     TWO_56
54:             POP     DS                 ;RESTORE REGISTERS
55:             POP     DX
56:             POP     CX
57:             POPF                       ;RESTORE FLAGS
58:             RET                        ;RETURN (RANDOM)
59: RANDOM      ENDP                       ;END RANDOM
60: CODE        ENDS
61:*            END
```

0 (line 10), and the label TRUE is equated to the constant 1 (line 11). The EQU pseudo-operations are directives to the assembler to indicate that the label FALSE is to be treated as the constant 0, and the label TRUE is to be treated as the constant 1. FALSE and TRUE are *not* symbolic names to be associated with memory locations. Whenever the assembler encounters the name FALSE in this assembly module, it is to substitute the constant 0. Similarly, it is to substitute 1 for the name TRUE. For example, the instruction

```
MOV  FIRST_CALL, FALSE
```

is really the instruction

```
MOV  FIRST_CALL, 0
```

in this assembly module.

The local data segment for the procedure is defined in lines 12–24. The actual definition of the segment begins with the SEGMENT pseudo-operation in line 15. The SEED of the random number generator is defined in line 17. It has a type attribute of WORD and is uninitialized. It receives an initial value on first invocation of the random number generator. The multiplier used in the formula to compute the new SEED value is defined in line 18. It is given an initial value of 3621 and is treated as a constant by the random number generator. If the SEED variable is going to be given an initial value on the first call to the random number generator, then the random number generator must be able to detect its first call. To accomplish this task, a Boolean variable and the two Boolean constants, True and False, are defined. The Boolean constants are defined in lines 10 and 11. The Boolean variable FIRST_CALL is defined in line 20. It has type attribute BYTE and is initialized to TRUE (1). Two additional constants are defined in lines 21 and 22. TWO_56 is the constant 256 and TEN_THOU is the constant 10,000. These constants actually are defined as variables with type attribute WORD and given the initial values 256 and 10,000, respectively. However, their values remain constant during execution. TWO_56 and TEN_THOU must be defined as variables, because they are going to be used as the operands of DIV and MUL instructions, respectively. DIV and MUL instructions cannot have an immediate operand, and a constant is an immediate operand. This situation is true even when the constant is given a name using the EQU pseudo-operation. The local data segment definition terminates with the ENDS pseudo-operation in line 24.

The function procedure that returns the pseudo-random integer is defined in a code segment that begins with the SEGMENT pseudo-operation in line 28 and ends with the ENDS pseudo-operation in line 60. In addition to the random number generator procedure, the code segment contains two pseudo-operations:

1. The ASSUME pseudo-operation in line 29 instructs the assembler to assume that when the procedure is executed, the CS-register will point to the code segment containing the procedure and the DS-register will point to the local data segment, RAND_DATA. The CS-register will automatically be set by execution of the CALL instruction that invokes

the procedure, however, the DS-register has to be set by the called procedure itself.

2. The PUBLIC pseudo-operation in line 30 tells the assembler that the procedure RANDOM is to be invoked by procedures in code segments of other assembly modules.

The function procedure, called RANDOM, is defined in lines 31–59. The PROC pseudo-operation in line 31 defines the procedure to be a FAR procedure, since it is to be invoked by procedures defined in other code segments. The procedure begins by saving the flags and the registers that it will be using (lines 32–35). Included in the registers being saved is the DS-register, which will be used by the procedure to address the local data segment. The MOV instructions in lines 36 and 37 set the DS-register to point to the local data segment. This task must be done prior to executing any instruction that references an item defined in the local data segment.

The single alternative-decision structure in lines 39–45 tests the FIRST_CALL flag to see if it is the first call to the RANDOM procedure. If it is the first call (i.e., FIRST_CALL has the value TRUE), then the instructions in lines 41–44 are executed. The MOV instruction in line 41 sets the value of the FIRST_CALL flag to FALSE so that lines 41–44 are not executed on subsequent calls to RANDOM. The two instructions in lines 42 and 43 are the calling sequence for a BIOS function procedure that returns the current value of the IBM PC's time-of-day clock in the CX:DX register pair (which is why the CX-register must be saved and restored for the caller). The instruction in line 43 generates a software interrupt that causes the BIOS procedure that references the time-of-day clock to be executed. It can be viewed as a procedure call. The INT instruction executes similarly to a CALL instruction. The MOV instruction in line 42 sets up the input parameter for this BIOS procedure in the AH-register. An input parameter of 0 means read the current clock value. (Interrupts and interrupt service procedures are discussed in detail in Chapter 9.) The MOV instruction in line 44 sets the initial SEED value to the lower half of the time-of-day clock value returned by the BIOS procedure, which means that each time a program that uses this random number generator is executed, it starts the SEED at a different initial value.

The instructions in lines 46–49 compute the new value of the SEED using the following formula:

$$SEED = ((SEED * MULTIPLIER) + 1) \bmod 65536$$

The MUL instruction in line 47 produces a 32-bit product in the DX:AX register pair. To obtain the remainder of this 32-bit value divided by 65,536 (i.e., the result of the mod operation), the program simply saves the lower 16 bits of the 32-bit value. The MOV instruction in line 49 essentially accomplishes the mod operation as it saves the new SEED value.

The instructions in lines 50–53 compute the pseudo-random integer to be returned to the caller. The integer is computed by the following formula:

$$RANDOM = SEED/256*10000/256$$

The MOV instruction in line 50 expands the 16-bit unsigned SEED value to 32 bits for division. The SEED is an unsigned integer in the range 0–65535. The divide by 256 (line 51) converts the 32-bit expanded SEED value to a 16-bit integer value in the range 0–255. The multiply by 10000 (line 52) converts this 16-bit integer value to a 32-bit integer value in the range 0–2,550,000. The divide by 256 (line 53) converts this 32-bit integer value to a 16-bit integer value in the range 0–9999. This value is in the AX-register and is the value that is returned to the caller.

The instructions in lines 54–57 restore the registers for the caller, and the RET instruction in line 58 returns control to the caller with the pseudo-random integer in the AX-register. The ENDP pseudo-operation in line 59 marks the end of the definition of the RANDOM procedure.

Beginning with an initial SEED value 21,845, the first 12 computed values of SEED and the corresponding random integers are as follow:

Seed	Random Integer
64330	9804
23987	3632
21728	3281
33889	5156
28678	4375
34015	5156
26172	3984
3757	546
38146	5820
42315	6445
64984	9882
32825	5000

5.6 Additional Capabilities in the IBM PC-AT Assembly Language

The IBM PC-AT Assembly language provides a single instruction to save the contents of all eight general registers onto the stack and a single instruction to restore the contents of all eight general registers by popping the top eight stack items into these registers. These two instructions are the PUSHA and POPA instructions (see Chapter 2), which are 1-byte instructions. In the IBM PC Assembly language, it takes eight 1-byte instructions to push the values of all eight general registers onto the stack and another eight 1-byte instructions to restore the values of the eight general registers. That is, two 1-byte instructions in the IBM PC-AT Assembly language can do the job of 16 1-byte instructions in the IBM PC Assembly language. If a subprocedure must save and restore a small number of general registers, say three or less, then the individual PUSH and POP instructions could be used in the IBM PC-AT Assembly language to avoid using more stack locations than are needed. However, if a subprocedure must save and restore four or more of the general registers, then the PUSHA and POPA instructions could be used, since the savings in instruction bytes compensates for the unneeded stack locations that are used. It should be noted that instruction bytes represent permanent storage, and stack locations represent temporary storage. A savings in instruction bytes often is worth the use of extra stack locations.

5.7   Assembler Macros

The assembler's macro feature is a programming tool that provides the capability for programmers to define operation codes in terms of existing machine operations. For example, the MUL and IMUL instructions do not allow an immediate operand. To multiply the unsigned integer value in the AX-register by 7, the following instructions might be used:

```
MOV BX, 7
MUL BX
```

The macro feature provides the capability to assign an operation code to represent this sequence of instructions. Each time the assembler encounters the user-defined operation code, it substitutes in the corresponding sequence of instructions. User-defined operation codes can have operands, which allows the operands in the corresponding sequence of instructions to be different each time that operation code appears in the assembly module. In the case of the preceding multiply immediate example, the immediate operand can be different each time the multiply immediate operation code appears in the assembly module.

Macro Definition and Expansion

Two steps are involved in using macros: macro definition and macro expansion. **Macro definition** gives the macro a name (the user-defined operation code) and identifies the sequence of instructions that are represented by this name. **Macro expansion** occurs whenever the assembler encounters the macro name used as an operation code, at which time the assembler substitutes the sequence of instructions specified in the macro definition for the macro reference.

A macro definition has the following general form:

⟨*mac-name*⟩ MACRO ⟨*arg-list*⟩   [⟨*comment*⟩]
            ⟨*macro-body*⟩
            ENDM   [⟨*comment*⟩]

in which ⟨*mac-name*⟩ is the symbolic name of the macro (the user-defined operation code), ⟨*arg-list*⟩ is a list of dummy arguments separated by commas, and ⟨*macro-body*⟩ is the sequence of instructions that are represented by the ⟨*mac-name*⟩. The dummy arguments in the ⟨*arg-list*⟩ are symbolic names that can be used as operation codes or operands in the ⟨*macro-body*⟩ instructions.

These dummy arguments are replaced by actual arguments whenever macro expansion occurs.

A **macro reference** looks like a mnemonic representation of a machine instruction, and it has the following general form:

[⟨*label*⟩] ⟨*mac-name*⟩ ⟨*opnd-list*⟩ [⟨*comment*⟩]

in which ⟨*label*⟩ is the symbolic name to be associated with the memory location in which the macro body instructions are to begin, ⟨*mac-name*⟩ is the name of the macro to be expanded (the user-defined operation code), and ⟨*opnd-list*⟩ is the list of operands for the user-defined operation code. The number of operands in the ⟨*opnd-list*⟩ must agree with the number of dummy arguments in the ⟨*arg-list*⟩ of the macro definition. An operand in the ⟨*opnd-list*⟩ must be compatible with the corresponding dummy argument in the macro body of the macro definition. Otherwise, assembly errors occur at time of macro expansion.

When the assembler encounters a macro reference, it expands the macro by substituting the instructions of the macro body for the macro reference. Each dummy argument appearing in the macro body is replaced by the corresponding operand from the operand list in the macro reference. Operands are matched to dummy arguments by position.

EXAMPLES

The multiply immediate operation code for unsigned integers, mentioned previously, can be defined by the following macro definition:

```
muli MACRO const
     MOV   BX, const
     MUL   BX
     ENDM
```

The name of the macro is muli. It has one operand represented in the macro body by the dummy argument const. The macro body is the instruction sequence

```
     MOV   BX, const
     MUL   BX
```

On encountering the instruction

```
     muli  7
```

the assembler substitutes the instructions

```
     MOV   BX, 7
     MUL   BX
```

The dummy argument const is replaced by the operand 7 when the macro is expanded. On encountering the instruction

```
     muli  3
```

the assembler substitutes the instructions

```
     MOV   BX, 3
     MUL   BX
```

The dummy argument const is replaced by the operand 3 for this reference.

The preceding macro can be generalized to accommodate either signed or unsigned integers by using a dummy argument for the operation code of the second instruction in the macro body. The modified macro definition might be as follows:

```
muli MACRO op,const
     MOV   BX,const
     op    BX
     ENDM
```

On encountering the instruction

```
     muli  MUL,12
```

the assembler substitutes the instructions

```
     MOV   BX,12
     MUL   BX
```

On encountering the instruction

```
     muli  IMUL,-12
```

the assembler substitutes the instructions

```
     MOV   BX,-12
     IMUL  BX
```

Programming Example—Compute Date of Easter Sunday

Program Listing 5.5 is an implementation of an algorithm to compute the date of Easter Sunday (month and day) given the year. The following pseudocode describes the algorithm:

```
GET     YEAR
A       = YEAR mod 19
X       = (19A + 24) mod 30
B       = 2(YEAR mod 4)
C       = 4(YEAR mod 7)
Y       = (6X + 5 + B + C) mod 7
DATE    = Y + X + 22
IF      DATE > 31
THEN
        DATE = DATE - 31
        IF   DATE = 26
        THEN
             DATE = 19
        ENDIF
        DISPLAY 'APRIL' ,DATE
ELSE    DISPLAY 'MARCH' ,DATE
ENDIF
```

```
 1: ;                         PROGRAM LISTING 5.5
 2: ;
 3: ; PROGRAM  TO COMPUTE THE DATE OF
 4: ; EASTER  SUNDAY,  GIVEN THE YEAR
 5: ;
 6:                                         ;PROCEDURES TO
 7:             EXTRN    PUTSTRNG:FAR        ;DISPLAY CHARACTER STRING
 8:             EXTRN    GETDEC$:FAR         ;INPUT UNSIGNED DECIMAL INTEGER
 9:             EXTRN    PUTDEC$:FAR         ;DISPLAY UNSIGNED DECIMAL INT.
10:             EXTRN    NEWLINE:FAR         ;DISPLAY NEWLINE CHARACTER
11: ;
12: ; S T A C K   S E G M E N T   D E F I N I T I O N
13: ;
14: STACK       SEGMENT STACK
15:             DW       128 DUP(?)
16: STACK       ENDS
17: ;
18: ; D A T A   S E G M E N T   D E F I N I T I O N
19: ;
20: DATA        SEGMENT
21: ;
22: B           DW       ?
23: C           DW       ?
24: X           DW       ?
25: YEAR        DW       ?                   ;YEAR OF EASTER SUNDAY
26: PROMPT      DB       'ENTER YEAR - '
27: ANNOTATE    DB       'EASTER SUNDAY WILL BE ON '
28: MARCH       DB       'MARCH '
29: APRIL       DB       'APRIL '
30: ;
31: DATA        ENDS
32: ;-------------------------------------------------
33: ;
34: ; M A C R O   D E F I N I T I O N S
35: ;
36: ;-------------------------------------------------
37: ;FUNCTION  x mod y
38: ;                    x AND y CAN BE WORD REGISTER,
39: ;                    WORD MEMORY, OR IMMEDIATE.
40: ;                    USES AX, BX, AND DX REGISTERS
41: ;                    LEAVES x mod y IN AX-REGISTER
42: ;
43: mod         MACRO    x,y
44:             MOV      AX,x
45:             MOV      BX,y
46:             MOV      DX,0
47:             DIV      BX
48:             MOV      AX,DX
49:             ENDM
50: ;-------------------------------------------------
51: ;MULTIPLY IMMEDIATE (UNSIGNED)
52: ;
53: ;                    const SHOULD BE IMMEDIATE
54: ;                    USES BX-REGISTER
55: ;                    LEAVES PRODUCT IN DX:AX
56: ;
57: muli        MACRO    const
58:             MOV      BX,const
59:             MUL      BX
60:             ENDM
61: ;-------------------------------------------------
62:*;
```

```
 63: ;
 64: ;C O D E     S E G M E N T     D E F I N I T I O N
 65: ;
 66: CODE        SEGMENT
 67:             ASSUME    CS:CODE,SS:STACK,DS:DATA
 68: EASTER      PROC      FAR
 69:             PUSH      DS                      ;PUSH RETURN SEG ADDR ON STACK
 70:             SUB       AX,AX                   ;PUSH RETURN OFFSET 0 ON STACK
 71:             PUSH      AX
 72:             MOV       AX,SEG DATA             ;SET DS AND ES REGISTERS TO
 73:             MOV       DS,AX                   ;POINT TO DATA SEGMENT
 74:             MOV       ES,AX
 75:             LEA       DI,PROMPT               ;PROMPT FOR YEAR
 76:             MOV       CX,13
 77:             CALL      PUTSTRNG
 78:             CALL      GETDEC$                 ;GET YEAR
 79:             MOV       YEAR,AX
 80:             LEA       DI,ANNOTATE             ;DISPLAY ANNOTATION
 81:             MOV       CX,25
 82:             CALL      PUTSTRNG
 83:             mod       AX,19                   ;A = YEAR mod 19
 84:             muli      19                      ;X = (19A + 24) mod 30
 85:             ADD       AX,24
 86:             mod       AX,30
 87:             MOV       X,AX
 88:             mod       YEAR,4                  ;B = 2(YEAR mod 4)
 89:             muli      2
 90:             MOV       B,AX
 91:             mod       YEAR,7                  ;C = 4(YEAR mod 7)
 92:             muli      4
 93:             MOV       C,AX
 94:             MOV       AX,X                    ;Y = (6X + 5 + B + C) mod 7
 95:             muli      6
 96:             ADD       AX,5
 97:             ADD       AX,B
 98:             ADD       AX,C
 99:             mod       AX,7
100:             ADD       AX,X                    ;DATE = Y + X + 22
101:             ADD       AX,22
102:             CMP       AX,31                   ;IF    DATE > 31
103:             JLE       ELSE
104:             SUB       AX,31                   ;THEN DATE = DATE - 31
105:             CMP       AX,26                   ;     IF    DATE = 26
106:             JNE       _ENDIF
107:             MOV       AX,19                   ;        THEN DATE = 19
108: _ENDIF:                                       ;        ENDIF
109:             LEA       DI,APRIL                ;        DISPLAY 'APRIL '
110:             JMP       ENDIF
111: ELSE:                                         ;ELSE
112:             LEA       DI,MARCH                ;     DISPLAY 'MARCH '
113: ENDIF:                                        ;ENDIF
114:             MOV       CX,6
115:             CALL      PUTSTRNG
116:             CALL      PUTDEC$                 ;DISPLAY DATE
117:             CALL      NEWLINE
118:             RET                               ;RETURN
119: EASTER      ENDP
120: CODE        ENDS
121:*            END       EASTER
*
```

The algorithm contains several multiplications by a constant; therefore, the previously defined multiply immediate macro is useful. The algorithm also contains several instances of the mod function; therefore, a mod function macro is also useful.

The assembly module in Program Listing 5.5 implements this algorithm. A complete description is not provided here. Only the use of macros in this implementation is discussed.

The multiply immediate macro is defined in lines 57–60 (which is the same macro definition that was presented in a previous example). The prologue in lines 51–56 explains the macro's function, specifies the type of operand expected, identifies the registers used by the macro, and indicates where the macro leaves its result. This information is provided mainly for instructional purposes. However, it is extremely helpful to provide this information for any macro that is to be used in more than one program or by more than one programmer.

The mod function macro is defined in lines 43–49. The macro has two operands that are represented in the macro body by the symbolic names x and y. The macro body instruction sequence divides the unsigned integer value of the dummy argument x by the unsigned integer value of the dummy argument y, and then the instruction sequence moves the remainder of that division (the value x mod y) into the AX-register. The prologue in lines 37–42 provides important information about the macro for users.

The program input is the year, entered via the keyboard. The GETDEC$ procedure (line 78) accepts the input from the keyboard. The MOV instruction in line 79 replaces the value of the variable YEAR with a copy of this input value. At the beginning of the computation, the AX-register and the variable YEAR both contain a copy of the input value.

The computation appears in lines 83–113. The mod instruction in line 83 implements the assignment

```
A  =  YEAR mod 19
```

leaving the result in the AX-register. This instruction is a macro reference that is expanded by the assembler to the following instruction sequence:

```
MOV AX, AX
MOV BX, 19
MOV DX, 0
DIV BX
MOV AX, DX
```

This sequence divides the value in the AX-register (the year) by 19, leaving the remainder in the AX-register. Note that the first instruction of the macro body is

```
MOV AX, x
```

and the first operand in the macro reference

```
MOV AX, 19
```

is the register designator AX. Thus, the assembler substitutes the operand AX for the dummy argument x, producing the redundant instruction

```
MOV AX,AX
```

This instruction is legal, as it does exactly what it says it does; it moves a copy of the contents of the AX-register into the AX-register.

The instructions in lines 84–87 implement the assignment

```
X = (19A + 24) mod 30
```

The muli instruction in line 84 multiplies the value in the AX-register (the value of the pseudocode variable A) by 19, leaving the result in the DX:AX register pair. This instruction is a macro reference expanded by the assembler to the following instruction sequence:

```
MOV BX,19
MUL BX
```

Given any reasonable value for the year, none of the computations in this algorithm can cause overflow. Therefore, it is safe to assume that the product of this multiplication fits in the AX-register. The ADD instruction in line 85 adds 24 to the product in the AX-register. The instructions generated for the macro reference in line 86 cause the value in the AX-register (19A + 24) to be divided by 30 and the remainder of the division ((19A + 24) mod 30) to be moved to the AX-register. The MOV instruction in line 87 stores this remainder as the value of variable X.

The instructions in lines 88–90 implement the assignment

```
B = 2(YEAR mod 4)
```

The instructions generated for the macro reference in line 88 divide the value of the variable YEAR by 4 and move the remainder of that division to the AX-register. The instructions generated for the macro reference in line 89 multiply this remainder (YEAR mod 4) by 2, leaving the product in the DX:AX register pair. Again, this product fits in the AX-register. The MOV instruction in line 90 stores this product as the value of variable B.

The instructions in lines 91–93 implement the assignment

```
C = 4(YEAR mod 7)
```

The instructions generated for the macro reference in line 91 compute the value YEAR mod 7, leaving the result in the AX-register. The instructions generated for the macro reference in line 92 multiply this value by 4, leaving the product in the AX-register. The MOV instruction in line 93 stores this product as the value of variable C.

The instructions in lines 94–99 implement the assignment

```
Y  =  (6X + 5 + B + C) mod 7
```

The MOV instruction in line 94 loads the AX-register with the value of variable X. The instructions generated for the macro reference in line 95 multiply this value by 6, leaving the result in the AX-register. The ADD instructions in lines 96–98 add the constant 5, the value of variable B, and the value of variable C to this result, leaving the value 6X + 5 + B + C in the AX-register. The instructions generated for the macro reference in line 99 divide this value by 7 and move the remainder of that division to the AX-register. At this point, the AX-register contains the value of the pseudocode variable Y.

The instructions in lines 100 and 101 implement the assignment

```
DATE = Y + X + 22
```

The value of the pseudocode variable DATE is left in the AX-register and is an integer in the range 22–57, inclusive. A value in the range 22–31 represents a date in March. A value greater than 31 represents a date in April and must be decremented by 31. Note that Easter cannot fall after April 25, but the formula can produce April 26 as a date. The year 1981 is an example: If this situation occurs, then the correct date for Easter Sunday is April 19. The nested decision structure in lines 102–113 makes the appropriate adjustments to the pseudocode variable DATE and displays the appropriate month.

The following are the results from some sample executions of this program:

```
A > b: ex_5_5
ENTER YEAR - 1980
EASTER SUNDAY WILL BE ON APRIL 6

A > b: ex_5_5
ENTER YEAR - 1981
EASTER SUNDAY WILL BE ON APRIL 19

A > b: ex_5_5
ENTER YEAR - 1982
EASTER SUNDAY WILL BE ON APRIL 18

A > b: ex_5_5
ENTER YEAR - 1986
EASTER SUNDAY WILL BE ON MARCH 30

A > b: ex_5_5
ENTER YEAR - 1987
EASTER SUNDAY WILL BE ON APRIL 19

A > b: ex_5_5
ENTER YEAR - 1988
EASTER SUNDAY WILL BE ON APRIL 3
```

Assembler Listing 5.6 shows the first two pages of the assembler-generated listing for Program Listing 5.5. The TITLE and PAGE pseudo-operations have been added for the purpose of generating this listing. Note: no machine code is shown for the macro definition. The macro definition simply identifies, to the assembler, the sequence of instructions that is to be substituted each time the macro name is encountered as an operation code. Also note: Each reference to the macro is followed by the Assembly language instructions generated for that reference. Each instruction of the expansion is preceded by a plus sign (+) in the

```
The Microsoft MACRO Assembler , Version 1.27        Page    1-1
ASSEMBLER LISTING 5.6                                        09-24-87


                            TITLE   ASSEMBLER LISTING 5.6
                            PAGE    80,132
                        ; PROGRAM  TO COMPUTE THE DATE OF
                        ; EASTER  SUNDAY,  GIVEN THE YEAR
                        ;
                                                        ;PROCEDURES TO
                            EXTRN   PUTSTRNG:FAR        ;DISPLAY CHARACTER STRING
                            EXTRN   GETDEC$:FAR         ;INPUT UNSIGNED DECIMAL INTEGER
                            EXTRN   PUTDEC$:FAR         ;DISPLAY UNSIGNED DECIMAL INT.
                            EXTRN   NEWLINE:FAR         ;DISPLAY NEWLINE CHARACTER
                        ;
                        ;S T A C K   S E G M E N T   D E F I N I T I O N
                        ;
0000                    STACK     SEGMENT STACK
0000    80 [                      DW      128 DUP(?)
             ????
                  ]

0100                    STACK     ENDS
                        ;
                        ;D A T A   S E G M E N T   D E F I N I T I O N
                        ;
0000                    DATA      SEGMENT
                        ;
0000  ????             B         DW      ?
0002  ????             C         DW      ?
0004  ????             X         DW      ?
0006  ????             YEAR      DW      ?                   ;YEAR OF EASTER SUNDAY
0008  45 4E 54 45 52 20 PROMPT   DB      'ENTER YEAR - '
      59 45 41 52 20 2D
      20
0015  45 41 53 54 45 52 ANNOTATE DB      'EASTER SUNDAY WILL BE ON '
      20 53 55 4E 44 41
      59 20 57 49 4C 4C
      20 42 45 20 4F 4E
      20
002E  4D 41 52 43 48 20 MARCH    DB      'MARCH '
0034  41 50 52 49 4C 20 APRIL    DB      'APRIL '
                        ;
003A                    DATA      ENDS
                        ;----------------------------------------------
                        ;
                        ;M A C R O   D E F I N I T I O N S
                        ;
                        ;----------------------------------------------
                        ;FUNCTION  x mod y
                        ;                 x AND y CAN BE WORD REGISTER,
                        ;                 WORD MEMORY, OR IMMEDIATE.
                        ;                 USES AX, BX, AND DX REGISTERS
                        ;                 LEAVES x mod y IN AX-REGISTER
                        ;
                        mod       MACRO   x,y
                                  MOV     AX,x
                                  MOV     BX,y
                                  MOV     DX,0
                                  DIV     BX
                                  MOV     AX,DX
                                  ENDM
                        ;----------------------------------------------
                        ;MULTIPLY IMMEDIATE (UNSIGNED)
                        ;
                        ;                 const SHOULD BE IMMEDIATE
                        ;                 USES BX-REGISTER
                        ;                 LEAVES PRODUCT IN DX:AX
                        ;
                        muli      MACRO   const
                                  MOV     BX,const
                                  MUL     BX
                                  ENDM
                        ;----------------------------------------------
                        ;
                        ;
                        ;C O D E   S E G M E N T   D E F I N I T I O N
                        ;
0000                    CODE      SEGMENT
```

The Microsoft MACRO Assembler , Version 1.27   Page   1-2
ASSEMBLER LISTING 5.6   09-24-87

```
                                        ASSUME  CS:CODE,SS:STACK,DS:DATA
0000                            EASTER  PROC    FAR
0000  1E                                PUSH    DS              ;PUSH RETURN SEG ADDR ON STACK
0001  2B C0                             SUB     AX,AX           ;PUSH RETURN OFFSET 0 ON STACK
0003  50                                PUSH    AX
0004  B8 ---- R                         MOV     AX,SEG DATA     ;SET DS AND ES REGISTERS TO
0007  8E D8                             MOV     DS,AX           ;POINT TO DATA SEGMENT
0009  8E C0                             MOV     ES,AX
000B  8D 3E 0008 R                      LEA     DI,PROMPT       ;PROMPT FOR YEAR
000F  B9 000D                           MOV     CX,13
0012  9A 0000 ---- E                    CALL    PUTSTRNG
0017  9A 0000 ---- E                    CALL    GETDEC$         ;GET YEAR
001C  A3 0006 R                         MOV     YEAR,AX
001F  8D 3E 0015 R                      LEA     DI,ANNOTATE     ;DISPLAY ANNOTATION
0023  B9 0019                           MOV     CX,25
0026  9A 0000 ---- E                    CALL    PUTSTRNG
                                        mod     AX,19           ;A = YEAR mod 19
002B  8B C0                     +       MOV     AX,AX
002D  BB 0013                   +       MOV     BX,19
0030  BA 0000                   +       MOV     DX,0
0033  F7 F3                     +       DIV     BX
0035  8B C2                     +       MOV     AX,DX
                                        muli    19              ;X = (19A + 24) mod 30
0037  BB 0013                   +       MOV     BX,19
003A  F7 E3                     +       MUL     BX
003C  05 0018                           ADD     AX,24
                                        mod     AX,30
003F  8B C0                     +       MOV     AX,AX
0041  BB 001E                   +       MOV     BX,30
0044  BA 0000                   +       MOV     DX,0
0047  F7 F3                     +       DIV     BX
0049  8B C2                     +       MOV     AX,DX
004B  A3 0004 R                         MOV     X,AX
                                        mod     YEAR,4          ;B = 2(YEAR mod 4)
004E  A1 0006 R                 +       MOV     AX,YEAR
0051  BB 0004                   +       MOV     BX,4
0054  BA 0000                   +       MOV     DX,0
0057  F7 F3                     +       DIV     BX
0059  8B C2                     +       MOV     AX,DX
                                        muli    2
005B  BB 0002                   +       MOV     BX,2
005E  F7 E3                     +       MUL     BX
0060  A3 0000 R                         MOV     B,AX
                                        mod     YEAR,7          ;C = 4(YEAR mod 7)
0063  A1 0006 R                 +       MOV     AX,YEAR
0066  BB 0007                   +       MOV     BX,7
0069  BA 0000                   +       MOV     DX,0
006C  F7 F3                     +       DIV     BX
006E  8B C2                     +       MOV     AX,DX
                                        muli    4
0070  BB 0004                   +       MOV     BX,4
0073  F7 E3                     +       MUL     BX
0075  A3 0002 R                         MOV     C,AX
0078  A1 0004 R                         MOV     AX,X            ;Y = (6X + 5 + B + C) mod 7
                                        muli    6
007B  BB 0006                   +       MOV     BX,6
007E  F7 E3                     +       MUL     BX
0080  05 0005                           ADD     AX,5
0083  03 06 0000 R                      ADD     AX,B
0087  03 06 0002 R                      ADD     AX,C
                                        mod     AX,7
008B  8B C0                     +       MOV     AX,AX
008D  BB 0007                   +       MOV     BX,7
0090  BA 0000                   +       MOV     DX,0
0093  F7 F3                     +       DIV     BX
0095  8B C2                     +       MOV     AX,DX
0097  03 06 0004 R                      ADD     AX,X            ;DATE = Y + X + 22
009B  05 0016                           ADD     AX,22
009E  3D 001F                           CMP     AX,31           ;IF   DATE > 31
00A1  7E 12                             JLE     ELSE
00A3  2D 001F                           SUB     AX,31           ;THEN DATE = DATE - 31
00A6  3D 001A                           CMP     AX,26           ;    IF   DATE = 26
00A9  75 03                             JNE     _ENDIF          ;       THEN DATE = 19
00AB  B8 0013                           MOV     AX,19           ;       THEN DATE = 19
00AE                            _ENDIF:                         ;    ENDIF
```

listing. As well, note that it is the instructions of the expansion that are translated to machine language. No machine code is shown for the macro reference itself. The substitution of the macro body for the macro reference takes place before the translation to machine language.

INCLUDE Pseudo-Operation

One macro may be useful in a number of programs or procedures; for example, the Assembly language subprocedures appearing in this book save and restore registers for their callers. The subprocedure in Program Listing 5.4 has four instructions (lines 32–35) for saving register values on the stack and four instructions (lines 54–57) for restoring register values from the stack. The IBM PC-AT Assembly language provides a single instruction (the PUSHA instruction) for saving the values of all eight general registers on the stack and another, single instruction (the POPA instruction) for restoring the values of all eight general registers from the stack (see also Section 2.6 and Section 5.6). These instructions do not exist in the IBM PC Assembly language, but a similar capability can be provided by using macros.

The macros in Program Listing 5.7 provide a capability similar to that provided by the PUSHA and POPA instructions of the IBM PC-AT Assembly language, with two important differences:

1. The PUSHA and POPA instructions include the SP-register, but the macros in Program Listing 5.7 do not.

```
 1: ;                   PROGRAM LISTING 5.7
 2: ;
 3: ; MACRO TO PUSH ALL GENERAL REGISTERS (EXCEPT SP) AND THE FLAGS REGISTER
 4: ;
 5: PUSHA      MACRO
 6:            PUSH     AX
 7:            PUSH     BX
 8:            PUSH     CX
 9:            PUSH     DX
10:            PUSH     DI
11:            PUSH     SI
12:            PUSH     BP
13:            PUSHF
14:            ENDM
15: ;
16: ; MACRO TO POP  THE FLAGS REGISTER AND ALL GENERAL REGISTERS (EXCEPT SP)
17: ;
18: POPA       MACRO
19:            POPF
20:            POP      BP
21:            POP      SI
22:            POP      DI
23:            POP      DX
24:            POP      CX
25:            POP      BX
26:            POP      AX
27:*           ENDM
```

2. The macros in Program Listing 5.7 include the flags register, but the PUSHA and POPA instructions do not.

Since the PUSHA and POPA macros would be used only once in a sub-procedure, using the macros in Program Listing 5.7 might lead to more work than using the individual PUSH and POP instructions. Consider again Program Listing 5.4 that contains the definition of one procedure, the random number generator. Using the PUSHA and POPA macros in this assembly module would replace eight lines (lines 32–35 and lines 54–57) with a minimum of 22 lines (10 for the definition of PUSHA, 10 for the definition of POPA, and two for the references to the two macros).

In an assembly module like Program Listing 5.4, the INCLUDE pseudo-operation makes it feasible to use macros like PUSHA and POPA. The **INCLUDE pseudo-operation** provides the capability to embed text from one source code file into the text of another source code file during the assembly process. The pseudo-operation has the following general form:

INCLUDE ⟨ *file-spec* ⟩   [⟨*comment*⟩]

in which ⟨ *file-spec* ⟩ is an explicit file specification that identifies the disk drive and the filename. When the assembler encounters an INCLUDE pseudo-operation it replaces that pseudo-operation with the text from the file specified by the ⟨ *file-spec* ⟩ operand.

EXAMPLE

Suppose the macro definitions shown in Program Listing 5.7 are on the diskette in drive B under the filename PUSHPOP.MAC. On encountering the pseudo-operation

INCLUDE B:PUSHPOP.MAC

in an assembly module, the assembler substitutes the definitions of the PUSHA and POPA macros that appear in the file PUSHPOP.MAC.

Labels in Macros

The need to use labels in macros leads to the need for a special kind of label. Consider the following macro definition that is designed to compute the absolute value of the contents of a general register or memory location and to leave the result as the new value of that register or memory location:

```
abs       MACRO num
          CMP    num,0
          JGE    ENDABS
          NEG    num
ENDABS:
          ENDM
```

If this macro is referenced more than once in the assembly module, then the label ENDABS is generated more than once. The assembler generates two error messages at each definition of the ENDABS label after the first:

```
Error --- 4:Redefinition of Symbol
Error --- 5:Symbol is multi-defined
```

The assembler also generates the error message

```
Error --- 26:Reference to mult defined
```

for each instruction that references the multidefined label.

If labels are to be allowed in macros, then there must be a way to direct the assembler to generate unique labels during macro expansion. The **LOCAL pseudo-operation** provides this capability and has the following general form:

```
LOCAL ⟨dummy-label-list⟩   [⟨comment⟩]
```

in which ⟨*dummy-label-list*⟩ is a list of dummy labels separated by commas. At the time of macro expansion, the LOCAL pseudo-operation directs the assembler to generate a unique label for each dummy label in the ⟨*dummy-label-list*⟩ and substitute that unique label for each occurrence of the corresponding dummy label in the macro body. The labels generated by the assembler are the labels in the range ??0000 through ??FFFF. The LOCAL pseudo-operation cannot be used outside a macro definition, and it must appear between the MACRO pseudo-operation that marks the beginning of the macro definition and the first instruction of the macro body.

EXAMPLE

The following macro definition corrects the absolute value macro defined earlier:

```
abs     MACRO num
        LOCAL ENDABS
        CMP   num,0
        JGE   ENDABS
        NEG   num
ENDABS:
        ENDM
```

If the first reference to the macro is

```
abs X
```

then the instruction sequence substituted by the assembler might be as follows:

```
        CMP X,0
        JGE ??0000
        NEG X
??0000:
```

If the second reference to the macro is

```
abs BX
```

then the instruction sequence substituted by the assembler might be as follows:

```
     CMP BX, O
     JGE ??0001
     NEG BX
??0001:
```

The actual code generated would depend on the existence of other macros with local labels. On encountering a reference to the abs macro, the assembler selects the next available label from the list ??0000 through ??FFFF and substitutes it for the dummy label ENDABS in the expansion.

Conditional Assembly

It is possible in an assembly module to identify a sequence of instructions and pseudo-operations that is to be included in or omitted from the assembly depending on the value of a constant expression—which is known as **conditional assembly**. A conditional assembly specification has the following general form:

```
IFxxxx ⟨argument⟩
       ⟨block⟩
[ELSE
       ⟨block⟩]
ENDIF
```

in which IFxxxx is one of the conditional pseudo-operations from Table 5.1,

TABLE 5.1
Conditional pseudo-operations

Pseudo-Operation		Explanation
IF	⟨expr⟩	True if the constant expression (⟨expr⟩) evaluates to a nonzero value.
IFE	⟨expr⟩	True if the constant expression (⟨expr⟩) evaluates to zero.
IFDEF	⟨symbol⟩	True if the symbolic name (⟨symbol⟩) is defined or has been declared as external by the EXTRN pseudo-operation.
IFNDEF	⟨symbol⟩	True if the symbolic name (⟨symbol⟩) is not defined and has not been declared as external by the EXTRN pseudo-operation.
IFB	⟨⟨arg⟩⟩	The pointed brackets around ⟨arg⟩ are required. Usually used inside a macro definition. True in a specific macro expansion if the operand corresponding to the dummy argument (⟨arg⟩) is blank.
IFNB	⟨⟨arg⟩⟩	The pointed brackets around ⟨arg⟩ are required. Usually used inside a macro definition. True in a specific macro expansion if the operand corresponding to the dummy argument (⟨arg⟩) is not blank.

⟨*argument*⟩ is a constant expression or symbolic name depending on the conditional pseudo-operation, and ⟨*block*⟩ is a sequence of instructions and pseudo-operations to be included in or omitted from the assembly.

Note that the clause

```
[ELSE
      ⟨block⟩]
```

is optional. The ⟨*block*⟩ in this clause is included in the assembly if the conditional pseudo-operation selects to omit the required ⟨*block*⟩. The required ⟨*block*⟩ is included in the assembly if the specified condition is True; it is omitted from the assembly if the condition is False. Table 5.1 explains some of the conditional pseudo-operations.

Conditional assembly is especially useful in macros. For a specific expansion, the decision to include or omit some of the instructions in the macro body can be based on the operand associated with a specific dummy argument.

EXAMPLE

Consider the following macro definition that generates the calling sequence for the PUTSTR procedure:

```
putstr MACRO  string,lngth
       LEA    DI,string
       MOV    CX,lngth
       CALL   PUTSTRNG
       ENDM
```

The macro reference

```
putstr PROMPT,25
```

would be expanded to the instruction sequence

```
LEA DI,PROMPT
MOV CX,25
CALL PUTSTRNG
```

Some references to the PUTSTRNG procedure are followed by a reference to the NEWLINE procedure and others are not. With a conditional assembly specification in the macro body, the assembler can determine whether or not to generate the call to NEWLINE as part of macro expansion. Consider the following alternate definition of the putstr macro:

```
putstr MACRO  string,lngth,flag
       LEA    DI,string
       MOV    CX,lngth
       CALL   PUTSTRNG
       IF     flag
       CALL   NEWLINE
       ENDIF
       ENDM
```

The dummy argument, flag, is used to control whether or not the call to NEW-LINE is to be generated during macro expansion. If the operand associated with flag is nonzero, then the call to NEWLINE is generated. However, if the value is zero, then the call to NEWLINE is not generated. The macro reference

```
putstr PROMPT,25,1
```

would be expanded to the instruction sequence

```
LEA  DI,PROMPT
MOV  CX,25
CALL PUTSTRNG
CALL NEWLINE
```

The macro reference

```
putstr MSG,12,0
```

would be expanded to the instruction sequence

```
LEA  DI,MSG
MOV  CX,12
CALL PUTSTRNG
```

Programming Example—Compute Dates of 21 Easter Sundays

Program Listing 5.8 implements an algorithm to compute the dates of 21 consecutive Easter Sundays given the starting year. The assembly module contains the definition of the stack segment for the program (lines 17–22), the definition of a data segment for the main procedure (lines 23–31), and the definition of the main procedure (lines 37–56). The main procedure prompts for and accepts from the keyboard a value for the beginning year (lines 44–45) and then enters a REPEAT-UNTIL loop (lines 47–54). The loop executes 21 times, once for each of 21 consecutive years beginning with the year that was input via the keyboard. The body of the loop displays the year (line 50), invokes the external procedure EASTER (line 51) to compute and display the date of Easter Sunday for that year, and then increments to the next year (line 52). The year is maintained in the AX-register.

The assembly module in Program Listing 5.9 contains the definition of a data segment for the subprocedure EASTER (lines 10–22) and the definition of the subprocedure EASTER (lines 62–105). The EASTER procedure computes and displays the date of an Easter Sunday given the year. The year is passed to the EASTER procedure via the AX-register. The date of Easter Sunday for that year (month and day) is displayed on the screen beginning at the current cursor position. The EASTER procedure in Program Listing 5.9 implements the same algorithm as the EASTER procedure in Program Listing 5.5. The main difference between the two implementations is the interface: The EASTER

```
 1: ;                   PROGRAM LISTING 5.8
 2: ;
 3: ; PROGRAM  TO  COMPUTE  THE  DATE  OF 21
 4: ; EASTER SUNDAYS GIVEN THE STARTING YEAR
 5: ;
 6:                                         ;PROCEDURES TO
 7:              EXTRN    EASTER:FAR         ;COMPUTE AND DISPLAY DATE OF
 8:                                         ;EASTER SUNDAY GIVEN YEAR
 9:              EXTRN    GETDEC$:FAR        ;INPUT UNSIGNED DECIMAL INTEGER
10:              EXTRN    NEWLINE:FAR        ;DISPLAY NEWLINE CHARACTER
11:              EXTRN    PUTDEC$:FAR        ;DISPLAY UNSIGNED DECIMAL INT.
12:              EXTRN    PUTSTRNG:FAR       ;DISPLAY CHARACTER STRING
13: ;
14: ; M A C R O   D E F I N I T I O N S
15: ;
16:              INCLUDE B:PUTSTR.MAC
17: ;
18: ; S T A C K   S E G M E N T   D E F I N I T I O N
19: ;
20: STACK        SEGMENT STACK
21:              DB       256 DUP(?)
22: STACK        ENDS
23: ;
24: ; D A T A   S E G M E N T   D E F I N I T I O N
25: ;
26: DATA         SEGMENT
27: ;
28: PROMPT       DB       'ENTER YEAR - '
29: ANNOTATE     DB       'EASTER SUNDAYS:'
30: ;
31: DATA         ENDS
32: ;
33: ; C O D E   S E G M E N T   D E F I N I T I O N
34: ;
35: CODE         SEGMENT
36:              ASSUME   CS:CODE,SS:STACK,DS:DATA
37: DATES        PROC     FAR
38:              PUSH     DS                 ;PUSH RETURN SEG ADDR ON STACK
39:              SUB      AX,AX              ;PUSH RETURN OFFSET 0 ON STACK
40:              PUSH     AX
41:              MOV      AX,SEG DATA        ;SET DS AND ES REGISTERS TO
42:              MOV      DS,AX              ;POINT TO DATA SEGMENT
43:              MOV      ES,AX
44:              putstr   PROMPT,13,0        ;PROMPT FOR YEAR
45:              CALL     GETDEC$            ;GET YEAR
46:              putstr   ANNOTATE,15,1      ;DISPLAY ANNOTATION
47:              MOV      CX,21              ;LOOP_COUNT = 21
48:              MOV      BH,-1
49: LOOP_TOP:                               ;REPEAT
50:              CALL     PUTDEC$            ;   DISPLAY YEAR
51:              CALL     EASTER             ;   DISPLAY EASTER DATE FOR YEAR
52:              INC      AX                 ;   YEAR = YEAR + 1
53:              LOOP     LOOP_TOP           ;   DECREMENT LOOP COUNT
54:                                          ;UNTIL LOOP_COUNT = 0
55:              RET                         ;RETURN
56: DATES        ENDP
57: CODE         ENDS
58:*             END      DATES
```

```
 1: ;                        PROGRAM LISTING 5.9
 2: ;
 3: ; PROCEDURE  TO  COMPUTE THE DATE
 4: ; OF EASTER SUNDAY GIVEN THE YEAR
 5: ;
 6:                                         ;PROCEDURES TO
 7:             EXTRN    PUTSTRNG:FAR        ;DISPLAY CHARACTER STRING
 8:             EXTRN    PUTDEC$:FAR         ;DISPLAY UNSIGNED DECIMAL INT.
 9:             EXTRN    NEWLINE:FAR         ;DISPLAY NEWLINE CHARACTER
10: ;
11: ;D A T A   S E G M E N T   D E F I N I T I O N
12: ;
13: DATA        SEGMENT
14: ;
15: B           DW       ?
16: C           DW       ?
17: X           DW       ?
18: YEAR        DW       ?                   ;YEAR OF EASTER SUNDAY
19: MARCH       DB       'MARCH '
20: APRIL       DB       'APRIL '
21: ;
22: DATA        ENDS
23: ;------------------------------------------------
24: ;
25: ; M A C R O   D E F I N I T I O N S
26: ;
27: ;------------------------------------------------
28: ;FUNCTION  x mod y
29: ;                    x AND y CAN BE WORD REGISTER,
30: ;                    WORD MEMORY, OR IMMEDIATE.
31: ;                    USES AX, BX, AND DX REGISTERS
32: ;                    LEAVES x mod y IN AX-REGISTER
33: ;
34: mod         MACRO    x,y
35:             MOV      AX,x
36:             MOV      BX,y
37:             MOV      DX,O
38:             DIV      BX
39:             MOV      AX,DX
40:             ENDM
41: ;------------------------------------------------
42: ;MULTIPLY IMMEDIATE (UNSIGNED)
43: ;
44: ;                    const SHOULD BE IMMEDIATE
45: ;                    USES BX-REGISTER
46: ;                    LEAVES PRODUCT IN DX:AX
47: ;
48: muli        MACRO    const
49:             MOV      BX,const
50:             MUL      BX
51:             ENDM
52: ;------------------------------------------------
53:             INCLUDE B:PUSHPOP.MAC
54:             INCLUDE B:PUTSTR.MAC
55: ;------------------------------------------------
56:*;
57: ;
58: ;C O D E   S E G M E N T   D E F I N I T I O N
```

*

```
59: ;
60: CODE       SEGMENT
61:            ASSUME   CS:CODE,ES:DATA
62: EASTER     PROC     FAR                 ;PROCEDURE EASTER(YEAR)
63:            PUBLIC   EASTER
64:            pusha                         ;SAVE REGISTERS AND FLAGS
65:            PUSH     ES                   ;SAVE ES-REGISTER
66:            MOV      BX,SEG DATA          ;SET ES-REG TO ADDRESS
67:            MOV      ES,BX                ;LOCAL DATA SEGMENT
68:            MOV      YEAR,AX
69:            mod      AX,19                ;A = YEAR mod 19
70:            muli     19                   ;X = (19A + 24) mod 30
71:            ADD      AX,24
72:            mod      AX,30
73:            MOV      X,AX
74:            mod      YEAR,4               ;B = 2(YEAR mod 4)
75:            muli     2
76:            MOV      B,AX
77:            mod      YEAR,7               ;C = 4(YEAR mod 7)
78:            muli     4
79:            MOV      C,AX
80:            MOV      AX,X                 ;Y = (6X + 5 + B + C) mod 7
81:            muli     6
82:            ADD      AX,5
83:            ADD      AX,B
84:            ADD      AX,C
85:            mod      AX,7
86:            ADD      AX,X                 ;DATE = Y + X + 22
87:            ADD      AX,22
88:            CMP      AX,31                ;IF   DATE > 31
89:            JLE      ELSE
90:            SUB      AX,31                ;THEN DATE = DATE - 31
91:            CMP      AX,26                ;     IF   DATE = 26
92:            JNE      _ENDIF
93:            MOV      AX,19                ;        THEN DATE = 19
94: _ENDIF:                                 ;        ENDIF
95:            putstr   APRIL,6,0            ;     DISPLAY 'APRIL '
96:            JMP      ENDIF
97: ELSE:                                   ;ELSE
98:            putstr   MARCH,6,0            ;     DISPLAY 'MARCH '
99: ENDIF:                                  ;ENDIF
100:           CALL     PUTDEC$              ;DISPLAY DATE
101:           CALL     NEWLINE
102:           POP      ES                   ;RESTORE ES-REGISTER
103:           popa                          ;RESTORE FLAGS AND REGISTERS
104:           RET                           ;RETURN
105: EASTER    ENDP                       ;END EASTER
106: CODE      ENDS
107:*          END      EASTER
```

procedure in Program Listing 5.9 is a subprocedure that receives its input from the AX-register, and the EASTER procedure in Program Listing 5.5 is a main procedure that receives its input via the keyboard.

Program Listings 5.8 and 5.9 are two parts of a single program that uses four macros. Two of these macros (mod and muli) are defined in Program Listing 5.9 (lines 23–51) and were discussed and illustrated in Program Listing 5.5. The other two macros are defined in separate source code files: The file

B:PUSHPOP.MAC contains the definitions of the PUSHA and POPA macros in Program Listing 5.7, and the file B:PUTSTR.MAC contains the macro definition shown in Program Listing 5.10 (which was discussed in the preceding section).

The INCLUDE pseudo-operation incorporates the definitions of the putstr, pusha, and popa macros into the assembly modules in Program Listings 5.8 and 5.9. The INCLUDE pseudo-operation in line 16 in Program 5.8 causes the assembler to replace line 16 with the text contained in file PUTSTR.MAC on the diskette in drive B. The INCLUDE pseudo-operations in lines 53 and 54 in Program Listing 5.9 cause the assembler to replace lines 53 and 54 with the text contained in files PUSHPOP.MAC and PUTSTR.MAC on the diskette in drive B.

Assembler Listing 5.11 shows the first two pages of the assembler-generated listing for the assembly module in Program Listing 5.8. The TITLE and PAGE pseudo-operations have been added for the purpose of generating this listing. Note that the INCLUDE pseudo-operation is immediately followed by the lines of text from the PUTSTR.MAC file, and that in the listing, each of these lines is preceded by the letter C. Note also that no machine code is generated for these lines. Each line from the INCLUDE file is either a comment line or part of a macro definition. Assembler Listing 5.11 shows the expansion for each reference to the putstr macro. The first reference

```
putstr   PROMPT,13,0
```

was expanded to the instruction sequence

```
LEA    DI,PROMPT
MOV    CX,13
CALL   PUTSTRNG
```

and the second reference

```
putstr   ANNOTATE,15,1
```

```
 1: ;                    PROGRAM LISTING 5.10
 2: ;
 3: ; CALLING SEQUENCE FOR PROCEDURE PUTSTRNG
 4: ;
 5: ;                string SHOULD BE A BYTE ARRAY NAME
 6: ;                lngth  CAN BE WORD REGISTER,  WORD
 7: ;                       MEMORY, OR IMMEDIATE
 8: ;                flag   NONZERO => CALL NEWLINE
 9: ;                       ZERO    => NO CALL TO NEWLINE
10: ;                USES DI-REGISTER and CX-REGISTER
11: ;
12: PUTSTR     MACRO    string,lngth,flag
13:            LEA      DI,string
14:            MOV      CX,lngth
15:            CALL     PUTSTRNG
16:            IF       flag
17:            CALL     NEWLINE
18:            ENDIF
19:*           ENDM
```

```
The Microsoft MACRO Assembler , Version 1.27          Page    1-1
ASSEMBLER LISTING 5.11                                         09-24-87


                          TITLE    ASSEMBLER LISTING 5.11
                          PAGE     80,132
                      ;
                      ;
                      ; PROGRAM  TO  COMPUTE  THE  DATE  OF 21
                      ; EASTER SUNDAYS GIVEN THE STARTING YEAR
                      ;
                                                    ;PROCEDURES TO
                          EXTRN   EASTER:FAR        ;COMPUTE AND DISPLAY DATE OF
                                                    ;EASTER SUNDAY GIVEN YEAR
                          EXTRN   GETDEC$:FAR       ;INPUT UNSIGNED DECIMAL INTEGER
                          EXTRN   NEWLINE:FAR       ;DISPLAY NEWLINE CHARACTER
                          EXTRN   PUTDEC$:FAR       ;DISPLAY UNSIGNED DECIMAL INT.
                          EXTRN   PUTSTRNG:FAR      ;DISPLAY CHARACTER STRING
                      ;
                      ; M A C R O   D E F I N I T I O N S
                      ;
   C                      INCLUDE B:PUTSTR.MAC
   C  ;
   C  ; CALLING SEQUENCE FOR PROCEDURE PUTSTRNG
   C  ;
   C  ;                      string SHOULD BE A BYTE ARRAY NAME
   C  ;                      lngth  CAN BE WORD REGISTER,  WORD
   C  ;                             MEMORY, OR IMMEDIATE
   C  ;                      flag   NONZERO => CALL NEWLINE
   C  ;                             ZERO    => NO CALL TO NEWLINE
   C  ;                      USES DI-REGISTER and CX-REGISTER
   C  ;
   C  PUTSTR      MACRO    string,lngth,flag
   C              LEA      DI,string
   C              MOV      CX,lngth
   C              CALL     PUTSTRNG
   C              IF       flag
   C              CALL     NEWLINE
   C              ENDIF
   C              ENDM
                      ;
                      ; S T A C K   S E G M E N T   D E F I N I T I O N
                      ;
0000                  STACK       SEGMENT STACK
0000  0100 [          DB          256 DUP(?)
        ??
             ]

0100                  STACK       ENDS
                      ;
                      ; D A T A   S E G M E N T   D E F I N I T I O N
                      ;
0000                  DATA        SEGMENT

0000  45 4E 54 45 52 20   PROMPT   DB     'ENTER YEAR - '
      59 45 41 52 20 2D
      20
000D  45 41 53 54 45 52   ANNOTATE DB     'EASTER SUNDAYS:'
      20 53 55 4E 44 41
      59 53 3A

001C                  DATA        ENDS
                      ;
                      ; C O D E   S E G M E N T   D E F I N I T I O N
                      ;
0000                  CODE        SEGMENT
                                  ASSUME  CS:CODE,SS:STACK,DS:DATA
0000                  DATES       PROC    FAR
0000  1E                          PUSH    DS            ;PUSH RETURN SEG ADDR ON STACK
0001  2B C0                       SUB     AX,AX         ;PUSH RETURN OFFSET 0 ON STACK
0003  50                          PUSH    AX
0004  B8 ---- R                   MOV     AX,SEG DATA   ;SET DS AND ES REGISTERS TO
0007  8E D8                       MOV     DS,AX         ;POINT TO DATA SEGMENT
0009  8E C0                       MOV     ES,AX
                                  putstr  PROMPT,13,0   ;PROMPT FOR YEAR
000B  8D 3E 0000 R         +      LEA     DI,PROMPT
000F  B9 000D             +      MOV     CX,13
0012  9A 0000 ---- E      +      CALL    PUTSTRNG
0017  9A 0000 ---- E             CALL    GETDEC$       ;GET YEAR
```

```
001C  8D 3E 000D R        +        putstr   ANNOTATE,15,1        ;DISPLAY ANNOTATION
                                   LEA      DI,ANNOTATE
0020  B9 000F             +        MOV      CX,15
0023  9A 0000 ---- E      +        CALL     PUTSTRNG
0028  9A 0000 ---- E      +        CALL     NEWLINE
002D  B9 0015                      MOV      CX,21                ;LOOP_COUNT = 21
0030  B7 FF                        MOV      BH,-1
0032                      LOOP_TOP:                              ;REPEAT
0032  9A 0000 ---- E               CALL     PUTDEC$              ;   DISPLAY YEAR
0037  9A 0000 ---- E               CALL     EASTER               ;   DISPLAY EASTER DATE FOR YEAR
003C  40                           INC      AX                   ;   YEAR = YEAR + 1
003D  E2 F3                        LOOP     LOOP_TOP             ;   DECREMENT LOOP COUNT
                                                                ;UNTIL LOOP_COUNT = 0
003F  CB                           RET                          ;RETURN
0040                      DATES    ENDP
0040                      CODE     ENDS
                                   END      DATES
```

was expanded to the instruction sequence

```
LEA    DI,ANNOTATE
MOV    CX,15
CALL   PUTSTRNG
CALL   NEWLINE
```

Note that in the expansion for the second reference, a call to the NEWLINE procedure was generated, but in the expansion for the first reference, a call to the NEWLINE procedure was not generated.

The following is the result from a sample execution of the program of Program Listings 5.8 and 5.9:

```
ENTER YEAR - 1980
EASTER SUNDAYS:
1980 APRIL 6
1981 APRIL 19
1982 APRIL 11
1983 APRIL 3
1984 APRIL 22
1985 APRIL 7
1986 MARCH 30
1987 APRIL 19
1988 APRIL 3
1989 MARCH 26
1990 APRIL 15
1991 MARCH 31
1992 APRIL 19
1993 APRIL 11
1994 APRIL 3
1995 APRIL 16
1996 APRIL 7
1997 MARCH 30
1998 APRIL 12
1999 APRIL 4
2000 APRIL 23
```

5.8   Macro Versus Subprocedure

The subprocedure and the macro are both important tools in Assembly language programming and important concepts for the beginning Assembly language programmer to master. One key to proficiency in Assembly language programming is having a good library of suprocedures and macros available. From the viewpoint of a beginning Assembly language programmer, a subprocedure and a macro may appear to be quite similar. In both cases, a block of instructions is written once by the programmer but can be used in many places in the program. However, the two are quite different with respect to memory space and execution time.

The difference between macros and subprocedures can be viewed from the standpoint of when certain events occur during program translation and execution. The subprocedure instructions appear only once in a machine language program. When the assembler encounters a subprocedure definition, it translates the subprocedure instructions to machine language. Each time the assembler encounters a reference to that subprocedure, for example, a CALL instruction that names the subprocedure, it translates that instruction to a machine language call instruction. During program execution, execution of the machine language call instruction causes control to be transferred to the single copy of the machine language instructions of the subprocedure. Subsequent execution of a return instruction should return control to the instruction that immediately follows the call instruction. The memory space required for subprocedure instructions is not dependent on the number of times the subprocedure is referenced (called).

A macro's instructions may appear more than once in a machine language program. When the assembler encounters a macro definition, no translation to machine language takes place. However, each time the assembler encounters a reference to the macro (i.e., the macro name used as an operation code), the macro body instructions are translated to machine language. The memory space required for the macro instructions is dependent on the number of times the macro is referenced.

Some extra processing is required to execute a subprocedure that is not required to execute macro instructions. There are usually instructions in the calling procedure to set up the inputs for the subprocedure. There is a call instruction to transfer control to the subprocedure. There are usually instructions in the subprocedure to save and restore the state of the processor for the caller. There is a return instruction to transfer control back to the caller. All these instructions require extra memory space and increase execution time, which is referred to as the **overhead** of using a subprocedure.

The decision of whether to use a macro or a subprocedure is often based on the tradeoff of memory space per copy of the macro versus the subprocedure overhead. The macro was chosen for the multiply immediate and mod operations of the Easter Sunday algorithm because the overhead of a subprocedure was considered to equal or exceed the memory space required for the macro instructions. For the display of signed decimal integer capability, provided by the

PUTDEC procedure, a subprocedure was chosen because the memory requirements for a macro were felt to be too restrictive for large programs in which signed decimal output is frequently needed. Effective use of macros and subprocedures makes Assembly language programming more feasible.

PROGRAMMING EXERCISES

5.1 In Programming Exercise 4.1, the notion of an Ulam sequence and its length was introduced. Design a subalgorithm to accept a positive integer as input and to return the length of the Ulam sequence for that integer as output. As well, design a main algorithm that uses the subalgorithm to find an integer in the range 1–100 whose Ulam sequence has the largest length. The algorithm is to output that integer and the length of its Ulam sequence. The main algorithm is to reference the subalgorithm 100 times, once for each integer in the range 1–100.

Implement your subalgorithm with an IBM PC Assembly language NEAR function procedure. The input to your procedure should be a positive integer passed in the AX-register. The length of the Ulam sequence for the input integer should be returned to the caller in the AX-register. Implement your main algorithm with an IBM PC Assembly language program that uses your NEAR subprocedure to compute the length of the Ulam sequence for each of the integers in the given range. There is no input to your program. Your output should be the integer whose Ulam sequence has the largest length and that largest length value. The two integers are to be displayed on the screen.

5.2 Design an algorithm to perform integer exponentiation. Your input to the algorithm should be a signed integer value that represents the BASE and an unsigned integer value that represents the positive exponent. Your output should be the value of BASE raised to the EXPONENT. For example, if the inputs are BASE = 2 and EXPONENT = 5, then the output should be $2^5 = 32$. Your algorithm must detect overflow.

Implement your algorithm with an IBM PC Assembly language FAR procedure. The input to your procedure should be an 8-bit signed integer value in the AL-register that represents the BASE and an 8-bit unsigned integer value in the AH-register that represents the EXPONENT. Your procedure is to return the result, a 16-bit signed integer value, in the AX-register and to return an overflow indicator in the BL-register (BL-register = 0 implies no overflow).

Your procedure must save and restore all registers used for purposes other than procedure output. The registers being saved and restored must include the flags register and the BH-register, if it is being used.

5.3 Program Listing 5.4 shows an external procedure called RANDOM that returns pseudo-random integers in the range 0–9999. The procedure uses a local data segment to maintain a SEED for the random number generator function used and contains some logic to initialize the SEED value at the time of first invocation of the procedure.

Remove the first call logic from the RANDOM procedure. Instead, provide a second FAR procedure called RESEED that is defined in the same code segment. The RESEED procedure simply sets the SEED value as specified by the caller. Your input to the RESEED procedure should be a code in the BL-register and possibly a 16-bit unsigned integer value in the AX-register. The interpretation for the code in the BL-register is as follows:

BL = 0 → Use the lower half of the time-of-day clock as the new SEED value

BL ≠ 0 → Use the value in the AX-register as the new SEED value

Design an algorithm that uses RANDOM and RESEED to perform the following tasks:

1. Call RANDOM 200 times to produce a sequence of 200 pseudo-random integers.

2. Call RESEED prior to the first call to RANDOM to initialize the SEED value to 5555 hexadecimal.

3. Call RESEED after the one-hundredth call to RANDOM to reinitialize the SEED value to the value in the lower half of the time-of-day clock.

4. Display the sequence of random integers on the screen, 10 per line.

5. Count the number of integers in the sequence that are (a) odd, (b) even, (c) high (i.e., in the range 5000–9999), and (d) low (i.e., in the range 0000–4999).

6. Display the results of the four preceding counts on the screen.

Implement your algorithm with an IBM PC Assembly language program. There is no input to your program. Link your program with RANDOM, RESEED, and the local data segment to produce a complete, executable program. Your output should look something like the following:

```
9804 3632 3281 5156 4375 5156 3984  546 5820 6445
9882 5000 6484 4140 9648 6445 1210 7539 4335 5351
7382 8359 7578 4687 4804  742 5390 9921 5820 1484
6445 9062 5312 9765 1796 2539  546 7304 5078 3359
1445 8320 2304 6914  351 9570 2148 1250 2031  234
5664 6796 3906 2031 6484 6523 5781 9179  625 5937
   0 8437 6757 2968 1445 8984 5937 8085 7382 2539
1757 4257 7734 3359  351 6953 4804 8085  273 4179
3476 6015 2617 6367 1054 8828  976 6523 7382  781
1484   39 4804 8515 2695 4960 8164 1328 5703 1718
 742 9375  273 7226 8515 5507 6132 9492 8984 5273
1796 8437 1953 2929 3281 9570 9765 5117 9257  820
7304 1132  781 2656 1875 2656 1484 8046 3320 3945
7382 2500 3984 1640 7148 3945 8710 5039 1835 2851
4882 5859 5078 2187 2304 8242 2890 7421 3320 8984
3945 6562 2812 7265 9296   39 8046 4804 2578  859
8945 5820 9804 4414 7851 7070 9648 8750 9531 7734
3164 4296 1406 9531 3984 4023 3281 6679 8125 3437
7500 5937 4257  468 8945 6484 3437 5585 4482   39
9257 1757 5234  859 7851 4453 2304 5585 7773 1679
ODD = 95     EVEN = 105    HIGH = 101    LOW = 99
```

5.4 In Programming Exercise 4.6 Euclid's algorithm for finding the greatest common divisor (GCD) of two positive integers was introduced. Implement Euclid's algorithm with an IBM PC Assembly language FAR function procedure called GCD. Your input should be two 16-bit unsigned integers in the AX and BX registers. Your procedure should return the GCD of these two integers in the AX-register. Your procedure must protect all registers used.

The programs in Programming Exercises 5.5 or 5.6 can be used to demonstrate your procedure.

5.5 In Programming Exercise 4.9, the notion of Pythagorean triples was introduced. Your solution probably produced some Pythagorean triples that were integer multiples of other triples produced. For example, the triple (6, 8, 10) is an integer multiple of the triple (3, 4, 5).

If each pair of integers in the triple is relatively prime, then the triple is not an integer multiple of some other triple. Two positive integers are relatively prime if their GCD is 1.

$$GCD(3, 4) = GCD(3, 5) = GCD(4, 5) = 1$$

Therefore, (3, 4, 5) is not a multiple.

$$GCD(6, 8) = GCD(6, 10) = GCD(8, 10)$$
$$= 2$$

Therefore, (6, 8, 10) is a multiple.

Modify your solution to Programming Exercise 4.9 to eliminate the display of triples that are integer multiples of other triples. Use your GCD procedure from Programming Exercise 5.4 to determine if a given triple is a multiple. Increase the range of integers considered from 1–50 to 1–100.

5.6 Programming Exercises 4.9 and 5.5 involve algorithms for producing Pythagorean triples. Your solution to these problems probably included three nested loops. You probably noticed some hesitation in the display of the triples, especially in the second version that considered a wider range of integers. The following algorithm contains only two nested loops and is a much more efficient algorithm for computing Pythagorean triples:

```
ALGORITHM:
    U = 2
    REPEAT
        IF   U is even
        THEN
            V = 1
        ELSE
            V = 2
```

```
            ENDIF
            REPEAT
                  IF   GCD(U,V) = 1
                  THEN
                              CALL TRIPLE(U,V)
                  ENDIF
                  V = V + 2
            UNTIL V > U
            U = U + 1
      UNTIL U = 10

SUBALGORITHM:
      TRIPLE(U,V)
            Z = U*U + V*V
            Y = U*U - V*V
            X = 2*U*V
            IF   X > Y
            THEN
                        INTERCHANGE X & Y
            ENDIF
            DISPLAY X, Y, Z
            RETURN
      END TRIPLE
```

It is based on the following result:

> Given positive integers U and V, such that either U or V is odd and the other is even, and that U and V are relatively prime, the triple $(2UV, U^2 - V^2, U^2 + V^2)$ is a unique Pythagorean triple and is not an integer multiple of some other Pythagorean triple.

Implement this algorithm with an IBM PC Assembly language program. There is no input to your program. Your output should be a list of the Pythagorean triples displayed on the screen, one triple per line. Implement the subalgorithm with an IBM PC Assembly language NEAR procedure. Your input should be the two positive integers U and V in the BX and CX registers, respectively. Your output should be the Pythagorean triple displayed on the screen on a line by itself. Your program should also include your GCD procedure from Programming Exercise 5.4.

5.7 In Programming Exercise 4.8 the notion of an insipid integer was introduced. Design a Boolean subalgorithm to accept a positive integer as input and to return True if that integer is insipid; otherwise, it should return False. Design a main algorithm to find and output all positive integers in the range 1–1500 that are insipid. Your algorithm is to use your Boolean subalgorithm to determine if a given integer is insipid.

Implement your subalgorithm with an IBM PC Assembly language NEAR Boolean function procedure. Your input should be a positive integer passed in the AX-register. The Boolean result should be returned to the BL-register (0 for False, 1 for True).

Implement your main algorithm with an IBM PC Assembly language program that uses your NEAR procedure to test each of the integers in the range 1–1500 to see if it is insipid. There is no input to your program. Your output should be the list of insipid integers in the range 1–1500. The integers are to be displayed on the screen, 10 per line.

5.8 The mod function macro used in Program Listing 5.5 will fail if the operand associated with the dummy argument y is the AX-register. Why? Rewrite the mod function macro to eliminate this problem. Your solution should not create the same problem with a different register. (*Hint*: Consider use of the stack and/or data storage embedded in the macro.)

5.9 In Programming Exercise 4.6, Euclid's algorithm for finding the GCD of two positive integers was introduced. Implement Euclid's algorithm with an IBM PC Assembly language macro named GCD. The macro is to compute the GCD of the two 16-bit unsigned integers in the AX and BX registers, leaving the result in the AX-register. Complete Programming Exercises 5.5 or 5.6 with the GCD macro replacing the GCD subprocedure.

5.10 Rewrite the multiply immediate macro used in Program Listing 5.5 to perform either byte or word multiplication depending on the operand associated with a second dummy argument called byte:

$$byte = 0$$

means perform word multiplication

$$byte = 1$$

means perform byte multiplication

For example, the macro reference

```
muli 7,0
```

should generate the instructions

```
MOV BX,7
MUL BX
```

and the macro reference

```
muli 12,1
```

should generate the instructions

```
MOV BL,12
MUL BL
```

5.11 Modify the PUSHA and POPA macros defined in Program Listing 5.7 to include two dummy arguments, ef and df, to be used as flags to indicate whether PUSH ES (POP ES) and/or PUSH DS (POP DS) should be generated in addition to the other PUSH and POP instructions.

6

BIT MANIPULATION

In Assembly language programming, you often need to perform operations on individual bits. For example, the solution to Programming Exercise 4.1 requires that you determine whether an integer is odd or even. To do so, you can test that integer's least-significant bit (the remainder of division by 2 yields the least-significant bit of an integer) and determine if that bit value is 1 or 0. As a second example, the PUTBIN procedure in Program Listing 5.1 isolates each bit of an 8-bit or 16-bit integer by repeatedly dividing by 2. Each remainder represents one bit of the binary number. This technique produces the bits of a binary number in right-to-left order. To display the bits in left-to-right order, PUTBIN had to reverse them.

Bit manipulation instructions provide access to an individual bit or a group of bits in a binary number. With these instructions, a programmer can inspect, change, or make a decision based on the value of an individual bit or group of bits. This chapter discusses the two types of bit manipulation instructions available in the IBM PC Assembly language, shift instructions and logical instructions, and presents alternative solutions to the problems previously identified.

6.1 Shift Operations

A **shift operation** is the bit-to-bit movement of the contents of a register or memory location. Figure 6.1 depicts both a byte and a word with the individual bits numbered from right to left, according to the convention used in the IBM PC documentation. The most-significant bit (MSB) is bit 7 for a byte and bit 15 for a word. The least-significant bit (LSB) is bit 0.

FIGURE 6.1
Byte and word with
individual bits
numbered

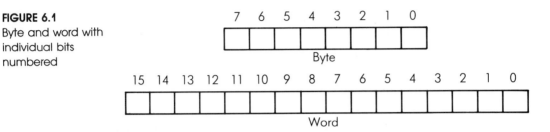

A 1-bit left-shift operation moves bit i to bit $i + 1$ ($14 \leqslant i \leqslant 0$ for word shifts; $6 \leqslant i \leqslant 0$ for byte shifts). The MSB is shifted into the CF bit of the flags register. The bit value that is shifted into the LSB depends on the type of shift operation. A multibit, left-shift operation behaves like a sequence of single-bit, left-shift operations.

A 1-bit right-shift operation moves bit i to bit $i - 1$ ($15 \leqslant i \leqslant 1$ for word shifts; $7 \leqslant i \leqslant 1$ for byte shifts). The LSB is shifted into the CF bit of the flags register. The bit value that is shifted into the MSB depends on the type of shift operation. A multibit, right-shift operation behaves like a sequence of single-bit, right-shift operations.

All shift operations affect the OF bit in the flags register in the same way. If the MSB changes with the 1-bit shift, then the OF bit in the flags register is set; otherwise, the OF bit is cleared. Since a multibit shift operation behaves like a sequence of single-bit shift operations, the OF bit in the flags register reflects a change in the MSB on the last bit shifted.

The **shift instructions** in the IBM PC Assembly language have the following general form:

[⟨*label*⟩] ⟨*op code*⟩ ⟨*destination*⟩, ⟨*shift-count*⟩   [⟨*comment*⟩]

in which ⟨*op code*⟩ is one of the following operation codes: SAR, SHR, ROR, RCR, SAL, SHL, ROL, or RCL; ⟨*destination*⟩ specifies the register or memory location containing the value to be shifted; and ⟨*shift-count*⟩ is either the constant 1 or the register designator CL. The constant 1 specifies a single-bit shift; the register designator CL specifies a multibit shift, with the shift count being the value in the CL-register.

Execution of a shift instruction that uses the CL-register as a shift count does *not* alter the value in the CL-register. The value is used but *not* changed.

Arithmetic Shift

There are three types of shift operations: the *arithmetic shift*, the *logical shift*, and the *rotate*. An **arithmetic shift** operation treats the operand as a signed binary number in two's complement form. The operation code for an **arithmetic right-shift** is SAR. With the SAR instruction, the bit value that is shifted into the MSB is a copy of the sign bit (Figure 6.2). Note in the figure that the sign bit does not change during the shift, which means that the overflow flag is always

FIGURE 6.2
SAR instruction

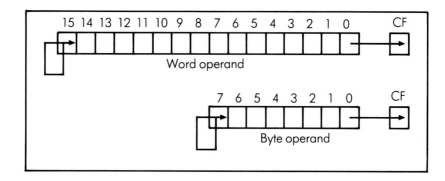

cleared by execution of a SAR instruction. The SAR instruction extends the sign bit as it shifts right.

Given a signed integer value, x, an arithmetic right-shift of n bits produces the signed integer value $\lfloor x/2^n \rfloor$ in which $\lfloor y \rfloor$ (read floor of y) is the greatest integer that is less than or equal to y. If y is an integer, then $\lfloor y \rfloor = y$.

EXAMPLES

			CF
Value before shift	00101000 =	40	?
After right-shift of 1	00010100 =	20 = 40/2	0
After right-shift of 2	00001010 =	10 = 40/4	0
After right-shift of 3	00000101 =	5 = 40/8	0
After right-shift of 4	00000010 =	2 = $\lfloor 40/16 \rfloor$	1

			CF
Value before shift	11011000 =	-40	?
After right-shift of 1	11101100 =	$-20 = -40/2$	0
After right-shift of 2	11110110 =	$-10 = -40/4$	0
After right-shift of 3	11111011 =	$-5 = -40/8$	0
After right-shift of 4	11111101 =	$-3 = \lfloor -40/16 \rfloor$	1

The operation code for an **arithmetic left-shift** operation is SAL. With the SAL instruction, the bit value that is shifted into the LSB is always 0 (Figure 6.3). Given a signed integer value, x, an arithmetic left-shift of n bits produces the signed integer value $x \times 2^n$.

If the sign bit changes on the last bit shifted, then the OF bit in the flags register is set; otherwise, the OF bit is cleared. For an arithmetic left-shift of 1, the OF bit in the flags register is a true indication of overflow when dealing with signed two's complement integer values. For a multibit left-shift of a signed integer value, if the sign bit ever changes during the shift, then overflow has occurred. Therefore, the OF bit in the flags register is *not* a true indication of overflow when dealing with a multibit left-shift of a signed integer value.

FIGURE 6.3
SAL and SHL
instructions

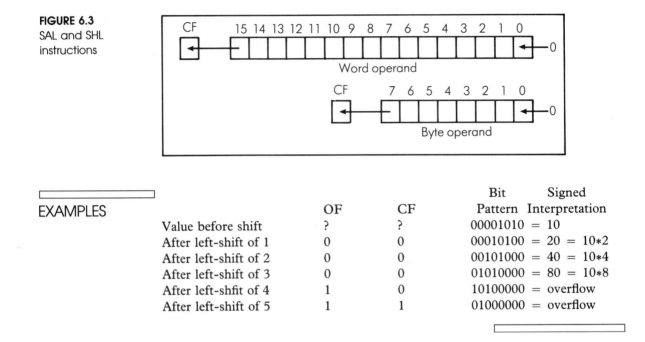

EXAMPLES

	OF	CF	Bit Pattern		Signed Interpretation
Value before shift	?	?	00001010	=	10
After left-shift of 1	0	0	00010100	=	20 = 10*2
After left-shift of 2	0	0	00101000	=	40 = 10*4
After left-shift of 3	0	0	01010000	=	80 = 10*8
After left-shfit of 4	1	0	10100000	=	overflow
After left-shift of 5	1	1	01000000	=	overflow

The arithmetic shift operation provides an extremely efficient method for multiplying and dividing signed integer values by powers of 2. To double a signed integer value, simply perform an arithmetic left-shift of 1 bit. For signed integer values, the OF bit in the flags register will correctly reflect whether or not an overflow occurred because of the shift operation. To divide a signed integer value in half, simply perform an arithmetic right-shift of 1 bit. The CF bit in the flags register is the remainder of this division by 2.

In addition to the CF and OF bits, the arithmetic shift instructions affect the SF, ZF, AF, and PF bits in the flags register:

If the result of the shift operation has the MSB (sign bit) set, then the SF bit in the flags register is set following execution of an arithmetic shift instruction; otherwise, the SF bit is cleared.

If the result of the arithmetic shift operation is zero, then the ZF bit in the flags register is set; otherwise, the ZF bit is cleared.

The AF bit in the flags register is undefined following execution of an arithmetic shift instruction.

The PF bit in the flags register reflects the parity of the low-order 8 bits of the result of the arithmetic shift operation.

Logical Shift

A **logical shift** operation treats the operand as an unsigned integer value. The operation code for a **logical right-shift** is SHR. With the SHR instruction, the

FIGURE 6.4
SHR instruction

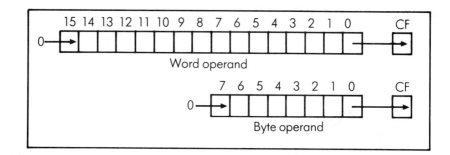

FIGURE 6.4
SHR instruction

bit that is shifted into the MSB is always 0 (Figure 6.4). Given an unsigned integer value, x, a logical right-shift of n bits produces the unsigned integer value $\lfloor x/2^n \rfloor$.

EXAMPLES

				CF
Value before shift	00101000 =	40		?
After right-shift of 1	00010100 =	20 =	40/2	0
After right-shift of 2	00001010 =	10 =	40/4	0
After right-shift of 3	00000101 =	5 =	40/8	0
After right-shift of 4	00000010 =	2 =	$\lfloor 40/16 \rfloor$	1

				CF
Value before shift	11011000 =	216		?
After right-shift of 1	01101100 =	108 =	216/2	0
After right-shift of 2	00110110 =	54 =	216/4	0
After right-shift of 3	00011011 =	27 =	216/8	0
After right-shift of 4	00001101 =	13 =	$\lfloor 216/16 \rfloor$	1

The operation code for a **logical left-shift** operation is SHL, which behaves exactly like a SAL instruction (Figure 6.3). In fact, SAL and SHL are two operation codes that produce exactly the same machine language instruction.

The logical shift operation provides an extremely efficient method for multiplying and dividing unsigned integer values by powers of 2. To double an unsigned integer value, simply perform a logical left-shift of 1 bit. The CF bit in the flags register will correctly reflect overflow. For a multibit left-shift of an unsigned integer value, if the CF bit in the flags register ever receives a 1 during the shift operation, even though its final value may not be a 1, then overflow has occurred. Therefore, the CF bit in the flags register is *not* a true indication of overflow in the case of the multibit left-shift of an unsigned integer.

The following example shows a sequence of single-bit, left-shift operations on an 8-bit value. Both signed and unsigned integer interpretations are given, and the effect on the OF and CF bits of the flags register is shown.

EXAMPLE	OF	CF		Signed Interpretation	Unsigned Interpretation
	0	0	00001010	= 10	= 10
	0	0	00010100	= 20 = 10*2	= 20 = 10*2
	0	0	00101000	= 40 = 10*4	= 40 = 10*4
	0	0	01010000	= 80 = 10*8	= 80 = 10*8
	1	0	10100000	= overflow	= 160 = 10*16
	1	1	01000000	= overflow	= overflow

To divide an unsigned integer value in half, simply perform a logical right-shift of 1 bit. The CF bit in the flags register is the remainder of this division by 2.

In addition to the CF and OF bits, the logical shift instructions affect the SF, ZF, AF, and PF bits in the flags register:

If the result of the shift operation has the MSB set, then the SF bit in the flags register is set following execution of a logical shift instruction; otherwise, the SF bit is cleared.

If the result of the logical shift operation is zero, then the ZF bit in the flags register is set; otherwise, the ZF bit is cleared.

The AF bit in the flags register is undefined following execution of a logical shift instruction.

The PF bit in the flags register reflects the parity of the low-order 8 bits of the result of the logical shift operation.

Rotate

A **rotate** operation treats the operand as if it were a circular collection of bits. That is, it treats the MSB as if it were physically adjacent to the LSB. Bit values shifted from one end of the operand are shifted back into the other end. The IBM PC Assembly language has two types of rotate operations: the *straight rotate* and the *rotate-through-carry flag*.

Straight Rotate

A **straight rotate** operation treats the carry flag as if it were separate from the operand itself. The carry flag is used to record the last bit rotated from one end of the operand and into the other end. The operation code for a **right rotate** instruction is ROR. With the ROR instruction, the bit value that is shifted into the MSB is the bit value that was shifted from the LSB (Figure 6.5).

The operation code for a **left rotate** instruction is ROL. With the ROL instruction, the bit value that is shifted into the LSB is the bit value that was shifted from the MSB (Figure 6.6).

FIGURE 6.5
ROR instruction

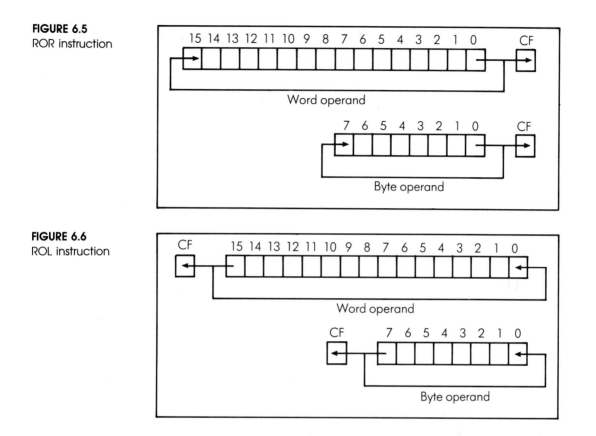

FIGURE 6.6
ROL instruction

Rotate-through-Carry Flag

A **rotate-through-carry flag** operation treats the carry flag as a 1-bit extension of the operand. The carry flag is treated as a bit that lies between the MSB and the LSB of the operand. The operation code for the **right rotate-through-carry** operation is RCR. With the RCR instruction, the bit value that is shifted out of the LSB is shifted into the carry flag, and the bit value that is shifted from the carry flag is shifted into the MSB (Figure 6.7).

The operation code for the **left rotate-through-carry** operation is RCL. With the RCL instruction, the bit value that is shifted from the MSB is shifted into the carry flag, and the bit that is shifted from the carry flag is shifted into the LSB (Figure 6.8).

Programming Example—Shift Instructions

Program Listing 6.1 demonstrates the various shift operations in the IBM PC Assembly language. The program places a value in the AX-register and then moves through a sequence of shift operations. After each shift operation, a call to the PUTBIN procedure is made to display the resulting register value in binary form.

FIGURE 6.7
RCR instruction

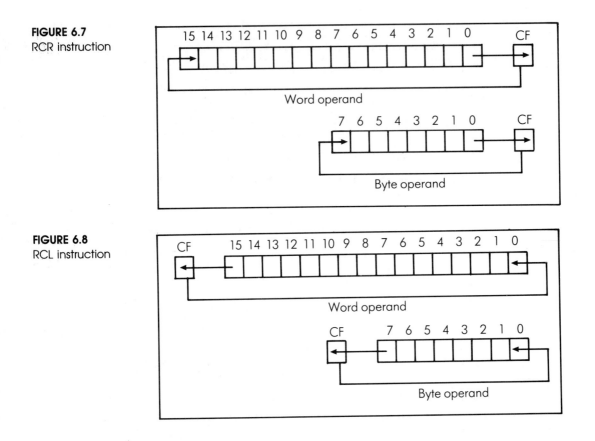

Word operand

Byte operand

FIGURE 6.8
RCL instruction

Word operand

Byte operand

The MOV instruction in line 23 sets the display code for the PUTBIN procedure to request WORD output. Since the BL-register is not used for any other purpose in the program, and since the BL-register value is protected by all external procedures referenced, this MOV operation only has to be performed once. That is, the BL-register value remains constant as far as this program is concerned, and therefore, it does not have to be set up for subsequent calls to PUTBIN.

The MOV instruction in line 24 initializes the AX-register value to AAAB hexadecimal. The two CALL instructions in lines 28 and 29 cause the value 1010101010101011 to be displayed in binary on a line by itself.

The ROL instruction in line 30, which is a rotate operation, shifts this value left 1 bit position, thus the bit shifted out on the left (1) is shifted back into the vacated bit position on the right. The bit rotated out on the left and back in on the right (1) is also recorded in the CF bit of the flags register. The two CALL instructions in lines 34 and 35 display the resulting value, 0101010101010111, by itself on the next line of the display screen.

The MOV instruction in line 36 sets the CL-register to 3 in preparation for a 3-bit shift operation. The ROR instruction in line 37, which is a

```
 1: ;                      PROGRAM LISTING 6.1
 2: ;
 3: ;PROGRAM TO DEMONSTRATE SHIFT AND ROTATE INSTRUCTIONS
 4: ;
 5:                                         ;PROCEDURES TO
 6:             EXTRN    PUTBIN:FAR          ;DISPLAY BINARY INTEGER
 7:             EXTRN    NEWLINE:FAR         ;DISPLAY NEWLINE CHARACTER
 8: ;
 9: ; S T A C K   S E G M E N T   D E F I N I T I O N
10: ;
11: STACK       SEGMENT STACK
12:             DB       256 DUP(?)
13: STACK       ENDS
14: ;
15: ; C O D E   S E G M E N T   D E F I N I T I O N
16: ;
17: CODE        SEGMENT
18: EX_6_1      PROC     FAR
19:             ASSUME   CS:CODE,SS:STACK
20:             PUSH     DS                  ;PUSH RETURN SEG ADDR ON STACK
21:             MOV      AX,0               ;PUSH RETURN OFFSET OF ZERO
22:             PUSH     AX                  ;ON STACK
23:             MOV      BL,1               ;DISPLAY CODE - WORD OUTPUT
24:             MOV      AX,0AAABH          ;LOAD AX WITH
25:                                         ;
26:                                         ;1010101010101011
27:                                         ;
28:             CALL     PUTBIN             ;DISPLAY CONTENTS OF AX
29:             CALL     NEWLINE            ;DISPLAY NEWLINE CHARACTER
30:             ROL      AX,1               ;LEFT ROTATE AX 1 GIVING
31:                                         ;
32:                                         ;0101010101010111
33:                                         ;
34:             CALL     PUTBIN             ;DISPLAY CONTENTS OF AX
35:             CALL     NEWLINE            ;DISPLAY NEWLINE CHARACTER
36:             MOV      CL,3               ;MOVE SHIFT COUNT TO CL
37:             ROR      AX,CL              ;RIGHT ROTATE AX 3 GIVING
38:                                         ;
39:                                         ;1110101010101010
40:                                         ;
41:             CALL     PUTBIN             ;DISPLAY CONTENTS OF AX
42:             CALL     NEWLINE            ;DISPLAY NEWLINE CHARACTER
43:             SAR      AX,1               ;ARITH SHIFT RIGHT 1 GIVING
44:                                         ;
45:                                         ;1111010101010101
46:                                         ;
47:             CALL     PUTBIN             ;DISPLAY CONTENTS OF AX
48:             CALL     NEWLINE            ;DISPLAY NEWLINE CHARACTER
49:             SAL      AX,CL              ;ARITH SHIFT LEFT 3 GIVING
50:                                         ;
51:                                         ;1010101010101000
52:                                         ;
53:             CALL     PUTBIN             ;DISPLAY CONTENTS OF AX
54:             CALL     NEWLINE            ;DISPLAY NEWLINE CHARACTER
55:*;


56: ;
57:             MOV      CL,2               ;MOVE SHIFT COUNT TO CL
58:             SHR      AX,CL              ;LOG. SHIFT RIGHT 2 GIVING
```

```
 59:                                        ;
 60:                                        ;0010101010101010
 61:                                        ;
 62:              CALL      PUTBIN           ;DISPLAY CONTENTS OF AX
 63:              CALL      NEWLINE          ;DISPLAY NEWLINE
 64:              MOV       CL,3             ;MOVE SHIFT COUNT TO CL
 65:              SHL       AX,CL            ;LOG.SHIFT LEFT 3 GIVING
 66:                                        ;
 67:                                        ;0101010101010000
 68:                                        ;
 69:                                        ;AND CARRY FLAG = 1
 70:              CALL      PUTBIN           ;DISPLAY CONTENTS OF AX
 71:              CALL      NEWLINE          ;DISPLAY NEWLINE CHARACTER
 72:              RCL       AX,1             ;LEFT ROTATE AX 1 THROUGH
 73:                                        ;CARRY GIVING
 74:                                        ;
 75:                                        ;1010101010100001
 76:                                        ;
 77:                                        ;AND CARRY FLAG = 0
 78:              CALL      PUTBIN           ;DISPLAY CONTENTS OF AX
 79:              CALL      NEWLINE          ;DISPLAY NEWLINE CHARACTER
 80:              MOV       CL,2             ;
 81:              RCR       AX,CL            ;RIGHT ROTATE AX 2 THROUGH
 82:                                        ;CARRY GIVING
 83:                                        ;
 84:                                        ;1010101010101000
 85:                                        ;
 86:              CALL      PUTBIN           ;DISPLAY CONTENTS OF AX
 87:              CALL      NEWLINE          ;DISPLAY NEWLINE CHARACTER
 88:              MOV       CL,4             ;MOVE SHIFT COUNT TO CL
 89:              SAR       AL,CL            ;ARITH RIGHT SHIFT AL 4 GIVING
 90:                                        ;
 91:                                        ;1010101011111010
 92:                                        ;
 93:              CALL      PUTBIN           ;DISPLAY CONTENTS OF AX
 94:              CALL      NEWLINE          ;DISPLAY NEWLINE CHARACTER
 95:              ROL       AL,CL            ;LEFT ROTATE AL 4 GIVING
 96:                                        ;
 97:                                        ;1010101010101111
 98:                                        ;
 99:              CALL      PUTBIN           ;DISPLAY CONTENTS OF AX
100:              CALL      NEWLINE          ;DISPLAY NEWLINE CHARACTER
101:              RET                        ;RETURN
102: EX_6_1       ENDP
103: CODE         ENDS
104:*             END       EX_6_1
```

rotate operation, shifts the value in the AX-register right 3 bit positions, thus the three bits shifted out on the right (111) are shifted back into the vacated bit positions on the left. The last bit rotated out on the right and back in on the left (1) is also recorded in the CF bit of the flags register. The resulting value, 1110101010101010, in the AX-register is displayed by itself on the next line of the display screen (lines 41 and 42).

The SAR instruction in line 43, an arithmetic right-shift operation, shifts this value right 1 bit position, thus the bit shifted out on the right (0) is recorded in the CF bit of the flags register, and a copy of the sign bit (1) is shifted into the vacated bit position on the left. The resulting value in the AX-register, 1111010101010101, is displayed by itself on the next line of the display screen (lines 47 and 48).

Since the value in the CL-register is still 3, the SAL instruction in line 49, an arithmetic left-shift operation, shifts the value in the AX-register left 3 bit positions, thus the three bits (111) shifted out on the left are lost (except for the last one [1], which is recorded in the CF bit of the flags register), and zeros are shifted into the vacated bit positions on the right. The resulting value in the AX-register, 1010101010101000, is displayed by itself on the next line of the display screen (lines 53 and 54).

The MOV instruction in line 57 sets the CL-register to 2 in preparation for a 2-bit shift operation. The SHR instruction in line 58, a logical right-shift operation, shifts the value in the AX-register right 2 bit positions, thus the first zero shifted out on the right is lost, the second zero shifted out on the right is recorded in the CF bit of the flags register, and zeros are shifted into the vacated bit positions on the left. The resulting value in the AX-register, 0010101010101010, is displayed by itself on the next line of the display screen (lines 62 and 63).

The MOV instruction in line 64 sets the CL-register to 3 in preparation for a 3-bit shift operation. The SHL instruction in line 65, a logical left-shift operation, shifts the value in the AX-register left 3 bit positions, thus the three bits (001) shifted out on the left are lost (except for the last bit [1], which is recorded in the CF bit of the flags register), and zeros are shifted into the vacated bit positions on the right. The resulting value in the AX-register, 0101010101010000, is displayed by itself on the next line of the display screen (lines 70 and 71).

Since the last bit shifted out on the previous shift operation (line 65) was a 1, and since PUTBIN and NEWLINE save and restore the flags register for the caller, the value in the CF bit of the flags register is a 1 just prior to execution of the RCL instruction in line 72. This instruction, a rotate-through-carry operation, shifts the value in the AX-register left 1 bit position, thus the value in the CF bit of the flags register (1) is shifted into the vacated bit position on the right, and the bit shifted out on the left (0) is recorded in the CF bit of the flags register. The resulting value in the AX-register, 1010101010100001, is displayed by itself on the next line of the display screen (lines 78 and 79).

The MOV instruction in line 80 sets the CL-register to 2 in preparation for a 2-bit shift operation. The CF bit in the flags register is zero, the result of the previous shift operation. The RCR instruction in line 81 shifts the value in the AX-register (extended to include the CF bit of the flags register) right 2 bit positions. The 17-bit value being shifted is 0 1010101010100001. Since this is a rotate operation, the two bits rotated out on the right (01) are rotated into the vacated bit positions on the left. (The 1 goes into bit 15 of the AX-register, and the 0 goes into the CF bit of the flags register.) The resulting value in the AX-register, 1010101010101000, is displayed by itself on the next line of the display screen (lines 86 and 87).

The MOV instruction in line 88 sets the CL-register to 4 in preparation for a 4-bit shift operation. The SAR instruction in line 89, an arithmetic right-shift operation, shifts the value in the AL-register right 4 bit positions, thus the last bit (1) of the 1000 shifted out on the right is recorded in the CF bit of the flags register, and a copy of the sign bit (1) is copied into the 4 vacated bit positions on the left. Since this is an AL-register shift, the value in the AH-register is unchanged by execution of this instruction. The resulting value in the AX-register, 1010101011111010, is displayed by itself on the next line of the display screen (lines 93 and 94).

The ROL instruction in line 95, a rotate operation, shifts the value in the AL-register left 4 bit positions, thus the 4 bits rotated out on the left (1111) are rotated back into the vacated bit positions on the right. The last bit rotated out on the left and back in on the right (1) is also recorded in the CF bit of the flags register. Since this is a shift of the AL-register, the AH-register is not changed by execution of this instruction. The resulting value in the AX-register, 1010101010101111, is displayed by itself on the next line of the display screen (lines 99 and 100).

The complete output for this program is as follows:

```
1010101010101011
0101010101010111
1110101010101010
1111010101010101
1010101010101000
0010101010101010
0101010101010000
1010101010100001
1010101010101000
1010101011111010
1010101010101111
```

To see this program's operation more vividly, especially with regard to the setting of the CF bit of the flags register, trace its execution using the DEBUG utility program.

6.2   Logical Operations

The **logical operations** treat each bit of an operand as a **Boolean value**. A bit value of zero represents the Boolean value False, and a bit value of one represents the Boolean value True. In the IBM PC Assembly language, the logical instructions provide the Boolean operations AND, Inclusive OR, Exclusive OR and NOT.

The AND operation is provided by the **AND instruction**, which has the following general form:

[⟨*label*⟩] AND ⟨*destination*⟩, ⟨*source*⟩ [⟨*comment*⟩]

Execution of an AND instruction ANDs each bit of the destination operand with the corresponding bit of the source operand, replacing that bit in the destination operand with the result. Table 6.1 is a truth table that defines the AND operation.

Figure 6.9 shows the possible combinations of destination and source operands for the AND instruction. If the destination operand is a general register, then the source operand can be either a general register, a memory location, or an immediate value. If the destination operand is a memory location, then the source operand can be either a general register or an immediate value. The types of the two operands must match (i.e., both must be byte, or both must be word).

TABLE 6.1
Definition of the AND operation

Source Bit	Destination Bit	AND
0	0	0
0	1	0
1	0	0
1	1	1

FIGURE 6.9
Allowable operands for AND, OR, and XOR instructions

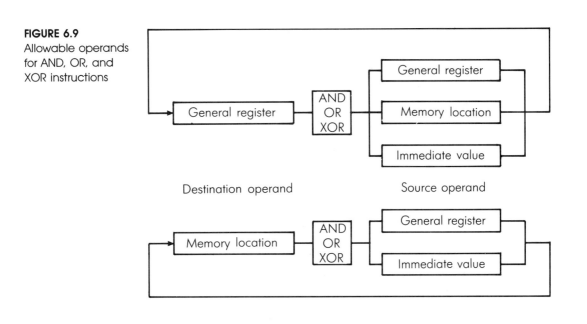

AND AL,BL   AND each bit in the AL-register with the corresponding bit in
             the BL-register, leaving the result in that bit of the AL-register.
00110011   AL-register before execution of AND
01010101   BL-register
00010001   AL-register after execution of AND

The inclusive OR operation is provided by the **OR instruction**, which has the following general form:

[⟨*label*⟩] OR ⟨*destination*⟩,⟨*source*⟩   [⟨*comment*⟩]

Execution of an OR instruction performs the inclusive OR of each bit of the destination operand with the corresponding bit of the source operand, replacing that bit in the destination operand with the result. Table 6.2 is a truth table that defines the inclusive OR operation. Figure 6.9 also shows the possible combinations of destination and source operands for the OR operation. The types of the two operands must match (i.e., both must be byte, or both must be word).

OR AL,55H   OR each bit in the AL-register with the corresponding bit in the
             immediate value 01010101, leaving the result in that bit of the
             AL-register.
00110011   AL-register before execution of OR
01010101   Immediate operand
01110111   AL-register after execution of OR

The exclusive OR operation is provided by the **XOR instruction**, which has the following general form:

[⟨*label*⟩] XOR ⟨*destination*⟩, ⟨*source*⟩   [⟨*comment*⟩]

Execution of an XOR instruction performs the exclusive OR of each bit of the destination operand with the corresponding bit of the source operand, replacing that bit in the destination operand with the result. Table 6.3 is a truth table that

TABLE 6.2
Definition of the OR operation

Source Bit	Destination Bit	OR
0	0	0
0	1	1
1	0	1
1	1	1

TABLE 6.3
Definition of the
XOR operation

Source Bit	Destination Bit	XOR
0	0	0
0	1	1
1	0	1
1	1	0

defines the exclusive OR operation. Figure 6.9 also shows the possible combinations of destination and source operands for the XOR operation. The types of the two operands must match (i.e., both must be byte, or both must be word).

EXAMPLE

XOR AL,33H	Exclusive OR each bit in the AL-register with the corresponding bit in the immediate value 00110011, leaving the result in that bit of the AL-register.
01010101	AL-register before execution of XOR
00110011	Immediate operand
01100110	AL-register after execution of XOR

The AND, OR, and XOR instructions affect the OF, SF, ZF, AF, PF, and CF bits of the flags register:

The OF bit in the flags register is cleared by the execution of an AND, OR, or XOR instruction.

If the result of the logical operation has the MSB set, then the SF bit in the flags register is set; otherwise, the SF bit is cleared.

If the result of the logical operation is zero, then the ZF bit in the flags register is set; otherwise, the ZF bit is cleared.

The AF bit in the flags register is undefined following execution of an AND, OR, or XOR instruction.

If the low-order 8 bits of the result of the logical operation have an even number of 1 bits, then the PF bit in the flags register is set; otherwise, the PF bit is cleared.

The CF bit in the flags register is cleared by execution of an AND, OR, or XOR instruction.

The AND operation is frequently used to isolate a bit or group of bits (i.e., to clear out the bits that are not needed). The OR operation is frequently used to set certain bits or to merge bits together.

EXAMPLE

Suppose the byte value in the variable COUNTS represents two 4-bit mod 16 counters. A mod 16 counter is one that counts from 0 to 15 and back to 0 again, producing the following sequence of binary counts:

```
0000
0001
0010
0011
    .
    .
    .
1101
1110
1111
0000
0001
0010
0011
    .
    .
    .
```

The following sequence of instructions will increment the counter in the low-order 4 bits (right nibble), leaving the counter in the high-order 4 bits (left nibble) unchanged:

```
MOV AL, COUNTS
INC AL
AND AL, ØFH
AND COUNTS, ØFØH
OR  COUNTS, AL
```

The first instruction moves a copy of the two counters into the AL-register. The second instruction increments the counter in the right nibble of the AL-register, which may cause an overflow into the counter in the left nibble of the AL-register, but the counter in the right nibble has been correctly incremented in a mod 16 fashion. The third instruction clears the left nibble of the AL-register, which now has its left nibble clear, and its right nibble contains the incremented low-order counter. The fourth instruction clears the counter in the right nibble of the variable COUNTS, which now has its right nibble clear, and its left nibble has the high-order counter unchanged. The last instruction merges the two counters into the two nibbles of the variable COUNTS.

Traces of this instruction sequence for two initial values of COUNTS are given:

```
                    COUNTS   AL-Register
                    0110 0101
MOV AL, COUNTS      0110 0101 0110 0101
INC AL              0110 0101 0110 0110
AND AL, ØFH         0110 0101 0000 0110
AND COUNTS, ØFØH    0110 0000 0000 0110
OR  COUNTS, AL      0110 0110 0000 0110
```

```
                              COUNTS   AL-Register
                              0011 1111
MOV  AL, COUNTS               0011 1111 0011 1111
INC  AL                       0011 1111 0100 0000
AND  AL, ØFH                  0011 1111 0000 0000
AND  COUNTS, ØFØH  0011 0000 0000 0000
OR   COUNTS, AL    0011 0000 0000 0000
```

The NOT operation is provided by the **NOT instruction**, which has the following general form:

[⟨*label*⟩] NOT ⟨*destination*⟩   [⟨*comment*⟩]

Execution of the NOT instruction inverts each bit of the destination operand, thus performing the one's complement operation. Table 6.4 is a truth table that defines the NOT operation. The destination operand can be either a general register or a memory location, and it can be either byte or word. None of the flags are affected by execution of this instruction.

EXAMPLE

NOT AL   Inverts each bit in the AL-register
00110101   AL-register before execution of NOT
11001010   AL-register after execution of NOT

The NOT operation inverts every bit of a bit pattern, and the XOR instruction can be used to invert certain bits of a bit pattern.

EXAMPLE

Suppose the PF bit in the flags register is to be inverted. The following instructions invert the PF bit, leaving the other flag bits unchanged:

```
PUSHF
POP   AX
XOR   AX, 0004H
PUSH  AX
POPF
```

The first two instructions copy the flags register into the AX-register. The third instruction inverts bit 2 of the AX-register. Bit 2 of the flags register is the PF bit. The last two instructions copy the modified flags from the AX-register to the flags register.

TABLE 6.4
Definition of the NOT operation

Destination Bit	NOT
0	1
1	0

The AND operation can be used to test a single bit to see if it is set. For example, to determine if an integer is odd or even, a test of the least-significant bit (LSB) can be made: If the LSB is 1, then the integer is odd; if the LSB is 0, then the integer is even. To determine if the value in the AX-register is odd or even, the following instructions can be used:

```
AND AX, 0001
JZ  EVEN
```

If the jump is taken, then the number that was in the AX-register just before execution of the AND instruction was even; if the jump is *not* taken, then that number was odd. The value in the AX-register is modified by execution of the AND instruction. However, that value may be needed in one or both decision alternatives.

The IBM PC Assembly language provides a bit test instruction, the **TEST instruction**, that behaves like the AND instruction except that the destination operand is not modified (i.e., the result is not saved). This instruction has the following general form:

[⟨*label*⟩] TEST ⟨*destination*⟩, ⟨*source*⟩   [⟨*comment*⟩]

Execution of a TEST instruction ANDs each bit of the destination operand with the corresponding bit of the source operand and sets the flags to reflect the result. Neither the source operand nor the destination operand is modified. Note that the TEST instruction relates to the AND instruction in the same way that the CMP instruction relates to the SUB instruction.

Figure 6.10 shows the possible combinations of destination and source operands for the TEST instruction. If the destination operand is a general

FIGURE 6.10
Allowable operands for the TEST instruction

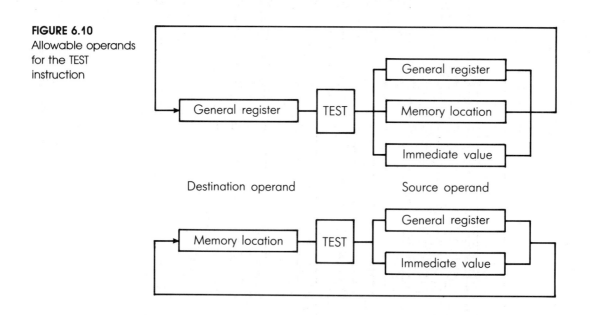

register, then the source operand can be either a general register, a memory location, or an immediate value. If the destination operand is a memory location, then the source operand can be either a general register or an immediate value. The types of the two operands must match (i.e., both must be byte, or both must be word). The bits of the flags register are affected in exactly the same way as they are for the AND instruction.

EXAMPLE

To test the value in the AX-register to determine if it is odd or even, without changing this value, the following instructions can be used:

```
TEST AX,0001
JZ   EVEN
```

If the jump is taken, then the value in the AX-register is even; if the jump is *not* taken, then the value in the AX-register is odd. In either case, the value in the AX-register is not modified by this decision.

Programming Example—Logical Instructions

Program Listing 6.2 demonstrates the various logical operations in the IBM PC Assembly language. The program places a value in the AX-register and then goes through a sequence of logical operations, each involving the AX-register. After each logical operation, a call to the PUTBIN procedure is made to display the resulting value in binary form.

The MOV instruction in line 23 sets the display code for the PUTBIN procedure to request word output. This value will remain in the BL-register throughout program execution, and does not have to be reestablished prior to each call to PUTBIN.

The MOV instruction in line 25 initializes the AX-register value to 5555 hexadecimal. The two CALL instructions in lines 27 and 28 cause the value 0101010101010101 to be displayed on a line by itself.

The MOV instruction in line 30 loads the CX-register with the value 3F3F hexadecimal, which is 0011111100111111 in binary. The AND instruction in line 31 ANDs the AX-register value with the CX-register value, leaving the result in the AX-register. The operation performed is shown as follows:

$$
\begin{array}{rl}
\text{AX-register} & 0101010101010101 \\
\text{AND CX-register} & \underline{0011111100111111} \\
\text{AX-register} & 0001010100010101
\end{array}
$$

The two CALL instructions in lines 34 and 35 cause the resulting value, 0001010100010101, to be displayed on a line by itself.

The OR instruction in line 37 ORs the AX-register value with the immediate value 4343 hexadecimal, which is 0100001101000011 in binary, leaving the result

```
 1: ;                   PROGRAM LISTING 6.2
 2: ;
 3: ; PROGRAM TO DEMONSTRATE LOGICAL INSTRUCTIONS
 4: ;
 5:                                         ;PROCEDURES TO
 6:             EXTRN    PUTBIN:FAR          ;DISPLAY BINARY NUMBERS
 7:             EXTRN    NEWLINE:FAR         ;DISPLAY NEWLINE CHARACTER
 8: ;
 9: ; S T A C K   S E G M E N T   D E F I N I T I O N
10: ;
11: STACK       SEGMENT STACK
12:             DB       256 DUP(?)
13: STACK       ENDS
14: ;
15: ; C O D E   S E G M E N T   D E F I N I T I O N
16: ;
17: CODE        SEGMENT
18: EX_6_2      PROC     FAR
19:             ASSUME   CS:CODE,SS:STACK
20:             PUSH     DS                 ;PUSH RETURN SEG ADDR ON STACK
21:             MOV      AX,0               ;PUSH RETURN OFFSET OF ZERO
22:             PUSH     AX                 ;ON STACK
23:             MOV      BL,1               ;MOVE CODE FOR WORD OUTPUT TO BL
24:                                         ;
25:             MOV      AX,5555H           ;LOAD AX WITH 0101010101010101
26:                                         ;
27:             CALL     PUTBIN             ;DISPLAY CONTENTS OF AX
28:             CALL     NEWLINE            ;SKIP TO NEXT LINE
29:                                         ;
30:             MOV      CX,3F3FH           ;LOAD CX WITH 0011111100111111
31:             AND      AX,CX              ;AND AX WITH CX
32:                                         ;GIVING        0001010100010101
33:                                         ;
34:             CALL     PUTBIN             ;DISPLAY CONTENTS OF AX
35:             CALL     NEWLINE            ;SKIP TO NEXT LINE
36:                                         ;
37:             OR       AX,4343H           ;OR AX WITH    0100001101000011
38:                                         ;GIVING        0101011101010111
39:                                         ;
40:             CALL     PUTBIN             ;DISPLAY CONTENTS OF AX
41:             CALL     NEWLINE            ;SKIP TO NEXT LINE
42:                                         ;
43:             XOR      AX,33CCH           ;EXCLUSIVE OR AX WITH
44:                                         ;
45:                                         ;              0011001111001100
46:                                         ;GIVING        0110010010011011
47:                                         ;
48:             CALL     PUTBIN             ;DISPLAY CONTENTS OF AX
49:             CALL     NEWLINE            ;SKIP TO NEXT LINE
50:                                         ;
51:             NOT      AX                 ;TAKE 1'S COMPLEMENT OF AX
52:                                         ;GIVING        1001101101100100
53:                                         ;
54:             CALL     PUTBIN             ;DISPLAY CONTENTS OF AX
55:             CALL     NEWLINE            ;SKIP TO NEXT LINE
56:                                         ;
57:             OR       AH,AL              ;OR AH WITH AL
58:                                         ;GIVING        1111111101100100
59:                                         ;
60:             CALL     PUTBIN             ;DISPLAY CONTENTS OF AX
61:             CALL     NEWLINE            ;SKIP TO NEXT LINE
```

```
62:              RET                               ;RETURN
63: EX_6_2      ENDP
64: CODE        ENDS
65:*            END        EX_6_2
*
```

in the AX-register. The operation performed is shown as follows:

$$
\begin{array}{ll}
\text{AX-register} & 0001010100010101 \\
\text{OR immediate} & \underline{0100001101000011} \\
\text{AX-register} & 0101011101010111
\end{array}
$$

The two CALL instructions in lines 40 and 41 cause the resulting value, 0101011101010111, to be displayed on a line by itself.

The XOR instruction in line 43 performs the bit-by-bit exclusive OR of the AX-register value with the immediate value 33CC hexadecimal, which is 0011001111001100 in binary, leaving the result in the AX-register. The operation performed is shown as follows:

$$
\begin{array}{ll}
\text{AX-register} & 0101011101010111 \\
\text{XOR immediate} & \underline{0011001111001100} \\
\text{AX-register} & 0110010010011011
\end{array}
$$

The two CALL instructions in lines 48 and 49 cause the resulting value, 0110010010011011, to be displayed on a line by itself.

The NOT instruction in line 51 inverts every bit of the value in the AX-register, leaving the result, 1001101101100100, in the AX-register. The two CALL instructions in lines 54 and 55 cause the resulting value, 1001101101100100, to be displayed on a line by itself.

The OR instruction in line 57 ORs the AH-register value with the AL-register value, leaving the result in the AH-register. The AL-register value is not modified by execution of this instruction. The operation performed is shown as follows:

$$
\begin{array}{ll}
\text{AH-register} & 10011011 \\
\text{OR AL-register} & \underline{01100100} \\
\text{AH-register} & 11111111
\end{array}
$$

The two CALL instructions in lines 60 and 61 cause the entire AX-register value, 1111111101100100, to be displayed on a line by itself.

The complete output of this program is as follows:

```
0101010101010101
0001010100010101
0101011101010111
0110010010011011
1001101101100100
1111111101100100
```

To see this program's operation more vividly, trace its execution using the DEBUG utility program.

6.3 Flag Bit Operations

Some applications require direct manipulation of certain bits in the flags register. As will be seen in Chapter 8, a group of IBM PC Assembly language instructions, called string instructions, automatically update an index register to address the next (or previous) character in a string or element in an array. The DF bit in the flags register is used to determine whether this automatic update is an increment or a decrement to the next character or array element. The program, therefore, must be able to set or clear the DF bit in the flags register directly.

As will be seen in Chapter 9, the IF bit in the flags register indicates whether or not external interrupts are enabled. Interrupt service procedures and input/output procedures must be able to set or clear the IF bit in the flags register directly.

Seven instructions provide for direct manipulation of bits in the flags register, and they have the following general form:

[⟨*label*⟩] ⟨*op code*⟩   [⟨*comment*⟩]

in which ⟨*op code*⟩ is one of the following seven operation codes: CMC, CLC, CLD, CLI, STC, STD, or STI.

> The **CMC instruction** complements the CF bit of the flags register.
> The **CLC instruction** clears the CF bit in the flags register.
> The **STC instruction** sets the CF bit in the flags register.
> The **CLD instruction** clears the DF bit in the flags register.
> The **STD instruction** sets the DF bit in the flags register.
> The **CLI instruction** clears the IF bit in the flags register.
> The **STI instruction** sets the IF bit in the flags register.

Only the indicated flag bit is affected by execution of one of these instructions. All other bits in the flags register remain unchanged.

To manipulate any of the other bits in the flags register, the flags register value must first be loaded into one of the general registers. The flags register value can be copied into the AX-register with the following sequence of instructions:

```
PUSHF
POP   AX
```

Once the flags register value has been copied into one of the general registers, the individual bits of this copy can be manipulated using shift and logical instructions. This modified copy of the flags register can then be copied back to the flags register, replacing the previous value of the flags register. The AX-register value can be copied into the flags register with the following sequence of instructions:

```
PUSH AX
POPF
```

The IBM PC Assembly language provides two additional instructions for moving values between the flags register and the accumulator register

(AX-register), the **LAHF** and **SAHF instructions**, which have the following general forms:

[⟨*label*⟩] LAHF   [⟨*comment*⟩]

[⟨*label*⟩] SAHF   [⟨*comment*⟩]

The LAHF instruction loads the AH-register with a copy of the value in the low-order half of the flags register, which is diagrammed in Figure 6.11. The SAHF instruction copies the AH-register value into the low-order half of the flags register.

These two instructions are provided in the Intel 8086/8088 machine language for compatibility with the Intel 8080/8085 microprocessors. They are not very useful for beginning IBM PC Assembly language programmers.

FIGURE 6.11
Low-order half of flags register

7	6	5	4	3	2	1	0
SF	ZF		AF		PF		CF

Programming Example—Display Binary Integer (PUTBIN Version 2)

6.4

Program Listing 6.3 shows an external procedure, called PUT_BIN, that displays an 8- or 16-bit integer in binary form. From a functional standpoint, this procedure behaves exactly like the external subprocedure in Program Listing 5.3. It accepts a code in the BL-register that specifies whether 8-bit (BL = 0) or 16-bit (BL ≠ 0) output is desired. It also accepts the value to be displayed in either the AL-register (8-bit display) or the AX-register (16-bit display). It displays the input value in binary form on the screen beginning at the current cursor position.

This version of the PUT_BIN procedure implements an algorithm different from the version in Program Listing 5.3. The previous version repeatedly divides by 2, saving the remainder each time until either 8 or 16 remainders have been produced. The remainders (0s and 1s) are displayed in the reverse order from which they are produced. The version in Program Listing 6.3 tests each individual bit of the input value, displaying a 1 if the bit is set and a 0 if the bit is not set.

Except for the algorithm itself, Program Listing 6.3 looks like Program Listing 5.3, and this discussion thus concentrates on the algorithm being implemented. The procedure begins by saving the registers it uses (lines 20–24). The double-alternative decision structure in lines 25–33 tests the input code in the BL-register (line 25). If the BL-register value is 0 (byte output), then the value to be displayed is shifted to the upper half of the AX-register (lines 27–28), and the bit count in the CX-register is set to 8 (line 29). If the BL-register value is nonzero, then the bit count in the CX-register is set to 16 (line 32). The rest of

```
 1: ;                      PROGRAM LISTING 6.3
 2: ;
 3: ; PROCEDURE TO DISPLAY AN 8- OR 16-BIT VALUE IN BINARY FORM
 4: ;
 5: ; INPUT:   AL-REG  8-BIT  VALUE TO BE DIAPLAYED
 6: ;          BL=0    CODE FOR  8-BIT DISPLAY
 7: ;              OR
 8: ;          AX-REG  16-BIT VALUE TO BE DISPLAYED
 9: ;          BL<>0   CODE FOR 16-BIT DISPLAY
10: ;
11: ; OUTPUT:  INPUT VALUE DISPLAYED IN BINARY FORM ON THE
12: ;          SCREEN BEGINNING AT CURRENT CURSOR POSITION
13: ;
14:                                        ;PROCEDURE TO
15:            EXTRN    PUTDEC:FAR          ;DISPLAY DECIMAL INTEGER
16: CODE       SEGMENT
17:            ASSUME   CS:CODE
18:            PUBLIC   PUT_BIN
19: PUT_BIN    PROC     FAR              ;PROCEDURE PUT_BIN(NUMBER,CODE)
20:            PUSH     AX                 ;SAVE REGISTERS
21:            PUSH     BX
22:            PUSH     DX
23:            PUSH     CX
24:            PUSHF                       ;SAVE FLAGS
25:            CMP      BL,0               ;IF   CODE = BYTE (BL=0)
26:            JNZ      ELSE
27:            MOV      CL,8               ;THEN LEFT JUSTIFY 8-BIT NUMBER
28:            SHL      AX,CL              ;     IN 16-BIT AX-REGISTER
29:            MUV      CX,8               ;        BIT_COUNT = 8
30:            JMP      ENDIF
31: ELSE:                                 ;ELSE
32:            MOV      CX,16              ;        BIT_COUNT = 16
33: ENDIF:                                ;ENDIF
34:            MOV      DX,AX              ;SAVE NUMBER IN DX
35:            MOV      BH,0               ;<PUTDEC DISPLAY CODE>
36: NEXT_BIT:                             ;REPEAT
37:            TEST     DX,8000H           ;   IF   BIT 15 OF NUMBER = 0
38:            JNZ      ONE
39:            MOV      AX,0               ;     THEN DISPLAY 0
40:            JMP      DISPLAY
41: ONE:                                  ;     ELSE
42:            MOV      AX,1               ;          DISPLAY 1
43: DISPLAY:
44:            CALL     PUTDEC             ;   ENDIF
45:            ROL      DX,1               ;   ROTATE NUMBER LEFT 1 BIT
46:                                        ;   TO GET NEXT BIT IN POS. 15
47:            LOOP     NEXT_BIT           ;   DECREMENT BIT_COUNT
48:                                        ;UNTIL BIT_COUNT = 0
49:            POPF                        ;RESTORE FLAGS
50:            POP      CX                 ;RESTORE REGISTERS
51:            POP      DX
52:            POP      BX
53:            POP      AX
54:            RET                         ;RETURN
55: PUT_BIN    ENDP                     ;END PUT_BIN
56: CODE       ENDS
57:*           END
```
*

the algorithm tests and displays the first 8 or 16 bits of the AX-register depending on the value of the bit count in the CX-register.

The input number is moved to the DX-register (line 34). The DX-register is used as the working register, since the AX-register is needed for displaying individual bits. The external PUTDEC procedure is used to display the individual bits. The display code, an input to the PUTDEC procedure, is placed in the BH-register (line 35), which causes each bit to be displayed as a single digit with no leading or trailing blanks.

The REPEAT-UNTIL loop in lines 36–48 tests and displays the first 8 or 16 bits of the DX-register. The double-alternative decision structure in lines 37–44 tests the next bit in the DX-register and displays a 1 or a 0 depending on whether or not the bit is set. The TEST instruction in line 37 checks to see if bit 15 of the DX-register (the next bit of the input number) is set. If it is set, then the jump in line 38 is taken, and the instruction in line 42 moves the value 1 into the AX-register; if it is reset, then the jump in line 38 is *not* taken, and the instruction in line 39 moves the value 0 into the AX-register. In both cases, a CALL is made to PUTDEC (line 44) to display the value just moved into the AX-register (0 or 1) with no leading or trailing blanks. The rotate instruction in line 45 shifts the next bit of the input number into bit position 15 of the DX-register in preparation for the next iteration of the REPEAT-UNTIL loop. The TEST instruction in line 37 always tests bit 15 of the DX-register. The ROL instruction in line 45 ensures that a different bit (the next bit) of the input number is in bit position 15 on each iteration of the loop. The LOOP instruction in line 47 decrements the bit count and transfers control to the top of the loop, if the bit count has not reached zero.

The procedure ends by restoring the registers that it used (lines 49–53) and returning control to the caller (line 54).

In the preceding algorithm, the bit pattern used for the test remains constant (1000000000000000). The value being displayed is rotated on each iteration to get its next bit into bit position 15 for testing. An alternative approach would be to keep the input number constant and to vary the bit pattern being used for the test. To accomplish such a task, place a

```
PUSH DI
```

instruction after line 22 in Program Listing 6.3, place a

```
POP  DI
```

instruction after line 50, and change lines 36–46 to the following code:

```
          MOV   DI,8000H    ;I = 15
NEXT_BIT:                   ;REPEAT
          TEST  DX,DI       ;   IF BIT I OF NUMBER=0
          JNZ   ONE
          MOV   AX,0        ;   THEN DISPLAY 0
          JMP   DISPLAY
ONE:                        ;   ELSE
          MOV   AX,1        ;       DISPLAY 1
```

```
DISPLAY:
          CALL PUTDEC    ;   ENDIF
          SHR  DI,1      ;   I = I - 1
```

The bit manipulation instructions are quite useful in certain character string operations and in operations involving BCD numbers. Character strings and BCD numbers are covered in detail in Chapters 8 and 11, respectively.

PROGRAMMING EXERCISES

6.1 Design a subalgorithm to compute the parity of a 16-bit integer value. Implement your algorithm with an IBM PC Assembly language external FAR procedure called PARITY. Your input should be a 16-bit value in the AX-register. Your output should be reflected in the PF bit of the flags register, in which

> PF = 1 implies that the parity of the input value is even.
>
> PF = 0 implies that the parity of the input value is odd.

Your procedure should save and restore all registers used including the flags register, except for the PF bit of the flags register that is used for the procedure output.

6.2 Write an IBM PC external FAR procedure called PUTFLAGS to display the flags register value. Your input should be the flags register. Your output should have the following form:

```
OF DF IF TF SF ZF AF PF CF
×1 ×2 ×3 ×4 ×5 ×6 ×7 ×8 ×9
```

in which xi is 0 or 1 depending on whether the corresponding flag bit is cleared or set.

6.3 Write an IBM PC Assembly language program to demonstrate your procedures from Programming Exercises 6.1 and 6.2. Your program should perform the following steps in sequence:

a. Accept a 16-bit integer input via the keyboard.
b. Display the input value in binary.
c. Call PUTFLAGS to display the flags register value.
d. Call PARITY to compute the parity of the input value.
e. Call PUTFLAGS to display the flags register. The PF bit in the flags register should correctly reflect the parity of the input value. All other flag bits should remain unchanged from the previous call to PUTFLAGS.

Demonstrate your program and subprocedures with the following inputs: 0, 32767, 33023, 33024, 21845, and 54613.

6.4 Modify Program Listing 6.1 to use your PUT-FLAGS procedure from Programming Exercise 6.2 to display the flags register prior to the display of each binary value. To obtain the entire output on one screen, display the binary value at the end of the second line of the flags display.

6.5 Design an algorithm to convert an n-bit binary number

$$b_1 b_2 b_3 \ldots b_n$$

to an n-bit gray code number

$$g_1 g_2 g_3 \ldots g_n$$

The following formulas describe this conversion process:

$$g_1 = b_1$$
$$g_i = b_i \oplus b_{i-1} \qquad \text{for } 2 \leq i \leq n$$

in which $\oplus$ is the exclusive OR operation. Implement your algorithm with an IBM PC Assembly language external FAR procedure called BIN_GRAY. Your input should be a 16-bit binary integer in the AX-register. Your output should be the corresponding gray code integer in the AX-register.

6.6 Design an algorithm to convert an n-bit gray code number

$$g_1 g_2 g_3 \ldots g_n$$

to an n-bit binary number

$$b_1 b_2 b_3 \ldots b_n$$

The following formulas describe this conversion process:

$$b_1 = g_1$$
$$b_i = g_i \oplus b_{i-1} \quad \text{for } 2 \leqslant i \leqslant n$$

in which $\oplus$ is the exclusive OR operation. Implement your algorithm with an IBM PC Assembly language external FAR procedure called GRAY_BIN. Your input should be a 16-bit gray code integer in the AX-register. Your output should be the corresponding binary integer in the AX-register.

6.7 Write an IBM PC Assembly language program to demonstrate your procedures from Programming Exercises 6.5 and 6.6. Your program should perform the following steps in sequence.

a. Accept a 16-bit integer input via the keyboard in decimal.
b. Call the PUTBIN procedure to display the input integer in binary.
c. Call your BIN_GRAY procedure to convert the input integer to gray code.
d. Call the PUBTIN procedure to display the gray code number.
e. Call your GRAY_BIN procedure to convert the integer back to binary.
f. Call the PUTBIN procedure to display the binary number.

Demonstrate your program and subprocedures with the following inputs: 5A0F, 00FF, 694B, and 33CC.

6.8 If the IBM PC were a one's complement machine rather than a two's complement machine, then the SAL instruction might execute as follows for a 1-bit shift of a 16-bit operand:

Bit i is shifted into bit $i + 1$ for $14 \leqslant i \leqslant 0$.
Bit 15 is shifted into the CF bit of the flags register and replaces the vacated bit, bit 0. If the sign bit (bit 15) changes, then the OF bit in the flags register is set; otherwise, the OF bit is cleared. All other flags are handled the same as for the two's complement SAL instruction.

A multiple-bit shift would behave like a sequence of 1-bit shift operations. The SAL

instruction for an 8-bit operand would execute in a similar manner.

Write an IBM PC external FAR procedure called SAL_1C to perform the left-shift of a signed integer in one's complement form according to the preceding specifications. Your inputs should be as follows:

AX-register contains the 16-bit value to be shifted.
BL-register contains a nonzero value to specify a word shift.
CL-register contains the shift count, or
AL-register contains the 8-bit value to be shifted.
BL-register contains 0 to specify a byte shift.
CL-register contains the shift count.

Your outputs should be the shifted value in the AX-register (AL-register), and the flags register should be modified according to the preceding specifications. All registers used by your procedure, except the ones used for procedure output, must be saved and restored.

6.9 The Boolean operator implication, denoted by the operator symbol $\Rightarrow$, is defined by the following truth table:

A	B	A $\Rightarrow$ B
0	0	1
0	1	1
1	0	0
1	1	1

Note that the implication operation is not commutative.

Write an IBM PC external FAR procedure to perform the implication operation on two 8-bit or two 16-bit operands. Your inputs should be as follows:

AX-register contains the 16-bit left operand.
DX-register contains the 16-bit right operand.
BL-register contains a nonzero value to specify a word operation, or
AL-register contains the 8-bit left operand.

AH-register contains the 8-bit right operand.

BL-register contains zero to specify a byte operation.

Your output should be the result of the implication operation in the AX-register (AL-register) with the flags register affected the same way as for the AND, OR, and XOR instructions.

All registers used by your procedure, except the ones used for procedure output, must be saved and restored.

6.10 Write a macro named STF that sets bit i of the flags register, in which i is the operand for the macro. Your macro can assume that i is an immediate value in the range 0–15, inclusive. That is, the macro reference

```
STF 11
```

should generate the code to set the OF bit of the flags register.

Write a macro named CLF that clears bit i of the flags register, in which i is the operand for the macro. Your macro can assume that i is an immediate value in the range 0–15, inclusive. That is, the macro reference

```
CLF 11
```

should generate the code to clear the OF bit of the flags register.

7 MULTIPLE PRECISION INTEGER ARITHMETIC USING THE CARRY FLAG

Chapter 3 introduced 8-bit and 16-bit integer arithmetic in the IBM PC. The ranges of integers that can be manipulated by these instructions are summarized in Table 7.1(a). The solution to a specific problem might require a larger range of integer values. For example, Program Listings 3.2 and 4.1 show programs that compute the sum of the first n cubes. The largest value of n that can be accommodated by the 16-bit integer arithmetic of these programs is 22. But, suppose the sum of the first 300 cubes is required. If the program could be modified to perform 32-bit integer arithmetic, then the largest value of n that could be accommodated would be over 300. Table 7.1(b) shows the signed and unsigned integer ranges for 32-bit binary numbers.

This chapter presents techniques for storing and performing arithmetic on integers that are larger than 16 bits. It introduces addition and subtraction instructions designed to aid in performing multiple precision integer arithmetic operations. The shift operations presented in Chapter 6 are expanded to accommodate integers whose size is a multiple of 8 or 16 bits.

7.1 Addition and Subtraction Using Carry/Borrow Flag

The CF bit of the flags register is used to record the carry out of the most-significant bit on an addition operation and to record the borrow into the most-significant bit on a subtraction operation, and it is required for multiple precision addition and subtraction operations. To add two 32-bit binary integers

TABLE 7.1
Integer ranges: (a)
8- and 16-bit
integer ranges and
(b) 32-bit integer
ranges

(a)

	Unsigned Integers	Signed Two's Complement
8-Bit	0–255	− 128–127
16-Bit	0–65535	− 32768–32767

(b)

	Unsigned Integers	Signed Two's Complement
32-Bit	0–4294967295	− 2147483648– + 2147483647

using 16-bit integer arithmetic, the following procedure can be used:

1. Add the low-order 16 bits of one operand to the low-order 16 bits of the second operand, producing the low-order 16 bits of the sum and the carry out of bit 15 into bit 16.

2. Add the high-order 16 bits of one operand, the high-order 16 bits of the other operand, and the carry from the addition of the low-order halves of the two operands. This addition produces the high-order 16 bits of the sum and the carry out of its most-significant bit (MSB).

Figure 7.1 illustrates this procedure giving hexadecimal and decimal equivalences. Note that the carry out of the MSB is zero, which means that overflow does not occur for the unsigned integer interpretation. The result (2148309336 decimal) is within the 32-bit unsigned integer range specified in Table 7.1. Note also that the carry into the MSB (1) differs from the carry out of the MSB (0), which means that overflow does occur for the signed integer interpretation. The result (2148309336 decimal) is not within the 32-bit signed integer range specified in Table 7.1.

FIGURE 7.1
32-bit addition

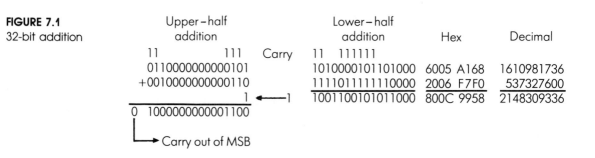

To subtract two 32-bit binary integers using 16-bit integer arithmetic, the following procedure can be used:

1. Subtract the low-order 16 bits of the subtrahend from the low-order 16 bits of the minuend, producing the low-order 16 bits of the difference and the borrow from bit 16 into bit 15.

2. Subtract from the high-order 16 bits of the minuend, the high-order 16 bits of the subtrahend, and the borrow into the low-order half of the subtraction. This subtraction produces the high-order 16 bits of the difference and the borrow into the MSB.

Figure 7.2 illustrates this procedure giving hexadecimal and decimal equivalences. The subtraction operations are shown as complement and add operations. Note that the borrow into the MSB is zero for the high-order half of the subtraction, which means that overflow does not occur for the unsigned integer interpretation. The result (1073654136) is within the 32-bit unsigned integer range specified in Table 7.1. Note also that on both upper-half additions the carry into the MSB is the same as the carry out of the MSB, which means that overflow does not occur for the signed integer interpretation. The result (1073654136) is within the 32-bit signed integer range specified in Table 7.1.

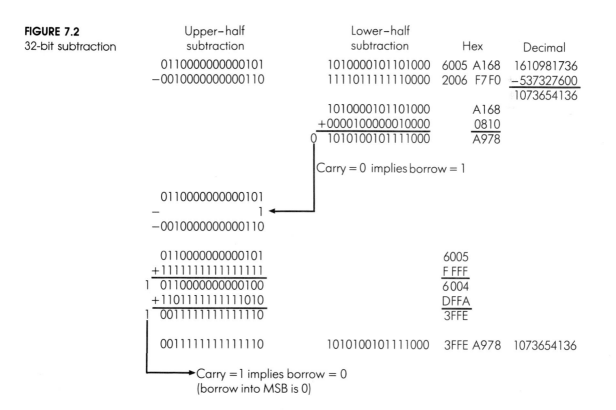

FIGURE 7.2
32-bit subtraction

The IBM PC Assembly language includes an addition instruction and a subtraction instruction that are useful in multiple precision integer arithmetic operations: the ADd with Carry (ADC) instruction and the SuBtract with Borrow (SBB) instruction. The **ADC instruction** has the following general form:

[⟨*label*⟩] ADC ⟨*destination*⟩, ⟨*source*⟩ [⟨*comment*⟩]

This instruction causes the source operand, the destination operand, and the CF bit of the flags register to be added together, producing a sum that replaces the value of the destination operand.

The **SBB instruction** has the following general form:

[⟨*label*⟩] SBB ⟨*destination*⟩, ⟨*source*⟩ [⟨*comment*⟩]

This instruction causes the source operand and the CF bit of the flags register to be subtracted from the destination operand, producing a difference that replaces the value of the destination operand. Figure 7.3 shows the possible combinations of destination and source operands for the ADC and SBB instructions. If the destination operand is a general register, then the source operand can be either a general register, a memory location, or an immediate value. If the destination operand is a memory location, then the source operand can be either a general register or an immediate value. The types of the two operands must match (i.e., both must be word, or both must be byte).

FIGURE 7.3
Allowable operands for ADC and SBB instructions

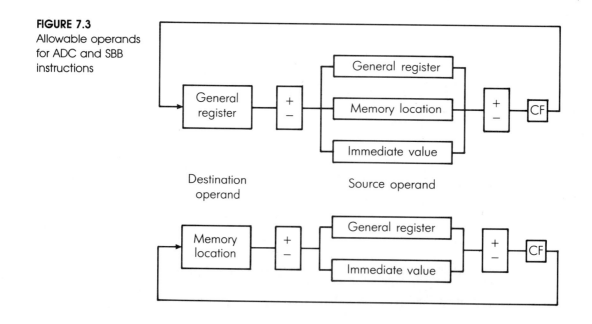

The OF, SF, ZF, AF, PF, and CF bits of the flags register are all affected by execution of ADC and SBB instructions:

If the carry into the MSB differs from the carry out of the MSB on the addition operation, then the OF bit is set; otherwise, the OF bit is cleared. (Recall that subtraction is performed by complement and addition.) If the two operands represent signed two's complement integers, then the OF bit reflects whether or not execution of the ADC or SBB instruction resulted in an overflow.

The SF bit is a copy of the MSB of the result of the addition or subtraction operation. If the two operands represent signed two's complement numbers, then the SF bit reflects the sign of the result.

If the result of the addition or subtraction operation is zero, then the ZF bit is set; otherwise, the ZF bit is cleared.

The PF bit is set to reflect the parity of the low-order 8 bits of the result.

If an addition operation produces a carry of 1 from the MSB (bit 7 for byte addition; bit 15 for word addition), or if a subtraction operation requires a borrow into the MSB, then the CF bit is set; otherwise, the CF bit is cleared. If the two operands represent unsigned integer values, then the CF bit reflects whether or not execution of the ADC or SBB instruction resulted in an overflow.

The AF bit is handled in a manner similar to the CF bit. However, the AF bit reflects the carry out of or borrow into bit 3.

The ADC and SBB instructions are used primarily for multiple precision integer arithmetic. Suppose there is a 32-bit variable defined in the data segment as follows:

```
TIME DW ?,?
```

The value for this variable is stored in memory beginning at the location identified by the symbolic name TIME. This 32-bit value could be interpreted as shown in Figure 7.4. To give this variable an initial value of 1, the data definition could be

```
TIME DW 1,0
```

To add the 32-bit value of TIME to the 32-bit value in the DX:AX register pair leaving the result in that register pair, the following sequence of instructions could be used:

```
ADD AX,TIME
ADC DX,TIME+2
```

The ADD instruction adds the low-order halves of the two operands, leaving the result in the AX-register. The ADC instruction adds the high-order halves of the two operands along with the carry from the addition of the low-order halves,

FIGURE 7.4
Storage for a 32-bit integer

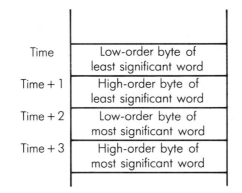

Time	Low-order byte of least significant word
Time + 1	High-order byte of least significant word
Time + 2	Low-order byte of most significant word
Time + 3	High-order byte of most significant word

leaving the result in the DX-register. The organization of the bits for this 32-bit addition is shown in Figure 7.5.

To subtract the 32-bit value beginning at the memory location specified by the symbolic name TIME from the 32-bit value in the DX:AX register pair leaving the result in that register pair, the following sequence of instructions could be used:

```
SUB AX,TIME
SBB DX,TIME+2
```

The SUB instruction subtracts the low-order half of the 32-bit value beginning at the memory location identified by the label TIME from the low-order half of the DX:AX register pair, leaving the result in the AX-register. The SBB instruction subtracts from the high-order half of the DX:AX register pair the high-order half of the 32-bit value of TIME and the borrow into the subtraction of the low-order halves, leaving the result in the DX-register.

These techniques can be extrapolated to techniques for performing addition and subtraction operations involving integers whose lengths are any multiple of 8 or 16 bits.

FIGURE 7.5
Organization of bits for a 32-bit addition of the variable TIME to DX:AX

```
31      24 23      16 15       8 7         0
┌──────────┬──────────┬──────────┬──────────┐
│    DH    │    DL    │    AH    │    AL    │
│    DX-register      │     AX-register     │
└─────────────────────┴─────────────────────┘

31      24 23      16 15       8 7         0
┌──────────┬──────────┬──────────┬──────────┐
│ TIME + 3 │ TIME + 2 │ TIME + 1 │   TIME   │
│  Word at TIME + 2   │    Word at TIME     │
└─────────────────────┴─────────────────────┘

31      24 23      16 15       8 7         0
┌──────────┬──────────┬──────────┬──────────┐
│    DH    │    DL    │    AH    │    AL    │
│    DX-register      │     AX-register     │
└─────────────────────┴─────────────────────┘
```

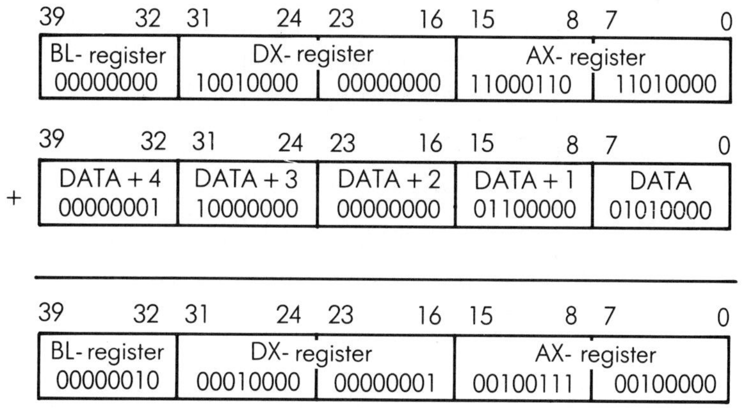

FIGURE 7.6
Organization of bits
for a 40-bit addition
of variable DATA to
the BL:DX:AX register
group

39	32	31	24	23	16	15	8	7	0
BL- register		DX- register				AX- register			
00000000		10010000		00000000		11000110		11010000	

39	32	31	24	23	16	15	8	7	0
DATA + 4		DATA + 3		DATA + 2		DATA + 1		DATA	
00000001		10000000		00000000		01100000		01010000	

+

39	32	31	24	23	16	15	8	7	0
BL- register		DX- register				AX- register			
00000010		00010000		00000001		00100111		00100000	

EXAMPLE

Consider the following definition for a 40-bit variable named DATA:

```
DATA DW 6050H, 8000H

     DB 1H
```

The initial value of variable data is 0180006050 hex or 6442475600 decimal. To add the 40-bit value of DATA to the 40-bit value in the BL:DX:AX register group, the following sequence of instructions could be used:

```
ADD AX, DATA
ADC DX, DATA+2
ADC BL, BYTE PTR DATA+4
```

The result of the addition is in the BL:DX:AX register group. The BYTE PTR operators are required in the second ADC instruction because the symbolic name DATA is defined with a type attribute of word, but the reference DATA + 4 is used to access a byte. Figure 7.6 shows the bit organization for this addition using the hexadecimal values shown:

$$
\begin{array}{rl}
\text{BL:DX:AX} & \text{009000C6D0} \\
+ \quad \text{DATA} & \text{0180006050} \\
\hline
\text{BL:DX:AX} & \text{0210012720}
\end{array}
$$

7.2 Multiple Register Shifts

In multiple precision integer arithmetic operations, it is often necessary to perform shift operations on multiple precision values. Recall from Chapter 6 that a left-shift operation is like multiplication by a power of 2 and a right-shift operation is like division by a power of 2. Multiplication and division by a power of 2 can be performed much more efficiently by a shift operation than by the multiplication and division instructions. In multiple precision integer arithmetic, multiplication and division must be performed by some algorithm. If the multiplication or division operation is by a power of 2, then the multiple precision shift operation is by far the most efficient approach.

It is important to remember two things in the implementation of multiple precision shift operations:

1.   With any shift or rotate instruction, the last bit shifted out is recorded in the CF bit of the flags register.

2.   There are two rotate instructions that include the CF bit of the flags register as part of the value being rotated: the rotate-through-carry instructions presented in Section 6.1.

Suppose the 32-bit signed integer value in the DX:AX register pair must be shifted right 1 bit position. The value in the DX-register is first shifted right 1 bit position using an arithmetic shift operation. The bit shifted from the low-order end of the DX-register is recorded in the CF bit of the flags register. The value in the AX-register is then shifted right 1 bit position using a rotate-through-carry operation. The value of the CF bit in the flags register (i.e., the bit shifted from the low-order end of the DX-register) is rotated into the MSB of the AX-register as the bits of the AX-register are shifted right 1 bit position. The bit shifted from the low-order end of the AX-register is recorded in the CF bit of the flags register. This arithmetic right-shift of the 32-bit value in the DX:AX register pair is performed by the following two instructions:

```
SAR DX,1
RCR AX,1
```

These instructions divide the signed integer value in the DX:AX register pair by 2, leaving the quotient in the DX:AX register pair and the remainder (0 or 1) in the CF bit of the flags register. Figure 7.7 shows the operation of these two instructions for the 32-bit value 1111111100001001 0110100111110000.

Suppose the 32-bit signed integer value in the DX:AX register pair must be shifted right 3 bit positions. In multiple precision shift operations, the CL-register cannot be used as a shift count for the individual shift instructions, because a shift of 1 bit position requires multiple shift operations. It is these multiple shift operations (e.g., the two shift instructions shown previously) that must be repeated to implement the multibit, multiple precision shift operation.

FIGURE 7.7
32-bit arithmetic
right-shift operation

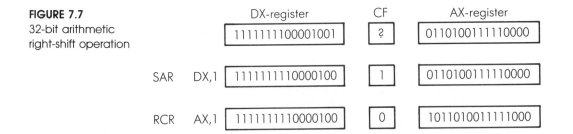

	DX-register	CF	AX-register
	1111111100001001	?	0110100111110000
SAR DX,1	1111111110000100	1	0110100111110000
RCR AX,1	1111111110000100	0	1011010011111000

A loop can be used to repeat the multiple shift operations the desired number of times. The following loop shifts the 32-bit signed integer value in the DX:AX register pair right 3 bit positions:

```
            MOV   CX,3
SHFT_LOOP:
            SAR   DX,1
            RCR   AX,1
            LOOP  SHFT_LOOP
```

Figure 7.8 shows the operation of this loop for the 32-bit value 1111111111110101 0000110000000110.

Note that when a multibit, right-shift operation is used for division by a power of 2, the remainder of the division is not available. The most-significant bit of the remainder appears in the CF bit of the flags register, but the other bits of the remainder are lost during the shift. The preceding loop can be modified so that the remainder is shifted into another register and, therefore, not lost (see Programming Exercise 7.12 at the end of this chapter).

Multiple precision left-shift operations are implemented in a similar manner. To shift the 32-bit signed integer value in the DX:AX register pair left 1 bit position, the following sequence of instructions can be used:

```
SAL AX,1
RCL DX,1
```

FIGURE 7.8
32-bit arithmetic
right-shift by 3 bit
positions

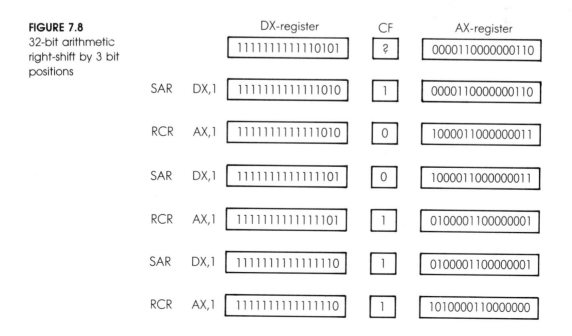

To shift the 32-bit signed integer value in the DX:AX register pair left 3 bit positions, these instructions can be placed in the body of a loop as follows:

```
          MOV CX,3
SHFT_LOOP:
          SAL   AX,1
          RCL   DX,1
          LOOP SHFT_LOOP
```

A left-shift of a signed integer value is like a multiplication by a power of 2, and it can, therefore, produce an overflow. The RCL instruction affects the OF bit in the flags register as follows:

> If the sign bit changes on the last bit shifted, then the OF bit in the flags register is set.

> If the sign bit does *not* change on the last bit shifted, then the OF bit in the flags register is cleared.

For a single bit, multiple precision shift (i.e., a multiply by 2), the OF bit in the flags register correctly reflects signed integer overflow. However, for a multibit, multiple precision shift, the OF bit does *not* correctly reflect signed integer overflow. For a multibit shift, if the sign bit ever changes during the shift, then overflow has occurred. However, if the sign bit *never* changes during the shift, then overflow has *not* occurred.

EXAMPLE

Consider the 32-bit value

0100000000000010 0110100111000011   (4002 69C3 hex)

interpreted as a signed integer value. Figure 7.9 shows the steps of a 3-bit left-shift of this value. At the end of this 3-bit shift operation, the OF bit of the flags register is cleared. The sign bit of the DX-register did not change on the last bit shifted, and the OF bit was cleared. However, the sign bit (MSB of DX-register) changed from 0 to 1 on the first bit shifted. The OF bit was set at that point, correctly reflecting the signed integer overflow.

To detect overflow during the 3-bit left-shift of the 32-bit signed integer value in the DX:AX register pair, the following loop can be used:

```
          MOV   OVERFLO,0
          MOV   CX,3
SHFT_LOOP:
          SAL   AX,1
          RCL   DX,1
          JNO   SLOOP_END
          MOV   OVERFLO,1
SLOOP_END:
          LOOP SHFT_LOOP
```

FIGURE 7.9
32-bit left-shift by 3
bit positions

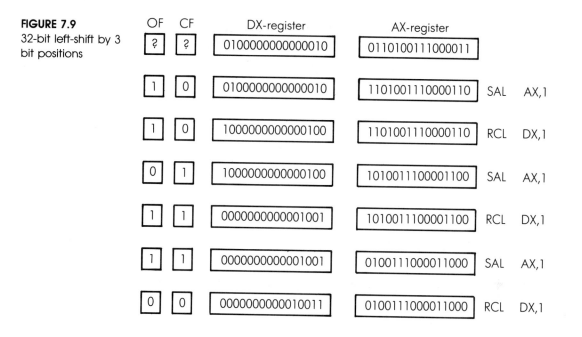

If the sign bit ever changed during the shift, then the variable OVERFLO has the value 1 at loop exit; otherwise, OVERFLO has the value 0 at loop exit.

For multiple precision shifts of unsigned integer values, simply replace SAR and SAL instructions with SHR and SHL instructions, respectively, in each of the preceding examples except the overflow detection example. Recall that the SAL and SHL instructions are equivalent. For the single-bit, left-shift of a multiple precision unsigned integer value, the CF bit in the flags register correctly reflects overflow. However, for a multibit, multiple precision shift, the CF bit does *not* correctly reflect an unsigned integer overflow. For a multibit, left-shift of a multiple precision unsigned integer value, if the CF bit in the flags register is ever set to 1 during the shift, then overflow has occurred.

EXAMPLE

Consider again the 32-bit value

0100000000000010 0110100111000011   (4002 69C3 hex)

interpreted as an unsigned integer value. Figure 7.9 shows the steps of a 32-bit left-shift of this value. At the end of this 32-bit left-shift operation, the CF bit of the flags register is cleared. The last bit shifted from the DX-register (0) was recorded in the CF bit. However, a significant bit was shifted from the MSB of the DX-register on the second bit shifted. The CF bit was set at that point, correctly reflecting the unsigned integer overflow.

To detect overflow during the 3-bit left-shift of the 32-bit unsigned integer value in the DX:AX register pair, the following loop can be used:

```
            MOV    OVERFLO,0
            MOV    CX,3
SHFT_LOOP:
            SHL    AX,1
            RCL    DX,1
            JNC    SLOOP_END
            MOV    OVERFLO,1
SLOOP_END:
            LOOP   SHFT_LOOP
```

If the CF bit in the flags register was ever set during the shift (i.e., a significant bit was shifted out), then the variable OVERFLO has the value 1 at loop exit; otherwise, OVERFLO has the value 0 at loop exit.

These procedures can be extrapolated to procedures for performing shift operations involving integers whose lengths are any multiple of 8 or 16 bits. For example, to shift the 40-bit signed integer value in the BL:DX:AX register group right 3 bit positions, the following loop can be used:

```
            MOV    CX,3
SHFT_LOOP:
            SAR    BL,1
            RCR    DX,1
            RCR    AX,1
            LOOP   SHFT_LOOP
```

7.3 Programming Examples

The programming examples in this chapter present two implementations of an algorithm for performing integer multiplication using addition and shift operations. The goal is to produce a procedure to perform 32-bit integer multiplication. The algorithm used in these example programs is known as the Russian Peasant's Method. The first implementation of this algorithm is an internal procedure for performing 16-bit unsigned integer multiplication. The second implementation is an external procedure for performing 32-bit signed integer multiplication.

The programming exercises at the end of this chapter introduce other algorithms for multiplication and an algorithm for division. Algorithms for multiplication and division are presented for two reasons:

1. Such algorithms are needed to perform multiple precision multiplication and division operations.

2. Some microprocessors do not have multiplication and division instructions in their machine language. A software algorithm is, therefore, needed to perform these operations.

The Russian Peasant's Method can be explained through examination of the standard multiplication method taught in elementary schools. The following is an example of the multiplication of two 6-bit unsigned binary integers using the long multiplication method that is normally used when two decimal numbers are multiplied using pencil and paper.

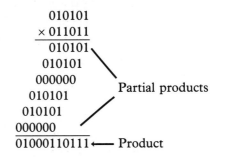

```
      010101
   ×  011011
      010101
      010101
      000000
      010101
      010101
      000000
   01000110111 ◄── Product
```
Partial products

Note that a given partial product is either 000000 or a copy of the multiplicand (010101) shifted left the appropriate number of bit positions necessary to place its least-significant bit under the multiplier bit that produced it. Recall from Chapter 6 that shifting an unsigned binary integer value left n-bit positions is the equivalent to multiplying that value by 2^n. The partial products can be rewritten as shown:

$$
\begin{array}{ll}
\quad\quad 010101 & \\
\times\ 011011 & \\
\hline
\quad\quad 010101 & (2^0 \times \text{multiplicand}) \times 1 \\
\quad\ 0101010 & (2^1 \times \text{multiplicand}) \times 1 \\
\quad 00000000 & (2^2 \times \text{multiplicand}) \times 0 \\
\ 010101000 & (2^3 \times \text{multiplicand}) \times 1 \\
0101010000 & (2^4 \times \text{multiplicand}) \times 1 \\
00000000000 & (2^5 \times \text{multiplicand}) \times 0 \\
\hline
01000110111 & \longleftarrow \text{Product}
\end{array}
$$

The interpretation states each successive partial product as the next higher power of 2 (starting with 2^0) multiplied by the multiplicand, which is multiplied by the next higher multiplier bit (starting with the LSB).

In general, the product of a 6-bit unsigned binary integer multiplicand and a 6-bit unsigned binary integer multiplier, M5 M4 M3 M2 M1 M0, can be computed by summing the following six partial products:

$$2^0 \times \text{multiplicand} \times \text{M0}$$

$$2^1 \times \text{multiplicand} \times \text{M1}$$

$$2^2 \times \text{multiplicand} \times \text{M2}$$

$$2^3 \times \text{multiplicand} \times \text{M3}$$

$$2^4 \times \text{multiplicand} \times \text{M4}$$

$$2^5 \times \text{multiplicand} \times \text{M5}$$

Note that the only partial products that need to be summed are those that are produced by a multiplier bit (Mi) of 1. The ith bit of the multiplier from the right will be a 1 only if the multiplier / 2^i is odd.

This process leads to the following algorithm, the Russian Peasant's Method, for computing the product of two unsigned binary integers:

```
FUNCTION MULTIPLY (MULTIPLICAND, MULTIPLIER)
    PRODUCT = 0
    WHILE   MULTIPLIER > 0
      IF   MULTIPLIER IS ODD
      THEN PRODUCT = PRODUCT + MULTIPLICAND
      ENDIF
      MULTIPLICAND = MULTIPLICAND * 2
      MULTIPLIER = MULTIPLIER / 2
                    truncated to an integer
    ENDWHILE
    RETURN (PRODUCT)
  END MULTIPLY
```

Table 7.2 shows a trace, in both binary and decimal, of this algorithm for the two values (21 a.id 27) used in the preceding binary examples.

TABLE 7.2
Trace of Russian Peasant's Method algorithm

Step	Multiplier Conditions >0	Odd	Multiplicand	Multiplier	Product
Enter function			000000010101 (21)	011011 (27)	
Product = 0					000000000000 (000)
Loop test	T				
Decision test		T			
Product = Product + Multiplicand					000000010101 (21)
Multiplicand = Multiplicand * 2			000000101010 (42)		
Multiplier = Multiplier / 2				001101 (13)	
Loop test	T				
Decision test		T			
Product = Product + Multiplicand					000000111111 (63)

TABLE 7.2
Continued

Step	Multiplier Conditions >0	Odd	Multiplicand	Multiplier	Product
Multiplicand = Multiplicand * 2			000001010100 (84)		
Multiplier = Multiplier / 2				000110 (6)	
Loop test	T				
Decision test		F			
Multiplicand = Multiplicand * 2			000010101000 (168)		
Multiplier = Multiplier / 2				000011 (3)	
Loop test	T				
Decision test		T			
Product = Product + Multiplicand					000011100111 (231)
Multiplicand = Multiplicand * 2			000101010000 (336)		
Multiplier = Multiplier / 2				000001 (1)	
Loop test	T				
Decision test		T			
Product = Product + Multiplicand					001000110111 (567)
Multiplicand = Multiplicand * 2			001010100000 (672)		
Multiplier = Multiplier / 2				000000 (0)	
Loop test	F				
Return					001000110111 (567)

Russian Peasant's Multiply—16-bit Implementation

Program Listing 7.1 shows a program that contains an internal subprocedure that is an implementation of the Russian Peasant's Method algorithm for 16-bit unsigned integers and a main procedure that demonstrates the subprocedure. This discussion concentrations on the subprocedure defined in lines 62–108 of Program Listing 7.1.

```
 1: ;                        PROGRAM LISTING 7.1
 2: ;
 3: ;PROGRAM TO DEMONSTRATE RUSSIAN PEASANT MULTIPLY PROCEDURE
 4: ;
 5:                                         ;PROCEDURES TO
 6:               EXTRN   GETDEC$:FAR       ;GET UNSIGNED DECIMAL INTEGER
 7:               EXTRN   NEWLINE:FAR       ;DISPLAY NEWLINE CHARACTER
 8:               EXTRN   PUTSTRNG:FAR      ;DISPLAY CHARACTER STRING
 9:               EXTRN   PUTDC32$:FAR      ;DISPLAY 32-BIT UNSIGNED INTEGER
10: ;
11: ; S T A C K   S E G M E N T   D E F I N I T I O N
12: ;
13: STACK         SEGMENT STACK
14:               DB      256 DUP(?)
15: STACK         ENDS
16: ;
17: ; D A T A   S E G M E N T   D E F I N I T I O N
18: ;
19: DATA          SEGMENT
20: ;
21: PROMPT1       DB      'ENTER MULTIPLICAND (POSITIVE) '
22: PROMPT2       DB      'ENTER MULTIPLIER   (POSITIVE) '
23: ;
24: ANNOTATE      DB      'PRODUCT = '
25: ;
26: DATA          ENDS
27: ;
28: ; C O D E   S E G M E N T   D E F I N I T I O N
29: ;
30: CODE          SEGMENT
31: EX_7_1        PROC    FAR
32:               ASSUME  CS:CODE,DS:NOTHING,SS:STACK,ES:DATA
33:               PUSH    DS                ;PUSH RETURN SEG ADDR ON STACK
34:               MOV     AX,0              ;PUSH RETURN OFFSET OF ZERO
35:               PUSH    AX                ;ON STACK
36:               MOV     AX,SEG DATA       ;INITIALIZE ES-REGISTER
37:               MOV     ES,AX             ;TO ADDRESS DATA SEGMENT
38:               CALL    NEWLINE
39:               LEA     DI,PROMPT1        ;PROMPT FOR MULTIPLICAND
40:               MOV     CX,30
41:               CALL    PUTSTRNG
42:               CALL    GETDEC$           ;GET MCAND
43:               MOV     BX,AX             ;MULTIPLICAND TO BX
44:               CALL    NEWLINE
45:               LEA     DI,PROMPT2        ;PROMPT FOR MULTIPLIER
46:               MOV     CX,30
47:               CALL    PUTSTRNG
48:               CALL    GETDEC$           ;GET MPLIER
49:               CALL    NEWLINE
50:               CALL    MULTIPLY          ;PRODUCT = MULTIPLY(MCAND,MPLIER)
51:               LEA     DI,ANNOTATE       ;DISPLAY 'PRODUCT = '
52:               MOV     CX,10
53:               CALL    PUTSTRNG
54:               MOV     BH,-1             ;DISPLAY CODE = LEFT JUSTIFY
55:               JNC     LEFT              ;IF   PRODUCT OVERFLOWED 16 BITS
56:               MOV     BH,1              ;THEN DISPLAY CODE = RIGHT JUST.
57: LEFT:                                   ;ENDIF
58:               CALL    PUTDC32$          ;DISPLAY PRODUCT ACCORDING TO
59:               CALL    NEWLINE           ;                DISPLAY CODE
60:               RET                       ;RETURN
61: EX_7_1        ENDP
62:*;
```

*

```
 63: ;
 64: ; PROCEDURE TO PERFORM 16-BIT UNSIGNED INTEGER MULTIPLICATION
 65: ; USING THE RUSSIAN PEASANT'S METHOD.
 66: ;
 67: ; INPUTS:    AX-REGISTER - MULTIPLIER
 68: ;            BX-REGISTER - MULTIPLICAND
 69: ; OUTPUTS:   DX:AX-REGISTER - PRODUCT
 70: ;            OF AND CF BITS OF FLAGS REGISTER SET TO REFLECT OVERFLOW
 71: ;
 72: MULTIPLY    PROC     NEAR               ;FUNCTION MULTIPLY (MULTIPLICAND,
 73:                                         ;                        MULTIPLIER)
 74:             PUSH     BX                   ;SAVE REGISTERS
 75:             PUSH     BP
 76:             PUSH     CX
 77:             PUSHF                         ;SAVE FLAGS
 78:             MOV      BP,AX
 79:             MOV      CX,0               ;EXPAND MULTIPLICAND INTO CX:BX
 80:             MOV      DX,CX              ;PRODUCT (DX:AX) = 0
 81:             MOV      AX,DX
 82: LOOPTOP:                               ;WHILE MULTIPLIER > 0
 83:             CMP      BP,0
 84:             JE       LOOPEND
 85:             SHR      BP,1              ;   IF   MULTIPLIER IS ODD
 86:             JNC      UPDATE
 87:             ADD      AX,BX             ;      THEN PRODUCT = PRODUCT +
 88:             ADC      DX,CX             ;                     MULTIPLICAND
 89: UPDATE:                               ;      ENDIF
 90:             SAL      BX,1              ;      MULTIPLICAND = MULTIPLICAND*2
 91:             RCL      CX,1
 92:                                       ;      MULTIPLIER = MULTIPLIER / 2
 93:                                       ;      (DONE IN IF TEST ABOVE)
 94:             JMP      LOOPTOP
 95: LOOPEND:                              ;ENDWHILE
 96:             POP      BX                ;FLAGS = SAVED FLAGS
 97:             AND      BX,0F7FEH         ;CLEAR OF AND CF IN FLAGS
 98:             CMP      DX,0              ;IF   UPPER HALF OF PRODUCT <> 0
 99:             JE       RESTORE
100:             OR       BX,0801H          ;THEN SET OF AND CF IN FLAGS
101: RESTORE:                              ;ENDIF
102:             PUSH     BX                ;SAVED FLAGS = FLAGS
103:             POPF                       ;RESTORE FLAGS
104:             POP      CX                ;RESTORE REGISTERS
105:             POP      BP
106:             POP      BX
107:             RET                        ;RETURN (PRODUCT)
108: MULTIPLY    ENDP                     ;END MULTIPLY
109: CODE        ENDS
110:*           END      EX_7_1
```

The subprocedure begins with a prologue in lines 62–71 that explains the function of and the interface for the procedure. The 16-bit unsigned integer multiplicand is expected in the BX-register, and the 16-bit unsigned integer multiplier is expected in the AX-register. The 32-bit unsigned integer product is returned in the DX:AX register pair. The OF and CF bits of the flags register are set to reflect whether or not the product overflows 16 bits. If the high-order 16 bits of the product are zero, then the OF and CF bits are cleared. However, if there is a 1 anywhere in the high-order 16 bits of the product, then the OF and CF bits are set. Note that both the OF and CF bits are affected, which was done to make the MULTIPLY procedure consistent with the MUL instruction. However, there is a slight inconsistency between the MUL instruction and the MULTIPLY procedure. The MUL instruction leaves the AF, PF, SF, and ZF bits of the flags register undefined, and the MULTIPLY procedure leaves them unchanged.

The subprocedure definition begins with the PROC pseudo-operation in line 72 and terminates with the ENDP pseudo-operation in line 108. The subprocedure itself begins by saving registers (lines 74–76) and flags (line 77).

The MOV instruction in line 78 stores the input multiplier as the value of the BP-register. The MOV instruction in line 79 expands the input multiplicand to 32 bits in the CX:BX register pair by setting the upper 16 bits (CX-register) to zero. The MOV instructions in lines 80 and 81 initialize the 32-bit product in the DX:AX register pair to zero. Since the product of two 16-bit integers is a 32-bit integer, the product is maintained by the procedure as a 32-bit value. Since the product is accumulated by adding powers of 2 multiplied by the multiplicand, the multiplicand is maintained by the procedure as a 32-bit value. The 32-bit multiplicand is doubled on each iteration of the WHILE loop.

The WHILE loop in lines 82–95 computes the product of the multiplicand and the multiplier. The instructions in lines 83 and 84 provide the loop test. While the multiplier is greater than zero, there are still nonzero partial products to be added to the product sum, so the loop body is executed. When the multiplier becomes zero, there are no further nonzero partial products to be added to the product sum, so the loop is terminated (i.e., the jump in line 84 is taken). The loop body consists of the instructions in lines 85–91.

The single-alternative decision structure in lines 85–89 tests the current value of the multiplier to see if it is odd: If it is odd, then the current value of the multiplicand is added to the product sum; if it is even, then nothing is added to the product sum (i.e., the partial product for the current multiplier bit is zero). The SHR instruction in line 85 performs two functions. It tests the current value of the multiplier to see if it is odd, and it divides the multiplier by 2, discarding the remainder, in preparation for the next loop test and the next iteration of the loop body. A logical right-shift of 1 divides an unsigned integer by 2. The bit shifted from the right is recorded in the CF bit of the flags register. The bit shifted out is actually the remainder of the division by 2. If this remainder is 1 (i.e., CF = 1), then the value of the multiplier was odd prior to the division operation. If this remainder is 0 (i.e., CF = 0), then the value of the multiplier was even prior to the division operation. The JNC instruction in line 86 makes the decision based on this condition. If the CF bit in the flags register is 1, then the jump is not taken, and the instructions in lines 87 and 88 are executed. If the CF bit in the flags register is zero, then the instructions in lines 87 and 88 are skipped.

The two instructions in lines 87 and 88 add the 32-bit value in the CX:BX register pair (the current value of the multiplicand) to the 32-bit value in the DX:AX register pair (the current value of the product sum), leaving the result in the DX:AX register pair (the new value of the product sum). The ADD instruction in line 87 adds the low-order halves of the two 32-bit operands, leaving the result in the AX-register. The ADC instruction in line 88 adds the high-order halves of the two operands plus the carry from the addition of the low-order halves, leaving the result in the DX-register.

Following the single-alternative decision structure, the 32-bit value of the multiplicand in the CX:BX register pair is multiplied by 2. This task is accomplished by the double-register, left-shift operation in lines 90 and 91. The SAL instruction in line 90 shifts the BX-register left 1 bit position. The value shifted from the MSB of the BX-register is recorded in the CF bit of the flags register. The RCL instruction in line 91 shifts the CX-register value left 1 bit position, shifting the CF bit of the flags register into the LSB of the CX-register. The bit shifted from the MSB of the CX-register is recorded in the CF bit of the flags register and will always be 0; that is, the 32-bit multiplicand does not overflow during the computation. This situation occurs because the high-order 16 bits are initially 0 (line 79), and the double-register, left-shift occurs, at most, 16 times before the multiplier reduces to zero. The comments in lines 92 and 93 indicate that the division of the multiplier by 2 was performed by the SHR instruction in line 85.

The JMP instruction in line 94 returns control to the WHILE loop test beginning in line 83. At the time of loop exit, the instructions in lines 96–107 are executed, and the completed product is in the DX:AX register pair.

The instructions in lines 96–102 set the OF and CF bits in the flags register to reflect whether or not the product overflows 16 bits. If the high-order half of the product is nonzero, then the OF and CF bits in the flags register are set; if the high-order half of the product is zero, then the OF and CF bits in the flags register are cleared. Again, both bits are affected for consistency with the MUL instruction that is being simulated. The POP instruction in line 96 pops the flags register value, which is saved on entry to the subprocedure, from the stack into the BX-register. The AND instruction in line 97 clears the OF and CF bits in this flags register value. The single-alternative decision structure in lines 98–101 set the OF and CF bits in this flags register value, if the upper half of the product is nonzero. The CMP instruction in line 98 tests the DX-register (the high-order half of the product) to see if it is nonzero. The JE instruction in line 99 makes the decision based on this condition: If the DX-register does not contain zero, then the jump is not taken, and the OR instruction in line 100 is executed. The OR instruction sets the OF and CF bits in the flags register value in the BX-register. Following the single-alternative decision structure, the PUSH instruction in line 102 is executed, which pushes the modified flags register value back on the stack.

The subprocedure ends by restoring the registers for the caller (lines 103–106) and returning control to the caller (line 107). The unsigned integer product is returned in the DX:AX register pair. Note that the OF and CF bits, in the saved and restored flags register value, have been modified by this subprocedure. All other bits in the flags register have been preserved. This subprocedure simulates the IBM PC Assembly language MUL instruction for 16-bit operands. However, it does not leave the SF, ZF, AF, and PF bits in the flags register undefined, as does the MUL instruction.

The main procedure defined in lines 31–61 in Program Listing 7.1 performs the following steps:

1. Prompts for the multiplicand (lines 38–41).
2. Accepts the input value for the multiplicand in the AX-register (line 42).
3. Moves the multiplicand to the BX-register (line 43).
4. Prompts for the multiplier (lines 44–47).
5. Accepts the input value for the multiplier in the AX-register (line 48).
6. Calls the MULTIPLY subprocedure to compute the product of the multiplicand and the multiplier (line 50).
7. Displays the product left-justified in an 11-character field if the product did not overflow 16 bits, right-justified in an 11-character field if the product overflowed 16 bits (lines 51–59).

The following results are from some sample executions of this program:

```
ENTER MULTIPLICAND (POSITIVE) 2400
ENTER MULTIPLIER   (POSITIVE) 12
PRODUCT = 28800

ENTER MULTIPLICAND (POSITIVE) 32767
ENTER MULTIPLIER   (POSITIVE) 2
PRODUCT = 65534

ENTER MULTIPLICAND (POSITIVE) 32767
ENTER MULTIPLIER   (POSITIVE) 3
PRODUCT =        98301

ENTER MULTIPLICAND (POSITIVE) 32767
ENTER MULTIPLIER   (POSITIVE) 32767
PRODUCT =  1073676289
```

Note that in the first two executions the product is displayed immediately after the annotation message (i.e., left-justified in the 11-character field), and in the last two executions it is separated from the annotation message by some spaces (i.e., right-justified in the 11-character field). These differences demonstrate the setting of the CF bit by the MULTIPLY procedure.

Russian Peasant's Multiply— 32-Bit Implementation

A slight change to the Russian Peasant's Method algorithm produces an algorithm that handles signed integer values, as follows:

```
FUNCTION MULTIPLY (MULTIPLICAND,MULTIPLIER)
    SIGN = +1
    IF    MULTIPLICAND < 0
    THEN
          SIGN = - SIGN
          MULTIPLICAND = - MULTIPLICAND
    ENDIF
```

```
      IF    MULTIPLIER < O
      THEN
            SIGN = - SIGN
            MULTIPLIER = - MULTIPLIER
      ENDIF
      PRODUCT = O
      WHILE   MULTIPLIER > O
         IF   MULTIPLIER IS ODD
         THEN
               PRODUCT = PRODUCT+MULTIPLICAND
         ENDIF
         MULTIPLICAND = MULTIPLICAND*2
         MULTIPLIER = MULTIPLIER/2
      ENDWHILE
      IF    SIGN = -1
      THEN  PRODUCT = - PRODUCT
      ENDIF
      RETURN (PRODUCT)
END MULTIPLY
```

The two, single-alternative decision structures that appear before the WHILE loop set both the multiplicand and multiplier to positive and set a sign flag to indicate the required sign of the product. The WHILE loop is the same as in the previous algorithm: It produces a positive product from a positive multiplicand and a positive multiplier. The single-alternative decision structure that appears after the WHILE loop negates the product, if the sign flag indicates that the product should be negative.

The assembly module in Program Listing 7.3 contains an external sub-procedure that is an implementation of the modified Russian Peasant's Method algorithm for 32-bit signed binary integers in two's complement form. The assembly module in Program Listing 7.2 contains a main procedure that demonstrates the external subprocedure. This section concentrates on the subprocedure and concludes with a brief discussion of the main procedure.

The assembly module in Program Listing 7.3 begins with a prologue in lines 1–11 that describes the function of the external subprocedure defined in the assembly module and describes the interface requirements for that subprocedure. The subprocedure multiplies two 32-bit signed integers, producing a 64-bit signed integer product. The subprocedure expects the 32-bit multiplicand in the DX:AX register pair, and it expects the 32-bit multiplier in the DI:SI register pair. The product is returned to the caller in the DI:SI:DX:AX register group. Both the product and the multiplicand are maintained by the subprocedure as 64-bit values. Each time the multiplicand is added to the product, a 64-bit addition operation is performed.

The assembly module contains the definition of a local data segment (lines 13–23). The data in this local data segment are referenced by the MULTIPLY procedure defined in the same assembly module. Two variables are defined in the local data segment: MPCAND and MPLIER. MPCAND is defined in lines 16–19 as four consecutive 16-bit words (i.e., 64 bits). MPLIER is defined in lines

```
 1: ;
 2: ;
 3: ;                      PROGRAM LISTING 7.2
 4: ;
 5: ;PROGRAM TO DEMONSTRATE RUSSIAN PEASANT MULTIPLY PROCEDURE
 6: ;
 7:                                       ;PROCEDURES TO
 8:             EXTRN    GETDEC32:FAR      ;GET 32-BIT SIGNED DEC. INT.
 9:             EXTRN    MULTIPLY:FAR      ;PERFORM 32-BIT MULTIPLY
10:                                       ;USING RUSSIAN PEASANT'S METHOD
11:             EXTRN    NEWLINE:FAR       ;DISPLAY NEWLINE CHARACTER
12:             EXTRN    PUTBIN:FAR        ;DISPLAY BINARY INTEGER
13:             EXTRN    PUTDEC32:FAR      ;DISPLAY 32-BIT SIGNED DEC. INT.
14:             EXTRN    PUTSTRNG:FAR      ;DISPLAY CHARACTER STRING
15: ;
16: ; S T A C K   S E G M E N T   D E F I N I T I O N
17: ;
18: STACK       SEGMENT STACK
19:             DB       256 DUP(?)
20: STACK       ENDS
21: ;
22: ; D A T A   S E G M E N T   D E F I N I T I O N
23: ;
24: DATA        SEGMENT
25: ;
26: PROMPT1     DB       'ENTER MULTIPLICAND '
27: PROMPT2     DB       'ENTER MULTIPLIER   '
28: ANNOTATE    DB       'PRODUCT = '
29: ;
30: DATA        ENDS
31: ;
32: ; C O D E   S E G M E N T   D E F I N I T I O N
33: ;
34: CODE        SEGMENT
35: EX_7_2      PROC     FAR
36:             ASSUME   CS:CODE,DS:NOTHING,SS:STACK,ES:DATA
37:             PUSH     DS                ;PUSH RETURN SEG ADDR ON STACK
38:             MOV      AX,0              ;PUSH RETURN OFFSET OF ZERO
39:             PUSH     AX                ;ON STACK
40:             MOV      AX,SEG DATA       ;INITIALIZE ES-REGISTER
41:             MOV      ES,AX             ;TO POINT TO DATA SEGMENT
42:*           CALL     NEWLINE

43: ;
44:             LEA      DI,PROMPT2        ;PROMPT FOR MPLIER
45:             MOV      CX,19
46:             CALL     PUTSTRNG
47:             CALL     GETDEC32          ;GET MPLIER
48:             MOV      BL,1              ;PUTBIN CODE = WORD
49:             XCHG     DX,AX             ;DISPLAY MPLIER IN BINARY
50:             CALL     PUTBIN
51:             XCHG     DX,AX
52:             CALL     PUTBIN
53:             CALL     NEWLINE
54:             CALL     NEWLINE
55:             MOV      DI,DX             ;<MPLIER IN DI:SI>
56:             MOV      SI,AX
57:             PUSH     DI
58:             LEA      DI,PROMPT1        ;PROMPT FOR MCAND
59:             MOV      CX,19
60:             CALL     PUTSTRNG
```

```
61:             POP      DI
62:             CALL     GETDEC32              ;GET MCAND
63:             XCHG     DX,AX                 ;DISPLAY MCAND IN BINARY
64:             CALL     PUTBIN
65:             XCHG     DX,AX
66:             CALL     PUTBIN
67:             CALL     NEWLINE
68:             CALL     NEWLINE
69:             CALL     MULTIPLY              ;PRODUCT = MULTIPLY(MCAND,MPLIER)
70:             PUSH     DI
71:             LEA      DI,ANNOTATE           ;DISPLAY 'PRODUCT = '
72:             MOV      CX,10
73:             CALL     PUTSTRNG
74:             POP      DI
75:             MOV      BL,1                  ;PUTBIN CODE = WORD
76:             JNO      ELSE                  ;IF   OVERFLOW
77:             PUSH     AX                    ;THEN
78:             MOV      AX,DI                 ;        DISPLAY BITS 63 - 48
79:             CALL     PUTBIN                ;                 OF PRODUCT
80:             MOV      AX,SI                 ;        DISPLAY BITS 47 - 32
81:             CALL     PUTBIN                ;                 OF PRODUCT
82:             MOV      AX,DX                 ;        DISPLAY BITS 31 - 16
83:             CALL     PUTBIN                ;                 OF PRODUCT
84:             POP      AX                    ;        DISPLAY BITS 15 - 00
85:             CALL     PUTBIN                ;                 OF PRODUCT
86:             JMP      ENDIF
87: ELSE:                                     ;ELSE
88:             MOV      BH,0                  ;        DISPLAY PRODUCT IN DECIMAL
89:             CALL     PUTDEC32
90: ENDIF:                                    ;ENDIF
91:             CALL     NEWLINE
92:             RET                            ;RETURN
93: EX_7_2      ENDP
94: CODE        ENDS
95:*           END      EX_7_2
```
*

```
 1: ;
 2: ;
 3: ;                     PROGRAM LISTING 7.3
 4: ;
 5: ; PROCEDURE TO PERFORM 32-BIT SIGNED INTEGER MULTIPLICATION
 6: ; USING THE RUSSIAN PEASANT'S METHOD.
 7: ;
 8: ; INPUTS:   DX:AX REGISTER PAIR CONTAINS MULTIPLICAND
 9: ;           DI:SI REGISTER PAIR CONTAINS MULTIPLIER
10: ; OUTPUTS:  DI:SI:DX:AX REGISTER GROUP CONTAINS PRODUCT
11: ;           OF AND CF BITS OF FLAGS REGISTER SET TO REFLECT OVERFLOW
12: ;
13: ; L O C A L   D A T A   S E G M E N T   D E F I N I T I O N
14: ;
15: DATA        SEGMENT
16: MPCAND      DW       ?                     ;64-BIT EXPANDED MULTIPLICAND
17:             DW       ?
18:             DW       ?
19:             DW       ?
20: MPLIER      DW       ?                     ;32-BIT MULTIPLIER
21:             DW       ?
22: SIGN        DB       1                     ;SIGN OF PRODUCT (INIT +1)
23: DATA        ENDS
```

```
24: ;
25: ; M A C R O   D E F I N I T I O N
26: ;
27: NEG32        MACRO    msreg,lsreg        ;NEGATE 32-BIT INTEGER
28:              NOT      msreg
29:              NOT      lsreg
30:              ADD      lsreg,1
31:              ADC      msreg,0
32:              ENDM
33: ;
34: ; C O D E   S E G M E N T   D E F I N I T I O N
35: ;
36: CODE         SEGMENT
37:              ASSUME   CS:CODE,DS:DATA
38:              PUBLIC   MULTIPLY
39: MULTIPLY     PROC     FAR                ;FUNCTION MULTIPLY (MPCAND,MPLIER)
40:              PUSH     BX                   ;SAVE REGISTERS
41:              PUSH     DS
42:              PUSHF                       ;SAVE FLAGS
43:              MOV      BX,SEG DATA        ;SET DS-REGISTER TO POINT
44:              MOV      DS,BX              ;TO DATA SEGMENT
45:              CMP      DX,0               ;IF   MPCAND < 0
46:              JGE      EXPAND
47:              NEG      SIGN               ;THEN SIGN = - SIGN
48:              NEG32    DX,AX              ;     MPCAND = - MPCAND
49: EXPAND:                                 ;ENDIF
50:              MOV      MPCAND,AX          ;EXPAND MPCAND TO 64-BITS
51:              MOV      MPCAND+2,DX
52:              MOV      MPCAND+4,0
53:              MOV      MPCAND+6,0
54:              CMP      DI,0               ;IF   MPLIER < 0
55:              JGE      ENDIF
56:              NEG      SIGN               ;THEN SIGN = - SIGN
57:              NEG32    DI,SI              ;     MPLIER = - MPLIER
58: ENDIF:                                  ;ENDIF
59:              MOV      MPLIER,SI
60:*             MOV      MPLIER+2,DI

61: ;
62:              MOV      AX,0               ;PRODUCT = 0
63:              MOV      DX,AX
64:              MOV      SI,AX
65:              MOV      DI,AX
66: LOOPTOP:                                ;WHILE MPLIER > 0
67:              CMP      MPLIER,0
68:              JNE      CONTINUE
69:              CMP      MPLIER+2,0
70:              JE       LOOPEND
71: CONTINUE:
72:              SHR      MPLIER+2,1         ;   IF   MPLIER IS ODD
73:              RCR      MPLIER,1
74:              JNC      UPDATE
75:              ADD      AX,MPCAND          ;   THEN PRODUCT = PRODUCT +
76:              ADC      DX,MPCAND+2        ;                     MPCAND
77:              ADC      SI,MPCAND+4
78:              ADC      DI,MPCAND+6
79: UPDATE:                                 ;   ENDIF
80:              SAL      MPCAND,1           ;   MPCAND = MPCAND * 2
81:              RCL      MPCAND+2,1
82:              RCL      MPCAND+4,1
83:              RCL      MPCAND+6,1
```

```
 84:                                              ;    MPLIER = MPLIER / 2
 85:                                              ;    (DONE IN IF TEST ABOVE)
 86:             JMP      LOOPTOP
 87: LOOPEND:                                     ;ENDWHILE
 88:             POP      BX                       ;FLAGS = SAVED FLAGS
 89:             AND      BX,OF7FEH                ;CLEAR OF AND CF IN FLAGS
 90:             CMP      DI,0                     ;IF    UPPER 33 BITS OF PRODUCT
 91:             JNE      SET_OF                   ;         NOT ZERO
 92:             CMP      SI,0
 93:             JNE      SET_OF
 94:             TEST     DX,8000H
 95:             JE       RESTORE
 96: SET_OF:
 97:             OR       BX,0801H                 ;THEN SET OF AND CF IN FLAGS
 98: RESTORE:                                      ;ENDIF
 99:             PUSH     BX                       ;SAVED FLAGS = FLAGS
100:             CMP      SIGN,0                   ;IF   SIGN < 0
101:             JG       RETURN
102:             NOT      DI                       ;THEN PRODUCT = - PRODUCT
103:             NOT      SI
104:             NOT      DX
105:             NOT      AX
106:             ADD      AX,1
107:             ADC      DX,0
108:             ADC      SI,0
109:             ADC      DI,0
110: RETURN:                                       ;ENDIF
111:             POPF                              ;RESTORE FLAGS
112:             POP      DS                       ;RESTORE REGISTERS
113:             POP      BX
114:             RET                               ;RETURN (PRODUCT)
115: MULTIPLY    ENDP                         ;END MULTIPLY
116: CODE        ENDS
117:*            END
```
*

20 and 21 as two consecutive 16-bit words (i.e., 32 bits). The physical order of the storage of the 8 bytes of MPCAND and the 4 bytes of MPLIER is shown in Figure 7.10. The bytes are stored in reverse order. The local data segment also contains a SIGN flag that is initialized to $+1$ (line 22). The flag indicates whether the final product should be positive or negative.

The macro definition in lines 27–32 is that of a user-defined operation code to negate a 32-bit value. The high-order half of the value to be negated is identified by the first macro operand (msreg), and the low-order half is identified by the second macro operand (lsreg). For example, the macro reference

```
NEG32 DX,AX
```

generates the instructions to negate the 32-bit value in the DX:AX register pair. The macro body appears in lines 28–31. Recall that the two's complement of a binary integer is equivalent to the one's complement of the binary integer plus 1. The two NOT instructions in lines 28 and 29 perform the one's complement of the 32-bit value in msreg:lsreg, leaving the result in msreg:1sreg. The ADD and ADC instructions add one to this value, completing the two's complement operation.

FIGURE 7.10
Organization of
local data segment

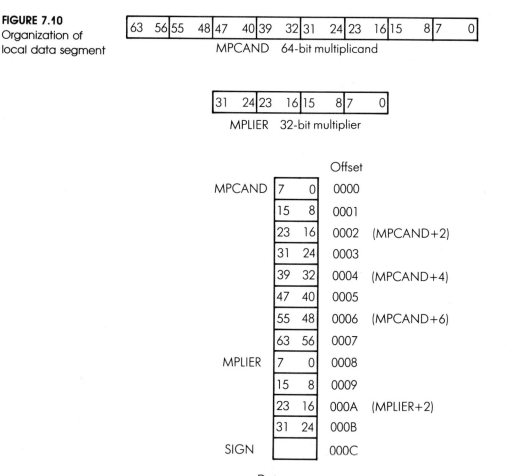

Data segment

The external subprocedure, MULTIPLY, is defined in lines 39–115. It begins by saving registers (lines 40 and 41) and flags (line 42) for its caller. The MOV instructions in lines 43 and 44 set the DS-register to the origin of the local data segment.

The single-alternative decision structure in lines 45–49 tests the multiplicand in the DX:AX register pair to see if it is negative: If it is negative, then the instructions in lines 47 and 48 are executed; if it is nonnegative, then these instructions are skipped. The NEG instruction in line 47 negates the value of the SIGN flag. The instructions generated by the macro reference in line 48 negate the value of the multiplicand in the DX:AX register pair.

Note that the 32-bit negation operation is designed to convert the multiplicand from signed two's complement form to unsigned integer form, with the sign maintained separately. Recall that the range of integers that can be represented with 32-bit binary numbers in two's complement form is $-2,147,483,648$ to $+2,147,483,647$. Thus, the 32-bit signed integer value $-2,147,483,648$ cannot successfully be negated, since the integer $+2,147,483,648$ cannot be represented in the 32-bit two's complement number system. However, this integer can be represented in 32-bit unsigned integer form, and the 32-bit negation operation is performed to convert it from signed form to unsigned form. The value $-2,147,483,648$ is represented in 32-bit two's complement form by the hexadecimal value 80000000. Taking the two's complement of this value produces the same hexadecimal value 80000000, which is the 32-bit unsigned integer representation of $+2,147,483,648$. This situation means that any negative integer in two's complement form can be converted to the corresponding positive integer in unsigned form by performing the negation (two's complement) operation on that negative integer.

The four MOV instructions in lines 50–53 expand the 32-bit unsigned integer multiplicand now in the DX:AX register pair to a 64-bit value beginning at the memory location specified by the symbolic name MPCAND. The first two MOV instructions move the 32-bit contents of the DX:AX register pair to the lower 32 bits of MPCAND. The last two MOV instructions set the upper 32 bits of MPCAND to zero.

The single-alternative decision structure in lines 54–58 tests the multiplier in the DI:SI register pair to see if it is negative: If it is negative, then the instructions in lines 56 and 57 are executed; if it is nonnegative, then these instructions are skipped. The NEG instruction in line 56 negates the value of the SIGN flag. The instructions generated by the macro reference in line 57 negate the value of the multiplier in the DI:SI register pair. Again, this negation operation is performed by taking the one's complement of the value in the DI:SI register pair and then adding 1 to that result.

The two MOV instructions in lines 59 and 60 move a copy of the 32-bit value of the multiplier to the four consecutive bytes of memory that begin at the memory location specified by the symbolic name MPLIER. The first MOV instruction moves a copy of the contents of the SI register to the lower 16 bits of MPLIER. The second MOV instruction moves a copy of the contents of the DI-register to the upper 16 bits of MPLIER.

At this point, the variable MPCAND contains a 64-bit unsigned integer multiplicand, and the variable MPLIER contains a 32-bit unsigned integer multiplier. The SIGN flag indicates whether or not the unsigned integer product, to be produced by the Russian Peasant's Method algorithm, will need to be negated to produce the correct signed integer product. The SIGN flag is initialized to $+1$ (line 22). If the original multiplicand and multiplier are both nonnegative, then neither of the NEG instructions (lines 47 and 56) are executed, and the value of SIGN remains at 1. If the multiplicand and multiplier are both negative, then both NEG instructions are executed. The first instruction changes the value of SIGN to -1, and the second returns the value of SIGN to $+1$. If the multiplicand and the multiplier do not have the same sign (i.e., one is negative, and one is nonnegative), then exactly one of the two NEG instructions is executed, setting SIGN to -1, which indicates that the product must be negated.

The four MOV instructions in lines 62–65 initialize the product in the DI:SI:DX:AX register group to zero. The MOV instruction in line 62 moves the immediate value zero to the AX-register. The three MOV instructions in lines 63–65 copy zero from the AX-register to the DX, SI, and DI registers, respectively. The register-to-register moves are 2-byte instructions, and the immediate-to-register move is a 3-byte instruction. That is, the sequence

```
MOV AX,0
MOV DX,AX
MOV SI,AX
MOV DI,AX
```

requires three fewer instruction bytes than does the sequence

```
MOV AX,0
MOV DX,0
MOV SI,0
MOV DI,0
```

In addition to the memory savings, a register-to-register move executes faster than an immediate-to-register move.

The WHILE loop in lines 66–87 computes the product of the multiplicand and the multiplier. The instructions in lines 67–70 provide the loop test. The two 16-bit halves of the multiplier have to be compared to zero separately. As long as the multiplier is nonzero, there are still nonzero, partial products to be added *to the product* sum—thus the loop body is executed. When both halves of the multiplier become zero, no further nonzero partial products are to be added to the product sum, so the loop is terminated (i.e., the jump in line 70 is taken). The loop body consists of the instructions in lines 72–83.

The single-alternative decision structure in lines 72–79 tests the current value of the multiplier to see if it is odd: If it is odd, then the current value of the multiplicand is added to the product sum; if it is even, then nothing is added to the product sum (i.e., the partial product for the current multiplier bit is zero). The SHR and RCR instructions in lines 72 and 73 perform two functions. They test the current value of the 32-bit multiplier to see if it is odd, and they divide the 32-bit multiplier by 2 in preparation for the next loop test and the next iteration of the loop body. The bit shifted from the right of the 32-bit operand, MPLIER, is recorded in the CF bit of the flags register. The bit shifted out is the remainder of the division by 2, and it indicates whether the value of the 32-bit multiplier was odd or even prior to the division operation. The JNC instruction in line 74 makes the decision based on this condition: If the CF bit in the flags register is 1, then the jump is not taken, and the instructions in lines 75–78 are executed; if the CF bit in the flags register is zero, then the instructions in lines 75–78 are skipped.

The four instructions in lines 75–78 perform a 64–bit addition operation. They add the 64-bit value of the MPCAND variable (the current value of the multiplicand) to the 64-bit value in the DI:SI:DX:AX register group (the current value of the product sum), leaving the result in the DI:SI:DX:AX register group (the new value of the product sum). The ADD instruction in line 75 adds bits 15 to 0 of the two 64-bit operands, leaving the result in the AX-register. The

ADC instruction in line 76 adds bits 31 to 16 of the two 64-bit operands and the carry from bit 15, leaving the result in the DX-register. The ADC instruction in line 77 adds bits 47 to 32 of the two 64-bit operands and the carry from bit 31, leaving the result in the SI-register. The ADC instruction in line 78 adds bits 63 to 48 of the two 64-bit operands and the carry from bit 47, leaving the result in the DI-register. The carry out of bit 63 (the MSB) is recorded in the CF bit of the flags register.

Following the single-alternative decision structure, the 64-bit value of MPCAND, the current value of the multiplicand, is multiplied by 2. This task is accomplished by the multiple-word, left-shift operation in lines 80–83. The comments in lines 84 and 85 indicate that the division of the multiplier by 2 was performed by the SHR and RCR instructions in lines 72 and 73.

The JMP instruction in line 86 returns control to the WHILE loop test beginning in line 66. At loop exit, the instructions in lines 88–114 are executed, and the complete unsigned integer product is in the DI:SI:DX:AX register group.

The instructions in lines 88–98 set the OF and CF bits in the flags register to reflect whether or not the product overflows 32 bits. If the high-order 33 bits of the product are not all zero, then the unsigned integer product will not fit into 32 bits when converted to a signed integer product, and the CF and OF bits in the flags register are set. If the high-order 33 bits of the product are all zero, then the OF and CF bits in the flags register are cleared. The POP instruction in line 88 pops the flags register value, saved on entry to the subprocedure, into the BX-register. The AND instruction in line 89 clears the OF and CF bits in this flags register value.

The single-alternative decision structure in lines 90–98 set the OF and CF bits in the flags register value in the BX-register, if the upper 33 bits of the product are not all zero. The CMP instruction in line 90 tests the DI-register, the CMP instruction in 92 tests the SI-register, and the TEST instruction in line 94 tests the MSB of the DX-register. The JNE instructions in lines 91 and 93 and the JE instruction in line 95 make decisions based on these preceding conditions. If any of the bits tested are nonzero, then the OR instruction in line 97 is executed. If all of the bits tested are zero, then the OR instruction is skipped. The OR instruction sets the OF and CF bits in the flags register value in the BX-register. Following this single-alternative decision structure, the PUSH instruction in line 99 is executed, which pushes the modified flags register value back onto the stack.

The single-alternative decision structure in lines 100–110 negates the 64-bit product in the DI:SI:DX:AX register group, if the SIGN flag indicates that this is required. The CMP instruction in line 100 tests the SIGN flag, and the JG instruction in line 101 makes the decision based on the condition of the SIGN flag: If the SIGN flag has the value -1, then the instructions in lines 102–109 are executed; otherwise, these instructions are skipped. The instructions in lines 102–109 perform the two's complement of the 64-bit value in the DI:SI:DX:AX register group. The four NOT instructions perform the one's complement of this 64-bit value, and the four addition instructions add 1 to the one's complement, producing the two's complement. The resulting 64-bit signed integer product is left in the DI:SI:DX:AX register group.

The subprocedure ends by restoring the registers for the caller (lines 111–113) and returning control to the caller (line 114). The signed integer product is returned in the DI:SI:DX:AX register group. The OF and CF bits in the saved and restored flags register value have been modified. All other bits in the flags register have been preserved.

The main procedure defined in lines 35–93 in Program Listing 7.2 performs the following steps:

1. Prompts for the multiplier (lines 44–46).
2. Accepts the input value for the multiplier in the DX:AX register pair (line 47).
3. Displays the multiplier in binary form (lines 48–54).
4. Moves the multiplier to the DI:SI register pair (lines 55–56).
5. Prompts for the multiplicand (lines 57–61).
6. Accepts the input value for the multiplicand in the DX:AX register pair (line 62).
7. Displays the multiplicand in binary form (lines 63–68).
8. Calls the MULTIPLY subprocedure to compute the product of the multiplicand and the multiplier (line 69).
9. Displays the product in binary form if the product overflowed 32 bits, in decimal if the product did not overflow 32 bits (lines 70–91).

The following results are from some sample executions of this program:

```
ENTER MULTIPLICAND 32767
00000000000000000111111111111111

ENTER MULTIPLIER  -32767
11111111111111111000000000000001


PRODUCT = -1073676289


ENTER MULTIPLICAND 62100
00000000000000001111001010010100

ENTER MULTIPLIER      -12
11111111111111111111111111110100

PRODUCT = -745200


ENTER MULTIPLICAND 65535
00000000000000001111111111111111

ENTER MULTIPLIER  -65535
11111111111111110000000000000001

PRODUCT =
1111111111111111111111111111111100000000000000001111111111111111
```

```
ENTER MULTIPLICAND -65536
11111111111111110000000000000000

ENTER MULTIPLIER -65536
11111111111111110000000000000000

PRODUCT =
00000000000000000000000000000001000000000000000000000000000000000
```

PROGRAMMING EXERCISES

7.1 In Programming Exercise 4.1, the notion of an Ulam sequence and its length was introduced. Programming Exercise 5.1 also involved Ulam sequences. This exercise expands Programming Exercise 5.1.

Design a subalgorithm to accept a positive integer as input and to return the length of the Ulam sequence for that integer as output. Design a main algorithm that uses the subalgorithm to find the integer in the range 1–65,535 whose Ulam sequence has the largest length. The algorithm is to output that integer and the length of its Ulam sequence. The main algorithm will reference the subalgorithm 65,535 times, once for each integer in the range 1–65,535.

Implement your subalgorithm with an IBM PC Assembly language external FAR function procedure. Your input should be a 16-bit unsigned integer in the AX-register. The length of the Ulam sequence for the input integer will be returned to the caller in the AX-register. Use 32-bit arithmetic in your subprocedure to accommodate large integers in the Ulam sequence. (*Hint*: You can avoid the need for a 32-bit multiply by using $3x + 1 = 2x + x + 1$.) In the event that 32-bit arithmetic is not sufficient for all integers in the given range, your subprocedure should return an Ulam length of zero, if overflow is detected during computation of the Ulam sequence.

Implement your main algorithm with an IBM PC Assembly language program that uses your external subprocedure to compute the length of the Ulam sequence for each of the integers in the given range. There is no input to your program. Your output should be a list of integers whose Ulam sequence produced an integer that overflowed 32 bits and the integer whose Ulam sequence had the largest length along with that largest length. The output is to be displayed on the screen. *Warning*: Allow approximately five minutes for this program to execute.

7.2 Design an algorithm to perform integer exponentiation. Your inputs should be a signed integer value that represents the BASE and an unsigned integer value that represents the positive EXPONENT. Your output should be the value of BASE raised to EXPONENT. For example, if the inputs are BASE = −2 and EXPONENT = 5, then the output should be $(-2)^5 = -32$. Your algorithm must detect overflow.

Implement your algorithm with an IBM PC Assembly language external FAR procedure. Your input should be an 8-bit signed integer value in the AL-register that represents BASE and an 8-bit unsigned integer value in the AH-register that represents EXPONENT. Your procedure is to return the result, a 32-bit signed integer, in the DX:AX register pair and an overflow indicator in the BL-register (BL-register = 0 implies no overflow).

Your procedure must save and restore all registers used for purposes other than procedure output. These registers must include the flags register and the BH-register if it is used.

7.3 The MULTIPLY procedure presented in Program Listing 7.3 contains two known bugs:

    a. The overflow flag is not set correctly for a product of − 2,147,483,648. Execute the program with the following inputs: 65,536 and − 32,768. You will find that the product is displayed in binary, which means that the OF and CF bits in the flags register were set by

the MULTIPLY procedure. However, − 2,147,483,648 does *not* overflow 32 bits. Thus, the value should
have been displayed in decimal.

b. The procedure may not execute correctly if called more than once from
another procedure. For example, if
MULTIPLY is called with inputs of
− 12 and + 16 and then called a
second time with inputs of − 12 and
+ 16, the product from the second call
will be + 192. Use the main procedure
in Program Listing 7.4 and see what
happens.

Repair the bugs in Program Listing 7.3.
Demonstrate the modified procedure by using
the main procedure in Program Listing 7.4 with
the inputs in Table 7.3.

TABLE 7.3   Inputs for Programming Exercises
7.3–7.6

Multiplicand	Multiplier
0	5281
150	150
− 160	− 160
32767	− 1
− 32768	32767
65536	− 32768
− 16384	− 131072
20	− 102261127

7.4 The following algorithm is an alternative to the
algorithm for signed integer multiplication
presented in the section "Russian Peasant's
Multiply—32-Bit Implementation":

```
FUNCTION MULTIPLY(MULTIPLICAND,MULTIPLIER)
    IF      MULTIPLIER <0
    THEN
            MULTIPLICAND = - MULTIPLICAND
            MULTIPLIER  = - MULTIPLIER
    ENDIF
    PRODUCT = 0
    WHILE    MULTIPLIER > 0
      IF     MULTIPLIER IS ODD
      THEN
             PRODUCT = PRODUCT + MULTIPLICAND
      ENDIF
      MULTIPLICAND = MULTIPLICAND*2
      MULTIPLIER =   MULTIPLIER/2
    ENDWHILE
    RETURN (PRODUCT)
END MULTIPLY
```

Implement this algorithm with an IBM PC
Assembly language external FAR procedure.
Your input should be a 32-bit signed integer
multiplicand in the DX:AX register pair and a
32-bit signed integer multiplier in the DI:SI
register pair. Your output should be the 64-bit
signed integer product in the DI:SI:DX:AX
register group, with the OF and CF bits of the
flags register set to reflect whether or not the
product overflows 32 bits. Your procedure must
save and restore all registers used for purposes
other than procedure output. All flags register
bits other than the OF and CF bits must be saved
and restored.

Use the main procedure in Program Listing
7.4 to demonstrate your subprocedure, and use
the inputs in Table 7.3 in your demonstration.

7.5 The following algorithm, the Shift and Add
Method, is an alternative to the Russian Peasant's
Method for performing signed integer multi-
plication:

```
FUNCTION MULTIPLY(MULTIPLICAND,MULTIPLIER)
    EXP_MPCAND = MULTIPLICAND EXPANDED TO 2N BITS
    PARTIAL_PRODUCT = 0
    IF   MSB OF MULTIPLIER = 1
    THEN
         PARTIAL_PRODUCT = 2'S COMPLEMENT OF EXP_MPCAND
    ENDIF
    BIT_COUNT = N-1
    REPEAT
      SHIFT PARTIAL_PRODUCT LEFT 1 BIT POSITION
      SHIFT MULTIPLIER LEFT 1 BIT POSITION
      IF   MSB OF MULTIPLIER = 1
      THEN
           PARTIAL_PRODUCT = PARTIAL_PRODUCT + EXP_MPCAND
      ENDIF
      BIT_COUNT = BIT_COUNT - 1
    UNTIL BIT_COUNT = 0
    RETURN (PARTIAL_PRODUCT)
END MULTIPLY
```

It accepts an n-bit multiplicand and an n-bit
multiplier and produces a $2n$-bit product. Implement this algorithm with an IBM PC Assembly
language external FAR procedure. Your input
should be a 32-bit signed integer multiplicand in
the DX:AX register pair and a 32-bit signed
integer multiplier in the DI:SI register pair.
Your output should be the 64-bit signed integer
product in the DI:SI:DX:AX register group,
with the OF and CF bits of the flags register set
to reflect whether or not the product overflows 32
bits. Your procedure must save and restore all
registers used for purposes other than procedure

```
 1: ;
 2: ;
 3: ;                    PROGRAM LISTING 7.4
 4: ;
 5: ;PROGRAM TO DEMONSTRATE MULTIPLY PROCEDURES
 6: ;
 7:                                        ;PROCEDURES TO
 8:              EXTRN    GETDEC32:FAR     ;GET 32-BIT SIGNED DEC. INT.
 9:              EXTRN    MULTIPLY:FAR     ;PERFORM 32-BIT MULTIPLY
10:                                        ;USING RUSSIAN PEASANT'S METHOD
11:              EXTRN    NEWLINE:FAR      ;DISPLAY NEWLINE CHARACTER
12:              EXTRN    PUTBIN:FAR       ;DISPLAY BINARY INTEGER
13:              EXTRN    PUTDEC32:FAR     ;DISPLAY 32-BIT SIGNED DEC. INT.
14:              EXTRN    PUTSTRNG:FAR     ;DISPLAY CHARACTER STRING
15: ;
16: ; S T A C K    S E G M E N T    D E F I N I T I O N
17: ;
18: STACK        SEGMENT STACK
19:              DB       256 DUP(?)
20: STACK        ENDS
21: ;
22: ; D A T A    S E G M E N T    D E F I N I T I O N
23: ;
24: DATA         SEGMENT
25: ;
26: PROMPT1      DB       'ENTER MULTIPLICAND '
27: PROMPT2      DB       'ENTER MULTIPLIER   '
28: ANNOTATE     DB       'PRODUCT = '
29: ;
30: DATA         ENDS
31: ;
32: ; C O D E    S E G M E N T    D E F I N I T I O N
33: ;
34: CODE         SEGMENT
35: EX_7_4       PROC     FAR
36:              ASSUME   CS:CODE,DS:NOTHING,SS:STACK,ES:DATA
37:              PUSH     DS               ;PUSH RETURN SEG ADDR ON STACK
38:              MOV      AX,0             ;PUSH RETURN OFFSET OF ZERO
39:              PUSH     AX               ;ON STACK
40:              MOV      AX,SEG DATA      ;INITIALIZE ES-REGISTER
41:              MOV      ES,AX            ;TO POINT TO DATA SEGMENT
42:*             CALL     NEWLINE


43: ;
44:              LEA      DI,PROMPT2       ;PROMPT FOR MPLIER
45:              MOV      CX,19
46:              CALL     PUTSTRNG
47:              CALL     GETDEC32         ;GET MPLIER
48:              MOV      BL,1             ;PUTBIN CODE = WORD
49:              XCHG     DX,AX            ;DISPLAY MPLIER IN BINARY
50:              CALL     PUTBIN
51:              XCHG     DX,AX
52:              CALL     PUTBIN
53:              CALL     NEWLINE
54:              CALL     NEWLINE
55:              MOV      DI,DX            ;<MPLIER IN DI:SI>
56:              MOV      SI,AX
57:              PUSH     DI
58:              LEA      DI,PROMPT1       ;PROMPT FOR MCAND
59:              MOV      CX,19
```

```
 60:              CALL    PUTSTRNG
 61:              POP     DI
 62:              CALL    GETDEC32          ;GET MCAND
 63:              XCHG    DX,AX             ;DISPLAY MCAND IN BINARY
 64:              CALL    PUTBIN
 65:              XCHG    DX,AX
 66:              CALL    PUTBIN
 67:              CALL    NEWLINE
 68:              CALL    NEWLINE
 69:              PUSH    DX                ;SAVE MULTIPLICAND
 70:              PUSH    AX
 71:              PUSH    DI                ;SAVE MULTIPLIER
 72:              PUSH    SI
 73:              CALL    MULTIPLY          ;PRODUCT = MULTIPLY(MCAND,MPLIER)
 74:              POP     SI                ;RESTORE MULTIPLIER
 75:              POP     DI
 76:              POP     AX                ;RESTORE MULTIPLICAND
 77:              POP     DX
 78:              CALL    MULTIPLY          ;PRODUCT = MULTIPLY(MCAND,MPLIER)
 79:              PUSH    DI
 80:              LEA     DI,ANNOTATE       ;DISPLAY 'PRODUCT = '
 81:              MOV     CX,10
 82:              CALL    PUTSTRNG
 83:              POP     DI
 84:              MOV     BL,1              ;PUTBIN CODE = WORD
 85:              JNO     ELSE              ;IF    OVERFLOW
 86:              PUSH    AX                ;THEN
 87:              MOV     AX,DI             ;          DISPLAY BITS 63 - 48
 88:              CALL    PUTBIN            ;                  OF PRODUCT
 89:              MOV     AX,SI             ;          DISPLAY BITS 47 - 32
 90:              CALL    PUTBIN            ;                  OF PRODUCT
 91:              MOV     AX,DX             ;          DISPLAY BITS 31 - 16
 92:              CALL    PUTBIN            ;                  OF PRODUCT
 93:              POP     AX                ;          DISPLAY BITS 15 - 00
 94:              CALL    PUTBIN            ;                  OF PRODUCT
 95:              JMP     ENDIF
 96: ELSE:                                 ;ELSE
 97:              MOV     BH,0              ;          DISPLAY PRODUCT IN DECIMAL
 98:              CALL    PUTDEC32
 99: ENDIF:                                ;ENDIF
100:              CALL    NEWLINE
101:              RET                       ;RETURN
102: EX_7_4       ENDP
103: CODE         ENDS
104:*             END     EX_7_4
*
```

output. All flags register bits other than the OF and CF bits must be saved and restored.

Use the main procedure in Program Listing 7.4 to demonstrate your subprocedure, and use the inputs in Table 7.3 in your demonstration.

7.6 The following algorithm, the Add and Shift Method, is another alternative for performing signed integer multiplication:

```
FUNCTION MULTIPLY(MULTIPLICAND,MULTIPLIER)
  PARTIAL_PRODUCT = 0
  BIT_COUNT = N-1
  REPEAT
      IF    LSB OF MULTIPLIER = 1
      THEN  ADD MULTIPLICAND TO UPPER HALF OF PARTIAL_PRODUCT
            IF    OVERFLOW
            THEN SHIFT PARTIAL_PRODUCT RIGHT 1 BIT SHIFTING
                 IN CARRY
            ELSE
                 SHIFT PARTIAL PRODUCT
                 RIGHT 1 BIT SHIFTING
                 IN COPY OF SIGN
            ENDIF
      ELSE
            SHIFT PARTIAL_PRODUCT RIGHT 1 BIT SHIFTING IN COPY
            OF SIGN
      ENDIF
```

```
        SHIFT MULTIPLIER RIGHT 1 BIT POSITION
        BIT_COUNT = BIT_COUNT - 1
   UNTIL   BIT_COUNT = 0
   IF    LSB OF MULTIPLIER = 1
   THEN
        ADD 2'S COMPLEMENT OF MULTIPLICAND TO UPPER HALF OF
        PARTIAL_PRODUCT
   ENDIF
   SHIFT PARTIAL_PRODUCT RIGHT 1 BIT SHIFTING IN COPY OF SIGN
   IF    PARTIAL_PRODUCT = -2^{2N-2}
   THEN
             PARTIAL_PRODUCT = +2^{2N-2}
   ENDIF
   RETURN (PARTIAL_PRODUCT)
END MULTIPLY
```

It accepts an n-bit multiplicand and an n-bit multiplier and produces a $2n$-bit product. Implement this algorithm with an IBM PC Assembly language external FAR procedure. Your input should be a 32-bit signed integer multiplicand in the DX:AX register pair and a 32-bit signed integer multiplier in the DI:SI register pair. Your output should be the 64-bit signed integer product in the DI:SI:DX:AX register group, with the OF and CF bits of the flags register set to reflect whether or not the product overflows 32 bits. Your procedure must save and restore all registers used for purposes other than procedure output. All flags register bits other than the OF and CF bits must be saved and restored.

Use the main procedure in Program Listing 7.4 to demonstrate your subprocedure, and use the inputs in Table 7.3 in your demonstration.

7.7 The following algorithm, the Restoring Method, provides a method for performing signed integer division:

```
PROCEDURE DIVIDE (DIVIDEND,DIVISOR,QUOTIENT,REMAINDER)
   QUOTIENT = 0
   IF  SIGN OF DIVIDEND ≠ SIGN OF DIVISOR
   THEN
        TRIAL_DIV = DIVISOR
        RESTORE = - DIVISOR
   ELSE
        TRIAL_DIV = - DIVISOR
        RESTORE = DIVISOR
   ENDIF
   SIGN = SIGN OF DIVIDEND
   EXP_DIV = DIVIDEND EXPANDED TO 2N BITS
   BIT_COUNT = N
   REPEAT
      SHIFT EXP_DIV LEFT 1 BIT POSITION
      ADD TRIAL_DIV TO UPPER HALF OF EXP_DIV
      SHIFT QUOTIENT LEFT 1 BIT POSITION
      IF    EXP_DIV = 0 OR
            SIGN = SIGN OF EXP_DIV
      THEN
            QUOTIENT = QUOTIENT + 1
```

```
      ENDIF
      BIT_COUNT = BIT_COUNT - 1
   UNTIL BIT_COUNT = 0
   REMAINDER = UPPER HALF OF EXP_DIV
   IF   SIGN OF DIVIDEND ≠ SIGN OF DIVISOR
   THEN
             QUOTIENT = - QUOTIENT
   ENDIF
   RETURN
END DIVIDE
```

The algorithm accepts an n-bit dividend and an n-bit divisor and produces an n-bit quotient and an n-bit remainder. Implement this algorithm with an IBM PC Assembly language external FAR procedure. Your input should be a 32-bit signed integer dividend in the DX:AX register pair and a 32-bit signed integer divisor in the CX:BX register pair. Your output should be the 32-bit signed integer quotient in the DX:AX register pair and the 32-bit signed integer remainder in the CX:BX register pair. Your procedure must save and restore all registers used for purposes other than procedure output, including the flags register.

Use the main procedure in Program Listing 7.5 to demonstrate your subprocedure, and use the following inputs in your demonstration:

Dividend	Divisor
2147483635	117
2147483635	− 117
− 2147483635	117
− 2147483635	− 117
0	− 123456789
123456789	1
− 20	2
− 23	4
2147483647	− 2147483648
− 2147493648	2147483647

7.8 The following sequence of positive integers, 1, 1, 2, 3, 5, 8, 13, 21, 34, 55, 89 . . . , is called the Fibonacci sequence. The first number in the sequence, F_1, is 1. The second number in the sequence, F_2, is 1. Each subsequent number in the sequence, F_i, is the sum of the two numbers previous to it in the sequence. That is,

$$F_i = F_{i-1} + F_{i-2} \quad \text{for } i > 2$$

Design an algorithm to find and display the largest value of i for which F_i can be represented as a 64-bit unsigned binary integer.

Implement your algorithm with an IBM PC Assembly language program. There is no input to your program. Your output should be the appropriate value of i displayed in decimal and the corresponding value of F_i displayed in binary.

7.9 The factorial of a nonnegative integer, n, can be defined as follows:

$$n! = 1 \qquad \text{if } n = 0$$

$$n! = (n)(n - 1)(n - 2) \ldots (2)(1) \quad \text{if } n > 0$$

That is, $n!$ is the product of the first n positive integers, for $n > 0$.

Design an algorithm to find the largest value of n for which $n!$ can be represented as a 32-bit unsigned binary integer. Implement your algorithm with an IBM PC Assembly language program. There is no input to your program. Your output should be the appropriate value of n and the corresponding value of $n!$ displayed in decimal on the screen.

You will need a 32-bit unsigned integer multiply procedure in your program. The assembly module in Program Listing 7.3 with slight modifications can satisfy this need.

7.10 Write an IBM PC Assembly language macro, named ROL32, to perform a left rotate operation on a 32-bit value in the DX:AX register pair. Your macro should have one operand, an immediate value that specifies the shift count. It should affect the flags register in exactly the same way that the ROL instruction affects the flags register.

It also should protect registers for the user.

Write an IBM PC Assembly language macro, named ROR32, to perform a right rotate operation on a 32-bit value in the DX:AX register pair. Your macro should have one operand, an immediate value that specifies the shift count. It should affect the flags register in exactly the same way that the ROR instruction affects the flags register. It also should protect registers for the user.

7.11 Write a 32-bit version of the PUT_BIN procedure in Program Listing 6.3. Use the same basic algorithm as in Program Listing 6.3, eliminating the logic that tests the code in the BL-register. You *may not* call the PUTBIN procedure in your solution. Your procedure should be named PUTBIN32. Your input should be a 32-bit value in the DX:AX register pair. Your procedure should display the value in binary form on the screen beginning at the current cursor position.

7.12 Write an IBM PC Assembly language macro, named SHR32, to perform a logical right-shift of the 32-bit value in the DX:AX register pair. This macro is to be used for division by a power of 2, so your macro should leave the remainder of the division (the bits shifted from the DX:AX register pair) in the BX:CX register pair (right-justified). It should have one operand, an immediate value that specifies the shift count. You may assume that the shift count will be in the range 1–32.

```
 1: ;
 2: ;
 3: ;                    PROGRAM LISTING 7.5
 4: ;
 5: ;PROGRAM TO DEMONSTRATE INTEGER DIVISION SUBPROCEDURE
 6: ;
 7:                                       ;SUBPROCEDURES TO
 8:            EXTRN    DIVIDE:FAR         ;PERFORM 32-BIT SIGNED DIVISION
 9:            EXTRN    GETDEC32:FAR       ;GET 32-BIT SIGNED DECIMAL INT.
10:            EXTRN    NEWLINE:FAR        ;DISPLAY NEWLINE CHARACTER
11:            EXTRN    PUTDEC32:FAR       ;DISPLAY 32-BIT SIGNED DEC INT
12:            EXTRN    PUTSTRNG:FAR       ;DISPLAY CHARACTER STRING
13: ;
14: ; S T A C K   S E G M E N T   D E F I N I T I O N
15: ;
16: STACK      SEGMENT STACK
17:            DB       128 DUP(0)
```

```
18: STACK      ENDS
19: ;
20: ; D A T A   S E G M E N T   D E F I N I T I O N
21: ;
22: DATA       SEGMENT
23: ;
24: DVDEND     DW      ?                       ;DIVIDEND
25:            DW      ?
26: DVISOR     DW      ?                       ;DIVISOR
27:            DW      ?
28: PROMPT1    DB      'ENTER DIVIDEND  '
29: PROMPT2    DB      'ENTER DIVISOR   '
30: OUTPUT1    DB      'DIVIDEND   =  '
31: OUTPUT2    DB      'DIVISOR    =  '
32: OUTPUT3    DB      'QUOTIENT   =  '
33: OUTPUT4    DB      'REMAINDER  =  '
34: ;
35: DATA       ENDS
36: ;
37: ; C O D E   S E G M E N T   D E F I N I T I O N
38: ;
39: CODE       SEGMENT
40: EX_7_5     PROC    FAR
41:            ASSUME  CS:CODE,DS:DATA,SS:STACK,ES:DATA
42:            PUSH    DS                      ;PUSH RETURN SEG ADDR ON STACK
43:            MOV     AX,0                    ;PUSH RETURN OFFSET OF ZERO
44:            PUSH    AX                      ;ON STACK
45:                                            ;ON STACK
46:            MOV     AX,SEG DATA             ;SET DS AND ES REGISTERS TO
47:            MOV     DS,AX                   ;POINT TO DATA SEGMENT
48:*           MOV     ES,AX
49: ;
50:            LEA     DI,PROMPT1              ;PROMPT FOR DIVIDEND
51:            MOV     CX,16
52:            CALL    PUTSTRNG
53:            CALL    GETDEC32                ;GET DIVIDEND
54:            MOV     DVDEND,AX               ;SAVE DIVIDEND
55:            MOV     DVDEND+2,DX
56:            CALL    NEWLINE
57:            LEA     DI,PROMPT2              ;PROMPT FOR DIVISOR
58:            MOV     CX,16
59:            CALL    PUTSTRNG
60:            CALL    GETDEC32                ;GET DIVISOR
61:            MOV     DVISOR,AX               ;SAVE DIVISOR
62:            MOV     DVISOR+2,DX
63:            CALL    NEWLINE
64:            MOV     AX,DVDEND               ;CALL DIVIDE (DIVIDEND,DIVISOR,
65:            MOV     DX,DVDEND+2             ;            QUOTIENT,REMAINDER)
66:            MOV     BX,DVISOR
67:            MOV     CX,DVISOR+2
68:            CALL    DIVIDE
69:            PUSH    BX                      ;SAVE REMAINDER
70:            PUSH    CX
71:            PUSH    AX                      ;SAVE QUOTIENT
72:            PUSH    DX
73:            LEA     DI,OUTPUT1              ;OUTPUT DIVIDEND
74:            MOV     CX,14
75:            CALL    PUTSTRNG
76:            MOV     AX,DVDEND
7(:            MOV     DX,DVDEND+2
78:            MOV     BH,0
```

```
 79:                CALL    PUTDEC32
 80:                CALL    NEWLINE
 81:                LEA     DI,OUTPUT2              ;OUTPUT DIVISOR
 82:                MOV     CX,14
 83:                CALL    PUTSTRNG
 84:                MOV     AX,DVISOR
 85:                MOV     DX,DVISOR+2
 86:                CALL    PUTDEC32
 87:                CALL    NEWLINE
 88:                LEA     DI,OUTPUT3             ;OUTPUT QUOTIENT
 89:                MOV     CX,14
 90:                CALL    PUTSTRNG
 91:                POP     DX
 92:                POP     AX
 93:                CALL    PUTDEC32
 94:                CALL    NEWLINE
 95:                LEA     DI,OUTPUT4             ;OUTPUT REMAINDER
 96:                MOV     CX,14
 97:                CALL    PUTSTRNG
 98:                POP     DX
 99:                POP     AX
100:                CALL    PUTDEC32
101:                CALL    NEWLINE
102: RETURN:        RET                            ;RETURN
103: EX_7_5         ENDP
104: CODE           ENDS
105:*               END     EX_7_5
*
```

8

ARRAYS AND
CHARACTER STRINGS

The example programs presented in the preceding chapters have primarily involved single-valued data items, called *scalars*. They have included character strings, but these were used exclusively to display messages to the program's user. This chapter introduces one type of multivalued data item, the *array*. The *character string*, which is a special kind of array, is also discussed in more detail. This book assumes you are already familiar with one- and two-dimensional arrays in some high-level language. This book explores how arrays are stored in a computer's memory and the machine-level techniques that are used to manipulate an array's elements. This discussion is restricted to one-dimensional arrays. (Two-dimensional arrays are covered in Chapter 13.)

8.1 One-Dimensional Array

An **array** is an ordered list of homogeneous data items, called the **array elements**. The term "ordered" refers to the fact that the list has a first element, a second element, a third element, and so on. The term "homogeneous" means that all elements in the list are of the same data type; that is, an array is a list of integers, a list of real numbers, a list of characters, a list of arrays (i.e., a multidimensional array). A **character string** is a special kind of array—it is an array of characters.

Figure 8.1 shows the logical arrangement of the elements of an *n*-element array. Representing an array in computer memory is quite natural. Its elements are stored in contiguous memory locations, with the first element stored first, immediately followed by the second element, immediately followed by the third element, and so on. Figure 8.1 can be viewed as a block of contiguous memory. The address of the first element of the array, called the **base address** of the

FIGURE 8.1
Organization of
array elements

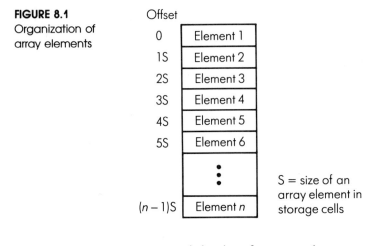

array, and the size of an array element are the only items needed to compute an element's address. The address of a given element is computed from an offset relative to the base address. Figure 8.1 shows the offset for each element relative to the base address. Memory itself can be viewed as an array of storage cells. In fact, the segment-offset approach to memory addressing is based on this viewpoint: The segment portion of the address is a base address, and the offset portion is an offset relative to that base address.

The example programs in this chapter illustrate arrays of integers (word arrays) and character strings (byte arrays). One program introduces BCD numbers (nibble arrays). BCD numbers and BCD arithmetic are discussed in detail in Chapter 11.

8.2   Defining and Initializing Arrays

In the IBM PC Assembly language, arrays are defined and initialized with DB and DW pseudo-operations. Recall that the DB and DW pseudo-operations have the following general forms:

```
[⟨label⟩]   DB   ⟨byte constant-list⟩   [⟨comment⟩]
[⟨label⟩]   DW   ⟨word constant-list⟩   [⟨comment⟩]
```

in which ⟨constant-list⟩ is a list of constants (named constants, literal constants, or the null constant) separated by commas. Also, recall that a list of constants that contains a constant or group of constants that is repeated in a sequence can be abbreviated with a duplicate clause (see Section 2.2).

In array definitions, the DB and DW pseudo-operations specify the name of the array. The ⟨constant-list⟩ defines the size of the array and the initial values of the array's elements. The following data segment definition provides some examples of array definitions along with the translation listing generated by the assembler (note that the array elements are stored in a contiguous sequence of memory locations):

```
0000                                  DATA     SEGMENT
0000      64 [                        TABLE    DW    100 DUP(?)
                ????
                        ]
00C8      32 [                        COUNTS   DW    50 DUP(0)
                0000
                        ]
012C      0000 0001 0002 0003  ARRAY  DW    0, 1, 2, 3, 4, 5, 6, 7, 8, 9
          0004 0005 0006 0007
          0008 0009
0140      54 48 49 53 20 49   STRING  DB    'THIS IS A STRING'
          53 20 41 20 53 54
          52 49 4E 47
0150      28 [                INSTRNG  DB    40 DUP(' ')
               20
                        ]
0178                          DATA     ENDS
                                       END
```

TABLE is defined as a word array with 100 elements (64 hex) whose elements are not initialized. COUNTS is defined as a word array with 50 elements (32 hex) whose elements are all initialized to zero. ARRAY is defined as a word array with 10 elements whose first element is initialized to 0 and whose second element is initialized to 1. In general, the nth element is initialized to $n - 1$. STRING is defined as a byte array with 16 elements whose first element is initialized to "T" (ASCII code 54 hex) and whose second element is initialized to "H." The sixteenth element of STRING is initialized to "G." INSTRNG is defined as a byte array with 40 elements (28 hex) whose elements are all initialized to the character SPACE (ASCII code 20 hex). Note that 40 DUP (20H) or 40 DUP (32) could also have been used for definition of INSTRNG.

8.3   Accessing Array Elements

Array elements can be accessed by specifying an index (offset) relative to the base address (start address) of the array or by using a special set of IBM PC Assembly language instructions called *string instructions*.

Indexing into Arrays

To select and use an array element, an operation known as **subscripting** (or **indexing**) is used. A **subscript** is an offset that is added to the base address of the array, thus providing the address of a specific element. The base address of an array is the address of the first element. In array definition examples given previously, the name in the label field of the DB or DW pseudo-operation is the name of the array. It is actually the symbolic name of the memory location where contiguous storage for the array elements begins; that is, it is the symbolic name for the array's first element. Therefore, this name is used symbolically to specify the base address of the array. **Index registers** are used to hold offsets from this base address. In the IBM PC Assembly language, the BX, DI, SI, and BP registers are used for indexing (subscripting) into arrays. Note: The BP-register is designed for use as an auxiliary pointer in the stack segment. However, it can also be used as an index register for a static array. Its use is discussed further in Section 8.4. If an operand is to be subscripted, then the index register name appears in square brackets following the operand. Such notation indicates that the value in the index register is to be added to the address specified by the operand, which then provides the address of the desired array element.

EXAMPLES

Suppose a byte array is defined by

```
TABLE   DB   10 DUP(0)
```

This byte array is described in Figure 8.2(a). TABLE is the symbolic name associated with the first element of the array, the element with index 0. The ith element is indexed by the integer $i - 1$, that is, to reach the ith element, $i - 1$ must be added to the array's base address, which is associated with the symbolic name TABLE.

Suppose the AL-register contains 17 hex and that the BX-register contains 3 hex. Then the instruction

```
MOV   TABLE[BX],AL
```

will move 17 hex into the fourth element of TABLE (Figure 8.2(b)). The offset portion of the effective address specified by the operand TABLE[BX] is the

FIGURE 8.2(a)
Byte array
table before
MOV TABLE[BX],AL

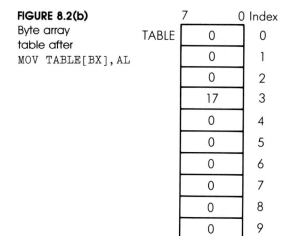

FIGURE 8.2(b)
Byte array
table after
`MOV TABLE[BX],AL`

	7 0	Index
TABLE	0	0
	0	1
	0	2
	17	3
	0	4
	0	5
	0	6
	0	7
	0	8
	0	9

offset of TABLE plus the contents of the BX-register. The segment portion of the effective address is the address of the segment that contains the TABLE definition.

Suppose TABLE had been defined as a word array:

```
TABLE   DW   10 DUP(0)
```

This word array is described in Figure 8.3(a). TABLE is the symbolic name associated with the first element (word) of the array (bytes 0 and 1). The ith element is the word in bytes $2(i - 1)$ and $2(i - 1) + 1$ of the array.

Therefore, the ith element is the word indexed by the integer $2(i - 1)$; that is, to reach the ith element of a word array, $2(i - 1)$ must be added to the base address of the array, the address associated with the symbolic name TABLE.

FIGURE 8.3(a)
Word array
table before
`MOV TABLE[BX],AX`

	15 0	Index	Bytes
TABLE	0	0	1–0
	0	2	3–2
	0	4	5–4
	0	6	7–6
	0	8	9–8
	0	10	11–10
	0	12	13–12
	0	14	15–14
	0	16	17–16
	0	18	19–18

FIGURE 8.3(b)
Word array
table after
`MOV TABLE[BX],AX`

TABLE	15 ... 0	Index	Bytes
	0	0	1–0
	0	2	3–2
	0	4	5–4
	17	6	7–6
	0	8	9–8
	0	10	11–10
	0	12	13–12
	0	14	15–14
	0	16	17–16
	0	18	19–18

Suppose the AX-register contains 17 hex and the BX-register contains 6 hex. Then the instruction

```
MOV   TABLE[BX],AX
```

will move 17 hex into the fourth element of TABLE (Figure 8.3(b)).

To perform some function on every element of an array, a loop can be used. The loop body can execute once for each element in the array. Each time through the loop body, the array index is incremented (or decremented) to move to the next element.

EXAMPLE

Consider the following array definitions:

```
BTABLE   DB   100 DUP(?)
WTABLE   DW   100 DUP(?)
```

BTABLE is defined as a byte array of 100 elements, and WTABLE is defined as a word array of 100 elements. To initialize both arrays to the values 1, 2, 3, 4, . . . , 99, 100, the following loop could be used:

```
          MOV   CX,100            ;LOOP_CNT = 100
LOOPTOP:                          ;REPEAT
          MOV   BX,CX             ;    I = LOOP_CNT - 1
          DEC   BX
          MOV   BTABLE[BX],CL     ;    BTABLE[I] = LOOP_CNT
          SAL   BX,1              ;    I = I*2
          MOV   WTABLE[BX],CX     ;    WTABLE[I] = LOOP_CNT
          LOOP  LOOPTOP           ;    DECREMENT LOOP_CNT
                                  ;UNTIL LOOP_CNT = 0
```

The first instruction sets the loop count to 100. Each iteration of the loop initializes one element in each array. The label LOOPTOP marks the top of the loop. The loop body consists of the five instructions that follow the label LOOP-TOP. LOOPTOP is actually the label of the first instruction of the loop body. The first two instructions in the loop body set the index to the loop count minus 1. As the loop count moves from 100 to 1, the index moves from 99 to 0. The third instruction in the loop body stores the low-order 8 bits of the loop count in the BTABLE element specified by the index in the BX-register. The fourth instruction in the loop body converts the BX-register value from a byte index to a word index, which is done by shifting the BX-register left 1 bit position (i.e., multiplying it by 2). The last instruction in the loop body stores the loop count in the WTABLE element specified by the index in the BX-register. The LOOP instruction that follows the loop body performs the loop test: It decrements the loop count by 1 and returns to LOOPTOP if the resulting value of the loop count is nonzero. Table 8.1 traces the first few and last few iterations of the loop.

TABLE 8.1
Iterations of BTABLE/WTABLE initialization loop

Loop Count	Byte Index	BTABLE Store	Word Index	WTABLE Store
100	99	BTABLE(99) = 100	198	WTABLE(99) = 100
99	98	BTABLE(98) = 99	196	WTABLE(98) = 99
98	97	BTABLE(97) = 98	194	WTABLE(97) = 98
.	.	.	.	.
.	.	.	.	.
.	.	.	.	.
3	2	BTABLE(2) = 3	4	WTABLE(2) = 3
2	1	BTABLE(1) = 2	2	WTABLE(1) = 2
1	0	BTABLE(0) = 1	0	WTABLE(0) = 1

IBM PC String Instructions

The **string instructions** in the IBM PC Assembly language are really a set of array instructions that operate on either byte arrays (e.g., character strings) or word arrays. With these instructions, the following conventions are used:

1. Source array elements are addressed by the DS:SI register pair.

2. Destination array elements are addressed by the ES:DI register pair.

3. The SI and/or DI register(s) is (are) automatically updated at the end of execution of a string instruction, which allows for addressing of the next array element in sequence. This update is an increment (decrement) by 2 for word arrays or an increment (decrement) by 1 for byte arrays.

4. The direction flag (DF bit in the flags register) is used to determine whether the SI/DI register update is an increment or a decrement: If the DF bit in the flags register is 0, then the update is an increment; if the DF bit is 1, then the update is a decrement.

Two instructions in the IBM PC Assembly language manipulate the DF bit in the flags register: the CLD and STD instructions. The **CLD instruction** *clears* the DF bit in the flags register to denote incrementing. The **STD instruction** *sets* the DF bit in the flags register to denote decrementing. The general forms for these two instructions are as follow:

```
[⟨label⟩]    CLD                    [⟨comment⟩]
[⟨label⟩]    STD                    [⟨comment⟩]
```

Only the DF bit in the flags register is affected by execution of a CLD or an STD instruction.

Move, Load, and Store String Instructions

There are two move string instructions: MOVSB and MOVSW. The **MOVSB instruction** has the following general form:

```
[⟨label⟩]    MOVSB                  [⟨comment⟩]
```

It causes the processor to replace the byte addressed by the ES:DI register pair with a copy of the byte addressed by the DS:SI register pair and then to update the DI and SI registers to point to the next byte in their respective strings. If the DF bit in the flags register is 0, then DI and SI are both incremented by 1. If the DF bit in the flags register is 1, then DI and SI are both decremented by 1.

The **MOVSW instruction** has the following general form:

```
[⟨label⟩]    MOVSW                  [⟨comment⟩]
```

It causes the processor to replace the word addressed by the ES:DI register pair with a copy of the word addressed by the DS:SI register pair and then to update the DI and SI registers to point to the next word in their respective arrays. If the DF bit in the flags register is 0, then DI and SI are both incremented by 2. If the DF bit in the flags register is 1, then DI and SI are both decremented by 2.

EXAMPLES

Consider the segments DATA and EXTRA defined and illustrated in Figure 8.4. Suppose the DS-register contains 0926 hex (the base address of segment DATA) and the ES-register contains 0927 hex (the base address of segment EXTRA).

Suppose the SI-register contains 000A (the offset of string COUNTRY within segment DATA), and the DI-register contains 0000 (the offset of string CITY within segment EXTRA). That is, the DS:SI register pair specifies the base address of byte array COUNTRY (0926:000A), and the ES:DI register pair specifies the base address of byte array CITY (0927:0000). Suppose further that the DF bit of the flags register is zero (for automatic incrementing). The

FIGURE 8.4
DATA and EXTRA
segment definitions
for string instruction
examples

```
DATA        SEGMENT
TABLE       DW          100, 200, 300, 400, 500
COUNTRY     DB          'POLAND'
DATA        ENDS

EXTRA       SEGMENT
CITY        DB          'KRAKOW'
LIST        DW          200, 400, 600, 800, 1000
EXTRA       ENDS
```

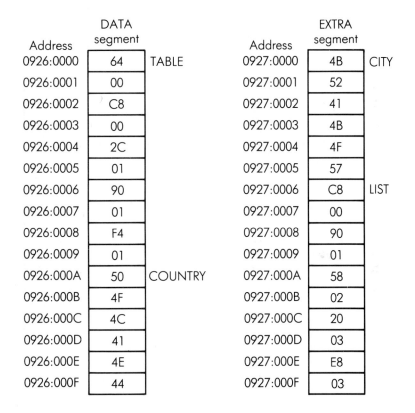

	DATA segment			EXTRA segment	
Address			Address		
0926:0000	64	TABLE	0927:0000	4B	CITY
0926:0001	00		0927:0001	52	
0926:0002	C8		0927:0002	41	
0926:0003	00		0927:0003	4B	
0926:0004	2C		0927:0004	4F	
0926:0005	01		0927:0005	57	
0926:0006	90		0927:0006	C8	LIST
0926:0007	01		0927:0007	00	
0926:0008	F4		0927:0008	90	
0926:0009	01		0927:0009	01	
0926:000A	50	COUNTRY	0927:000A	58	
0926:000B	4F		0927:000B	02	
0926:000C	4C		0927:000C	20	
0926:000D	41		0927:000D	03	
0926:000E	4E		0927:000E	E8	
0926:000F	44		0927:000F	03	

instruction MOVSB moves a copy of the byte addressed by the DS:SI register pair (50 hex, the ASCII code for P) to the byte addressed by the ES:DI register pair, and then it increments the DI and SI registers by 1. The result is shown in Figure 8.5. The DS:SI register pair now addresses the second element of array COUNTRY (0926:000B), and the ES:DI register pair now addresses the second element of array CITY (0927:0001).

Suppose the SI-register contains 0004, the DI-register contains 000C, and the DF bit of the flags register is set to 1. That is, the DS:SI register pair specifies the address of the third element of word array TABLE (0926:0004), the ES:DI

FIGURE 8.5
DATA and EXTRA segments after `MOVSB`

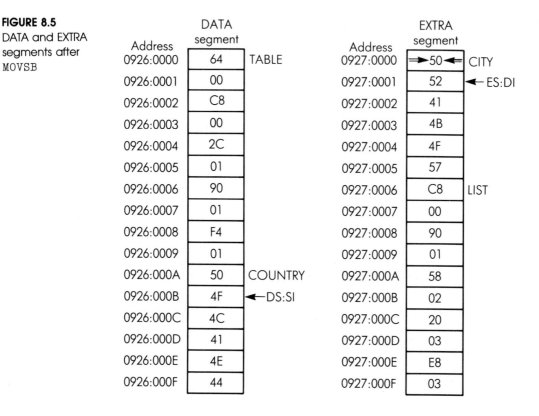

register pair specifies the address of the fourth element of word array LIST (0927:000C), and the direction flag is set for automatic decrementing. The instruction MOVSW replaces the word addressed by the ES:DI register pair with the word addressed by the DS:SI register pair, and then it decrements the DI and SI registers by 2 (one word). The result is shown in Figure 8.6. The DS:SI register pair now addresses the second element of array TABLE (0926:0002), and the ES:DI register pair now addresses the third element of array LIST (0927:000A).

There are two load string instructions: LODSB and LODSW. The **LODSB instruction** has the following general form:

[⟨*label*⟩]   LODSB   [⟨*comment*⟩]

It causes the processor to load the AL-register with a copy of the byte addressed by the DS:SI register pair and then to update the SI-register to point to the next byte in the string. If the DF bit in the flags register is 0, then the SI-register is incremented by 1. If the DF bit in the flags register is 1, then the SI-register is decremented by 1.

FIGURE 8.6
DATA and EXTRA
segments after
MOVSW

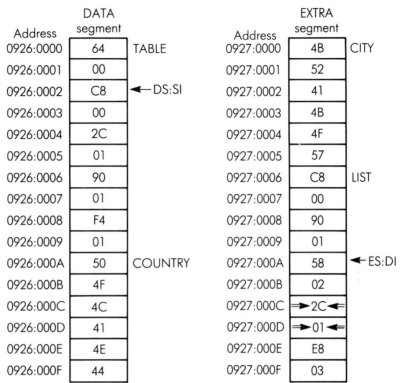

The **LODSW instruction** has the following general form:

[⟨*label*⟩]   LODSW   [⟨*comment*⟩]

It causes the processor to load the AX-register with a copy of the word addressed by the DS:SI register pair and then to update the SI-register to point to the next word in the array. If the DF bit in the flags register is 0, then the SI-register is incremented by 2. If the DF bit in the flags register is 1, then the SI-register is decremented by 2.

There are two store string instructions: STOSB and STOSW. The **STOSB instruction** has the following general form:

[⟨*label*⟩]   STOSB   [⟨*comment*⟩]

It causes the processor to replace the byte addressed by the ES:DI register pair with a copy of the byte in the AL-register and then to update the DI-register to point to the next byte in the string. If the DF bit in the flags register is 0, then the DI-register is incremented by 1. If the DF bit in the flags register is 1, then the DI-register is decremented by 1.

The **STOSW instruction** has the following general form:

[⟨*label*⟩]   STOSW   [⟨*comment*⟩]

It causes the processor to replace the word addressed by the ES:DI register pair with a copy of the word in the AX-register and then to update the DI-register to point to the next word in the array. If the DF bit in the flags register is 0, then the DI-register is incremented by 2. If the DF bit in the flags register is 1, then the DI-register is decremented by 2.

EXAMPLES

Consider again the segments DATA and EXTRA defined and illustrated in Figure 8.4.

Suppose the DS:SI register pair contains 0926:000C (the address of the third element of byte array COUNTRY), and the DF bit of the flags register is zero. The instruction LODSB loads the AL-register with a copy of the byte addressed by the DS:SI register pair (4C hex, the ASCII code for L) and then increments the SI-register by 1. The result is shown in Figure 8.7. The DS:SI register pair now addresses the fourth element of array COUNTRY (0926:000D).

FIGURE 8.7
DATA and EXTRA segments after LODSB

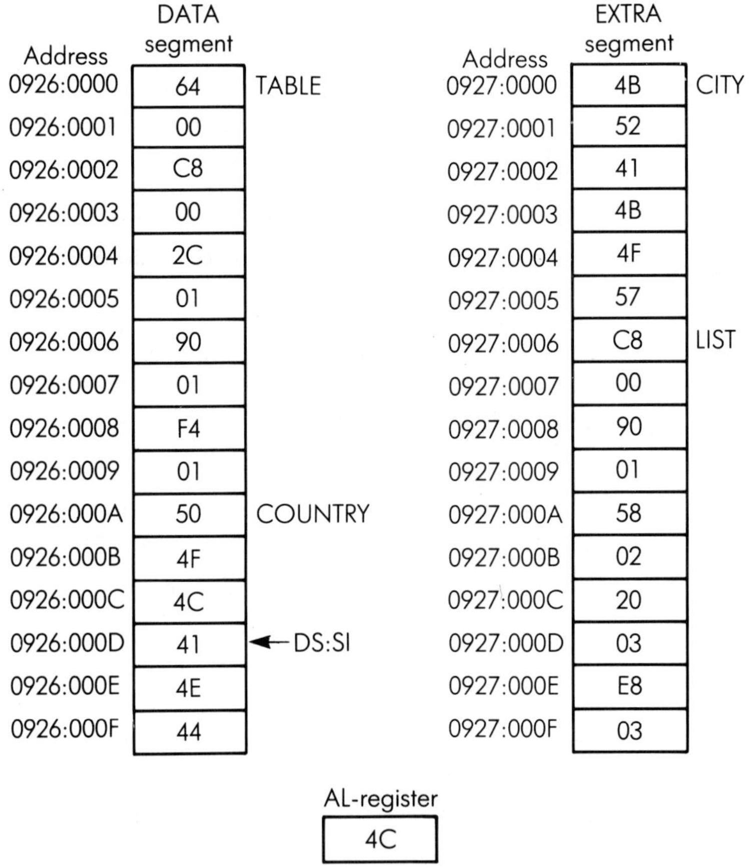

Address	DATA segment		Address	EXTRA segment	
0926:0000	64	TABLE	0927:0000	4B	CITY
0926:0001	00		0927:0001	52	
0926:0002	C8		0927:0002	41	
0926:0003	00		0927:0003	4B	
0926:0004	2C		0927:0004	4F	
0926:0005	01		0927:0005	57	
0926:0006	90		0927:0006	C8	LIST
0926:0007	01		0927:0007	00	
0926:0008	F4		0927:0008	90	
0926:0009	01		0927:0009	01	
0926:000A	50	COUNTRY	0927:000A	58	
0926:000B	4F		0927:000B	02	
0926:000C	4C		0927:000C	20	
0926:000D	41	←DS:SI	0927:000D	03	
0926:000E	4E		0927:000E	E8	
0926:000F	44		0927:000F	03	

AL-register
4C

FIGURE 8.8

DATA and EXTRA segments after STOSW

	DATA segment	
Address		
0926:0000	64	TABLE
0926:0001	00	
0926:0002	C8	
0926:0003	00	
0926:0004	2C	
0926:0005	01	
0926:0006	90	
0926:0007	01	
0926:0008	F4	
0926:0009	01	
0926:000A	50	COUNTRY
0926:000B	4F	
0926:000C	4C	
0926:000D	41	
0926:000E	4E	
0926:000F	44	

	EXTRA segment	
Address		
0927:0000	4B	CITY
0927:0001	52	
0927:0002	41	
0927:0003	4B	
0927:0004	4F	
0927:0005	57	
0927:0006	C8	LIST
0927:0007	00	
0927:0008	90	← ES:DI
0927:0009	01	
0927:000A	⇒ AC ⇐	
0927:000B	⇒ 12 ⇐	
0927:000C	20	
0927:000D	03	
0927:000E	E8	
0927:000F	03	

Suppose the ES:DI register pair contains 0927:000A (the address of the third element of word array LIST), the DF bit of the flags register is set to 1, and the AX-register contains the hexadecimal value 12AC. The instruction STOSW replaces the word addressed by the ES:DI register pair (0258) with a copy of the AX-register value (12AC), and it then decrements the DI-register by 2. The result is shown in Figure 8.8. The ES:DI register pair now addresses the second element of array LIST (0927:0008).

None of the flag bits in the flags register are affected by execution of a move, load, or store string instruction.

Compare and Scan String Instructions

There are two compare string instructions: CMPSB and CMPSW. The **CMPSB instruction** has the following general form:

[⟨*label*⟩]   CMPSB   [⟨*comment*⟩]

It causes the processor to compare the byte addressed by the DS:SI register pair to the byte addressed by the ES:DI register pair, to set the flags to reflect this relationship, and then to update the DI and SI registers to point to the next byte in their respective strings. If the DF bit in the flags register is 0, then the DI and SI registers are both incremented by 1. If the DF bit in the flags register is 1, then the DI and SI registers are both decremented by 1. To perform the comparison, the processor subtracts the byte addressed by the ES:DI register pair from the byte addressed by the DS:SI register pair and sets the bits in the flags register to reflect the result. Neither byte is modified by execution of this instruction.

The **CMPSW instruction** has the following general form:

[⟨*label*⟩]   CMPSW   [⟨*comment*⟩]

It causes the processor to compare the word addressed by the DS:SI register pair to the word addressed by the ES:DI register pair, to set the flags to reflect this relationship, and then to update the DI and SI registers to point to the next word in their respective arrays. If the DF bit in the flags register is 0, then the DI and SI registers are both incremented by 2. If the DF bit in the flags register is 1, then the DI and SI registers are both decremented by 2. To perform the comparison, the processor subtracts the word addressed by the ES:DI register pair from the word addressed by the DS:SI register pair and sets the bits in the flags register to reflect the result. Neither word is modified by execution of this instruction.

It is important to note that the CMPSB and CMPSW string instructions follow a different philosophy than does the CMP compare instruction. CMP compares the destination to the source operand; that is, it sets the flags to reflect the value destination operand minus source operand. CMPSB and CMPSW compare the item addressed by the DS:SI register pair (source operand) to the item addressed by the ES:DI register pair (destination operand); that is, they set the flags to reflect the value source operand minus destination operand.

There are two scan string instructions: SCASB and SCASW. The **SCASB instruction** has the following general form:

[⟨*label*⟩]   SCASB   [⟨*comment*⟩]

It causes the processor to compare the byte in the AL-register to the byte addressed by the ES:DI register pair, to set the flags to reflect this relationship, and then to update the DI-register to point to the next byte in the string. If the direction flag is zero, then the DI-register is incremented by 1. If the direction flag is 1, then the DI-register is decremented by 1. To perform the comparison, the processor subtracts the byte addressed by the ES:DI register pair from the byte in the AL-register and sets the flags to reflect the result. Neither byte is modified by execution of this instruction.

The **SCASW instruction** has the following general form:

[⟨*label*⟩]   SCASW   [⟨*comment*⟩]

It causes the processor to compare the word in the AX-register to the word addressed by the ES:DI register pair, to set the flags to reflect this relationship, and then to update the DI-register to point to the next word in the array. If the direction flag is zero, then the DI-register is incremented by 2. If the direction flag is 1, then the DI-register is decremented by 2. To perform the comparison, the processor subtracts the word addressed by the ES:DI register pair from the word in the AX-register and sets the flags to reflect the result. Neither word is modified by execution of this instruction.

The OF, SF, ZF, AF, PF, and CF bits in the flags register are affected by execution of a compare or scan string instruction:

If the subtraction operation results in a signed integer, arithmetic overflow, then the OF bit in the flags register is set; otherwise, the OF bit in the flags register is cleared.

The SF bit in the flags register will contain a copy of the sign bit of the result of the subtraction operation. That is, if the result of the subtraction is negative, then the SF bit in the flags register is set; otherwise, the SF bit is cleared.

If the result of the subtraction operation is zero, then the ZF bit in the flags register is set; otherwise, the ZF bit is cleared.

If the result of the subtraction operation has an even number of 1 bits in the low-order byte, then the PF bit in the flags register is set; if the result has an odd number of 1 bits in the low-order byte, then the PF bit in the flags register is cleared.

If the subtraction operation requires a borrow into the most-significant bit, then the CF bit in the flags register is set; otherwise, the CF bit is cleared.

The AF bit in the flags register is set if there is a borrow into bit 3 during the subtraction operation; otherwise, the AF bit is cleared.

EXAMPLES

Consider again the segments DATA and EXTRA defined and illustrated in Figure 8.4.

Suppose the DS:SI register pair contains 0926:0000 (the address of the first element of word array TABLE), the ES:DI register pair contains 0927:0006 (the address of the first element of word array LIST), and the DF bit of the flags register is zero. The instruction CMPSW subtracts the word addressed by the ES:DI register pair (00C8) from the word addressed by the DS:SI register pair (0064), sets the flags to reflect the result, and then increments the DI and SI registers by 2. The subtraction performed is

$$
\begin{array}{rr}
0064 & 0064 \\
-\ 00C8 & +\ FF38 \\
\hline
& FF9C
\end{array}
$$

The six flags affected are set as follows:

```
OF  SF  ZF  AF  PF  CF
 0   1   0   1   1   1
```

The DS:SI register pair now addresses the second element of array TABLE (0926:0002), and the ES:DI register pair now addresses the second element of array LIST (0927:0008). Neither array is modified.

Suppose the ES:DI register pair contains 0927:0005 (the address of the last element of byte array CITY), the DF bit of the flags register is 1, and the AL-register contains 59 hex. The instruction SCASB subtracts the byte addressed by the ES:DI register pair (57 hex) from the byte in the AL-register (59 hex), sets the flags to reflect the result, and decrements the DI-register by 1. The subtraction performed is

$$
\begin{array}{r}
59 \text{ hex} \\
- \underline{57 \text{ hex}} \\
02 \text{ hex}
\end{array}
$$

The six flags affected are set as follows:

```
OF   SF   ZF   AF   PF   CF
 0    0    0    0    0    0
```

The ES:DI register pair now addresses the fifth element of array CITY (0927:0004). Neither the array nor the AL-register is modified.

Generic Forms for String Instructions

Note that there is also a generic form for each of the five string instructions previously discussed:

[⟨*label*⟩]   MOVS   ⟨*destination*⟩,⟨*source*⟩   [⟨*comment*⟩]

[⟨*label*⟩]   LODS   ⟨*source*⟩   [⟨*comment*⟩]

[⟨*label*⟩]   STOS   ⟨*destination*⟩   [⟨*comment*⟩]

[⟨*label*⟩]   CMPS   ⟨*source*⟩,⟨*destination*⟩   [⟨*cor:ment*⟩]

[⟨*label*⟩]   SCAS   ⟨*destination*⟩   [⟨*comment*⟩]

An operand in the generic form of a string instruction is the symbolic name of an array. When two operands are required (i.e., with MOVS or CMPS), the type attributes of the two operands must match (i.e., both must be byte, or both must be word). When the generic form of a string instruction is used, the assembler generates the code for one of the two corresponding standard string instructions depending on the type attribute of the operand(s). For example, when the generic form MOVS is used, the assembler generates the machine code for either MOVSB or MOVSW depending on the type attribute of the two operands. The explicit statement of the operands provides several advantages:

1. By explicitly identifying the arrays involved, the program is better documented.
2. It allows the assembler to check the types of the operands.
3. It allows the assembler to check the accessibility of the operands. That is, the assembler can check to see that the arrays identified by the explicit operands are in the proper segments for the specified string instruction.

It is important to realize, however, that the string instructions use the ES:DI register pair and/or the DS:SI register pair (not the explicit operands) to locate the array elements. The operands in the generic string instructions are there only to provide type- and accessibility-checking information for the assembler; that is, the operands could be incorrect, and yet the instruction generated by the assembler might be the instruction desired.

<hr>

EXAMPLE

Consider the following data segment definition shown with its assembler-generated output:

```
0000                        DATA    SEGMENT
0000  50 4F 4C 41 4E 44      COUNTRY DB      'POLAND'
0006  4B 52 41 4B 4F 57      CITY    DB      'KRAKOW'
000C  0014 0028 003C 0050    LIST    DW      20,40,60,80,100
      0064
0016                        DATA    ENDS
```

Suppose the assembler has already encountered the statement

```
ASSUME  DS:DATA,ES:DATA
```

and the instructions

```
MOV   AX,SEG DATA
MOV   DS,AX
MOV   ES,AX
```

which, at execution time, initialize the DS and ES segment registers to address the segment DATA. The ASSUME pseudo-operation instructs the assembler as to how the segment registers are to be used during execution, and the three MOV instructions actually initialize the segment registers during execution.

The following sequence of instructions is designed to move a SPACE character to each element of array CITY:

```
          CLD
          LEA   DI,CITY
          MOV   CX,6
          MOV   AL,' '
LOOPTOP:
          STOSB
          LOOP  LOOPTOP
```

The STOSB instruction could be replaced by the generic form

```
STOS  CITY
```

and the assembler would generate exactly the same code. The assembler would use the symbolic name CITY to verify that the named array (CITY) is defined in the segment ASSUMEd to be addressed by the ES-register (the register used by a store string instruction). The assembler would then generate the machine code for an STOSB instruction, since CITY is defined with type attribute byte.

The STOSB instruction could also be replaced by the generic form

```
STOS  COUNTRY
```

and again the assembler would generate exactly the same code. The assembler would use the symbolic name COUNTRY to verify that the named array (COUNTRY) is defined in the segment ASSUMEd to be addressed by the ES-register (the register used by a store string instruction). The assembler would then generate the machine code for an STOSB instruction, since COUNTRY is defined with type attribute byte.

At execution time, the store string operation uses the ES:DI register pair to identify the array element. With both generic forms given previously, the translated program is exactly the same. However, in one case, the documentation is consistent with the array used:

```
LEA    DI,CITY
       .
       .
       .
STOS   CITY
```

In the other case, it is not consistent with the array used:

```
LEA    DI,CITY
       .
       .
       .
STOS   COUNTRY
```

The generic forms of the string instructions are generally not used in the example programs of this book.

Repeat Prefixes

The string instructions operate on a single character of a string or on a single element of an array, although there are times you may wish to perform some operation on every character in a string or on every element of an array. To accomplish this task, a repeat prefix can be placed on a string instruction to specify that the instruction is to be repeated some number of times. With a repeat prefix, the CX-register is used as a counter to control the number of times the string instruction is to be executed.

There are three repeat prefixes that can be used with the string instructions: REP, REPE/REPZ, and REPNE/REPNZ.

REP

The **REP prefix** has the following general form:

[⟨*label*⟩]   REP   ⟨*string-op*⟩   ⟨*operands*⟩   [⟨*comment*⟩]

in which ⟨*string-op*⟩ is the operation code of one of the string instructions and ⟨*operands*⟩ is the operand list (if any) for the string instruction. The REP prefix

FIGURE 8.9
REP prefix

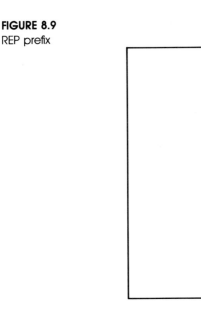

on a string instruction causes the processor to execute the string instruction the number of times specified by the value in the CX-register, which is decremented after each execution of the string instruction. The REP prefix on a string instruction causes the following loop to be executed:

```
REPEAT
     Execute string instruction (updating DI and/or SI)
     Decrement CX-register by 1
UNTIL  CX-register is 0
```

This loop is given in flowchart form in Figure 8.9. Note that each time the string instruction is executed, the SI and/or DI register is automatically updated so that a different array element (different array elements) is (are) processed on each execution of the string instruction.

The REP prefix should only be used with the move, load, and store string instructions. If it is used with the compare or scan string instructions, it behaves exactly like REPE/REPZ (which is discussed in the next section).

EXAMPLE

Suppose a character string is defined in a static data segment as follows:

```
STRING  DB  40 DUP(?)
```

Also suppose the ES segment register currently specifies the address of the origin of this data segment. The following code sets every character in STRING to an asterisk (*):

```
        CLD
        LEA     DI,STRING
        MOV     CX,40
        MOV     AL,'*'
REP     STOSB
```

The CLD instruction clears the DF bit in the flags register, so that the store string instruction automatically increments the DI-register. The LEA instruction sets the DI-register to the offset of STRING, which means that the ES:DI register pair now specifies the address of the first element of array STRING. The first MOV instruction sets the CX-register to 40, the number of elements in array STRING. The string instruction that contains the REP prefix is to be executed 40 times, once for each element in array STRING. The second MOV instruction places the ASCII representation of the character * in the AL-register, which is the value that is to be stored in each element of array STRING.

 The store string instruction is executed 40 times. The REP prefix causes the store string instruction to be executed repeatedly as the CX-register counts from 40 to 0. Each time the store string instruction is executed, the DI-register is automatically incremented by 1, so that the ES:DI register pair specifies the address of the next character (byte) of the string (array). On each execution of the store string instruction, an * character is stored in the byte addressed by the ES:DI register pair.

 On the first execution of the store string instruction, the first character of STRING is replaced by *. On the second execution of the store string instruction, the second character of STRING is replaced by *. In general, on the nth execution of the store string instruction, the nth character of STRING is replaced by *. On the last execution of the store string instruction, the fortieth character of STRING is replaced by *.

REPE/REPZ

The **REPE/REPZ prefix** has the following general form (either form is acceptable):

[⟨*label*⟩] REPE ⟨*strng-op*⟩ ⟨*operands*⟩ [⟨*comment*⟩]

[⟨*label*⟩] REPZ ⟨*strng-op*⟩ ⟨*operands*⟩ [⟨*comment*⟩]

in which ⟨*strng-op*⟩ is the operation code of one of the string instructions and ⟨*operands*⟩ is the operand list (if any) for the string instruction. The REPE or REPZ prefix on a string instruction causes the processor to execute the string instruction repeatedly as long as the ZF bit in the flags register is set. The value in the CX-register specifies the maximum number of times that the string instruction is to be executed, which is decremented after each execution of the string instruction. The REPE/REPZ prefix on a string instruction causes the

FIGURE 8.10
REPE/REPZ prefix

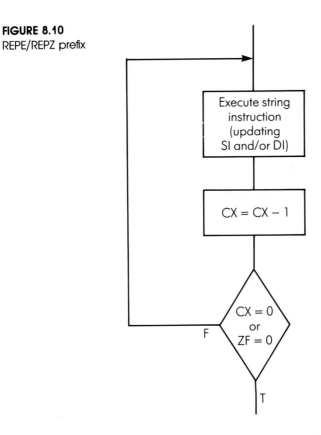

following loop to be executed:

```
REPEAT
    Execute string instruction (updating SI and/or DI)
    Decrement CX-register by 1
UNTIL  CX-register is 0 or ZF = 0
```

This loop is given in flowchart form in Figure 8.10.

The prefix REPE/REPZ should only be used with the compare and scan string instructions. If it is used with a move, load, or store string instruction, then it behaves exactly like REP (which has already been discussed). That is, the ZF bit of the flags register has no effect when a REPE/REPZ is used with a move, load, or store string instruction.

EXAMPLE

Suppose a character string is defined in a static data segment as follows:

```
STRING  DB  40  DUP(?)
```

Also suppose the ES segment register currently specifies the address of the origin of this data segment, and STRING has been given a value.

The following code is designed to set the ES:DI register pair to address the first nonblank character in STRING:

```
        CLD
        LEA    DI,STRING
        MOV    CX,40
        MOV    AL,' '
REPE    SCASB
        JE     ALL_BLANKS
        DEC    DI
```

The CLD instruction clears the DF bit in the flags register, so that the scan string instruction automatically increments the DI-register. The LEA instruction sets the DI-register to the offset of STRING, which means that the ES:DI register pair now specifies the address of the first element of array STRING. The first MOV instruction sets the CX-register to 40, the number of elements in array STRING. The scan string instruction is to be executed a maximum of 40 times. The second MOV instruction places the ASCII code for SPACE in the AL-register.

The scan string instruction repeatedly executes as long as the character being scanned is a space (blank), up to a maximum of 40 times. It terminates if either a nonblank character is found or all 40 characters of STRING have been scanned.

Following the repeated execution of the scan string instruction, it must be determined which of the two conditions caused the instruction to terminate execution: The JE instruction makes this determination. If the ZF bit in the flags register is still set, then the CX-register must have reached zero, causing the scan string instruction to terminate; that is, the jump is taken when all 40 characters are scanned without finding a character that is not equal to blank. However, if the ZF bit in the flags register is not set, then the last character scanned was a nonblank character, and the ES:DI register pair has already been updated to specify the address of the byte immediately following that nonblank character. Therefore, if the jump fails, the DI-register must be decremented, so that the ES:DI register pair specifies the address of the byte containing the first nonblank character in STRING: This is accomplished by the DEC instruction.

REPNE/REPNZ

The **REPNE/REPNZ prefix** has the following general form (either form is acceptable):

[⟨*label*⟩]   REPNE   ⟨*strng-op*⟩   ⟨*operands*⟩   [⟨*comment*⟩]

[⟨*label*⟩]   REPNZ   ⟨*strng-op*⟩   ⟨*operands*⟩   [⟨*comment*⟩]

in which ⟨*strng-op*⟩ is the operation code of one of the string instructions and ⟨*operands*⟩ is the operand list (if any) for the string instruction. The REPNE or

REPNZ prefix on a string instruction causes the processor to execute the string instruction repeatedly as long as the ZF bit in the flags register is *not* set. The value in the CX-register specifies the maximum number of times that the string instruction is to be executed, which is decremented after each execution of the string instruction. The REPNE/REPNZ prefix on a string instruction causes the following loop to be executed:

```
REPEAT
     Execute string instruction (updating DI and/or SI )
     Decrement CX-register by 1
UNTIL  CX-register is 0 or ZF = 1
```

This loop is given in flowchart form in Figure 8.11.

The prefix REPNE/REPNZ should only be used with the compare and scan string instructions. If it is used with a move, load, or store string instruction, then it behaves exactly like REP (which has already been discussed). That is, the ZF bit of the flags register has no effect when a REPNE/REPNZ prefix is used with a move, load, or store string instruction.

FIGURE 8.11
REPNE/REPNZ prefix

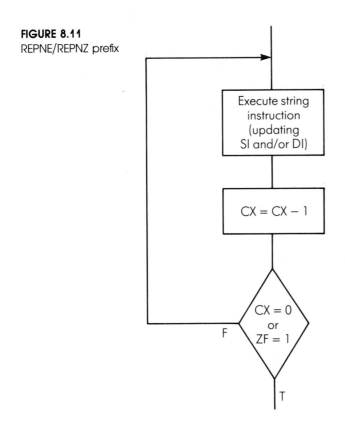

EXAMPLE

Suppose a word array is defined in a static data segment as follows:

```
ARRAY       DW  99 DUP(?)
ARRAYEND    DW  ?
```

Note that ARRAY is defined as a word array of size 100 and that each element is left uninitialized. ARRAY is the symbolic name associated with the first array element, and ARRAYEND is the symbolic name associated with the last (one-hundredth) array element. This setup allows for sequential processing to begin at either end of the array.

Suppose the DS and ES registers currently specify the address of the origin of this data segment, and also suppose the elements of ARRAY have been given values. The following code is designed to set the ES:DI register pair to address the last element of ARRAY that has a value of zero:

```
        STD
        LEA    DI,ARRAYEND
        MOV    CX,100
        MOV    AX,0
REPNE   SCASW
        JNE    NOT_FOUND
        INC    DI
        INC    DI
```

The STD instruction sets the DF bit in the flags register, so that the scan string instruction automatically decrements the DI-register. The LEA instruction sets the DI-register to the offset of ARRAYEND, the last word in the array, which means that the ES:DI register pair now specifies the address of the last element of the array. The first MOV instruction sets the CX-register to 100, the number of elements in ARRAY. The scan string instruction containing the REPNE prefix is executed a maximum of 100 times (i.e., at most once for each element of ARRAY). The second MOV instruction places the value zero in the AX-register.

The scan string instruction repeatedly executes as long as the value being scanned is *not* zero, up to a maximum of 100 times. It terminates if either a value of zero is found or all 100 elements of ARRAY have been scanned. Since the scan is from the last element to the first element in the array, the first element found whose value is zero is the last element in the array whose value is zero.

Following repeated execution of the scan string instruction, it must be determined which of the two conditions caused the instruction to terminate execution: the JNE instruction makes this determination. If the ZF bit in the flags register is still cleared, then the CX-register must have reached zero, causing the scan string instruction to terminate; that is, the jump is taken when all 100 elements are scanned without finding a zero value. However, if the ZF bit in the flags register is set, then the last element scanned was zero, and the ES:DI register pair has already been updated to specify the address of the word immediately preceding that zero value. Therefore, if the jump fails, then the DI-register must be incremented by 2 (2 bytes or 1 word), so that the ES:DI register pair specifies the address of the word found to be zero: This is accomplished by the two INC instructions. The instruction

```
ADD   DI,2
```

could replace the two INC instructions. The two INC instructions require less memory space than the single ADD instruction. However, the ADD instruction executes faster than the two INC instructions.

The repeat prefixes translate to 1111001Z in machine code, in which Z = 1 for REP and REPE/REPZ and Z = 0 for REPNE/REPNZ. For the move, load, and store string instructions, the repeat prefix causes the string instruction to be repeated until the CX-register counts down to zero, regardless of the value of Z. For the scan and compare string instructions, the repeat prefix causes the string instruction to be repeated until the ZF bit in the flags register is not equal to Z or the CX-register counts down to zero.

None of the flags are affected by a repeat prefix. However, the string instruction being repeated affects the flags in the normal manner.

Programming Example—BCD-to-ASCII Conversion

It is possible to store numbers in the computer in decimal rather than in binary form and to perform computations on those decimal numbers. To do so, a binary code is used to represent the individual digits of a decimal number. One such code is called **binary coded decimal (BCD)**. The BCD code for each of the 10 decimal digits is given in Table 8.2, in which each decimal digit is represented by a 4-bit binary code. Note that the six 4-bit codes (1010, 1011, 1100, 1101, 1110, 1111) are not used, and in fact they are illegal in the BCD number system. To represent a 5-digit decimal number, a total of 20 bits (4 per digit) are needed.

TABLE 8.2
BCD codes

Decimal Digit	BCD Code
0	0000
1	0001
2	0010
3	0011
4	0100
5	0101
6	0110
7	0111
8	1000
9	1001

TABLE 8.3
Examples of corresponding numbers in the BCD, decimal, and binary number systems

BCD	Decimal	Binary
0000 0000 0000 0000	0000	0
1001 1001 1001 1001	9999	10011100001111
1000 0001 1001 0001	8191	1111111111111
0010 0111 0011 0101	2735	101010101111
0100 0110.0010 0101	46.25	101110.01

Table 8.3 shows some 4-digit BCD numbers, the corresponding 4-digit decimal numbers, and the corresponding binary numbers.

Program Listing 8.1 shows an implementation of an algorithm to convert a BCD number to an ASCII character string for output. The input is a packed array of BCD digits and a count of the number of BCD digits in the array. A **packed array** is one in which the BCD digits are packed 2 per byte. This kind of array is also called a **nibble array**, because each element of the array is a 4-bit nibble (one-half a byte). The output of the algorithm is a character string (i.e., an ASCII array). Figure 8.12 shows the hexadecimal contents of a BCD array and the corresponding ASCII array. Each of the two arrays in the figure contain the 7-digit decimal number 2147483.

Program Listing 8.1 shows an external subprocedure that performs this BCD-to-ASCII conversion. The prologue (lines 5–14) explains the function of the procedure and its interface requirements. On entry to the subprocedure, the DS:SI register pair must specify the base address of the BCD array, the ES:DI register pair must specify the base address of the array in which the ASCII character string is to be stored, and the CX-register must contain a count of the number of digits in the BCD array. On return to the caller, the array addressed by the ES:DI register pair will contain an ASCII number equivalent to the BCD number in the array addressed by the DS:SI register pair.

The subprocedure begins by saving the registers it is going to use (lines 20–25). Note that the DI and SI are among the registers that are saved. They are

FIGURE 8.12
BCD and ASCII arrays for 7-digit number 2147483

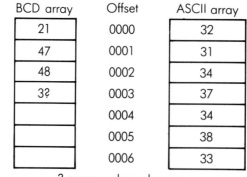

BCD array	Offset	ASCII array
21	0000	32
47	0001	31
48	0002	34
3?	0003	37
	0004	34
	0005	38
	0006	33

? means value unknown

```
 1: ;
 2: ;
 3: ;                     PROGRAM LISTING 8.1
 4: ;
 5: ; PROCEDURE TO CONVERT A BCD NUMBER TO ASCII
 6: ;
 7: ; INPUT:   DS:SI POINTS TO ARRAY CONTAINING BCD   NUMBER
 8: ;          ES:DI POINTS TO ARRAY TO CONTAIN ASCII NUMBER
 9: ;          CX    CONTAINS SIZE OF BCD NUMBER (DIGIT_COUNT)
10: ;
11: ; OUTPUT: UPON RETURN, THE ARRAY POINTED TO BY ES:DI WILL
12: ;          CONTAIN AN ASCII NUMBER EQUIVALENT  TO  THE BCD
13: ;          NUMBER IN THE ARRAY POINTED TO BY DS:SI.
14: ;
15: CODE       SEGMENT
16:            ASSUME  CS:CODE
17:            PUBLIC  BCDASCII
18: BCDASCII   PROC    FAR              ;PROCEDURE BCDASCII (DIGIT_COUNT,
19:                                     ;                  DS:SI,ES:DI)
20:            PUSHF                       ;SAVE FLAGS
21:            PUSH    AX                  ;SAVE REGISTERS
22:            PUSH    CX
23:            PUSH    DX
24:            PUSH    DI
25:            PUSH    SI
26:            CLD                         ;SET DF FOR INCREMENTING
27:            MOV     DX,-1               ;LR_FLAG = LEFT
28: LOOP_TOP:                             ;REPEAT
29:            PUSH    CX               ;    SAVE DIGIT_COUNT
30:            CMP     DX,0             ;    IF   LR_FLAG = LEFT
31:            JG      ELSE
32:            LODSB                    ;      THEN PAIR = DS:SI -> BYTE
33:                                     ;           SI = SI + 1
34:            MOV     AH,AL
35:            MOV     CL,4             ;           CHAR = LEFT NIBBLE
36:            SHR     AL,CL            ;                  OF PAIR
37:            JMP     ENDIF
38: ELSE:                              ;      ELSE
39:            MOV     AL,AH
40:            AND     AL,0FH           ;           CHAR = RIGHT NIBBLE
41:                                     ;                  OF PAIR
42: ENDIF:                             ;      ENDIF
43:            ADD     AL,'0'           ;      CHAR = CHAR + ASCII(0)
44:            STOSB                    ;      ES:DI -> BYTE = CHAR
45:                                     ;      DI = DI + 1
46:            NEG     DX               ;      REVERSE LR_FLAG
47:            POP     CX               ;      RESTORE DIGIT_COUNT
48:            LOOP    LOOP_TOP         ;      DECREMENT DIGIT_COUNT
49:                                     ;UNTIL DIGIT_COUNT = 0
50:            POP     SI               ;RESTORE REGISTERS
51:            POP     DI
52:            POP     DX
53:            POP     CX
54:            POP     AX
55:            POPF                        ;RESTORE FLAGS
56:            RET                         ;RETURN
57: BCDASCII   ENDP              ;END BCDASCII
58: CODE       ENDS
59:*          END
```
*

updated as the procedure works its way through the two arrays. The DS:SI register pair always specifies the address of the next pair of BCD digits to be fetched from the BCD array. The ES:DI register pair always specifies the address of the ASCII array element where the next ASCII character is to be stored. On return to the caller, the DS:SI register pair and the ES:DI register pair must once again specify the base addresses of the respective arrays.

The CLD instruction in line 26 clears the DF bit in the flags register, so that string instructions automatically increment the DI and/or SI registers. The MOV instruction in line 27 initializes a LEFT/RIGHT flag to LEFT, and this flag is maintained in the DX-register. The LEFT/RIGHT flag indicates whether the BCD digit currently being processed is from the left or right nibble of a byte; that is, each byte extracted from the BCD array contains two BCD digits, one in the left nibble and one in the right nibble. The flag indicates which of the two is currently being converted to ASCII.

The body (lines 29–47) of the REPEAT-UNTIL loop (lines 28–49) executes once for each digit in the BCD array. The digit count, input to the subprocedure in the CX-register, controls execution of this loop. Each iteration of the loop translates one BCD digit to ASCII and stores the result in the ASCII array. A byte is extracted from the BCD array on every odd iteration of the loop (i.e., every time a left nibble is to be translated).

The PUSH instruction in line 29 saves the digit count, so that the CL-register can be used as a shift count within the loop body. The double-alternative decision structure in lines 30–42 selects the next BCD digit to be translated. The selection is based on the LEFT/RIGHT flag. The CMP instruction in line 30 tests the flag. If the flag indicates LEFT, then the instructions in lines 32–37 are executed. The LODSB instruction in line 32 extracts the next two BCD digits from the BCD array (the byte pointed to by the DS:SI register pair) and increments the SI-register by 1, so that the DS:SI register pair addresses the next byte in the BCD array. The byte just extracted is in the AL-register. The MOV instruction in line 34 saves a copy of this byte in the AH-register for use in the next iteration of the loop. This iteration of the loop translates the left nibble of the byte just extracted, and the next iteration, if needed, translates the right nibble of the byte just extracted. The instructions in lines 35 and 36 shift the byte in the AL-register right 4 bit positions, pushing out the right nibble and right-justifying the left nibble; that is, the leftmost BCD digit of the byte is now in the rightmost 4 bits of the AL-register. If the flag indicates RIGHT, then the instructions in lines 39 and 40 are executed. The MOV instruction in line 39 moves the copy (saved in line 34) of the byte extracted from the BCD array on the last iteration of the loop from the AH-register to the AL-register. The AND instruction in line 40 clears the left nibble of the byte, leaving the right nibble in the rightmost 4 bits of the AL-register. When the ENDIF is reached (line 42), the AL-register contains a single BCD digit.

The ADD instruction in line 43 converts the BCD digit in the AL-register to ASCII by adding the ASCII code for zero to the BCD code. The STOSB instruction in line 44 stores the ASCII code in the ASCII array at the address specified by the ES:DI register pair, and then it increments the DI-register by 1, so that the ES:DI register pair addresses the next byte in the ASCII array.

The NEG instruction in line 46 reverses the direction of the LEFT/ RIGHT flag for the next iteration of the loop. The POP instruction in line 47 restores the digit count to the CX-register. The LOOP instruction in line 48 decrements the digit count in the CX-register by 1, and if the resulting digit count is nonzero, it transfers control to the top of the loop (line 28). Otherwise, the loop is terminated. At loop exit, the caller's registers are restored (lines 50–55), and control is returned to the caller (line 56).

8.4 Addressing Modes

The one-dimensional array is a good vehicle for studying the various addressing modes available in the IBM PC Assembly language. An instruction such as MOV or ADD specifies the addresses of operands to be used in execution of the instruction. Such an operand may be the contents of a general register, an immediate value (i.e., a value contained in the instruction itself), or the contents of a memory location. The example programs in previous chapters dealt exclusively with **scalar** (single-valued) data items. Three addressing modes were used in those example programs.

Register Addressing   With register addressing, the operand is the contents of one of the 8-bit or 16-bit registers. A specific register is addressed by coding its 2-character symbolic name into the operand field of the instruction. For example:

```
INC   AL
MOV   BX,DX
```

Register addressing can be used for either the source operand, the destination operand, or both.

Direct Addressing   With direct addressing, the operand is the 8-bit contents of a memory location or the 16-bit contents of two consecutive memory locations. A specific memory location is addressed directly by coding its symbolic name into the operand field of the instruction. For example:

```
INC   COUNT
MOV   SUM,0
```

Direct addressing can be used for either the source operand or the destination operand, but not both.

With a direct address, the symbolic name identifies both a segment and an offset within the segment, thus identifying a unique memory location. In most cases, the symbolic name used in a direct address is completely defined in the same assembly module. The assembler knows the segment in which the symbolic name is defined, and through the ASSUME pseudo-operation, it knows which segment register is to contain the base address of that segment during program execution. The segment register is specified (implicitly or explicitly) in the machine language representation of the instruction. The offset associated with the symbolic name is dependent on the order in which items are defined in the segment that contains the symbolic name. Therefore, the assembler has the information to determine the offset within the segment. The offset is also part of the machine language representation of the instruction.

Immediate Addressing   With immediate addressing, the operand is an 8- or 16-bit constant that is contained in the machine language representation of the instruction. A specific immediate value is referenced by coding its literal in the operand field of the instruction. For example:

```
MOV   COUNT,16
CMP   CHAR,'*'
ADD   AX,-4
```

An immediate value can only be a source operand; it cannot be a destination operand.

Memory Addressing Modes

With register and immediate addressing modes, the operands are directly accessible by the execution unit of the Intel 8088 microprocessor (see Figure 1.17). The general registers are part of the EU, and the immediate operands are contained in the instruction queue. Memory operands, on the other hand, are only accessible through the bus interface unit of the microprocessor. The EU directs the BIU to perform a data fetch or data store operation, and it provides the offset portion of the address. The offset portion is also called the **effective address**. The BIU adds the shifted contents of the appropriate segment register to the effective address, producing a 20-bit physical memory address. The BIU then performs the appropriate bus operations to fetch or replace the contents of the memory location identified by the physical address.

The effective address, a 16-bit unsigned integer, is computed by the EU according to information contained in the second byte of the machine language instruction. The second byte of a memory referencing instruction has the form shown in Figure 8.13. The effective address is computed from one or more of the following components:

> An 8-bit or 16-bit displacement contained in the third or the third and fourth bytes of the machine language instruction
>
> The 16-bit contents of an index register, either the DI-register or the SI-register
>
> The 16-bit contents of a base register, either the BX-register or the BP-register

Table 8.4 shows the various ways that the effective address can be computed by the EU of the Intel 8088 microprocessor. It also states the addressing mode and

FIGURE 8.13

Second byte of memory referencing instruction

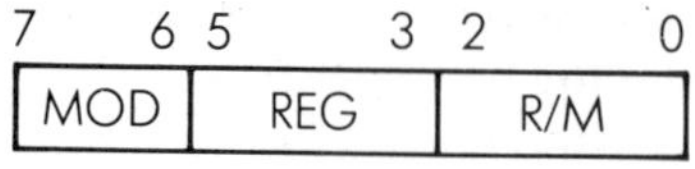

TABLE 8.4
Effective address computations for memory addressing modes

MOD	R/M	Effective Address Computation	Addressing Mode
00	110	EA = DISP_16	Direct
00	100	EA = (SI)	Register indirect
00	101	EA = (DI)	Register indirect
00	111	EA = (BX)	Register indirect
01	100	EA = (SI) + DISP_8	Indexed
01	101	EA = (DI) + DISP_8	Indexed
10	100	EA = (SI) + DISP_16	Indexed
10	101	EA = (DI) + DISP_16	Indexed
01	110	EA = (BP) + DISP_8	Base
01	111	EA = (BX) + DISP_8	Base
10	110	EA = (BP) + DISP_16	Base
10	111	EA = (BX) + DISP_16	Base
00	000	EA = (BX) + (SI)	Base indexed
00	001	EA = (BX) + (DI)	Base indexed
00	010	EA = (BP) + (SI)	Base indexed
00	011	EA = (BP) + (DI)	Base indexed
01	000	EA = (BX) + (SI) + DISP_8	Base indexed
01	001	EA = (BX) + (DI) + DISP_8	Base indexed
01	010	EA = (BP) + (SI) + DISP_8	Base indexed
01	011	EA = (BP) + (DI) + DISP_8	Base indexed
10	000	EA = (BX) + (SI) + DISP_16	Base indexed
10	001	EA = (BX) + (DI) + DISP_16	Base indexed
10	010	EA = (BP) + (SI) + DISP_16	Base indexed
10	011	EA = (BP) + (DI) + DISP_16	Base indexed

gives the MOD and R/M field encodings for each of the possible address computations.

Direct Addressing

Direct addressing is one of several memory addressing modes. With direct addressing, the effective address of the memory operand is the 16-bit displacement contained in the third and fourth bytes of the machine language representation of the instruction. In the Assembly language representation of an instruction, a direct address is specified by encoding the symbolic name of the memory location in the appropriate operand field of the instruction.

EXAMPLE

```
MOV  CX, COUNT
```

The offset portion of the address of the memory location associated with symbolic name COUNT is the displacement stored in the third and fourth bytes of the machine language representation of the instruction.

Register Indirect Addressing

With **register indirect addressing**, the effective address of the memory operand is the 16-bit contents of the BX, DI, or SI register. The segment portion of the address is assumed to be the shifted contents of the DS-register. In the Assembly language representation of an instruction, a register indirect address is specified by enclosing the 2-character symbolic name of the register (BX, DI, or SI) in square brackets in the appropriate operand field of the instruction.

EXAMPLE

Suppose character strings are represented with byte arrays whose first byte contains the length of the string and whose subsequent bytes contain the ASCII characters of the string. The 8-character string JOHN DOE would be represented as shown in Figure 8.14.

Also suppose a subprocedure is entered with the DS:SI register pair pointing to the base of such an array (i.e., the address of the byte containing the length of the string). To move the length of the string to the CX-register, the following instruction can be used:

```
MOV  CX, [SI]
```

The instruction

```
INC  SI
```

would then update the SI-register, so that the DS:SI register pair would point to the first character of the string.

Now suppose a subprocedure is entered with the ES:DI register pair pointing to the base of such an array. To move the length of the string to the CX-register, the following instruction could be used:

```
MOV  CX, ES: [DI]
```

The prefix, ES:, is called a **segment override prefix**. When the BX, DI, or SI register is used as an indirect address, the DS-register contents are assumed to specify the segment portion of the address, unless a segment override prefix explicitly specifies the use of another segment register.

FIGURE 8.14
Hexadecimal representation of character string JOHN DOE with length as first byte

08
4A
4F
48
4E
20
44
4F
45

Indexed Addressing

With **indexed addressing**, the effective address of the memory operand is the sum of the displacement contained in the machine language representation of the instruction and the 16-bit contents of an index register (DI or SI register). In the Assembly language representation of an instruction, an indexed address can be specified by encoding the symbolic name of a memory location followed by the 2-character designator for an index register enclosed in square brackets.

EXAMPLE

Suppose the following array is defined in the data segment:

```
TABLE   DW   100 DUP(?)
```

The instruction

```
ADD   TABLE[DI],3
```

adds 3 to the nth element of array TABLE if $2(n-1)$ is the value in the DI-register.

The offset of TABLE within the data segment (i.e., the offset of the base address of array TABLE) is the displacement in the machine language representation of the instruction. The effective address is the sum of the displacement and the contents of the DI-register, an offset relative to the base address of array TABLE.

Base Addressing

With **base addressing**, the effective address of the memory operand is the sum of the displacement contained in the machine language representation of the instruction and the 16-bit contents of a base register (BX or BP register). In the Assembly language representation of an instruction, a base address can be specified by encoding a constant followed by the 2-character designator for a base register, which is enclosed in square brackets.

EXAMPLE

Arguments to a subprocedure can be passed via the stack. Suppose a subprocedure named SUBPROC requires the following calling sequence:

```
PUSH   ⟨arg 1⟩
PUSH   ⟨arg 2⟩
CALL   SUBPROC
```

Figure 8.15 shows the state of the stack at time of entry to the SUBPROC procedure. Suppose the first two instructions in SUBPROC are the following:

```
PUSH   BP
MOV    BP,SP
```

Figure 8.16 shows the state of the stack just after execution of these two instructions. The SS:BP register pair is not modified by further PUSH and POP

FIGURE 8.15
Stack at entry to
SUBPROC

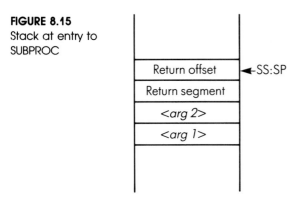

operations. It provides a reference point in the stack. An offset relative to this reference point is the technique for referencing the two arguments. To move a copy of the second argument, $\langle arg\ 2 \rangle$, to the DX-register, the following instruction can be used:

```
MOV  DX, 6[BP]
```

The value 6 is the 8-bit displacement in the Assembly language representation of the instruction. The effective address is the sum of the displacement, sign extended to 16 bits, and the contents of the BP-register. When the BP-register is used as a base address, the SS-register is assumed to be the segment register. If the BX-register had been used throughout this example instead of the BP-register, then a segment override prefix of SS: would have been required. That is, the preceding MOV instruction would have been

```
MOV  DX, 6SS:[BX]
```

The following are some alternative forms for the same instruction:

```
MOV  DX, [BP]+6
MOV  DX, [BP+6]
```

FIGURE 8.16
Stack just after
initialization of the
BP-register

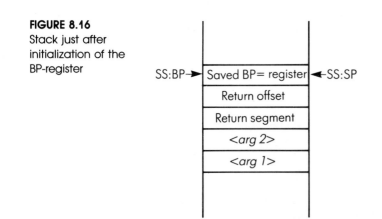

FIGURE 8.17
Stack just after
initialization of the
BP-register

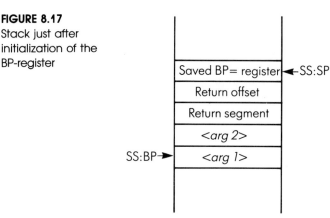

The displacement can also be a negative value. Suppose the first three instructions in the SUBPROC procedure are the following:

```
PUSH   BP
MOV    BP,SP
ADD    BP,8
```

Figure 8.17 shows the state of the stack just after execution of these three instructions. To move a copy of the second argument to the DX-register, the following instruction can be used:

```
MOV    DX,-2[BP]
```

Base Indexed Addressing

With **base indexed addressing**, the effective address of the memory operand is one of the following sums:

> The sum of the 16-bit contents of a base register (BX or BP) and the 16-bit contents of an index register (DI or SI)
> The sum of the displacement contained in the machine language representation of the instruction, the 16-bit contents of a base register (BX or BP), and the 16-bit contents of an index register (DI or SI).

In the Assembly language representation of an instruction, a base indexed address can be specified in any of the following forms:

⟨*name*⟩[⟨*base*⟩][⟨*index*⟩]

[⟨*base*⟩ + ⟨*constant*⟩][⟨*index*⟩]

[⟨*base*⟩][⟨*index*⟩ + ⟨*constant*⟩]

[⟨*base*⟩ + ⟨*index*⟩ + ⟨*constant*⟩]

[⟨*base*⟩ + ⟨*constant*⟩ + ⟨*index*⟩]

in which ⟨*name*⟩ is the symbolic name associated with a memory location, ⟨*base*⟩ is the 2-character designator of a base register (BX or BP), ⟨*index*⟩ is the 2-character designator of an index register (DI or SI), and ⟨*constant*⟩ is any legal 8-bit or 16-bit constant. Base indexed addressing can be used to access the elements of two-dimensional arrays and is discussed further in Chapter 13.

Programming Example—BCD to ASCII Conversion Revisited

Program Listing 8.2 is an alternate implementation of the algorithm previously discussed that converts a BCD number to an ASCII character string. The only difference between Program Listing 8.1 and Program Listing 8.2 is that the former uses string instructions, and the latter does not. The changes between the two implementations are summarized:

1. The CLD instruction in line 26 in Program Listing 8.1 has been eliminated in Program Listing 8.2. Since the string instructions are not being used in this implementation, there is no need for the direction flag.

2. The LODSB instruction in line 32 in Program Listing 8.1 is replaced by the two instructions in lines 31 and 32 in Program Listing 8.2. The MOV instruction in line 31 moves to the AL-register a copy of the byte in the BCD array addressed by the DS:SI register pair (an example of register indirect addressing). The prefix, DS:, is not required, because the default segment register for the SI-register is the DS-register. The INC instruction in line 32 increments the SI-register by 1, so that the DS:SI register pair addresses the next byte in the BCD array. These two instructions perform the same function as the LODSB instruction, except INC affects the flags, and LODSB does not affect the flags.

3. The STOSB instruction in line 44 in Program Listing 8.1 is replaced by the two instructions in lines 43 and 44 in Program Listing 8.2. The MOV instruction in line 43 moves to the byte in the ASCII array addressed by the ES:DI register pair a copy of the byte in the AL-register (an example of register indirect addressing with a segment override prefix). The prefix, ES:, is required, because the default segment register for the DI-register is the DS-register. The INC instruction in line 44 increments the DI-register by 1, so that the ES:DI register pair addresses the next byte in the ASCII array. These two instructions perform the same function as the STOSB instruction, except INC affects the flags, but STOSB does not affect the flags.

```
 1: ;
 2: ;
 3: ;                       PROGRAM LISTING 8.2
 4: ;
 5: ; PROCEDURE TO CONVERT A BCD NUMBER TO ASCII
 6: ;
 7: ; INPUT:   DS:SI POINTS TO ARRAY CONTAINING BCD   NUMBER
 8: ;          ES:DI POINTS TO ARRAY TO CONTAIN ASCII NUMBER
 9: ;          CX    CONTAINS SIZE OF BCD NUMBER (DIGIT_COUNT)
10: ;
11: ; OUTPUT: UPON RETURN, THE ARRAY POINTED TO BY ES:DI WILL
12: ;          CONTAIN AN ASCII NUMBER EQUIVALENT  TO  THE BCD
13: ;          NUMBER IN THE ARRAY POINTED TO BY DS:SI.
14: ;
15: CODE        SEGMENT
16:             ASSUME  CS:CODE
17:             PUBLIC  BCDASCII
18: BCDASCII    PROC    FAR              ;PROCEDURE BCDASCII (DIGIT_COUNT,
19:                                      ;                    DS:SI,ES:DI)
20:             PUSHF                       ;SAVE FLAGS
21:             PUSH    AX                  ;SAVE REGISTERS
22:             PUSH    CX
23:             PUSH    DX
24:             PUSH    DI
25:             PUSH    SI
26:             MOV     DX,-1               ;LR_FLAG = LEFT
27: LOOP_TOP:                               ;REPEAT
28:             PUSH    CX                  ;    SAVE DIGIT_COUNT
29:             CMP     DX,0                ;    IF   LR_FLAG = LEFT
30:             JG      ELSE
31:             MOV     AL,DS:[SI]          ;      THEN PAIR = DS:SI -> BYTE
32:             INC     SI                  ;           SI = SI + 1
33:             MOV     AH,AL
34:             MOV     CL,4                ;           CHAR = LEFT NIBBLE
35:             SHR     AL,CL               ;                    OF PAIR
36:             JMP     ENDIF
37: ELSE:                                   ;      ELSE
38:             MOV     AL,AH
39:             AND     AL,0FH              ;           CHAR = RIGHT NIBBLE
40:                                         ;                    OF PAIR
41: ENDIF:                                  ;      ENDIF
42:             ADD     AL,'0'              ;      CHAR = CHAR + ASCII(0)
43:             MOV     ES:[DI],AL          ;      ES:DI -> BYTE = CHAR
44:             INC     DI                  ;      DI = DI + 1
45:             NEG     DX                  ;      REVERSE LR_FLAG
46:             POP     CX                  ;      RESTORE DIGIT_COUNT
47:             LOOP    LOOP_TOP            ;      DECREMENT DIGIT_COUNT
48:                                         ;UNTIL DIGIT_COUNT = 0
49:             POP     SI                  ;RESTORE REGISTERS
50:             POP     DI
51:             POP     DX
52:             POP     CX
53:             POP     AX
54:             POPF                        ;RESTORE FLAGS
55:             RET                         ;RETURN
56: BCDASCII    ENDP                     ;END BCDASCII
57: CODE        ENDS
58:*           END
```

*

8.5 | Programming Examples

This section contains three example programs that demonstrate most of the topics discussed in this chapter: character strings, integer word arrays, and integer byte arrays. As well, many of the addressing modes described are illustrated in these examples.

Secret Message Translation

Program Listing 8.3 is an implementation of an algorithm to translate a secret message, in which the input is an encoded message and the output is the decoded message. The translation scheme is as follows:

Encoded alphabet: JEKPQBWALR. MSCUTDVNFZGYHIOX$

Decoded alphabet: ABCDEFG. HIJKLMNO PQRSTUVWXYZ

The algorithm accepts an encoded message such as KTCVYGQFDZKRQUKQ and decodes and displays the decoded message: COMPUTER SCIENCE. The decoding is accomplished by translating the K to a C, the T to an O, the C to an M, and so forth. The translation algorithm places an asterisk ($*$) in the decoded message for any character in the encoded message that is not in the encoded alphabet.

Program Listing 8.3 shows a program for performing this translation. The data segment is defined in lines 21–32. The array SECRTMSG defined in line 23 is a 40-character string whose characters are uninitialized, and it is used to hold the input encoded string. The array TRANSMSG defined in line 24 is a 40-character string whose characters are uninitialized, and it is used to build the decoded string.

The array DECODED defined in line 25 is a 28-character string that is initialized to contain the characters of the decoded alphabet. The array ENCODED defined in line 26 is also a 28-character string that is initialized to contain the characters of the encoded alphabet. The two strings ENCODED and DECODED have been initialized in such a way that the ith character of the ENCODED string translates to the ith character of the DECODED string. For each character of SECRTMSG, the algorithm searches the encoded string for the same character. If the character is found in the ENCODED string, then the corresponding character in the DECODED string is copied into the next position of TRANSMSG. If the character is not found in the ENCODED string, then an asterisk is copied into the next position of TRANSMSG.

The array PROMPT and the array TMSG defined in lines 27 and 28 are prompt and annotation messages, respectively. Character strings have been used for these purposes in example programs throughout this book. The ASCII characters 0D hex and 0A hex are RETURN and line feed, respectively. These two characters are displayed by the NEWLINE subprocedure.

```
 1: ;
 2: ;
 3: ;                    PROGRAM LISTING 8.3
 4: ;
 5: ;PROGRAM TO TRANSLATE A SECRET MESSAGE
 6: ;
 7: ;
 8:                                          ;PROCEDURES TO
 9:           EXTRN    GETSTRNG:FAR          ;INPUT A CHARACTER STRING
10:           EXTRN    PUTSTRNG:FAR          ;DISPLAY CHARACTER STRING
11:           EXTRN    NEWLINE:FAR           ;DISPLAY NEWLINE CHARACTER
12: ;
13: ; S T A C K   S E G M E N T   D E F I N I T I O N
14: ;
15: STACK     SEGMENT STACK
16:           DB       256 DUP(?)
17: STACK     ENDS
18: ;
19: ; D A T A   S E G M E N T   D E F I N I T I O N
20: ;
21: DATA      SEGMENT
22: ;
23: SECRTMSG  DB       40 DUP(?)             ;SECRET MESSAGE
24: TRANSMSG  DB       40 DUP(?)             ;TRANSLATED MESSAGE
25: DECODED   DB       'ABCDEFG.HIJKLMNO PQRSTUVWXYZ'
26: ENCODED   DB       'JEKPQBWALR.MSCUTDVNFZGYHIOX$'
27: PROMPT    DB       'ENTER SECRET MESSAGE',0DH,0AH
28: TMSG      DB       'TRANSLATED MESSAGE',0DH,0AH
29: COUNT     DW       ?                     ;CHARACTER COUNT OF MESSAGE
30: CODE_LNGTH EQU     28                    ;LENGTH OF CODE STRINGS
31: ;
32: DATA      ENDS
33: ;
34: ; C O D E   S E G M E N T   D E F I N I T I O N
35: ;
36: CODE      SEGMENT
37: EX_8_3    PROC     FAR
38:           ASSUME   CS:CODE,DS:DATA,SS:STACK,ES:DATA
39:           PUSH     DS                    ;PUSH RETURN SEG ADDR ON STACK
40:           SUB      AX,AX                 ;PUSH RETURN OFFSET OF ZERO
41:           PUSH     AX                    ;ON STACK
42:           MOV      AX,SEG DATA           ;SET DS AND ES REGISTERS
43:           MOV      DS,AX                 ;TO POINT TO DATA SEGMENT
44:           MOV      ES,AX
45:*          CALL     NEWLINE

46: ;
47:           LEA      DI,PROMPT             ;PROMPT FOR SECRET_MSG
48:           MOV      CX,22
49:           CALL     PUTSTRNG
50:           LEA      DI,SECRTMSG           ;GET SECRET_MSG AND MSG_LENGTH
51:           MOV      CX,40
52:           CALL     GETSTRNG
53:           CALL     NEWLINE
54:           CLD                            ;SET DF FOR INCREMENTING
55:           MOV      COUNT,CX              ;COUNT = MSG_LENGTH
56:           MOV      BX,0                  ;INDEX = 0
57: NEXT_CHAR:                              ;REPEAT
58:           MOV      AL,SECRTMSG[BX]       ;    CHAR = SECRET_MSG (INDEX)
59:           PUSH     CX                    ;    SAVE MSG_LENGTH
```

*

```
60:                  MOV      CX,CODE_LNGTH        ;   SEARCH_COUNT = CODE_LNGTH
61:                  LEA      DI,ENCODED           ;   SET ES:DI TO POINT TO
62:                                                ;   BEGINNING OF ENCODED STRING
63:           REPNE  SCASB                         ;   FOUND = FALSE
64:                                                ;   REPEAT
65:                                                ;      IF   ES:DI->BYTE = CHAR
66:                                                ;      THEN FOUND = TRUE
67:                                                ;      ENDIF
68:                                                ;      DI = DI + 1
69:                                                ;      DECREMENT SEARCH_COUNT
70:                                                ;   UNTIL FOUND OR SEARCH_COUNT=0
71:                  JE       FOUND                ;   IF   NOT FOUND
72:                  MOV      TRANSMSG[BX],'*'      ;   THEN TRANSMSG(INDEX) = *
73:                  JMP      LOOPEND              ;
74: FOUND:                                         ;   ELSE
75:                  DEC      DI                   ;      DI = DI - 1
76:                  MOV      SI,DI                ;      SI = DI
77:                  SUB      SI,OFFSET ENCODED    ;         - OFFSET OF ENCODED
78:                  ADD      SI,OFFSET DECODED    ;         + OFFSET OF DECODED
79:                  LODSB                         ;      TRANSMSG(INDEX) =
80:                  MOV      TRANSMSG[BX],AL      ;         DS:SI->BYTE
81: LOOPEND:                                       ;   ENDIF
82:                  INC      BX                   ;   INDEX = INDEX + 1
83:                  POP      CX                   ;   RESTORE MSG_LENGTH
84:                  LOOP     NEXT_CHAR            ;   DECREMENT MSG_LENGTH
35:                                                ;UNTIL MSG_LENGTH = 0
86:                  LEA      DI,TMSG              ;DISPLAY TRANS_MSG
87:                  MOV      CX,20
88:                  CALL     PUTSTRNG
89:                  LEA      DI,TRANSMSG
90:                  MOV      CX,COUNT             ;MSG_LENGTH = COUNT
91:                  CALL     PUTSTRNG
92:                  CALL     NEWLINE
93:                  RET                           ;RETURN
94: EX_8_3           ENDP
95: CODE             ENDS
96:*                 END      EX_8_3
```

The scalar variable COUNT defined in line 29 holds the length of the secret message. The named constant CODE_LNGTH defined in line 30 is the fixed length of the encoded and decoded alphabets.

The program begins in the standard manner by saving the return address for DOS (lines 39–41) and initializing the segment registers (lines 42–44). The instructions in lines 47–49 display the prompt message that asks the user to enter a secret message. The instructions in lines 50–52 are the calling sequence for the GETSTRNG procedure, the procedure that accepts a character string from the keyboard and returns it to the caller. GETSTRNG expects two inputs: the ES:DI register pair that points to the array that is to receive the input string and the CX-register that contains the size of that array. The LEA instruction in line 50 sets up the first of these two inputs, and the MOV instruction in line 51 sets up the second. The GETSTRNG procedure returns the input character string to the caller in the caller's array, with the actual length of the string in the CX-register.

The instructions in lines 54–56 perform initialization for the loop that translates the characters of the secret message, one character per loop iteration.

The CLD instruction in line 54 clears the DF bit in the flags register, so that string instructions automatically increment the index registers. The MOV instruction in line 55 saves the input string length as the value of variable COUNT. The string length in the CX-register controls the loop that translates the secret message. The value of variable COUNT restores the string length when the translated message is displayed. The MOV instruction in line 56 initializes to zero the index for arrays SECRTMSG and TRANSMSG.

The REPEAT-UNTIL loop in lines 57–85 translates the secret message. Each iteration of the loop translates one character of the message. The MOV instruction in line 58 copies the next character of the secret message into the AL-register (an example of base addressing). The effective address is the sum of the offset of symbolic name SECRTMSG and the contents of the BX-register, which is an index from the base address of array SECRTMSG.

The instructions in lines 59–61 perform initialization for the loop that searches the encoded alphabet for the character just extracted from the secret message. The PUSH instruction in line 59 saves the outer loop counter, the remaining message length, so that the CX-register can be used to control the inner loop. The MOV instruction in line 60 initializes the CX-register to the length of the encoded alphabet. This CX-register value defines the maximum number of times that the inner loop body is to be executed. The LEA instruction in line 61 sets the ES:DI register pair to address the first character of the string ENCODED.

The entire inner loop is implemented by the SCASB instruction that contains the REPNE prefix (line 63). The comments in lines 63–70 describe the loop that is implemented by this repeated instruction. The SCASB instruction repeatedly executes until a character is found in the encoded string that matches the character in the AL-register or until all characters of the encoded string have been scanned. That is, the SCASB instruction terminates for either one of the following two reasons:

> A match is found between the character just scanned in ENCODED and the character in the AL-register. In this case, the ZF bit in the flags register is set.

> The CX-register reaches zero, meaning that the entire ENCODED string has been scanned. In this case, the ZF bit in the flags register is cleared, unless the character is found to match the last character of ENCODED.

On termination of the inner loop, the program must determine which of the two reasons caused the loop exit.

The double-alternative decision structure in lines 71–81 determines the condition that caused the loop exit and performs the appropriate translation based on this condition. The JE instruction in line 71 makes the decision based on this condition: If the character from SCRETMSG was not found in the ENCODED string, then the jump is not taken, and the instructions in lines 72 and 73 are executed. The MOV instruction in line 72 stores an asterisk in the string TRANSMSG. The BX-register is used as an index into the string TRANSMSG. This index is the same as that for the string SECRTMSG (line

58), which means that the translated character is inserted at the same position in TRANSMSG as the character being translated appeared in SECRTMSG. The JMP instruction in line 73 causes the second alternative of the double-alternative decision structure to be skipped.

If the character from SECRTMSG is found in the ENCODED string, then the jump in line 71 is taken, and the instructions in lines 75–80 are executed. Since the SCASB instruction updates the DI-register after the comparison is made, the ES:DI register pair addresses the character in ENCODED that immediately follows the one that matches the character from SECRTMSG. The DEC instruction in line 75 sets the ES:DI register pair to address the character in ENCODED that matches the character from SECRTMSG. The instructions in lines 76–78 set the DS:SI register pair to address the character in DECODED that corresponds to the character in ENCODED that is addressed by the ES:DI register pair. Figure 8.18 shows an example of this address conversion. The MOV instruction in line 76 copies the offset from the DI-register to the SI-register. At this point in the program, the ES:DI register pair and the DS:SI register pair address the same character in ENCODED. The SI-register contains the offset of this character relative to the origin of the data segment (Figure 8.18(a)). The SUB instruction in line 77 subtracts the offset of the origin of the string

FIGURE 8.18

Computation to convert the address of the character in the ENCODED string to the address of the corresponding character in the DECODED string

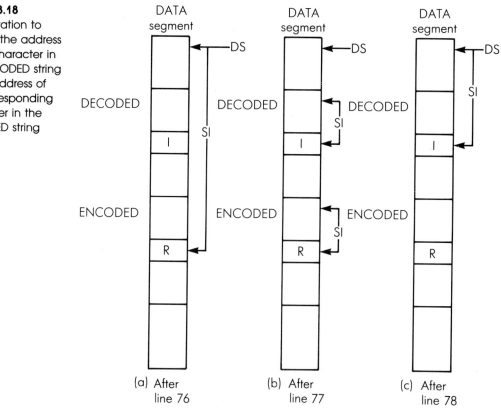

(a) After line 76

(b) After line 77

(c) After line 78

ENCODED from the offset in the SI-register. The SI-register now contains the offset of the matching character in ENCODED relative to its origin (Figure 8.18(b)), which is also the offset of the corresponding character in DECODED relative to its origin (Figure 8.18(b)). The ADD instruction in line 78 adds the offset of the origin of the string DECODED to the offset in the SI-register. The SI-register now contains the offset of the corresponding character in DECODED relative to the origin of the data segment (Figure 8.18(c)); that is, the DS:SI register pair now addresses the character in DECODED that is the translation of the character from SECRTMSG. The LODSB instruction in line 79 loads the character addressed by the DS:SI register pair into the AL-register, and the MOV instruction in line 80 stores this character in the string TRANSMSG. Again, the BX-register is used as the index into the string TRANSMSG.

When line 81 is reached, which is the end of the double-alternative decision structure, a new character has been inserted into the string TRANSMSG in the same position as that of the character extracted from SECRTMSG in line 58. Following the double-alternative decision structure, some loop maintenance operations are performed. The INC instruction in line 82 increments the index into SECRTMSG and TRANSMSG for the next iteration of the outer loop. The POP instruction in line 83 restores the value of the outer loop counter, the remaining message length, to the CX-register. The LOOP instruction in line 84 decrements the loop counter in the CX-register and transfers control to the top of the loop (line 57), if the resulting value is nonzero.

On termination of the outer loop, the translated message is displayed on the video screen. The instructions in lines 86–88 display the annotation message, and the instructions in lines 89–91 display the translated message itself. The LEA instruction in line 89 sets the ES:DI register pair to address the origin of TRANSMSG. The MOV instruction in line 90 loads the saved length of the secret message (i.e., the length of the translated message) into the CX-register. The call to the PUTSTRNG procedure in line 91 then causes the translated message to be displayed on the screen.

The following results are from some sample executions of this program:

```
*

A>B: EX_8_3

ENTER SECRET MESSAGE
VJYSDFYUURTU

TRANSLATED MESSAGE
PAUL RUNNION

A>B: EX_8_3

ENTER SECRET MESSAGE
JUPXDTFDMKDPYQDGTDJFFRHQDRUDPQKQCEQF

TRANSLATED MESSAGE
ANDY OR KC DUE TO ARRIVE IN DECEMBER

A>
```

Sieve of Eratosthenes

Program Listing 8.4 is an implementation of an algorithm to compute prime numbers. The algorithm is called the Sieve of Eratosthenes. The algorithm can be stated as follows:

> Fill the sieve with the consecutive integers from 2 through *n*.
> Repeat.
> Find the smallest integer in the sieve. It is a prime number, so display it.
> Remove this prime number and remove all multiples of this prime number from the sieve.
> Until sieve is empty.

Program Listing 8.4 shows part of an implementation of this algorithm. It uses two internal subprocedures for the purpose of modularity: One of the subprocedures finds the next prime number (the smallest integer left) in the sieve, and the other removes a given prime number and all of its multiples from the sieve. An integer array is used for the sieve.

The data segment for the program is defined in lines 22–29. The named constant, SIZE$ (defined in line 24), defines the size of the sieve in words: Its value here is 15,999. To modify the program to process a different size sieve, you only need to modify the value of SIZE$. The named constant, MAX_INDEX (defined in line 25), is the index of the last word in the sieve. Its value here is two times the value of SIZE$. The sieve itself is defined in line 26, and it is a word array of length SIZE$ (15,999 in the implementation shown). It is initialized by the main procedure to contain the integers 2–16,000. As stated in the prologue (lines 5 and 6), the program displays the prime numbers that are less than 16,000. The character string defined in line 27 is displayed at the end of each page of display. The program pauses at the end of each page of display to allow the user to print a hard copy of the display.

The code segment definition begins in line 33 and contains a main procedure and two internal, NEAR subprocedures. The two subprocedures are used to divide the problem into simpler subproblems. The 15,999-element array that represents the sieve is initialized to contain the consecutive integers 2–16,000. To remove a prime and its multiples from the sieve, the SIFTSIEVE subprocedure replaces those values with zeros. The subprocedure performs this removal process given the index in the sieve of a prime number. To find the next prime number in the sieve, a search, using the FINDPRIM subprocedure, is performed for the next nonzero element. The search can begin at the position (index) of the last prime number found and removed from the sieve.

The SIFTSIEVE subprocedure is defined in lines 91–116. The prologue in lines 91–98 states the interface requirements for the procedure, which expects a prime number in the AX-register and the sieve index of that prime number in the BX-register. The procedure sets the indexed sieve element to zero and also sets to zero any sieve element that is a multiple of that prime number.

The subprocedure begins by saving the registers that it uses (lines 100–101). The MOV instruction in line 102 removes the prime number from the sieve by setting to zero the element of SIEVE that is indexed by the value in the

```
 1: ;
 2: ;
 3: ;                        PROGRAM LISTING 8.4
 4: ;
 5: ; PROGRAM TO DISPLAY THE PRIME NUMBERS THAT ARE LESS THAN 16000.
 6: ; THE PROGRAM USES THE SIEVE OF ERATOSTHENES.
 7: ;
 8: ;                                           ;PROCEDURES TO
 9:                                             ;DISPLAY NEWLINE CHARACTER
10:            EXTRN      NEWLINE:FAR            ;DISPLAY NEWLINE CHARACTER
11:            EXTRN      PAUSE:FAR              ;PAUSE UNTIL KEYSTROKE
12:            EXTRN      PUTDEC$:FAR            ;DISPLAY UNSIGNED DECIMAL INT.
13: ;
14: ; S T A C K    S E G M E N T    D E F I N I T I O N
15: ;
16: STACK      SEGMENT STACK
17:            DB         256 DUP(?)
18: STACK      ENDS
19: ;
20: ; D A T A    S E G M E N T    D E F I N I T I O N
21: ;
22: DATA       SEGMENT
23: ;
24: SIZE$      EQU        15999
25: MAX_INDEX  EQU        2*SIZE$
26: SIEVE      DW         SIZE$ DUP(?)
27: PAUSE_MSG  DB         'PRESS ANY KEY TO CONTINUE'
28: ;
29: DATA       ENDS
30: ;
31: ; C O D E    S E G M E N T    D E F I N I T I O N
32: ;
33: CODE       SEGMENT
34: EX_8_4     PROC       FAR
35:            ASSUME     CS:CODE,SS:STACK,DS:DATA,ES:DATA
36:            PUSH       DS                     ;PUSH RETURN SEG ADDR ON STACK
37:            SUB        AX,AX                  ;PUSH RETURN OFFSET OF ZERO
38:            PUSH       AX                     ;ON STACK
39:            MOV        AX,SEG DATA            ;SET ES AND DS REGISTERS TO
40:            MOV        DS,AX                  ;POINT TO DATA SEGMENT
41:            MOV        ES,AX
42:                                              ;<INITIALIZE SIEVE>
43:            CLD                               ;SET DF FOR INCREMENTING
44:            MOV        CX,SIZE$               ;LOOP_COUNT = SIZE OF SIEVE
45:            LEA        DI,SIEVE               ;SET ES:DI TO BASE ADDRESS
46:                                              ;                OF SIEVE
47:            MOV        AX,2                   ;VALUE = 2
48: LOADLOOP:                                    ;REPEAT
49:            STOSW                             ;    ES:DI -> WORD = VALUE
50:                                              ;    DI = DI + 2
51:            INC        AX                     ;    VALUE = VALUE + 1
52:            LOOP       LOADLOOP               ;    LOOP_COUNT = LOOP_COUNT - 1
53:                                              ;UNTIL LOOP_COUNT = 0
54:            MOV        BX,0                   ;INDEX = 0
55:            MOV        CX,0                   ;PRIME_COUNT = 0
56:*           CALL       FINDPRIM               ;CALL FINDPRIME(INDEX,PRIME)

57: ;
58: PRIMELOOP:                                   ;REPEAT
59:            CALL       SIFTSIEVE              ;    CALL SIFTSIEVE(PRIME,INDEX)
```

*

```
60:                                             ;   <SIFT OUT MULTIPLES OF PRIME>
61:             PUSH    BX                      ;   SAVE SIEVE INDEX
62:             MOV     BH,1                    ;   DISPLAY PRIME
63:             CALL    PUTDEC$
64:             INC     CX                      ;   PRIME_COUNT = PRIME_COUNT + 1
65:             MOV     AX,CX                   ;   IF    PRIME_COUNT mod 10 = 0
66:             MOV     DX,0
67:             MOV     BX,10
68:             DIV     BX
69:             CMP     DX,0
70:             JNE     NEXTPRIME
71:             CALL    NEWLINE                 ;       THEN DISPLAY NEWLINE CHAR
72:             MOV     DX,0                    ;           IF    PRIME_COUNT mod 240
73:             MOV     BX,24                   ;               = 0
74:             DIV     BX
75:             CMP     DX,0
76:             JNE     NEXTPRIME
77:             PUSH    CX                      ;               THEN
78:             LEA     DI,PAUSE_MSG            ;                   PAUSE FOR PRINT
79:             MOV     CX,25                   ;                   OF DISPLAY SCREEN
80:             CALL    PAUSE
81:             POP     CX
82:                                             ;               ENDIF
83: NEXTPRIME:                                  ;   ENDIF
84:             POP     BX                      ;   RESTORE SIEVE INDEX
85:             CALL    FINDPRIM                ;   CALL FINDPRIME(INDEX,PRIME)
86:             CMP     AX,0
87:             JNE     PRIMELOOP               ;UNTIL SIEVE IS EMPTY
88:             CALL    NEWLINE
89:             RET                             ;RETURN
90: EX_8_4      ENDP
91: ;
92: ; SIFT MULTIPLES OF PRIME OUT OF SIEVE
93: ;
94: ; INPUT:   AX-REG CONTAINS PRIME NUMBER
95: ;          BX-REG CONTAINS SIEVE INDEX OF PRIME NUMBER
96: ;
97: ; OUTPUT: SIEVE WITH MULTIPLES OF PRIME REMOVED
98: ;
99: SIFTSIEVE   PROC    NEAR                    ;PROCEDURE SIFTSIEVE(PRIME,INDEX)
100:            PUSH    AX                      ;SAVE REGISTERS
101:            PUSH    BX
102:            MOV     SIEVE[BX],0             ;SIEVE(INDEX) = 0
103:            SAL     AX,1                    ;OFFSET = PRIME * 2
104:                                            ;<OFFSET BETWEEN MULTIPLES
105:                                            ;            OF PRIME>
106: SIFTLOOP:                                  ;WHILE (INDEX+OFFSET) < MAX_INDEX
107:            ADD     BX,AX                   ;   INDEX = INDEX + OFFSET
108:            CMP     BX,MAX_INDEX
109:            JAE     RETURN1
110:            MOV     SIEVE[BX],0             ;   SIEVE(INDEX) = 0
111:            JMP     SIFTLOOP
112: RETURN1:                                   ;ENDWHILE
113:            POP     BX                      ;RESTORE REGISTERS
114:            POP     AX
115:            RET                             ;RETURN
116:*SIFTSIEVE  ENDP                            ;END SIFTSIEVE
*
```

BX-register. The SAL instruction in line 103 computes the offset (i.e., difference in index) between consecutive multiples of the prime number just removed. Since this is a word array, the prime number is multiplied by 2 to compute this offset.

The WHILE loop in lines 106–112 removes the multiples of the specified prime number from the sieve. On each iteration of the loop, the index of the next multiple is computed from the index of the multiple removed on the previous iteration, and the multiple at this new index is replaced with zero (i.e., removed). The ADD instruction in line 107 computes the index of the next multiple by adding the offset between multiples (computed in line 103) to the index in the BX-register. Figure 8.19 shows several iterations of this index computation for the prime number 3. The CMP instruction in line 108 performs the loop test, and the JAE instruction in line 109 makes the decision based on this test: If the new index is less than or equal to the index of the last element in the sieve (MAX_INDEX), then the jump is not taken and the loop continues; if the new index is greater than the maximum index, the jump is taken, and the loop is terminated. The MOV instruction in line 110 sets to zero the element of array SIEVE that is indexed by the value of the BX-register. This step removes the current multiple of the specified prime number. The JMP instruction in line 111 returns control to the top of the loop (line 106).

FIGURE 8.19

Computation of the sieve index of the next multiple of a prime from the index of the current multiple of the prime

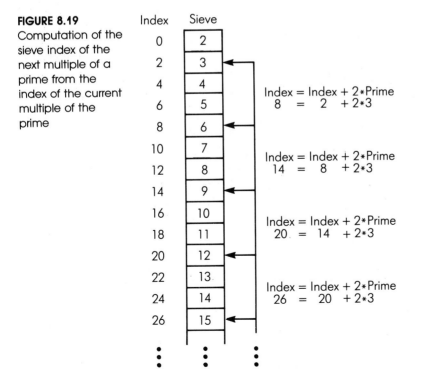

At loop exit, the registers are restored for the caller (lines 113 and 114), and control is returned to the caller (line 115).

The subprocedure FINDPRIM is not shown in Program Listing 8.4 (the task is left for you as Programming Exercise 8.10), although the interface requirements of FINDPRIM are discussed here. The FINDPRIM procedure expects a sieve index in the BX-register. This index specifies the position in array SIEVE at which the search for the prime number is to begin. The procedure starts at the specified position and searches for the first nonzero element. If a nonzero element is found, then the sieve index of that element is returned in the BX-register, and the element itself (i.e., the next prime number) is returned in the AX-register. If the end of array SIEVE is reached without finding a nonzero element, then zero is returned in the AX-register, which indicates to the caller that the sieve is empty.

The main procedure for this program is defined in lines 34–90 of Program Listing 8.4. The program begins in the standard manner by saving the return address for DOS (lines 36–38) and initializing the segment registers (lines 39–41). Both the ES and the DS registers specify the address of the origin of the data segment.

The instructions in lines 43–47 perform initialization for the loop that initializes SIEVE. The CLD instruction in line 43 clears the DF bit of the flags register, so that string instructions increment their way through the sieve. The MOV instruction in line 44 sets the loop counter, the CX-register, to the size of the sieve. The LEA instruction in line 45 sets the ES:DI register pair to specify the base address of array SIEVE. The MOV instruction in line 47 sets the AX-register to 2, the first value in the range of integers to be placed in the sieve.

The REPEAT-UNTIL loop in lines 48–52 places the consecutive integers 2–16,000 into consecutive locations of array SIEVE. The STOSW instruction in line 49 copies the value of the AX-register into the word of array SIEVE addressed by the ES:DI register pair, and then it increments the DI-register by 2, so that the ES:DI register pair addresses the next element in array SIEVE. The INC instruction in line 51 increments the value in the AX-register by 1, producing the value to be stored in that next element of array SIEVE. The LOOP instruction in line 52 performs the loop test: It decrements the loop count in the CX-register by 1, and if the resulting value is nonzero, then it transfers control to the top of the loop (line 48).

At loop exit, the instructions in lines 54–56 are executed. These instructions perform initialization for the loop that finds and displays the prime numbers. The MOV instruction in line 54 initializes the BX-register, the index into array SIEVE, to zero. At this point, the address expression, SIEVE[BX], addresses the first element of array SIEVE. The MOV instruction in line 55 initializes the count of prime numbers displayed to zero. This count is maintained in the CX-register. The CALL instruction in line 56 invokes the FINDPRIM procedure to locate the first prime number in the sieve. FINDPRIM returns with the first prime number, 2, in the AX-register and with the BX-register set to the index within SIEVE of that prime number. Since the first prime number in the sieve is the first element in array SIEVE, FINDPRIM finds that element immediately. In fact, the CALL instruction could be replaced by the instruction

```
MOV   AX,SIEVE[BX]
```

obviously rendering the program more efficient.

The REPEAT-UNTIL loop in lines 58–87 finds and displays the prime numbers, one prime number per iteration. At the beginning of each iteration of the loop body, the AX-register contains the next prime number in the sieve, and the BX-register contains the index within array SIEVE of that prime number. The CALL instruction in line 59 invokes the SIFTSIEVE procedure to remove that prime number and its multiples from the sieve. On return from the SIFT-SIEVE procedure, the AX-register still contains the prime number, and the BX-register still contains the index within array SIEVE. That index is used as the starting point for the search of array SIEVE for the next prime number. The PUSH instruction in line 61 saves the sieve index, so that the BX-register can be used for other purposes. The two instructions in lines 62 and 63 display the prime number, and the INC instruction in line 64 increments the count of prime numbers displayed. The nested, single-alternative decision structures in lines 65–83 handle line and page control for the display of the prime numbers. This nested structure is discussed in detail shortly.

On completion of the nested decision structure, the sieve index is restored (line 84). The CALL to FINDPRIM in line 85 locates the next prime number in the sieve, if the sieve is not empty. On return from the FINDPRIM procedure, either the AX-register contains the next prime number in the sieve, or it contains zero, indicating that the sieve is empty. If the AX-register contains a prime number, then the BX-register contains the index within array SIEVE of that prime number. The CMP instruction in line 86 performs the loop test, and the JNE instruction in line 87 makes the decision based on this test: If a prime number is in the AX-register, then the jump is taken to the top of the REPEAT-UNTIL loop (line 58); however, if the AX-register contains zero, then the sieve is empty, and the loop is terminated. At loop exit, control is returned to DOS (line 89).

The prime numbers are displayed on the screen 10 per line. Each number is displayed right-justified in a 6-character field (lines 62 and 63). After each 24 lines of display, a pause is made to allow the user to print the display screen. The continuation of the display is under user control. The display control is performed by the nested, single-alternative decision structures in lines 65–83. The instructions in lines 65–69 test to see if the count of primes displayed (CX-register value) is divisible by 10, and the JNE instruction in line 70 makes the decision based on this test: If the count is not divisible by 10 (i.e., remainder of division by 10 is nonzero), then the jump is taken to the end of the nested decision structure (line 83); if the count is divisible by 10, then a display line has just been completed, and the instructions in lines 71–82 are executed. The call to the NEWLINE procedure in line 71 moves the cursor to the beginning of the next line on the display. Lines 72–82 implement the inner decision structure.

The inner decision structure determines whether a page of display has been completed. The quotient of the division of the count by 10 (line 68) represents a line count. The instructions in lines 72–75 test to see if the line count is divisible by 24, and the JNE instruction in line 76 makes the decision based on this test: If the line count is not divisible by 24 (i.e., the remainder of the division by 24 is nonzero), then the jump is taken to the end of the nested decision structure (line 83); if the line count is divisible by 24, then a display page has just been completed, and the instructions in lines 77–81 are executed. The PUSH instruction in line 77 saves the CX-register value, the count of primes displayed, so that the CX-register can be used for input to the PAUSE procedure. The instructions in lines 78–80 are the calling sequence for the PAUSE procedure. The input requirements for PAUSE are the same as those for PUTSTRNG. In fact, PAUSE calls PUTSTRNG to display the specified message beginning at the current cursor position. The PAUSE procedure then clears the input buffer and waits for a keystroke. When the keystroke is received, the PAUSE procedure calls the NEWLINE procedure to move the cursor to the beginning of the next display line and then returns to the caller. On return from PAUSE, the count of primes displayed is restored in the CX-register (line 81), and the end of the decision structure is reached (line 83). Output Listing 8.5 is a printout of the first two pages of the display generated by this program.

Large Integer Values

Program Listing 8.6 demonstrates a technique for processing decimal integers that are too large to be represented directly in binary with 8, 16, or even 32 bits. The technique is demonstrated using a program that computes large factorial values.

Given an integer, n, the factorial of n (denoted by $n!$) is the product of the first n positive integer:

$$n! = n(n - 1)(n - 2) \ldots (3)\,(2)\,(1)$$

One interesting property of the factorial function is the rate at which $n!$ grows as n gets larger: The limit for 8-bit unsigned integers is $5! = 120$; the limit for 16-bit unsigned integers is $8! = 40,320$; and the limit for 32-bit unsigned integers is $12! = 479,001,600$. The value of $20!$ requires 19 decimal digits and 63 binary digits.

To compute arbitrarily large factorial values, a byte array is used to represent a single decimal integer. Each element of the array represents one decimal digit of the integer value. The number of decimal digits in the integer value being represented is limited only by the array size. Program Listing 8.6 uses a 60-byte array called FAC to represent a factorial value. The factorial value is represented in the following way:

FAC(0)   *contains the most-significant digit*
FAC(1)   *contains the next most-significant digit*

    .
    .
    .

FAC(57)   *contains the hundreds digit*
FAC(58)   *contains the tens digit*
FAC(59)   *contains the units digit*

OUTPUT LISTING 8.5

```
   2      3      5      7     11     13     17     19     23     29
  31     37     41     43     47     53     59     61     67     71
  73     79     83     89     97    101    103    107    109    113
 127    131    137    139    149    151    157    163    167    173
 179    181    191    193    197    199    211    223    227    229
 233    239    241    251    257    263    269    271    277    281
 283    293    307    311    313    317    331    337    347    349
 353    359    367    373    379    383    389    397    401    409
 419    421    431    433    439    443    449    457    461    463
 467    479    487    491    499    503    509    521    523    541
 547    557    563    569    571    577    587    593    599    601
 607    613    617    619    631    641    643    647    653    659
 661    673    677    683    691    701    709    719    727    733
 739    743    751    757    761    769    773    787    797    809
 811    821    823    827    829    839    853    857    859    863
 877    881    883    887    907    911    919    929    937    941
 947    953    967    971    977    983    991    997   1009   1013
1019   1021   1031   1033   1039   1049   1051   1061   1063   1069
1087   1091   1093   1097   1103   1109   1117   1123   1129   1151
1153   1163   1171   1181   1187   1193   1201   1213   1217   1223
1229   1231   1237   1249   1259   1277   1279   1283   1289   1291
1297   1301   1303   1307   1319   1321   1327   1361   1367   1373
1381   1399   1409   1423   1427   1429   1433   1439   1447   1451
1453   1459   1471   1481   1483   1487   1489   1493   1499   1511
PRESS ANY KEY TO CONTINUE

1523   1531   1543   1549   1553   1559   1567   1571   1579   1583
1597   1601   1607   1609   1613   1619   1621   1627   1637   1657
1663   1667   1669   1693   1697   1699   1709   1721   1723   1733
1741   1747   1753   1759   1777   1783   1787   1789   1801   1811
1823   1831   1847   1861   1867   1871   1873   1877   1879   1889
1901   1907   1913   1931   1933   1949   1951   1973   1979   1987
1993   1997   1999   2003   2011   2017   2027   2029   2039   2053
2063   2069   2081   2083   2087   2089   2099   2111   2113   2129
2131   2137   2141   2143   2153   2161   2179   2203   2207   2213
2221   2237   2239   2243   2251   2267   2269   2273   2281   2287
2293   2297   2309   2311   2333   2339   2341   2347   2351   2357
2371   2377   2381   2383   2389   2393   2399   2411   2417   2423
2437   2441   2447   2459   2467   2473   2477   2503   2521   2531
2539   2543   2549   2551   2557   2579   2591   2593   2609   2617
2621   2633   2647   2657   2659   2663   2671   2677   2683   2687
2689   2693   2699   2707   2711   2713   2719   2729   2731   2741
2749   2753   2767   2777   2789   2791   2797   2801   2803   2819
2833   2837   2843   2851   2857   2861   2879   2887   2897   2903
2909   2917   2927   2939   2953   2957   2963   2969   2971   2999
3001   3011   3019   3023   3037   3041   3049   3061   3067   3079
3083   3089   3109   3119   3121   3137   3163   3167   3169   3181
3187   3191   3203   3209   3217   3221   3229   3251   3253   3257
3259   3271   3299   3301   3307   3313   3319   3323   3329   3331
3343   3347   3359   3361   3371   3373   3389   3391   3407   3413
PRESS ANY KEY TO CONTINUE
```

```
 1: ;
 2: ;
 3: ;                     PROGRAM LISTING 8.6
 4: ;
 5: ;PROGRAM TO COMPUTE LARGE FACTORIAL VALUES.   A LARGE INTEGER IS
 6: ;REPRESENTED BY A BYTE ARRAY. EACH ELEMENT OF THE ARRAY CONTAINS
 7: ;ONE DIGIT OF THE LARGE INTEGER. A TABLE OF FACTORIAL VALUES  IS
 8: ;DISPLAYED.   THE USER ENTERS THE LARGEST VALUE OF N FOR WHICH N!
 9: ;IS TO BE DISPLAYED
10: ;
11:                                     ;PROCEDURES TO
12:             EXTRN   GETDEC$:FAR     ;GET UNSIGNED DECIMAL INTEGER
13:             EXTRN   PUTDEC$:FAR     ;DISPLAY UNSIGNED DECIMAL INT.
14:             EXTRN   NEWLINE:FAR     ;DISPLAY NEWLINE CHARACTER
15:             EXTRN   PUTSTRNG:FAR    ;DISPLAY CHARACTER STRING
16:             EXTRN   PUTLGINT:FAR    ;DISPLAY LARGE INTEGERS
17: ;
18: ; S T A C K   S E G M E N T   D E F I N I T I O N
19: ;
20: STACK       SEGMENT STACK
21:             DB      256 DUP(?)
22: STACK       ENDS
23: ;
24: ; D A T A   S E G M E N T   D E F I N I T I O N
25: ;
26: DATA        SEGMENT
27: ;
28: SIZE$       EQU     60
29: FAC         DB      (SIZE$-1) DUP(O)
30: FAC_END     DB      1
31: CARRY       DW      ?
32: N           DW      ?
33: MAXN        DW      ?
34: COUNT       DB      ?
35: PROMPT      DB      'ENTER LARGEST VALUE',0DH,0AH
36:             DB      'FOR WHICH TO COMPUTE',0DH,0AH
37:             DB      'FACTORIAL',0DH,0AH
38: ;
39: DATA        ENDS
40:*;
```
*
```
41: ;
42: ; C O D E   S E G M E N T   D E F I N I T I O N
43: ;
44: CODE        SEGMENT
45: EX_8_6      PROC    FAR
46:             ASSUME  CS:CODE,SS:STACK,ES:DATA
47:             PUSH    DS              ;PUSH RETURN SEG ADDR ON STACK
48:             SUB     AX,AX           ;PUSH RETURN OFFSET OF ZERO
49:             PUSH    AX              ;ON STACK
50:             MOV     AX,SEG DATA     ;SET ES-REG TO POINT TO
51:             MOV     ES,AX           ;DATA SEGMENT
52:             LEA     DI,PROMPT       ;PROMPT FOR MAXN
53:             MOV     CX,54
54:             CALL    PUTSTRNG
55:             CALL    GETDEC$         ;GET MAXN
56:             MOV     MAXN,AX
57:             MOV     CX,MAXN         ;OUTER_LOOP_COUNT = MAXN
58: OUTERLOOP:                          ;REPEAT
59:             MOV     BX,CX           ;    N = MAXN - OUTER_LOOP_COUNT
60:             NEG     BX              ;        + 1
```

```
61:                ADD     BX,1
62:                ADD     BX,MAXN
63:                MOV     N,BX
64:                MOV     CARRY,0            ;   CARRY = 0
65:                LEA     DI,FAC_END         ;   SET ES:DI TO ADDR OF FAC(59)
66:                STD                        ;   SET DF FOR DECREMENTING
67:                MOV     COUNT,SIZE$        ;   INNER_LOOP_COUNT = SIZE$
68: INNERLOOP:                               ;   REPEAT
69:                MOV     AL,BYTE PTR ES:[DI]
70:                MOV     AH,0               ;      CARRY = (ES:DI->BYTE * N
71:                MUL     N                  ;                   + CARRY) / 10
72:                ADD     AX,CARRY
73:                MOV     DX,0
74:                MOV     BX,10
75:                DIV     BX                 ;      ES:DI->BYTE =
76:                MOV     CARRY,AX           ;          (ES:DI->BYTE * N
77:                XCHG    AX,DX              ;              + CARRY) mod 10
78:                STOSB                      ;      DI = DI - 1
79:                DEC     COUNT              ;      DECR INNER_LOOP_COUNT
80:                JNZ     INNERLOOP          ;   UNTIL INNER_LOOP_COUNT = 0
81:                PUSH    CX                 ;   SAVE OUTER_LOOP_COUNT
82:                LEA     DI,FAC             ;   DISPLAY FACTORIAL VALUE
83:                MOV     CX,SIZE$
84:                CALL    PUTLGINT
85:                MOV     BH,1
86:                MOV     AX,N               ;   DISPLAY N
87:                CALL    PUTDEC$
88:                CALL    NEWLINE
89:                POP     CX                 ;   RESTORE OUTER_LOOP_COUNT
90:                LOOP    OUTERLOOP          ;   DECR OUTER_LOOP_COUNT
91:                                           ;UNTIL OUTER_LOOP_COUNT = 0
92:                RET                        ;RETURN
93: EX_8_6         ENDP
94: CODE           ENDS
95:*               END     EX_8_6
*
```

The program computes a table of factorial values of the consecutive integers 1–n. For simplification, the program makes use of the relationship $n! = n(n - 1)!$. That is, each factorial value can be computed from the previous factorial value. For example:

$$10! = 3,628,800$$

$$11! = 11(10!) = 11(3,628,800) = 39,916,800$$

The series of diagrams in Figure 8.20 demonstrates the technique that is used in Program Listing 8.6 for computing one factorial value from the previous factorial value. The figure shows the computing of 11! from 10!. Starting with the last digit of array FAC (i.e., starting with the least-significant digit of the 10! value) and working toward the beginning of the array (i.e., toward the most-significant digit of the 10! value), the following operations are performed on each digit in turn:

1. The digit is multiplied by 11, and the carry from the previous digit is added.

FIGURE 8.20
Computation of 11!
from 10!

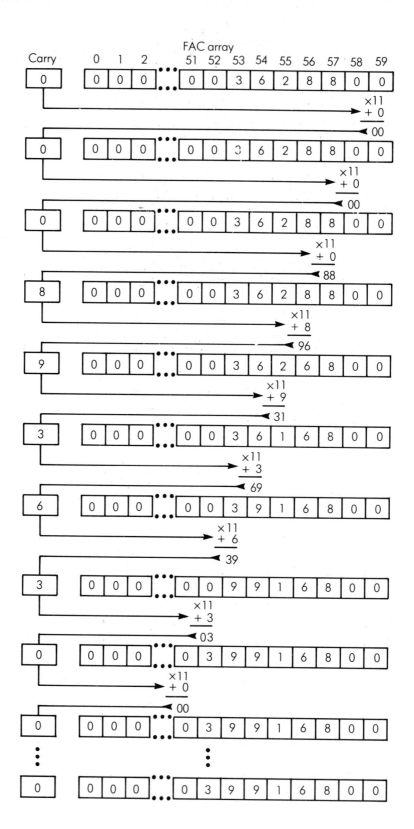

2. The result of step 1 is divided by 10.
3. The remainder of the division in step 2 (i.e., the rightmost digit of the result of step 1) is the new digit for this position of the number.
4. The quotient of the division in step 2 (i.e., the result of step 1 with its rightmost digit removed) is the carry into the next digit position.

Figure 8.20 shows these steps being performed on the rightmost nine digits of 10!, producing the rightmost nine digits of 11!. The other 51 iterations of these steps simply produce 51 leading zeros.

Program Listing 8.6 is an implementation of the technique just described. It references a subprocedure called PUTLGINT (see the EXTRN pseudo-operation in line 16) that displays a large integer that is stored in a byte array, one digit per byte, beginning with the most-significant digit. The PUTLGINT procedure expects the ES:DI register pair to specify the base address of the array that contains the integer to be displayed and the CX-register to contain the size in bytes of that array. The procedure displays blanks for leading zeros, so that the integer contained in an n-element array is displayed right-justified in an n-character field. The PUTLGINT procedure is left as Programming Exercise 8.12.

The data segment is defined in lines 26–39. The named constant defined in line 28 is the size of the FAC array (i.e., the number of decimal digits in the large integer). To modify the program to handle a different size factorial value, simply change the value of this named constant. The FAC array is defined in lines 29 and 30 as a 60-byte array with symbolic names for both the first and last elements: FAC is the symbolic name for the first element, and FAC_END is the symbolic name for the last element. Such labeling makes it easy to begin sequential processing from either end of the array. The elements of array FAC are initialized to zero, except for the last element (the last-significant digit) that is initialized to 1—initializing the factorial value to 0! = 1.

The word variable CARRY (line 31) holds the carry from one digit position to the next in the computation of a factorial value from the previous factorial value. The word variable N (line 32) holds the integer whose factorial is currently being computed. The word variable MAXN (line 33) holds the input value that specifies the largest value for which the factorial is to be computed (i.e., the maximum value for N). The byte variable COUNT (line 34) is used for the inner loop count, which computes one factorial value from the previous factorial value.

The character string defined in lines 35–37 is a prompt message that is displayed on the screen to prompt the user to enter the maximum value for N. The string is 54 characters in length and is displayed on three lines.

The program begins in the standard manner by saving the return address for DOS (lines 47–49) and initializing the segment register (lines 50–51). The ES-register is used to address the data segment, because the ES:DI register pair must address PROMPT for input to the PUTSTRNG procedure (lines 52–54), and the ES:DI register pair must address array FAC for input to the PUTLGINT procedure (lines 82–84). However, the machine language program requires less memory space if the DS-register also addresses the data segment. A memory referencing instruction such as

```
MOV   MAXN, AX
```

implicitly specifies the DS-register as the segment register, unless a 1-byte segment override prefix explicitly appears in memory immediately preceding the machine language representation of the instruction. The ASSUME pseudo-operation in line 46 tells the assembler to use the ES-register for any reference to a variable in the segment called DATA. Therefore, for instructions like

```
MOV   MAXN, AX
```

and

```
ADD   BX, MAXN
```

the assembler has to tack the ES segment register prefix onto the front of the machine language representation of the instruction, increasing the length of the machine language representation of such instructions by 1 byte. To eliminate these prefix bytes, you can make the following changes to Program Listing 8.6:

1. Add the operand

    ```
    , DS: DATA
    ```

    to the ASSUME pseudo-operation in line 46.
2. Add the instruction

    ```
    MOV   DS, AX
    ```

    following line 51.

You can use DEBUG before and after making these modifications to see the difference in the machine language representation of the memory referencing instructions in this program.

The instructions in lines 52–54 prompt the user for the maximum value for which to compute the factorial. The GETDEC$ procedure is called (line 55) to perform the input. The value received from the keyboard by GETDEC$ is returned in the AX-register. The MOV instruction in line 56 stores the input value as the value of variable MAXN.

The program contains nested REPEAT-UNTIL loops. The outer loop executes once for each factorial value computed. It is controlled by a counter that counts from MAXN (the input value) to zero. On each iteration of the outer loop, a factorial value is computed and displayed. The MOV instruction in line 57 initializes the outer loop counter to the value of variable MAXN. The CX-register maintains the outer loop counter, so that the LOOP instruction can be used for the loop test. The body of the outer loop appears in lines 58–89.

The inner loop performs the computation illustrated in Figure 8.20. It computes a new factorial value from the previous factorial value and executes once for each element of array FAC. It is controlled by a counter that counts from SIZE$ (the size of the FAC array) to zero. The instructions at the beginning of the outer loop body (lines 59–67) perform the initialization for the inner loop. The instructions in lines 59–63 compute and store the value of variable N, the integer whose factorial is about to be computed by the inner loop. The value of N is computed from MAXN and the outer loop counter. Table 8.5 shows the relationship between the value of the outer loop counter and the value of N. N is computed by the formula

$$N = MAXN - \text{outer loop counter} + 1$$

The MOV instruction in line 64 initializes the carry from the previous digit to zero (i.e., the carry into the least-significant digit position is always zero). The LEA instruction in line 65 sets the ES:DI register pair to address the last element of array FAC (i.e., the least-significant digit of the previous factorial value). The STD instruction in line 66 sets the DF bit in the flags register, so that string instructions automatically decrement the DI register. This step allows processing to proceed from the end of array FAC toward the beginning. The MOV instruction in line 67 initializes the inner loop counter to the size of array FAC, and it is maintained as the value of variable COUNT.

The inner loop body appears in lines 68–79. The MOV instruction in line 69 copies to the AL-register the digit of the FAC array that is addressed by the ES:DI register pair, and the MOV instruction in line 70 expands that digit to a 16-bit value in the AX-register. The MUL instruction in line 71 multiplies the digit by the value of the variable N, and the ADD instruction in line 72 adds the carry from the previous digit position. The instructions in lines 73–75 divide the result by 10 to separate the new digit for this position from the carry into the next digit position. The quotient of this division is the carry into the next digit position and is stored as the value of variable CARRY (line 76). The remainder of this division is the new digit for this position. The STOSB instruction in line 78 stores this new digit in the byte of array FAC addressed by the ES:DI register pair, and it decrements the DI-register, so that the ES:DI register pair addresses the previous element of array FAC (the next higher digit of the previous factorial

TABLE 8.5

Relationship between the value of the outer loop counter and the value of N

Outer Loop Counter	N = MAXN − Outer Loop Counter + 1
MAXN	N = MAXN − MAXN + 1 = 1
MAXN − 1	N = MAXN − (MAXN − 1) + 1 = 2
MAXN − 2	N = MAXN − (MAXN − 2) + 1 = 3
MAXN − 3	N = MAXN − (MAXN − 3) + 1 = 4
.	.
.	.
.	.
3	N = MAXN − 3 + 1 = MAXN − 2
2	N = MAXN − 2 + 1 = MAXN − 1
1	N = MAXN − 1 + 1 = MAXN

value). The DEC instruction in line 79 decrements the outer loop counter, and the JNZ instruction in line 80 transfers control to the top of the inner loop (line 68), if the inner loop count is nonzero. If the decrement operation leaves the inner loop counter at zero, then the inner loop is terminated.

On termination of the inner loop, the new factorial value, just computed by the inner loop, and the value of N are displayed. The PUSH instruction in line 81 saves the outer loop counter, so that the CX-register can be used for input to the PUTLGINT procedure. The instructions in lines 82–84 cause the factorial value to be displayed, and the instructions in lines 85–87 cause the value of N to be displayed. The POP instruction in line 89 restores the outer loop counter. The LOOP instruction in line 90 decrements the outer loop counter, and if the result is nonzero, transfers control to the top of the outer loop (line 58). If the decrement operation leaves the outer loop counter at zero, then the outer loop is terminated. On termination of the outer loop, control is returned to DOS (line 92). The following results are from a sample execution of the program:

```
ENTER LARGEST VALUE
FOR WHICH TO COMPUTE
FACTORIAL
19
```

```
                          1      1
                          2      2
                          6      3
                         24      4
                        120      5
                        720      6
                       5040      7
                      40320      8
                     362880      9
                    3628800     10
                   39916800     11
                  479001600     12
                 6227020800     13
                87178291200     14
              1307674368000     15
             20922789888000     16
            355687428096000     17
           6402373705728000     18
         121645100408832000     19
```

PROGRAMMING EXERCISES

8.1   Design an algorithm to accept as input a byte array that contains an ASCII number and to produce as output a byte array that contains the same number in packed BCD form (2 BCD digits per byte). The size of the array is also an input to the algorithm.

Implement your algorithm with an IBM PC Assembly language external FAR procedure. The name of your procedure should be ASCIIBCD. Your inputs should be as follows:

DS:SI—register pair addresses the beginning of the array that contains the ASCII number

ES:DI—register pair addresses the beginning of the array that is to contain the result (i.e., the corresponding BCD number)

CX-register—contains the number of digits in the ASCII number

On return from your procedure, the array addressed by the ES:DI register pair should contain the BCD number equivalent of the ASCII number in the array addressed by the DS:SI register pair. Your procedure should save and restore all registers used.

8.2 Design an algorithm to accept a character string as input and to return as output the input string with all nonletters removed.

Implement your algorithm with an IBM PC Assembly language external FAR procedure called REMOVE. Your inputs should be as follows:

DS:SI—register pair addresses the first character of the input string
CX-register—contains the length of the input string
ES:DI—register pair addresses the first character of the output string

(Note that DS:SI and ES:DI may address the same string.)

On return to the calling procedure, the output string is to contain the input string with all nonalphabetic characters removed, and the CX-register is to contain the length of the output string. Your procedure should save and restore all registers used, except for the CX-register that is used for procedure output.

8.3 Design an algorithm to accept a character string as input and to return as output the input string with each lowercase letter converted to the corresponding uppercase letter.

Implement your algorithm with an IBM PC Assembly language FAR procedure called UP_SHIFT. Your inputs should be as follows:

DS:SI—register pair addresses the first character of the input string
CX-register—contains the length of the input string
ES:DI—register pair addresses the first character of the output string

(Note that DS:SI and ES:DI may address the same string.)

On return to the calling procedure, the output string is to contain the input string with all lowercase letters converted to uppercase letters. Your procedure should save and restore all registers used.

8.4 Design an algorithm to accept a character string as input and to return as output the reverse of the input string. Implement your algorithm with an IBM PC Assembly language external FAR procedure called REVERSE. Your inputs should be as follows:

DS:SI—register pair addresses the first character of the input string
CX-register—contains the length of the input string
ES:DI—register pair addresses the first character of the output string

(Note that DS:SI and ES:DI may address the same string.)

On return to the calling procedure, the output string is to contain the reverse of the input string. Your procedure should save and restore all registers used.

8.5 Design an algorithm to accept two character strings as input, compare the two strings, and return the result of the comparison to the caller. The algorithm should allow for the fact that the two strings may be of different lengths. In the case of different string lengths, the smaller string is to be viewed as being padded on the right-hand side with blanks.

Implement your algorithm with an IBM PC Assembly language external FAR procedure called CMP_STR. Your inputs should be as follows:

ES:DI—register pair addresses the first character of the destination string
DS:SI—register pair addresses the first character of the source string
CH-register—contains the length of the destination string
CL-register—contains the length of the source string

Your procedure should return to the caller with the SF and ZF bits of the flags register set to reflect the relationship of the source string to the destination string. As well, your procedure should save and restore all registers used.

8.6 A palindrome is a word, sentence, or phrase that is spelled the same backward as forward. The following are several palindromes: Madam I'm Adam; Able was I ere I saw Elba; A man, a plan, a canal, Panama!

Design and implement in IBM PC Assembly language an algorithm that uses the subalgorithms of Programming Exercises 8.2–8.5 to detect palindromes. Your algorithm should perform the following steps.

a. Use GETSTRNG to input a character string from the keyboard.

b. Call REMOVE to remove all nonalphabetic characters from the input string.

c. Call UP_SHIFT to convert the letter string produced in (b) to an uppercase letter string.

d. Call REVERSE to obtain the reverse of the uppercase letter string.

e. Call CMP_STR to compare the uppercase letter string in (c) to the reverse string in (d).

f. Display the string

        THE STRING IS A PALINDROME

or the string

        THE STRING IS NOT A PALINDROME

depending on the outcome of (e).

8.7 Design an algorithm to find the first occurrence of a source string within a destination string. Your inputs should be the two byte arrays that contain the two character strings. The first byte in each array contains the length of the string contained in the subsequent bytes of the array. Your output should be the index within the destination string's array of the first character of the first occurrence of the source string. The algorithm should return an index of 0 if the source string does not appear in the destination string.

Implement your algorithm with an IBM PC external FAR procedure called INDEX. Your inputs should be as follows:

ES:DI—register pair addresses the first byte of the destination string's array
DS:SI—register pair addresses the first byte of the source string's array

On return to the caller, the BX-register should contain the index within the destination string's array of the first occurrence of the source string. The BX-register should contain zero, if the source string does not appear within the destination string. Your procedure should save and restore all registers used, except the BX-register that is used for procedure output.

8.8 The sequence of positive integers that begins 1, 1, 2, 3, 5, 8, 13, 21, 34, 55, 89 . . . is called the Fibonacci sequence. The first number in the sequence, F_1, is 1. The second number in the sequence, F_2, is 1. Each subsequent number in the sequence, F_i, is the sum of the two numbers previous to it in the sequence. That is,

$$F_i = F_{i-1} + F_{i-2} \quad \text{for } i > 2$$

This sequence grows at a fairly rapid pace. The fourteenth number in the sequence, 377, is too large for 8-bit unsigned integers. The twenty-fifth number in the sequence, 75,025, is too large for 16-bit unsigned integers. The fiftieth number in the sequence, 12,586,269,025, is too large for 32-bit unsigned integers.

Design an algorithm to compute arbitrarily large Fibonacci numbers. Use the technique presented in Section 8.5 for maintaining large integers. Your input should be an integer value of n, and your output should be the nth integer in the Fibonacci sequence.

Implement your algorithm with an IBM PC Assembly language program. Your input value for n should be entered via the keyboard. The nth Fibonacci number is to be displayed on the video screen. Your program should be able to produce Fibonacci numbers up to 72 digits in length.

8.9 Design an algorithm to simulate the following procedure:

a. Place 500 cups in a row, and number the cups consecutively from 1 to 500.

b. Place a marble in each cup.

c. Remove the marble from every other cup beginning with cup 2.

d. Check every third cup beginning with cup 3. If the cup contains a marble, then remove it; otherwise, place a marble in the cup.

e. Check every fourth cup beginning with cup 4. If the cup contains a marble, then remove it; otherwise, place a marble in the cup.

f. Continue this process until every five-hundredth cup is checked beginning with cup 500.

g. Display the number of each cup that contains a marble.

Implement your algorithm with an IBM PC Assembly language program. There is no input to your program. Your output should be the list of cup numbers displayed on the screen.

8.10 Complete Program Listing 8.4 by implementing the internal procedure FINDPRIM with interface specifications as described in Section 8.5. If your implementation requires the size of the sieve or the maximum index within array SIEVE, be sure to use the named constants defined in lines 24 and 25 of Program Listing 8.4.

Assemble, link, and execute the completed program in Program Listing 8.4. Change the value of SIZE$ in line 24 to 1199, and then assemble, link, and execute the program once again. Again change the value of SIZE$ in line 24 to 3099, and assemble, link, and execute the program one more time.

8.11 Design an algorithm to compute and display a table of the first 64 powers of 2. Use the technique presented in Section 8.5 to maintain large integers. Implement your algorithm with an IBM PC Assembly language program. There is no input to your program. Your output should be the table of powers of 2 displayed one entry per line, 16 lines per page. Each line should contain a value for n followed by the value of 2^n, which should be right-justified.

8.12 Design an algorithm to display a large integer that is stored in a byte array using the technique described in Section 8.5. Your input should be the base address and size of the array. Your output should be the large integer displayed, on the screen, right-justified in an n-character field, in which n is the size of the input array. Leading zeros are to be replaced by spaces in the output.

Implement your algorithm with an IBM PC Assembly language external FAR procedure called PUTLGINT. Your input should be the address of the array in the ES:DI register pair and the size of the array in the CX-register. Your output should be displayed on the video screen as described previously. The PUTDEC or PUTDEC$ procedure can be used to display the integer's individual digits.

9

INTERRUPTS
AND INPUT/OUTPUT

In the example programs presented in the preceding chapters, input/output operations were performed by a set of input/output subprocedures. To use these subprocedures, you only had to know the interface requirements for each. From the standpoint of a user, how a given subprocedure performs its function is of no concern. This chapter introduces input/output operations at a lower level, the machine level. To understand machine-level I/O operations, an understanding of interrupts is required, and this chapter discusses interrupts in general and the interrupt structure of the IBM PC in particular.

Input/output operations have already been viewed from the user level. In this chapter, I/O operations are studied from two lower levels. The read-only memory (ROM) in the IBM PC contains a set of primitive input/output procedures, known as the Basic Input/Output System (BIOS), that can be invoked from IBM PC Assembly language programs via software interrupts. The I/O subprocedures used in preceding chapters were implemented using I/O procedures of the BIOS level. The interface requirements for a number of BIOS procedures are discussed in this chapter, and several additional I/O subprocedures are presented.

The IBM PC Assembly language has two instructions that provide for direct communication between a program and I/O devices. The chapter introduces the BIOS procedures, which are implemented using these machine-level I/O instructions.

9.1 | Interrupts

An **interrupt** is an external request for service—a request for the processor to stop executing a procedure and to begin executing a procedure that has been previously designated to service interrupts of the designated type. On completion of the interrupt service procedure, the processor normally is instructed to resume execution of the interrupted procedure. An interrupt can be viewed as an unscheduled procedure invocation.

Interrupts often signal some event (e.g., the completion of an I/O operation, the end of a time interval, or an attempt to divide by zero). It is said to be **maskable** if it can be ignored by the hardware or **nonmaskable** if it must be acknowledged by the hardware. All interrupts can be ignored by software, by writing an interrupt service procedure that simply returns control to the interrupted procedure.

Three hardware mechanisms are required for the handling of interrupts:

1. The mechanism for recognizing interrupt requests
2. The mechanism for stopping the currently executing procedure and initiating a designated procedure to service the external request
3. The mechanism for restoring the state of the processor, so that the interrupted procedure can continue execution once the interrupt service procedure has performed its function

In the Intel 8088 microprocessor, each interrupt has associated with it an integer in the range 0–255 that is called the **interrupt type** and is used to identify the procedure that is to be executed to service an interrupt. The first 1024 bytes of memory (addresses 00000–003FF) are reserved for **interrupt vectors**, which are the addresses (segment and offset) of interrupt service procedures. The interrupt vector for the Type 0 interrupt is stored in the 4 bytes at memory locations 00000–00003. The interrupt vector for the Type 1 interrupt is stored in the 4 bytes at memory locations 00004–00007. In general, the interrupt vector for the Type t interrupt is stored in the 4 bytes at memory locations $4t$–$4t + 3$. Each interrupt vector requires 4 bytes (two words): The first two bytes hold the offset portion of the address of the interrupt service procedure, and the last two bytes hold the segment portion.

The Intel 8088 checks for pending interrupts at the end of most instruction executions. When an interrupt is detected, the following steps are performed by the processor:

1. The flags register is pushed onto the stack.
2. The trap flag and the interrupt flag are cleared.
3. The CS-register is pushed onto the stack.
4. The location of the interrupt vector is computed from the interrupt type.
5. The second word of the interrupt vector is loaded into the CS-register.
6. The IP-register is pushed onto the stack.
7. The first word of the interrupt vector is loaded into the IP-register.

Steps 1, 3, and 6 save the return address and the flags register for the interrupted procedure. Any general registers and/or segment registers used by the interrupt service procedure must be saved and restored by the interrupt service procedure itself. Step 2 ensures that the interrupt service procedure will not execute in the single-step mode and that the interrupt service procedure will not be interrupted. Steps 4, 5, and 7 set the CS:IP register pair to address the beginning of the interrupt service procedure, which transfers control to that procedure. The next instruction to be executed is the first instruction of the interrupt service procedure.

The interrupt service procedure returns control to the interrupted procedure by executing an **IRET instruction**, which has the following general form:

.[⟨*label*⟩   IRET   [⟨*comment*⟩]

Its execution causes the processor to pop the top-of-stack item into the IP-register, pop the new top-of-stack item into the CS-register, and then pop the new top-of-stack item into the flags register. This sequence returns control to the interrupted procedure. The next instruction to be executed, then, is the instruction that logically follows the instruction that was executed just prior to detection of the interrupt.

Interrupts can be classified as being external or internal. An *external interrupt* is generated by some event that occurs external to the microprocessor. An *internal interrupt* is generated by some event that occurs within the microprocessor itself. The Intel 8088 microprocessor provides for both external and internal interrupts.

External Interrupts

An **external interrupt** is generated by a device that is external to the microprocessor in order to request some service by the microprocessor. For example, when a key is pressed on the keyboard, an interrupt is generated to tell the microprocessor that a key has been pressed and that the **key identifier code** (called a **scan code**) is available at the input port. The BIOS keyboard interrupt service procedure in the IBM PC accepts the scan code, converts it to an extended ASCII code, and stores both codes in the next available location in its keyboard input buffer. It can queue up to 15 scan code:character code pairs in its input buffer.

Except for the Type 2 interrupt (discussed shortly), all external interrupts are maskable. To disable external interrupts, clear the IF bit in the flags register by using the CLI instruction. To enable external interrupts, set the IF bit in the flags register by using the STI instruction.

The 8088 microprocessor has two lines that can be used for signaling external interrupts: the **nonmaskable interrupt line (NMI)** and the **interrupt request line (INTR).** Interrupts arriving on the NMI line cannot be disabled by clearing the interrupt flag (IF bit of the flags register). The IBM PC uses the NMI line to report memory and I/O parity errors. Interrupts arriving on the INTR line are enabled and disabled by the IF bit in the flags register. In the IBM PC, the INTR line is driven by an interrupt controller, the Intel 8259 interrupt controller, which is programmed to provide the interrupt type when the interrupt is acknowledged by the microprocessor. The interrupt controller can report interrupts from eight different devices. In the IBM PC, these interrupts are identified with interrupt Types 8–15.

Internal Interrupts

An **internal interrupt** is generated within the microprocessor itself, and it can be generated in any of the following ways:

An internal interrupt is generated when execution of a DIV or IDIV instruction produces a quotient that is too large to fit in the AL-register (byte division) or AX-register (word division). For unsigned integer division, overflow occurs if the divisor is not greater than the high-order half of the double-length dividend. For signed integer division, overflow occurs if the n-bit divisor is not greater in magnitude than the high-order $n + 1$ bits of the dividend, in which $n = 8$ for byte division and $n = 16$ for word division. Division by zero is one case that causes a divide overflow.

An internal interrupt is generated following execution of most instructions when the microprocessor is in the single-step mode. The microprocessor is in the single-step mode when the trap flag (i.e., the TF bit in the flags register) is set. The single-step interrupt is discussed in detail in Section 9.2.

An internal interrupt is generated by execution of an **INT instruction**, which has the following general form:

[⟨*label*⟩]   INT   ⟨*int-type*⟩   [⟨*comment*⟩]

in which ⟨*int-type*⟩ is an integer in the range 0–255 that specifies the specific interrupt being generated. Execution of an INT instruction causes an interrupt of Type ⟨*int-type*⟩ to be generated. The microprocessor immediately acknowledges the interrupt by performing the seven steps described previously.

Internal interrupts have many uses in Assembly language programming. The single-step interrupt can be used to trace program execution, one instruction at a time. The DEBUG program uses this single-step feature to implement its T (trace) command. Internal interrupts can also be used to provide a set of system software procedures, such as the **Basic Input/Output System (BIOS)**, for general use in Assembly language programs. BIOS is a set of primitive input/output procedures that appear in the read-only memory (ROM) of the IBM PC. Each BIOS procedure can be invoked by execution of an INT instruction. Interrupt Types 10 hexadecimal through 1C hexadecimal are assigned to specific BIOS procedures. Another use of internal interrupts is the simulation of external interrupts. Any external interrupt can be simulated by execution of an INT instruction with the appropriate interrupt type.

Internal interrupts are nonmaskable. That is, the IF bit in the flags register has no effect on internal interrupts.

IBM PC Interrupt Assignments

Interrupts in the Intel 8088 microprocessor can be classified as predefined interrupts or 8088 user-defined interrupts. *Predefined interrupts* are those that were defined by Intel at the time the 8088 microprocessor was designed. *8088 user-defined interrupts* are those that are available for definition by the user of the 8088 microprocessor. In the case of the IBM PC, the user is the IBM Corporation. The 8088 user-defined interrupts can be further classified as system-defined interrupts or IBM PC user-defined interrupts. *System-defined interrupts* are those assigned to the various system software packages, such as BIOS and DOS. IBM PC *user-defined interrupts* are those available to Assembly language programmers. Table 9.1 summarizes the interrupt assignments in the IBM PC, IBM PC-XT, and IBM PC-AT.

Predefined Interrupts

Interrupt Types 0–7 are reserved by Intel for **predefined interrupts**, of which five of these are currently defined and all are nonmaskable.

Type 0 Interrupt—Divide Overflow   A Type 0 interrupt is generated whenever a divide operation results in a quotient that is too large to be represented in the number of bits allocated. With unsigned integer division, overflow occurs if the divisor is not greater than the high-order half of the double-length dividend. With signed two's complement integer division, overflow occurs if the n-bit divisor is not greater in magnitude than the high-order $n + 1$ bits of the dividend. DOS provides an interrupt service procedure for the Type 0 interrupt, and it displays the message: Divide Overflow and then returns control to DOS rather than to the interrupted procedure.

Type 1 Interrupt—Single Step   When the TF bit in the flags register is set, a Type 1 interrupt is generated following most instruction executions. This interrupt allows a program to be executed in the single-step mode, which means that a program can be executed one instruction at a time with program intervention between instruction executions. The program that intervenes is the Type 1 interrupt service procedure. Recall that when an interrupt occurs, the flags register is saved, and the IF and TF bits are cleared in the flags register; this sequence means that the single-step interrupt service procedure will *not* be executing in the single-step mode. However, when the IRET instruction is executed to return control to the interrupted procedure, the flags register is restored, resetting the TF bit in the flags register. Thus, the interrupted procedure executes one instruction before being interrupted again by the Type 1 interrupt. DOS masks the Type 1 interrupt by providing an interrupt service procedure that contains only the IRET instruction. The DEBUG program substitutes its own service procedure for the Type 1 interrupt to implement its trace (T) command.

TABLE 9.1
IBM PC interrupt assignments

Type	Vector	Class	PC	PC-XT	PC-AT
0	0–3	Predefined		Divide overflow	
1	4–7			Single-step	
2	8–B			Nonmaskable	
3	C–F			Breakpoint	
4	10–13			Overflow	
5	14–17			Print screen	
6	18–1B			Reserved	
7	1C–1F			Reserved	
8	20–23	System-		Time of day	
9	24–27	defined		Keyboard	
A	28–2B	hardware		Reserved	
B	2C–2F			Communications	
C	30–33			Communications	
D	34–37			Fixed Disk	ALT printer
E	38–3B			Diskette	
F	3C–3F			Printer	
10 | 1F	40–43 | 7C–7F	System- defined software	BIOS	BIOS	BIOS
20 | 3F	80–83 | FC–FF	System- defined software	DOS	DOS	DOS
40 | 5F	100–103 | 17C–17F	System- defined	Reserved	Reserved	Reserved
60 | 6F	180–183 | 1BC–1BF	User- defined software			
70 | 77	1C0–1C3 | 1DC–1DF	System defined	Not used	Not used	BIOS
78 | 7F	1E0–1E3 | 1FC–1FF	System defined	Not used	Not used	Not used
80 | F0	200–203 | 3C0–3C3	System- defined software	Basic	Basic	Basic
F1 | FF	3C4–3C7 | 3FC–3FF	User- defined software			

Type 2 Interrupt—Nonmaskable Interrupt   The Type 2 interrupt is the highest priority interrupt in the Intel 8088. In the IBM PC, it is generated whenever a memory or I/O parity error occurs. BIOS provides an interrupt service procedure for the Type 2 interrupt, and it displays the message PARITY ERROR 1 for memory parity errors and PARITY ERROR 2 for I/O parity errors.

Type 3 Interrupt—Breakpoint   A Type 3 interrupt is generated on execution of an INT 3 instruction. The INT instruction is normally a 2-byte instruction, one byte for the INT operation code and one byte for the interrupt type. The INT 3 instruction has a special operation code: It is a 1-byte instruction that can be used temporarily to replace the first byte of any instruction in the Intel 8088 instruction set for the purpose of setting a breakpoint. DOS masks the Type 3 interrupt by providing an interrupt service procedure that contains only the IRET instruction. The DEBUG program substitutes its own service procedure for the Type 3 interrupt to implement its GO (G) command. When the command G ⟨*offset*⟩ is issued to DEBUG, it replaces the instruction byte at address CS:⟨*offset*⟩ with an INT 3 instruction. Note that CS:⟨*offset*⟩ must be the address of the first byte of an instruction. When the INT 3 instruction is executed and the breakpoint interrupt occurs, the interrupt service procedure (part of DEBUG) restores the instruction byte at address CS:⟨*offset*⟩. DEBUG then produces a current register display and retains control, awaiting another command from the user.

Type 4 Interrupt—Overflow   If the OF bit in the flags register is set, then the execution of an INT 4 instruction generates a Type 4 interrupt. If the OF bit is not set, then this instruction performs no operation. There is an abbreviated form of the INT 4, which has the following general form:

[⟨*label*⟩] INTO   [⟨*comment*⟩]

DOS masks the Type 4 interrupt by providing an interrupt service procedure that contains only the IRET instruction. The Type 4 interrupt feature can be used in any IBM PC Assembly langauge program for detecting and handling arithmetic overflow in signed integer computations. To use this facility, a program must contain the following:

> An interrupt service procedure that performs the desired function for the case of arithmetic overflow
> The logic to save the Type 4 interrupt vector for DOS.
> The logic to load the Type 4 interrupt vector with the address of the user's interrupt service procedure
> An INTO instruction immediately following each instruction that can cause arithmetic overflow
> The logic to restore the Type 4 interrupt vector before returning to DOS

The notion of substituting a user-defined interrupt service procedure for the one provided by DOS or BIOS is demonstrated later in Program Listing 9.1.

Interrupt Types 5–7 are reserved by Intel for future use. Although the IBM PC makes use of the Type 5 interrupt, and BIOS provides a service procedure for the Type 5 interrupt. The procedure performs the same function as does the SHIFT-PRTSC key combination but performs it under program control. That is, execution of an INT 5 instruction causes the cursor position to be saved, the contents of the video screen to be transmitted to the printer, and the cursor position to be restored. On return from the Type 5 interrupt service procedure, memory address 00500 hex contains the status of the print screen operation: A status value of zero indicates that the print operation was successful; a status value of FF hex indicates that an error occurred during the print operation. This status byte contains the value 01 while the print operation is in progress.

System-Defined Interrupts

Interrupt Types 8–F hex are **system-defined hardware interrupts** that arrive at the Intel 8088 via the INTR line under control of the Intel 8259 interrupt controller. Most of these hardware interrupts, the events that cause them, and the procedures that service them are beyond the scope of this book. However, two of them, the timer interrupt and the keyboard interrupt, are discussed briefly. The system-defined hardware interrupts are enabled and disabled by the IF bit of the flags register.

Type 8 Interrupt—System Timer   The Intel 8253 programmable timer is a chip in the IBM PC that is programmed to generate an interrupt every 54.9254 milliseconds (approximately 18.2 times per second). BIOS provides an interrupt service procedure for the Type 8 interrupt that keeps a 32-bit count of Type 8 interrupts that DOS uses to keep track of the time of day.

Type 9 Interrupt—Keyboard Interrupt   Each time a key is pressed at the keyboard, a Type 9 interrupt is generated. BIOS provides an interrupt service procedure for the Type 9 interrupt that accepts the scan code from the port, converts it to an extended ASCII code, and stores both codes in the next available location in its keyboard input buffer. The service procedure can queue up to 15 scan code:character code pairs.

Interrupt Types 10 hex–1F hex are system-defined software interrupts assigned to BIOS. Many are BIOS entry points. These interrupts are generated by execution of an INT instruction with the appropriate interrupt type. The service procedures for these interrupts provide primitive device-level I/O operations. The BIOS services are discussed in detail in Section 9.3.

Interrupt Types 20 hex–3F hex are system-defined software interrupts assigned to DOS. Many of these are used to provide additional I/O services for user programs. The DOS services are not discussed in detail in this book. For a summary of DOS services, see the *DOS Reference Manual*.

Interrupt Types 40 hex–5F hex are reserved for system use. Interrupt Type 40 hex and interrupt Type 41 hex are used in the IBM PC-XT and the IBM PC-AT versions of BIOS for support of fixed-disk operations.

Interrupt Types 70 hex–7F hex are also reserved for system use. None of these are currently used in the IBM PC or IBM PC-XT. Interrupt Types 70 hex–77 hex are used by the IBM PC-AT version of BIOS.

Interrupt Types 80 hex–F0 hex are system-defined interrupts assigned to the BASIC interpreter.

IBM PC User-Defined Interrupts

Interrupt Types 60 hex–67 hex are reserved for use in **user-defined software**. Interrupt Types 68 hex–6F hex and interrupt Types F1 hex–FF hex are classified in the various IBM PC technical reference manuals as "not used." These interrupts could, therefore, be used in user-defined software. However, they could be assigned for other purposes in the future. Interrupt Types 60 hex–67 hex are the only interrupts actually reserved for user-defined software interrupts.

Example Program—Divide Overflow

Program Listing 9.1 demonstrates the notion of substituting a user-defined interrupt service procedure for one provided by DOS. A Type 0 interrupt is generated whenever execution of a DIV or an IDIV instruction produces a quotient that is too large to fit in the AL-register (byte division) or the AX-register (word division). DOS provides an interrupt service procedure for the Type 0 interrupt. The service procedure displays the message Divide Overflow and then returns control to DOS instead of to the interrupted procedure. Suppose a specific application requires that control be returned to the interrupted procedure following the handling of a divide overflow.

Program Listing 9.1 demonstrates the operation of signed integer division. It prompts the user for a dividend and a divisor, accepts the dividend and divisor from the keyboard, and performs the division. The program repeats this process until the division operation produces no overflow. On execution of a valid division operation, the program displays the dividend, divisor, quotient, and remainder, and then it returns control to the operating system.

The user-defined interrupt service procedure that handles the divide overflow interrupt appears in lines 39–53 of Program Listing 9.1. The symbolic name for the service procedure is ZERO_DIV (line 42). The service procedure begins by saving the registers that it uses (lines 43–44). It then displays a message to the user (lines 45–48). The message displayed,

```
DIVIDE OVERFLOW
TRY ANOTHER SET OF INPUTS
```

is defined in the program's data segment (line 32). The service procedure sets the BX-register to 1 (line 49). The BX-register serves as an overflow flag for the program. The service procedure then restores the registers it used (lines 50–51) and returns to the interrupted procedure (line 52).

The program must set the Type 0 interrupt vector to the address of this local interrupt service procedure. The program must also save and restore the

```
 1: ;
 2: ;
 3: ;                     PROGRAM LISTING 9.1
 4: ;
 5: ;PROGRAM TO DEMONSTRATE INTEGER DIVISION
 6: ;
 7:                                            ;PROCEDURES TO
 8:             EXTRN   GETDEC:FAR             ;GET DECIMAL INTEGER
 9:             EXTRN   NEWLINE:FAR            ;DISPLAY NEWLINE CHARACTER
10:             EXTRN   PUTSTRNG:FAR           ;DISPLAY CHARACTER STRING
11:             EXTRN   PUTDEC:FAR             ;DISPLAY DECIMAL INTEGER
12: ;
13: ; S T A C K   S E G M E N T   D E F I N I T I O N
14: ;
15: STACK       SEGMENT STACK
16:             DB      256 DUP(?)
17: STACK       ENDS
18: ;
19: ; D A T A   S E G M E N T   D E F I N I T I O N
20: ;
21: DATA        SEGMENT
22: DVDEND      DW      ?
23: DVISOR      DW      ?
24: QUOTIENT    DW      ?
25: REMAINDR    DW      ?
26: PROMPT1     DB      'ENTER DIVIDEND  '
27: PROMPT2     DB      'ENTER DIVISOR   '
28: OUTPUT1     DB      'DIVIDEND   =  '
29: OUTPUT2     DB      'DIVISOR    =  '
30: OUTPUT3     DB      'QUOTIENT   =  '
31: OUTPUT4     DB      'REMAINDER  =  '
32: DIVO_MSG    DB      'DIVIDE OVERFLOW',0DH,0AH,'TRY ANOTHER SET OF INPUTS'
33: DATA        ENDS
34: ;
35: ; C O D E   S E G M E N T   D E F I N I T I O N
36: ;
37: CODE        SEGMENT
38:             ASSUME  CS:CODE,DS:DATA,SS:STACK,ES:DATA
39: ;_____
40: ;ZERO DIVIDE INTERRUPT SERVICE ROUTINE
41: ;
42: ZERO_DIV:
43:             PUSH    CX                    ;SAVE REGISTERS
44:             PUSH    DI
45:             LEA     DI,DIVO_MSG           ;DISPLAY ERROR MESSAGE
46:             MOV     CX,42
47:             CALL    PUTSTRNG
48:             CALL    NEWLINE
49:             MOV     BX,1                  ;OVRFLO = TRUE
50:             POP     DI                    ;RESTORE REGISTERS
51:             POP     CX
52:             IRET                          ;RETURN FROM INTERRUPT
53: ;_____
54: EX_9_1      PROC    FAR
55:             PUSH    DS                    ;PUSH RETURN SEG ADDR ON STACK
56:             SUB     AX,AX                 ;PUSH RETURN OFFSET OF ZERO
57:             PUSH    AX                    ;ON STACK
58:             MOV     DI,0                  ;DI = 0 <OFFSET WITHIN INTERRUPT
59:                                           ;         VECTOR TABLE OF
60:                                           ;         INT 0 INTERRUPT VECTOR>
61:             MOV     ES,DI                 ;ES = 0 <ADDRESS OF INTERRUPT
```

```
 62:                                          ;            VECTOR TABLE>
 63:              PUSH     ES:[DI]            ;PUSH INT 0 VECTOR ON STACK
 64:*             PUSH     ES:[DI+2]          ;      (DIVIDE OVERFLOW)
*
 65: ;
 66:              MOV      AX,OFFSET ZERO_DIV ;SET INT 0 VECTOR TO POINT TO
 67:              MOV      ES:[DI],AX         ;LOCAL INTERRUPT SERVICE ROUTINE
 68:              MOV      AX,SEG ZERO_DIV
 69:              MOV      ES:[DI+2],AX
 70:              MOV      AX,SEG DATA        ;SET DS AND ES REGISTERS
 71:              MOV      DS,AX              ;TO POINT TO DATA SEGMENT
 72:              MOV      ES,AX
 73: REPEAT:                                 ;REPEAT
 74:              MOV      BX,0              ;    OVRFLO = FALSE
 75:              CALL     NEWLINE
 76:              LEA      DI,PROMPT1        ;    PROMPT FOR DIVIDEND
 77:              MOV      CX,16
 78:              CALL     PUTSTRNG
 79:              CALL     GETDEC            ;    GET DIVIDEND
 80:              MOV      DVDEND,AX
 81:              CALL     NEWLINE
 82:              LEA      DI,PROMPT2        ;    PROMPT FOR DIVISOR
 83:              MOV      CX,16
 84:              CALL     PUTSTRNG
 85:              CALL     GETDEC            ;    GET DIVISOR
 86:              MOV      DVISOR,AX
 87:              CALL     NEWLINE
 88:              MOV      AX,DVDEND
 89:              CWD                        ;    EXPAND DIVIDEND TO DBL LENGTH
 90:              IDIV     DVISOR            ;    DIVIDE DIVIDEND BY DIVISOR
 91:                                         ;    GIVING QUOTIENT AND REMAINDER
 92:              CMP      BX,0
 93:              JNE      REPEAT            ;UNTIL NOT OVERFLOW
 94:              MOV      QUOTIENT,AX        ;SAVE QUOTIENT
 95:              MOV      REMAINDR,DX        ;SAVE REMAINDER
 96:              LEA      DI,OUTPUT1         ;OUTPUT DIVIDEND
 97:              MOV      CX,14
 98:              CALL     PUTSTRNG
 99:              MOV      AX,DVDEND
100:              CALL     PUTDEC
101:              CALL     NEWLINE
102:              LEA      DI,OUTPUT2         ;OUTPUT DIVISOR
103:              CALL     PUTSTRNG
104:              MOV      AX,DVISOR
105:              CALL     PUTDEC
106:              CALL     NEWLINE
107:              LEA      DI,OUTPUT3         ;OUTPUT QUOTIENT
108:              CALL     PUTSTRNG
109:              MOV      AX,QUOTIENT
110:              CALL     PUTDEC
111:              CALL     NEWLINE
112:              LEA      DI,OUTPUT4         ;OUTPUT REMAINDER
113:              CALL     PUTSTRNG
114:              MOV      AX,REMAINDR
115:              CALL     PUTDEC
116:              CALL     NEWLINE
117: RETURN:      MOV      DI,0              ;DI = 0 <OFFSET WITHIN INTERRUPT
118:                                         ;          VECTOR TABLE OF
119:                                         ;          INT 0 INTERRUPT VECTOR>
120:              MOV      ES,DI             ;ES = 0 <ADDRESS OF INTERRUPT
121:                                         ;          VECTOR TABLE>
```

```
122:                    POP     ES:[DI+2]            ;POP INT 0 VECTOR FROM STACK
123:                    POP     ES:[DI]              ;    (DIVIDE OVERFLOW)
124:                    RET                          ;RETURN
125: EX_9_1             ENDP
126: CODE               ENDS
127:*                   END     EX_9_1
```
*

Type 0 interrupt vector that exists on entry to the program. In this manner, programs that are executed after this one will have the DOS interrupt service procedure for a divide overflow. The Type 0 interrupt vector appears in memory locations 00000–00003. Locations 00000 and 00001 contain the offset portion of the address of the Type 0 interrupt service procedure, and locations 00002 and 00003 contain the segment portion. The MOV instructions in lines 58 and 61 set the ES:DI register pair to the address of this interrupt vector. Both registers are set to zero, which means that the ES:DI register pair addresses memory location 00000, the location at which the Type 0 interrupt vector begins. The PUSH instructions in lines 63 and 64 save the 4 bytes of the DOS Type 0 interrupt vector on the stack. The two MOV instructions in lines 66 and 67 set the first word (first 2 bytes) of the Type 0 interrupt vector to the offset portion of the memory address associated with symbolic name ZERO_DIV. The two MOV instructions in lines 68 and 69 set the second word (last 2 bytes) of the Type 0 interrupt vector to the segment portion of the memory address associated with symbolic name ZERO_DIV. The Type 0 interrupt vector now addresses the interrupt service procedure appearing in lines 42–52.

The REPEAT-UNTIL loop in lines 73–93 accepts the inputs (dividend and divisor) and performs the division. At the beginning of the loop (line 74), the overflow flag (BX-register) is cleared to zero. If the IDIV instruction in line 90 results in a divide overflow, then the Type 0 interrupt is generated, and the local interrupt service procedure is executed. The interrupt service procedure displays the diagnostic message and sets the overflow flag (BX-register) to 1. The CMP instruction in line 92 is the loop test that tests the value of the overflow flag (BX-register). If the flag is set, then the jump (line 93) is taken to the top of the loop, which gives the user an opportunity to enter different values for the dividend and divisor. If the flag is not set, then the jump is not taken, and the results are displayed (lines 94–116).

Before returning to DOS, the program must restore the DOS Type 0 interrupt vector. The MOV instructions in lines 117 and 120 set the ES:DI register pair to again address the Type 0 interrupt vector. The POP instructions in lines 122 and 123 restore the 4 bytes of the DOS Type 0 interrupt vector.

The following results are from a sample execution of this program:

```
ex_9_1

ENTER DIVIDEND -32768

ENTER DIVISOR  -1

DIVIDE OVERFLOW
TRY ANOTHER SET OF INPUTS
```

```
ENTER DIVIDEND -32768

ENTER DIVISOR  -17

DIVIDEND   =  -32768
DIVISOR    =  -17
QUOTIENT   =  1927
REMAINDER  =  -9

ex_9_1

ENTER DIVIDEND 127

ENTER DIVISOR  0

DIVIDE OVERFLOW
TRY ANOTHER SET OF INPUTS

ENTER DIVIDEND 127

ENTER DIVISOR -17

DIVIDEND   = 127
DIVISOR    = -17
QUOTIENT   = -7
REMAINDER  = 8
```

In general, to set the ES:DI register pair to the address of the Type t interrupt vector, set the ES-register to zero (the origin of the interrupt vector table) and the DI-register to $4t$ (the offset within the interrupt vector table of the Type t interrupt vector). Note that the DS-register could be used for the segment register, and either the SI-register or the BX-register could be used for the index register.

9.2   Single-Step Mode

The Intel 8088 microprocessor is in the single-step mode when the TF bit of the flags register is set to 1. When in the single-step mode, the microprocessor generates a Type 1 interrupt following execution of most instructions. A Type 1 interrupt is *not* generated following execution of an instruction that modifies a segment register (e.g., MOV ES,AX), a prefix instruction (e.g., REP), or a WAIT instruction.

There are no instructions in the IBM PC Assembly language that directly manipulate the TF bit of the flags register. To set the TF bit, the following sequence of instructions can be used:

```
PUSHF
POP   AX
OR    AX,0100H
PUSH  AX
POPF
NOP
```

The first single-step interrupt thus occurs after execution of the instruction that immediately follows the NOP instruction. When the trap flag is set with a POPF instruction, two instructions are executed before the first single-step interrupt is generated.

Recall that when an interrupt is detected by the microprocessor, the IF and TF bits of the flags register are cleared before transferring control to the interrupt service procedure; thus, the procedure that services the single-step interrupt will *not* be executing in the single-step mode. The interrupt service procedure should return to the interrupted procedure by executing an IRET instruction, which causes the flags register to be restored to its value at the point at which the interrupt occurred. This sequence resets the TF bit in the flags register. When the trap flag is set with an IRET instruction, one instruction is executed before the next single-step interrupt is generated.

To clear the TF bit of the flags register, the following sequence of instructions can be used:

```
PUSHF
POP     AX
AND     AX, 0FEFFH
PUSH    AX
POPF
```

The last single-step interrupt occurs immediately after execution of the POPF instruction. When the trap flag is cleared with a POPF instruction, one more single-step interrupt occurs.

The DEBUG utility program uses the single-step mode to implement its trace (T) command. The interrupt service procedure for the single-step interrupt is an entry point within the DEBUG program. The single-step interrupt can also be used to perform some function after each instruction of a program. Program Listing 9.2 demonstrates such an application of the single-step mode.

Example Program—Demonstrates Shift and Rotate Instructions

Program Listing 6.1 was designed to demonstrate shift and rotate instructions in the IBM PC Assembly language. It loads a value into the AX-register and then performs a series of shifts and rotates. Following each shift and rotate instruction, a call is made to the PUTBIN procedure to display the resulting AX-register in binary form.

The program of Program Listing 9.2 performs the same function as that of Program Listing 6.1, however, Program Listing 9.2 uses a single-step interrupt service procedure to display the result of each shift operation. In addition to displaying the AX-register value, the single-step interrupt service procedure also displays the value of the carry flag. This discussion concentrates on the changes made to Program Listing 6.1 that produce Program Listing 9.2.

The calls to the PUTBIN procedure and the NEWLINE procedure in Program Listing 6.1 have all been removed from Program Listing 9.2. The

```
 1: ;
 2: ;
 3: ;                     PROGRAM LISTING 9.2
 4: ;
 5: ;PROGRAM TO DEMONSTRATE SHIFT AND ROTATE INSTRUCTIONS
 6: ;
 7:                                       ;PROCEDURES TO
 8:             EXTRN    PUTBIN:FAR       ;DISPLAYT BINARY INTEGER
 9:             EXTRN    PUTDEC:FAR       ;DISPLAY DECIMAL INTEGER
10:             EXTRN    NEWLINE:FAR      ;DISPLAY NEWLINE CHARACTER
11: ;
12: ; S T A C K   S E G M E N T   D E F I N I T I O N
13: ;
14: STACK       SEGMENT STACK
15:             DB       256 DUP(?)
16: STACK       ENDS
17: ;
18: ; C O D E   S E G M E N T   D E F I N I T I O N
19: ;
20: CODE        SEGMENT
21: EX_9_2      PROC     FAR
22:             ASSUME   CS:CODE,SS:STACK
23:             PUSH     DS               ;PUSH RETURN SEG ADDR ON STACK
24:             MOV      AX,0             ;PUSH RETURN OFFSET OF ZERO
25:             PUSH     AX               ;ON STACK
26:             MOV      DI,4             ;DI = 4 <OFFSET WITHIN INTERRUPT
27:                                       ;        VECTOR TABLE OF INT 1
28:                                       ;        INTERRUPT VECTOR>
29:             MOV      AX,0             ;EI = 0 <ADDRESS OF INTERRUPT
30:             MOV      ES,AX            ;        VECTOR TABLE>
31:             PUSH     ES:[DI]          ;PUSH INT 1 VECTOR ON STACK
32:             PUSH     ES:[DI+2]        ;    (SINGLE STEP)
33:             MOV      AX,OFFSET S_STEP ;SET INT 1 VECTOR TO POINT TO
34:             MOV      ES:[DI],AX       ;LOCAL INTERRUPT SERVICE ROUTINE
35:             MOV      AX,SEG S_STEP
36:             MOV      ES:[DI+2],AX
37:             PUSHF                     ;SET TF BIT IN FLAGS REGISTER
38:             POP      AX
39:             OR       AX,0100H
40:             PUSH     AX
41:             POPF
42:             NOP
43:             MOV      AX,0AAABH        ;LOAD AX WITH
44:                                       ;
45:                                       ;1010101010101011
46:                                       ;
47:             ROL      AX,1             ;LEFT ROTATE AX 1 GIVING
48:                                       ;
49:                                       ;0101010101010111
50:                                       ;
51:             MOV      CL,3             ;MOVE SHIFT COUNT TO CL
52:             ROR      AX,CL            ;RIGHT ROTATE AX 3 GIVING
53:                                       ;
54:                                       ;1110101010101010
55:                                       ;
56:             SAR      AX,1             ;ARITH SHIFT RIGHT 1 GIVING
57:                                       ;
58:                                       ;1111010101010101
59:                                       ;
60:             SAL      AX,CL            ;ARITH SHIFT LEFT 3 GIVING
61:                                       ;
```

```
62:                                              ;1010101010101000
63:*                                             ;
 *

64: ;
65:                MOV      CL,2                  ;MOVE SHIFT COUNT TO CL
66:                SHR      AX,CL                 ;LOG. SHIFT RIGHT 2 GIVING
67:                                               ;
68:                                               ;0010101010101010
69:                                               ;
70:                MOV      CL,3                  ;MOVE SHIFT COUNT TO CL
71:                SHL      AX,CL                 ;LOG.SHIFT LEFT 3 GIVING
72:                                               ;
73:                                               ;0101010101010000
74:                                               ;
75:                                               ;AND CARRY FLAG = 1
76:                RCL      AX,1                  ;LEFT ROTATE AX 1 THROUGH
77:                                               ;CARRY GIVING
78:                                               ;
79:                                               ;1010101010100001
80:                                               ;
81:                                               ;AND CARRY FLAG = O
82:                MOV      CL,2
83:                RCR      AX,CL                 ;RIGHT ROTATE AX 2 THROUGH
84:                                               ;CARRY GIVING
85:                                               ;
86:                                               ;1010101010101000
87:                                               ;
88:                MOV      CL,4                  ;MOVE SHIFT COUNT TO CL
89:                SAR      AL,CL                 ;ARITH RIGHT SHIFT AL 4 GIVING
90:                                               ;
91:                                               ;1010101011111010
92:                                               ;
93:                ROL      AL,CL                 ;LEFT ROTATE AL 4 GIVING
94:                                               ;
95:                                               ;1010101010101111
96:                                               ;
97:                PUSHF                          ;CLEAR TF BIT IN FLAGS REGISTER
98:                POP      AX
99:                AND      AX,OFEFFH
100:               PUSH     AX
101:               POPF
102:               POP      ES:[DI+2]             ;RESTORE INT 1 VECTOR FROM STACK
103:               POP      ES:[DI]               ;         (SINGLE STEP)
104:               RET                            ;RETURN
105: ;_____
106: ;
107: ; S I N G L E - S T E P   I N T E R R U P T   S E R V I C E
108: ;
109: S_STEP:                                      ;TYPE 1 INTERRUPT SERVICE ROUTINE
110:               PUSH     AX                    ;SAVE REGISTERS
111:               PUSH     BX
112:               MOV      BL,1                  ;PUTBIN CODE = 1
113:               CALL     PUTBIN                ;DISPLAY AX REGISTER IN BINARY
114:               MOV      BH,1                  ;PUTDEC CODE = RIGHT JUSTIFY
115:               RCL      AX,1                  ;DISPLAY CARRY FLAG
116:               AND      AX,1
117:               CALL     PUTDEC
118:               CALL     NEWLINE               ;DISPLAY NEWLINE CHARACTER
119:               POP      BX                    ;RESTORE REGISTERS
120:               POP      AX
```

```
121:                IRET                              ;RETURN TO INTERRUPTED PROC
122:                                                  ;END TYPE 1 INTERRUPT SERVICE
123: ;_____
124: ;
125: EX_9_2         ENDP
126: CODE           ENDS
127:*               END      EX_9_2
```
*

function performed by these calls is now achieved with a single-step interrupt service procedure (lines 105–123). This procedure begins by saving the two registers that it uses (lines 110 and 111), which is vital, since the interrupted procedure has no method of saving them. The PUTBIN procedure is invoked (lines 112 and 113) to display the AX-register value in binary form. The RCL instruction in line 115 moves the CF bit of the flags register to bit 0 of the AX-register. The AND instruction in line 116 clears bits 1–15 of the AX-register. The PUTDEC procedure is invoked (lines 114 and 117) to display the CF bit (now in bit 0 of the AX-register) right-justified in a 6-character field. The call to the NEWLINE procedure (line 118) moves the cursor to the beginning of the next line of the display. The service procedure ends by restoring the registers it used (lines 119 and 120) and performing an interrupt return (line 121). The IRET instruction causes the flags register to be restored and control to be returned to the interrupted procedure. Restoring the flags register resets the trap flag. The interrupted procedure will have its next instruction executed, and then another single-step interrupt will occur.

The Type 1 interrupt vector is stored in locations 00004–00007 of memory. The offset portion of the address of the interrupt service procedure is stored in locations 00004 and 00005, and the segment portion of the address is stored in locations 00006 and 00007. The instructions in lines 26, 29, and 30 set the ES:DI register pair to address memory location 00004, the start of the single-step interrupt vector. The instructions in lines 31 and 32 save the current Type 1 interrupt vector on the stack. The instructions in lines 33 and 34 set the first word of the Type 1 interrupt vector (locations 00004 and 00005) to the offset portion of the address of the local interrupt service procedure. And the instructions in lines 35 and 36 set the second word of the Type 1 interrupt vector (locations 00006 and 00007) to the segment portion of the address of the local interrupt service procedure. At this point, the Type 1 interrupt vector addresses the interrupt service procedure defined in lines 105–123.

The instructions in lines 37–42 set the trap flag (bit 8) of the flags register. The PUSHF instruction in line 37 pushes a copy of the flags register onto the stack. The POP instruction in line 38 pops this copy of the flags into the AX-register. The OR instruction in line 39 sets bit 8 in this copy of the flags. Bit 8 corresponds to the TF bit in the flags register. The PUSH instruction in line 40 pushes this modified copy of the flags onto the stack, and the POPF instruction in line 41 pops it into the flags register. The TF bit in the flags register is now set. The other bits of the flags register are the same as they were before execution of the instruction in line 37. The NOP instruction in line 42 ensures that the first single-step interrupt will occur following the MOV instruction in line 43.

Since the interrupt service procedure returns to the interrupted procedure via an IRET instruction, a single-step interrupt will occur after each subsequent instruction in the main procedure, until the trap flag is cleared by the procedure. The instructions in lines 97–101 clear the TF bit of the flags register. The instructions in lines 97 and 98 copy the flags register value into the AX-register. The AND instruction in line 99 clears the TF bit (bit 8) in this copy of the flags register value. It preserves all of the other bits in this value. The instructions in lines 100 and 101 copy this modified value in the AX-register to the flags register. The TF bit in the flags register is now zero. The other bits of the flags register are the same as they were before execution of the instruction in line 97. The last single-step interrupt occurs after execution of the POPF instruction in line 101.

The two POP instructions in lines 102 and 103 restore the Type 1 interrupt vector to the value that it was prior to program execution. That is, the Type 1 interrupt vector is restored by the value that was placed on the stack by the two PUSH instructions in lines 31 and 32. Note that when the instruction in line 102 is reached, the ES:DI register pair still contains the address of the Type 1 interrupt vector. This value was set by the MOV instructions in lines 26–30, and there are no instructions in between that modify either the ES or the DI registers.

The output of this program appears as follows:

```
1010101010101011   0
0101010101010111   1
0101010101010111   1
1110101010101010   1
1111010101010101   0
1010101010101000   1
1010101010101000   1
0010101010101010   0
0010101010101010   0
0101010101010000   1
1010101010100001   0
1010101010100001   0
1010101010101000   0
1010101010101000   0
1010101011111010   1
1010101010101111   1
1010101010101111   1
1111001110000111   1
1111001010000111   0
1111001010000111   0
1111001010000111   1
```

The first line of output shows the value in the AX-register and the value of the CF bit of the flags register just after execution of the MOV instruction in line 43. The AX-register value is AAAB hex, and the CF bit of the flags register is zero. The sixteenth line of output shows the value in the AX-register and the value of the CF bit of the flags register just after execution of the ROL instruction in line 93. The AX-register value is AAAF hex, and the CF bit of the flags register is 1. The seventeenth line of output shows these values just after execution of the PUSHF instruction in line 97. Its output is identical to the preceding output line. A PUSHF instruction modifies neither the AX-register nor the flags register. The eighteenth line of output shows the value in the AX-register and the value of the CF bit of the flags register just after execution of the POP instruction in line 98. The AX-register value, F387 hex, is a copy of the flags register value. Note that bit 8 (corresponding to the TF bit) is set to 1. The CF bit of the flags register is still 1, as the POP instruction has no effect on the flags register. The nineteenth line of output shows the AX-register value, F287 hex, and the value of the carry flag, 0, just after execution of the AND instruction in line 99. Note that bit 8 of the AX-register has been cleared to zero and that the CF bit of the flags register has been cleared to zero by execution of the AND instruction. The twentieth line of output reflects the values of the AX-register and the carry flag just after execution of the PUSH instruction in line 100. Its output is identical to the preceding output line. A PUSH instruction modifies neither the AX-register nor the flags register. The last line of output reflects the values of the AX-register and the carry flag just after execution of the POPF instruction in line 101. The AX-register value was not changed by execution of this instruction, but the CF bit of the flags register was restored to its value at the time of execution of the PUSHF instruction in line 97. The TF bit in the flags register is now zero. Therefore, no further single-step interrupts occur, and no further output is produced by the program.

9.3   Input/Output

There are two levels at which I/O operations are considered here. The first level is that provided by the BIOS subprocedures. At this level, BIOS controls the actual communication between the microprocessor and the I/O devices. The BIOS routines are accessible from IBM PC Assembly language programs via software interrupts. Two example procedures demonstrate the use of BIOS procedures to implement more general I/O operations. The second level, the most primitive level, is that provided by the machine language. At this level, the Assembly language program itself controls the communication between the microprocessor and the I/O devices. A simple example of direct device communication is given.

BIOS Service Procedures

BIOS provides a set of subprocedures that removes the burden of direct device communication from the Assembly language programmer. These procedures are accessible from Assembly language programs via software interrupt Types 10 hex–1C hex. Table 9.2 summarizes these services, and several are described in the following sections.

TABLE 9.2
BIOS software
interrupt services

Interrupt Type (Hex)	Service
10	Video I/O
11	Equipment check
12	Memory size
13	Diskette I/O
14	Communications I/O
15	Cassette I/O
16	Keyboard I/O
17	Printer I/O
18	ROM BASIC
19	Power-on reset
1A	Time of day
1B	Control break
1C	Timer (user supplied)

Video I/O (Interrupt 10H)

Video I/O services are provided through software interrupt Type 10 hex. The BIOS subprocedure that services interrupt Type 10 hex uses the value in the AH-register as a function code. It is via the AH-register that the caller requests the specific video operation to be performed. Depending on the function code in the AH-register, other registers are used for input to and output from the BIOS service procedure. Table 9.3 summarizes the function codes recognized by the BIOS interrupt Type 10 hex service procedure and the other registers used for procedure input and output.

TABLE 9.3 BIOS interrupt Type 10H subfunctions

AH	Function	Procedure Inputs	Procedure Outputs
0	Set video mode	AL = video mode 0–40 × 25 B/W 1–40 × 25 color text 2–80 × 25 B/W 3–80 × 25 color text 4–320 × 200 color graphics 5–320 × 200 B/W graphics 6–640 × 200 B/W graphics	None
1	Set cursor type	CH = start line numbers 0–12 CL = end line numbers 0–12	None
2	Set cursor position	BH = page number (0–3) DH = row of cursor 0–24 DL = column of cursor 0–79	None

TABLE 9.3   Continued

AH	Function	Procedure Inputs	Procedure Outputs
3	Read cursor type and position	BH = page number (0–3)	CH = start line number CL = end line number DH = row of cursor DL = column of cursor
4	Read light pen position	None	AH = status code 0—disabled 1—enabled BX = pixel column CH = raster line DH = row of light pen DL = column of light pen
5	Select active display page	AL = new page number 0–3	None
6	Scroll up of active page	AL = number of lines BH = display attribute for blank lines CH = upper-left row of scroll window CL = upper-left column of scroll window DH = lower-right row of scroll window DL = lower right column of scroll window	None
7	Scroll down of active page	AL = number of lines BH = display attribute for blank lines CH = upper-left row of scroll window CL = upper-left column of scroll window DH = lower-right row of scroll window DL = lower-right column of scroll window	None
8	Read attribute/character at current cursor position	BH = page number (0–3)	AL = ASCII character AH = attribute of character in AL
9	Write attribute/character beginning at current cursor position	BH = page number (0–3) BL = attribute of character AL = character to write CX = count of times to write character	None

TABLE 9.3   Continued

AH	Function	Procedure Inputs	Procedure Outputs
10	Write character beginning at current cursor position	BH = page number (0–3) AL = character to write CX = count of times to write character	None
11	Set color for background/border	BH = 0 BL = color code	None
	Set graphics color palette	BH = 1 BL = 0 green/red/yellow = 1 cyan/magenta/white	None
12	Plot graphics pixel	AL = color DX = row CX = column	None
13	Read graphics pixel	DX = row CX = column	AL = color
14	Write character and advance cursor	AL = character to write BH = page number (0–3) BL = character color	None
15	Read current video state	None	AL = video mode (see AH = 0) AH = screen width BH = active page number

Programming Example—PUTBIN

Program Listing 9.3 illustrates the use of BIOS interrupt Type 10 hex with the PUTBIN procedure from the author's I/O subprocedure library. In Chapters 5 and 6, implementations of algorithms to display 8- or 16-bit integers in binary were presented (see Program Listings 5.1 and 5.3 and Program Listing 6.3). Program Listing 9.3 implements the same algorithm as does the procedure in Program Listing 6.3, with the main difference between the two implementations being that Program Listing 6.3 uses the PUTDEC procedure to display the individual bits, and Program Listing 9.3 uses BIOS interrupt Type 10 hex to display the individual bits. This discussion concentrates on the I/O procedure differences in Program Listing 9.3.

The STI instruction in line 26 ensures that external interrupts are enabled. This step is simply a precautionary measure performed by all of the author's I/O subprocedures in the library. External interrupts are always enabled when a user program is placed into execution under DOS control. Unless the user program

```
 1: ;
 2: ;
 3: ;                       PROGRAM LISTING 9.3
 4: ;
 5: CODE          SEGMENT PARA 'IO_CODE'
 6:               ASSUME  CS:CODE
 7:               PUBLIC  PUTBIN
 8: ;
 9: ; PROCEDURE TO DISPLAY AN 8- OR 16-BIT VALUE IN BINARY FORM
10: ;
11: ; INPUT:   AL-REG  8-BIT  VALUE TO BE DISPLAYED
12: ;          BL=0    CODE FOR  8-BIT DISPLAY
13: ;                OR
14: ;          AX-REG  16-BIT VALUE TO BE DISPLAYED
15: ;          BL<>0   CODE FOR 16-BIT DISPLAY
16: ;
17: ; OUTPUT: INPUT VALUE DISPLAYED IN BINARY FORM ON THE
18: ;         SCREEN BEGINNING AT CURRENT CURSOR POSITION
19: ;
20: PUTBIN        PROC    FAR                    ;PROCEDURE PUTBIN (NUMBER,CODE)
21:               PUSH    AX                       ;SAVE REGISTERS
22:               PUSH    DX
23:               PUSH    BX
24:               PUSH    CX
25:               PUSHF                            ;SAVE FLAGS
26:               STI                              ;ENABLE INTERRUPTS
27:               CMP     BL,0                     ;IF   CODE = BYTE (BL=0)
28:               JNZ     ELSE
29:               MOV     AH,AL                  ;THEN LEFT JUSTIFY 8-BIT NUMBER
30:                                              ;     IN 16-BIT AX-REGISTER
31:               MOV     CX,8                   ;     BIT_COUNT = 8
32:               JMP     ENDIF
33: ELSE:                                        ;ELSE
34:               MOV     CX,16                  ;     BIT_COUNT = 16
35: ENDIF:                                       ;ENDIF
36:               MOV     DX,AX                  ;<NUMBER NOW IN DX-REG>
37:               MOV     AH,15                  ;READ ACTIVE DISPLAY PAGE
38:               INT     10H                    ; NUMBER INTO BH-REGISTER
39: PRINT:                                       ;REPEAT
40:               TEST    DX,8000H               ;   IF   BIT 15 OF NUMBER = 0
41:               JNZ     ONE
42:               MOV     AH,14                  ;     THEN DISPLAY 0
43:               MOV     AL,'0'
44:               INT     10H
45:               JMP     ROTATE
46: ONE:          MOV     AH,14                  ;     ELSE
47:               MOV     AL,'1'                 ;          DISPLAY 1
48:               INT     10H                    ;     ENDIF
49: ROTATE:       ROL     DX,1                   ;   ROTATE NUMBER LEFT 1 BIT
50:                                              ;   TO GET NEXT BIT IN POS. 15
51:               LOOP    PRINT                  ;   DECREMENT BIT_COUNT
52:                                              ;UNTIL BIT_COUNT = 0
53:               POPF                           ;RESTORE FLAGS
54:               POP     CX                     ;RESTORE REGISTERS
55:               POP     BX
56:               POP     DX
57:               POP     AX
58:               RET                            ;RETURN
59: PUTBIN        ENDP                         ;END PUTBIN
60: CODE          ENDS
61:*              END
```

disables external interrupts for some reason, the user program executes with external interrupts enabled. Thus, in case an I/O subprocedure is called when external interrupts are disabled, each I/O procedure performs an STI instruction.

The MOV instruction in line 37 places the subfunction code for BIOS interrupt Type 10 hex in the AH-register. A subfunction code of 15 causes BIOS to return the current status of the video display (Table 9.3). The INT instruction in line 38 calls the BIOS interrupt Type 10 hex service procedure into execution. This call is made to find the current active display page number, which BIOS returns in the BH-register. If the IBM PC on which the program is executing has a monochrome display, then this call is unnecessary as the monochrome display has only one page. However, if the IBM PC on which the program is executing has a color display, then this step is vital as the color display has four pages, numbered 0–3. The active display page is the one that currently appears on the video screen. It is selected by subfunction 5 of BIOS interrupt Type 10 hex (Table 9.3). The active display page number is read into the BH-register by subfunction 15 of BIOS interrupt Type 10 hex. The PUTBIN procedure reads the current active display page number, so that it can display the binary number on the active display page. This process makes PUTBIN compatible with both the monochrome display and the color display.

The loop in lines 39–52 displays the 8- or 16-bit binary number based on the loop count determined by the double-alternative decision structure in lines 27–35. The loop body contains a double-alternative decision structure (lines 40–48) that determines whether the next bit of the number is 0 or 1 and displays the appropriate ASCII character. The TEST instruction in line 40 tests bit 15 of the number, and the JNZ instruction in line 41 makes the decision based on this test: If the bit is 0, then the instructions in lines 42–44 are executed; if the bit is 1, then the instructions in lines 46–48 are executed. The rotate instruction in line 49 ensures that the next most-significant digit of the number is in bit position 15 for the next iteration of the loop.

The instructions in lines 42–44 display a 0 at the current cursor position on the active display page and advance the cursor to the next character position. The MOV instruction in line 42 places the subfunction code for BIOS interrupt Type 10 hex in the AH-register. A subfunction code of 14 causes BIOS to display the ASCII character in the AL-register on the screen at the current cursor position and then to advance the cursor to the next character position. The MOV instruction in line 43 loads the AL-register with the ASCII representation for the digit 0, the character to be displayed. The BH-register already contains the active display page number. It was set as a result of the BIOS call in line 38, and there are no instructions in the loop body that will change the value in the BH-register. The INT instruction in line 44 calls the BIOS interrupt Type 10 hex service procedure into execution.

The instructions in lines 46–48 display a 1 at the current cursor position on the active display page and advance the cursor to the next character position. The MOV instruction in line 46 places the subfunction code for BIOS interrupt Type 10 hex in the AH-register. The MOV instruction in line 47 loads the

AL-register with the ASCII representation for the digit 1, the character to be displayed. The BH-register already contains the active display page number. The INT instruction in line 48 calls the BIOS interrupt Type 10 hex service procedure into execution.

Equipment Check (Interrupt 11H)

By using software interrupt Type 11 hex, BIOS provides a method for an Assembly language program to determine the kinds and capacities of resources that are attached to the PC. If programs are being written for a specific personal computer configuration, then this service is of no value. However, if programs are being written to execute on a variety of PC configurations, then this BIOS service allows the program to determine its environment. The BIOS procedure that services the Type 11 hex interrupt returns a value in the AX-register that summarizes the equipment that is available on the PC. Table 9.4 shows the interpretation for each bit in the AX-register value that is returned by the interrupt Type 11 hex service procedure.

Memory Size (Interrupt 12H)

By using software interrupt Type 12 hex, BIOS provides a method for an Assembly language program to determine the amount of RAM memory in the PC. This quantity includes both memory on the system board and the add-on memory accessible through I/O ports. The BIOS procedure that services the Type 12 hex interrupt returns in the AX-register a count of the number of 1K RAM memory blocks. For a PC with 256K of RAM, the value returned in the AX-register is 0100 hexadecimal (256 decimal).

Keyboard Input (Interrupt 16H)

Each time a key is pressed at the keyboard, a Type 9 interrupt is generated. The BIOS procedure that services the Type 9 interrupt, accepts the scan code from the keyboard input port, converts it to an extended ASCII code, and stores both codes in the next available location in its keyboard input buffer. The Type 9 interrupt service procedure can queue up to 15 scan code:character code pairs in its input buffer. If a Type 9 interrupt occurs and the keyboard input buffer is full, then the interrupt service procedure sends a tone to the speaker on the PC, and the input scan code is discarded. The beep indicates to the user that the keyboard input was not accepted. Because of the BIOS Type 9 interrupt service procedure, Assembly language programs do not have to interface directly with the keyboard. BIOS creates a different keyboard interface for Assembly language programs.

    Keyboard input services are provided through software interrupt Type 16 hex. The BIOS subprocedure that services interrupt Type 16 hex uses the value in the AH-register as a function code. It is via the AH-register that the caller requests the specific keyboard operation to be performed. Depending on the function code in the AH-register, certain registers are used for output from the

TABLE 9.4

Interpretation of the AX-register value returned by the Type 11 hex interrupt service procedure

15	14	13	12	11	10	9	8	7	6	5	4	3	2	1	0

Bit #	Interpretation
0	0 ⇒ PC has no diskette drives 1 ⇒ PC has at least one diskette drive
1	Not used
3–2	Amount of read/write memory on system board 00 ⇒ 16K 01 ⇒ 32K 10 ⇒ 48K 11 ⇒ 64K
5–4	Initial video mode 00 ⇒ not used 01 ⇒ 40 × 25 B/W using color card 10 ⇒ 80 × 25 B/W using color card 11 ⇒ 80 × 25 B/W using B/W card
7–6	Number of diskette drives (if bit 0 = 1) 00 ⇒ 1 01 ⇒ 2 10 ⇒ 3 11 ⇒ 4
8	Not used
11–9	Number of RS-232 communication cards attached
12	0 ⇒ no device attached to game I/O port 1 ⇒ device attached to game I/O port
13	Not used
15–14	Number of printers attached

BIOS service procedure. Table 9.5 summarizes the function codes recognized by the BIOS interrupt Type 16 hex service procedure and the registers used for procedure output.

To obtain a character from the keyboard, an Assembly language program invokes the interrupt Type 16 hex service procedure with a subfunction code of zero in the AH-register. That is, to obtain a character from the keyboard, execute the following two Assembly language instructions:

```
MOV AH,O
INT 16H
```

The interrupt Type 16 hex service procedure returns the next scan code:character code pair from its keyboard input buffer: The scan code is returned in the

TABLE 9.5

BIOS interrupt Type
16H subfunctions

AH	Function	Procedure Outputs
0	Read character	AH-register contains scan code of next keyboard character AL-register contains extended ASCII code of next keyboard character Character is deleted from keyboard input buffer

1	Read buffer status	ZF = 0 implies input buffer is not empty
		    AH-register contains scan code of next keyboard character
		    AL-register contains extended ASCII code of next keyboard character
		    Character remains in keyboard input buffer
		ZF = 1 implies input buffer is empty

2	Read Keyboard status	AL-register contains keyboard status byte

7	6	5	4	3	2	1	0

Bit	Meaning
7	Status of INSERT 0 ⇒ INSERT mode off 1 ⇒ INSERT mode on
6	Status of CAPS LOCK 0 ⇒ CAPS LOCK off 1 ⇒ CAPS LOCK on
5	Status of NUM LOCK 0 ⇒ NUM LOCK off 1 ⇒ NUM LOCK on
4	Status of SCROLL LOCK 0 ⇒ SCROLL LOCK off 1 ⇒ SCROLL LOCK on
3	0 ⇒ ALT not depressed 1 ⇒ ALT depressed
2	0 ⇒ CTRL not depressed 1 ⇒ CTRL depressed
1	0 ⇒ LEFT-SHIFT not pressed 1 ⇒ LEFT-SHIFT depressed
0	0 ⇒ RIGHT-SHIFT not pressed 1 ⇒ RIGHT-SHIFT depressed

AH-register, and the extended ASCII character code is returned in the AL-register. If the keyboard input buffer is empty when the interrupt Type 16 hex service procedure is invoked, then the service procedure goes into an idle loop, waiting until a scan code:character code pair is in its input buffer. The keyboard input buffer is handled as a true **first-in-first-out** (FIFO) queue, so that Assembly language programs receive keyboard characters in the same order as they were depressed at the keyboard.

Programming Example—GETSTRNG

Program Listing 9.4 illustrates the use of BIOS interrupt Type 16 hex with the GETSTRNG procedure from the author's I/O subprocedure library. GETSTRNG also illustrates BIOS interrupt Type 10 hex, since each character entered via the keyboard is echoed to the video screen. The program shows the assembly module that contains the GETSTRNG procedure.

The prologue in lines 9–23 explains the function of the GETSTRNG procedure and states its interface requirements. The caller sets the ES:DI register pair to address the first location of the byte array in which the input character string is to be stored, sets the CX-register to the length of this byte array, and then calls GETSTRNG. GETSTRNG accepts characters from the keyboard and stores their extended ASCII codes in the specified byte array until either a RETURN is received or n characters have been received, in which n is the value input to GETSTRNG via the CX-register. That is, the value input in the CX-register instructs GETSTRNG as to the maximum number of characters that the byte array can hold, and therefore, the maximum size string that GETSTRNG should accept from the keyboard. GETSTRNG returns to the caller with the input character string stored in the specified array, the ES:DI register pair again addressing the first byte of that array, and the CX-register set to the actual length of the input string.

When entering a character string, the user may wish to erase part of the string already entered. The GETSTRNG procedure uses BACKSPACE to provide this capability. Entering a BACKSPACE erases the last character entered into the string; thus, entering m consecutive BACKSPACE characters erases the last m characters entered into the string. GETSTRNG not only removes the characters from the string, but it also erases them from the echoed copy on the video screen.

The GETSTRNG procedure begins by saving the registers that it uses (lines 25–29). The STI instruction in line 30 enables external interrupts, which ensures that the keyboard interrupt will be enabled. The CLD instruction in line 31 sets the DF bit of the flags register for incrementing through the byte array. GETSTRNG uses the STOSB string instruction to store characters in the byte array.

The two instructions in lines 32 and 33 generate a software interrupt Type 10 hex with a subfunction code of 15, which requests the BIOS video I/O service procedure to read the current video state. This step is taken to read the active display page number into the BH-register. GETSTRNG echoes the character string input to the active page of the video screen. Since no other program instructions modify the BH-register value, the active display page number is held in the BH-register until that register is restored (line 72) just prior to return to the caller.

```
 1: ;
 2: ;
 3: ;                     PROGRAM LISTING 9.4
 4: ;
 5: CODE          SEGMENT PARA 'IO_CODE'
 6:               ASSUME  CS:CODE
 7:               PUBLIC  GETSTRNG
 8: ;
 9: ; PROCEDURE TO INPUT A CHARACTER STRING FROM THE KEYBOARD.
10: ; CHARACTERS  WILL  BE ACCEPTED UNTIL THE USER PRESSES THE
11: ; RETURN  KEY  OR N CHARACTERS HAVE BEEN ENTERED,  WHERE N
12: ; IS SUPPLIED BY THE CALLER.
13: ;
14: ; INPUT:  ES:DI POINTS TO THE BUFFER THAT  IS  TO  RECEIVE
15: ;               THE STRING
16: ;         CX    CONTAINS  THE  LENGTH OF THE INPUT  BUFFER
17: ;
18: ; OUTPUT: CX    CONTAINS THE ACTUAL  LENGTH  OF  THE INPUT
19: ;               STRING
20: ;         THE  SPECIFIED  BUFFER  CONTAINS  THE  CHARACTER
21: ;         STRING THAT WAS ENTERED.
22: ;
23: ;
24: GETSTRNG      PROC    FAR                 ;PROCEDURE GETSTRNG (PTR,SIZE)
25:               PUSH    AX                    ;SAVE REGISTERS
26:               PUSH    BX
27:               PUSH    DI
28:               PUSH    DX
29:               PUSHF                         ;SAVE FLAGS
30:               STI                           ;ENABLE INTERRUPTS
31:               CLD                           ;SET DF FOR INCREMENTING
32:               MOV     AH,15                 ;READ ACTIVE DISPLAY PAGE
33:               INT     10H                   ;NUMBER INTO BH-REGISTER
34:               MOV     DX,0                  ;KEY_COUNT = 0
35: LOOP_TOP:                                   ;REPEAT
36:               MOV     AH,0            ;    READ CHAR FROM KEYBOARD
37:               INT     16H
38:               CMP     AL,0DH          ;    IF   CHAR IS CARRIAGE RETURN
39:               JE      LOOP_END        ;<- THEN EXIT
40:                                       ;    ENDIF
41:               STOSB                   ;    PTR->BYTE = CHAR
42:                                       ;    PTR = PTR + 1
43:               INC     DX              ;    KEY_COUNT = KEY_COUNT + 1
44:               MOV     AH,14           ;    DISPLAY CHAR
45:               INT     10H             ;    <ECHO CHAR TO SCREEN>
46:               CMP     AL,08H          ;    IF   CHAR IS BACKSPACE
47:               JNE     LOOP_TEST
48:               SUB     DX,2            ;    THEN KEY_COUNT = KEY_COUNT-2
49:               SUB     DI,2            ;         PTR = PTR - 2
50:               ADD     CX,2            ;         SIZE = SIZE + 2
51:               MOV     AH,14           ;         DISPLAY BLANK
52:               MOV     AL,' '
53:               INT     10H
54:               MOV     AH,14           ;         DISPLAY BACKSPACE
55:               MOV     AL,08H
56:               INT     10H
57: LOOP_TEST:                            ;    ENDIF
58:               LOOP    LOOP_TOP        ;    SIZE = SIZE - 1
59: LOOP_END:                             ;UNTIL SIZE = 0
60:*             MOV     CX,DX            ;SIZE = KEY_COUNT
```

*

```
61: ;
62: ;
63:             MOV    AH,14              ;DISPLAY CARRIAGE RETURN
64:             MOV    AL,0DH
65:             INT    10H
66:             MOV    AH,14              ;DISPLAY LINE FEED
67:             MOV    AL,0AH
68:             INT    10H
69:             POPF                      ;RESTORE FLAGS
70:             POP    DX                 ;RESTORE REGISTERS
71:             POP    DI
72:             POP    BX
73:             POP    AX
74:             RET                       ;RETURN
75: GETSTRNG    ENDP               ;END GETSTRNG
76: CODE        ENDS
77:*            END
```

The GETSTRNG procedure returns to its caller a count of the number of characters in the input string, and the DX-register maintains this count. The MOV instruction in line 34 initializes this key count to 0.

The REPEAT-UNTIL loop in lines 35–58 reads the characters from the keyboard and stores them in the caller's byte array, one character per loop iteration. The loop body executes until a RETURN is received or the length of the input string has reached the maximum allowed, as specified by the value input to GETSTRNG via the CX-register. The CX-register value is used as a loop counter to control the maximum number of characters that can be stored in the caller's byte array.

The two instructions in lines 36 and 37 generate a software interrupt Type 16 hex with a subfunction code of 0, which requests the BIOS keyboard service procedure to obtain a character from the keyboard. The ASCII character code is returned in the AL-register. The CMP instruction in line 38 tests the input character to see if it is a RETURN (OD hex is the ASCII code for a RETURN). The JE instruction in line 39 makes the decision based on this test: If the character is a RETURN, then the jump is taken to line 59, thus exiting the loop body; if the character is not a RETURN, then the jump is not taken, and the loop body is continued.

The STOSB instruction in line 41 stores the character in the caller's byte array and then increments the DI-register by 1, so that the ES:DI register pair addresses the next byte in the array. The INC instruction in line 43 increments the key count in the DX-register to reflect the character just stored.

The two instructions in lines 44 and 45 generate a software interrupt Type 10 hex with a subfunction code of 14, which requests the BIOS video I/O service procedure to display the character in the AL-register at the current cursor position, on the display page indicated by the value in the BH-register, and then to advance the cursor position. This process echoes the character just stored in the caller's byte array to the video screen.

The single-alternative decision structure in lines 46–57 detects the input of a BACKSPACE and performs the necessary adjustments. The CMP instruction in line 46 tests the input character to see if it is a BACKSPACE (08 hex is the ASCII code for a BACKSPACE). The JNE instruction in line 47 makes the decision based on this test: If the character is a BACKSPACE, then the instructions in lines 48–56 are executed; otherwise, these instructions are skipped.

If the input character is a BACKSPACE, then two characters must be logically removed from the caller's byte array: the BACKSPACE just stored and the character stored previous to the BACKSPACE. The SUB instruction in line 48 decrements the key count by 2. The SUB instruction in line 49 decrements the DI-register by 2, so that the ES:DI register pair addresses the location in the byte array of the character being erased, which means that the next character entered replaces the one being erased in the byte array. Note that erased characters are not actually removed from the byte array, but logically, they are no longer a part of the input string. The loop counter in the CX-register (i.e., the maximum number of remaining characters that can be stored in the byte array) is incremented by 2 (line 50). Since two characters have been removed from the array, two more iterations of the loop are now possible before the array becomes full.

The echoed character string on the video screen must also be modified to reflect the effect of the BACKSPACE. The instructions in lines 51–56 ensure this modification. When the BACKSPACE was echoed to the screen by the instructions in lines 44 and 45, the result was that the cursor backed up under the character to be erased. To erase this character from the screen, a blank is displayed (lines 51–53). Displaying the blank character also advances the cursor. The cursor now must be backed up again, so that the next character entered will be echoed in the position where the blank was displayed. This step is accomplished by displaying a BACKSPACE (lines 54–56).

The LOOP instruction in line 58 decrements the loop counter in the CX-register and returns to the top of the loop (line 35) if the count is nonzero. If the count is zero, then the caller's byte array is full, and no more characters can be accepted. Loop exit can occur for one of two reasons: RETURN was entered or the caller's byte array was filled.

On loop exit, the key count, the actual length of the input string, is moved to the CX-register (line 60) for procedure output. Next, a RETURN and a LINE FEED are displayed on the video screen (lines 63–68), which means that the echoed input string terminates a line on the display. The GETSTRNG procedure ends by restoring registers for the caller (lines 69–73) and returning control to the caller (line 74). (The GETSTRNG procedure shown in Program Listing 9.4 contains one known bug, which is addressed in Programming Exercise 9.8.)

Printer Output (Interrupt 17H)

Printer I/O services are provided through software interrupt Type 17 hex. The BIOS subprocedure that services interrupt Type 17 hex uses the value in the AH-register as a function code. It is via the AH-register that the caller requests the specific printer operation to be performed. Table 9.6 summarizes the function codes recognized by the BIOS interrupt Type 17 hex service procedure and the other registers used for procedure input and output.

TABLE 9.6
BIOS interrupt Type
17H subfunctions

AH	Function	Procedure Inputs	Procedure Outputs
0	Print character	AL = Character to print DX = Printer number (0, 1, 2)	AH = status byte
1	Initialize printer	DX = Printer number (0, 1, 2)	AH = status byte
2	Read printer status	DX = Printer number (0, 1, 2)	AH = status byte

Subfunction 0 causes the ASCII character in the AL-register to be output to the printer. Unless the ASCII character is a control character, the character is printed in the next position on the current line. Control characters are discussed in the following paragraphs. Subfunction 1 causes the printer to be initialized, which means a RETURN is output to the printer, and the current line is established as the top of page. Subfunction 2 causes no output to the printer, but it is simply a request for the current printer status. For all three subfunctions, the DX-register specifies the printer number (0, 1, or 2). BIOS can provide service for up to three printers via interrupt Type 17 hex. For all three subfunctions, the printer status is returned to the caller in the AH-register.

Table 9.7 shows the interpretation for each bit of the printer status byte returned in the AH-register. The key bits of interest for the IBM PC Graphics

TABLE 9.7
Interpretation of
printer status byte

	7	6	5	4	3	2	1	0

Bit	Meaning
7	Printer busy 1 implies printer is busy
6	Acknowledge 1 implies printer acknowledged receipt of data
5	Out of paper 1 implies printer is out of paper
4	Selected 0 implies printer is offline 1 implies printer is online
3	I/O error 1 implies an I/O error occurred on the requested print operation
2	Not used
1	Not used
0	Timeout error 1 implies timeout error occurred on the requested print operation (printer busy for too long a time)

TABLE 9.8
Printer status for IBM
PC graphics printer

Status of printer	Bit 7	Bit 5	Bit 4	Bit 3
Printer power switch is off	1	0	0	1
Printer power switch is on Printer has paper Printer is offline	0	0	0	1
Printer power switch is on Printer is out of paper	0	1	0	1
Printer power switch is on Printer has paper Printer is online	1	0	1	0

Printer are bits 7, 5, 4, and 3. Table 9.8 summarizes the settings for these bits
for various printer conditions.

The IBM PC Graphics Printer has several modes. The standard print
mode prints 80 characters per line, 6 lines per inch (66 lines per page). The
compressed mode prints 132 characters per line, 6 lines per inch. The double-
width mode prints 40 characters per line, 6 lines per inch. The number of lines
per inch can be changed from 6 to 8, which is convenient when printing in the
compressed mode. To change the printer mode, set the number of lines per inch,
or perform carriage control operations at the printer, special control characters
are transmitted to the printer.

The extended ASCII character set contains both printable and control
characters. When a printable character is transmitted to the Graphics Printer, it
is stored in a buffer in the printer. The characters are not actually printed until
a complete print line has been received by the printer. The characters in the
buffer are printed when a RETURN, a LINE FEED, or a FORM FEED
character is received, or a printable character is received and the printer buffer
is full. The printer buffer can hold up to 80 characters in the standard mode, 132
characters in the compressed mode, and 40 characters in the double-width mode.
When a line is printed because of a full printer buffer, a RETURN and a LINE
FEED are automatically performed. When a control character is transmitted to
the Graphics Printer, the printer performs the requested control operation (e.g.,
changes mode, advances to top of next page). Table 9.9 summarizes the more
useful printer control characters, and a complete set is discussed in the *Guide to
Operations Manual for the IBM PC*. The characters in Table 9.9 are standard
ASCII characters, so their interpretations apply to most printers. Illustrations of
printer I/O operations are left as programming exercises.

Time of Day (Interrupt 1AH)

DOS computes the time of day from a count of the number of timer interrupts
(Type 8 interrupts) since midnight. This count is initialized to 0 (i.e., time of day

TABLE 9.9
Printer control
characters

ASCII Code	Interpretation
07 hex	Sounds a beep at the printer
09 hex	Horizontal TAB TAB stops initialized to every eight columns on IBM PC graphics printer
0A hex	Line feed (advance to next line)
0B hex	Vertical TAB Acts like line feed on IBM PC graphics printer
0C hex	FORM FEED (advance to top of next page)
0D hex	RETURN (return to left margin)
0E hex	Turn on double-width print mode (40 characters per line)
0F hex	Turn on compressed print mode (132 characters per line)
12 hex	Turn off compressed print mode
14 hex	Turn off double-width print mode
18 hex	Clear printer buffer

is initialized to midnight) at time of system startup. When DOS is loaded, it prompts the user for the correct date and time. DOS accepts the time of day entered by the user, converts it to a count of timer interrupts since midnight, and reinitializes the count. This count of timer interrupts is maintained by BIOS as a 32-bit value. A program can read or set this count by using software interrupt Type 1A hex.

The BIOS procedure that services interrupt Type 1A hex uses the value in the AH-register as a subfunction code. Table 9.10 summarizes the function codes recognized by the Type 1A interrupt service procedure.

The time-of-day interrupt can be used to compute program execution time. Immediately on entry to the program, the program reads and saves the value of the timer count. Just before exit from the program, the program reads the value of the timer count and computes the difference between the value just read and

TABLE 9.10
BIOS interrupt Type
1AH subfunctions

AH	Function	Procedure Input	Procedure Output
0	Read count of timer interrupts	None	CX:DX register pair contains timer count
1	Set count of timer interrupts	CX:DX register pair contains timer count	None

the value saved at the beginning of the program. This difference is the number of timer interrupts (Type 8 interrupts) that occurred during program execution. Since the timer interrupt occurs approximately once every 55 milliseconds, multiplying this difference by 55 gives the approximate number of milliseconds that elapsed during program execution.

The time-of-day interrupt can also be used to provide a delay in a program. The timer interrupt occurs approximately 18.2 times per second. In 5 seconds, the timer interrupt occurs approximately 91 times. To perform a 5-second delay, the following instructions could be used:

```
        MOV CX,O
        MOV DX,O
        MOV AH,1
        INT 1AH

REPEAT:

        MOV AH,O
        INT 1AH
        CMP DX,91
        JB  REPEAT
```

The first four instructions set the time count to 0. The last four instructions repeatedly read the timer count until the timer count is found to be 91 or above. The one problem with this delay loop is that it destroys the system's time of day. Some other possibilities for delay loops are considered in the programming exercises at the end of the chapter.

Timer Subfunction (Interrupt 1CH)

BIOS provides the capability for a user program to perform some function on every timer interrupt. The BIOS procedure that services the Type 8 interrupt generates a Type 1C hex software interrupt. BIOS provides an interrupt service procedure for the Type 1C interrupt that contains only an IRET instruction. To perform some function on every timer interrupt, the user program must provide its own Type 1C interrupt service procedure. External interrupts should be disabled while modifying the Type 1C interrupt vector. If a timer interrupt is allowed to occur between setting the segment and offset portions of the interrupt vector, then a bogus Type 1C interrupt service procedure is invoked. (The author muddled over that problem for several months.)

Direct Input/Output

Direct input/output involves accessing the I/O ports in the IBM PC. The set of I/O ports is like a set of byte registers that holds data that are being transmitted between the microprocessor and an external device (e.g., keyboard, video display). The main difference between a processor register and a port is that a port has an electrical connection to some external device. A port may be used for transmitting data to or from a device, transmitting control information to a device, or receiving status information from a device.

The IBM PC has 65,536 ports, numbered 0–65,535. A specific port is addressed by its unique port number. Addressing a port opens the electrical connection between the port and its external device to allow data to flow from the device to the port or from the port to the device.

There are two Assembly language instructions for accessing the ports in the IBM PC: the IN instruction and the OUT instruction. The **IN instruction** has the following general form:

[⟨*label*⟩] IN ⟨*accumulator*⟩, ⟨*port*⟩   [⟨*comment*⟩]

in which ⟨*accumulator*⟩ is either register designator AL or AX and ⟨*port*⟩ is either an immediate value in the range 0–255 or the register designator DX. If the ⟨*accumulator*⟩ operand is AL, then the IN instruction transfers the byte from the port addressed by the value of the ⟨*port*⟩ operand to the AL-register. If the ⟨*accumulator*⟩ operand is AX, then the IN instruction transfers the byte from the port addressed by the value of the ⟨*port*⟩ operand to the AL-register and transfers the byte from the port addressed by the value of the ⟨*port*⟩ operand plus 1 to the AH-register.

The **OUT instruction** has the following general form:

[⟨*label*⟩] OUT ⟨*port*⟩,⟨*accumulator*⟩   [⟨*comment*⟩]

in which ⟨*port*⟩ is either an immediate value in the range 0–255 or the register designator DX and ⟨*accumulator*⟩ is either register designator AL or AX. If the ⟨*accumulator*⟩ operand is AL, then the OUT instruction transfers the byte from the AL-register to the port addressed by the value of the ⟨*port*⟩ operand. If the ⟨*accumulator*⟩ operand is AX, then the OUT instruction transfers the byte from the AL-register to the port addressed by the value of the ⟨*port*⟩ operand and transfers the byte from the AH-register to the port addressed by the value of the ⟨*port*⟩ operand plus 1.

EXAMPLES

The instruction

```
IN AL, 2BH
```

transfers the byte from port 2B hex to the AL-register. The instructions

```
MOV DX, 3E2H
OUT DX, AX
```

transfer the byte in the AL-register to port 3E2 hex and the byte in the AH-register to port 3E3 hex.

The port assignments in the IBM PC are summarized in the I/O address map in the IBM PC Technical Reference manual. A few of the ports are discussed here to give examples of IN and OUT instructions. One example that has been used several times in this chapter is that of keyboard input. When a Type 9 interrupt (keyboard interrupt) occurs, the BIOS service procedure reads the scan code for the key by executing the instruction

```
IN  AL, 60H
```

Execution of the IN instruction opens the connection between the keyboard and port 60 hex, allowing the scan code to be transferred to the port, and then copies the scan code from the port to the AL-register. The interrupt service procedure then converts the scan code to an extended ASCII character and stores both codes in the keyboard input buffer.

Programming Example—Demonstrates HLT, IN, and OUT Instructions

Program Listing 9.5 gives a simple illustration of the IN and OUT instructions. It also uses the HLT instruction that halts instruction executions in the microprocessor. The **HLT instruction** has the following general form.

```
[⟨label⟩]  HLT                 [⟨comment⟩]
```

It causes the microprocessor to halt its instruction execution cycle and wait for an interrupt to occur. When an interrupt occurs, instruction execution resumes with the appropriate interrupt service procedure. On return from the interrupt service procedure, execution continues with the instruction immediately following the HLT instruction.

Suppose an HLT instruction has just been executed and that the microprocessor is in the halt state. If all external interrupts are enabled, then the next timer interrupt (Type 8 interrupt) will bring the microprocessor out of the halt state. Suppose that there is a need to lock out the timer interrupt, so that a keyboard interrupt can be used to awaken the microprocessor from the halt state. If the IF bit of the flags register is used to lock out the timer interrupt, then all other external interrupts, including the keyboard interrupts, are locked out as well. A method is needed for selectively locking out the external interrupts.

The eight external interrupts (Types 8–F hex) are under control of the Intel 8259A interrupt controller. The microprocessor communicates with the interrupt controller via port 20 hex and port 21 hex. The byte at port 21 hex enables or disables each of the eight external interrupts individually, and each bit controls one of the eight external interrupts: Bit 0 controls interrupt Type 8, bit 1 controls interrupt Type 9, bit 2 controls interrupt Type A, and so forth. A 1 in the bit means that the corresponding interrupt type is disabled, and a 0 means that the interrupt is enabled. Therefore, the timer interrupt can be individually disabled by setting bit 0 at port 21 hex.

Program Listing 9.5 demonstrates execution of an HLT instruction with the timer interrupt disabled. The IN instruction in line 25 reads the current value of port 21 hex into the AL-register. The call to the PUTBIN procedure

```
 1: ;
 2: ;
 3: ;                         PROGRAM LISTING 9.5
 4: ;
 5: ; PROGRAM TO DEMONSTRATE HLT, IN, AND OUT INSTRUCTIONS
 6: ;
 7:                                         ;SUBROUTINES TO
 8:            EXTRN    NEWLINE:FAR          ;DISPLAY NEWLINE CHARACTER
 9:            EXTRN    PUTBIN:FAR           ;DISPLAY BYTE OR WORD IN BINARY
10: ;
11: ; S T A C K    S E G M E N T    D E F I N I T I O N
12: ;
13: STACK      SEGMENT STACK
14:            DB       256 DUP(?)
15: STACK      ENDS
16: ;
17: ; C O D E    S E G M E N T    D E F I N I T I O N
18: ;
19: CODE       SEGMENT
20:            ASSUME   CS:CODE,SS:STACK
21: HLT_TEST   PROC     FAR
22:            PUSH     DS                   ;PUSH RETURN SEG ADDR ON STACK
23:            SUB      AX,AX                ;PUSH RETURN OFFSET OF ZERO
24:            PUSH     AX                   ;ON STACK
25:            IN       AL,21H               ;READ INTERRUPT MASK REGISTER
26:            MOV      BL,0                 ;PUTBIN CODE = BYTE
27:            CALL     PUTBIN               ;DISPLAY INTERRUPT MASK REGISTER
28:            CALL     NEWLINE
29:            OR       AL,1                 ;MASK TIMER INTERRUPT
30:            OUT      21H,AL
31:            HLT                           ;HALT --> WAIT FOR INTERRUPT
32:            CALL     PUTBIN               ;DISPLAY INTERRUPT MASK REGISTER
33:            AND      AL,0FEH              ;ENABLE TIMER INTERRUPT
34:            OUT      21H,AL
35:            RET                           ;RETURN
36: HLT_TEST   ENDP
37: CODE       ENDS
38:*           END      HLT_TEST
```

(lines 26–27) displays this byte value in binary. The OR instruction in line 29 sets bit 0 of this byte value in the AL-register, leaving all other bits unchanged. The OUT instruction in line 30 copies this modified byte value to port 21 hex. This instruction disables the timer interrupt, leaving the status of the other seven external interrupts unchanged. The HLT instruction in line 31 places the microprocessor into the halt state. The microprocessor then remains in the halt state until an interrupt occurs. A timer interrupt will not occur, because the program has disabled the timer interrupt. Keyboard interrupts are still enabled, so pressing a key at the keyboard will awaken the microprocessor from the halt state.

On awakening from the halt state, the program displays the value in the AL-register (line 32), which is the value that was transmitted to the interrupt controller via port 21 hex. It is the same value as the value read from port 21 hex (line 25) and displayed earlier (line 27), except that bit 0 is set to 1. The AND instruction in line 33 clears bit 0 of this byte value, leaving all other bits unchanged. The OUT instruction in line 34 transmits this modified byte value to port 21 hex. This instruction enables the timer interrupt once again, leaving the status of the other seven external interrupts unchanged.

When executed on an IBM PC-XT, the program displays the value 10111100 and then halts. When a key is pressed at the keyboard, the program displays the value 10111101 and then returns control to DOS. If the user sets the system time to the correct time before executing this program and waits 2 minutes after the first display before pressing a key, then the system time, after program execution, will be approximately 2 minutes slow.

9.4   Additional Capabilities in the IBM PC-AT Assembly Language

The IBM PC-AT Assembly language has two kinds of string instructions, input string instructions and output string instructions, that provide the capability for transmitting arrays between memory and the ports.

There are two input string instructions; INSB and INSW. The **INSB instruction** has the following general form:

[⟨*label*⟩]   INSB   [⟨*comment*⟩]

It causes the byte at the port addressed by the value of the DX-register to replace the byte in memory addressed by the ES:DI register pair and then causes the value of the DI-register to be updated so that the ES:DI register pair addresses the next byte of the string. If the DF bit in the flags register is 0, then the DI-register is incremented by 1; if the DF bit in the flags register is 1, then the DI-register is decremented by 1.

The **INSW instruction** has the following general form:

[⟨*label*⟩]   INSW   [⟨*comment*⟩]

It causes the word at the port addressed by the value of the DX-register to replace the word in memory addressed by the ES:DI register pair and then causes the value of the DI-register to be updated so that the ES:DI register pair addresses the next word of the array. If the DF bit in the flags register is 0, then the DI-register is incremented by 2; if the DF bit in the flags register is 1, then the DI-register is decremented by 2.

There is a generic form for the input string instructions:

[⟨*label*⟩]   INS ⟨*destination*⟩, DX   [⟨*comment*⟩]

in which ⟨*destination*⟩ is the symbolic name of an array. When this form is used, the assembler generates the code for either INSB or INSW depending on the type attribute of the ⟨*destination*⟩ operand.

There are two output string instructions: OUTSB and OUTSW. The **OUTSB instruction** has the following general form:

[⟨*label*⟩]   OUTSB   [⟨*comment*⟩]

It causes the byte in memory addressed by the DS:SI register pair to be transmitted to the port addressed by the value of the DX-register and then causes the value of the SI-register to be updated, so that the DS:SI register pair addresses the next byte of the string. If the DF bit in the flags register is 0, then the SI-register is incremented by 1; if the DF bit in the flags register is 1, then the SI-register is decremented by 1.

The **OUTSW instruction** has the following general form:

```
[⟨label⟩] OUTSW                    [⟨comment⟩]
```

It causes the word in memory addressed by the DS:SI register pair to be transmitted to the port addressed by the value of the DX-register and then causes the value of the SI-register to be updated, so that the DS:SI register pair addresses the next word of the array. If the DF bit in the flags register is 0, then the SI-register is incremented by 2; if the DF bit in the flags register is 1, then the SI-register is decremented by 2.

There is a generic form for the output string instructions:

```
[⟨label⟩]  OUTS   DX,⟨source⟩  [⟨comment⟩]
```

in which ⟨source⟩ is the symbolic name of an array. When this form is used, the assembler generates the code for either OUTSB or OUTSW depending on the type attribute of the ⟨source⟩ operand. None of the flags are affected by input and output string instructions. As well, since these are string instructions, the REP prefix can be used. But, such use causes a high rate of data transfers, and it should be noted that not all I/O devices can handle such a high rate.

PROGRAMMING EXERCISES

Programming Exercises 9.1–9.7 are designed to provide a series of printer I/O subprocedures similar to the video I/O subprocedures in the author's I/O subprocedure library.

9.1 Implement three printer carriage control procedures defined as follows:

    a. Implement a procedure called FORM-FEED that accepts a printer number in the DX-register and sends a FORM FEED to the designated printer.

    b. Implement a procedure called LINEFEED that accepts a printer number in the DX-register and sends a LINE FEED character to the designated printer.

    c. Implement a procedure called SAMELINE that accepts a printer number in the DX-register and sends a RETURN to the designated printer.

9.2 Implement a procedure called PRTSTAT to test the printer status. Your input should be the printer number in the DX-register. The procedure should loop, testing printer status until the printer is ready. If printer power is turned off or the printer is offline, then the procedure should display the message

```
PRINTER TURNED OFF OR OFF LINE
PRESS ANY KEY WHEN PRINTER IS READY
```

on the video screen and then pause until a keystroke is received. If the printer is out of paper, then the procedure should display the message

```
PRINTER OUT OF PAPER
PRESS ANY KEY WHEN PRINTER IS READY
```

on the video screen and then pause until a keystroke is received. The procedure should not return to the caller until the printer is ready for output.

9.3 Design and implement a procedure called PRTSTRNG to print a character string at the line printer. Your inputs should be the following:

a. ES:DI register pair addresses the first character of the string.

b. CX-register contains the length of the string.

c. DX-register contains the printer number.

The procedure should print the designated string at the specified line printer beginning at the current print position.

9.4 Design and implement a procedure called PRTBIN to print an 8- or 16-bit integer in binary form at the line printer. Your inputs should be the following:

a. AL-register contains the value to be printed for a byte print; AX-register contains the value to be printed for a word print.

b. BL-register contains the print code: Zero implies byte print; nonzero implies word print.

c. DX-register contains the printer number.

The procedure should print the binary value at the specified printer beginning at the current print position.

9.5 Design and implement a procedure called PRTHEX to print an 8- or 16-bit integer in hexadecimal form at the line printer. Your inputs should be the following:

a. AL-register contains the value to be printed for a byte print; AX-register contains the value to be printed for a word print.

b. BL-register contains the print code: Zero implies byte print; nonzero implies word print.

c. DX-register contains the printer number.

The procedure should print the hexadecimal value at the specified printer beginning at the current print position.

9.6 Design and implement a procedure called PRTDEC$ to print a 16-bit integer in unsigned decimal form at the line printer. Your inputs should be the following:

a. AX-register contains the value to be printed.

b. BH-register contains the print code: BH < 0 implies that the value is to be printed left-justified in a 6-character field. BH = 0 implies that the value is to be printed with no leading or trailing blanks. BH > 0 implies that the value is to be printed right-justified in a 6-character field.

c. DX-register contains the printer number.

The procedure should print the unsigned decimal value at the specified printer beginning at the current print position.

9.7 Design and implement a procedure called PRTDEC to print a 16-bit integer in signed decimal form on the line printer. Your inputs should be the following:

a. AX-register contains the value to be printed.

b. BH-register contains the print code: BH < 0 implies that the value is to be printed left-justified in a 6-character field. BH = 0 implies that the value is to be printed with no leading or trailing blanks. BH > 0 implies that the value is to be printed right-justified in a 6-character field.

c. DX-register contains the printer number.

The procedure should print the signed decimal value at the specified printer beginning at the current print position.

9.8 The version of the GETSTRNG procedure shown in Program Listing 9.4 contains one known bug: A BACKSPACE erases a character whether or not the byte array contains a character to be erased; that is, if a BACKSPACE is the first character entered, then the next character entered is placed in the byte of memory just prior to the beginning of specified byte array and will not actually be part of the string. In fact, it may destroy some useful data in the caller's environment. Modify Program Listing 9.4 to eliminate this bug.

9.9 The program of Program Listing 9.6 locks out external interrupts and then enters a delay loop. The delay loop executes for approximately 5 minutes. After the delay loop, the program enables external interrupts. Execute this program displaying the time of day immediately before and after execution. The difference in the time of day will be only a few seconds, even

```
;
;
;                     PROGRAM LISTING 9.6
;
; S T A C K   S E G M E N T   D E F I N I T I O N
;
STACK         SEGMENT STACK
              DB      256 DUP(?)
STACK         ENDS
;
; C O D E   S E G M E N T   D E F I N I T I O N
;
CODE          SEGMENT
              ASSUME  CS:CODE,SS:STACK
LOCKOUT       PROC    FAR
              PUSH    DS                    ;PUSH RETURN SEG ADDR ON STACK
              SUB     AX,AX                 ;PUSH RETURN OFFSET OF ZERO
              PUSH    AX                    ;ON STACK
              CLI                           ;LOCKOUT INTERRUPTS
              MOV     CX,750                ;COUNT1 = 750
LOOP1:                                      ;REPEAT
              PUSH    CX                    ;    SAVE COUNT1
              MOV     CX,65535              ;    COUNT2 = 65535
LOOP2:        NOP                           ;    REPEAT
              LOOP    LOOP2                 ;        COUNT2 = COUNT2 - 1
                                            ;    UNTIL COUNT2 = 0
              POP     CX                    ;    RESTORE COUNT1
              LOOP    LOOP1                 ;    COUNT1 = COUNT1 - 1
                                            ;UNTIL COUNT1 = 0
              STI                           ;ENABLE INTERRUPTS
              RET                           ;RETURN
LOCKOUT       ENDP
CODE          ENDS
              END     LOCKOUT

A>
```

though the program was executing for approximately 5 minutes. With interrupts disabled, the periodic timer interrupt (Type 8) does not get through to the microprocessor, and BIOS does not update the time of day.

9.10 Implement a procedure called DELAY that executes for a specified number of timer interrupts. Your input should be a count in the AX-register that specifies the number of timer interrupts to delay. The procedure should repeatedly read the timer counter, decrementing the value in the AX-register each time the count changes. When the AX-register value reaches zero, the procedure should return to the caller.

9.11 Implement a procedure called DELAY that executes for a specified number of timer interrupts. Your input should be a count in the AX-register that specifies the number of timer interrupts to delay. The procedure should provide a Type 1C interrupt service procedure that decrements the AX-register value on each timer interrupt. When the AX-register value reaches zero, the procedure should restore the Type 1C interrupt vector and return control to the caller.

9.12 Modify your solution to Programming Exercise 4.2 to use a Type 4 interrupt service procedure and the INTO instruction to handle the case of arithmetic overflow.

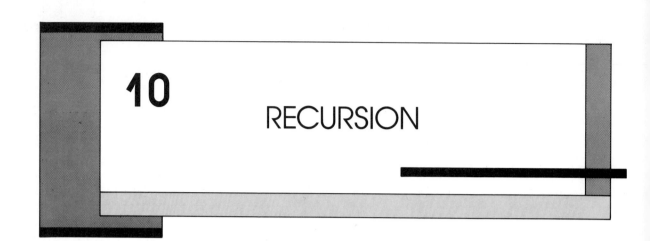

10 RECURSION

Chapter 5 presented subprocedures as a programming tool. The PUT_BIN subprocedure in Program Listing 5.3 contains a call to another subprocedure, PUTDEC, which also makes reference to other subprocedures. This chapter deals with a special kind of procedure, a recursive procedure, which is one that can call itself as a subprocedure. The chapter discusses recursion as a programming tool and shows how recursive algorithms are implemented at the machine level.

10.1 Recursive Definitions

A thing is said to be **recursive** if it partially consists of itself or is defined in terms of itself.

EXAMPLES

"A descendant of a person is a son or daughter of the person, or a descendant of a son or daughter." *Elementary Pascal* by Henry Ledgard and Andrew Singer, Science Research Associates, Inc., 1982

An arithmetic expression can be defined as (a) a variable reference by itself, (b) a constant by itself, (c) a function reference by itself, or (d) if x and y are arithmetic expressions, then so are the following: $x + y$, $x*y$, (x), $-x$, $x - y$, x/y, $x**y$, and $+x$.

In the first example, the term *descendant* is used in its definition: A son of a daughter of a daughter of a person is a descendant of that person. In the second example, (d) is the recursive portion of the definition. Part (a) says that the variables x and y are arithmetic expressions, and (b) says that the constant 2 is an arithmetic expression. The recursive portion of the definition, (d), then says that $x + y$ and $x - y$ are arithmetic expressions. It thus follows that $(x + y)$ and $(x - y)$ are arithmetic expressions, that $(x + y)**2$ and $(x - y)**2$ are arithmetic expressions, that $(x + y)**2/(x - y)**2$ is an arithmetic expression, and so on.

With recursion, an infinite set of objects can be defined using a finite statement. An infinite number of arithmetic expressions can be constructed from the definition given.

10.2 Recursive Algorithms

Recursion can often be used in algorithm design. A **recursive algorithm** is one that makes reference to itself. In this section, several recursive algorithms are considered.

Compute 2^n

Consider the trivial problem of calculating 2 to the nth power for some integer value of n:

$$2^n = 2 \times 2^{n-1} = 2^{n-1} + 2^{n-1}$$

The problem of computing 2^{n-1} and adding the result to itself can be substituted for the problem of computing 2^n, which has been restated in a form that is similar to but simpler than the original problem. Continuing in this manner, the problem can be reduced to one that is so simple that it can be solved directly. The original problem is therefore solved:

$$2^n = 2 \times 2^{n-1} = 2^{n-1} + 2^{n-1}$$
$$2^{n-1} = 2 \times 2^{n-2} = 2^{n-2} + 2^{n-2}$$
$$2^{n-2} = 2 \times 2^{n-3} = 2^{n-3} + 2^{n-3}$$
$$\cdot \qquad\qquad \cdot$$
$$\cdot \qquad\qquad \cdot$$
$$\cdot \qquad\qquad \cdot$$
$$2^3 = 2 \times 2^2 = 2^2 + 2^2$$
$$2^2 = 2 \times 2^1 = 2^1 + 2^1$$
$$2^1 = 2 \times 2^0 = 2^0 + 2^0$$

The preceding problem leads to the following recursive algorithm for computing 2^n:

```
TWO_TO_N (N):
            IF    N > 0
            THEN
                  RESULT = TWO_TO_N (N-1)
                  RESULT = RESULT + RESULT
            ELSE
                  RESULT = 1
            ENDIF
            RETURN (RESULT)
```

Fibonacci Numbers

The following sequence of numbers

$$1, 1, 2, 3, 5, 8, 13, 21, 34, 55, 89, \ldots$$

is called the **Fibonacci sequence**. The first number in the sequence is 1, the second number in the sequence is 1, and each subsequent number in the sequence is equal to the sum of the two numbers previous to it in the sequence. Consider the problem of finding the nth number in the Fibonacci sequence given a positive integer value for n. The nth Fibonacci number can be defined recursively as follows:

$$F(1) = 1$$

$$F(2) = 1$$

$$F(n) = F(n - 1) + F(n - 2) \quad \text{for } n > 2$$

This definition is captured by the following recursive algorithm:

```
FIBONACCI (N):
            IF    N ≤ 2
            THEN
                  RESULT = 1
            ELSE
                  RESULT = FIBONACCI(N-1) + FIBONACCI(N-2)
            ENDIF
            RETURN (RESULT)
```

Termination of Recursive Algorithms

Like looping constructs, recursive algorithms introduce the possibility of non-terminating computations. The basic technique for demonstrating that a repetition terminates is to define a function, $F(x)$, such that $F(x) \leq 0$ implies loop termination, and to prove that $F(x)$ decreases during each repetition of the loop. This same technique can be used to ensure termination of a recursive algorithm: Define for the recursive subprocedure a parameter, n, such that $n > 0$ implies that the subprocedure is to be called recursively with $n - 1$ as the value of the parameter, and $n \leqslant 0$ implies that no recursive call is to be made. This technique is the same as that used in both of the algorithms presented in the two previous sections.

10.3 Implementation of Recursive Algorithms

A subprocedure can be classified as nonreusable, serially reusable, reentrant, or recursive. A **nonreusable** subprocedure can be called only once in an executable program. After its first execution, it leaves itself in such a state that a subsequent execution might produce incorrect results. The MULTIPLY subprocedure in Program Listing 7.3 is an example of a nonreusable subprocedure. The procedure that was used to demonstrate the MULTIPLY subprocedure (procedure EX_7_2 of Listing 7.2) referenced MULTIPLY only once. Using EX_7_2, the subprocedure MULTIPLY consistently produces the same product when presented with the same multiplicand and multiplier. However, as pointed out in Programming Exercise 7.3, the MULTIPLY subprocedure does not produce consistent results when called more than once in a program. Using the EX_7_4 procedure from Program Listing 7.4, the MULTIPLY subprocedure might produce two different products if called twice with the same inputs.

A **serially reusable** subprocedure can be used more than once in a program as long as one execution of the subprocedure terminates before another execution of the subprocedure begins. The MULTIPLY subprocedure in Program 7.3 is nonreusable, because the flag variable SIGN is initialized as part of the data segment definition (line 22). This initialization is performed only once, just prior to execution of the program. The variable SIGN is conditionally modified during execution of MULTIPLY (lines 47 and 56). On a subsequent call to MULTIPLY, the variable SIGN may or may not be properly initialized. By moving the initialization from the data segment to the code segment, it is performed on each invocation of MULTIPLY. By changing line 22 of Program Listing 7.3 to

```
SIGN   DB   ?   ;SIGN OF PRODUCT
```

and inserting the line

```
MOV   SIGN,1   ;SIGN = +1
```

after line 44, the MULTIPLY procedure is changed from a nonreusable subprocedure to a serially reusable subprocedure.

Consider the RANDOM subprocedure in Program Listing 5.4. This subprocedure is one for which initialization is performed only once. The

FIRST_CALL flag (line 20) is initialized prior to execution of the program that contains the subprocedure. The variable SEED is initialized on the first execution of the RANDOM procedure (lines 39–45). Even though the RANDOM subprocedure does not reinitialize itself on each call, it is considered a serially reusable subprocedure. The FIRST_CALL flag is used so that an initial value for variable SEED is selected only on the first execution of RANDOM. The variable SEED is not reinitialized on subsequent executions of RANDOM, so that a new value for SEED can be computed from the value that was computed for SEED on the previous execution of RANDOM. In this case, the subprocedure is supposed to compute a potentially different result (i.e., a potentially different random integer) on each execution.

A **reentrant** subprocedure is one that does not modify itself. The important characteristic of reentrant procedures is that multiple instances of one procedure can be executing at the same time without having multiple copies of the subprocedure. This type of subprocedure is important in large, time-shared computer systems. With such systems, multiple users have simultaneous access to the same software resources: they can be using the text editor or the Pascal compiler simultaneously, for example. Having multiple copies of the text editor or the Pascal compiler (one per user) would consume too much storage space—instead, each user shares a common copy. As long as this common copy is reentrant, then one user has no effect on other users of the common copy. However, each instance of the text editor must be able to edit a different text file, and each instance of the compiler must be able to compile a different source code file. This task is accomplished by dividing the shared program into two parts: a fixed part (code and nonchanging data) and a changeable part (changing data). The fixed portion is reentrant, and a single copy of it is shared by all instances of the procedure. The changeable portion is called an **activation record**, and each instance of the procedure must have its own separate activation record. The activation record contains the information that makes one instance of the shared procedure different from other instances of the shared procedure. For a compiler, the activation record might include the following information:

> The information needed to return control to the operating system (i.e., the return address)
> The name of the file that contains the source code being compiled (i.e., an input argument)
> The mass storage address of the file that contains the source code
> The compile options selected (i.e., input arguments)
> The name of the file to receive the object code (i.e., an input argument)
> The mass storage address of the object code file

The operating system tracks each instance of execution of a shared procedure by a set of **state variables** (one state variable for each instance) (Figure 10.1). The state variable for a given instance contains two pointers: a code pointer (CP) and a data pointer (DP). The **code pointer** is the address within the fixed part of the next instruction to be executed for this instance of the shared procedure. The **data pointer** is the base address of the activation record

FIGURE 10.1
Reentrant
procedure with
three instances

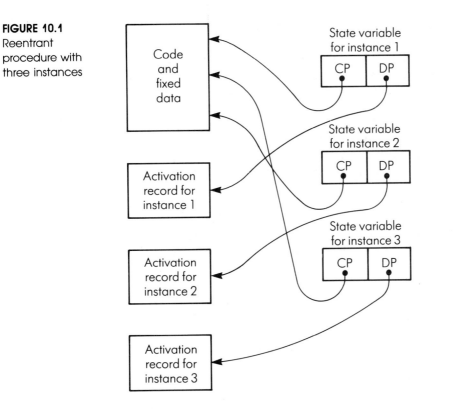

for this instance of execution of the shared procedure. As long as the fixed portion is reentrant (i.e., does not modify itself), the execution of one instance has no effect on other instances.

The MULTIPLY procedure in Program Listing 7.3, even with the corrections specified in Programming Exercise 7.3, is not a reentrant procedure. It modifies itself by changing the variables in the data segment (e.g., the variable SIGN). Multiple instances of the MULTIPLY procedure could not be allowed, because the variables would need to be maintained separately for different instances. Programming Exercise 10.11 at the end of the chapter deals with a method for changing MULTIPLY into a reentrant procedure.

A recursive subprocedure is one that creates multiple instances of itself by calling itself. A procedure, A, is said to contain a **direct reference** to procedure B if it contains an explicit call to procedure B. A procedure, A, is said to contain an **indirect reference** to procedure B if a procedure, X, exists such that procedure A contains a direct reference to procedure X, and procedure X contains a direct or indirect reference to procedure B. A subprocedure is said to be **directly recursive** if it contains an explicit call to itself. A subprocedure is said to be **indirectly recursive** if it contains a direct reference to some other procedure that contains a direct or indirect reference to the first procedure. Note that recursion was used in the definitions of indirect reference and indirectly recursive.

Tools for Implementing Recursive Algorithms

Recursive subprocedures are generally implemented as reentrant subprocedures. The items that are different from one invocation of a subprocedure to another include the return address, the arguments passed to the subprocedure, the registers saved for the caller, and local variables used by the subprocedure. These items must be part of the activation record for a reentrant procedure. It is easy to implement a reentrant procedure on a machine that provides a stack: The activation record for a given instance of the procedure can be pushed onto the stack at the beginning of the procedure and popped off at the point of return from the procedure.

In execution of a sequential program, the life span of an instance of execution of one subprocedure cannot overlap the life span of an instance of execution of another subprocedure. That is, the life span of an instance of a subprocedure must be completely contained within the life span of its caller. For example, if the main procedure calls subprocedure A, which in turn calls subprocedure B, then B must return to A before A can return to the main procedure. This sequence must be true for recursive subprocedures as well: If the main procedure calls subprocedure A and subprocedure A calls itself recursively, then the recursive instance of A must return to the original instance of A before the original instance of A can return to the main procedure. This last-called-first-to-return nature of subprocedures coincides with the last-in-first-out (LIFO) nature of the stack (Figure 10.2). The activation record for an instance of the recursive subprocedure is pushed onto the stack as that instance begins execution. The activation record at the top of the stack always corresponds to the latest instance of the subprocedure, the one that has execution control of the processor. This instance is the **active instance**, since it is the one that is actually executing instructions in the recursive procedure. As the active instance of the subprocedure returns to its caller, its activation record is popped from the stack. If the caller is a previous instance of the same subprocedure, then the activation record for that instance (the now active instance) is once again at the top of the stack.

The subprocedure and the stack are the two tools sufficient to implement recursive algorithms. The subprocedure allows a block of instructions to be given a name by which it can be invoked. The stack allows data storage to be allocated and deallocated dynamically, which means that there can be more than one instance of a procedure currently in a state of execution and that each such instance can have its own private set of local objects (i.e., its own activation record). Each instance has its own return address (to a previous instance or to the original caller), its own set of arguments, its own set of saved registers for its caller, and its own set of local variables.

The maximum number of instances of a recursive subprocedure that occur at one time during execution of an executable program containing that subprocedure is called the **depth of recursion**. Obviously, to ensure termination, the depth of recursion must be finite, and to be practical, it must not only be

FIGURE 10.2
Relationship of activation records on the stack to instances of a recursive subprocedure

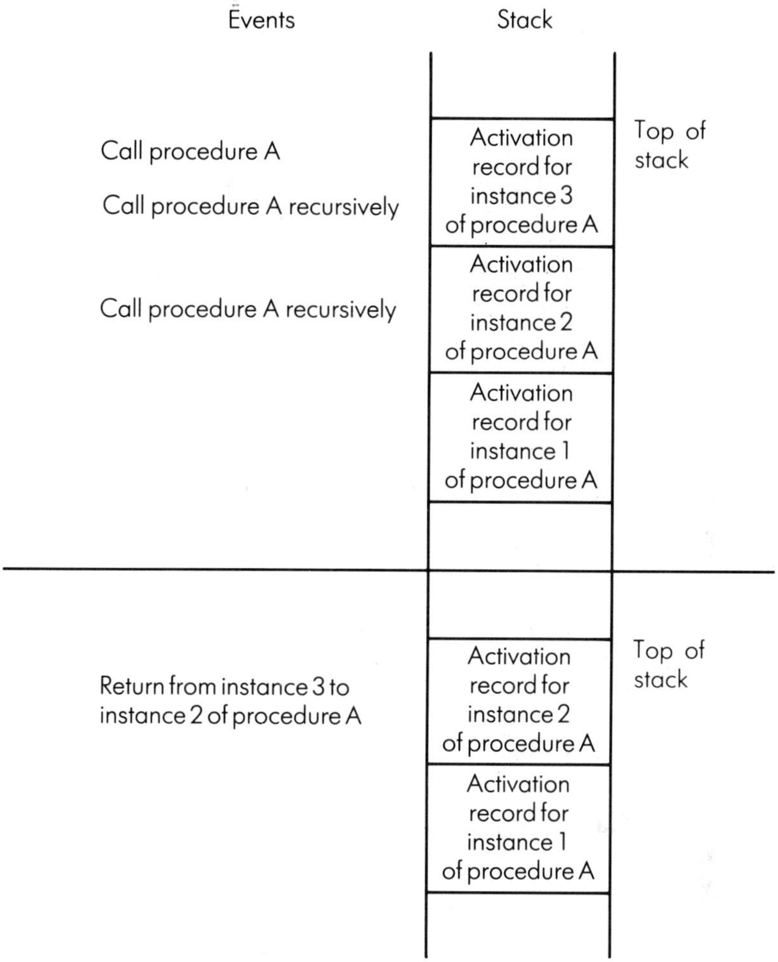

Events	Stack	
Call procedure A	Activation record for instance 3 of procedure A	Top of stack
Call procedure A recursively		
Call procedure A recursively	Activation record for instance 2 of procedure A	
	Activation record for instance 1 of procedure A	
Return from instance 3 to instance 2 of procedure A	Activation record for instance 2 of procedure A	Top of stack
	Activation record for instance 1 of procedure A	

finite, it must also be small. On each invocation of a recursive procedure, some amount of dynamic storage is required for the activation record. The amount of storage space consumed and the execution time needed to allocate and deallocate dynamic storage space can be significant with a large depth of recursion. It can be even more significant when indirect recursion is involved.

Passing Parameters via the Stack

As mentioned in Chapter 5 and discussed in Section 8.4, parameters can be passed to a subprocedure via the stack. The caller pushes the arguments onto the stack just prior to calling the subprocedure, which uses the BP-register as a pointer into the stack and addresses the arguments relative to that pointer. As part of procedure return, the subprocedure pops the arguments from the stack and discards them. Since the return address for the caller is on the stack above the arguments, the popping of the arguments from the stack must be done as part of the return. Recall that the RET instruction has the following general form:

[⟨*label*⟩] RET [⟨*pop-value*⟩]   [⟨*comment*⟩]

The ⟨*pop-value*⟩ is an immediate operand that specifies the value that is to be added to the SP-register after the return address is popped from the stack and before the return to the caller is performed. That is, ⟨*pop-value*⟩ is the number of argument bytes to be popped from the stack and discarded.

An example parameter passing procedure was discussed in Section 8.4. The state of the stack segment must be the same just prior to return from a sub-procedure as it was on entry to the subprocedure. In the case of the example in Section 8.4, the state of the stack just prior to return from SUBPROC should be the same as that shown in Figure 8.15. This state is also shown in Figure 10.3, and it was produced by the following calling sequence:

```
PUSH ⟨arg 1⟩
PUSH ⟨arg 2⟩
CALL SUBPROC
```

To return from SUBPROC and discard the arguments, the instruction

```
RET 4
```

is used. This return instruction pops the return address from the stack and adds 4 to the SP-register, which, in effect, pops and discards two additional words from the stack—the arguments.

Programming Example—Compute Fibonacci Numbers

Program Listing 10.1 shows an implementation of the recursive algorithm to compute the *n*th number in the Fibonacci sequence. The program consists of a main procedure and a recursive subprocedure. The main procedure prompts the user for a value for *n* and accepts the input value from the keyboard. It calls the subprocedure, FIBONACCI, to compute the *n*th Fibonacci number and displays the result. The FIBONACCI subprocedure implements the recursive algorithm in Section 10.2.

FIGURE 10.3
Stack prior to return from SUBPROC

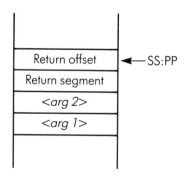

| Return offset | ◄—SS:PP |
| Return segment |
| ⟨arg 2⟩ |
| ⟨arg 1⟩ |

```
 1: ;                      PROGRAM LISTING 10.1
 2: ;
 3: ; PROGRAM TO COMPUTE FIBONACCI NUMBERS
 4: ;
 5:                                           ;PROCEDURES TO
 6:            EXTRN    GETDEC$:FAR           ;GET UNSIGNED DECIMAL INTEGER
 7:            EXTRN    NEWLINE:FAR           ;DISPLAY NEWLINE CHARACTER
 8:            EXTRN    PUTDEC$:FAR           ;DISPLAY UNSIGNED DEC INTEGER
 9:            EXTRN    PUTSTRNG:FAR          ;DISPLAY CHARACTER STRING
10: ;
11: ; S T A C K   S E G M E N T   D E F I N I T I O N
12: ;
13: STACK      SEGMENT STACK
14:            DB       10000  DUP(?)
15: STACK      ENDS
16: ;
17: ; E X T R A   S E G M E N T   D E F I N I T I O N
18: ;
19: EXTRA      SEGMENT
20: ;
21: PROMPT     DB       'COMPUTE N-TH FIBONACCI NUMBER',0DH,0AH
22:            DB       'ENTER VALUR FOR N',0DH,0AH
23: ANNOTATE   DB       'FIBONACCI NUMBER = '
24: ;
25: EXTRA      ENDS
26: ;
27: ; C O D E   S E G M E N T   D E F I N I T I O N
28: ;
29: CODE       SEGMENT
30:            ASSUME   CS:CODE,SS:STACK,ES:EXTRA
31: EX_10_1    PROC     FAR
32:            PUSH     DS                    ;PUSH RETURN SEG ADDR ON STACK
33:            SUB      AX,AX                 ;PUSH RETURN OFFSET
34:            PUSH     AX                    ;OF ZERO ON STACK
35:            MOV      AX,SEG EXTRA          ;SET ES-REGISTER TO
36:            MOV      ES,AX                 ;POINT TO EXTRA SEGMENT
37: ;
38:            LEA      DI,PROMPT             ;PROMPT FOR N
39:            MOV      CX,50
40:            CALL     PUTSTRNG
41:            CALL     GETDEC$               ;GET N
42:            PUSH     AX
43:            CALL     FIBONACCI             ;COMPUTE FIBONACCI(N)
44:            LEA      DI,ANNOTATE
45:            MOV      CX,19
46:            CALL     PUTSTRNG
47:            MOV      BH,0
48:            CALL     PUTDEC$               ;DISPLAY N-TH FIBONACCI NUMBER
49:            CALL     NEWLINE
50:            RET                            ;RETURN
51: EX_10_1    ENDP
52:*;
53: ;
54: ; RECURSIVE SUBROUTINE TO COMPUTE N-TH FIBONACCI NUMBER
55: ; GIVEN A VALUE FOR N. N-TH FIBONACCI NUMBER IS DEFINED
56: ; RECURSIVELY AS FOLLOWS:
57: ;                    F(1) = 1
58: ;                    F(2) = 1
59: ;                    F(N) = F(N-2) + F(N-1)   FOR N > 2
```

```
60: ; CALLING SEQUENCE
61: ;         PUSH    <N>
62: ;         CALL    FIBONACCI
63: ;
64: ; THE RESULT IS RETURNED IN THE AX REGISTER
65: ;
66: FIBONACCI  PROC    NEAR                ;FUNCTION FIBONACCI(N)
67:            PUSH    BP                    ;SAVE REGISTERS
68:            MOV     BP,SP                 ;INITIALIZE ARGUMENT POINTER
69:            CMP     WORD PTR [BP+4],2   ;IF    N <= 2
70:            JG      NGTONE
71:            MOV     AX,1                ;THEN RESULT = 1
72:            JMP     RETURN
73: NGTONE:                                ;ELSE
74:            DEC     WORD PTR [BP+4]
75:            PUSH    [BP+4]
76:            CALL    FIBONACCI
77:            PUSH    AX                  ;      TEMP = FIBONACCI(N-1)
78:            DEC     WORD PTR [BP+4]
79:            PUSH    [BP+4]
80:            CALL    FIBONACCI
81:            POP     BX                  ;      RESULT = TEMP
82:            ADD     AX,BX               ;              + FIBONACCI(N-2)
83: RETURN:                                ;ENDIF
84:            POP     BP                  ;RESTORE REGISTERS
85:            RET     2                   ;POP ARGUMENTS
86: ;                                       ;RETURN (RESULT)
87: FIBONACCI  ENDP                        ;END FIBONACCI
88: CODE       ENDS
89:*          END     EX_10_1
```

The program's stack segment is defined in lines 13–15. It has been defined as quite large, because recursive algorithms tend to require a large stack. Although, this size is an overkill, because the depth of recursion for this algorithm is not that large. The actual needs of the stack are analyzed later in this section.

The main program (lines 1–51) is rather straightforward and, for the most part, is not discussed here. The portion of the main program that is of interest in this discussion of recursion is the subprocedure interface, lines 41–43. The call to the GETDEC$ procedure in line 41 accepts the positive integer value for n into the AX-register. Lines 42 and 43 contain the calling sequence for the recursive procedure. The instruction in line 42 pushes the argument, the value of n, onto the stack. In line 43, the call is made to the recursive procedure, FIBONACCI. On return, the nth Fibonacci number will be in the AX-register. Figure 10.4 describes the state of the stack segment just prior to execution of the CALL instruction in line 43. It assumes an input value of 4, as do all subsequent figures in this section.

The recursive procedure, FIBONACCI, is defined in lines 52–87. Lines 54–65 contain the procedure's prologue, which explains the procedure's function. It also gives the calling sequence for the procedure and specifies how the value of the function is to be returned to the caller. The calling sequence is explicitly shown, because the stack is being used to pass the arguments to the

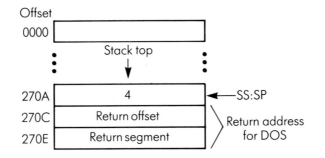

procedure. This explanation is especially useful when more than one argument is being passed via the stack, because it explicitly shows the order in which the arguments must be pushed onto the stack.

Line 66 defines the recursive procedure FIBONACCI as a NEAR procedure, which means that only the offset of the return address is pushed onto the stack by execution of the CALL instruction. Figure 10.5 shows the state of the stack segment just after invocation of the FIBONACCI procedure and just before execution of the PUSH instruction in line 67. For ease in hand-tracing the program, the return address offset is shown as a line number and a procedure name; it identifies the position within Program Listing 10.1 of the instruction that follows the CALL instruction.

The instructions in lines 67 and 68 save the value in the BP-register for the caller and set it up to point to the beginning of the stack segment block that contains the local objects for the current instance of the FIBONACCI procedure. Figure 10.6 shows the state of the stack segment following execution of these two instructions. Note that the figure shows the word in the stack segment that is pointed to by the SS:SP register pair as well as the word that is pointed to by the SS:BP register pair. The SS:SP register pair always points to the current top-of-stack entry. The SS:BP register pair is used to point to the beginning of the stack segment block that contains the set of local objects (i.e., the activation record) for the active instance of FIBONACCI.

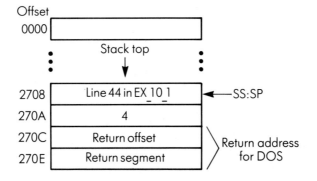

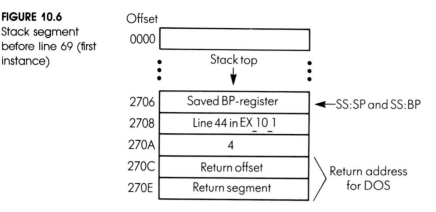

The activation record for the active instance of the FIBONACCI procedure contains the following three items:

1. The saved BP-register (at offset 2706 within the stack segment)
2. The return address offset (at offset 2708)
3. The input argument (at offset 270A)

Since the BP-register was set to point to the beginning of this block, the address expression for referencing the input argument is SS:[BP + 4]. Since the SS-register is the default segment register for the BP-register, the SS: can be omitted; thus, the address expression becomes [BP + 4].

The instructions in lines 69 and 70 test the input argument to see if it is less than or equal to 2. If the CMP instruction in line 69 had been written as

CMP [BP + 4],2

then the assembler would generate the error message

```
E r r o r --- 35:Operand must have size
```

The reason for the error is that the assembler does not know the type attribute of the two operands. The address expression [BP + 4] could specify the address of either a byte operand or a word operand. The type attribute of the immediate value 2 is automatically chosen by the assembler to be the same as the type attribute of the destination operand. Therefore, the assembler must be supplied with the type attribute of the destination operand. The two operators WORD and PTR that precede the address expression inform the assembler that the address expression is a PoinTeR to a WORD operand. In this case, the input argument is greater than 2, so the instruction in line 70 causes a jump to the instruction with label NGTONE (lines 73 and 74).

The instructions in lines 74–76 carry out the first recursive call to the FIBONACCI procedure. The instruction in line 74 decrements the value of the input argument from 4 to 3, and the instruction in line 75 pushes that value onto the stack as the argument for the recursive call to FIBONACCI. Figure 10.7

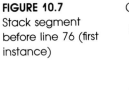

FIGURE 10.7
Stack segment before line 76 (first instance)

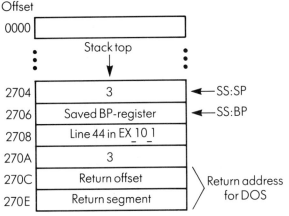

Offset

0000		

Stack top

2704	3	←SS:SP
2706	Saved BP-register	←SS:BP
2708	Line 44 in EX_10_1	
270A	3	
270C	Return offset	} Return address
270E	Return segment	for DOS

shows the state of the stack segment just prior to execution of the CALL instruction in line 76.

The recursive call to FIBONACCI in line 76 causes the offset of the return address (the offset of line 77 in FIBONACCI) to be pushed onto the stack and the FIBONACCI procedure to be entered for the second time. On entry to the procedure, the value in the BP-register is saved for the caller (line 67) and is set up to point to the beginning of the stack segment block that contains the activation record for this second instance of FIBONACCI (line 68). Figure 10.8 shows the state of the stack segment just prior to execution of line 69 in the second instance of the FIBONACCI procedure. Note that there are two activation records on the stack for FIBONACCI: the one pointed to by the SS:BP register pair and the one pointed to by the saved BP-register (SS:2706). The activation record currently in use is *always* the one at the top of the stack.

FIGURE 10.8
Stack segment before line 69 (second instance)

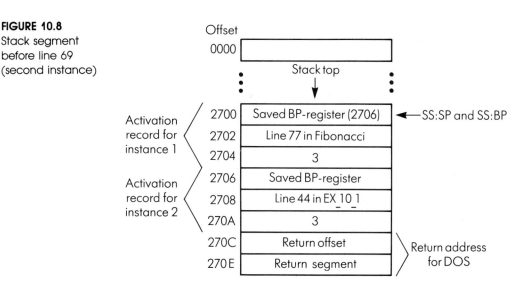

Offset

0000		

Stack top

Activation record for instance 1	2700	Saved BP-register (2706)	←SS:SP and SS:BP
	2702	Line 77 in Fibonacci	
	2704	3	
Activation record for instance 2	2706	Saved BP-register	
	2708	Line 44 in EX_10_1	
	270A	3	
	270C	Return offset	} Return address
	270E	Return segment	for DOS

FIGURE 10.9
Stack segment
before line 76
(second instance)

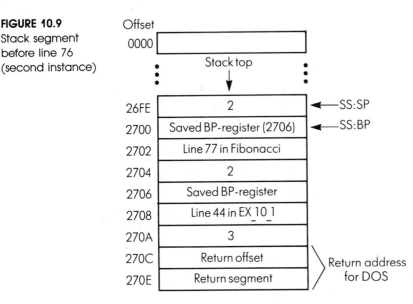

The value of the input argument for the second instance (3) is greater than 2 (lines 69 and 70), so the jump is made to the instruction in lines 73 and 74. The instruction in line 74 decrements the value of the input argument from 3 to 2, and the instruction in line 75 pushes that value onto the stack as the argument for the next recursive call to FIBONACCI. Figure 10.9 shows the state of the stack segment just prior to execution of the CALL instruction in line 76.

The recursive call to FIBONACCI in line 76 causes the offset of the return address (the offset of line 77 in FIBONACCI) to be pushed onto the stack and the procedure FIBONACCI to be entered for the third time. On entry to the procedure, the value in the BP-register is saved for the caller (line 67) and is set to point to the beginning of the stack segment block that contains the activation record for the third instance of FIBONACCI (line 68). Figure 10.10 shows the state of the stack segment just prior to execution of line 69 in the third invocation of FIBONACCI.

Note that there are now three activation records on the stack for the FIBONACCI procedure. The one at the top of the stack is the one currently in use. The saved BP-register in each activation record is a partial pointer to the activation record for the previous instance (the caller). It is a partial pointer because it must be combined with the value in the stack segment register to become a complete pointer.

The value of the input argument for the third instance (2) is not greater than 2 (line 69 and 70), so the jump in line 70 is not taken, and the instruction in line 71 is executed. This instruction moves 1, the value of F(2), into the AX-register. The instruction in line 72 causes an unconditional jump to the instruction with label RETURN (lines 83 and 84). The instruction in line 84 restores the BP-register in preparation for a return to the caller, the second

FIGURE 10.10
Stack segment before line 69 (third instance)

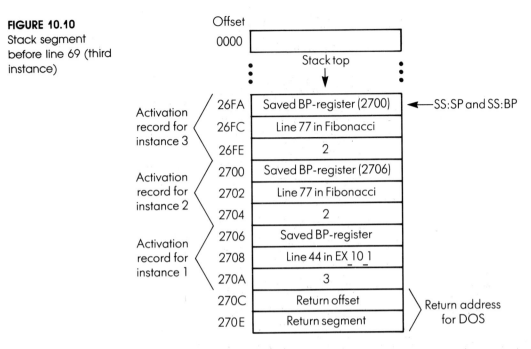

instance of FIBONACCI. The SS:BP register pair again points to the activation record for the second instance of FIBONACCI. Figure 10.11 shows the state of the stack segment just prior to execution of the RET instruction (line 85) in the third instance of FIBONACCI. The value in the AX-register at this point is 1, the value of F(2).

FIGURE 10.11
Stack segment before line 85 (third instance)

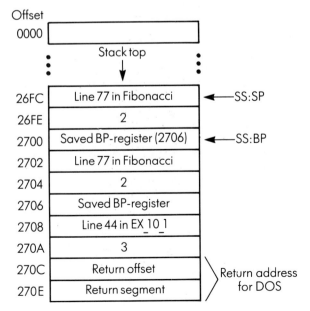

Execution of the RET instruction in line 85 causes the following sequence of events:

1.   The offset of the return address (the offset of line 77 in FIBONACCI) is popped from the stack.
2.   The value 2 is added to the SP-register, which, in effect, pops and discards the input argument from the stack.
3.   A transfer of control is made to the instruction in line 77 in the previous instance of FIBONACCI with the output value (F(2) = 1) in the AX-register.

Figure 10.12 shows the state of the stack segment just prior to execution of the instruction in line 77 in the second instance of FIBONACCI.

The instruction in line 77 pushes the result returned from the third instance of FIBONACCI (F(2) = 1) onto the stack. This value is saved so that it can be added to the result of the next recursive call to FIBONACCI, which produces the result of this, the second, instance of FIBONACCI. The instruction in line 78 decrements the input argument from 2 to 1, and the instruction in line 79 pushes that value onto the stack as the argument for the next recursive call to the FIBONACCI procedure. Figure 10.13 shows the state of the stack segment just prior to execution of the CALL instruction in line 80. The value at offset 26FE in the stack is the saved value of F(2), and the value at offset 26FC is the argument for the next recursive call to FIBONACCI.

The recursive call to FIBONACCI in line 80 causes the offset of the return address (the offset of line 81 in FIBONACCI) to be pushed onto the stack and the FIBONACCI procedure to be entered for the fourth time. On entry to the procedure, the value in the BP-register is saved for the caller (line 67) and is set to point to the beginning of the stack segment block that contains the activation record for this fourth instance of FIBONACCI (line 68). Figure 10.14 shows the

FIGURE 10.12
Stack segment
before line 77
(second instance)

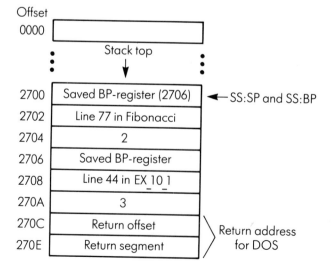

FIGURE 10.13
Stack segment
before line 80
(second instance)

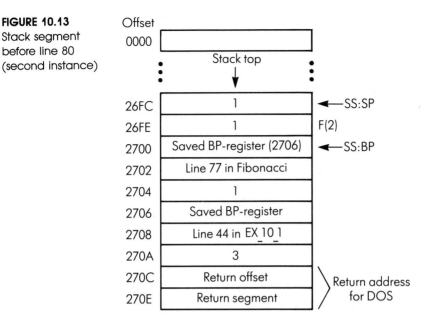

Offset
0000

Stack top

26FC	1	←—SS:SP
26FE	1	F(2)
2700	Saved BP-register (2706)	←—SS:BP
2702	Line 77 in Fibonacci	
2704	1	
2706	Saved BP-register	
2708	Line 44 in EX_10_1	
270A	3	
270C	Return offset	} Return address
270E	Return segment	for DOS

FIGURE 10.14
Stack segment
before line 69
(fourth instance)

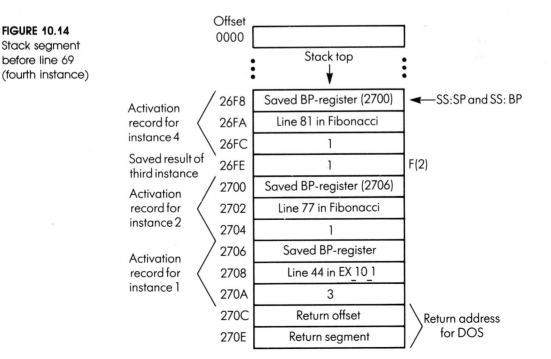

Offset
0000

Stack top

Activation record for instance 4	26F8	Saved BP-register (2700)	←—SS:SP and SS: BP
	26FA	Line 81 in Fibonacci	
	26FC	1	
Saved result of third instance	26FE	1	F(2)
Activation record for instance 2	2700	Saved BP-register (2706)	
	2702	Line 77 in Fibonacci	
	2704	1	
Activation record for instance 1	2706	Saved BP-register	
	2708	Line 44 in EX_10_1	
	270A	3	
	270C	Return offset	} Return address
	270E	Return segment	for DOS

state of the stack segment just prior to execution of the instruction in line 69 in the fourth instance of FIBONACCI. Note again that there are three activation records on the stack for the procedure FIBONACCI, one for each existing instance.

The value of the input argument for the fourth instance (1) is not greater than 2 (lines 69 and 70), so the jump in line 70 is not taken, and the instruction in line 71 is executed. This instruction moves 1, the value of F(1), into the AX-register. The instruction in line 72 causes an unconditional jump to the instruction with label RETURN (lines 83 and 84). The instruction in line 84 restores the BP-register in preparation for a return to the caller, the second instance of FIBONACCI. The SS:BP register pair again points to the activation record for the second instance of FIBONACCI. Figure 10.15 shows the state of the stack segment just prior to execution of the RET instruction (line 85) in the fourth instance of FIBONACCI. The value in the AX-register at this point is 1, the value of F(1).

Execution of the RET instruction in line 85 causes the following sequence of events:

1. The offset of the return address (the offset of line 81 in FIBONACCI) is popped from the stack.
2. The value 2 is added to the SP-register, which, in effect, pops and discards the input argument from the stack.
3. A transfer of control is made to the instruction in line 81 in the previous (second) instance of FIBONACCI with the output value (F(1) − 1) in the AX-register.

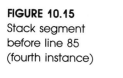

FIGURE 10.15
Stack segment before line 85 (fourth instance)

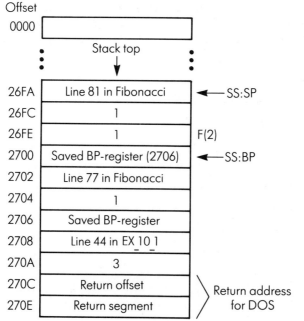

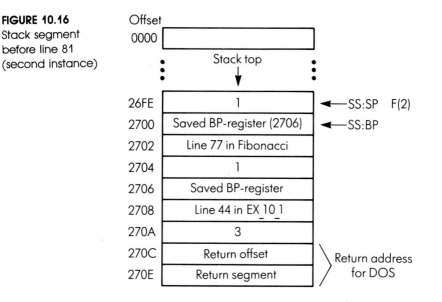

FIGURE 10.16
Stack segment
before line 81
(second instance)

Offset

0000	
	Stack top
26FE	1	←SS:SP F(2)
2700	Saved BP-register (2706)	←SS:BP
2702	Line 77 in Fibonacci
2704	1
2706	Saved BP-register
2708	Line 44 in EX_10_1
270A	3
270C	Return offset	Return address for DOS
270E	Return segment

Figure 10.16 shows the state of the stack segment just prior to execution of the instruction in line 81 in the second instance of FIBONACCI. At this point, the value of F(1) is in the AX-register, and the value of F(2) is at the top of the stack.

Execution of the POP instruction in line 81 places the value of F(2) in the BX-register. The instruction in line 82 adds the value of F(2) to the value of F(1) in the AX-register, producing the value of F(3). The instruction in line 84 restores the BP-register in preparation for a return to the caller, the first instance of FIBONACCI. The SS:BP register pair again points to the activation record for the first instance of FIBONACCI. Figure 10.17 shows the state of the stack

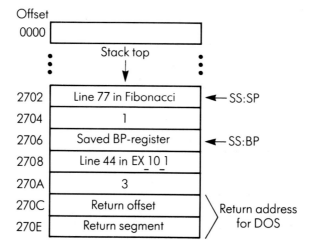

FIGURE 10.17
Stack segment
before line 85
(second instance)

Offset

0000	
	Stack top
2702	Line 77 in Fibonacci	←SS:SP
2704	1
2706	Saved BP-register	←SS:BP
2708	Line 44 in EX_10_1
270A	3
270C	Return offset	Return address for DOS
270E	Return segment

segment just prior to execution of the RET instruction (line 85) in the second instance of FIBONACCI. The value in the AX-register at this point is 2, the value of F(3).

Execution of the RET instruction in line 85 causes the return address offset (the offset of line 77 in FIBONACCI) to be popped from the stack, the input argument to be popped and discarded from the stack, and a transfer of control to be made to line 77 in the previous (first) instance of FIBONACCI. The value of F(3) is in the AX-register. Figure 10.18 shows the state of the stack segment just prior to execution of the instruction in line 77 in the first instance of FIBONACCI.

The instruction in line 77 pushes the result returned from the second invocation of FIBONACCI (F(3) = 2) onto the stack. Again, this value is saved so that it can be added to the result of the next recursive call to FIBONACCI, which produces the result of this, the original, instance of FIBONACCI. The instruction in line 78 decrements the input argument from 3 to 2, and the instruction in line 79 pushes that value onto the stack as the argument for the next recursive call to FIBONACCI. Figure 10.19 shows the state of the stack segment just prior to execution of the CALL instruction in line 80. The value at offset 2704 in the stack is the saved value of F(3), and the value at offset 2702 is the argument for the next recursive call to FIBONACCI.

The recursive call to FIBONACCI in line 80 causes the offset of the return address (the offset of line 81 in FIBONACCI) to be pushed onto the stack and the FIBONACCI procedure to be entered for the fifth time. On entry to the procedure, the value in the BP-register is saved for the caller (line 67) and is set to point to the beginning of the stack segment block that contains the activation record for the fifth instance of FIBONACCI (line 68). Figure 10.20 shows the state of the stack segment just prior to execution of the instruction in line 69 in the fifth instance of FIBONACCI.

The value of the input argument for the fifth instance (2) is not greater than 2 (lines 69 and 70), so the jump in line 70 is not taken, and the instruction in line 71 is executed. This instruction moves 1, the value of F(2), into the AX-register.

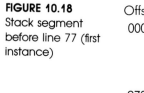

FIGURE 10.18
Stack segment before line 77 (first instance)

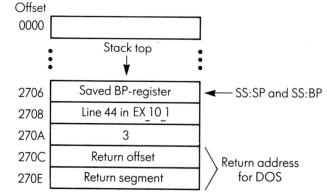

FIGURE 10.19
Stack segment
before line 80 (first
instance)

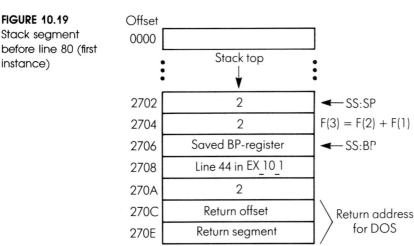

The instruction in line 72 causes an unconditional jump to the instruction with label RETURN (lines 83 and 84). The instruction in line 84 restores the BP-register in preparation for a return to the caller, the first instance of FIBONACCI. The SS:BP register pair again points to the activation record for the first instance of FIBONACCI. Figure 10.21 shows the state of the stack segment just prior to execution of the RET instruction (line 85) in the fifth instance of FIBONACCI. The value in the AX-register at this point is 1, the value of F(2).

Execution of the RET instruction in line 85 causes the return address offset (the offset of line 81 in FIBONACCI) to be popped from the stack, the input

FIGURE 10.20
Stack segment
before line 69 (fifth
instance)

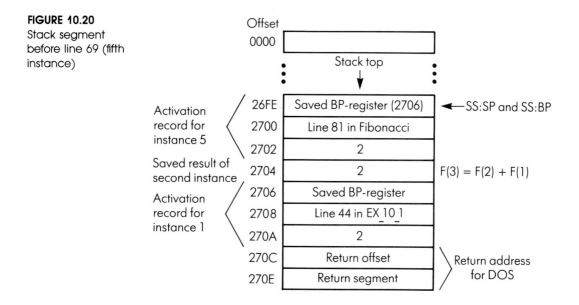

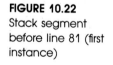

FIGURE 10.21
Stack segment
before line 85 (fifth
instance)

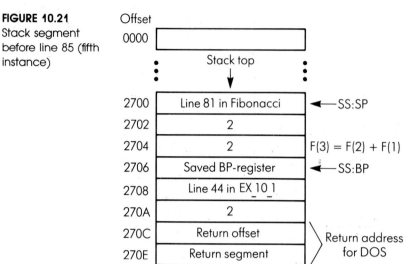

Offset

0000		

Stack top

2700	Line 81 in Fibonacci	◄—SS:SP
2702	2	
2704	2	F(3) = F(2) + F(1)
2706	Saved BP-register	◄—SS:BP
2708	Line 44 in EX_10_1	
270A	2	
270C	Return offset	} Return address
270E	Return segment	for DOS

argument to be popped from the stack and discarded, and a transfer of control to be made to line 81 in the previous (first) instance of FIBONACCI. Figure 10.22 shows the state of the stack segment just prior to execution of the instruction in line 81 in the original instance of FIBONACCI. At this point, the value of F(2) is in the AX-register, and the value of F(3) is at the top of the stack.

The instruction in line 81 pops the value of F(3) from the stack, and the instruction in line 82 adds this value to the value of F(2) in the AX-register, producing the value of F(4). The value of F(4) is the value requested by the original caller, the EX_10_1 procedure. The instruction in line 84 restores the BP-register for the caller (the main procedure), and the instruction in line 85 returns control to the instruction in line 44 in EX_10_1 with the output value (F(4) = 3) in the AX-register. The argument is popped from the stack as part of the return.

FIGURE 10.22
Stack segment
before line 81 (first
instance)

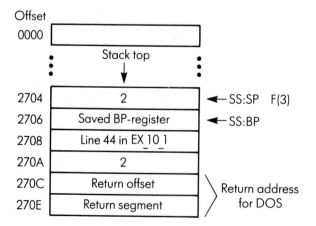

Offset

0000		

Stack top

2704	2	◄—SS:SP F(3)
2706	Saved BP-register	◄—SS:BP
2708	Line 44 in EX_10_1	
270A	2	
270C	Return offset	} Return address
270E	Return segment	for DOS

The following results are from some executions of this program:

```
COMPUTE N-TH FIBONACCI NUMBER
ENTER VALUE FOR N
4
FIBONACCI = 3

COMPUTE N-TH FIBONACCI NUMBER
ENTER VALUE FOR N
12
FIBONACCI = 144

COMPUTE N-TH FIBONACCI NUMBER
ENTER VALUE FOR N
22
FIBONACCI = 17711

COMPUTE N-TH FIBONACCI NUMBER
ENTER VALUE FOR N
23
FIBONACCI = 28657

COMPUTE N-TH FIBONACCI NUMBER
ENTER VALUE FOR N
24
FIBONACCI = 46368
```

Note that $n = 24$ is the largest input value that can be accommodated by this program without overflow. The twenty-fifth FIBONACCI number is

$$F(25) = F(24) + F(23) = 46,368 + 28,657 = 75,025$$

This number is greater than 65,535, the upper limit for 16-bit unsigned integers. Therefore, an input of $n = 25$ would create an arithmetic overflow in the computation. The program as it appears does nothing to detect arithmetic overflow.

The graph in Figure 10.23 is a binary tree that shows the hierarchy of recursive calls to the FIBONACCI procedure in the example execution that was

FIGURE 10.23

Tree of recursive calls in computing F(4)

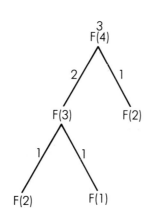

traced in Figures 10.4–10.22. The graph nodes are labeled with the function that is being performed by an invocation of FIBONACCI. The edges are labeled with the value being returned from an invocation back up to its caller. The order of call is that of a **preorder traversal** of the tree, which can be defined recursively by performing the following steps in sequence:

1.   Visit the root of the tree.
2.   Perform a preorder traversal of the left subtree.
3.   Perform a preorder traversal of the right subtree.

For the tree in Figure 10.23, a preorder traversal produces the following sequence of function calls: F(4), F(3), F(2), F(1), and F(2).

From the figure it can be seen that the depth of recursion for this example execution was 3. That depth was reached twice, on the third and fourth invocations (Figures 10.10 and 10.14). Program Listing 10.2 shows the same program with some modifications to compute and display the depth of recursion. A new annotation message appears in line 24, which is used to label the display of the depth of recursion. Two variables have been added in lines 25 and 26. DEPTH is used to track the current level of recursion. It is incremented on each entry to the FIBONACCI procedure (line 77), and it is decremented on each exit from FIBONACCI (line 98). That is, it counts the number of currently existing instances of FIBONACCI. Whenever the value of DEPTH becomes greater than the value of MAX_DEPTH, MAX_DEPTH is set to the current value of DEPTH (lines 93–96). Both DEPTH and MAX_DEPTH are initialized to 0 (lines 25 and 26). On return to the main program from FIBONACCI, MAX_DEPTH contains the true depth of recursion. The instructions in lines 53–57 display the value of MAX_DEPTH. The following results are from some executions of this version of the program:

```
COMPUTE N-TH FIBONACCI NUMBER
ENTER VALUE FOR N
4
FIBONACCI NUMBER = 3
DEPTH OF RECURSION = 3

COMPUTE N-TH FIBONACCI NUMBER
ENTER VALUE FOR N
12
FIBONACCI NUMBER = 144
DEPTH OF RECURSION = 11

COMPUTE N-TH FIBONACCI NUMBER
ENTER VALUE FOR N
22
FIBONACCI NUMBER = 17711
DEPTH OF RECURSION = 21

COMPUTE N-TH FIBONACCI NUMBER
ENTER VALUE FOR N
23
FIBONACCI NUMBER = 28657
DEPTH OF RECURSION = 22
```

```
COMPUTE N-TH FIBONACCI NUMBER
ENTER VALUE FOR N
24
FIBONACCI NUMBER = 46368
DEPTH OF RECURSION = 23
```

From these results and from drawing some graphs like the one in Figure 10.23, you can become convinced that the depth of recursion for computing $F(n)$, in which $n > 1$, is $n - 1$. You already have seen that the maximum value for n is 24. On each recursive call, a block of three local objects is pushed onto the stack, although a fourth value may be pushed onto the stack just prior to the call (line 77 in Program Listing 10.1). Therefore, each call causes a maximum of four

```
 1: ;                      PROGRAM LISTING 10.2
 2: ;
 3: ; PROGRAM TO COMPUTE FIBONACCI NUMBERS
 4: ;
 5:                                        ;PROCEDURES TO
 6:              EXTRN   GETDEC$:FAR        ;GET UNSIGNED DECIMAL INTEGER
 7:              EXTRN   NEWLINE:FAR        ;DISPLAY NEWLINE CHARACTER
 8:              EXTRN   PUTDEC$:FAR        ;DISPLAY UNSIGNED DEC INTEGER
 9:              EXTRN   PUTSTRNG:FAR       ;DISPLAY CHARACTER STRING
10: ;
11: ; S T A C K   S E G M E N T   D E F I N I T I O N
12: ;
13: STACK        SEGMENT STACK
14:              DB      10000  DUP(?)
15: STACK        ENDS
16: ;
17: ; E X T R A   S E G M E N T   D E F I N I T I O N
18: ;
19: EXTRA        SEGMENT
20: ;
21: PROMPT       DB      'COMPUTE N-TH FIBONACCI NUMBER',0DH,0AH
22:              DB      'ENTER VALUR FOR N',0DH,0AH
23: ANNOTATE     DB      'FIBONACCI NUMBER = '
24: DEPTH_MSG    DB      'DEPTH OF RECURSION = '
25: DEPTH        DW      0                  ;CURRENT DEPTH OF RECURSION
26: MAX_DEPTH    DW      0                  ;DEPTH OF RECURSION
27: ;
28: EXTRA        ENDS
29: ;
30: ; C O D E   S E G M E N T   D E F I N I T I O N
31: ;
32: CODE         SEGMENT
33:              ASSUME  CS:CODE,SS:STACK,ES:EXTRA
34: EX_10_2      PROC    FAR
35:              PUSH    DS                 ;PUSH RETURN SEG ADDR ON STACK
36:              SUB     AX,AX              ;PUSH RETURN OFFSET
37:              PUSH    AX                 ;OF ZERO ON STACK
38:              MOV     AX,SEG EXTRA       ;SET ES-REGISTER TO
39:              MOV     ES,AX              ;POINT TO EXTRA SEGMENT
40: ;
41:              LEA     DI,PROMPT          ;PROMPT FOR N
42:              MOV     CX,50
43:              CALL    PUTSTRNG
44:              CALL    GETDEC$            ;GET N
45:              PUSH    AX
```

```
 46:            CALL     FIBONACCI              ;COMPUTE FIBONACCI(N)
 47:            LEA      DI,ANNOTATE
 48:            MOV      CX,19
 49:            CALL     PUTSTRNG
 50:            MOV      BH,O
 51:            CALL     PUTDEC$               ;DISPLAY N-TH FIBONACCI NUMBER
 52:            CALL     NEWLINE
 53:            LEA      DI,DEPTH_MSG          ;DISPLAY DEPTH OF RECURSION
 54:            MOV      CX,21
 55:            CALL     PUTSTRNG
 56:            MOV      AX,MAX_DEPTH
 57:            CALL     PUTDEC$
 58:            RET                            ;RETURN
 59: EX_10_2    ENDP
 60:*;

 61: ;
 62: ; RECURSIVE SUBROUTINE TO COMPUTE N-TH FIBONACCI NUMBER
 63: ; GIVEN A VALUE FOR N. N-TH FIBONACCI NUMBER IS DEFINED
 64: ; RECURSIVELY AS FOLLOWS:
 65: ;                       F(1) = 1
 66: ;                       F(2) = 1
 67: ;                       F(N) = F(N-2) + F(N-1)    FOR N > 2
 68: ; CALLING SEQUENCE
 69: ;            PUSH     <N>
 70: ;            CALL     FIBONACCI
 71: ;
 72: ; THE RESULT IS RETURNED IN THE AX REGISTER
 73: ;
 74: FIBONACCI  PROC     NEAR             ;FUNCTION FIBONACCI(N)
 75:            PUSH     BP               ;SAVE REGISTERS
 76:            MOV      BP,SP            ;INITIALIZE ARGUMENT POINTER
 77:            INC      DEPTH            ;DEPTH = DEPTH + 1
 78:            CMP      WORD PTR [BP+4],2 ;IF   N <= 2
 79:            JG       NGTONE
 80:            MOV      AX,1             ;THEN RESULT = 1
 81:            JMP      CHK_DEPTH
 82: NGTONE:                             ;ELSE
 83:            DEC      WORD PTR [BP+4]
 84:            PUSH     [BP+4]
 85:            CALL     FIBONACCI
 86:            PUSH     AX               ;      TEMP = FIBONACCI(N-1)
 87:            DEC      WORD PTR [BP+4]
 88:            PUSH     [BP+4]
 89:            CALL     FIBONACCI
 90:            POP      BX               ;      RESULT = TEMP
 91:            ADD      AX,BX            ;              + FIBONACCI(N-2)
 92: CHK_DEPTH:                          ;ENDIF
 93:            MOV      BX,DEPTH         ;IF   DEPTH > MAX_DEPTH
 94:            CMP      BX,MAX_DEPTH
 95:            JLE      RETURN
 96:            MOV      MAX_DEPTH,BX     ;THEN MAX_DEPTH = DEPTH
 97: RETURN:                             ;ENDIF
 98:            DEC      DEPTH            ;DEPTH = DEPTH - 1
 99:            POP      BP               ;RESTORE REGISTERS
100:            RET      2                ;POP ARGUMENTS
101: ;                                   ;RETURN (RESULT)
102: FIBONACCI  ENDP                     ;END FIBONACCI
103: CODE       ENDS
104:*          END      ·EX_10_2
```

words (8 bytes) to be pushed onto the stack. With a maximum value of $n = 24$, the depth of recursion is 23, and a total of $23 * 8 = 184$ bytes are needed in the stack to support the FIBONACCI procedure. Four additional bytes are needed for the DOS return address. A stack segment of 200 bytes would be more than sufficient, which is far below the estimate of 10,000 bytes that was used. However, with a recursive program, it is much safer to begin with a large stack segment and then reduce it later if analysis shows that a reduction is advisable.

PROGRAMMING EXERCISES

10.1 The factorial function can be defined recursively as follows:

$$0! = 1$$

$$n! = n \times (n - 1)! \quad \text{for } n > 0$$

Design a recursive algorithm to compute $n!$ given a nonnegative integer value for n. Implement your algorithm with an IBM PC Assembly language recursive, external FAR procedure. Your calling sequence should be

```
PUSH ⟨n⟩
CALL FACT
```

Your procedure should return the value of $n!$ in the AX-register. Use a zero result to signify that an overflow occurred in the computation.

10.2 Design an algorithm to compute and display a table of nonnegative integers and their factorial values. Use the recursive subalgorithm in Programming Exercise 10.1 to compute the factorial values. Implement your algorithm with a complete IBM PC Assembly language program. The table displayed should begin with $n = 0$ and terminate with the first value of n that causes an arithmetic overflow in the factorial computation.

10.3 The binomial coefficients, $C(n, k)$, in which $n >= 0$, $k >= 0$, and $n >= k$, are given by the following recursive definition:

$$C(n, n) = 1$$

$$C(n, 0) = 1$$

$$C(n, k) = C(n - 1, k - 1) + C(n - 1, k)$$

$$\text{for } (0 < k < n) \text{ and } n > 1$$

Design a recursive algorithm to compute $C(n, k)$ given nonnegative integer values for n and k. Implement your algorithm with an IBM PC Assembly language recursive, external FAR procedure. Your calling sequence should be

```
PUSH ⟨n⟩
PUSH ⟨k⟩
CALL C
```

Your procedure should return the value of the binomial coefficient, $C(n, k)$, in the AX-register. Use a zero result to signify that an overflow occurred in the computation.

10.4 The first five rows of Pascal's triangle are shown:

$$
\begin{array}{ccccccccc}
& & & & 1 & & & & \\
& & & 1 & & 1 & & & \\
& & 1 & & 2 & & 1 & & \\
& 1 & & 3 & & 3 & & 1 & \\
1 & & 4 & & 6 & & 4 & & 1 \\
\end{array}
$$

The nth row of Pascal's triangle produces the $(a + b)^{n-1}$ coefficients of the expansion. For example, row 5 of Pascal's triangle produces the coefficients of

$$(a + b)^4 = a^4 + 4a^3b + 6a^2b^2 + 4ab^3 + b^4.$$

The elements in the nth row are the n binomial coefficients $C(n - 1, 0)$, $C(n - 1, 1)$, $C(n - 1, 2), \ldots, C(n - 1, n - 1)$. Design an algorithm to compute and display the first 13 rows of Pascal's triangle. Use the recursive subalgorithm in Programming Exercise 10.3 to compute the binomial coefficients. Implement your algorithm with a complete IBM PC Assembly language program.

10.5   The following recursive function, defined for nonnegative integers m and n, is called Ackermann's function:

$$A(m, n) = n + 1$$
$$\text{if } m = 0$$
$$A(m, n) = A(m - 1, 1)$$
$$\text{if } m > 0 \text{ and } n = 0$$
$$A(m, n) = A(m - 1, A(m, n - 1))$$
$$\text{if } m > 0 \text{ and } n > 0$$

Design an algorithm to compute and output the value of Ackermann's function given values for m and n. The actual computation of the function should be designed as a recursive sub-algorithm.

Implement your algorithm with a complete IBM PC Assembly language program. Your program should accept values for m and n from the keyboard and output to the display screen the value of Ackermann's function applied to m and n. Implement Ackermann's function with an IBM PC Assembly language recursive, internal NEAR procedure. The calling sequence for the recursive procedure is

```
PUSH ⟨m⟩
PUSH ⟨n⟩
CALL ACKERMAN
```

The result of the recursive procedure is to be returned in the AX-register. Demonstrate your program with the following computations: $A(0, 3)$, $A(3, 0)$, $A(3, 2)$, $A(3, 5)$, and $A(3, 9)$.

10.6   Ackermann's function has a large depth of recursion. To convince yourself of this, compute $A(3, 2)$ by hand. Now, modify your program from Programming Exercise 10.5 to compute and display the depth of recursion and the total number of calls to the recursive ACKERMAN procedure. Demonstrate your program with the same computations specified in Programming Exercise 10.5.

10.7   The Towers of Hanoi puzzle consists of three pegs and three or more disks of distinct diameters. The disks are all on one peg and are initially arranged in order of decreasing diameter from bottom to top. The object of the puzzle is to transfer all of the disks to another

peg by a sequence of moves. Each move involves a *single* disk, the topmost disk from any peg. That disk can be moved to any peg that is either empty or whose topmost disk is larger than the disk being moved. A disk can never be placed on top of a smaller disk. The series of diagrams in Figure 10.24 shows the sequence of moves necessary to transfer three disks from peg 1 to peg 2.

The key of stating an algorithm for solving the Towers of Hanoi puzzle is to realize the following requirement: Before the nth largest disk can be moved from peg X to peg Y, the $n - 1$ smaller disks must first be moved to the third peg, peg Z. Once done, it is trivial to move the nth largest disk from peg X to peg Y. The $n - 1$ smaller disks can then be moved from peg Z to peg Y using a sequence of moves that is similar to the sequence that moved them from peg X to peg Z. The preceding requirement gives rise to the following recursive algorithm for specifying the moves in the Towers of Hanoi puzzle:

```
MOVDSK (COUNT,FROMPEG,TOPEG):
        IF    COUNT = 1
        THEN
            DISPLAY 'move disk ',COUNT
            DISPLAY ' from peg ',FROMPEG
            DISPLAY ' to peg ',TOPEG
        ELSE
            OTHERPEG = 6 - FROMPEG - TOPEG
            MOVDSK (COUNT-1,FROMPEG,OTHERPEG)
            DISPLAY 'move disk ',COUNT
            DISPLAY ' from peg ',FROMPEG
            DISPLAY ' to peg ',TOPEG
            MOVDSK (COUNT-1,OTHERPEG,TOPEG)
        ENDIF
```

Implement this algorithm with an IBM PC Assembly language recursive, internal NEAR procedure. The calling sequence for the procedure is

```
PUSH ⟨count⟩
PUSH ⟨from-peg⟩
PUSH ⟨to-peg⟩
CALL MOVDSK
```

in which ⟨count⟩ specifies the number of disks to be moved, ⟨from-peg⟩ specifies the number of the peg that contains the disks, and ⟨to-peg⟩ specifies the number of the peg to which the disks are to be moved. Design and implement a main program to test this recursive procedure.

FIGURE 10.24
Sequence of moves
to transfer three
disks from peg 1 to
peg 2

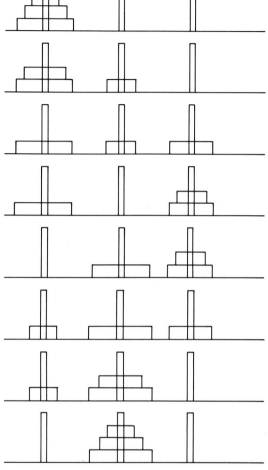

10.8 Euclid's algorithm for computing the greatest common divisor (GCD) of two positive integers can be stated recursively as follows:

$$GCD\ (x, y)\ =\ y$$

$$\text{if } x \bmod y = 0$$

$$GCD\ (x, y)\ =\ GCD\ (y, x \bmod y)$$

$$\text{if } x \bmod y \neq 0$$

Design a recursive algorithm that accepts two positive integers as input and returns the GCD of the input integers as output. Implement your algorithm with an IBM PC recursive, external FAR procedure called GCD. Your input should be two 16-bit unsigned integers in the AX and BX registers. Your procedure should return the GCD of these two integers in the AX-register and must protect all registers used. Programming Exercises 10.9 and 10.10 suggest main procedures that can be used to test your subprocedure.

10.9 The least common multiple (LCM) of two positive integers, x and y, is defined by

$$LCM\ (x, y)\ =\ \frac{xy}{GCD\ (x, y)}$$

Design an algorithm that accepts two positive integers, x and y, as input and outputs the least common multiple of the two input integers.

Assume the existence of a function sub-algorithm, GCD(X,Y), that accepts two positive integers as input and returns the greatest common divisor of those two integers. Implement your algorithm with an IBM PC Assembly language program that accepts two positive integers entered via the keyboard and displays the LCM of the two integers on the screen. Use your solution to Programming Exercise 10.8 as the implementation of the GCD subalgorithm. Demonstrate your program with the following sets of inputs:

x	y
108	60
190	34
12	30
504	540

10.10 Programming Exercises 5.5 and 5.6 involved programs that computed and displayed Pythagorean triples. Both of these programs required a subprocedure (see Programming Exercise 5.4) to compute the GCD of two positive integers.

The interface definition for that GCD procedure is the same as that for the GCD procedure in Programming Exercise 10.8. Substitute the recursive GCD subprocedure in Programming Exercise 10.8 for the one in Chapter 5 and then test the modified programs.

10.11 The corrected MULTIPLY procedure (i.e., the solution to Programming Exercise 7.3) can be converted to a reentrant procedure by passing arguments via the stack and maintaining all local variables in the stack rather than in a static data segment. Implement the MULTIPLY procedure as a reentrant subprocedure with the following calling sequence:

```
PUSH ⟨least-significant word of multiplicand⟩
PUSH ⟨most-significant word of multiplicand⟩
PUSH ⟨least-significant word of multiplier⟩
PUSH ⟨most-significant word of multiplier⟩
CALL MULTIPLY
```

The product is to be returned in the DI:SI:DX:AX register group. The OF and CF bits of the flags register are to reflect whether or not the product overflows 32 bits.

11

BCD OPERATIONS

Chapter 1 introduced the binary number system, the number system of the digital computer. Chapter 2 showed various methods for representing binary integers in the computer. It also discussed how text characters are represented in a computer using ASCII code. This chapter presents the binary coded decimal (BCD) code for representing the 10 decimal digits. As Chapter 2 presented various methods for using binary bit patterns to represent integers, in a similar manner, various methods can be used to represent decimal numbers with BCD codes. This chapter presents several of these representations.

Since the BCD number system is not the native number system of the digital computer, algorithms are required for performing arithmetic computations in BCD. This chapter presents algorithms for performing BCD arithmetic and provides IBM PC Assembly language implementations for some of the algorithms. The chapter also introduces a set of IBM PC Assembly language instructions that aid in implementing BCD arithmetic algorithms. Using the BCD code along with algorithms for performing computations with BCD-coded numbers, the machine is virtually transformed from a binary machine to a decimal machine.

The example programs in the preceding chapters have used I/O procedures like GETDEC and PUTDEC to perform integer I/O operations. The GETDEC procedure converts an input, signed ASCII digit string to a binary integer in two's complement form. The PUTDEC procedure converts a two's complement binary integer to a signed ASCII digit string for output. To perform BCD I/O operations, procedures are needed to convert between BCD and ASCII codes. A procedure for output is provided in this chapter.

11.1 Decimal Encoding

In Chapter 2, an algorithm for converting a fraction from decimal to binary was presented. One example of this algorithm (see Table 1.6) showed that the fraction .1 in decimal is a repeating fraction in binary, which means that the decimal fraction .1 cannot be represented exactly with a finite number of bits. Many such fractions occur in decimal that become infinite fractions when converted to binary.

Consider the problem of representing monetary values (dollars and cents) in the computer. If the binary number system is used, then a value like $45.10 cannot be represented precisely—the value stored in the computer is an approximation of $45.10. Each time this value is used in a computation, the error is compounded. To see the effect of representational error compounded by computation, try the following experiment:

> In a high-level language such as FORTRAN or Pascal that provides the data type real, perform the following two computations and print the results to nine decimal places:
>
> 1.   Multiply 0.1 by 1000.
> 2.   Using a loop, add 0.1 to an initially zero sum 1000 times.
>
> In both cases, the result should be 100. In most high-level language systems, however, neither of the two values will be exactly 100, although the first computation produces a value that is closer to 100 than does the second computation. This situation occurs because the first computation uses an approximation of 0.1 in only one computation, but the second uses the approximation in 1000 operations. Following each of the 1000 additions, a rounding off occurs. Each computation and rounding off compounds the error.

To eliminate the representational error caused by conversions between the decimal and binary number systems, a binary code can be used to represent decimal digits in the computer. With such a code, each digit of a decimal number is represented separately and precisely, and a collection of such digit codes represents a complete number.

With n-bit binary numbers, 2^n different objects can be represented. Taking the opposite view, if m objects are to be represented, then a minimum of

$$B = \lceil \log_2 m \rceil$$

bits are needed to represent those objects. The notation, $\lceil x \rceil$, called the **ceiling** of x, is the smallest integer that is greater than or equal to x. The act of selecting m of the 2^B possible bit patterns to represent the m objects (one bit pattern represents one object) is called **encoding** the objects. The set of bit patterns chosen, along with their interpretations, is called a **binary code**.

There are 10 decimal digits (0, 1, 2, 3, 4, 5, 6, 7, 8, and 9) so

$$\lceil \log_2 10 \rceil \ = \ \lceil 3.3219281 \rceil \ = \ 4$$

bits are required for a binary code. One such code, **binary coded decimal (BCD)**, is presented in this chapter.

11.2 | BCD Number System

Binary coded decimal (BCD) is a 4-bit code that is used to represent the 10 digits of the decimal number system. Table 11.1 shows the 4-bit BCD code. Note that six codes (1010, 1011, 1100, 1101, 1110, and 1111) are not used, and in fact they are illegal in the BCD number system. To represent a 5-digit decimal number using BCD code, a total of 20 bits (4 bits per decimal digit) are needed. Table 11.2 shows some 4-digit BCD numbers, the corresponding 4-digit decimal number, and the corresponding binary number. From the examples in Table 11.2, you can observe the following:

1. The largest number that can be represented with 4-digit BCD (16 bits) is 9999. In the binary number system, only 14 bits are required to represent the integer 9999.

2. Using the binary number system with 13 bits, the decimal numbers in the range 0–8191 can be represented. However, 16 bits (4 BCD digits) are required to represent this same range in the BCD number system.

3. The decimal number 45.10 can be represented precisely in the BCD number system using a minimum of 16 bits. However, 45.10 cannot be represented precisely in the binary number system with any finite number of bits.

TABLE 11.1
BCD code

BCD Bit Pattern	Decimal Digit
0000	0
0001	1
0010	2
0011	3
0100	4
0101	5
0110	6
0111	7
1000	8
1001	9

TABLE 11.2
Examples of corresponding numbers in the BCD, decimal, and binary number systems

BCD	Decimal	Binary
0000 0000 0000 0000	0000	0
1001 1001 1001 1001	9999	10011100001111
1000 0001 1001 0001	8191	1111111111111
0010 0111 0011 0101	2735	101010101111
0100 0101.0001 0000	45.10	101101.0001100110011 . . .

The BCD number system requires more bits to represent a number than does the binary number system. However, the BCD number system provides a more accurate representation for fractions.

With n BCD digits ($4n$ bits), the nonnegative, decimal integers in the range 0 to $10^n - 1$ can be represented. That is, the integers in the modulo 10^n number system can be represented.

Ten's Complement Representation

To represent both negative and nonnegative integers, the ten's complement number system can be used. The **ten's complement number system** for decimal integers is analogous to the two's complement number system for binary integers. With n BCD digits ($4n$ bits), decimal integers in the range $-5(10^{n-1})$ to $+5(10^{n-1}) - 1$ can be represented using the ten's complement number system.

In the n-digit BCD, ten's complement number system, negating an integer is a two-step process:

1. Subtract each digit in the number from 1001 (9 in decimal).
2. Add 1 to the result of step 1 using modulo 10^n BCD addition. (BCD addition is discussed shortly.)

An alternate method for negating an integer in the n-digit BCD, ten's complement number system is the following:

Start with the rightmost digit of the BCD number and work left. Copy all BCD digits up to but not including the first nonzero digit. Subtract this first nonzero digit from 1010 (10 in decimal). Subtract all of the remaining BCD digits to the left from 1001 (9 in decimal).

The subtractions in these two methods are straight, 4-bit binary subtractions.

EXAMPLE

$n = 5$

| 0 | 3 | 7 | 0 | 0 | Decimal |

0000 0011 0111 0000 0000   BCD

```
                                                   C ⇒ copy BCD digit
   N    N    T    C    C    Operation ──→ T ⇒ subtract from 1010
                                                   N ⇒ subtract from 1001
 1001 0110 0011 0000 0000   BCD ten's complement

   9    6    3    0    0    Decimal ten's complement
```

Table 11.3 shows the range of decimal integers that can be represented using 4 BCD digits (16 bits) with both the modulo 10,000 and the ten's complement number systems. Note that in the ten's complement number system, the leftmost digit of an integer is an indication of its sign. Nonnegative integers begin with a digit 0–4, (0000–0100 in BCD), and negative integers begin with a digit 5–9 (0101–1001 in BCD).

BCD Arithmetic

Arithmetic in the BCD number system is not as straightforward as it is in the binary number system. This situation occurs because digits in one number system (decimal) are being represented by digits in another number system (binary). Performing arithmetic in BCD requires that you simulate decimal arithmetic using binary arithmetic. In this section, algorithms for BCD addition and subtraction are presented. An algorithm for BCD multiplication is presented in the programming exercises at the end of the chapter.

BCD Addition

To add the n-digit BCD number $A_{n-1}A_{n-2} \ldots A_2A_1A_0$ to the n-digit BCD number $B_{n-1}B_{n-2} \ldots B_2B_1B_0$, the following algorithm can be performed:

```
CARRY = 0
I = 0
WHILE I < n
     CARRY: S_I = A_I + B_I + CARRY
     IF    CARRY = 1 or S_I > 1001
     THEN
             S_I = S_I + 0110
             CARRY = 1
     ENDIF
     I = I + 1
ENDWHILE
```

The output of this algorithm is the n-digit BCD sum $S_{n-1}S_{n-2} \ldots S_2S_1S_0$ and the carry out, CARRY, of the most-significant digit position. The expression

```
CARRY: S_I = A_I + B_I + CARRY
```

TABLE 11.3
Range of integer values for modulo 10,000, 4-digit BCD, and ten's complement number systems

4-Digit BCD Integer	Modulo 10,000 Interpretation	Ten's Complement Interpretation
0000 0000 0000 0000	0000	0000
0000 0000 0000 0001	0001	0001
0000 0000 0000 0010	0002	0002
0000 0000 0000 0011	0003	0003
0000 0000 0000 0100	0004	0004
0000 0000 0000 0101	0005	0005
0000 0000 0000 0110	0006	0006
0000 0000 0000 0111	0007	0007
0000 0000 0000 1000	0008	0008
0000 0000 0000 1001	0009	0009
0000 0000 0001 0000	0010	0010
0000 0000 0001 0001	0011	0011
.	.	.
.	.	.
.	.	.
0100 1001 1001 0100	4994	4994
0100 1001 1001 0101	4995	4995
0100 1001 1001 0110	4996	4996
0100 1001 1001 0111	4997	4997
0100 1001 1001 1000	4998	4998
0100 1001 1001 1001	4999	4999
0101 0000 0000 0000	5000	− 5000
0101 0000 0000 0001	5001	− 4999
0101 0000 0000 0010	5002	− 4998
0101 0000 0000 0011	5003	− 4997
0101 0000 0000 0100	5004	− 4996
0101 0000 0000 0101	5005	− 4995
.	.	.
.	.	.
.	.	.
1001 1001 1000 1000	9988	− 0012
1001 1001 1000 1001	9989	− 0011
1001 1001 1001 0000	9990	− 0010
1001 1001 1001 0001	9991	− 0009
1001 1001 1001 0010	9992	− 0008
1001 1001 1001 0011	9993	− 0007
1001 1001 1001 0100	9994	− 0006
1001 1001 1001 0101	9995	− 0005
1001 1001 1001 0110	9996	− 0004
1001 1001 1001 0111	9997	− 0003
1001 1001 1001 1000	9998	− 0002
1001 1001 1001 1001	9999	− 0001

is the straight binary sum of two 4-bit BCD digits plus a 1-bit carry from the previous digit position, producing a 4-bit BCD digit, S_I, and a carry into the next digit position. The result, CARRY:S_I, can be viewed as a 5-bit binary number in the range 00000–10011. If this result is less than or equal to 01001 (9 in decimal), then S_I is a legal BCD digit, the next BCD sum digit, and there is a carry of 0 into the next digit position. If the result is greater than 01001, then S_I has gone beyond 9 (in decimal) and therefore should wrap around to zero and produce a carry of 1 into the next digit position. However, there are six illegal BCD codes (mentioned earlier) that the straight binary sum must count through before the lower 4 bits (the BCD digit) wrap around to zero and produce a carry into the next BCD digit position. To allow the sum to count through the six illegal codes and produce the correct BCD sum digit and carry, 0110 (6 in decimal) is added to S_I.

EXAMPLE

```
                    BCD                              Decimal
        1      0      1    ←── Carry       1  0  1   ←── Carry
      0010   1001   0110   0100            2  9  6  4
      0000   1000   0001   0110            0  8  1  6
      ─────  ─────  ─────  ─────           ─────────
      00011  10001  01000  01010           3  7  8  0
             0110          0110                    ↑
             ─────         ─────                   │
             10111         10000                   │
                                                   │
    0   0011   0111   1000   0000 ─────────────────┘

    └──→ Carry
```

BCD Subtraction

To subtract the n-digit BCD number $B_{n-1}B_{n-2} \ldots B_2B_1B_0$ from the n-digit BCD number $A_{n-1}A_{n-2} \ldots A_2A_1A_0$, the steps of the following algorithm can be performed:

```
BORROW = 0
I = 0
WHILE I < n
        BORROW: D_I = A_I - B_I - BORROW
        IF    BORROW = 1
        THEN
                D_I = D_I - 0110
        ENDIF
        I = I + 1
ENDWHILE
```

The output of this algorithm is the n-digit BCD difference $D_{n-1}D_{n-2}\ldots D_2D_1D_0$ and the borrow into, BORROW, the most-significant digit position. The expression

```
BORROW: D_I = A_I - B_I - BORROW
```

is the straight binary sum of the 4-bit BCD digit A_I, the two's complement of the 4-bit BCD digit B_I, and the 4-bit two's complement of the 1-bit borrow. This binary sum produces a 4-bit BCD digit, D_I, and a carry into the fifth bit position. The borrow into the I-th BCD digit position is this carry inverted.

If the borrow is 0, then the digit D_I is a valid BCD digit and is the correct I-th digit of the difference. However, if the borrow is 1, then the digit D_I is either an invalid BCD digit or the wrong BCD digit for the I-th digit of the difference. The borrow means that the difference has gone below 0 in this digit position and

TABLE 11.4
BCD subtraction with both modulo 10,000 and ten's complement interpretations

BCD Subtraction				Modulo 10,000 Interpretation	Ten's Complement Interpretation
0010	1001	0110	0100	2964	2964
− 0000	1000	0001	0110	−0816	−(+0816)
				2148	
1	1	0			
0010	1001	0110	0100		2964
+ 1001	0001	1000	0100		+(−0816)
01100	01011	01110	01000		2148
0110	0110	0110			
10010	10001	10100			
1 0010	0001	0100	1000		

  → Borrow = 0

1000	0100	0110	0011	8463	−1537
− 0001	0010	1000	0000	−1280	−(+1280)
				7183	
1	0	0			010
1000	0100	0110	0011		−1537
+ 1000	0111	0010	0000		+(−1280)
10001	01011	01000	00011		−2817
0110	0110				
10111	10001				
1 0111	0001	1000	0011		

  → Borrow = 0

should wrap around to 9. However, six illegal BCD codes discussed earlier must be skipped to wrap around to the legal BCD codes. Therefore, when there is a borrow into the I-th digit position, the value 1010 (-6 in decimal) must be added to D_I to produce the correct I-th digit of the difference.

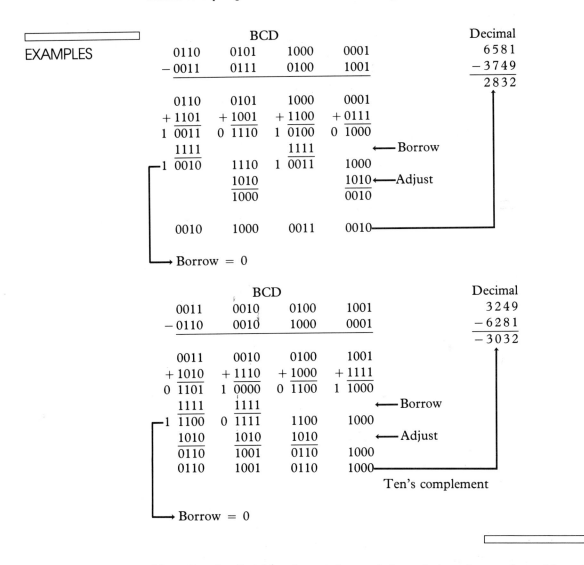

EXAMPLES					
		BCD			Decimal

Note that the algorithm leaves the result in ten's complement form. Note also that the subtraction of each pair of BCD digits and each adjustment of a BCD digit is performed as a binary subtraction; that is, the two's complement of the subtrahend digit is added to the minuend digit.

There is an alternative method for subtracting two BCD numbers: They can be subtracted by adding the ten's complement of the subtrahend to the minuend. Table 11.4 (p. 454) shows some examples of 4-digit BCD subtractions, with interpretations for both modulo 10,000 and the ten's complement number systems.

11.3 Internal BCD Representations

There are several ways to store BCD numbers in the memory of an IBM PC. Each digit of a decimal number is represented by a 4-bit code. The 4-bit codes that make up a BCD number can be stored one per byte (unpacked) or two per byte (packed). The packed or unpacked BCD digits can be stored in sign magnitude form or in ten's complement form. The following sections discuss several internal representations for BCD numbers.

Unpacked BCD Sign Magnitude Representation

A BCD number, entered via the keyboard, appears to a program as a string of ASCII characters stored in a byte array. The GETSTRNG subprocedure can be used to enter an ASCII signed digit string. Figure 11.1 shows the ASCII sign magnitude representation of the decimal number −1,328,745. The ASCII values shown in the figure are given in hexadecimal. The characters are stored in the array in the same order as they would be entered via the keyboard: sign followed by the digits from most-significant digit (MSD) to least-significant digit (LSD).

To convert this ASCII number to unpacked, BCD sign magnitude form, the following steps can be performed:

1. Convert the sign byte to 00 for positive, 80 for negative.
2. Convert each ASCII digit to its BCD equivalent by subtracting 30 hex from the ASCII code for the digit.

FIGURE 11.1
ASCII sign magnitude representation of −1,328,745

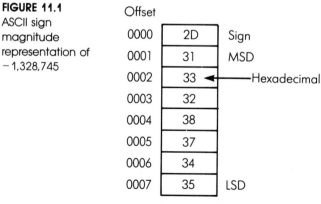

Offset		
0000	2D	Sign
0001	31	MSD
0002	33	◄───Hexadecimal
0003	32	
0004	38	
0005	37	
0006	34	
0007	35	LSD

FIGURE 11.2
Unpacked BCD sign magnitude representation of −1,328,745

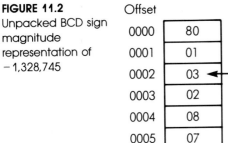

Offset		
0000	80	Sign
0001	01	MSD
0002	03	◀──── Hexadecimal
0003	02	
0004	08	
0005	07	
0006	04	
0007	05	LSD

Figure 11.2 shows the unpacked BCD sign magnitude representation of the decimal number −1,328,745.

Packed BCD Sign Magnitude Representation

With the BCD number system, each digit of a decimal number is represented by a 4-bit binary code. When a BCD number is stored in the memory of the IBM PC, two 4-bit BCD codes can be packed into each 8-bit byte of the array that holds the number, which utilizes memory space more efficiently. Figure 11.3(a) shows the packed BCD sign magnitude representation of the decimal number

FIGURE 11.3
Packed BCD sign magnitude representations of (a) −1,328,745 and (b) $+d_6 d_5 d_4 d_3 d_2 d_1 d_0$

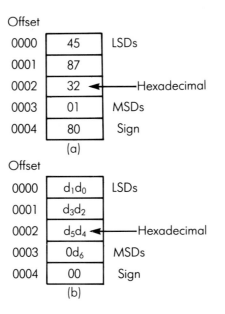

Offset		
0000	45	LSDs
0001	87	
0002	32	◀──── Hexadecimal
0003	01	MSDs
0004	80	Sign

(a)

Offset		
0000	$d_1 d_0$	LSDs
0001	$d_3 d_2$	
0002	$d_5 d_4$	◀──── Hexadecimal
0003	$0 d_6$	MSDs
0004	00	Sign

(b)

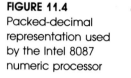

FIGURE 11.4
Packed-decimal
representation used
by the Intel 8087
numeric processor

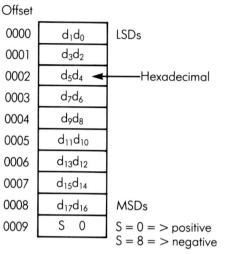

Offset

0000	d_1d_0	LSDs
0001	d_3d_2	
0002	d_5d_4	◄———Hexadecimal
0003	d_7d_6	
0004	d_9d_8	
0005	$d_{11}d_{10}$	
0006	$d_{13}d_{12}$	
0007	$d_{15}d_{14}$	
0008	$d_{17}d_{16}$	MSDs
0009	S 0	S = 0 = > positive
		S = 8 = > negative

– 1,328,745. Note the number is now being stored in reverse order. The least-significant pair of digits, 45, is stored in the first byte of the array, the next more-significant pair of digits, 87, is stored in the second byte of the array, and so forth. Figure 11.3(b) relates digit positions within a decimal number to positions within the array used to store the number. In general, the I-th digit (the LSD is the 0-th digit) is stored in the right nibble of the byte whose index is the floor of I/2 if I is even, or in the left nibble of the byte whose index is the floor of I/2 if I is odd. The number is stored in reverse order for compatibility with the Intel 8087 numeric processor. The Intel 8087 represents decimal numbers with a 10-byte array (Figure 11.4).

Note also that a packed BCD number has an even number of digits. A leading zero is added to convert a BCD number of odd length to one of even length.

Packed BCD Ten's Complement Representation

A packed BCD number also can be stored in ten's complement form rather than in sign magnitude form to facilitate arithmetic computation involving BCD numbers. Figure 11.5 shows the 10-digit, packed BCD ten's complement

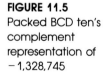

FIGURE 11.5
Packed BCD ten's
complement
representation of
– 1,328,745

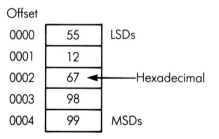

Offset

0000	55	LSDs
0001	12	
0002	67	◄———Hexadecimal
0003	98	
0004	99	MSDs

representation of the decimal number − 1,328,745. Again, the number is stored in reverse order.

Defining Packed BCD Data

BCD variables whose initial values are in any of the three forms described in the preceding sections can be defined using the DB pseudo-operation described in Chapter 2. Consider the following data segment definition:

```
DATA       SEGMENT
UNPACKED DB      80H, 01H, 03H, 02H, 08H, 07H, 04H, 05H
PACKSMAG DB      45H, 87H, 32H, 01H, 80H
PACKTENS DB      55H, 12H, 67H, 98H, 99H
DATA       ENDS
```

Figure 11.6 shows the 18-byte memory segment generated by this definition. UNPACKED is defined as a byte array of size 8. Its initial value is the unpacked BCD sign magnitude representation of the decimal number − 1,328,745. PACKSMAG is defined as a byte array of size 5. Its initial value is the packed BCD sign magnitude representation of the decimal number − 1,328,745.

FIGURE 11.6
BCD data
segment—DB
pseudo-operation

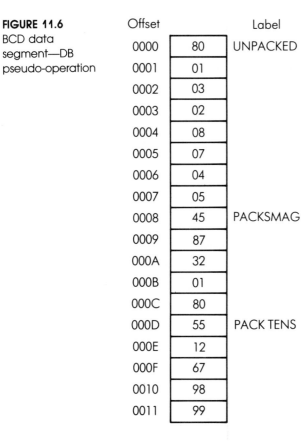

Offset		Label
0000	80	UNPACKED
0001	01	
0002	03	
0003	02	
0004	08	
0005	07	
0006	04	
0007	05	
0008	45	PACKSMAG
0009	87	
000A	32	
000B	01	
000C	80	
000D	55	PACK TENS
000E	12	
000F	67	
0010	98	
0011	99	

PACKTENS is defined as a byte array of size 5. Its initial value is the packed BCD ten's complement representation of the decimal number $-1,328,745$.

The IBM PC Assembly language also provides the **DT** (define 10 byte) **pseudo-operation** to facilitate the definition of packed BCD numbers that are compatible with the Intel 8087 numeric processor, and it has the following general form:

[⟨*name*⟩] DT ⟨*dec-constant-list*⟩   [⟨*comment*⟩]

in which ⟨*name*⟩ is the symbolic name to be associated with the memory location at which the byte array is to begin and ⟨*dec-constant-list*⟩ is a list of decimal constants separated by commas. A ⟨*dec-constant*⟩ is one of the following:

A signed or unsigned string of up to 18 decimal digits.

A question mark (?) that indicates that 10 bytes of storage are to be allocated but that an initial value is not being specified.

Each ⟨*dec-constant*⟩ specifies the allocation of 10 consecutive bytes of storage, with the value of the constant being the initial value of the 10-byte array, which is stored in the array using the packed BCD sign magnitude representation.

EXAMPLE

The following data segment definition generates the 20-byte memory segment shown in Figure 11.7:

```
DATA   SEGMENT
ALPHA  DT      1234567890
BETA   DT      -1234567890
DATA   ENDS
```

Programming Examples

Each of the internal BCD representations presented previously may be useful in the implementation of algorithms requiring decimal computations: The ASCII sign magnitude representation is useful in input/output operations; the packed sign magnitude representation provides for compatibility with the Intel 8087 numeric processor; and the packed ten's complement representation is useful in performing arithmetic computations. The need often arises for conversion of a BCD number from one of these representations to another. Procedures for two such conversions are presented in this section. Two additional conversion procedures are left as programming exercises at the end of the chapter.

Conversion from Packed Ten's Complement to Packed Sign Magnitude

The FAR procedure defined in Program Listing 11.1 is a PUBLIC procedure, called TENSSMAG, that converts a packed BCD number from ten's comple-

FIGURE 11.7
BCD data
segment—DT
pseudo-operation

Offset		Label
0000	90	ALPHA
0001	78	
0002	56	
0003	34	
0004	12	
0005	00	
0006	00	
0007	00	
0008	00	
0009	00	
000A	90	BETA
000B	78	
000C	56	
000D	34	
000E	12	
000F	00	
0010	00	
0011	00	
0012	00	
0013	80	

ment form to sign magnitude form. The prologue in lines 4–16 describes the function of the procedure and explains its interface requirements. On entry to the procedure, the ES:DI register pair must address the first byte of the array that contains the ten's complement BCD number, and the CX-register must contain the number of digits in the BCD number. The number of digits must be even, since the BCD number is stored in packed form. On return to the caller, the array addressed by the ES:DI register pair contains the packed sign magnitude equivalent of the input BCD number. An additional byte is required on the input array to accommodate the sign.

The TENSSMAG procedure references one subprocedure, the procedure NEGBCD (line 19). The NEGBCD procedure performs the ten's complement of a packed BCD number. On entry to NEGBCD, the ES:DI register pair must address the first byte of an array that contains a packed BCD number, and the CX-register must contain the number of digits in the BCD number. Again, the number of digits must be even. When NEGBCD returns to its caller, the array addressed by the ES:DI register pair contains the ten's complement of the input BCD number.

```
 1: ;
 2: ;                          PROGRAM LISTING 11.1
 3: ;
 4: ; PROCEDURE TO CONVERT A PACKED BCD NUMBER
 5: ; FROM TEN'S COMPLEMENT FORM TO SIGN MAGNITUDE FORM
 6: ;
 7: ; INPUTS:  ES:DI  POINTS TO ARRAY CONTAINING TEN'S COMPLEMENT BCD NO.
 8: ;                 CX-REG CONTAINS SIZE OF BCD NUMBER          (MUST BE EVEN)
 9: ;
10: ; OUTPUTS: UPON RETURN, THE ARRAY POINTED TO BY ES:DI WILL CONTAIN  A
11: ;                 SIGN MAGNITUDE, PACKED BCD NUMBER EQUIVALENT TO THE   TEN'S
12: ;                 COMPLEMENT, PACKED BCD NUMBER THAT IT CONTAINED UPON ENTRY
13: ;
14: ;                 CAUTION: ONE BYTE IS ADDED TO THE BCD ARRAY FOR THE   SIGN.
15: ;                          HOWEVER, THE SIZE (BCD DIGIT COUNT)   REMAINS   THE
16: ;                          SAME.
17: ;
18:                                          ;PROCEDURE TO
19:               EXTRN    NEGBCD:FAR         ;NEGATE A PACKED BCD NUMBER
20: ;
21: CODE          SEGMENT
22:               ASSUME   CS:CODE
23: TENSSMAG      PROC     FAR               ;PROCEDURE TENSSMAG (DPTR,DIGIT_COUNT)
24:               PUBLIC   TENSSMAG
25:               PUSH     SI                ;SAVE REGISTERS
26:               PUSHF                      ;SAVE FLAGS
27:               MOV      SI,CX             ;PTR = DPTR + DIGIT_COUNT/2 - 1
28:               SHR      SI,1
29:               DEC      SI
30:               ADD      SI,DI
31:               CMP      BYTE PTR ES:[SI],50H;IF   PTR -> BYTE >= 50H
32:               JB       ELSE
33:               CALL     NEGBCD            ;THEN CALL NEGBCD (DPTR,
34:                                          ;                  DIGIT_COUNT)
35:               INC      SI                ;      PTR = PTR + 1
36:               MOV      BYTE PTR ES:[SI],80H;     PTR -> BYTE = 80H
37:               JMP      ENDIF
38: ELSE:                                    ;ELSE
39:               INC      SI                ;      PTR = PTR + 1
40:               MOV      BYTE PTR ES:[SI],0 ;      PTR->BYTE = 0
41: ENDIF:                                   ;ENDIF
42:               POPF                       ;RESTORE FLAGS
43:               POP      SI                ;RESTORE REGISTERS
44:               RET                        ;RETURN
45: TENSSMAG      ENDP                  ;END TENSSMAG
46: CODE          ENDS
47:*             END
```
*

The TENSSMAG procedure begins by saving the registers that it uses (lines 25 and 26). The SI-register and the flags register are the only registers that are modified by the procedure. On entry to the procedure, the ES:DI register pair addresses the first byte of the array that holds the BCD number. The instructions in lines 27–30 set the SI-register to the offset of the last byte of the BCD number, which means that the ES:SI register pair now addresses the byte of the BCD number whose left nibble indicates the sign of the number. Recall that packed BCD numbers are stored with digit pairs in reverse order. The MOV instruction in line 27 moves the digit count to the SI-register. The SHR instruction in line 28 divides the digit count by 2, producing a byte count. The DEC instruction in line 29 decrements the byte count in the SI-register by 1, producing the offset of the last byte in the BCD array relative to the offset of the first byte. The ADD instruction in line 30 adds the offset of the first byte of the BCD array, producing the offset of the last byte of the BCD array relative to the beginning of the segment. The ES:SI register pair now addresses the last byte of the BCD array.

If the left nibble of the most-significant digit pair is one of the digits in the range 5–9, then the ten's complement BCD number is negative. If it is one of the digits in the range 0–4, then the BCD number is positive. The double-alternative decision structure in lines 31–41 determines whether the ten's complement BCD number is positive or negative. The CMP instruction in line 31 tests the left nibble of the most-significant BCD digit pair; that is, it tests the left nibble of the digit pair addressed by the ES:SI register pair. The JB instruction in line 32 makes the decision based on this test: If the left nibble is a BCD digit in the range 5–9, then the instructions in lines 33–37 are executed; if the left nibble is a BCD digit in the range 0–4, then the instructions in lines 38–40 are executed.

The THEN branch of the double-alternative decision structure (lines 33–37) handles the case of a negative BCD number. The call to NEGBCD in line 33 converts the negative BCD number to the corresponding positive BCD number. The INC instruction in line 35 adjusts the ES:SI register pair so that it addresses the next byte of the BCD array, the byte at which the sign is to be placed. The MOV instruction in line 36 sets the sign bit in this sign byte. The JMP instruction in line 37 causes the ELSE portion of the double-alternative decision structure to be skipped.

The ELSE branch of the double-alternative decision structure (lines 38–40) handles the case of a positive BCD number. The INC instruction in line 39 adjusts the ES:SI register pair to address the next byte of the BCD array, the byte at which the sign is to be placed. The MOV instruction in line 40 clears the sign bit in this sign byte.

On completion of the double-alternative decision structure, the registers are restored for the caller (lines 42 and 43), and control is returned to the caller (line 44). If the address of the array shown in Figure 11.5 is passed to procedure TENSMAG with a digit count of 10, then the array is converted to the sign magnitude form shown in Figure 11.8.

The NEGBCD subprocedure provides a significant portion of this conversion, and it is discussed in detail in Section 11.4.

Conversion from Packed BCD Sign Magnitude to ASCII Sign Magnitude

The FAR procedure defined in Program Listing 11.2 is a PUBLIC procedure, called BCDASCII, that converts a packed BCD sign magnitude number to ASCII sign magnitude form. It is similar to the BCDASCII procedure in

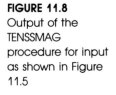

FIGURE 11.8
Output of the
TENSSMAG
procedure for input
as shown in Figure
11.5

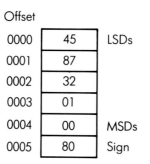

```
 1: ;
 2: ;                      PROGRAM LISTING 11.2
 3: ;
 4: ; PROCEDURE TO CONVERT A SIGN MAGNITUDE, PACKED BCD NUMBER TO ASCII
 5: ;
 6: ; INPUT:   DS:SI POINTS TO ARRAY CONTAINING BCD   NUMBER
 7: ;          ES:DI POINTS TO ARRAY TO CONTAIN ASCII NUMBER
 8: ;          CX    CONTAINS SIZE OF BCD NUMBER (MUST BE EVEN)
 9: ;
10: ; OUTPUT: UPON RETURN, THE ARRAY POINTED TO BY ES:DI WILL
11: ;         CONTAIN AN ASCII NUMBER EQUIVALENT   TO  THE BCD
12: ;         NUMBER IN THE ARRAY POINTED TO BY DS:SI.
13: ;
14: CODE       SEGMENT
15:            ASSUME  CS:CODE
16:            PUBLIC  BCDASCII
17: BCDASCII   PROC    FAR              ;PROCEDURE BCDASCII (DIGIT_COUNT,
18:                                     ;                    DPTR,SPTR)
19:            PUSHF                     ;SAVE FLAGS
20:            PUSH    AX                ;SAVE REGISTERS
21:            PUSH    CX
22:            PUSH    DX
23:            PUSH    SI
24:            PUSH    DI
25:            MOV     DX,CX             ;SPTR = SPTR + (DIGIT_COUNT/2)
26:            SHR     DX,1
27:            ADD     SI,DX
28:            STD                       ;SET DF FOR DECREMENTING
29:            LODSB                     ;SIGN = SPTR -> BYTE
30:                                      ;SPTR = SPTR - 1
31:            CMP     AL,0              ;IF   LEFT NIBBLE OF SIGN <> 0
32:            JZ      ELSE1
33:            MOV     AL,'-'            ;THEN SIGN = '-'
34:            JMP     ENDIF1
35: ELSE1:                              ;ELSE
36:            MOV     AL,' '            ;     SIGN = ' '
37: ENDIF1:                             ;ENDIF
38:            CLD                       ;SET DF FOR INCREMENTING
39:            STOSB                     ;DPTR -> BYTE = SIGN
40:                                      ;DPTR = DPTR + 1
41:*;
```
*

```
42: ;
43:              MOV     DX,-1             ;LR_FLAG = LEFT
44: LOOP_TOP:                             ;REPEAT
45:              CMP     DX,0             ;    IF    LR_FLAG = LEFT
46:              JG      ELSE             ;    THEN SET DF FOR DECR.
47:              STD                      ;         PAIR = DPTR -> BYTE
48:              LODSB                    ;         SPTR = SPTR - 1
49:                                       ;
50:              MOV     AH,AL            ;
51:              PUSH    CX               ;         SAVE DIGIT_COUNT
52:              MOV     CL,4             ;         DIGIT = LEFT NIBBLE
53:              SHR     AL,CL            ;                 OF PAIR
54:              POP     CX               ;         RESTORE DIGIT_COUNT
55:              JMP     ENDIF            ;
56: ELSE:                                ;    ELSE
57:              MOV     AL,AH            ;
58:              AND     AL,0FH           ;             DIGIT = RIGHT NIBBLE
59:                                       ;                     OF PAIR
60: ENDIF:                               ;    ENDIF
61:              ADD     AL,'0'           ;    CHAR = DIGIT + ASCII(0)
62:              CLD                      ;    SET DF FOR INCREMENTING
63:              STOSB                    ;    SPTR -> BYTE = CHAR
64:                                       ;    DPTR = DPTR + 1
65:              NEG     DX               ;    REVERSE LR_FLAG
66:              LOOP    LOOP_TOP         ;    DECREMENT DIGIT_COUNT
67:                                       ;UNTIL DIGIT_COUNT = 0
68:              POP     DI               ;RESTORE REGISTERS
69:              POP     SI
70:              POP     DX
71:              POP     CX
72:              POP     AX
73:              POPF                     ;RESTORE FLAGS
74:              RET                      ;RETURN
75: BCDASCII     ENDP                     ;END BCDASCII
76: CODE         ENDS
77:*             END
```

Program Listing 8.1, although there are two major differences between the procedures.

1. The procedure in Program Listing 11.2 allows for a sign, and the procedure in Program Listing 8.1 does not.
2. The procedure in Program Listing 11.2 reverses the order of the digits as part of the conversion process, and the procedure in Program Listing 8.1 does not. The procedure in Program Listing 11.2 assumes that the packed BCD number is stored in the form described in Figure 11.3, and it converts the BCD number to an ASCII number in the form described in Figure 11.1.

The prologue in lines 3–13 in Program Listing 11.2 describes the function of procedure BCDASCII and explains its interface requirements. On entry to the procedure, the DS:SI register pair must address the first byte of the array that contains the packed BCD number, the ES:DI register pair must address the first byte of the array that is to contain the corresponding ASCII number, and the CX-register must contain the number of digits in the BCD number. The number of digits must be even, since the BCD number is stored in packed form. On return to the caller, the array addressed by the ES:DI register pair contains the ASCII sign magnitude equivalent of the input BCD number addressed by the DS:SI register pair.

The BCDASCII procedure begins by saving the registers that it uses (lines 19–24). The instructions in lines 25–27 set the DS:SI register pair to address the last byte in the input BCD array (the sign byte). The procedure works from the end to the beginning of the BCD array, and it works from the beginning to the end of the ASCII array; thus, it processes both arrays in the following order: sign then digits from MSD to LSD.

The instructions in lines 28–40 perform the sign conversion. The STD instruction in line 28 sets the direction flag for decrementing through the BCD array. The LODSB instruction in line 29 loads the sign byte of the BCD number into the AL-register and then decrements the SI-register, so that the DS:SI register pair addresses the most-significant pair of BCD digits. The single-alternative decision structure in lines 31–37 tests the sign byte in the AL-register and then sets it to the ASCII representation of the appropriate sign character: − for negative (line 33) and blank for positive (line 36). The CLD instruction in line 38 clears the direction flag for incrementing through the ASCII array. The STOSB instruction in line 39 stores the ASCII character for the sign in the first byte of the ASCII array and then increments the DI-register, so that the ES:DI register pair addresses the second byte of the ASCII array.

The MOV instruction in line 43 initializes a LEFT/RIGHT flag (maintained in the DX-register) to LEFT. The LEFT/RIGHT flag is used to indicate whether the BCD digit currently being processed is from the left or right nibble of a byte. That is, each byte extracted from the BCD array contains two BCD digits, one in the left nibble and one in the right nibble. The flag indicates which of the two is currently being converted to ASCII.

The body (lines 45–65) of the REPEAT-UNTIL loop in lines 44–67 executes once for each digit in the BCD array. The digit count, input to the subprocedure in the CX-register, controls execution of this loop. Each iteration of the loop translates one BCD digit to ASCII and stores the result in the ASCII array. A byte is extracted from the BCD array on every odd iteration of the loop (i.e., every time a left nibble is to be translated).

The double-alternative decision structure in lines 45–60 selects the next BCD digit to be translated. The selection is based on the LEFT/RIGHT flag. The CMP instruction in line 45 tests the flag. If the flag indicates LEFT, then the instructions in line 47–55 are executed. The STD instruction in line 47 sets the direction flag for decrementing through the BCD array. The LODSB instruction in line 48 extracts the next two BCD digits from the BCD array (the byte addressed by the DS:SI register pair) and decrements the SI-register by 1, so that the DS:SI register pair addresses the previous byte in the BCD array. The byte extracted is placed in the AL-register, and the MOV instruction in line 50 saves a copy of this byte in the AH-register for use in the next iteration of the loop. This iteration of the loop translates the left nibble of the byte just extracted, and the next iteration translates the right nibble of the byte just extracted. The

PUSH instruction in line 51 saves the digit count so that the CL-register can be used as a shift count. The instructions in lines 52 and 53 shift the byte in the AL-register right 4 bit positions, which pushes out the right nibble and right-justifies the left nibble; that is, the leftmost BCD digit of the byte is now in the rightmost 4 bits of the AL-register. The POP instruction in line 54 restores the digit count in the CX-register. The JMP instruction in line 55 skips the ELSE portion of the double-alternative decision structure. If the flag indicates RIGHT, then the instructions in lines 57 and 58 are executed. The MOV instruction in line 57 moves the copy (saved in line 50) of the byte extracted from the BCD array on the last iteration of the loop from the AH-register back to the AL-register. The AND instruction in line 58 clears the left nibble of the byte, leaving the right nibble in the rightmost 4 bits of the AL-register. When the ENDIF is reached (line 60), the AL-register contains a single BCD digit.

The ADD instruction in line 61 converts the BCD digit in the AL-register to ASCII by adding the ASCII code for zero to the BCD code. The CLD instruction in line 62 clears the direction flag for incrementing through the ASCII array. The STOSB instruction in line 63 stores the ASCII code in the ASCII array at the address specified by the ES:DI register pair, and then it increments the DI-register by 1, so that the ES:DI register pair addresses the next byte in the ASCII array.

The NEG instruction in line 65 reverses the direction of the LEFT/RIGHT flag for the next iteration of the loop. The LOOP instruction in line 66 decrements the digit count in the CX-register by 1, and if the resulting digit count is nonzero, it transfers control to the top of the loop (line 44). Otherwise, the loop is terminated.

At loop exit, the registers are restored for the caller (lines 68–73), and control is returned to the caller (line 74). If the address of the array shown in Figure 11.3(a) is passed to the BCDASCII procedure with a digit count of 8, then the output ASCII array will have the values shown in Figure 11.9.

FIGURE 11.9
Output of the
BCDASCII procedure
for input as shown
in Figure 11.3(a)

Offset		
0000	2D	Sign
0001	30	MSD
0002	31	
0003	33	
0004	32	
0005	38	
0006	37	
0007	34	
0008	35	LSD

11.4 | BCD Arithmetic Instructions

Arithmetic in the BCD number system was discussed in Section 11.2 and its subsections. The algorithm presented use straight binary addition (or subtraction) to add (or subtract) corresponding digits of two BCD numbers. The result sum (or difference) digit requires an adjustment under certain conditions. This adjustment is an addition (or subtraction) of 0110 (6 in decimal), which is used to skip the six illegal codes. The IBM PC Assembly language provides six instructions for performing these adjustment operations: Four adjust the result of an arithmetic operation involving unpacked BCD digits, and two adjust the result of an arithmetic operation involving packed BCD digits.

Four of the six BCD adjustment instructions in the IBM PC Assembly language make use of the AF bit of the flags register, which is a copy of the carry from bit 3 to bit 4 after an addition operation and is a copy of the borrow from bit 4 into bit 3 after a subtraction operation. That is, the AF bit reflects the carry from the low nibble into the high nibble for a byte addition operation, and it reflects the borrow from the high nibble into the low nibble for a byte subtraction.

Unpacked BCD Arithmetic Instructions

There are four instructions in the IBM PC Assembly language that aid in performing arithmetic with unpacked BCD numbers: the **ASCII Adjust instructions**. The **ASCII Adjust for addition (AAA)** instruction has the following general form:

[⟨*label*⟩] AAA   [⟨*comment*⟩]

The AAA instruction has no explicit operand. The implicit operand is the contents of the AL-register. The AAA instruction should follow an ADD or ADC instruction that adds two unpacked BCD digits and leaves the result in the AL-register. It adjusts the AL-register to contain a valid, unpacked BCD digit. The carry from this digit is added to the AH-register and is recorded in the CF bit of the flags register. The AAA instruction causes the following steps to be performed:

IF   *((AL-REG and OF hex) > 9) or (AF = 1)*

THEN
      AL-REG is incremented by 6
      AH-REG is incremented by 1
      AF is set to 1
ENDIF
AF is copied into CF
Upper nibble of AL-REG is cleared

EXAMPLES

Suppose the AL-register contains 1001 (BCD code for 9) and the BL-register contains 0101 (BCD code for 5) before the following two instructions are executed:

```
ADD AL, BL
AAA
```

The ADD instruction performs the following addition:

$$\begin{array}{r} 1 \longleftarrow \text{Carry} \\ 00001001 \\ 00000101 \\ \hline 00001110 \end{array}$$

The carry from bit 3 into bit 4 is 0, so the AF bit of the flags register is cleared to 0 by the ADD instruction.

The AAA instruction performs the following operation:

1. Since the lower nibble of the AL-register is greater than 9, the value 0110 is added to the AL-register:

$$\begin{array}{r} 111 \longleftarrow \text{Carry} \\ 00001110 \\ 00000110 \\ \hline 00010100 \end{array}$$

The AH-register is incremented by 1, and the AF bit of the flags register is set to 1.
2. The CF bit of the flags register is set to 1.
3. The upper nibble of the AL-register is cleared leaving the value 00000100. The result in the AL-register is the BCD code for 4, the correct BCD sum digit, and the CF bit of the flags register is 1, the correct carry into the next BCD digit position.

Suppose the AL-register contains 00111001 (ASCII code for 9) and the BL-register contains 00110111 (ASCII code for 7) before the following two instructions are executed:

```
ADD AL, BL
AAA
```

The ADD instruction performs the following addition:

$$\begin{array}{r} 111111 \longleftarrow \text{Carry} \\ 00111001 \\ 00110111 \\ \hline 01110000 \end{array}$$

The carry from bit 3 into bit 4 is 1, so the AF bit of the flags register is set to 1 by the ADD instruction.

The AAA instruction performs the following operations:

1. Since the AF bit of the flags register is set, the value 0110 is added to the AL-register:

$$
\begin{array}{r}
01110000 \\
00000110 \\
\hline
01110110
\end{array}
$$

the AH-register is incremented by 1, and the AF bit of the flags register is set to 1.

2. The CF bit of the flags register is set to 1.

3. The upper nibble of the AL-register is cleared leaving the value 00000110. The result in the AL-register is the BCD code for 6, the correct BCD sum digit, and the CF bit of the flags register is 1, the correct carry into the next BCD digit position.

Note that the AAA instruction adjusts for the addition of ASCII digits as well as for the addition of unpacked BCD digits. When the sum of two ASCII digits is adjusted, the resulting sum digit is an unpacked BCD digit. To convert this unpacked BCD digit to ASCII, simply add 30 hex to the AL-register. The following loop then adds the ASCII number in the array addressed by the DS:SI register pair to the ASCII number in the array addressed by the ES:DI register pair, leaving the ASCII sum in the array addressed by the ES:DI register pair. The CX-register contains the size of the two ASCII numbers. The addition is ten's complement addition.

```
        MOV     BX,CX
        DEC     BX
        ADD     DI,BX       ;DPTR = DPTR + (SIZE - 1)
        ADD     SI,BX       ;SPTR = SPTR + (SIZE - 1)
        STD                 ;SET DF FOR DECREMENTING
        CLC                 ;CARRY = 0
REPEAT:                     ;REPEAT
        MOV     AL,ES:[DI] ;   DIGIT = DPTR→ASCII
        ADC     AL,DS:[SI] ;         + SPTR→ASCII
        AAA                 ;         + CARRY
        PUSHF               ;      PUSH CARRY FROM ADDITION
        ADD     AL,30H      ;      CHAR = DIGIT + 30 HEX
        POPF                ;      POP CARRY
        STOSB               ;      DPTR→ASCII = CHAR
                            ;      DPTR = DPTR - 1
        DEC     SI          ;      SPTR = SPTR - 1
        LOOP    REPEAT      ;      SIZE = SIZE - 1
                            ;UNTIL SIZE = 0
```

Figure 11.10(a) shows a possible configuration of the two arrays prior to execution of these instructions, and Figure 11.10(b) shows the result after execution.

FIGURE 11.10
ASCII addition loop
(a) before
execution and (b)
after execution

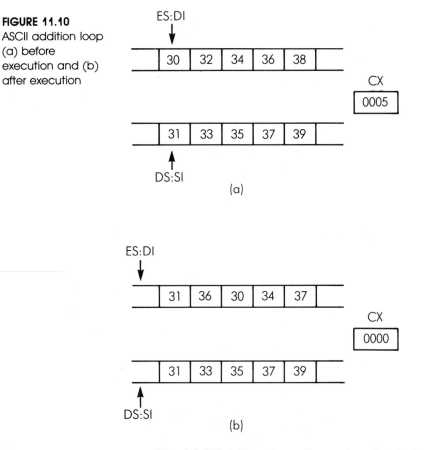

The **ASCII Adjust for subtraction (AAS)** instruction has the following general form:

[⟨*label*⟩]   AAS   [⟨*comment*⟩]

The AAS instruction has no explicit operand. The implicit operand is the contents of the AL-register. The AAS instruction should follow an SUB or SBB instruction that subtracts two unpacked BCD digits and leaves the result in the AL-register. It adjusts the AL-register to contain a valid, unpacked BCD digit. The borrow into this digit is subtracted from the AH-register and is recorded in the CF bit of the flags register. The AAS instruction causes the following steps to be performed.

IF   *((AL-REG and 0F hex) > 9) or (AF = 1)*
THEN
        AL-REG is decremented by 6
        AH-REG is decremented by 1
        AF is set to 1
ENDIF
AF is copied into CF
Upper nibble of AL-REG is cleared

EXAMPLE

Suppose the AL-register contains 0101 (BCD code for 5) and the BL-register contains 0111 (BCD code for 7) before the following two instructions are executed:

```
SUB AL,BL
AAS
```

The SUB instruction performs the following subtraction:

$$\begin{array}{r} 00000101 \\ 00000111 \\ \hline \end{array}$$

which is performed by a complement, and add:

$$\begin{array}{r} 1 \longleftarrow \text{Carry} \\ 00000101 \\ 11111001 \\ \hline 11111110 \end{array}$$

The carry from bit 3 into bit 4 is 0, thus the borrow from bit 4 into bit 3 is 1. Therefore, the AF bit of the flags register is set to 1 by execution of the SUB instruction.

The AAS instruction performs the following operations:

1. Since the AF bit of the flags register is set, the value 11111010 (− 6 in decimal) is added to the AL-register:

$$\begin{array}{r} 111111 \longleftarrow \text{Carry} \\ 11111110 \\ 11111010 \\ \hline 11111000 \end{array}$$

the AH-register is decremented by 1, and the AF bit of the flags register is set to 1.
2. The CF bit of the flags register is set to 1.
3. The upper nibble of the AL-register is cleared leaving the value 00001000. The result in the AL-register is the BCD code for 8, the correct BCD difference digit, and the CF bit of the flags register is 1, the correct borrow from the next BCD digit position.

The AAS instruction adjusts for the subtraction of ASCII digits as well as for the subtraction of unpacked BCD digits. When the difference between two ASCII digits is adjusted, the resulting difference digit is an unpacked BCD digit. To convert this unpacked BCD digit to ASCII, simply add 30 hex to the AL-register. The following loop subtracts the ASCII number in the array addressed by the DS:SI register pair from the ASCII number in the array addressed by the ES:DI register pair, leaving the ASCII difference in the array addressed by the ES:DI register pair. The CX-register contains the size of the two ASCII numbers. The subtraction is ten's complement subtraction.

```
            MOV     BX,CX
            DEC     BX
            ADD     DI,BX       ;DPTR = DPTR + (SIZE - 1)
            ADD     SI,BX       ;SPTR = SPTR + (SIZE - 1)
            STD                 ;SET DF FOR DECREMENTING
            CLC                 ;BORROW = 0
REPEAT:                         ;REPEAT
            MOV     AL,ES:[DI] ;   DIGIT = DPTR→ASCII
            SBB     AL,DS:[SI] ;       - SPTR→ASCII
            AAS                 ;           - BORROW
            PUSHF               ;   PUSH BORROW FROM SUBTRACT
            ADD     AL,30H      ;   CHAR = DIGIT + 30 HEX
            POPF                ;   POP BORROW
            STOSB               ;   DPTR→ASCII = CHAR
                                ;   DPTR = DPTR - 1
            DEC     SI          ;   SPTR = SPTR - 1
            LOOP    REPEAT      ;   SIZE = SIZE - 1
                                ;UNTIL SIZE = 0
```

Figure 11.11(a) shows a possible configuration of the two arrays prior to execution of these instructions, and Figure 11.11(b) shows the result after execution.

FIGURE 11.11
ASCII subtraction loop (a) before execution and (b) after execution

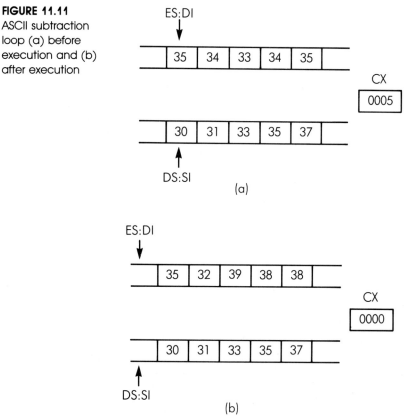

The **ASCII Adjust for multiplication (AAM)** instruction has the following general form:

[⟨*label*⟩] AAM   [⟨*comment*⟩]

The AAM instruction has no explicit operand. The implicit operand is the contents of the AX-register. The AAM instruction should follow a MUL instruction that multiplies two unpacked BCD digits and leaves the result in the AX-register. It divides the AX-register value by 10. The quotient (the high-order, unpacked BCD digit of the product) is placed in the AH-register. The remainder (the low-order, unpacked BCD digit of the product) is placed in the AL-register.

EXAMPLE

Suppose the AL-register contains 0110 (BCD code for 6) and the BL-register contains 0111 (BCD code for 7) before the following two instructions are executed:

```
MUL BL
AAM
```

The MUL instruction produces the product 0000000000101010 in the AX-register, the binary representation of the decimal value 42. The AAM instruction converts this binary product to the unpacked BCD digits 00000100 and 00000010 in the AH and AL registers, respectively.

An algorithm for the multiplication of two multidigit, unpacked BCD numbers is not considered here. An algorithm for the multiplication of two multidigit, packed BCD numbers is presented in Programming Exercises 11.6, 11.7, and 11.8.

The **ASCII Adjust for division (AAD)** instruction has the following general form:

[⟨*label*⟩]   AAD   [⟨*comment*⟩]

The AAD instruction has no explicit operand. The implicit operand is the two-digit, unpacked BCD number in the AX-register with the high-order digit in the AH-register and the low-order digit in the AL-register. The AAD instruction should precede a DIV instruction to adjust the dividend prior to division of a two-digit, unpacked BCD number by an unpacked BCD digit. The dividend to be adjusted is the two-digit, unpacked BCD number in the AX-register. The most-significant BCD digit (AH-register value) is multiplied by 10, and the least-significant BCD digit (AL-register value) is added to this product. The resulting binary integer is placed in the AL-register, and the AH-register is cleared.

EXAMPLE

Suppose the AX-register contains 0000010000000010 (unpacked BCD code for 42) and the BL-register contains 00001001 (unpacked BCD code for 9) before the following two instructions are executed:

```
AAD
DIV BL
```

The AAD instruction converts the two-digit BCD dividend in the AX-register to the binary integer 0000000000101010 in the AX-register. The division is then a binary division producing the quotient 00000100 (BCD code for 4) in the AL-register and the remainder 00000110 (BCD code for 6) in the AH-register.

An algorithm for the division of two multidigit, unpacked BCD numbers is not considered here.

Packed BCD Arithmetic Instructions

There are two instructions in the IBM PC Assembly language that aid in performing arithmetic with packed BCD numbers: the **Decimal Adjust instructions**. The **Decimal Adjust for addition (DAA)** instruction has the following general form:

[⟨*label*⟩] DAA   [⟨*comment*⟩]

The DAA instruction has no explicit operand. The implicit operand is the contents of the AL-register. The DAA instruction should follow an ADD or ADC instruction that adds two packed BCD digit pairs and leaves the result in the AL-register. It adjusts the AL-register to contain a valid pair of packed BCD digits. The carry from this digit pair is recorded in the CF bit of the flags register. The DAA instruction causes the following steps to be performed:

IF   *(lower nibble of AL-REG > 9) or (AF = 1)*
THEN

    AL-REG is incremented by 6
    AF is set to 1
ENDIF

IF   *(upper nibble of AL-REG > 9) or (CF = 1)*
THEN

    AL-REG is incremented by 60 hex
    CF is set to 1
ENDIF

EXAMPLE

Suppose the AL-register contains the value 10000101 (packed BCD code for 85) and the BL-register contains 10010110 (packed BCD code for 96) before the following two instructions are executed:

```
ADD AL, BL
DAA
```

The ADD instruction performs the following addition:

$$
\begin{array}{r}
1 \quad \longleftarrow \text{Carry} \\
10000101 \\
10010110 \\
\hline
1 \quad 00011011
\end{array}
$$

The carry from bit 3 into bit 4 is 0, thus the AF bit of the flags register is cleared to 0 by execution of the ADD instruction. The carry out of the most-significant bit is 1, thus the CF bit of the flags register is set to 1 by execution of the ADD instruction.

The DAA instruction performs the following operations:

1. Since the lower nibble of the AL-register (1011) is greater than 9 (1001), the value 00000110 is added to the AL-register:

$$
\begin{array}{r}
1111 \quad \longleftarrow \text{Carry} \\
00011011 \\
00000110 \\
\hline
00100001
\end{array}
$$

   and the AF bit of the flags register is set to 1. Note that this part of the adjustment caused a carry from the lower nibble into the upper nibble.

2. Since the CF bit of the flags register is set, the value 01100000 (60 hex) is added to the AL-register:

$$
\begin{array}{r}
11 \quad \longleftarrow \text{Carry} \\
00100001 \\
01100000 \\
\hline
10000001
\end{array}
$$

   and the CF bit of the flags register is set to 1.

The adjusted result is 10000001, which is the packed BCD code for 81 with a carry of 1 into the next higher digit pair.

The **Decimal Adjust for subtraction (DAS)** instruction has the following general form:

[⟨*label*⟩] DAS   [⟨*comment*⟩]

The DAS instruction has no explicit operand. The implicit operand is the contents of the AL-register. The DAS instruction should follow an SUB or SBB instruction that subtracts two packed BCD digit pairs and leaves the result in the AL-register. It adjusts the AL-register to contain a valid pair of packed BCD digits. The borrow into this digit pair is recorded in the CF bit of the flags register. The DAS instruction causes the following steps to be performed:

```
IF      (lower nibble of AL-REG > 9) or (AF = 1)
THEN
        AL-REG is decremented by 6
        AF is set to 1
ENDIF


IF      (upper nibble of AL-REG > 9) or (CF = 1)
THEN
        AL-REG is decremented by 60 hex
        CF is set to 1
ENDIF
```

EXAMPLE

Suppose the AL-register contains the value 01110010 (packed BCD code for 72) and the BL-register contains 00100101 (packed BCD code for 25) before the following two instructions are executed:

```
SUB AL, BL
DAS
```

The SUB instruction performs the following subtraction:

$$\begin{array}{r} 01110010 \\ - \ 00100101 \end{array}$$

which is performed by a complement, and add:

$$\begin{array}{r} 111 \quad 1 \ \longleftarrow \text{Carry} \\ 01110010 \\ + \ 11011011 \\ \hline 1 \quad 01001101 \end{array}$$

The carry from bit 3 into bit 4 is a 0, thus the borrow from bit 4 into bit 3 is a 1. Therefore, the AF bit of the flags register is set to 1 by execution of the SUB instruction. The carry out of the most-significant bit is a 1, thus the borrow into the MSB is 0. Therefore, the CF bit of the flags register is cleared to 0 by execution of the SUB instruction.

The DAS instruction performs the following operations:

1. Since the AF bit of the flags register is set, the value 11111010 (-6 in decimal) is added to the AL-register:

$$\begin{array}{r} 1111 \quad \longleftarrow \text{Carry} \\ 01001101 \\ + \ 11111010 \\ \hline 1 \quad 01000111 \end{array}$$

and the AF bit of the flags register is set to 1.

2. Since the upper nibble of the AL-register is not greater than 9 and the CF bit of the flags register is not set, no adjustment is required to the upper nibble of the AL-register.

The adjusted result is 01000111, which is the packed BCD code for 47 with no borrow from the next higher digit pair.

Arithmetic Overflow in BCD

With the packed BCD ten's complement representation presented in Section 11.3, BCD numbers can be interpreted as either unsigned numbers or signed ten's complement numbers. If the unsigned interpretation is used, then the range of integers that can be represented with n-digit BCD numbers is 0 to $10^n - 1$. If the signed interpretation is used, then the range of integers that can be represented with n-digit BCD numbers is $-5(10^{n-1})$ to $+5(10^{n-1}) - 1$. If an arithmetic operation produces a result that is outside the range of integers for that interpretation, then arithmetic overflow has occurred.

Detection of overflow depends on the interpretation used. With the unsigned integer interpretation, overflow occurs whenever a carry out of the MSD on addition or a borrow into the MSD on subtraction occurs. With the signed integer interpretation, overflow occurs on an addition whenever the signs of the two operands are the same and the sign of the sum is not the same as the signs of the operands. With the signed integer interpretation, overflow occurs on a subtraction operation whenever the signs of the minuend and subtrahend are different and the sign of the difference is not the same as the sign of the minuend. With the signed integer interpretation, overflow occurs on a negation operation whenever the sign of the result is the same as the sign of the operand, which occurs only when the negative number being negated has no corresponding positive number.

Programming Examples

Two BCD arithmetic procedures are presented in this section: The first performs the sum of two packed BCD numbers, and the second performs the ten's complement of a packed BCD number.

Procedure to Add Two Packed BCD Numbers

The FAR procedure defined in Program Listing 11.3 is a PUBLIC procedure, called ADDBCD, that adds two packed BCD numbers. The prologue in lines 3–19 describes the function of the procedure and explains its interface requirements. On entry to the procedure, the DS:SI register pair must address the source BCD number, the ES:DI register pair must address the destination BCD number, and the CX-register must contain the number of digits in the BCD numbers. The two BCD numbers must be the same size. On return to the caller, the array addressed by the ES:DI register pair contains the sum of the two input

```
 1: ;
 2: ;                   PROGRAM LISTING 11.3
 3: ;
 4: ; PROCEDURE TO ADD TWO PACKED BCD NUMBERS
 5: ;
 6: ; INPUTS:   DS:SI POINTS TO THE ARRAY CONTAINING
 7: ;                 THE SOURCE BCD NUMBER
 8: ;           ES:DI POINTS TO THE ARRAY CONTAINING
 9: ;                 THE DESTINATION BCD NUMBER
10: ;           CX    CONTAINS THE SIZE OF  THE   TWO
11: ;                 BCD NUMBERS (MUST BE EVEN)
12: ;
13: ; OUTPUTS: THE ARRAY POINTED TO BY ES:DI CONTAINS
14: ;              THE SUM OF THE TWO INPUT  BCD  NUMBERS
15: ;
16: ;              THE FOLLOWING FLAGS ARE SET TO REFLECT
17: ;              THE RESULT
18: ;                        OF  SF  ZF  CF
19: ;
20: ;
21: ; CODE SEGMENT
22: ;
23: CODE        SEGMENT
24:             ASSUME  CS:CODE
25: ADDBCD      PROC    FAR          ;PROCEDURE ADDBCD (SPTR,DPTR,DIGIT_COUNT)
26:             PUBLIC  ADDBCD
27:             PUSH    DI                      ;SAVE REGISTERS
28:             PUSH    SI
29:             PUSH    DX
30:             PUSH    CX
31:             PUSH    BX
32:             PUSH    AX
33:             PUSHF                           ;SAVE FLAGS
34:             SHR     CX,1                    ;LOOP_COUNT = DIGIT_COUNT/2
35:             CLD                             ;SET DF FOR INCREMENTING
36:             MOV     DX,0040H                ;ZERO_FLAG = 1
37:             CLC                             ;CLEAR CF BIT OF FLAGS REGISTER
38: REPEAT:                                     ;REPEAT
39:             MOV     BH,ES:[DI]              ;   D_SIGN = DPTR -> BYTE
40:             LODSB                           ;   SUM_PAIR = SPTR -> BYTE
41:             ADC     AL,ES:[DI]              ;                + DPTR -> BYTE
42:                                             ;                + CF
43:                                             ;   SPTR = SPTR + 1
44:             DAA                             ;   BCD_PAIR = ADJUSTED SUM_PAIR
45:             PUSHF                           ;   SAVE CF AND DF
46:             CMP     AL,0                    ;   IF   BCD_PAIR <> 0
47:             JE      END_ZERO
48:             SUB     DX,DX                   ;      THEN ZERO_FLAG = 0
49: END_ZERO:                                   ;   ENDIF
50:             POPF                            ;   RESTORE CF AND DF
51:             STOSB                           ;   DPTR -> BYTE = BCD_PAIR
52:                                             ;   DPTR = DPTR + 1
53:             LOOP    REPEAT                  ;   LOOP_COUNT = LOOP_COUNT - 1
54:                                             ;UNTIL LOOP_COUNT = 0
55:             PUSHF                           ;SAVE CF
56:             DEC     DI                      ;DPTR = DPTR - 1
57:             DEC     SI                      ;SPTR = SPTR - 1
58:                                             ;<SPTR AND DPTR NOW POINT TO
59:                                             ; THE HIGHEST PAIR OF DIGITS
60:                                             ; IN THEIR RESPECTIVE BCD NOS.>
61:*;
```

*

```
62: ;
63:                 CMP     BH,50H                      ;IF    D_SIGN = SIGN OF SOURCE
64:                 JAE     NEG                         ;              BCD NUMBER
65:                 CMP     BYTE PTR DS:[SI],50H
66:                 JAE     DIFF
67:                 JMP     SAME
68: NEG:
69:                 CMP     BYTE PTR DS:[SI],50H
70:                 JB      DIFF
71: SAME:                                               ;THEN
72:                 MOV     BL,1                        ;      CHECK_OVRFLO = TRUE
73:                 JMP     END_SIGN
74: DIFF:                                               ;ELSE
75:                 MOV     BL,0                        ;      CHECK_OVRFLO = FALSE
76: END_SIGN:                                           ;ENDIF
77: ;
78: ;<** S E T   F L A G S   F O R   O U T P U T **>
79: ;
80:                                                     ;CLEAR OUTPUT_FLAGS
81:                 POP     AX                          ;MOVE SAVED CF TO OUTPUT_FLAGS
82:                 AND     AX,0001
83:                 OR      AX,DX                       ;MOVE ZERO_FLAG TO OUTPUT_FLAGS
84:                 CMP     BYTE PTR ES:[DI],50H        ;IF    BCD SUM IS NEGATIVE
85:                 JB      END_SF
86:                 OR      AX,0080H                    ;THEN SET SF IN OUTPUT_FLAGS
87: END_SF:                                             ;ENDIF
88:                 CMP     BL,0                        ;IF    CHECK_OVRFLO
89:                 JE      END_OF
90:                 CMP     BH,50H                      ;THEN IF   D_SIGN NOT EQUAL
91:                 JB      POS                         ;              SIGN OF BCD SUM
92:                 CMP     BYTE PTR ES:[DI],50H
93:                 JAE     END_OF
94:                 JMP     SET_OF
95: POS:
96:                 CMP     BYTE PTR ES:[DI],50H
97:                 JB      END_OF
98: SET_OF:                                             ;      THEN
99:                 OR      AX,0800H                    ;              SET OF IN OUTPUT_FLAGS
100: END_OF:                                            ;          ENDIF
101:                                                    ;ENDIF
102:                 POP     CX                         ;TEMP = FLAGS SAVED UPON ENTRY
103:                 AND     CX,0F73EH                  ;CLEAR OF SF ZF ZND CF IN TEMP
104:                 OR      AX,CX                       ;MERGE TEMP WITH OUTPUT_FLAGS
105:                 PUSH    AX                         ;SAVE OUTPUT_FLAGS
106: ;
107:                 POPF                               ;RESTORE FLAGS
108:                 POP     AX                         ;RESTORE REGISTERS
109:                 POP     BX
110:                 POP     CX
111:                 POP     DX
112:                 POP     SI
113:                 POP     DI
114: ;
115:                 RET                                ;RETURN
116: ADDBCD          ENDP                  ;END ADDBCD
117: CODE            ENDS
118:*                END
```

BCD numbers, and the OF, SF, ZF, and CF bits of the flags register are set to reflect this BCD sum.

The ADDBCD procedure begins by saving the registers that it uses (lines 27–33) and performing initialization for the REPEAT-UNTIL loop that performs the packed BCD addition (lines 34–37). The SHR instruction in line 34 computes the loop count for the REPEAT-UNTIL loop. The loop count is one-half the digit count, since each iteration of the loop adds a pair of digits from the source BCD number to the corresponding pair of digits from the destination BCD number and adjusts the sum digit pair. The CLD instruction in line 35 clears the DF bit of the flags register for incrementing through the two BCD arrays from the least-significant digit pair to the most-significant digit pair. Bit 6 of the DX-register is used as a zero flag and is merged into the flags register value that is returned to the caller. The MOV instruction in line 36 initializes this zero flag to 1. It is cleared in the loop the first time that a nonzero sum digit pair is produced. If all sum digit pairs are zero (i.e., the sum of the two BCD numbers is zero), then the zero flag remains set to 1. The CLC instruction in line 37 clears the CF bit of the flags register, so that the carry into the least-significant digit position is zero. This operation allows the ADC instruction to be used for the addition of the least-significant digit pair as well as for the addition of all subsequent digit pairs.

The REPEAT-UNTIL loop in lines 38–54 performs the addition of the two BCD numbers. The loop body begins with the MOV instruction in line 39, which moves a copy of the digit pair addressed by the ES:DI register pair to the BH-register. At loop exit, the BH-register pair contains the most-significant pair of digits from the destination BCD array. The high-order digit of this digit pair indicates the sign of the destination BCD number. This sign would not otherwise be available at loop exit, because the sum digit pair replaces the destination BCD digit pair on each iteration of the loop.

The LODSB instruction in line 40 loads the AL-register with a pair of digits from the source BCD number (the pair of digits addressed by the DS:SI register pair) and increments the SI-register by 1, so that the DS:SI register pair addresses the next higher pair of digits in the source BCD number. The ADC instruction in line 41 adds to the digit pair in the AL-register the corresponding pair of digits from the destination BCD number (the pair of digits addressed by the ES:DI register pair) and the carry from the previous digit position. The DAA instruction in line 44 adjusts the sum in the AL-register to the correct pair of packed BCD digits and records the carry from this digit pair in the CF bit of the flags register. The PUSHF instruction in line 45 is used to save the CF bit of the flags register, which is needed in the addition operation in the next iteration of the loop body. Several instructions in the remainder of the loop body affect the CF bit of the flags register.

The single-alternative decision structure implemented in lines 46–49 tests the packed BCD digit pair in the AL-register (the sum digit pair) to see if it is nonzero. If it is nonzero, then the SUB instruction in line 48 is executed, which clears the zero flag in bit 6 of the DX-register.

The POPF instruction in line 50 restores the CF bit of the flags register. None of the remaining instructions in the loop affect the CF bit. The STOSB instruction in line 51 moves a copy of the sum digit pair in the AL-register to the destination BCD array, replacing the pair of digits addressed by the ES:DI register pair, and then increments the DI-register by 1, so that the ES:DI register pair addresses the next higher pair of digits in the destination BCD number. The LOOP instruction in line 53 decrements the loop count by 1, and if the loop count is nonzero, returns control to the top of the loop (line 38).

After the REPEAT-UNTIL loop, the procedure modifies the caller's saved flags to reflect the sum of the two BCD numbers. At loop exit, the destination BCD array contains the BCD sum, the CF bit of the flags register reflects the carry out of the MSD of the sum, and bit 6 of the DX-register reflects whether or not the sum is zero. The PUSHF instruction in line 55 saves the CF bit of the flags register, so that it can be merged into the caller's saved flags later in the procedure. The DEC instructions in lines 56 and 57 set the ES:DI register pair and the DS:SI register pair to address the most-significant pair of digits in their respective arrays. The single-alternative decision structure implemented in lines 63–76 determines whether or not overflow is possible. The sign of the destination BCD number, recorded in the BH-register on the last iteration of the REPEAT-UNTIL loop, and the sign of the source BCD number are compared to see if they are the same or different (lines 63–70). If the signs of the two input BCD numbers are the same, then the BL-register is set to 1 (line 72), indicating that overflow is possible and that a check for overflow must be made. If the two signs are not the same, then the BL-register is set to 0 (line 75), indicating that overflow is not possible and that a check for overflow is not to be made.

The instructions in lines 80–105 build in the AX-register an image of the OF, SF, ZF, and CF bits of the flags register that reflect the BCD sum. This image is then merged with the flags register value saved for the caller in line 33. The POP instruction in line 81 loads the AX-register with the image of the flags register that existed at exit from the REPEAT-UNTIL loop that was saved in line 55. The AND instruction in line 82 clears all bits except the CF bit in this image of the flags register. The OR instruction in line 83 merges the zero flag in bit 6 of the DX-register with the flag image in the AX-register. The single-alternative decision structure implemented in lines 84–87 sets the SF bit in the flags register image in the AX-register (line 86), if the MSD of the BCD sum is greater than or equal to 5. The single-alternative decision structure implemented in lines 88–101 tests the flag in the BL-register to see if an overflow check needs to be made. If the overflow check is required (BL-register = 1), then the single-alternative decision structure implemented in lines 90–100 is executed. This decision structure compares the sign of the destination BCD number (saved in the BH-register) with the sign of the BCD sum. If the two signs are not the same, then the OF bit in the flags register image in the AX-register is set to 1 (line 99). The POP instruction in line 102 loads the CX-register with the flags register image saved for the caller (line 33). The AND instruction in line 103 clears the OF, SF, ZF, and CF bits in the caller's flags register image in the CX-register. The OR instruction in line 104 merges the flags register image in the CX-register with the one in the AX-register. The PUSH instruction in line 105 pushes the caller's flags register image, modified to reflect the result of the BCD addition, back onto the stack. The instructions in lines 107–113 restore registers for the caller, and the RET instruction in line 115 returns control to the caller.

Procedure to Negate a Packed BCD Number

The FAR procedure defined in Program Listing 11.4 is a PUBLIC procedure, called NEGBCD, that performs the ten's complement of a packed BCD number. The prologue in lines 3–12 describes the function of the procedure and explains its interface requirements. On entry to the procedure, the ES:DI register pair must address the first byte of an array that contains a packed BCD number, and the CX-register must contain the number of digits in this BCD number. The digit count in the CX-register must be even. On return to the caller, the array addressed by the ES:DI register pair contains the ten's complement of the input BCD number, and the OF, SF, ZF, and CF bits of the flags register are set to reflect the BCD result. The algorithm used to perform the negation is an application of the alternate method described in Section 11.2.

    The procedure begins by saving the registers for the caller (lines 17–22) and performing loop initialization (lines 23–25). The SHR instruction in line 23 computes the loop count from the digit count input to the procedure in the CX-register. The loop count is one-half the digit count, since two digits are processed on each iteration of the loop. The CLD instruction in line 24 clears the

```
 1: ;
 2: ;                       PROGRAM LISTING 11.4
 3: ;
 4: ; PROCEDURE TO PERFORM TEN'S COMPLEMENT OF A PACKED BCD NUMBER
 5: ;
 6: ; INPUT:   ES:DI POINTS TO ARRAY CONTAINING PACKED BCD NUMBER
 7: ;          CX    CONTAINS SIZE OF BCD NUMBER   (MUST BE EVEN)
 8: ;
 9: ; OUTPUT:  THE ARRAY POINTED TO BY ES:DI CONTAINS   THE   TEN'S
10: ;          COMPLEMENT  OF  THE  NUMBER THAT IT CONTAINED UPON
11: ;          ENTRY TO THE PROCEDURE.
12: ;
13: CODE       SEGMENT
14:            ASSUME  CS:CODE
15: NEGBCD     PROC    FAR                 ;PROCEDURE NEGBCD (PTR,DIGIT_COUNT)
16:            PUBLIC  NEGBCD
17:            PUSH    AX                  ;SAVE REGISTERS
18:            PUSH    BX
19:            PUSH    CX
20:            PUSH    DX
21:            PUSH    DI
22:            PUSHF                       ;SAVE FLAGS
23:            SHR     CX,1                ;LOOP_COUNT = DIGIT_COUNT / 2
24:            CLD                         ;SET DF FOR INCREMENTING
25:            MOV     BX,0000             ;CLEAR OUTPUT_FLAGS
26:*;
```

```
27: ;
28:              MOV      AL,0                    ;FOUND = FALSE
29:      REPE    SCASB                            ;REPEAT
30:                                               ;    IF    PTR -> BYTE <> 0
31:                                               ;    THEN FOUND = TRUE
32:                                               ;    ENDIF
33:                                               ;    PTR = PTR + 1
34:                                               ;    LOOP_COUNT = LOOP_COUNT - 1
35:                                               ;UNTIL FOUND OR LOOP_COUNT = 0
36:              JE       NOTFOUND                ;IF    FOUND
37:              DEC      DI                      ;THEN PTR = PTR - 1
38:              OR       BX,0001                 ;     SET CF IN OUTPUT_FLAGS
39:              MOV      AL,ES:[DI]              ;     IF   RIGHT NIBBLE OF
40:              AND      AL,0FH                  ;          PTR -> BYTE = 0
41:              JNE      ELSE                    ;
42:              MOV      AL,0A0H                 ;     THEN PTR -> BYTE =
43:              JMP      SUBTRACT                ;          A0 HEX   PTR -> BYTE
44: ELSE:                                         ;     ELSE PTR -> BYTE =
45:              MOV      AL,9AH                  ;          9A HEX - PTR -> BYTE
46: SUBTRACT:                                     ;     ENDIF
47:              SUB      AL,ES:[DI]
48:              STOSB                            ;     PTR = PTR + 1
49:              JCXZ     LOOP_END                ;     WHILE LOOP_COUNT <> 0
50: LOOP_TOP:
51:              MOV      DL,ES:[DI]              ;        IN_SIGN = PTR -> BYTE
52:              MOV      AL,99H                  ;        PTR -> BYTE = 99 HEX
53:              SUB      AL,ES:[DI]              ;             - PTR -> BYTE
54:              STOSB                            ;        PTR = PTR + 1
55:              LOOP     LOOP_TOP                ;        DECREMENT LOOP_COUNT
56: LOOP_END:                                     ;     ENDWHILE
57:              DEC      DI                      ;     PTR = PTR - 1
58:                                               ;     PTR NOW POINTS TO FIRST
59:                                               ;     PAIR OF DIGITS IN BCD NUM
60:              CMP      BYTE PTR ES:[DI],50H;    IF   SIGN OF RESULT = -
61:              JB       OVRFLO_CHK
62:              OR       BX,0080H                ;     THEN SET SF IN OUTPUT_FLAGS
63: OVRFLO_CHK:                                   ;     ENDIF
64:              CMP      DL,ES:[DI]              ;     IF   IN_SIGN =
65:              JNE      MERGE_FLAGS             ;          SIGN OF RESULT
66:              OR       BX,0800H                ;     THEN SET OF IN OUTPUT_FLAGS
67:                                               ;     ENDIF
68:              JMP      MERGE_FLAGS
69: NOTFOUND:                                     ;ELSE
70:              OR       BX,0040H                ;     SET ZF IN OUTPUT_FLAGS
71: MERGE_FLAGS:                                  ;ENDIF
72:              POP      AX                      ;TEMP = FLAGS SAVED UPON ENTRY
73:              AND      AX,0F73EH               ;CLEAR OF SF ZF AND CF IN TEMP
74:              OR       AX,BX                   ;MERGE TEMP WITH OUTPUT_FLAGS
75:              PUSH     AX                      ;SAVE OUTPUT_FLAGS
76:              POPF                             ;RESTORE FLAGS
77:              POP      DI                      ;RESTORE REGISTERS
78:              POP      DX
79:              POP      CX
80:              POP      BX
81:              POP      AX
82:              RET                              ;RETURN
83: NEGBCD   ENDP                                 ;END NEGBCD
84: CODE     ENDS
85:*         END
```

*

DF bit of the flags register for incrementing through the BCD array from the least-significant digit pair to the most-significant digit pair. The flags register image for the OF, SF, ZF, and CF bits to be returned to the caller is built in the BX-register. The MOV instruction in line 25 initializes this flag image to zero.

The algorithm begins by copying digits from right to left up to but not including the first nonzero digit. The loop in lines 28 and 29 searches the BCD array for the first nonzero digit pair. Each time the string instruction in line 29 is executed, the DI-register is automatically incremented by 1, so that the ES:DI register pair addresses the next higher digit pair of the BCD array, and the loop count in the CX-register is automatically decremented by 1. The repetition of the string instruction in line 29 halts for one of two reasons: Either a nonzero digit pair is found, or the entire BCD array is scanned without finding a nonzero digit pair. The double-alternative decision structure implemented in lines 36–71 determines which of the two conditions caused the repetition of the string instruction to halt: If a nonzero digit pair were found, then the instructions in lines 37–68 (the THEN clause) are executed; otherwise, the instruction in line 70 (the ELSE clause) is executed.

The THEN clause of the double-alternative decision structure performs the remaining steps of the alternate method described in Section 11.2. The DEC instruction in line 37 adjusts the ES:DI register pair, so that it addresses the first nonzero digit pair in the BCD array. The OR instruction in line 38 sets the CF bit in the flags register image being built in the BX-register. For the purpose of setting flags, a negation is viewed as a subtraction from zero, and the subtraction of a nonzero value from zero always requires a borrow into the MSD. The double-alternative decision structure implemented in lines 39–46 determines whether the first nonzero digit is the left nibble or the right nibble of this digit pair. If the first nonzero digit is the left nibble, then the right nibble must be copied, and the left nibble must be subtracted from 1010 (10 in decimal); this step is accomplished by subtracting the digit pair from A0 hex (lines 42 and 47). If the first nonzero digit is the right nibble, then the right nibble must be subtracted from 1010 (10 in decimal), and the left nibble must be subracted from 1001 (9 in decimal); this step is accomplished by subtracting the digit pair from 9A hex (lines 45 and 47). The STOSB instruction in line 48 replaces the first nonzero digit pair in the BCD array with the result of this subtraction and increments the DI-register, so that the ES:DI register pair addresses the next higher digit pair in the BCD array.

The THEN clause continues with the WHILE loop implemented in lines 49–56. The WHILE loop subtracts all remaining BCD digits in the number from 1001 (9 in decimal). The JCXZ instruction (line 49) turns what would normally be a REPEAT-UNTIL loop into a WHILE loop. The loop body begins with the MOV instruction in line 51, which copies the digit pair addressed by the ES:DI register pair into the DL-register. At loop exit, the DL-register pair contains the most-significant pair of digits from the input BCD number. That digit indicates the sign of the input BCD number. The instructions in lines 52 and 53 subtract the digit pair addressed by the ES:DI register pair from 99 hex (10011001 binary), and the STOSB instruction in line 54 replaces the digit pair addressed by ES:DI with the result of this subtraction and then increments the DI-register, so that the ES:DI register pair addresses the next higher pair of BCD digits. The LOOP instruction in line 55 decrements the loop count by 1 the transfers control to the top of the loop (line 50), if the loop count is not zero. On exit from the WHILE loop, the proper settings for the SF and OF bits of the flags register are determined. The single-alternative decision structure implemented in lines 60–63 determines the sign of the result. If the result is negative, then the OR instruction in line 62 sets the SF bit in the flags register image being built in the BX-register. The single-alternative decision structure implemented in lines 64–67 compares the sign of the input BCD number (indicated by the digit pair in the DL-register) with the sign of the result. If the two signs are the same, then the OR instruction in line 66 sets the OF bit in the flags register image in the BX-register. This last step concludes the THEN clause of the double-alternative decision structure implemented in lines 36–71. The JMP instruction in line 68 skips the ELSE clause for this decision structure.

The ELSE clause of the double-alternative decision structure is executed, if the scan loop in lines 28 and 29 fails to find a nonzero digit pair in the input BCD array. In this case, the input BCD number is zero and its ten's complement is zero. The OR instruction in line 70 sets the ZF bit in the flags register image in the BX-register.

On completion of the double-alternative decision structure, the flags register image in the BX-register is merged with the flags register value that was saved for the caller. The POP instruction in line 72 loads the AX-register with the flags register value saved for the caller. The AND instruction in line 73 clears the OF, SF, ZF, and CF bits in this flags register image in the AX-register. The OR instruction in line 74 merges the flags register image in the BX-register with the one in the AX-register, which modifies the flags register image saved for the caller to reflect the result of the negation operation. The PUSH instruction in line 75 pushes this modified flags register image back onto the stack, and the POPF instruction in line 76 places this image in the flags register. The POP instructions in lines 77–81 restore the remainder of the caller's registers, and the RET instruction in line 82 returns control to the caller.

11.5 BCD Input/Output

When a BCD number includes both an integer and a fraction, the decimal point that separates the two portions of the number does not have to be part of the internal representation of the number. All BCD numbers can be stored internally as integers. The arithmetic computations performed with these BCD numbers can treat the numbers as integers. The decimal point is only considered in the interpretation of the BCD number. The interpretation is applied when a value is input for the BCD number or when the value represented by the BCD number is being output. This section discusses the interpretation of BCD numbers for input/output.

FIGURE 11.12
Packed BCD array—
value depends on
interpretation

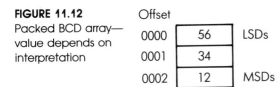

Offset

0000	56	LSDs
0001	34	
0002	12	MSDs

Interpretation of BCD Numbers for Input/Output

The internal representation of a BCD number does not have to have an explicit decimal point. The assumed decimal point can be in any position within the number. For example, consider the packed BCD array shown in Figure 11.12. This array represents the integer 123456, if the decimal point is assumed to follow the digit pair at offset 0000. It represents the real number 1234.56, if the decimal point is assumed to lie between the digit pair at offset 0001 and the digit pair at offset 0000. It represents the real number 1.23456, if the decimal point is assumed to lie between the left nibble and the right nibble of the digit pair at offset 0002.

The procedures that perform arithmetic computations on packed BCD numbers do not need to know whether their operands represent integers or real numbers. For example, the ADDBCD procedure discussed in Section 11.4 works correctly for real numbers as long as the assumed decimal point is in the same position in the two BCD operands. If so, then the position of the assumed decimal point in the sum is the same as its position in the two operands.

EXAMPLE

Consider the arrays in Figure 11.13(a). Suppose the destination array represents the number 14.5 and the source array represents the number 12.25. Then for the destination array, the assumed decimal point lies between the left and right nibbles of the digit pair at offset 0001, and for the source array, the assumed decimal point lies between the digit pair at offset 0001 and the digit pair at offset 0000. The two arrays are *not* compatible for addition, since the assumed decimal points are not in the same position. There is no interpretation that can be applied to the sum of these two BCD numbers that can produce the desired result (26.75).

Consider now the arrays in Figure 11.13(b). Suppose the destination array represents the number 14.5 and the source array represents the number 12.25. Then for both arrays the assumed decimal point lies between the digit pair at offset 0001 and the digit pair at offset 0000. The two arrays are compatible for addition, since the assumed decimal points are in the same position. If the decimal point is assumed to be in the same position in the sum array, then the correct sum (26.75) is produced.

FIGURE 11.13
Positions of
assumed decimal
points must match
for correct BCD
addition: (a) not
compatible and (b)
compatible

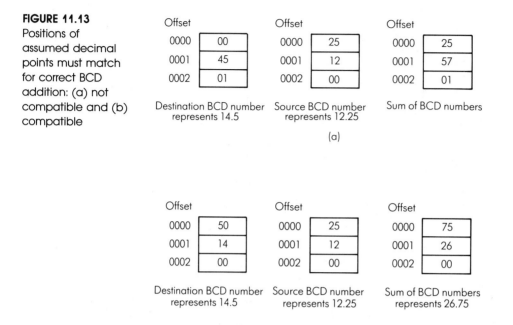

Offset	
0000	00
0001	45
0002	01

Destination BCD number
represents 14.5

Offset	
0000	25
0001	12
0002	00

Source BCD number
represents 12.25

Offset	
0000	25
0001	57
0002	01

Sum of BCD numbers

(a)

Offset	
0000	50
0001	14
0002	00

Destination BCD number
represents 14.5

Offset	
0000	25
0001	12
0002	00

Source BCD number
represents 12.25

Offset	
0000	75
0001	26
0002	00

Sum of BCD numbers
represents 26.75

(b)

Consistency is required in interpretation of operands supplied to and results received from procedures like ADDBCD. Consistency in interpretation is the responsibility of the caller. ADDBCD simply adds two BCD numbers without regard to interpretation.

Programming Example—BCD Output Procedure

The FAR procedure defined in Program Listing 11.5 is a PUBLIC procedure, called PUTBCD, that displays a packed BCD number in signed decimal form. The number is displayed on the screen beginning at the current cursor position. The prologue in lines 4–14 describes the function of the procedure and explains its interface requirements. On entry to the procedure, the DS:SI register pair must address the first byte of an array that contains a packed BCD number, the CH-register must contain the number of digits in this BCD number, and the CL-register must contain the number of digits that follow the assumed decimal point in this BCD number. The output of the procedure is the input BCD number displayed at the screen, in signed decimal form, beginning at the current cursor position. There are no outputs returned to the caller by the PUTBCD procedure.

The field width for the display of the BCD number depends on the count of the number of digits that follow the assumed decimal point. If the number of digits following the assumed decimal point is zero, then the number is displayed in a field of $n + 1$ character positions, in which n is the total number of digits

```
 1: ;
 2: ;
 3: ;                    PROGRAM LISTING 11.5
 4: ;
 5: ; PROCEDURE TO DISPLAY A PACKED BCD NUMBER IN SIGNED DECIMAL FORM
 6: ;
 7: ; INPUT:   DS:SI  POINTS TO ARRAY CONTAINING  PACKED BCD NUMBER IN
 8: ;                 TEN'S COMPLEMENT FORM
 9: ;          CH-REG CONTAINS SIZE OF BCD NUMBER        (MUST BE EVEN)
10: ;          CL-REG CONTAINS NUMBER OF FRACTIONAL DIGITS
11: ;
12: ; OUTPUT: INPUT BCD NUMBER DISPLAYED AT SCREEN IN SIGNED DECIMAL
13: ;         FORM BEGINNING AT THE CURRENT CURSOR POSITION
14: ;
15:                                       ;PROCEDURES TO
16:          EXTRN    BCDASCII:FAR        ;CONVERT BCD NUMBER TO ASCII
17:          EXTRN    FLT_SIGN:FAR        ;FLOAT SIGN IN ASCII NUMBER
18:          EXTRN    PUTSTRNG:FAR        ;DISPLAY A CHARACTER STRING
19:          EXTRN    TENSSMAG:FAR        ;CONVERT 10'S CMP BCD TO SIGN MAG
20: ;
21: ; D A T A   S E G M E N T   D E F I N I T I O N
22: ;
23: BCDDATA     SEGMENT COMMON
24: ;
25: SIGN        DB       ?                ;SIGN OF ASCII NUMBER
26: NUMBER      DB       255 DUP(?)       ;DIGITS OF ASCII NUMBER
27: DECIMAL_PT DB        '.'              ;DECIMAL POINT
28: BCD_NUM     DB       128 DUP(?)       ;BCD NUMBER
29: ;
30: BCDDATA     ENDS
31: ;
32: ; C O D E   S E G M E N T   D E F I N I T I O N
33: ;
34: CODE        SEGMENT
35:             PUBLIC  PUTBCD
36:             ASSUME  CS:CODE,ES:BCDDATA
37: PUTBCD      PROC    FAR        ;PUTBCD (SPTR,DIGIT_COUNT,FRAC_COUNT)
38:             PUSHF                             ;SAVE FLAGS
39:             PUSH    AX                        ;SAVE REGISTERS
40:             PUSH    BX
41:             PUSH    CX
42:             PUSH    DX
43:             PUSH    SI
44:             PUSH    DI
45:             PUSH    DS
46:             PUSH    ES
47:*;

48: ;
49:             MOV     AX,SEG BCDDATA    ;SET ES-REGISTER TO POINT
50:             MOV     ES,AX             ;TO BCD DATA SEGMENT
51:             MOV     BX,CX             ;<FRAC_COUNT IN BX>
52:             SUB     BH,BH
53:             XCHG    CL,CH             ;<DIGIT_COUNT IN CX>
54:             SUB     CH,CH
55:             MOV     DX,CX             ;INT_COUNT = DIGIT_COUNT
56:             SUB     DX,BX             ;          - FRAC_COUNT
57:                                       ;<INT_COUNT IN DX>
58:             PUSH    CX                ;SAVE DIGIT_COUNT
59:             SHR     CX,1              ;LOOP_COUNT = DIGIT_COUNT / 2
```

```
 60:            CLD                       ;SET DF FOR INCREMENTING
 61:            LEA     DI,BCD_NUM        ;DPTR = ADDRESS OF BCD_NUM
 62:    REP     MOVSB                     ;REPEAT
 63:                                      ;    DPTR->BYTE = SPTR->BYTE.
 64:                                      ;    DPTR = DPTR + 1
 65:                                      ;    SPTR = SPTR + 1
 66:                                      ;    LOOP_COUNT = LOOP_COUNT - 1
 67:                                      ;UNTIL LOOP_COUNT = 0
 68:            POP     CX                ;RESTORE DIGIT_COUNT
 69:            PUSH    ES                ;SET DS-REGISTER TO POINT
 70:            POP     DS                ;TO BCD DATA SEGMENT
 71:            LEA     DI,BCD_NUM        ;DPTR = ADDRESS OF BCD_NUM
 72:            CALL    TENSSMAG          ;CALL TENSSMAG(DPTR,DIGIT_COUNT)
 73:            LEA     SI,BCD_NUM        ;SPTR = ADDRESS OF BCD_NUM
 74:            LEA     DI,SIGN           ;DPTR = ADDRESS OF SIGN:NUMBER
 75:            CALL    BCDASCII          ;CALL BCDASCII (SPTR,DPTR,
 76:                                      ;                  DIGIT_COUNT)
 77:            MOV     CX,DX             ;CALL FLT_SIGN (DPTR,INT_COUNT)
 78:            CALL    FLT_SIGN
 79:            INC     CX                ;PRINT_COUNT = INT_COUNT + 1
 80:            CALL    PUTSTRNG          ;CALL PUTSTRNG(DPTR,PRINT_COUNT)
 81:            CMP     BX,0              ;IF   FRAC_COUNT > 0
 82:            JE      NO_FRAC
 83:            PUSH    CX                ;THEN
 84:            LEA     DI,DECIMAL_PT     ;      DISPLAY DECIMAL POINT
 85:            MOV     CX,1
 86:            CALL    PUTSTRNG
 87:            LEA     DI,SIGN           ;      DPTR = ADDRESS OF SIGN
 88:            POP     CX                ;            + PRINT_COUNT
 89:            ADD     DI,CX
 90:            MOV     CX,BX             ;      CALL PUTSTRNG (DPTR,
 91:            CALL    PUTSTRNG          ;                  FRAC_COUNT)
 92: NO_FRAC:                            ;ENDIF
 93:            POP     ES                ;RESTORE REGISTERS
 94:            POP     DS
 95:            POP     DI
 96:            POP     SI
 97:            POP     DX
 98:            POP     CX
 99:            POP     BX
100:            POP     AX
101:            POPF                      ;RESTORE FLAGS
102:            RET                       ;RETURN
103: PUTBCD     ENDP              ;END PUTBCD
104: CODE       ENDS
105:*           END
```

in the BCD number. The extra character position is for the sign. If the number of digits following the assumed decimal point is nonzero, then the number is displayed in a field of $n + 2$ character positions, in which n is the total number of digits in the BCD number. The two extra character positions are for the sign and the decimal point. The sign displayed with the BCD number is a blank for positive numbers and a minus sign $(-)$ for negative numbers. Leading zeros in the integer portion of the number are replaced with blanks for display. If the integer portion of the BCD number is zero, then one zero is displayed for the integer with blank fill to the left. If the BCD number has no integer portion (i.e., if the digit count in the CH-register is equal to the fractional digit count in the

FIGURE 11.14
PUTBCD display
formats: (a) packed
BCD array and (b)
strings displayed by
PUTDEC using the
packed BCD array
shown in (a) for
various digit counts

Offset

Offset		
0000	00	LSDs
0001	75	
0002	87	
0003	99	
0004	99	MSD's

(a)

Digit count	Fraction digit count	String displayed by PUTBCD
10	4	−12.2500
10	6	−0.122500
6	4	−12.2500
6	6	−.122500
6	0	−122500

(b)

CL-register), then no characters are displayed for the integer, and the decimal point immediately follows the sign. The sign is floated right in the field, so that it is displayed adjacent to the first digit displayed in the field. The specified number of fractional digits is displayed, including trailing zeros. Figure 11.14(a) shows a byte array that contains a packed BCD number. The digits of the number are 9999877500, which is the ten's complement of 0000122500. Figure 11.14(b) shows the string that would be displayed by PUTBCD for various interpretations of this BCD number specified by the digit count in the CH-register and the fractional digit count in the CL-register.

Four external subprocedures are referenced by the PUTBCD procedure and are identified by the EXTRN pseudo-operations in lines 16–19. The BCDASCII and TENSSMAG procedures are the same as those discussed earlier in the chapter. The PUTSTRNG procedure has been used in programming examples throughout the text. The FLT_SIGN procedure has not been used or discussed previously and is not presented here in detail. However, the function of the FLT_SIGN procedure and its interface requirements are discussed briefly. FLT_SIGN accepts a signed ASCII number as input and replaces leading zeros in the integer portion of that number with blanks. The sign of the ASCII number is floated through the field of blanks, so that it is adjacent to the first nonblank digit in the ASCII number. On entry to the FLT_SIGN procedure, the ES:DI register pair must address the first byte (i.e., the sign byte) of a byte array that contains an ASCII number, and the CX-register must contain a count of the number of digits in the integer portion of this ASCII number. This integer digit count may be zero. On return to the caller, the array addressed by the ES:DI register pair contains an ASCII number equivalent to the number it contained on entry, except that leading zeros in the integer portion have been replaced by blanks and the sign is adjacent to the first nonblank digit.

The PUTBCD procedure references a local data segment defined in lines 23–30. The data segment is defined as a COMMON data segment (see line 23), because the data segment is shared with the BCD input procedure GETBCD. COMMON data segments are discussed in detail in Chapter 12. The variables SIGN and NUMBER (lines 25 and 26) define a byte array of size 256 that is used to build the ASCII number from the input BCD number. Variable SIGN holds the ASCII character that represents the sign of the number, and array NUMBER holds the digits of the ASCII number. The byte variable DECIMAL_PT, defined in line 27, is a single-character string whose initial value is the ASCII code for a period. The variable BCD_NUM, defined in line 28, is a byte array of size 128 that holds a copy of the input packed BCD number. The PUTBCD procedure uses the TENSSMAG procedure to convert the BCD number from ten's complement to sign magnitude, and then it uses the BCDASCII procedure to convert the sign magnitude BCD number to ASCII. The local copy of the BCD number is used for the ten's complement–to–sign magnitude conversion to avoid modifying the BCD number in the caller's environment. (Recall that TENSSMAG returns its output in the same array in which it received its input.)

The PUTBCD procedure begins by saving the registers for the caller (lines 38–46) and initializing the ES-register to address the local data segment (lines 49–50). The procedure then isolates the three-digit counts that it needs: The count of the number of digits in the fractional portion of the number is moved from the CL-register to the BX-register (lines 51 and 52); the count of the total number of digits in the number is moved from the CH-register to the CX-register (lines 53 and 54); and the count of the number of digits in the integer portion of the number is computed and placed in the DX-register (lines 55 and 56).

The REPEAT-UNTIL loop implemented by the repeated string instruction in line 62 copies the input BCD number into array BCD_NUM in the local data segment. The PUSH instruction in line 58 saves the digit count, so that the CX-register can be used for the count that controls the loop. The SHR instruction in line 59 computes the loop count that is one-half the digit count. The loop count is the count of the number of bytes to be moved which is one-half the digit count, since the digits are packed two per byte. The CLD instruction in line 60 clears the direction flag so that the repeated string instruction increments through the two arrays. The DS:SI register pair already addresses the source array, the BCD array provided by the caller. The LEA instruction in line 61 initializes the DI-register, so that the ES:DI register pair addresses the array BCD_NUM in the local data segment. The MOVSB instruction in line 62 with the REP repeat prefix copies the BCD number from the caller's environment into the local environment. The POP instruction in line 68 restores the digit count in the CX-register. Now that the input BCD number has been copied into the local environment, both the ES and DS segment registers can be used to address the local data segment. The instructions in lines 69 and 70 copy the ES-register value to the DS-register. Recall that only one of the operands of a MOV instruction can be a segment register. To move from one segment register to another, PUSH and POP can be used.

PUTBCD uses a sequence of subprocedure references to convert the BCD number to an ASCII string for output. The instructions in lines 71 and 72 invoke the TENSSMAG procedure to convert the BCD number from ten's complement to sign magnitude form. TENSSMAG is entered with the ES:DI register pair addressing the local BCD array (BCD_NUM) and the CX-register containing the total digit count. The TENSSMAG procedure returns the sign magnitude version of the number in the same array (BCD_NUM). The instructions in lines 73–75 invoke the BCDASCII procedure to convert the sign magnitude BCD number to a sign magnitude ASCII string. BCDASCII is entered with the DS:SI register pair addressing the local BCD array (BCD_NUM), the ES:DI register pair addressing the local ASCII array (SIGN:NUMBER), and the CX-register containing the total digit count. The instructions in lines 77 and 78 invoke the FLT_SIGN procedure to replace leading zeros in the integer portion of the ASCII number with blanks and to float the sign through this field of blanks. FLT_SIGN is entered with the ES:DI register pair addressing the ASCII array (SIGN:NUMBER) and the CX-register containing the integer digit count (line 77). The ASCII string is now ready for output to the video screen.

The PUTBCD procedure displays the ASCII string in two parts. The instructions in lines 79 and 80 invoke the PUTSTRNG procedure to display the sign and the integer portion of the ASCII number. PUTSTRNG is entered with the ES:DI register pair addressing the ASCII array (SIGN:NUMBER) and the CX-register containing the integer digit count plus 1. The addition of 1 to the integer digit count (line 79) is performed to include the sign with the integer digits. The single-alternative decision structure, implemented in lines 81–92, displays the decimal point and the fractional portion of the ASCII number, if the fraction digit count is nonzero. The CMP instruction in line 81 tests the fraction digit count, and the JE instruction in line 82 makes the decision based on this test: If the fraction digit count is nonzero, then the instructions in lines 83–91 are executed; otherwise, these instructions are skipped. The PUSH instruction in line 83 saves the integer print count, so that the CX-register can be used for the display of the decimal point. The instructions in lines 84–86 invoke the PUTSTRNG procedure to display the single character string defined in line 27, the string that contains the decimal point. The instructions in lines 87–91 invoke PUTSTRNG to display the fractional portion of the ASCII number. PUTSTRNG is entered with the ES:DI register pair addressing the fractional portion of the ASCII number in array SIGN:NUMBER (lines 87–89) and the CX-register containing the fraction digit count (line 90).

On completion of the single-alternative decision structure, the caller's registers are restored (lines 93–101), and control is returned to the caller (line 102).

The object code for the TENSSMAG, BCDASCII, ADDBCD, NEGBCD, FLT_SIGN, and PUTBCD procedures are in a library named BCD.LIB on the diskette available for this book. This library also contains the object code for a procedure named GETBCD and for several subprocedures that it requires. The interface requirements for the GETBCD procedure are as follows:

1.   On entry to GETBCD, the ES:DI register pair must address the first byte of the BCD array that is to contain the BCD number entered via the keyboard, the CH-register is to contain the size (in nibbles) of the BCD array, and the CL-register is to contain the count of the number of digits that is to follow the assumed decimal point in the BCD array.
2.   On return to the caller, the specified BCD array contains the BCD number entered via the keyboard, aligned as specified by the inputs to GETBCD in the CX-register.

The programming exercises at the end of this chapter specify several other algorithms whose implementations can be added to this library.

11.6 Programming Example— Bank Account Transactions

Program Listing 11.6 displays a report regarding a sequence of transactions on a bank account and demonstrates the use of the subprocedures presented earlier in this chapter. The input data was embedded in the data segment for the program, so this discussion emphasizes computation and output involving BCD numbers. The prologue in line 4 briefly describes the program's function.

The subprocedures referenced by the main procedure are identified by the EXTRN pseudo-operations in lines 7–11. You should be familiar with all of these subprocedures.

The stack segment defined in lines 12–17 has been expanded from the 256-byte stack segment used in most of the example programs of this book. This modification accommodates the stack requirements of the BCD subprocedures.

The data segment for the program is defined in lines 18–45. The variable BALANCE (line 23) is a 6-byte (12-nibble) BCD array whose initial value is the beginning balance for the bank account. The initial value for BALANCE is 32550. The program interprets this value as $325.50, since it interprets all BCD numbers as having two digits following the assumed decimal point. The variable TRANSCOUNT (line 24) is a byte variable whose initial value (12) is a count of the number of transactions that have occurred on the bank account since the beginning balance was recorded. The variable TRANSACTN, defined in lines 25–36, is a data structure that contains the transactions. Each line defines one

```
 1: ;
 2: ;                    PROGRAM LISTING 11.6
 3: ;
 4: ; PROGRAM TO PRINT A REPORT OF BANK ACCOUNT TRANSACTIONS
 5: ;
 6:                                          ;PROCEDURES TO
 7:            EXTRN    ADDBCD:FAR           ;ADD     PACKED BCD NUMBERS
 8:            EXTRN    NEGBCD:FAR           ;NEGATE  PACKED BCD NUMBERS
 9:            EXTRN    NEWLINE:FAR          ;DISPLAY NEWLINE CHARACTER
10:            EXTRN    PUTBCD:FAR           ;DISPLAY PACKED BCD NUMBERS
11:            EXTRN    PUTSTRNG:FAR         ;DISPLAY CHARACTER STRINGS
12: ;
13: ; S T A C K    S E G M E N T    D E F I N I T I O N
14: ;
15: STACK      SEGMENT STACK
16:            DB       512 DUP(?)
17: STACK      ENDS
18: ;
19: ; D A T A    S E G M E N T    D E F I N I T I O N
20: ;
21: DATA       SEGMENT
22: ;
23: BALANCE    DB       50H,25H,03H,3 DUP(0)
24: TRANSCOUNT DB       12
25: TRANSACTN  DB       'W',00H,50H,00H,3 DUP(0)
26:            DB       'W',25H,25H,02H,3 DUP(0)
27:            DB       'D',00H,25H,00H,3 DUP(0)
28:            DB       'W',25H,75H,00H,3 DUP(0)
29:            DB       'W',50H,07H,00H,3 DUP(0)
30:            DB       'W',00H,20H,00H,3 DUP(0)
31:            DB       'D',00H,00H,01H,3 DUP(0)
32:            DB       'D',25H,50H,05H,3 DUP(0)
33:            DB       'W',50H,82H,00H,3 DUP(0)
34:            DB       'D',00H,50H,07H,3 DUP(0)
35:            DB       'W',45H,73H,02H,3 DUP(0)
36:            DB       'W',50H,27H,00H,3 DUP(0)
37: SERVICE    DB       6 DUP(0)
38: CHARGE     DB       65H,5 DUP(99H)
39: ;
40: HEADER     DB       '       DEPOSIT        WITHDRAWAL        BALANCE'
41: BLANKS     DB       '                              '
42: OVERDRAWN  DB       ' OVERDRAWN'
43: SERV_CHG   DB       ' SERVICE CHARGE'
44: ;
45: DATA       ENDS
46: ;
47: ; C O D E    S E G M E N T    D E F I N I T I O N
48: ;
49: CODE       SEGMENT
50:            ASSUME   CS:CODE,SS:STACK,DS:DATA,ES:DATA
51: BANKTRAN   PROC     FAR
52:            PUSH     DS                   ;PUSH RETURN SEG ADDR ON STACK
53:            SUB      AX,AX                ;PUSH RETURN OFFSET OF ZERO
54:            PUSH     AX                   ;ON STACK
55:            MOV      AX,SEG DATA          ;SET DS TO POINT TO DATA  SEG
56:            MOV      DS,AX
57:            MOV      ES,AX                ;SET ES TO POINT TO DATA  SEG
58:            LEA      DI,HEADER            ;DISPLAY HEADER
59:            MOV      CX,45
60:            CALL     PUTSTRNG
61:            CALL     NEWLINE              ;SKIP TO NEXT LINE
```

```
 62:             LEA      DI,BLANKS              ;DISPLAY 31 BLANKS
 63:             MOV      CX,31
 64::*           CALL     PUTSTRNG
*
 65: ;
 66:             LEA      SI,BALANCE             ;DISPLAY BEGINNING BALANCE
 67:             MOV      CX,0C02H
 68:             CALL     PUTBCD
 69:             CALL     NEWLINE                ;SKIP TO NEXT LINE
 70:             MOV      CL,TRANSCOUNT          ;LOOP_COUNT = TRANSCOUNT
 71:             MOV      CH,0
 72:             LEA      SI,TRANSACTN           ;PTR = ADDRESS OF TRANSACTN
 73: LOOP:                                      ;REPEAT
 74:             PUSH     CX                     ;   SAVE LOOP_COUNT
 75:             MOV      AL,[SI]                ;   CODE = PTR -> BYTE
 76:             INC      SI                     ;   PTR = PTR + 1
 77:             PUSH     SI                     ;   <PTR IS ADDRESS OF AMOUNT>
 78:             CMP      AL,'D'                 ;   IF   CODE = D
 79:             JNE      ELSE
 80:             LEA      DI,BALANCE             ;   THEN
 81:             MOV      CX,12                  ;         BALANCE = BALANCE
 82:             CALL     ADDBCD                 ;              + AMOUNT
 83:             MOV      CX,0C02H
 84:             CALL     PUTBCD                 ;         DISPLAY AMOUNT
 85:             LEA      DI,BLANKS              ;         DISPLAY 17 BLANKS
 86:             MOV      CX,17
 87:             CALL     PUTSTRNG
 88:             LEA      SI,BALANCE             ;         DISPLAY BALANCE
 89:             MOV      CX,0C02H
 90:             CALL     PUTBCD
 91:             JMP      SHORT ENDIF
 92: RELAY:      JMP      LOOP
 93: ELSE:                                      ;   ELSE
 94:             LEA      DI,BLANKS              ;         DISPLAY 16 BLANKS
 95:             MOV      CX,16
 96:             CALL     PUTSTRNG
 97:             MOV      CX,0C02H               ;         DISPLAY AMOUNT
 98:             CALL     PUTBCD
 99:             MOV      DI,SI
100:             MOV      CX,12                  ;         BALANCE = BALANCE
101:             CALL     NEGBCD                 ;              + (-AMOUNT)
102:             LEA      DI,BALANCE
103:             CALL     ADDBCD
104:             PUSHF                           ;         SAVE FLAGS
105:             LEA      DI,BLANKS              ;
106:             MOV      CX,1                   ;         DISPLAY A BLANK
107:             CALL     PUTSTRNG
108:             LEA      SI,BALANCE             ;         DISPLAY BALANCE
109:             MOV      CX,0C02H
110:             CALL     PUTBCD
111:             POPF                            ;         RESTORE FLAGS
112:             JGE      ENDIF_1                ;         IF   BALANCE < 0
113:             LEA      DI,OVERDRAWN           ;         THEN DISPLAY 'OVERDRAWN'
114:             MOV      CX,10
115:             CALL     PUTSTRNG
116: ENDIF_1:                                   ;         ENDIF
117:             LEA      DI,SERVICE             ;   SERVICE = SERVICE
118:             LEA      SI,CHARGE              ;              + CHARGE
119:             MOV      CX,12
120:             CALL     ADDBCD
121: ENDIF:                                     ;   ENDIF
```

```
122:              CALL    NEWLINE              ;    SKIP TO NEXT LINE
123:              POP     SI
124:              ADD     SI,6                 ;    PTR = PTR + 6
125:                                           ;    <PTR ADDRESSES NEXT CODE>
126:              POP     CX                   ;    RESTORE LOOP_COUNT
127:              LOOP    RELAY                ;    LOOP_COUNT = LOOP_COUNT - 1
128:*                                          ;UNTIL LOOP_COUNT = 0

129: ;
130:              LEA     DI,BALANCE           ;BALANCE = BALANCE + SERVICE
131:              LEA     SI,SERVICE
132:              MOV     CX,12
133:              CALL    ADDBCD
134:              LEA     DI,BLANKS            ;DISPLAY 31 BLANKS
135:              MOV     CX,31
136:              CALL    PUTSTRNG
137:              LEA     SI,BALANCE           ;DISPLAY BALANCE
138:              MOV     CX,0C02H
139:              CALL    PUTBCD
140:              MOV     CX,1
141:              CALL    PUTSTRNG             ;DISPLAY 1 BLANK
142:              LEA     SI,SERVICE           ;DISPLAY SERVICE
143:              MOV     CX,0C02H
144:              CALL    PUTBCD
145:              LEA     DI,SERV_CHG          ;DISPLAY 'SERVICE CHARGE'
146:              MOV     CX,15
147:              CALL    PUTSTRNG
148:              CALL    NEWLINE              ;SKIP TO NEXT LINE
149:              RET                          ;RETURN
150: BANKTRAN     ENDP
151: CODE         ENDS
152:*             END     BANKTRAN
```

transaction. A transaction is a one-character string followed by a 12-nibble BCD array. The initial value of the one-character string is either D, for deposit, or W, for withdrawal. The initial value of the BCD array is the amount of the transaction. The value is interpreted as having two digits that follow the assumed decimal point. For example, the transaction defined in line 28 is a withdrawal of $75.25. The variable SERVICE (line 37) is a 12-nibble BCD array whose initial value is zero. This value represents the total service charge to be deducted from the balance. The variable CHARGE (line 38) is a 12-nibble BCD array whose initial value is − 0.35, which is the amount of the service charge to be applied to each withdrawal from the account. Each time the program processes a withdrawal, it adds the value of CHARGE to SERVICE. At the end of the program, the value of SERVICE is added to BALANCE. Since CHARGE and SERVICE are negative, this addition to BALANCE represents a reduction of the BALANCE.

The remainder of the items in the data segment are character strings that are used to annotate the report. The string HEADER (line 40) is the column headers for the report. The report is displayed in three columns: one column for deposits, one column for withdrawals, and one column for the resulting balance. Each transaction fills one line of the report. If the transaction is a deposit, then the amount of the transaction is displayed under the DEPOSIT column, and the resulting balance is displayed under the BALANCE column. If the transaction is a withdrawal, then the amount of the transaction is displayed under the WITHDRAWAL column, and the resulting balance is displayed under the BALANCE column. To align values in specific columns, the program must output different size strings of blanks. The string BLANKS (line 41) is a string of 31 spaces. The string OVERDRAWN (line 42) is displayed next to any negative BALANCE. The string SERV_CHG (line 43) is displayed to annotate the service charge deduction on the last line of the report.

The code segment defined in lines 49–151 contains the definition of the main procedure for the program. The BANKTRAN procedure begins in the standard manner by saving the return address for the operating system (lines 52–54) and initializing the segment registers (lines 55–57). The program then displays the header for the report (lines 58–61) and the beginning balance (lines 62–69). The reference to the PUTSTRNG procedure (lines 62–64) displays 31 blanks. This step is taken so that the value of the beginning balance is displayed in the BALANCE column. The PUTBCD procedure is called (line 68) with the DS:SI register pair addressing the BCD array BALANCE (line 66), the CH-register containing the total digit count (12), and the CL-register containing the fraction digit count (2). The two digit counts are set up by the MOV instruction in line 67.

The REPEAT-UNTIL loop implemented in lines 73–128 processes the transactions. Each iteration of the loop processes one transaction and displays one line of the report. The initialization for the loop is performed by the instructions in lines 70–72. The count of the number of transactions is moved to the CX-register (lines 70 and 71), and the DS:SI register pair is set to address the beginning of the data structure that contains the transactions (line 72). At this point, the DS:SI register pair addresses the code for the first transaction. The loop body begins with the PUSH instruction in line 74. The loop count in the CX-register is saved, so that the register can be used for input to the PUTSTRNG and PUTBCD procedures referenced in the loop body. The MOV instruction in line 75 moves the code for the transaction to the AL-register. The INC instruction in line 76 increments the SI-register, so that the DS:SI register pair addresses the first byte of the transaction amount. The PUSH instruction in line 77 saves the SI-register, so that the current position within the transaction data structure is not lost when the SI-register is used for another purpose later in the loop.

The double-alternative decision structure implemented in lines 78–121 determines whether the transaction is a deposit or a withdrawal. The CMP instruction in line 78 tests the transaction code that was loaded into the AL-register by the MOV instruction in line 75, and the JNE instruction in line 79 makes the decision based on this test: If the transaction code is D, then the instructions in lines 80–91 (the THEN clause) are executed; if the transaction code is *not* D, then it is assumed to be W, and the instructions in lines 93–120 (the ELSE clause) are executed.

The THEN clause of the double-alternative decision structure processes a deposit transaction. The ADDBCD procedure is invoked (lines 80–82) to add the transaction amount (addressed by the DS:SI register pair) to the balance (addressed by the ES:DI register pair). The PUTBCD procedure is invoked (lines 83–84) to display the transaction amount (addressed by the DS:SI register pair) in the DEPOSIT column. The PUTSTRNG procedure is invoked (lines 85–87) to display 17 spaces, which skips the WITHDRAWAL column. The PUTBCD procedure is invoked (lines 88–90) to display the new balance (addressed by the DS:SI register pair) in the BALANCE column. The JMP instruction in line 91 causes the ELSE clause to be skipped.

The ELSE clause of the double-alternative decision structure processes a withdrawal transaction. The PUTSTRNG procedure is invoked (lines 94–96) to display 16 spaces, which skips the DEPOSIT column. The PUTBCD procedure is invoked (lines 97–98) to display the transaction amount (addressed by the DS:SI register pair) in the WITHDRAWAL column. The NEGBCD procedure is invoked (lines 99–101) to negate the transaction amount (addressed by the ES:DI register pair). The ADDBCD procedure is invoked (lines 102–103) to add the negated transaction amount (addressed by the DS:SI register pair) to the balance (addressed by the ES:DI register pair). Negating the transaction amount and adding the result to the balance is equivalent to subtracting the transaction amount from the balance. The implementation of a BCD subtraction procedure and its integration into this program is left as an exercise at the end of the chapter. The PUSHF instruction in line 104 saves the flags produced by this addition operation. The flags are used to determine if the account is overdrawn as a result of this withdrawal. The PUTSTRNG procedure is invoked (lines 105–107) to display a space. The PUTBCD procedure is invoked (lines 108–110) to display the new balance (addressed by the DS:SI register pair) in the BALANCE column. The POPF instruction in line 11 restores the flags (saved in line 104) to reflect the new balance. The single-alternative decision structure implemented in lines 112–116 displays the string 'OVERDRAWN', if the new balance is less than zero. Following this decision structure, the ADDBCD procedure is invoked (lines 117–120) to add the value of BCD array CHARGE (-0.35) to array SERVICE (the negative of the total service charge).

Following the double-alternative decision structure, preparations are made for the next iteration of the loop. The call to the NEWLINE procedure in line 122 terminates a line of the report. The POP instruction in line 123 restores the SI-register, so that the DS:SI register pair again addresses the transaction amount for the transaction just processed. The ADD instruction in line 124 increments the SI-register, so that the DS:SI register pair addresses the code for the next transaction to be processed. The POP instruction in line 126 restores the loop count in the CX-register. The LOOP instruction in line 127 decrements the loop count by 1 and transfers control to the top of the loop (line 73), if the resulting loop count is nonzero. The label LOOP in line 73 is outside the short label range (-128 to $+127$) from the instruction following the LOOP instruction in line 127. Therefore, the branch to the top of the loop requires a relay jump, and the LOOP instruction causes a branch to the line labeled RELAY (line 92). The instruction at that location is an unconditional jump to the top of the loop. Relay jumps are easily embedded in programs by placing them after any unconditional jump that is within range. The instruction immediately following an unconditional jump must be labeled; otherwise, there would be no way of reaching that instruction. The relay jump instruction can then be placed between that unconditional JUMP instruction (line 91 in this case) and the label of the next instruction (label ELSE in line 93 in this case) with no adverse effect on the program.

On exit from the REPEAT-UNTIL loop, the service charge line of the report is displayed. The ADDBCD procedure is invoked (lines 130–133) to add the value of BCD array SERVICE, the negative of the service charge, to the value of BCD array BALANCE, producing the ending balance for the account. The PUTSTRNG procedure is invoked (lines 134–136) to display 31 spaces, which skips the DEPOSIT and WITHDRAWAL columns. The PUTBCD procedure is invoked (lines 137–139) to display the ending balance in the BALANCE column. The PUTSTRNG procedure is again invoked (lines 140–141) to display a space. The PUTBCD procedure is invoked (lines 142–144) to display the value of BCD array SERVICE, the total service charge. The PUTSTRNG procedure is invoked (lines 145–147) to display the string 'SERVICE CHARGE'. The call to NEWLINE in line 148 terminates the last line of the report. The RET instruction in line 149 returns control to DOS.

The main procedure of this program consists largely of calling sequences for subprocedures. Most of the operations required for this program already exist in previously developed subprocedures. Assembly language programming becomes much more efficient once a good library of subprocedures has been developed. The following report was generated by this program:

```
A>b: ex_11_6


     DEPOSIT   WITHDRAWAL   BALANCE
                            325.50
               50.00        275.50
               225.25       50.25
     25.00                  75.25
               75.25        0.00
               7.50         -7.50  OVERDRAWN
               20.00        -27.50 OVERDRAWN
     100.00                 72.50
     550.25                 622.75
               82.50        540.25
     750.00                 1290.25
               273.45       1016.80
               27.50        989.30
                            986.50            -2.80 SERVICE CHARGE
A>
```

NUMERIC EXERCISES

11.1 Fill in the blanks in the following table:

4-Digit (16-Bit) BCD Bit Pattern	Modulo 10,000 Interpretation	Ten's Complement Interpretation
1000 0101 0111 0010		
0001 0100 0011 0110		
	6347	
		− 4095
	7200	

11.2 Perform the following additions involving 4-digit BCD integers in the ten's complement number system:

    a.   0001 1001 0010 0000
       + 0010 0011 1000 0101

    b.   1000 1001 0101 0100
       + 0000 0001 1000 0100

11.3 Perform the following subtractions involving 4-digit BCD integers in the ten's complement number system. Add the ten's complement of the subtrahend to the minuend.

    a.   0001 1001 0010 0000
      − 0010 0011 1000 0101

    b.   1000 1001 0101 0100
      − 0000 0001 1000 0100

PROGRAMMING EXERCISES

11.1 Design an algorithm to accept as input a nibble array that contains a packed BCD number in sign magnitude form and to produce as output a nibble array that contains the same packed BCD number in ten's complement form. The number of digits in the BCD number is also an input to the algorithm. Implement your algorithm with an IBM PC Assembly language FAR procedure. The name of your procedure should be SMAG-TENS. Your inputs should be as follows:

> The ES:DI register pair addresses the first byte of the packed BCD array.
> The CX-register contains a count of the number of digits in the BCD number (must be even).

On return from your procedure, the array addressed by the ES:DI register pair should contain the packed BCD number in ten's complement form that is equivalent to the sign magnitude number that the array contained on entry to the procedure. Your procedure should save and restore all registers used.

11.2 Design an algorithm to accept as input a byte array that contains an ASCII number in sign magnitude form and to produce as output a nibble array that contains the corresponding BCD number in sign magnitude form. The number of digits in the ASCII number is also an input to the algorithm. Implement your algorithm with an IBM PC Assembly language external FAR procedure. The name of your procedure should be ASCIIBCD. Your inputs should be as follows:

> The DS:SI register pair addresses the first byte of the array that contains the ASCII number.
> The ES:DI register pair addresses the first byte of the array that is to contain the corresponding BCD number.
> The CX-register contains a count of the number of digits in the ASCII number.

On return from your procedure, the array addressed by the ES:DI register pair should contain the packed BCD number in sign magnitude form that is equivalent to the ASCII number in the array addressed by the DS:SI register pair, and the CX-register should contain $n + (n \bmod 2)$, in which n is the input digit count. Your procedure should save and restore all registers used, except for the CX-register that is used for procedure output.

11.3 Design an algorithm to subtract two packed BCD numbers in ten's complement form. Do *not* use the complement-and-add method that was used in Program Listing 11.6. Instead, use the SBB and DAS instructions in a method analogous to that used in the procedure in Program Listing 11.3. Implement your algorithm with an IBM PC Assembly language external FAR procedure. The name of your procedure should be SUBBCD. Your inputs should be as follows:

> The DS:SI register pair addresses the first byte of the array that contains the souⅼce BCD number.
> The ES:DI register pair addresses the first byte of the array that contains the destination BCD number.
> The CX-register contains a count of the number of digits in one of the BCD numbers (must be even).

The size of the two BCD numbers must be the same.

On return from your procedure, the array addressed by the ES:DI register pair should contain the packed BCD difference of the two input BCD numbers (i.e., the difference replaces the destination BCD number), and the OF, SF, ZF, and CF bits of the flags register should reflect this difference. Your procedure should save and restore all registers used. Only the OF, SF, ZF, and CF bits of the flags register should be modified. Make your procedure a PUBLIC procedure and add it to the BCD subprocedure library BCD.LIB.

11.4 Modify Program Listing 11.6 to use your procedure SUBBCD (i.e., your solution to Programming Exercise 11.3) instead of using negate and add to process a withdrawal. Also, maintain the service charge as a positive number rather

than as a negative number, and use SUBBCD to deduct the service charge from the balance.

11.5 Design an algorithm to compare two packed BCD numbers in ten's complement form. Recall that a compare is like a subtraction in which the result is not saved. Implement your algorithm with an IBM PC Assembly language external FAR procedure. The name of your procedure should be CMPBCD. Your inputs should be as follows:

> The DS:SI register pair addresses the first byte of the array that contains the source BCD number.
> The ES:DI register pair addresses the first byte of the array that contains the destination BCD number.
> The CX-register contains the count of the number of digits in one of the BCD numbers (must be even).

The size of the two BCD numbers must be the same.

On return from your procedure, the OF, SF, ZF, and CF bits of the flags register should reflect the result of the subtraction: destination BCD number minus source BCD number. However, neither of the BCD numbers should be modified. Your procedure should save and restore all registers used. Only the OF, SF, ZF, and CF bits of the flags register should be modified. Make your procedure a PUBLIC procedure and add it to the BCD subprocedure library BCD.LIB.

11.6 Design an algorithm to multiply a packed BCD number in ten's complement form by 10. *Hint:* This exercise can be accomplished by shifting the number left one digit position. Implement your algorithm with an IBM PC Assembly language external FAR procedure. The name of your procedure should be MULBCD10. Your inputs should be as follows:

> The ES:DI register pair addresses the first byte of the array that contains the BCD number.
> The CX-register contains a count of the number of digits in the BCD number (must be even).

On return from your procedure, the array addressed by the ES:DI register pair should contain the product of the input BCD number and 10 (i.e., the product replaces the input BCD number), and the OF and CF bits of the flags register should reflect whether or not an overflow occurred. Your procedure should save and restore all registers used. Only the OF and CF bits of the flags register should be modified. Make your procedure a PUBLIC procedure, and add it to the BCD subprocedure library BCD.LIB.

11.7 Design an algorithm to divide a packed BCD number in ten's complement form by 10. *Hint*: This exercise can be accomplished by shifting the number right one digit position. The digit shifted out is the remainder of the division. Implement your algorithm with an IBM PC Assembly language external FAR procedure. The name of your procedure should be DIVBCD10. Your inputs should be as follows:

> The ES:DI register pair addresses the first byte of the array that contains the BCD number.
> The CX-register contains a count of the number of digits in the BCD number (must be even).

On return from your procedure, the array addressed by the ES:DI register pair should contain the quotient of the input BCD number and 10 (i.e., the quotient replaces the input BCD number), and the AL-register should contain the one-digit remainder. Your procedure should save and restore all registers used, except for the AL-register that is used for procedure output. Make your procedure a PUBLIC procedure and add it to the BCD subprocedure library BCD.LIB.

11.8 Using the MULBCD10 and DIVBCD10 procedures from Programming Exercises 11.6 and 11.7 and a modified version of the Russian Peasant's Method, a procedure can be developed to multiply two packed BCD numbers in ten's complement form. The algorithm is as follows:

```
PROCEDURE MULBCD (MPCAND,MPLIER)
   IF    MPLIER < 0
   THEN
          MPLIER = -MPLIER
          MPCAND = -MPCAND
   ENDIF
   PRODUCT = 0
   WHILE MPLIER > 0
        COUNT = MPLIER mod 10
        WHILE COUNT > 0
             PRODUCT = PRODUCT + MPCAND
             COUNT = COUNT - 1
        ENDWHILE
        MPCAND = MPCAND * 10
        MPLIER = MPLIER / 10
   ENDWHILE
   MPCAND = PRODUCT
END MULBCD
```

Implement this algorithm with an IBM PC Assembly language external FAR procedure. The name of your procedure should be MULBCD. Your inputs should be as follows:

> The ES:DI register pair addresses the first byte of the BCD array that contains the multiplicand.
> The DS:SI register pair addresses the first byte of the BCD array that contains the multiplier.
> The CH-register contains a count of the number of digits in the multiplicand (must be even).
> The CL-register contains a count of the number of digits in the multiplier (must be even).

On return from your procedure, the array addressed by the ES:DI register pair should contain the product of the two BCD numbers (i.e., the product replaces the multiplicand), and the OF and CF bits of the flags register should reflect whether or not overflow occurred. Your procedure should save and restore all registers used. Only the OF and CF bits of the flags register should be modified. Make your procedure a PUBLIC procedure and add it to the BCD subprocedure library BCD.LIB.

Note that when interpreting BCD numbers for output, the number of digits that follow the assumed decimal point in the product is the sum of the number of digits that follow the assumed decimal point in the multiplicand and the number of digits that follow the assumed decimal point in the multiplier. Note also that the number of digits that follow the assumed decimal point in the multiplier does not have to equal the number of digits that follow the assumed decimal point in the multiplicand.

11.9 Rewrite Program Listing 8.6 (the program to compute arbitrarily large factorial values) to use packed BCD numbers for the factorial values. The MULBCD procedure from Programming Exercise 11.8 is needed in the solution.

12

SEGMENT LINKING

Chapter 1 discussed the general form of an IBM PC assembly module and identified its three kinds of segment definitions. It also introduced the SEGMENT pseudo-operation that declares the beginning of a segment definition. As well, Chapter 1 introduced the Linkage Editor program (LINK) that organizes the corresponding machine language segments into an executable program module. The way in which the segments are organized in the executable program module depends on information provided by the SEGMENT pseudo-operations in the assembly modules that make up the corresponding Assembly language program.

In the example programs in the preceding chapters, the SEGMENT pseudo-operation appears in its most primitive form, which causes the LINK program to use default rules in organizing the machine language segments into an executable program. The SEGMENT pseudo-operation can have up to three operands that provide information to the LINK program. This information guides LINK in organizing the machine language segments into an executable program module. This chapter discusses the SEGMENT pseudo-operation and its operands in detail, demonstrating the advantages of some of the program segmentation features provided by the assembler and LINK.

12.1 Segment Pseudo-Operation

The SEGMENT pseudo-operation marks the physical beginning of a segment definition, indicates how that segment is to be aligned in memory, and specifies the relationship of the segment to other segments of the executable program. The **SEGMENT pseudo-operation** has the following general form:

⟨*seg name*⟩ SEGMENT [⟨*align*⟩] [⟨*combine*⟩] [⟨*class*⟩]

505

in which ⟨*seg name*⟩ is the symbolic name associated with the memory location at which the segment is to begin, ⟨*align*⟩ identifies the type of boundary for the beginning of the segment, ⟨*combine*⟩ indicates the way in which this segment is to be combined with other segments by the Linkage Editor program (LINK), and ⟨*class*⟩ is a symbolic name used to group segments at link time. All of the operands for the SEGMENT pseudo-operation are optional.

The ⟨*align*⟩ operand specifies how the segment is to be aligned in memory. The align type, if specified, must be one of the following: PAGE, PARA, WORD, or BYTE.

PAGE   An align type of **PAGE** specifies that the segment must begin on a page boundary, which is an address divisible by 256. That is, the start address for the segment must be an address of the hexadecimal form XXX00, in which X represents any hexadecimal digit. For example, the addresses 00000, 00100, and F3C00 all mark the beginning of a new page in memory.

PARA   An align type of **PARA** specifies that the segment must begin on a paragraph boundary, which is an address divisible by 16. That is, the start address for the segment must be an address of the hexadecimal form XXXX0, in which X represents any hexadecimal digit. For example, the addresses 00000, 00010, F3C00, and FF3E0 all mark the beginning of a new paragraph in memory. Note that any page boundary is also a paragraph boundary; however, a paragraph boundary is not necessarily a page boundary.

WORD   An align type of **WORD** specifies that the segment must begin on a word boundary, which is an even address. For example, 00000, 00002, 00004, and so forth are word boundary addresses.

BYTE   An align type of **BYTE** specifies that the segment is to begin at the next available byte in memory. That is, the start address for the segment can be any address in memory.

The default value for the align type is PARA; that is, unless otherwise specified, all segments begin on a paragraph boundary. Recall that all segments must begin on a paragraph boundary so that the start address of the segment can be stored in a 16-bit segment register. The only reason for using WORD or BYTE as the align type is to allow a segment to be combined with another segment without memory space being skipped.

The ⟨*combine*⟩ operand specifies the relationship between the segment being defined and other segments of the executable program. The combine type, if specified, must be one of the following: PUBLIC, STACK, COMMON, MEMORY, or AT ⟨*expr*⟩.

PUBLIC   A combine type of **PUBLIC** specifies that the segment is to be concatenated with other segments having the same ⟨*seg-name*⟩ and ⟨*class*⟩, producing a single physical segment.

STACK   A combine type of **STACK** specifies that the segment is to be concatenated with other segments having the same ⟨*seg-name*⟩ and ⟨*class*⟩, producing a single physical segment. This single segment is to be the run-time stack segment for the program. When program execution begins, the SS-register specifies the origin of this segment, and the SP-register contains the offset from this origin to the location immediately following the segment. This setup denotes that the run-time stack segment is empty.

After combining segments, if more than one segment is of combine type STACK, then the last segment encountered by the LINK program is the run-time stack segment for the program. This situation occurs when the segments with a combine type of STACK do not all have the same ⟨seg-name⟩ and ⟨class⟩.

COMMON   A combine type of **COMMON** specifies that the segment is to be overlayed with other segments having the same ⟨seg-name⟩ and ⟨class⟩, producing a single segment whose length is the length of the largest such common segment. Common segments allow procedures in separate assembly modules to reference the same physical data segment using a private set of symbolic names.

MEMORY   A combine type of **MEMORY** specifies that the segment is to be located at a higher memory address than any other segment of the executable program. If more than one segment being linked has a combine type of MEMORY, then only the first such segment encountered is to be treated in this way. Any subsequent segment with a combine type of MEMORY is to be treated as a COMMON segment. The Microsoft Linkage Editor (MS-LINK version 2.44) does not support the MEMORY combine type, and it treats the combine type MEMORY as if it were combine type PUBLIC.

AT ⟨expr⟩   A combine type of **AT ⟨expr⟩** specifies that the segment is to begin at the paragraph identified by the 16-bit value of the address expression, ⟨expr⟩. The AT combine type cannot be used to load values into fixed locations in memory. It is used to assign symbolic names to fixed offsets within fixed areas of memory (e.g., the video display buffer).

The default value for the combine type is **private**. That is, if the combine type is omitted, then the segment is to be logically separate from other segments, regardless of its placement relative to other segments. The combine type should not be mixed for segments with the same ⟨seg-name⟩ and ⟨class⟩.

The ⟨class⟩ operand is a symbolic name that is used to group segments at link time. (The class name must be enclosed in apostrophes.) All segments with the same class name are contiguous in memory.

12.2 Combining Segments

Combining several logical segments into one physical segment is done primarily to conserve memory space. Since each physical segment must begin on a paragraph boundary, segments consume memory in 16-byte (one-paragraph) units.

For example, if a data segment definition specifies 18 bytes of storage, the corresponding physical segment consumes 32 bytes (2 paragraphs), because the next contiguous segment cannot begin until the next paragraph boundary. The last paragraph of any physical segment is likely to include some unused storage cells. On the average, you can expect eight unused storage cells in the last paragraph of a physical segment. By combining n logical segments into one physical segment, the number of "last paragraphs" is reduced from n to 1, which reduces the expected number of unused storage cells from $8n$ to 8. In small programs, like the example programs in this book, the savings is insignificant. However, in large programs like a high-level language compiler, the savings can be quite significant.

Several segments can be combined into one physical segment by using the PUBLIC combine type. The segments being combined must all have the same segment name and class name. The first such segment encountered by the LINK program must have the PARA (default) align type, so that the physical segment begins on a paragraph boundary. All subsequent segments to be included in the same physical segment should have the BYTE align type to avoid embedded blocks of unused storage cells.

Programming Example—Simulate Tossing a Coin

Program Listings 12.1 and 12.2 show two parts of a single program that simulates the tossing of a coin. The program prompts the user for an integer that specifies the number of times to toss the coin, simulates tossing the coin the specified number of times, and displays a count of the number of heads and tails in the simulation. The assembly module in Program Listing 12.2 contains the definition of one subprocedure and the definition of a local data segment for that subprocedure. The subprocedure is the random number generator used in the simulation, which is the same random number generator presented in Program Listing 5.4). The assembly module in Program Listing 12.1 contains the definition of the main procedure and the definition of its data segment.

The main procedure uses the random number generator, which returns a nonnegative integer in the range 0–9999, to simulate a toss of the coin: An integer in the range 0–4999 represents tails; an integer in the range 5000–9999 represents heads. The detail of the main procedure is not discussed here as you should have no difficulty in following the logic of this program at this point in the text.

Program Listings 12.1 and 12.2 have two data segments. The data segment defined in Program Listing 12.1 (lines 16–22) requires 54 bytes of storage. The physical data segment corresponding to this definition consumes 4 paragraphs (64 bytes). The last 10 bytes in this 4-paragraph memory segment are unused. The data segment defined in Program Listing 12.2 (lines 13–24) requires 9 bytes of storage. The physical data segment corresponding to this definition consumes 1 paragraph (16 bytes). The last 7 bytes of this 1-paragraph memory segment are unused. A total of 17 bytes of unused space is encompassed in these two memory segments, which Load Map Listing 12.3 illustrates. The load map was generated

```
 1: ;                    PROGRAM LISTING 12.1
 2: ;
 3: ; PROGRAM TO SIMULATE THE TOSSING OF A COIN
 4:                                              ;PROCEDURES TO
 5:           EXTRN    GETDEC$:FAR              ;INPUT UNSIGNED DEC. INTEGER
 6:           EXTRN    PUTDEC$:FAR              ;DISPLAY UNSIGNED DEC. INTEGER
 7:           EXTRN    PUTSTRNG:FAR             ;DISPLAY A CHARACTER STRING
 8:           EXTRN    RANDOM:FAR              ;GENERATE PSEUDO-RANDOM NUMBER
 9: ;
10: ;<***** S T A C K    S E G M E N T    D E F I N I T I O N *****>
11: STACK     SEGMENT STACK
12:           DB       256 DUP(?)
13: STACK     ENDS
14: ;
15: ;<*****    D A T A    S E G M E N T    D E F I N I T I O N *****>
16: DATA      SEGMENT
17: HEADS     DW       0                      ;COUNT OF NUMBER OF HEADS
18: TAILS     DW       0                      ;COUNT OF NUMBER OF TAILS
19: PROMPT    DB       'ENTER NUMBER OF TIMES TO TOSS COIN '
20: HEADSMSG  DB       ' HEADS '
21: TAILSMSG  DB       ' TAILS'
22: DATA      ENDS
23: ;
24: ;<*****    C O D E    S E G M E N T    D E F I N I T I O N *****>
25: CODE      SEGMENT
26: COINTOSS  PROC     FAR
27:           ASSUME   CS:CODE,SS:STACK,DS:DATA,ES:DATA
28:           PUSH     DS                     ;PUSH RETURN SEG ADDR ON STACK
29:           SUB      AX,AX                  ;PUSH RETURN OFFSET OF ZERO
30:           PUSH     AX                     ;ON STACK
31:           MOV      AX,SEG DATA            ;SET DS AND ES REGISTERS
32:           MOV      DS,AX                  ;TO ADDRESS DATA SEGMENT
33:           MOV      ES,AX
34:           LEA      DI,PROMPT              ;PROMPT FOR NUMBER_OF_TOSSES
35:           MOV      CX,36
36:           CALL     PUTSTRNG
37:           CALL     GETDEC$                ;GET NUMBER_OF_TOSSES
38:           MOV      CX,AX                  ;LOOP_COUNT = NUMBER_OF_TOSSES
39: TOSS_COIN:                               ;REPEAT
40:           CALL     RANDOM                 ;   NUMBER = RANDOM()
41:           CMP      AX,5000                ;   IF    NUMBER >= 5000
42:           JL       CNT_TAILS
43:           INC      HEADS                  ;      THEN HEADS = HEADS + 1
44:           JMP      NEXT_TOSS
45: CNT_TAILS:                               ;      ELSE
46:           INC      TAILS                  ;         TAILS = TAILS + 1
47: NEXT_TOSS:                               ;      ENDIF
48:           LOOP     TOSS_COIN              ;   LOOP_COUNT = LOOP_COUNT - 1
49:                                          ;UNTIL LOOP_COUNT = 0
50:           MOV      BH,1
51:           MOV      AX,HEADS               ;DISPLAY HEADS
52:           CALL     PUTDEC$
53:           LEA      DI,HEADSMSG
54:           MOV      CX,8
55:           CALL     PUTSTRNG
56:           MOV      AX,TAILS               ;DISPLAY TAILS
57:           CALL     PUTDEC$
58:           LEA      DI,TAILSMSG
59:           MOV      CX,6
60:           CALL     PUTSTRNG
61:           RET                            ;RETURN
62: COINTOSS  ENDP
63: CODE      ENDS
64:*          END      COINTOSS
```

```
 1: ;                    PROGRAM LISTING 12.2
 2: ;
 3: ; r a n d o m   n u m b e r   g e n e r a t o r
 4: ;
 5: ; GENERATES PSEUDO-RANDOM INTEGERS IN THE RANGE
 6: ;                   0 TO 9999
 7: ;
 8: ; INPUT:  NONE
 9: ; OUTPUT: AX-REG CONTAINS RANDOM INTEGER
10: ;
11: ; D A T A    S E G M E N T
12: ;
13: RAND_DATA   SEGMENT
14: ;
15: SEED        DW      ?               ;SEED FOR RANDOM NUMBER GEN.
16: MULTIPLIER DW       3621            ;MULTIPLIER FOR LINEAR
17: ;                                   ;CONGRUENTIAL METHOD
18: FALSE       EQU     0               ;CONSTANT FALSE
19: TRUE        EQU     1               ;CONSTANT TRUE
20: FIRST_CALL DB       TRUE            ;FIRST CALL FLAG
21: TWO_56      DW      256             ;CONSTANT 256
22: TEN_THOU    DW      10000           ;CONSTANT 10000
23: ;
24: RAND_DATA   ENDS
25: ;
26: ; C O D E    S E G M E N T
27: ;
28: CODE        SEGMENT
29:             ASSUME  CS:CODE,DS:RAND_DATA
30:             PUBLIC  RANDOM
31: RANDOM      PROC    FAR
32:             PUSHF                   ;SAVE FLAGS
33:             PUSH    CX              ;SAVE REGISTERS
34:             PUSH    DX
35:             PUSH    DS
36:             MOV     AX,SEG RAND_DATA  ;SET DS-REGISTER TO POINT
37:             MOV     DS,AX           ;TO LOCAL DATA SEGMENT
38: ;
39:             CMP     FIRST_CALL,TRUE ;IF   FIRST_CALL
40:             JNE     ENDIF
41:             MOV     FIRST_CALL,FALSE ;THEN FIRST_CALL = FALSE
42:             MOV     AH,0            ;      SEED = LOWER HALF OF
43:             INT     1AH             ;              TIME OF DAY CLOCK
44:             MOV     SEED,DX
45: ENDIF:                             ;ENDIF
46:             MOV     AX,SEED         ;X = SEED * MULTIPLIER
47:             MUL     MULTIPLIER
48:             INC     AX              ;SEED = (X + 1) mod 65536
49:             MOV     SEED,AX
50:             MOV     DX,0
51:             DIV     TWO_56          ;RANDOM = SEED/256*10000/256
52:             MUL     TEN_THOU
53:             DIV     TWO_56
54:             POP     DS              ;RESTORE REGISTERS
55:             POP     DX
56:             POP     CX
57:             POPF                    ;RESTORE FLAGS
58:             RET                     ;RETURN (RANDOM)
59: RANDOM      ENDP
60: CODE        ENDS
61:*           END
```

```
 1:                      LOAD MAP LISTING 12.3
 2:
 3:
 4:    Start   Stop    Length  Name                      Class
 5:    00000H  000FFH  00100H  STACK
 6:    00100H  00135H  00036H  DATA
 7:    00140H  0019FH  00060H  CODE
 8:    001A0H  001A8H  00009H  RAND_DATA
 9:    001B0H  001EBH  0003CH  CODE
10:    001F0H  00246H  00057H  IO_DATA
11:    00250H  0026BH  0001CH  CODE                      IO_CODE
12:    00270H  00318H  000A9H  CODE                      IO_CODE
13:    00320H  00375H  00056H  CODE                      IO_CODE
14:    00380H  0039DH  0001EH  CODE                      IO_CODE
15:    003A0H  003F3H  00054H  CODE                      IO_CODE
16:    00400H  00412H  00013H  CODE                      IO_CODE
17:
18:    Origin    Group
19:
20:*Program entry point at 0014:0000
 *
```

when the object modules for this program were linked. The segment named DATA (defined in Program Listing 12.1) begins at zero-relative location 00100 hex and is 36 hex (54 decimal) bytes in length (line 6 in Load Map Listing 12.3). However, the next contiguous segment (the code segment for the main procedure) begins at zero-relative location 00140 hex, so the data segment actually consumes 40 hex (64 decimal) bytes of storage space. The segment named RAND-DATA (defined in Program Listing 12.2) begins at location 001A0 hex and is 9 bytes in length (line 8 in Load Map Listing 12.3). However, the next contiguous segment (the code segment for the random number generator) begins at location 001B0, so the data segment actually consumes 10 hex (16 decimal) bytes of storage space. The following listing shows some sample executions of the coin-toss simulation program:

```
A> EX_12_1
ENTER NUMBER OF TIMES TO TOSS COIN 10000
  4964 HEADS    5036 TAILS
A> EX_12_1
ENTER NUMBER OF TIMES TO TOSS COIN 10000
  5082 HEADS    4918 TAILS
A> EX_12_1
ENTER NUMBER OF TIMES TO TOSS COIN 10000
  5003 HEADS    4997 TAILS
A> EX_12_1
ENTER NUMBER OF TIMES TO TOSS COIN 10000
  4957 HEADS    5043 TAILS
```

Consider the modified version of this program defined in Program Listings 12.4 and 12.5. The assembly module in Program Listing 12.4 differs from the

```
 1: ;                      PROGRAM LISTING 12.4
 2: ;
 3: ; PROGRAM TO SIMULATE THE TOSSING OF A COIN
 4:                                     ;PROCEDURES TO
 5:          EXTRN    GETDEC$:FAR       ;INPUT UNSIGNED DEC. INTEGER
 6:          EXTRN    PUTDEC$:FAR       ;DISPLAY UNSIGNED DEC. INTEGER
 7:          EXTRN    PUTSTRNG:FAR      ;DISPLAY A CHARACTER STRING
 8:          EXTRN    RANDOM:FAR        ;GENERATE PSEUDO-RANDOM NUMBER
 9: ;
10: ;<***** S T A C K   S E G M E N T   D E F I N I T I O N *****>
11: STACK        SEGMENT STACK
12:          DB       256 DUP(?)
13: STACK        ENDS
14: ;
15: ;<*****   D A T A   S E G M E N T   D E F I N I T I O N *****>
16: DATA         SEGMENT PUBLIC
17: HEADS        DW       0                  ;COUNT OF NUMBER OF HEADS
18: TAILS        DW       0                  ;COUNT OF NUMBER OF TAILS
19: PROMPT       DB       'ENTER NUMBER OF TIMES TO TOSS COIN '
20: HEADSMSG     DB       ' HEADS '
21: TAILSMSG     DB       ' TAILS'
22: DATA         ENDS
23: ;
24: ;<*****   C O D E   S E G M E N T   D E F I N I T I O N *****>
25: CODE         SEGMENT
26: COINTOSS     PROC     FAR
27:          ASSUME   CS:CODE,SS:STACK,DS:DATA,ES:DATA
28:          PUSH     DS                ;PUSH RETURN SEG ADDR ON STACK
29:          SUB      AX,AX             ;PUSH RETURN OFFSET OF ZERO
30:          PUSH     AX                ;ON STACK
31:          MOV      AX,SEG DATA       ;SET DS AND ES REGISTERS
32:          MOV      DS,AX             ;TO ADDRESS DATA SEGMENT
33:          MOV      ES,AX
34:          LEA      DI,PROMPT         ;PROMPT FOR NUMBER_OF_TOSSES
35:          MOV      CX,36
36:          CALL     PUTSTRNG
37:          CALL     GETDEC$           ;GET NUMBER_OF_TOSSES
38:          MOV      CX,AX             ;LOOP_COUNT = NUMBER_OF_TOSSES
39: TOSS_COIN:                         ;REPEAT
40:          CALL     RANDOM            ;    NUMBER = RANDOM()
41:          CMP      AX,5000           ;    IF    NUMBER >= 5000
42:          JL       CNT_TAILS
43:          INC      HEADS             ;      THEN HEADS = HEADS + 1
44:          JMP      NEXT_TOSS
45: CNT_TAILS:                         ;      ELSE
46:          INC      TAILS             ;           TAILS = TAILS + 1
47: NEXT_TOSS:                         ;      ENDIF
48:          LOOP     TOSS_COIN         ;    LOOP_COUNT = LOOP_COUNT - 1
49:                                    ;UNTIL LOOP_COUNT = 0
50:          MOV      BH,1
51:          MOV      AX,HEADS          ;DISPLAY HEADS
52:          CALL     PUTDEC$
53:          LEA      DI,HEADSMSG
54:          MOV      CX,8
55:          CALL     PUTSTRNG
56:          MOV      AX,TAILS          ;DISPLAY TAILS
57:          CALL     PUTDEC$
58:          LEA      DI,TAILSMSG
59:          MOV      CX,6
60:          CALL     PUTSTRNG
61:          RET                        ;RETURN
62: COINTOSS     ENDP
63: CODE         ENDS
64:*          END      COINTOSS
```

```
 1: ;                      PROGRAM LISTING 12.5
 2: ;
 3: ; r a n d o m   n u m b e r   g e n e r a t o r
 4: ;
 5: ; GENERATES PSEUDO-RANDOM INTEGERS IN THE RANGE
 6: ;                 0 TO 9999
 7: ;
 8: ; INPUT:  NONE
 9: ; OUTPUT: AX-REG CONTAINS RANDOM INTEGER
10: ;
11: ; D A T A   S E G M E N T
12: ;
13: DATA        SEGMENT PUBLIC BYTE
14: ;
15: SEED        DW      ?                   ;SEED FOR RANDOM NUMBER GEN.
16: MULTIPLIER  DW      3621                ;MULTIPLIER FOR LINEAR
17: ;                                       ;CONGRUENTIAL METHOD
18: FALSE       EQU     0                   ;CONSTANT FALSE
19: TRUE        EQU     1                   ;CONSTANT TRUE
20: FIRST_CALL  DB      TRUE                ;FIRST CALL FLAG
21: TWO_56      DW      256                 ;CONSTANT 256
22: TEN_THOU    DW      10000               ;CONSTANT 10000
23: ;
24: DATA        ENDS
25: ;
26: ; C O D E   S E G M E N T
27: ;
28: CODE        SEGMENT
29:             ASSUME  CS:CODE,DS:DATA
30:             PUBLIC  RANDOM
31: RANDOM      PROC    FAR
32:             PUSHF                       ;SAVE FLAGS
33:             PUSH    CX                  ;SAVE REGISTERS
34:             PUSH    DX
35:             CMP     FIRST_CALL,TRUE     ;IF   FIRST_CALL
36:             JNE     ENDIF
37:             MOV     FIRST_CALL,FALSE    ;THEN FIRST_CALL = FALSE
38:             MOV     AH,0                ;     SEED = LOWER HALF OF
39:             INT     1AH                 ;              TIME OF DAY CLOCK
40:             MOV     SEED,DX
41: ENDIF:                                  ;ENDIF
42:             MOV     AX,SEED             ;X = SEED * MULTIPLIER
43:             MUL     MULTIPLIER
44:             INC     AX                  ;SEED = (X + 1) mod 65536
45:             MOV     SEED,AX
46:             MOV     DX,0
47:             DIV     TWO_56              ;RANDOM = SEED/256*10000/256
48:             MUL     TEN_THOU
49:             DIV     TWO_56
50:             POP     DX
51:             POP     CX
52:             POPF                        ;RESTORE FLAGS
53:             RET                         ;RETURN (RANDOM)
54: RANDOM      ENDP
55: CODE        ENDS
56:*           END
```

assembly module in Program Listing 12.1 in only one place: The DATA segment is defined with a combine type of PUBLIC (line 16 in Program Listing 12.4). The assembly module in Program Listing 12.5 differs from the assembly module in Program Listing 12.2 in several places. The name of the local data segment for the random number generator has been changed from RAND_DATA to DATA (line 13 in Program Listing 12.5). The names of the two data segments being combined must be the same. The local data segment for the random number generator is defined with a combine type of PUBLIC and an align type of BYTE (line 13 in Program Listing 12.5). This definition causes the LINK program to concatenate this segment with other PUBLIC segments that have the name DATA and have no class name. Since this piece of the segment has an align type of BYTE, it is concatenated with any existing portion of the segment, leaving no unused storage locations in between.

The assembly modules in Program Listings 12.2 and 12.5 also differ in the code segment. Since the local data segment for the random number generator in Program Listing 12.2 is physically separate from the caller's data segment, the random number generator must save the DS-register for the caller (line 35), set the DS-register to address its local data segment (lines 36 and 37), and restore the DS-register before returning to the caller (line 54). These lines have been removed from the random number generator in Program Listing 12.5. Since the local data for the random number generator is part of the caller's data segment, the DS-register has already been initialized by the caller (lines 31 and 32 in Program Listing 12.4) to address this shared data segment. Note the ASSUME pseudo-operation in line 29 in Program Listing 12.5. The assembler must know that the DS-register will address the DATA segment during execution of the RANDOM procedure, regardless of where the DS-register is actually initialized.

The load map for the second version of this program appears in Load Map Listing 12.6 and was produced in response to the following command:

```
LINK B:EX_12_4 B:EX_12_5,B:,B:,IO
```

```
 1:                    LOAD MAP LISTING 12.6
 2:
 3:
 4:  Start   Stop    Length  Name                    Class
 5:  00000H  000FFH  00100H  STACK
 6:  00100H  0013EH  0003FH  DATA
 7:  00140H  0019FH  00060H  CODE
 8:  001A0H  001D4H  00035H  CODE
 9:  001E0H  00236H  00057H  IO_DATA
10:  00240H  0025BH  0001CH  CODE                    IO_CODE
11:  00260H  00308H  000A9H  CODE                    IO_CODE
12:  00310H  00365H  00056H  CODE                    IO_CODE
13:  00370H  0038DH  0001EH  CODE                    IO_CODE
14:  00390H  003E3H  00054H  CODE                    IO_CODE
15:  003F0H  00402H  00013H  CODE                    IO_CODE
16:
17:  Origin    Group
18:
19:*Program entry point at 0014:0000
```

The load map was placed on the diskette in drive B under the name EX_12_4.MAP. Note that the two object modules must be presented to the LINK program in the order shown. The first part of the combined segment must be defined with align type PARA (the default), so that the physical segment begins on a paragraph boundary. All subsequent parts can be defined with align type BYTE. The segment named DATA, the shared data segment, begins at zero-relative location 00100 hex and is 3F hex (63 decimal) bytes in length (line 6 in Load Map Listing 12.6). Note that the length is the sum of the lengths of the two segments that were combined. The next contiguous segment (the code segment for the main procedure) begins at zero-relative location 00140 hex, so the data segment actually consumes 40 hex (64 decimal) bytes of storage space, which is the same amount of storage space consumed for segment DATA in Program Listing 12.1 (line 6 in Load Map 12.3). The storage space consumed by the data segment for the main procedure did not increase when the data required by the subprocedure was included. The paragraph consumed by the local data segment for the random number generator in the first version has been eliminated in the second version. Note that the second code segment (the code segment for the random number generator) and all subsequent segments begin one paragraph lower in Load Map Listing 12.6 than in Load Map Listing 12.3. The combining of data segments saved 1 paragraph (16 bytes) of storage.

Another observation can be made by comparing Load Map Listings 12.3 and 12.6. The length of the second code segment (the code segment for the random number generator) was reduced from 3C hex (60 decimal) bytes to 35 hex (53 decimal) bytes (line 9 in Load Map Listing 12.3 and line 8 in Load Map Listing 12.6). This reduction was due to the segment register initialization instructions that were removed from the random number generator when the two data segments were combined. The length of this code segment remains between 3 and 4 paragraphs, so the segment still consumes 4 paragraphs of storage space.

By combining segments, a program's storage requirements can be reduced. In the coin-toss illustration, combining the data segment for the random number generator with the data segment for the caller reduced the storage requirements of the program by 1 paragraph (16 bytes). The user of the random number generator must be familiar with the name of the random number generator's data segment and must use the same name for its data segment. The caller's data segment must also be defined with combine type PUBLIC. If the caller uses a different name for its data segment or defines its data segment as nonPUBLIC, then the data segment for the random number generator is physically separate and independent from the caller's data segment. In this case, the random number generator would execute with the DS-register addressing the caller's data segment rather than its local data segment, and the results would not be the desired results. Also, the data segment for the random number generator might not begin on a paragraph boundary as required for a physically separate segment. The reduction in storage requirements, achieved by combining segments, comes at the expense of a loss in flexibility for the random number generator.

Code segments can also be combined into a single physical segment, which is illustrated in Program Listing 12.9 and 12.10 later in this chapter.

12.3 Stack Segments

An IBM PC machine language program has exactly one run-time stack segment whose top-of-stack element is addressed by the SS:SP register pair. The various assembly modules from which the machine language program was generated can each contribute to the size of the run-time stack segment. All segments that have a combine type of STACK and have the same segment name and class name are combined into a single, physical segment by the LINK program. The length of this segment is the sum of the lengths of the segments being combined. At execution time, the SS-register is automatically initialized to specify the origin of this combined stack segment, and the SP-register is initialized to contain the offset, relative to the SS-register value, of the location immediately following the segment.

If the LINK program encounters segments with combine type STACK that have different segment and/or class names, then the run-time stack segment (i.e., the one addressed by the SS:SP register pair) is the last such segment encountered.

EXAMPLES

Table 12.1 specifies the order in which four segments with combine type STACK are encountered by the LINK program. LINK combines these four segments into two physical segments. The first segment, named STACK, is 192 bytes in length (offsets 0000–00BF hexadecimal). The second segment, named STAK, is 256 bytes in length (offsets 0000–00FF hexadecimal). Since the last segment encountered is a part of segment STAK, it is the run-time stack segment for the program. The SS-register is initialized to specify the origin of segment STAK, and the SP-register is initialized to the hexadecimal value 0100 (256 decimal).

Suppose the LINK program encountered the same segments in the order shown in Table 12.2. Since the last segment encountered is a part of segment STACK, it is the run-time stack segment for the program. The SS-register is initialized to specify the origin of segment STACK, and the SP-register is initialized to the hexadecimal value 00C0 (192 decimal).

TABLE 12.1
Stack segments being linked

Segment Name	Class Name	Combine Type	Size in Bytes
STACK	None	STACK	64
STAK	None	STACK	192
STACK	None	STACK	128
STAK	None	STACK	64

TABLE 12.2
Stack segments
being linked

Segment Name	Class Name	Combine Type	Size in Bytes
STACK	None	STACK	64
STAK	None	STACK	192
STAK	None	STACK	64
STACK	None	STACK	128

During program execution, the SS:SP register pair can be switched from one physical segment to another, but this technique is beyond the scope of this book.

The example programs used in this book contain one stack segment definition, and this stack segment definition appears in the assembly module that contains the definition of the main procedure. This one stack segment must be large enough to accommodate the stack needs for the entire program. An alternative would be to define a portion of the stack segment in each assembly module. The size of the portion defined in a given assembly module would depend on the needs of the procedures defined in that assembly module. With either approach, knowledge of the dynamic structure is required to define the size of the stack segment properly.

EXAMPLES

Suppose a program consists of a main procedure and four subprocedures named A, B, C, and D, and suppose the main procedure requires 4 words of the stack segment, procedure A requires 10 words of the stack segment, procedure B requires 12 words of the stack segment, procedure C requires 8 words of the stack segment, and procedure D requires 6 words of the stack segment.

Suppose the dynamic structure of the program is described by the graph in Figure 12.1. The main procedure references each of the subprocedures in sequence, and the subprocedures themselves do not call any subprocedures. In this case, the stack must be large enough to accommodate the main procedure and the subprocedure with the largest stack need. Therefore, the stack must be 16 words (4 for the main procedure and 12 for procedure B) in length.

FIGURE 12.1
Dynamic structure
of a program

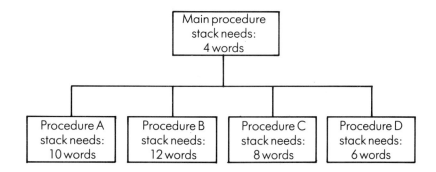

FIGURE 12.2
Dynamic structure
of a program

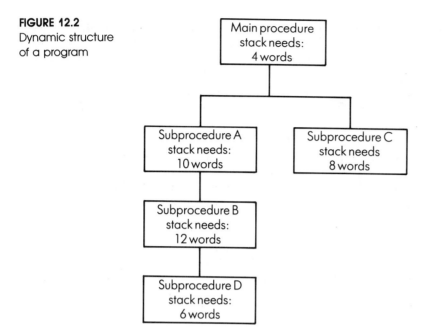

Suppose the dynamic structure of the program is described by the graph in Figure 12.2. The main procedure references subprocedures A and C in sequence. Subprocedure A calls subprocedure B, which in turn calls subprocedure D. In this case, the stack segment must be large enough to accommodate the main procedure and subprocedures A, B, and D at the same time. Therefore, the stack must be 32 words (4 for the main procedure, 10 for procedure A, 12 for procedure B, and 6 for procedure D) in length.

Twice as much stack space is required for the program structure of Figure 12.2 than is required for the structure of Figure 12.1.

Since you cannot know the dynamic structure nor the stack needs for the I/O subprocedures provided by the I/O subprocedure library that accompanies this text, it is suggested that a stack of at least 256 bytes be defined when using these subprocedures. Except for the example programs in Chapter 10, a 256-byte stack is sufficient for the example programs in this book; however, for a number of the programs, a stack of 128 bytes is not sufficient.

12.4 | Overlay Segments

In the IBM PC Assembly language, it is possible to define a data segment that is accessible to procedures in separate assembly modules. This accessibility is accomplished by having each assembly module define its own version of the common data segment. The various versions are overlayed on one another to produce one physical segment. The definition of the common data segment in a specific assembly module is simply a symbolic name template to be used by assembly module procedures in referencing the common data.

The combine type COMMON specifies that the segment being defined is to be overlayed with other COMMON segments that have the same segment name and class name. The segments being overlayed do not have to be the same size. The size of the physical segment produced is the same as the size of the largest of the segments being overlayed. Initial values for the storage cells in the common data segment can be specified in any of the segment definitions for the common segment. If more than one initial value is supplied for a specific storage cell, then the last value encountered by the LINK program is the one that prevails.

EXAMPLE

Suppose the following three segment definitions appear in separate assembly modules of an IBM PC Assembly language program:

Assembly module A:

```
DATA    SEGMENT COMMON
STRING DB       4 DUP(?)
V       DW      300
W       DW      500
DATA    ENDS
```

Assembly module B:

```
DATA    SEGMENT COMMON
STRING DB       4 DUP(' ')
X       DW      ?
Y       DW      ?
Z       DW      0
DATA    ENDS
```

Assembly module C:

```
DATA SEGMENT COMMON
        DB      4 DUP(?)
Z       DW      6
Y       DW      12
DATA ENDS
```

Table 12.3 shows the name template for use by procedures in each of the three assembly modules to reference the locations of the common data segment. The 4-byte string that begins at offset 0000 can be referenced by the name STRING in assembly modules A and B procedures. This string cannot be referenced by name in assembly module C procedures. The word variable that begins at offset 0006 can be referenced by the name Y in assembly modules B and C procedures and by the name W in assembly module A procedures.

TABLE 12.3
Label templates for
a common data
segment

Offset	Label for Use in Assembly Module A	Label for Use in Assembly Module B	Label for Use in Assembly Module C
0000	STRING	STRING	
0001			
0002			
0003			
0004	V	X	Z
0005			
0006	W	Y	Y
0007			
0008		Z	
0009			

Suppose the assembly modules are presented to the LINK program in the order shown previously (A followed by B followed by C). Table 12.4 shows the steps in building the common data segment from the three definitions. On encountering the data segment definition in assembly module A, the LINK program allocates 8 bytes for the data segment. No initial values are specified for the first 4 bytes. The fifth and sixth bytes are initialized to 2C hex and 01 hex, respectively, which is the word value 300 (012C hex). The seventh and eighth bytes are initialized to F4 hex and 01 hex, respectively, which is the word value 500 (01F4 hex). The status of the data segment at this point in the linking process is shown in Table 12.4(a).

On encountering the data segment definition in assembly module B, the LINK program appends two bytes to the common data segment. The data segment is now 10 bytes in length. Each of the first 4 bytes is initialized to the ASCII representation for a space (20 hex). No initial values are specified for the

TABLE 12.4
Common data
segment: (a) after
assembly module A,
(b) after assembly
module B, and (c)
after assembly
module C

(a)		(b)		(c)	
Offset	Value	Offset	Value	Offset	Value
0000	?	0000	20	0000	20
0001	?	0001	20	0001	20
0002	?	0002	20	0002	20
0003	?	0003	20	0003	20
0004	2C	0004	2C	0004	06
0005	01	0005	01	0005	00
0006	F4	0006	F4	0006	0C
0007	01	0007	01	0007	00
		0008	00	0008	00
		0009	00	0009	00

next 2 words (4 bytes), thus leaving the initial values specified by the data segment definition in assembly module A. The last 2 bytes (the 2 bytes just appended) are each initialized to 00. The status of the data segment at this point in the linking process is shown in Table 12.4(b).

On encountering the data segment definition in assembly module C, the LINK program makes no modification in the size of the common data segment, because the size specified by this definition (8 bytes) is smaller than the current size of the segment (10 bytes). No initial values are specified for the first 4 bytes, thus leaving the initial values specified by the data segment definition in assembly module B. The next 2 words are assigned the initial values 0006 and 000C hex, thus replacing the initial values specified by the data segment definition in assembly module A. The physical data segment produced by the complete linking process has the initial values shown in Table 12.4(c).

Programming Example—Sieve of Eratosthenes Revisited

The Sieve of Eratosthenes, introduced in Section 8.5, is a technique for computing prime numbers. Program Listing 8.4 shows part of an implementation of an algorithm for computing prime numbers using this technique. The assembly module contains a data segment definition (lines 22–29) that defines the sieve as a word array. It also contains the definition of a code segment that contains the definitions of a main procedure and two NEAR subprocedures. The program shows the definition of the main procedure (lines 34–90) and one of the subprocedures (lines 99–116). The definition of the other subprocedure was left as Programming Exercise 8.10.

Program Listings 12.7 and 12.8 illustrate an alternative approach for implementing the same algorithm: implementing the main procedure and the two NEAR subprocedures in separate assembly modules. The sieve is defined in a data segment that is common to the three assembly modules. Such a definition allows the subprocedure interface for the two NEAR subprocedures to remain the same. If the two subprocedures are to be NEAR subprocedures, then they must be defined in the same code segment as the main procedure. The code segments in the three assembly modules are given the same name and are defined with a combine type of PUBLIC, which causes the LINK program to combine the three code segments into one physical code segment containing all three procedures. Program Listings 12.7 and 12.8 show two of these three assembly modules. The third module is left as Programming Exercise 12.1.

The assembly module in Program Listing 12.7 contains the definition of the stack segment for the program (lines 19–21), a definition of the common data segment (lines 30–35), and the definition of the main procedure (lines 40–97). The main procedure references the two subprocedures: FINDPRIM and SIFT-SIEVE. Since the two subprocedures are external (i.e., defined in separate assembly modules), they must be identified to the assembler with the EXTRN

```
 1: ;
 2: ;
 3: ;                     PROGRAM LISTING 12.7
 4: ;
 5: ; PROGRAM TO DISPLAY THE PRIME NUMBERS THAT ARE LESS THAN 16000.
 6: ; THE PROGRAM USES THE SIEVE OF ERATOSTHENES.
 7: ;
 8: ;
 9:                                         ;PROCEDURES TO
10:         EXTRN    FINDPRIM:NEAR          ;FIND NEXT PRIME IN SIEVE
11:         EXTRN    NEWLINE:FAR            ;DISPLAY NEWLINE CHARACTER
12:         EXTRN    PAUSE:FAR              ;PAUSE UNTIL KEYSTROKE
13:         EXTRN    PUTDEC$:FAR            ;DISPLAY UNSIGNED DECIMAL INT.
14:         EXTRN    SIFTSIEVE:NEAR         ;SIFT MULTIPLES OF PRIME
15:                                         ;FROM SIEVE
16: ;
17: ; S T A C K   S E G M E N T   D E F I N I T I O N
18: ;
19: STACK        SEGMENT STACK
20:              DB      256 DUP(?)
21: STACK        ENDS
22: ;
23: ; C O N S T A N T   D E F I N I T I O N S
24: ;
25: SIZE$     EQU      15999
26: MAX_INDEX EQU      2*SIZE$
27: ;
28: ; D A T A   S E G M E N T   D E F I N I T I O N
29: ;
30: DATA         SEGMENT COMMON
31: ;
32: SIEVE        DW      SIZE$ DUP(?)
33: PAUSE_MSG    DB      'PRESS ANY KEY TO CONTINUE'
34: ;
35: DATA         ENDS
36: ;
37: ; CODE SEGMENT
38: ;
39: CODE         SEGMENT PUBLIC
40: EX_12_7      PROC    FAR
41:              ASSUME  CS:CODE,SS:STACK,DS:DATA,ES:DATA
42:              PUSH    DS             ;PUSH RETURN SEG ADDR ON STACK
43:              SUB     AX,AX          ;PUSH RETURN OFFSET OF ZERO
44:              PUSH    AX             ;ON STACK
45:              MOV     AX,SEG DATA    ;SET ES AND DS REGISTERS TO
46:              MOV     DS,AX          ;POINT TO DATA SEGMENT
47:              MOV     ES,AX
48:                                     ;<INITIALIZE SIEVE>
49:              CLD                    ;SET DF FOR INCREMENTING
50:              MOV     CX,SIZE$       ;LOOP_COUNT = SIZE OF SIEVE
51:              LEA     DI,SIEVE       ;SET ES:DI TO BASE ADDRESS
52:                                     ;           OF SIEVE
53:              MOV     AX,2           ;VALUE = 2
54: LOADLOOP:                          ;REPEAT
55:              STOSW                  ;   ES:DI -> WORD = VALUE
56:                                     ;   DI = DI + 2
57:              INC     AX             ;   VALUE = VALUE + 1
58:              LOOP    LOADLOOP       ;   LOOP_COUNT = LOOP_COUNT - 1
59:                                     ;UNTIL LOOP_COUNT = 0
60:              MOV     BX,0           ;INDEX = 0
61:              MOV     CX,0           ;PRIME_COUNT = 0
```

```
62:            CALL    FINDPRIM              ;CALL FINDPRIME(INDEX,PRIME)
63:*;

64: ;
65: PRIMELOOP:                              ;REPEAT
66:            CALL    SIFTSIEVE             ;    CALL SIFTSIEVE(PRIME,INDEX)
67:                                          ;    <SIFT OUT MULTIPLES OF PRIME>
68:            PUSH    BX                    ;    SAVE SIEVE INDEX
69:            MOV     BH,1                  ;    DISPLAY PRIME
70:            CALL    PUTDEC$
71:            INC     CX                    ;    PRIME_COUNT = PRIME_COUNT + 1
72:            MOV     AX,CX                 ;    IF   PRIME_COUNT mod 10 = 0
73:            MOV     DX,O
74:            MOV     BX,10
75:            DIV     BX
76:            CMP     DX,O
77:            JNE     NEXTPRIME
78:            CALL    NEWLINE               ;       THEN DISPLAY NEWLINE CHAR
79:            MOV     DX,O                  ;          IF   PRIME_COUNT mod 240
80:            MOV     BX,24                 ;             = O
81:            DIV     BX
82:            CMP     DX,O
83:            JNE     NEXTPRIME
84:            PUSH    CX                    ;             THEN
85:            LEA     DI,PAUSE_MSG          ;                PAUSE FOR PRINT
86:            MOV     CX,25                 ;                OF DISPLAY SCREEN
87:            CALL    PAUSE
88:            POP     CX
89:                                          ;             ENDIF
90: NEXTPRIME:                              ;       ENDIF
91:            POP     BX                    ;    RESTORE SIEVE INDEX
92:            CALL    FINDPRIM              ;    CALL FINDPRIME(INDEX,PRIME)
93:            CMP     AX,O
94:            JNE     PRIMELOOP             ;UNTIL SIEVE IS EMPTY
95:            CALL    NEWLINE
96:            RET                           ;RETURN
97: EX_12_7    ENDP
98: CODE       ENDS
99:*           END     EX_12_7
```

pseudo-operation (lines 10 and 14). These pseudo-operations notify the assembler that the symbolic names FINDPRIM and SIFTSIEVE, defined in other assembly modules, are used in this assembly module as NEAR procedure names. Since these are NEAR procedures, the code segments containing these procedures must be combined with the code segment for the main procedure, producing a single code segment for the three procedures.

Two named constants are defined in lines 25 and 26. The named constant, SIZE$, defines the word size of the sieve. To modify the program to process a different size sieve, you only need to modify the value of this named constant. Since this named constant appears in all three assembly modules, it must be consistent in all three. The name constant, MAX_INDEX, is the index of the last word in the sieve.

A definition of the common data segment appears in lines 30–35. The data segment is defined with combine type COMMON, so that it is overlayed with

```
 1: ;
 2: ;
 3: ;                        PROGRAM LISTING 12.8
 4: ;
 5: ; SIFT MULTIPLES OF PRIME OUT OF SIEVE
 6: ;
 7: ; INPUT:   AX-REG CONTAINS PRIME NUMBER
 8: ;          BX-REG CONTAINS SIEVE INDEX OF PRIME NUMBER
 9: ;
10: ; OUTPUT: SIEVE WITH MULTIPLES OF PRIME REMOVED
11: ;
12: ;
13: ; C O N S T A N T   D E F I N I T I O N S
14: ;
15: SIZE$        EQU      15999
16: MAX_INDEX    EQU      2*SIZE$
17: ;
18: ; D A T A   S E G M E N T   D E F I N I T I O N
19: ;
20: DATA         SEGMENT COMMON
21: ;
22: SIEVE        DW       SIZE$ DUP(?)
23: ;
24: DATA         ENDS
25: ;
26: ; C O D E   S E G M E N T   D E F I N I T I O N
27: ;
28: CODE         SEGMENT PUBLIC BYTE
29:              ASSUME  CS:CODE,DS:DATA
30:              PUBLIC  SIFTSIEVE
31: SIFTSIEVE    PROC    NEAR              ;PROCEDURE SIFTSIEVE(PRIME,INDEX)
32:              PUSH    AX                 ;SAVE REGISTERS
33:              PUSH    BX
34:              MOV     SIEVE[BX],0        ;SIEVE(INDEX) = 0
35:              SAL     AX,1               ;OFFSET = PRIME * 2
36:                                         ;<OFFSET BETWEEN MULTIPLES
37:                                         ;            OF PRIME>
38: SIFTLOOP:                               ;WHILE (INDEX+OFFSET) < MAX_INDEX
39:              ADD     BX,AX              ;   INDEX = INDEX + OFFSET
40:              CMP     BX,MAX_INDEX
41:              JAE     RETURN1
42:              MOV     SIEVE[BX],0        ;    SIEVE(INDEX) = 0
43:              JMP     SIFTLOOP
44: RETURN1:                                ;ENDWHILE
45:              POP     BX                 ;RESTORE REGISTERS
46:              POP     AX
47:              RET                        ;RETURN
48: SIFTSIEVE    ENDP                      ;END SIFTSIEVE
49: CODE         ENDS
50:*             END
```

the definitions appearing in the other assembly modules, producing a single data segment. The data segment contains the definition of the sieve (line 32) and the definition of a message to be displayed whenever the display screen is full (line 33).

The code segment (lines 39–98) is defined with combine type PUBLIC, which causes this code segment to be combined with other PUBLIC code segments having the same segment name and class name, producing a single code segment. The code segments containing the NEAR subprocedures must be defined in exactly the same way. The procedure defined in this code segment, the main procedure (lines 40–97), is exactly the same as the main procedure in Program Listing 8.4. The name of the procedure has been changed from EX_8_4 to EX_12_7.

The assembly module in Program Listing 12.8 contains a definition of the common data segment (lines 20–24) and the definition of the subprocedure SIFTSIEVE (lines 30–48). The named constants that were defined in the assembly module in Program Listing 12.7 are also defined in this assembly module (lines 15–16). Both constants are needed in the SIFTSIEVE procedure.

The data segment (lines 20–24) is defined with the combine type COMMON, so that it is overlayed with the data segment defined in the assembly module in Program Listing 12.7. Note that the same segment name is used in these two data segment definitions. The LINK program will not overlay COMMON segments that have different segment names. The version of the common data segment definition in Program Listing 12.8 only defines the sieve; it does not include the string that was defined in Program Listing 12.7. The SIFTSIEVE subprocedure does not use the character string, so it has no need for access to it. If the data segment definition in Program Listing 12.7 had been

```
DATA        SEGMENT COMMON
PAUSE_MSG DB        'PRESS ANY KEY TO CONTINUE'
SIEVE       DW       SIZE$ DUP(?)
DATA        ENDS
```

then the data segment definition in Program Listing 12.8 would have to be

```
DATA  SEGMENT COMMON
      DB       25 DUP(?)
SIEVE DW       SIZE$ DUP(?)
DATA  ENDS
```

Space needs to be allocated for the string, so that the sieve overlays properly. The name can be omitted, since the SIFTSIEVE procedure does not need to access the string. Its initial value has already been defined, so this definition must protect that initial value. The use of the question mark (?) protects any initial value that might have already been established.

The code segment is defined with the combine type PUBLIC, so that it is combined with the code segment defined in the assembly module in Program Listing 12.7. It is defined with the align type BYTE so that no unused storage space appears between the SIFTSIEVE procedure and the procedure that precedes it in the physical code segment. The code segment contains an ASSUME pseudo-operation (line 29) that notifies the assembler that the CS-register will address the code segment and the DS-register will address the data segment during execution of SIFTSIEVE. SIFTSIEVE does not have to be concerned with initialization of either of these registers. Since one code segment contains all three procedures, the CS-register is initialized on invocation of the main procedure, and it does not change when the SIFTSIEVE procedure is invoked. The main procedure initializes the DS-register to address the common data segment that is shared by the three procedures (lines 45 and 46 in Program Listing 12.7). The name SIFTSIEVE is declared as PUBLIC (line 30 in Program Listing 12.8), so that it is available for reference in other assembly modules. The definition of the SIFTSIEVE procedure (lines 31–48 in Program Listing 12.8) is exactly the same as the definition of the SIFTSIEVE procedure in Program Listing 8.4.

When the object modules for these assembly modules are presented to the LINK program, the object module for the assembly module in Program Listing 12.7 must be presented first because the PUBLIC code segment in that assembly module has align type PARA (the default), and the PUBLIC code segment must begin on a paragraph boundary. The other two object modules can be presented in any order.

12.5 Combining Code Segments with Data Segments

A code segment and a data segment can be combined into the same physical segment. This feature might be accomplished so that an external subprocedure can access its local data segment via the CS segment register rather than the DS or ES segment registers, which avoids having to save, initialize, and restore the DS or ES segment registers.

As an example, consider again the coin-toss simulation program. Program Listings 12.9 and 12.10 show a version of this program that specifies the combining of the main procedure, its data segment, the random number generator, and its data segment into one physical segment. Note that all four segments have the same name, PROG (lines 17 and 26 of Program Listing 12.9 and lines 13 and 28 of Program Listing 12.10). All four of these segments are defined with a combine type of PUBLIC: The first of these four segments, the data segment in Program Listing 12.9, is defined with an align type of PARA (the default); the other three are defined with an align type of BYTE.

Use of the DS-register has been eliminated from the program. The CS-register must be used to address the segment in order to access the procedures' instructions. It can also be used as the segment register for accessing the data items in the segment, which eliminates the need for the DS-register. The ASSUME pseudo-operation in line 28 in Program Listing 12.9 indicates that the main procedure uses both the CS and ES registers to address the segment PROG. The ES-register is needed because the PUTSTRNG procedure is being used: PUTSTRNG expects the address of the string to be displayed, to be in the ES:DI register pair. Note that only the ES-register is initialized (lines 32 and 33). Initialization of the DS-register has been eliminated. The ASSUME pseudo-operation in line 29 in Program Listing 12.10 indicates that the random number generator uses only the CS-register to address the segment PROG, which means that the CS-register is used by the random number generator to reference its data.

```
 1: ;                        PROGRAM LISTING 12.9
 2: ;
 3: ; PROGRAM TO SIMULATE THE TOSSING OF A COIN
 4: ;
 5:                                             ;PROCEDURES TO
 6:             EXTRN    GETDEC$:FAR            ;INPUT UNSIGNED DEC. INTEGER
 7:             EXTRN    PUTDEC$:FAR            ;DISPLAY UNSIGNED DEC. INTEGER
 8:             EXTRN    PUTSTRNG:FAR           ;DISPLAY A CHARACTER STRING
 9:             EXTRN    RANDOM:NEAR            ;GENERATE PSEUDO-RANDOM NUMBER
10: ;
11: ;<***** S T A C K    S E G M E N T    D E F I N I T I O N *****>
12: STACK       SEGMENT STACK
13:             DB       256 DUP(?)
14: STACK       ENDS
15: ;
16: ;<*****   D A T A    S E G M E N T    D E F I N I T I O N *****>
17: PROG        SEGMENT PUBLIC
18: HEADS       DW       0                     ;COUNT OF NUMBER OF HEADS
19: TAILS       DW       0                     ;COUNT OF NUMBER OF TAILS
20: PROMPT      DB       'ENTER NUMBER OF TIMES TO TOSS COIN '
21: HEADSMSG    DB       ' HEADS  '
22: TAILSMSG    DB       ' TAILS'
23: PROG        ENDS
24: ;
25: ;<*****   C O D E    S E G M E N T    D E F I N I T I O N *****>
26: PROG        SEGMENT PUBLIC BYTE
27: COINTOSS    PROC     FAR
28:             ASSUME   CS:PROG,SS:STACK,ES:PROG
29:             PUSH     DS                    ;PUSH RETURN SEG ADDR ON STACK
30:             SUB      AX,AX                 ;PUSH RETURN OFFSET OF ZERO
31:             PUSH     AX                    ;ON STACK
32:             MOV      AX,SEG PROG           ;SET ES-REGISTER TO ADDRESS
33:             MOV      ES,AX                 ;PROGRAM SEGMENT
34:             LEA      DI,PROMPT             ;PROMPT FOR NUMBER_OF_TOSSES
35:             MOV      CX,36
36:             CALL     PUTSTRNG
37:             CALL     GETDEC$               ;GET NUMBER_OF_TOSSES
38:             MOV      CX,AX                 ;LOOP_COUNT = NUMBER_OF_TOSSES
39: TOSS_COIN:                                 ;REPEAT
40:             CALL     RANDOM                ;    NUMBER = RANDOM()
41:             CMP      AX,5000               ;    IF   NUMBER >= 5000
42:             JL       CNT_TAILS
43:             INC      HEADS                 ;      THEN HEADS = HEADS + 1
44:             JMP      NEXT_TOSS
45: CNT_TAILS:                                 ;      ELSE
46:             INC      TAILS                 ;          TAILS = TAILS + 1
47: NEXT_TOSS:                                 ;    ENDIF
48:             LOOP     TOSS_COIN             ;    LOOP_COUNT = LOOP_COUNT - 1
49:                                            ;UNTIL LOOP_COUNT = 0
50:             MOV      BH,1
51:             MOV      AX,HEADS              ;DISPLAY HEADS
52:             CALL     PUTDEC$
53:             LEA      DI,HEADSMSG
54:             MOV      CX,8
55:             CALL     PUTSTRNG
56:             MOV      AX,TAILS              ;DISPLAY TAILS
57:             CALL     PUTDEC$
58:             LEA      DI,TAILSMSG
59:             MOV      CX,6
60:             CALL     PUTSTRNG
61:             RET                            ;RETURN
62: COINTOSS    ENDP
63: PROG        ENDS
64:*            END      COINTOSS
```

```
 1: ;                       PROGRAM LISTING 12.10
 2: ;
 3: ; r a n d o m    n u m b e r    g e n e r a t o r
 4: ;
 5: ; GENERATES PSEUDO-RANDOM INTEGERS IN THE RANGE
 6: ;            0 TO 9999
 7: ;
 8: ; INPUT:  NONE
 9: ; OUTPUT: AX-REG CONTAINS RANDOM INTEGER
10: ;
11: ; D A T A    S E G M E N T
12: ;
13: PROG          SEGMENT PUBLIC BYTE
14: ;
15: SEED          DW      ?               ;SEED FOR RANDOM NUMBER GEN.
16: MULTIPLIER DW         3621            ;MULTIPLIER FOR LINEAR
17: ;                                     ;CONGRUENTIAL METHOD
18: FALSE         EQU     0               ;CONSTANT FALSE
19: TRUE          EQU     1               ;CONSTANT TRUE
20: FIRST_CALL DB         TRUE            ;FIRST CALL FLAG
21: TWO_56        DW      256             ;CONSTANT 256
22: TEN_THOU      DW      10000           ;CONSTANT 10000
23: ;
24: PROG          ENDS
25: ;
26: ; C O D E    S E G M E N T
27: ;
28: PROG          SEGMENT PUBLIC BYTE
29:               ASSUME  CS:PROG
30:               PUBLIC  RANDOM
31: RANDOM        PROC    NEAR
32:               PUSHF                   ;SAVE FLAGS
33:               PUSH    CX              ;SAVE REGISTERS
34:               PUSH    DX
35:               CMP     FIRST_CALL,TRUE ;IF   FIRST_CALL
36:               JNE     ENDIF
37:               MOV     FIRST_CALL,FALSE;THEN FIRST_CALL = FALSE
38:               MOV     AH,0            ;     SEED = LOWER HALF OF
39:               INT     1AH             ;              TIME OF DAY CLOCK
40:               MOV     SEED,DX
41: ENDIF:                                ;ENDIF
42:               MOV     AX,SEED         ;X = SEED * MULTIPLIER
43:               MUL     MULTIPLIER
44:               INC     AX              ;SEED = (X + 1) mod 65536
45:               MOV     SEED,AX
46:               MOV     DX,0
47:               DIV     TWO_56          ;RANDOM = SEED/256*10000/256
48:               MUL     TEN_THOU
49:               DIV     TWO_56
50:               POP     DX
51:               POP     CX
52:               POPF                    ;RESTORE FLAGS
53:               RET                     ;RETURN (RANDOM)
54: RANDOM        ENDP
55: PROG          ENDS
56:*             END
```

*

The random number generator has been changed from a FAR procedure to a NEAR procedure in this version of the program (line 9 in Program Listing 12.9 and line 31 in Program Listing 12.10). There is no need for the random number generator to be a FAR procedure, since it is in the same code segment as its caller. By making it a NEAR procedure, the CALL instruction that invokes the NEAR procedure is 2 bytes shorter.

The following LINK command was used to create the executable module for this program:

```
LINK B:EX_12_9 B:EX_12_10,B:,B:,IO
```

The load map produced and stored on the diskette in drive B, under the name EX_12_9.MAP, is shown in Load Map Listing 12.11. The load map shows a segment named STACK (the stack segment for the program) and a segment named PROG (the combined data and code segment for the program). The remainder of the segments listed in the load map came from the I/O sub-procedure library. The segment PROG is DD hex (221 decimal) bytes in length.

The DEBUG session in DEBUG Listing 12.12 shows the four parts that make up the PUBLIC segment named PROG. The first command issued to DEBUG (the R command) requests a register display. The value of the CS-register (0928) indicates that segment PROG is loaded in memory beginning at location 09280 hexadecimal. The value of the IP-register (0036) indicates that the main procedure begins at offset 0036 within the segment.

The next command issued to DEBUG

```
D CS:0,35
```

requests a dump of the first 54 bytes of the segment addressed by the CS-register, which is the part of the segment produced from the data segment definition in Program Listing 12.9. The first two bytes (offsets 0000 and 0001) make up the memory word that contains the value of the variable HEADS, whose initial value is 0000. The next two bytes (offsets 0002 and 0003) make up the memory word

```
 1:                     LOAD MAP LISTING 12.11
 2:
 3:
 4:    Start   Stop    Length  Name                        Class
 5:    00000H  000FFH  00100H  STACK
 6:    00100H  001DCH  000DDH  PROG
 7:    001E0H  00236H  00057H  IO_DATA
 8:    00240H  0025BH  0001CH  CODE                        IO_CODE
 9:    00260H  00308H  000A9H  CODE                        IO_CODE
10:    00310H  00365H  00056H  CODE                        IO_CODE
11:    00370H  0038DH  0001EH  CODE                        IO_CODE
12:    00390H  003E3H  00054H  CODE                        IO_CODE
13:    003F0H  00402H  00013H  CODE                        IO_CODE
14:
15:    Origin    Group
16:
17:*Program entry point at 0010:0036
*
```

```
                         DEBUG LISTING 12.12
A>DEBUG B:EX_12_9.EXE
-R
AX=0000  BX=0000  CX=0403  DX=0000  SP=0100  BP=0000  SI=0000  DI=0000
DS=0908  ES=0908  SS=0918  CS=0928  IP=0036   NV UP DI PL NZ NA PO NC
0928:0036 1E             PUSH    DS
-D CS:0,35
0928:0000   00 00 00 00 45 4E 54 45-52 20 4E 55 4D 42 45 52   ....ENTER NUMBER
0928:0010   20 4F 46 20 54 49 4D 45-53 20 54 4F 20 54 4F 53    OF TIMES TO TOS
0928:0020   53 20 43 4F 49 4E 20 20-20 48 45 41 44 53 20 20   S COIN    HEADS
0928:0030   20 54 41 49 4C 53                                  TAILS
-U CS:36,95
0928:0036 1E             PUSH    DS
0928:0037 2BC0           SUB     AX,AX
0928:0039 50             PUSH    AX
0928:003A B82809         MOV     AX,0928
0928:003D 8EC0           MOV     ES,AX
0928:003F 8D3E0400       LEA     DI,[0004]
0928:0043 B92400         MOV     CX,0024
0928:0046 9A0000 3C09    CALL    093C:0000
0928:004B 9A0000 3E09    CALL    093E:0000
0928:0050 8BC8           MOV     CX,AX
0928:0052 E84A00         CALL    009F
0928:0055 3D8813         CMP     AX,1388
0928:0058 7C08           JL      0062
0928:005A 2E             CS:
0928:005B FF060000       INC     WORD PTR [0000]
0928:005F EB06           JMP     0067
0928:0061 90             NOP
0928:0062 2E             CS:
0928:0063 FF060200       INC     WORD PTR [0002]
0928:0067 E2E9           LOOP    0052
0928:0069 B701           MOV     BH,01
0928:006B 2E             CS:
0928:006C A10000         MOV     AX,[0000]
0928:006F 9A0000 4909    CALL    0949:0000
0928:0074 8D3E2800       LEA     DI,[0028]
0928:0078 B90800         MOV     CX,0008
0928:007B 9A0000 3C09    CALL    093C:0000
0928:0080 2E             CS:
0928:0081 A10200         MOV     AX,[0002]
0928:0084 9A0000 4909    CALL    0949:0000
0928:0089 8D3E3000       LEA     DI,[0030]
0928:008D B90600         MOV     CX,0006
0928:0090 9A0000 3C09    CALL    093C:0000
0928:0095 CB             RETF
-D CS:96,9E
0928:0096   00 00-25 0E 01 00 01 10 27                        ..%.....'
-U CS:9F,DC
0928:009F 9C             PUSHF
0928:00A0 51             PUSH    CX
0928:00A1 52             PUSH    DX
0928:00A2 2E             CS:
0928:00A3 803E9A0001     CMP     BYTE PTR [009A],01
0928:00A8 750F           JNZ     00B9
0928:00AA 2E             CS:
0928:00AB C6069A0000     MOV     BYTE PTR [009A],00
0928:00B0 B400           MOV     AH,00
0928:00B2 CD1A           INT     1A
0928:00B4 2E             CS:
0928:00B5 89169600       MOV     [0096],DX
```

```
0928:00B9 2E              CS:
0928:00BA A19600          MOV       AX,[0096]
0928:00BD 2E              CS:
0928:00BE F7269800        MUL       WORD PTR [0098]
0928:00C2 40              INC       AX
0928:00C3 2E              CS:
0928:00C4 A39600          MOV       [0096],AX
0928:00C7 BA0000          MOV       DX,0000
0928:00CA 2E              CS:
0928:00CB F7369B00        DIV       WORD PTR [009B]
0928:00CF 2E              CS:
0928:00D0 F7269D00        MUL       WORD PTR [009D]
0928:00D4 2E              CS:
0928:00D5 F7369B00        DIV       WORD PTR [009B]
0928:00D9 5A              POP       DX
0928:00DA 59              POP       CX
0928:00DB 9D              POPF
0928:00DC C3              RET
-Q

A>
```

that contains the value of the variable TAILS, whose initial value is 0000. The next 36 bytes (offsets 0004–0027 hex) are the bytes of the character string PROMPT. The ASCII interpretation at the right-hand side of the dump shows the actual characters of the string. The next eight bytes (offsets 0028–002F hex) are the bytes of the character string HEADSMSG. The next six bytes (offsets 0030–0035 hex) are the bytes of the character string TAILSMSG.

The next command issued to DEBUG

```
U CS:36,95
```

requests a dump of the next 96 bytes of the segment addressed by the CS-register. The command U means unassemble, which instructs the DEBUG program to interpret the bytes being dumped as machine language instruction bytes. DEBUG dumps each instruction in hexadecimal form and then unassembles that instruction to give an Assembly language interpretation of the instruction. The instruction bytes being dumped are the portion of the segment produced from the main procedure definition in Program Listing 12.9.

The next command issued to DEBUG

```
D CS:96,9E
```

requests a dump of the next nine bytes of the segment addressed by the CS-register, which is the portion of the segment produced from the data segment definition in Program Listing 12.10. The first two bytes (offsets 0096 and 0097) make up the memory word that contains the value of the variable SEED. No initial value is specified for SEED. The next two bytes (offsets 0098 and 0099) make up the memory word that contains the value of the variable MULTI-PLIER, whose initial value is 0E25 hexadecimal (3621 decimal). The next byte (offset 009A) contains the value of the variable FIRST_CALL, whose initial value is the constant TRUE (01). The next two bytes (offsets 009B and 009C) make up the memory word that contains the value of the variable TWO_56, whose initial value is 0100 hex (256 decimal). The next two bytes (offsets 009D and 009E) make up the memory word that contains the value of the variable TEN_THOU, whose initial value is 2710 hex (10000 decimal).

The next command issued to DEBUG

```
U CS:9F,DC
```

requests an instruction dump of the last 62 bytes of the segment addressed by the CS-register, which is the portion of the segment produced from the sub-procedure definition in Program Listing 12.10. The ninth instruction of this dump

```
0928:00B4 2E        CS:
0298:00B5 89169600 MOV [0096],DX
```

corresponds to the instruction

```
MOV SEED,DX
```

in line 40 in Program Listing 12.10. The variable SEED is located at offset 0096 hex within the segment addressed by the CS-register. The first byte of the instruction

```
0928:00B4 2E CS:
```

is called a segment override prefix. The machine language representation of a memory referencing instruction such as the instruction

```
MOV SEED,DX
```

indicates an offset relative to the paragraph address specified by the contents of the DS-register, unless this default segment register is overridden by a 1-byte segment prefix. That is, using the CS-register rather than the DS-register to address the data portions of segment PROG causes each memory referencing instruction to be expanded by 1 byte, the segment override prefix. Whether or not this override has an impact on the number of paragraphs consumed by segment PROG is left as an exercise.

This chapter has presented a number of the segmentation features provided by the assembler (MASM) in conjunction with the Linkage Editor (LINK). The discussion is by no means exhaustive, but it gives you a good basis from which to experiment further.

PROGRAMMING EXERCISES

12.1 Complete Program Listings 12.7 and 12.8 by implementing the NEAR procedure FIND-PRIM with interface specifications as described in Section 8.5. This procedure should be defined in a separate assembly module, which should also have a definition of the common data segment that contains the sieve. If your implementation requires the size of the sieve or the maximum index within the sieve, then use named constants similar to those defined in lines 25 and 26 in Program Listing 12.7. Assemble, link, and execute the completed program.

12.2 In Program Listings 12.7 and 12.8 and Programming Exercise 12.1, the named constants SIZE$ and MAX_INDEX appear in more than one assembly module. To change the size of the sieve, the value of SIZE$ must be changed in each assembly module. Modify this program so that the named constant SIZE$ appears in only one of the three assembly modules and so that only that one named constant needs to be modified to change the size of the sieve. Demonstrate the modified version of the program with sieve sizes 1199, 3099, and 15999. (This is a nontrivial problem.)

12.3 Modify Program Listings 12.9 and 12.10 to use the DS-register to address the data portions of segment PROG. Does this impact the number of paragraphs consumed by segment PROG?

12.4 Programming Exercises 8.2–8.6 make up the problem statement for a set of modules that are to solve for the detection of palindromes. Character strings are communicated from one procedure to another in this system by passing the addresses of character strings in the ES:DI register pair and/or DS:SI register pair and by passing the lengths of strings in the CX-register.

Redesign the procedures of this system so that all communication is handled through a common data segment. Make all of the procedures NEAR procedures, but define them in separate assembly modules.

13 TWO-DIMENSIONAL ARRAYS AND TEXT GRAPHICS

Chapter 8 introduced the notion of an array. It discussed methods for defining arrays in the data segment of an Assembly language program and presented various techniques for accessing an array's elements. This chapter explores a special kind of array, an array whose elements are themselves arrays—the notion of a multidimensional array, although the discussion here is restricted to two-dimensional arrays. The two classic methods of representing two-dimensional arrays in the linear memory of a computer are presented, along with the address calculations needed in each case to compute the memory address of a two-dimensional array element given its row and column position.

Chapter 9 discussed video input/output at the BIOS level (Section 9.3). The video monitor adapter is a circuit board that provides the hardware interface between the microprocessor and the video monitor. This adapter contains some memory space for a video buffer that holds the characters currently being displayed on the video screen. The video buffer can be viewed as a two-dimensional array with one element for each character position on the video screen. This chapter discusses direct access to the video buffer as an application involving a two-dimensional array.

13.1 One-Dimensional Array Revisited

Array applications often involve a translation process. When transferring text data from an IBM PC to an IBM mainframe, the data must be translated from ASCII code to EBCDIC code. Chapter 11 presented algorithms for translating numbers between ASCII and BCD code. The secret message program presented in Program Listing 8.3 performed a translation from one alphabet to another. The two alphabets were related by position. Translating a character of the secret message was a two-step process:

1.   Find the position of the character in the ENCODED alphabet.
2.   Extract the character in the same position of the DECODED alphabet.

The IBM PC Assembly language provides an instruction to aid in translations that are based on position, the **translate (XLAT) instruction**, which has the following general form:

[⟨*label*⟩] XLAT [⟨*source*⟩]   [⟨*comment*⟩]

in which ⟨*source*⟩ is the symbolic name of the byte array that is assumed to be addressed by the DS:BX register pair. Prior to execution of an XLAT instruction, the DS:BX register pair must be set up to address the first byte of the translation table, and the AL-register must be set up to contain the offset from this address to the translation table element of interest. Execution of the XLAT instruction replaces the AL-register value with the byte in the data segment, whose offset is specified by the contents of the BX-register plus the contents of the AL-register. Because the index into the translation table (i.e., the AL-register value) is an 8-bit index, the translation table can be a maximum of 256 bytes in length.

The optional ⟨*source*⟩ operand is provided for documentation and type-checking purposes. The assembler checks to see that it is a symbolic name defined in the segment to be addressed by the DS-register and that it has a type attribute of byte. The assembler does not attempt to determine whether or not, at execution time, the DS:BX register pair will correctly address the memory location associated with the symbolic name specified in the operand field of the XLAT instruction.

EXAMPLE

Consider the following hexadecimal-to-ASCII translation table:

```
HEX_ASCII DB '0123456789ABCDEF'
```

The 16-byte array HEX_ASCII is a character string whose characters are the ASCII representations of the 16 hexadecimal digits in numerical order (Figure 13.1). A 4-bit binary number serves as an index into this string. The contents of the byte indexed by a 4-bit binary number are the ASCII code for the hexadecimal digit that corresponds to that 4-bit binary number. The following instruction sequence translates the integer in the AL-register to a two-character ASCII string in the AH:AL register pair (AX-register). This code sequence assumes that the DS-register specifies the start address of the segment that contains the array HEX_ASCII:

```
LEA  BX,HEX_ASCII
MOV  AH,AL
MOV  CL,4
SHR  AL,CL
XLAT
XCHG AH,AL
AND  AL,0FH
XLAT HEX_ASCII
```

FIGURE 13.1

Array HEX_ASCII

Index	Contents
0	30
1	31
2	32
3	33
4	34
5	35
6	36
7	37
8	38
9	39
A	41
B	42
C	43
D	44
E	45
F	46

HEX_ASCII

The LEA instruction loads the BX-register with the offset within the data segment of the first byte of array HEX_ASCII. The DS:BX register pair now addresses the first byte of array HEX_ASCII.

Suppose the AL-register contains the integer 01011100 (5C hex). The first MOV instruction saves a copy of this value in the AH-register. The AX-register now contains the value 5C5C hex. The second MOV instruction loads the CL-register with a shift count of 4. The SHR instruction shifts the AL-register value 4 bit positions to the right, which isolates the left nibble (first hex digit) of the integer being translated. The AL-register now contains 00000101 (05 hex). The first XLAT instruction uses this AL-register value as an index into the translation table addressed by the DS:BX register pair (array HEX_ASCII). It loads the AL-register with the byte value at index 05 within array HEX_ASCII. The AL-register now contains 35 hex (the ASCII code for the digit 5). The XCHG instruction moves the 35-hex value to the AH-register and moves the saved copy of the integer being translated to the AL-register. The AND instruction isolates the right nibble (second hex digit) of the integer being translated. The AL-register now contains 00001100 (0C hex). The second XLAT instruction uses this AL-register value as an index into the translation table (HEX_ASCII). It loads the AL-register with the byte value at index 12 (0C hex) within array HEX_ASCII. The AL-register now contains 43 hex (the ASCII code for the letter C). The value in the AX-register is 3543 hex, which is the ASCII representation of the two-digit number 5C, which is the hexadecimal number that was in the AL-register at the beginning of the instruction sequence.

Note that the first XLAT instruction specifies no operand, and the second one specifies the operand HEX_ASCII. The two XLAT instructions translate to the same machine language instruction. In the case of the instruction

```
XLAT HEX_ASCII
```

the assembler provides some additional error checking: checking to see that HEX_ASCII is defined with type attribute byte and is defined in the segment that is to be addressed by the DS-register. Recall that the ASSUME pseudo-operation tells the assembler which segment register is to address a specific segment.

Programming Example—Secret Message Revisited

Consider again Program Listing 8.3 that translates a secret message. Program Listing 13.1 is an alternative implementation of this algorithm that uses the XLAT instruction to translate a character from the ENCODED alphabet to the DECODED alphabet. The stack segment and data segment definitions are the same for the two versions of the program, and both programs have the same basic structure. There is a REPEAT-UNTIL loop (lines 57–83 in Program Listing 13.1) that executes once for each character in the secret message; that is, each iteration of the loop body translates one character of the secret message. Nested within the REPEAT-UNTIL loop is a second REPEAT-UNTIL loop (lines 62–69). The inner REPEAT-UNTIL loop searches the ENCODED alphabet to find the occurrence of the character being translated, and it is followed by a double-alternative decision structure (lines 70–79) that determines whether or not the character being translated is found in the ENCODED alphabet. If it is not found, then an asterisk (*) is inserted into the translated message (line 71); if it is found, then the character in the same position of the DECODED alphabet is inserted into the translated message. The difference between Program Listing 13.1 and Program Listing 8.3 is in the ELSE clause of this double-alternative decision structure.

The ELSE clause (lines 74–78) translates a character from the ENCODED alphabet to the DECODED alphabet. On entry into the ELSE clause, the ES:DI register pair addresses the character of the ENCODED alphabet that immediately follows the occurrence of the character being translated. The DEC instruction in line 74 adjusts the DI-register, so that the ES:DI register pair addresses the character in the ENCODED alphabet that matches the character being translated. The DI-register is the offset of this ENCODED element relative to the beginning of the data segment. The MOV instruction in line 75 copies this offset to the AX-register. The SUB instruction in line 76 converts this offset to an index relative to the beginning of array ENCODED. This index is an integer in

```
 1: ;                    PROGRAM LISTING 13.1
 2: ;
 3: ;PROGRAM TO TRANSLATE A SECRET MESSAGE
 4: ;
 5: ;
 6:                                       ;PROCEDURES TO
 7:            EXTRN    GETSTRNG:FAR       ;INPUT A CHARACTER STRING
 8:            EXTRN    PUTSTRNG:FAR       ;DISPLAY CHARACTER STRING
 9:            EXTRN    NEWLINE:FAR        ;DISPLAY NEWLINE CHARACTER
10: ;
11: ; S T A C K    S E G M E N T    D E F I N I T I O N
12: ;
13: STACK      SEGMENT STACK
14:            DB       256 DUP(?)
15: STACK      ENDS
16: ;
17: ; D A T A    S E G M E N T    D E F I N I T I O N
18: ;
19: DATA       SEGMENT
20: ;
21: SECRTMSG   DB       40 DUP(?)          ;SECRET MESSAGE
22: TRANSMSG   DB       40 DUP(?)          ;TRANSLATED MESSAGE
23: DECODED    DB       'ABCDEFG.HIJKLMNO PQRSTUVWXYZ'
24: ENCODED    DB       'JEKPQBWALR.MSCUTDVNFZGYHIOX$'
25: PROMPT     DB       'ENTER SECRET MESSAGE',0DH,0AH
26: TMSG       DB       'TRANSLATED MESSAGE',0DH,0AH
27: COUNT      DW       ?                  ;CHARACTER COUNT OF MESSAGE
28: CODE_LNGTH EQU      28                 ;LENGTH OF CODE STRINGS
29: ;
30: DATA       ENDS
31: ;
32: ; C O D E    S E G M E N T    D E F I N I T I O N
33: ;
34: CODE       SEGMENT
35: EX_13_1    PROC     FAR
36:            ASSUME   CS:CODE,DS:DATA,SS:STACK,ES:DATA
37:            PUSH     DS                 ;PUSH RETURN SEG ADDR ON STACK
38:            SUB      AX,AX              ;PUSH RETURN OFFSET OF ZERO
39:            PUSH     AX                 ;ON STACK
40:            MOV      AX,SEG DATA        ;SET DS AND ES REGISTERS
41:            MOV      DS,AX              ;TO POINT TO DATA SEGMENT
42:            MOV      ES,AX
43:            CALL     NEWLINE
44:*;

45: ;
46:            LEA      DI,PROMPT          ;PROMPT FOR SECRET_MSG
47:            MOV      CX,22
48:            CALL     PUTSTRNG
49:            LEA      DI,SECRTMSG        ;GET SECRET_MSG AND MSG_LENGTH
50:            MOV      CX,40
51:            CALL     GETSTRNG
52:            CALL     NEWLINE
53:            CLD                         ;SET DF FOR INCREMENTING
54:            LEA      BX,DECODED
55:            MOV      COUNT,CX           ;COUNT = MSG_LENGTH
56:            MOV      SI,0               ;INDEX = 0
57: NEXT_CHAR:                            ;REPEAT
58:            MOV      AL,SECRTMSG[SI]    ;  CHAR = SECRET_MSG (INDEX)
59:            PUSH     CX                 ;  SAVE MSG_LENGTH
60:            MOV      CX,CODE_LNGTH      ;  SEARCH_COUNT = CODE_LNGTH
```

```
61:                 LEA      DI,ENCODED              ;  PTR = ADDRESS OF ENCODED
62:        REPNE SCASB                               ;  FOUND = FALSE
63:                                                  ;  REPEAT
64:                                                  ;     IF   PTR->BYTE = CHAR
65:                                                  ;     THEN FOUND = TRUE
66:                                                  ;     ENDIF
67:                                                  ;     PTR = PTR + 1
68:                                                  ;     DECREMENT SEARCH_COUNT
69:                                                  ;  UNTIL FOUND OR SEARCH_COUNT=0
70:                 JE       FOUND                   ;  IF   NOT FOUND
71:                 MOV      TRANSMSG[SI],'*'         ;  THEN TRANSMSG(INDEX) = *
72:                 JMP      LOOPEND
73: FOUND:                                           ;  ELSE
74:                 DEC      DI                       ;     PTR = PTR - 1
75:                 MOV      AX,DI                    ;     J = PTR - ADDRESS OF
76:                 SUB      AX,OFFSET ENCODED        ;                   ENCODED
77:                 XLAT                              ;     CHAR = DECODED(J)
78:                 MOV      TRANSMSG[SI],AL          ;     TRANSMSG(INDEX) = CHAR
79: LOOPEND:                                         ;  ENDIF
80:                 INC      SI                       ;  INDEX = INDEX + 1
81:                 POP      CX                       ;  RESTORE MSG_LENGTH
82:                 LOOP     NEXT_CHAR                ;  DECREMENT MSG_LENGTH
83:                                                  ;UNTIL MSG_LENGTH = 0
84:                 LEA      DI,TMSG                  ;DISPLAY TRANS_MSG
85:                 MOV      CX,20
86:                 CALL     PUTSTRNG
87:                 LEA      DI,TRANSMSG
88:                 MOV      CX,COUNT                 ;MSG_LENGTH = COUNT
89:                 CALL     PUTSTRNG
90:                 CALL     NEWLINE
91:                 RET                               ;RETURN
92: EX_13_1         ENDP
93: CODE            ENDS
94:*                END      EX_13_1
```

the range 0–27 in the AL-register. The character at the same index within array DECODED is the character to be inserted in the translated message. The XLAT instruction in line 77 loads the AL-register with a copy of this character from the DECODED alphabet. The MOV instruction in line 78 inserts this character into the appropriate position of the translated message.

The XLAT instruction in line 77 assumes that the DS:BX register pair addresses the first byte of a translation table, and it uses the AL-register value as an index into this table. At the time that the XLAT instruction is executed, the BX-register has already been set to the offset within the data segment of array DECODED. This initialization was accomplished by the LEA instruction in line 54. It is done outside the outer REPEAT-UNTIL loop to ensure that the LEA instruction is executed only once. Since the BX-register is used for no other purpose, the DS:BX register pair addresses array DECODED throughout the remainder of the program execution.

Note that the XLAT instruction in line 77 has no operand specified. The instruction

```
XLAT DECODED
```

could have been used. The machine language translation would have been exactly the same. However, the assembler would have verified that DECODED was defined in segment DATA with type attribute byte. The instruction

```
XLAT ENCODED
```

could also have been used. Again, the machine language translation would have been exactly the same. The array ENCODED is defined in segment DATA with type attribute byte. The program still executes correctly, since the DS:BX register pair correctly addresses array DECODED during execution. The incorrect operand on the XLAT instruction simply means that the program documentation is incorrect. Recall that a similar occurrence can happen with the generic form of the string instructions.

13.2 Two-Dimensional Arrays

A **two-dimensional array** is an ordered list of homogeneous data items that is logically arranged into rows and columns as shown in Table 13.1. The array in the table has m rows and n columns, and it is referred to as an m by n (written $m \times n$) array. Applications often involve data that are more conveniently viewed and processed from a two-dimensional standpoint. The grades of m students on each of n tests can be arranged in an $m \times n$ array. The element in row i, column j is the test score for student i on test j. To find the average test score for student i, simply sum all n elements of row i and divide this sum by n (the number of tests). To find the class average for test j, simply sum all m elements of column j and divide this sum by m (the number of students).

TABLE 13.1
Two-dimensional array

	Column 1	Column 2	Column 3	Column 4	. . .	Column n
Row 1	Row 1 Column 1	Row 1 Column 2	Row 1 Column 3	Row 1 Column 4	. . .	Row 1 Column n
Row 2	Row 2 Column 1	Row 2 Column 2	Row 2 Column 3	Row 2 Column 4	. . .	Row 2 Column n
Row 3	Row 3 Column 1	Row 3 Column 2	Row 3 Column 3	Row 3 Column 4	. . .	Row 3 Column n
Row 4	Row 4 Column 1	Row 4 Column 2	Row 4 Column 3	Row 4 Column 4	. . .	Row 4 Column n
. . .		.				.
Row m	Row m Column 1	Row m Column 2	Row m Column 3	Row m Column 4	. . .	Row m Column n

Linear Representations for Two-Dimensional Arrays

A computer's memory can be viewed as a one-dimensional array. In fact, the segment-offset approach to memory addressing is based on this viewpoint. A segment is like a byte array. The segment origin address, specified by the contents of a segment register, is the base address of the array. The offset is the index from this base address to the element (memory location) of interest.

Defining a two-dimensional array in terms of one-dimensional arrays leads to two natural ways of representing that array in the linear memory of a computer. A two-dimensional array can be defined as a one-dimensional array whose elements are each a row of the $m \times n$ array (an n-element, one-dimensional array). This view fits the definition of a one-dimensional array given in Chapter 8: It is an ordered list of data items; that is, there is a first element (the first row), a second element (the second row), and so forth. It is a list of homogeneous data an ordered list of data items; that is, there is a first element (the first row), a second element (the second row), and so forth. It is a list of homogeneous data items; that is, each element of the array is an n-element, one-dimensional array. This array of arrays can be stored in memory in the same way that a byte or word array is stored in memory. That is, the array elements are stored in contiguous memory locations beginning with the first element, followed immediately by the second element, followed immediately by the third element, and so forth. In the case of the $m \times n$ array, viewed as a one-dimensional array of rows, the elements can be stored by row as shown in Figure 13.2, which is known as **row-major order**.

The $m \times n$ array in Table 13.1 can also be viewed as an n-element, one-dimensional array, whose elements are each a column of the $m \times n$ array (an m-element, one-dimensional array). With this view, the elements can be stored by column as shown in Figure 13.3, which is known as **column-major order**.

Address Calculations

To select and use a specific element of a two-dimensional array, the subscripting operation is used. To identify an element of a two-dimensional array, two subscripts are needed: A row subscript identifies the row in which the element appears, and a column subscript identifies the column in which the element appears. An address calculaton is needed to translate the row and column position to a physical memory address. The formula used for the address calculation depends on whether the array is stored in row-major order or column-major order.

Consider the problem of computing the address of the element in row r, column c of an $m \times n$ array stored in row-major order. Assume that the array begins at address BASE, and each element is of size S bytes. To get to row r of the array, the first $(r - 1)$ rows must be skipped. There are $(r - 1)n$ elements in the first $(r - 1)$ rows, and each element is of size S bytes. Therefore, $(r - 1)nS$ bytes must be skipped to get to the rth row. That is, $(r - 1)nS$ is the

FIGURE 13.2

Two-dimensional array in row-major order (S is the size of an element: 1 for byte, 2 for word)

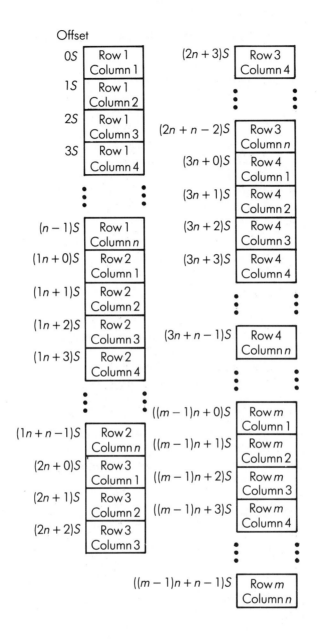

offset from the beginning of the array to the first element of the rth row. To get to column c within a given row, $(c - 1)$ elements must be skipped. Each element is of size S bytes. Therefore, $(c - 1)S$ bytes must be skipped to get to the cth column. That is, $(c - 1)S$ is the offset from the beginning of the rth row to the element in the cth column of the rth row. The sum of these two offsets produces the offset from the beginning of the array to the element in the rth row, cth column. Therefore, for an $m \times n$ array stored in row-major order, the address

FIGURE 13.3
Two-dimensional
array in column-
major order (S is the
size of an element:
1 for byte, 2 for
word)

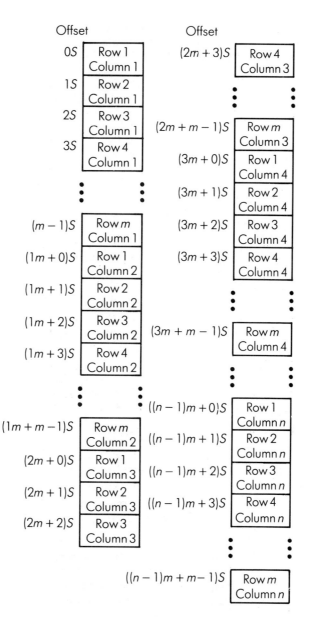

of the element at row r, column c is computed by either

$$\text{BASE} + (r - 1)nS + (c - 1)S$$

$$\text{BASE} + [(r - 1)n + (c - 1)]S$$

in which **BASE** is the base address of the array.

EXAMPLE

Consider the two-dimensional array in Table 13.1 stored in row-major order (Figure 13.2). The offset of the element in row 3, column 4, relative to the beginning of the array, is computed as follows:

$$[(r - 1)n + (c - 1)]S$$

$$[(3 - 1)n + (4 - 1)]S$$

$$(2n + 3)S$$

Compare this result to the offset shown for that element in Figure 13.2.

Consider now the problem of computing the address of the element in row r, column c of an $m \times n$ array stored in column-major order. Again, assume that the array begins at address BASE, and each element is of size S bytes. To get to column c of the array, the first $(c - 1)$ columns must be skipped. There are $(c - 1)m$ elements in the first $(c - 1)$ columns, and each element is of size S bytes. Therefore, $(c - 1)mS$ is the offset from the beginning of the array to the first element of the cth column. To get to the rth element of a column, $(r - 1)$ elements must be skipped. Therefore, $(r - 1)S$ is the offset from the beginning of the cth column to the element in the rth row of the cth column. For an $m \times n$ array stored in column-major order, the address of the element at row r, column c is computed by

$$\text{BASE} + [(c - 1)m + (r - 1)]S$$

in which BASE is the base address of the array.

EXAMPLE

Consider the two-dimensional array of Table 13.1 stored in column-major order (Figure 13.3). The offset of the element in row 3, column 4, relative to the beginning of the array, is computed as follows:

$$[(c - 1)m + (r - 1)]S$$

$$[(4 - 1)m + (3 - 1)]S$$

$$(3m + 2)S$$

Compare this result to the offset shown for that element in Figure 13.3.

Programming Example—Procedure to Compute the Address of a Two-Dimensional Array Element Given the Row and Column

The procedure presented in this section implements one of the formulas derived in the previous section: the address calculation formula for two-dimensional arrays stored in row-major order. This example introduces the notion of an

TABLE 13.2
Array descriptor

Byte(s)	Meaning
0–1	Segment portion of base address of array
2–3	Offset portion of base address of array
4	Type of array: $1 \Rightarrow$ byte array
	$2 \Rightarrow$ word array
5	Number of rows in array
6	Number of columns in array

array descriptor, which is a data structure that contains the information necessary to describe an array's characteristics. In this chapter, an array descriptor describes a two-dimensional array. It is a seven-byte data structure that has the general form shown in Table 13.2. The type of the array (byte 4 of the descriptor) describes the size in bytes of each element of the array. Integer values greater than 2 can be used for the type. For example, a type of 4 would be used for a two-dimensional array whose elements are 32-bit integer values. The number of rows and columns in the array (bytes 5 and 6 of the descriptor) describes the overall size of the array and can be used to check out-of-range subscripts.

EXAMPLE

The following data segment definition allocates storage for a 4 × 5 word array named SALES and defines a descriptor for this array:

```
DATA    SEGMENT
SALES   DW      20 DUP(?)
S_DSCR  DW      SEG SALES
        DW      OFFSET SALES
        DB      2
        DB      4
        DB      5
DATA    ENDS
```

The procedure in Program Listing 13.2 computes the address of a two-dimensional array element given the row and column position of the element and the address of the array descriptor. The prologue in lines 1–24 describes the function of the procedure, shows the general form of the array descriptor, and describes the procedure's interface requirements. On entry to the procedure, the DS:SI register pair must address the first byte of the array descriptor, the DH-register must contain the row number of the desired element, and the DL-register must contain the column number of the desired element. On return to the caller, the ES:DI register pair addresses the first element of the row that contains the desired element, the BP-register contains the offset within that row

```
 1: ;                     PROGRAM LISTING 13.2
 2: ; PROCEDURE TO COMPUTE THE ADDRESS OF A TWO-DIMENSIONAL ARRAY
 3: ; ELEMENT  GIVEN  THE  ROW  AND CLOUMN OF THE ELEMENT AND THE
 4: ; ARRAY DESCRIPTOR.  THE  ARRAY  DESCRIPTOR IS A 7-BYTE  DATA
 5: ; STRUCTURE THAT HAS THE FOLLOWING GENERAL FORM:
 6: ;
 7: ;      BYTE(S) : CONTENTS
 8: ;      +---------+-------------------------------------------------+
 9: ;      :   0-1   : SEGMENT PORTION OF BASE ADDRESS OF ARRAY - SEG  :
10: ;      :   2-3   : OFFSET  PORTION OF BASE ADDRESS OF ARRAY - OFFSET :
11: ;      :    4    : TYPE OF ARRAY : 1 => BYTE --------------- TYPE  :
12: ;      :         :                 2 => WORD                       :
13: ;      :    5    : NUMBER OF ROWS   IN ARRAY --------------- ROWS  :
14: ;      :    6    : NUMBER OF COLUMNS IN ARRAY --------------- COLS  :
15: ;      +---------+-------------------------------------------------+
16: ; INPUTS:  DS:SI  REGISTER PAIR CONTAINS BASE ADDRESS OF ARRAY DSCR
17: ;          DH-REG CONTAINS   ROW  NUMBER
18: ;          DL-REG CONTAINS COLUMN NUMBER
19: ; OUTPUTS: ES:DI  REGISTER PAIR ADDRESSES FIRST ELEMENT IN SPECIFIED
20: ;                 ROW OF ARRAY
21: ;          BP-REG CONTAINS  OFFSET  WITHIN  ROW  OF SPECIFIED COLUMN
22: ;          DX-REG CONTAINS DI-REGISTER OFFSET NEEDED TO MOVE  1  ROW
23: ;          OF-BIT OF FLAGS REGISTER IS SET TO 1 FOR AN OUT OF  RANGE
24: ;                 SUBSCRIPT
25: CODE      SEGMENT
26:           ASSUME  CS:CODE
27: ADDR      PROC    FAR     ;PROCEDURE ADDR(DSCR,ROW,COL,RPTR,COFF,RINC)
28:           PUBLIC  ADDR
29:           PUSH    AX                    ;SAVE REGISTERS
30:           PUSH    BX
31:           PUSHF                         ;SAVE FLAGS
32:           POP     BX          ;TEMP_FLAGS = SAVED FLAGS
33:           AND     BX,0F7FFH   ;CLEAR OF BIT IN TEMP_FLAGS
34:           CMP     DH,DS:[SI+5]  ;IF   ROW > DSCR.ROWS
35:           JA      THEN
36:           CMP     DL,DS:[SI+6]  ;   OR COL > DSCR.COLS
37:           JBE     ENDIF
38: THEN:                             ;THEN
39:           OR      BX,0800H    ;       SET OF BIT IN TEMP_FLAGS
40: ENDIF:                            ;ENDIF
41:           PUSH    BX          ;SAVED FLAGS = TEMP_FLAGS
42:           MOV     ES,DS:[SI]  ;ES-REG = DSCR.SEG
43:           MOV     AL,DS:[SI+4]  ;COFF = (COL - 1) * DSCR.TYPE
44:           DEC     DL
45:           MUL     DL
46:           MOV     BP,AX
47:           MOV     DI,DS:[SI+2]  ;RPTR = DSCR.OFFSET
48:           MOV     AL,DS:[SI+4]  ;     + (ROW - 1) * DSCR.TYPE
49:           DEC     DH            ;                 * DSCR.COLS
50:           MUL     DH
51:           MOV     DL,DS:[SI+6]
52:           MOV     DH,0
53:           MUL     DX
54:           ADD     DI,AX
55:           MOV     AL,DS:[SI+6]  ;RINC = DSCR.COLS * DSCR.TYPE
56:           MUL     BYTE PTR DS:[SI+4]
57:           MOV     DX,AX
58:           POPF                          ;RESTORE FLAGS
59:           POP     BX                    ;RESTORE REGISTERS
60:           POP     AX
61:           RET                           ;RETURN
62: ADDR      ENDP            ;END ADDR
63: CODE      ENDS
64:*          END
```

of the desired element, the DX-register contains the amount to be added to (or subtracted from) the DI-register to move one row in the array, and the OF bit of the flags register indicates whether the address generated is out of the bounds of the array. The range of legal row subscripts is from 1 to the number of rows, inclusive, and the range of legal column subscripts is from 1 to the number of columns, inclusive.

The procedure begins by saving the registers that it uses (lines 29–31) and checking the subscripts for an out-of-range condition (lines 32–41). The POP instruction in line 32 pops the flags register image, saved for the caller, into the BX-register. The AND instruction in line 33 clears the OF bit in this flags register image. The single-alternative decision structure in lines 34–40 sets the OF bit in this flags register image, if the row subscript (DH-register value) is greater than the number of rows (byte 5 of the descriptor) or the column subscript (DL-register value) is greater than the number of columns (byte 6 of the descriptor). The PUSH instruction in line 41 pushes this modified flags register image back onto the stack.

The instructions in lines 42–54 perform the address calculation. The MOV instruction in line 42 sets the ES-register to address the segment that contains the array. This segment address is obtained from bytes 0 and 1 of the descriptor. The operand DS:[SI] is an example of register indirect addressing (see Section 8.4).

The instructions in lines 43–46 implement the $(c - 1)S$ portion of the address calculation formula. The MOV instruction in line 43 loads the AL-register with the element size (the array type from byte 4 of the descriptor), which is the S in the formula. The DEC instruction in line 44 decrements the column subscript by 1, which is the $(c - 1)$ in the formula. The MUL instruction in line 45 computes the product of these two values, and the MOV instruction in line 46 copies this product into the BP-register. The BP-register now contains the offset from the beginning of a row to the element in the cth column of that row, in which c is the column subscript entered via the DL-register. The operand DS:[SI + 4] is an example of indexed addressing (see Section 8.4).

The instructions in lines 47–54 implement the $\text{BASE} + (r - 1)nS$ portion of the address calculation formula. The MOV instruction in line 47 loads the DI-register with the offset portion of the base address of the array (bytes 2 and 3 of the descriptor), which is the BASE in the formula. The MOV instruction in line 48 loads the AL-register with the element size (the array type from byte 4 of the descriptor), which is the S in the formula. The DEC instruction in line 49 decrements the row subscript by 1, which is the $(r - 1)$ in the formula. The MUL instruction in line 50 computes the product of these two values, which produces the $(r - 1)S$ in the formula and leaves it in the AX-register. The MOV instructions in lines 51 and 52 load the DX-register with the number of columns in the array (byte 6 of the descriptor), which is the n in the formula. The MUL instruction in line 53 computes the product of this value and the value in the AX-register, which produces the $(r - 1)nS$ portion of the formula. The ADD instruction in line 54 adds this value to the base address offset in the DI-register. The ES:DI register pair now addresses the first element of the rth row of the array, in which r is the row subscript entered via the DH-register.

The instructions in lines 55–57 compute the offset increment needed to move one complete row in the array (i.e., the number of bytes in one row of the array). The MOV instruction in line 55 loads the AL-register with the number of columns in the array (byte 6 of the descriptor). The MUL instruction in line 56 multiplies this value by the element size (the array type from byte 4 of the descriptor). The MOV instruction in line 57 copies this product (the number of bytes per row in the array) to the DX-register.

The procedure terminates by restoring the registers for the caller (lines 58–60) and returning control to the caller (line 61). The caller can access the specified array element by the operand ES:[DI][BP], which is an example of base indexed addressing with a segment override prefix (see Section 8.4). The operand ES:[DI][BP] addresses the element in row r, column c of the array, in which r is the row subscript and c is the column subscript passed to the ADDR procedure. To increment this address to the next element in the array, the instruction

```
ADD BP,DS:[SI + 4]
```

can be used, which adds the element size to the column offset in the BP-register. Similarly, to decrement this address to the previous element in the array, the instruction

```
SUB BP,DS:[SI + 4]
```

can be used. To increment this address to the corresponding element in the next row of the array, the instruction

```
ADD DI,DX
```

can be used, which adds the number of bytes per row to the row offset in the DI-register. Similarly, to decrement this address to the corresponding element in the previous row of the array, the instruction

```
SUB DI,DX
```

can be used. A procedure that uses ADDR is presented in Section 13.4.

13.3 Text Graphics (a Two-Dimensional Array Application)

The two standard video monitors for the IBM PC and PC-XT, the IBM Monochrome Display and the IBM Color Display, each require an adapter card. The display adapter is a circuit board that contains a video controller and some random access memory (RAM). The standard adapter for the monochrome display is the IBM Monochrome Display and Printer Adapter, and the standard adapter for the color display is the IBM Color/Graphics Adapter. Although other display adapters and video monitors are available for the IBM PC, only the two just mentioned are discussed here.

Both the monochrome adapter and the color/graphics adapter are capable of displaying text data on the monitor screen. The text data being displayed at any point in time is maintained in a display buffer in the adapter's RAM. This display buffer is organized as a two-dimensional word array with 25 rows and 80 columns. The 25 rows correspond to the 25 lines on the video screen, and the 80 columns correspond to the 80 character positions in each line on the video screen. Each word of this array contains the 8-bit ASCII code for a character to be displayed and an 8-bit attribute that indicates how the character is to be displayed (e.g., normal, blinking, with underscore). To display a character in the jth character position of the ith line on the screen, simply place the ASCII code and the desired attribute for the character in the word at row i, column j of this two-dimensional array.

The video controller on the adapter board contains the circuitry to convert a character : attribute pair to an array of dots and to display that array of dots at the appropriate position on the screen. This hardware includes a character generator and an attribute decoder: The **character generator** generates an array of dots from the ASCII code, and the **attribute decoder** determines exactly how that array of dots is to appear on the screen. The video controller displays the first character in the buffer in character position 1 of line 1, the second character in the buffer in character position 2 of line 1, and so forth. This method of display means that the character : attribute pairs are stored in the video buffer in row-major order. The video controller cycles through the video buffer approximately 50 times per second; that is, the complete display screen is refreshed approximately 50 times per second. This cycling virtually eliminates flicker on the screen. It also means that new data placed in the buffer are displayed almost immediately.

Graphics Symbols (Extended ASCII Character Set)

The ASCII code is a 7-bit code adopted by the American National Standards Institute (ANSI). With a 7-bit code, a total of 128 characters can be represented. The first 32 binary codes in the ASCII character set, 0000000–0011111 (00 hex–1F hex), represent control characters (e.g., form feed and line feed for the printer). The remaining binary codes, 0100000–1111111 (20 hex–7F hex), represent the printable characters, including the uppercase and lowercase letters, the decimal digits, and special characters such as $, ?, SPACE,], and /.

For the PC family of computers, IBM has extended the standard ASCII code to an 8-bit code called **Extended ASCII**. The first 128 codes in the Extended ASCII character set, 00000000–01111111 (00 hex–7F hex), represent the standard ASCII character set. The remaining 128 binary codes, 10000000–11111111 (80 hex–FF hex), represent a variety of symbols that include graphics symbols. In addition, the binary codes, 00000000–00011111 (00 hex–1F hex), are interpreted as special graphics symbols when the codes are output to the video monitor. For example, the binary code 00000011 displays a heart-shaped symbol. (See Appendix E for the complete set of symbols in the Extended ASCII character set.) Both the monochrome adapter and the color/graphics adapter are capable of generating the symbols of the Extended ASCII character set.

Video Buffer Organization

The video buffer in the adapter's RAM is organized as a 25 × 80, two-dimensional word array stored in row-major order. The number of elements in the array is 2000 (25 × 80), and the size of each element is 2 bytes. Therefore, 4000 bytes of memory are required for the video buffer. The address of the element at row r, column c is computed by

$$\text{BASE} + [(r - 1)80 + (c - 1)]2$$

Each element of the array contains a character : attribute pair. The first byte is the character and the second byte is the attribute. The size and location of the video memory and the interpretation of the attribute byte depend on whether the adapter is the monochrome or the color/graphics adapter.

Monochrome Video Buffer

The IBM Monochrome Display and Printer Adapter has 4K RAM (4096 bytes). This memory has physical addresses B0000 hex–B0FFF hex. The video buffer is normally the first 4000 bytes of this memory space, the bytes of addresses B0000 hex–B0F9F hex). The position of the 4000-byte video buffer within this 4096-byte memory space can be altered, as is shown later in this chapter. For now, the position of the video buffer is kept static. The address of the element at row r, column c of the video buffer is computed by

```
B0000 hex + [(r - 1)80 + (c - 1)]2
```

The attribute byte of the character : attribute pair indicates how the character is to be displayed. Table 13.3 shows the different ways that a character can be displayed on the monochrome display and, in each case, the attribute that can be used to display a character in that way. The attributes given in Table 13.3 are the ones typically used; however, any 8-bit pattern is legal as an attribute. Figure 13.4 shows the interpretations for all possible attribute bytes.

Color/Graphics Video Buffer

The IBM Color/Graphics Display Adapter has 16K RAM (16,384 bytes). This memory has physical addresses B8000 hex–BBFFF hex and houses four video buffers, one for each of four display pages (numbered 0–3). Only one of the four pages, called the **active display page**, is displayed at any point in time. The active display page is selectable via BIOS interrupt 10H. The four video buffers are normally the first 4000 bytes of each 4K block of this memory space. The physical addresses for these four video buffers are as follows: page 0, B8000–B8F9F; page 1, B9000–B9F9F; page 2, BA000–BAF9F; and page 3, BB000–

TABLE 13.3
Attributes for a
monochrome
adapter

Attribute (Hex)	Interpretation
00	No display
01	Normal video (green on black) with underscore beneath character
07	Normal video (green on black)
09	Intense normal video (green on black) with underscore beneath character
0F	Intense normal video (green on black)
70	Reverse video (black on green)
81	Normal video (green on black) with underscore beneath character and character and underscore blinking
87	Normal video (green on black) with character blinking
89	Intense normal video (green on black) with underscore beneath character and character and underscore blinking
8F	Intense normal video (green on black) with character blinking
F0	Reverse video (black on green) with character blinking

BBF9F. The position of the 4000-byte active display page within this 16K memory space can be altered, as is shown later in the chapter. For now, the positions of the four pages is kept static. The address of the element at row r, column c of the active display page is

$$\text{B8000 hex} + 4096\,(\text{page}\#) + [(r - 1)80 + (c - 1)]2$$

in which page# is the number of the active display page.

The attribute byte of the character : attribute pair indicates how the character is to be displayed, including the colors to be used in displaying the character. The bits of the attribute byte are interpreted as shown in Figure 13.5. The blink bit (bit 7) controls whether the character is displayed blinking (bit 7 = 1) or solid (bit 7 = 0).

The background color for the character is controlled by bits 6, 5, and 4 of the attribute byte: Bit 6 selects the color red (R), bit 5 selects the color green (G), and bit 4 selects the color blue (B). Combinations of these bits are used to select a color other than the three basic colors; for example, the color magenta (purple) is achieved by selecting both red and blue (bits 6 and 4). Figure 13.6 describes the background color produced for each possible combination of the RGB bits (bits 6–4) of the attribute byte.

The foreground color for the character (i.e., the color of the character itself) is controlled by bits 2, 1, and 0 of the attribute byte: Bit 2 selects the color red, bit 1 selects the color green, and bit 0 selects the color blue. Again, combinations

FIGURE 13.4
Complete
monochrome
attribute
interpretation

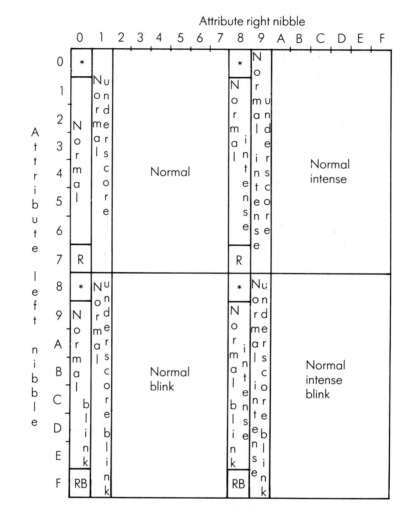

* — no display
R — reverse video (black on green)
RB — reverse video blinking

FIGURE 13.5
Attribute byte for
color/graphics
adapter

BL — blink bit
I — intensity bit (extends foreground colors)
R — red bit
G — green bit
B — blue bit

FIGURE 13.6

Color combinations available with IBM color/graphics adapter

R	G	B	Background color
0	0	0	Black
0	0	1	Blue
0	1	0	Green
0	1	1	Cyan
1	0	0	Red
1	0	1	Magenta
1	1	0	Brown
1	1	1	Light gray

I	R	G	B	Foreground color
0	0	0	0	Black
0	0	0	1	Blue
0	0	1	0	Green
0	0	1	1	Cyan
0	1	0	0	Red
0	1	0	1	Magenta
0	1	1	0	Brown
0	1	1	1	Light gray
1	0	0	0	Dark gray
1	0	0	1	Light blue
1	0	1	0	Light green
1	0	1	1	Light cyan
1	1	0	0	Light red
1	1	0	1	Light magenta
1	1	1	0	Yellow
1	1	1	1	White

of these bits are used to select a color other than the basic colors. In addition, the intensity bit (bit 3) is used to produce a lighter shade of the foreground color. Figure 13.6 describes the foreground color produced for each possible combination of the intense (I) RGB bits (bits 3–0) of the attribute byte.

Note that there is some amount of compatibility between the attribute byte for the color/graphics adapter and that for the monochrome adapter: Bit 7 is the blink bit, and bit 3 is the intensity bit in both cases. The color/graphics attribute for white on black is the same as the monochrome attribute for normal video (green on black). The color/graphics attribute for black on white is the same as the monochrome attribute for reverse video (black on green). These compatibilities make it easier to produce programs that are compatible with both monitors.

In Section 13.2, a procedure named ADDR was presented that computes the physical address of a two-dimensional array element given that element's row and column position. This procedure also requires the descriptor's address. If array descriptors are defined for the video buffers, then the ADDR procedure can be used to access the video buffers.

Program Listing 13.3 shows a data segment definition for a common data segment, named SCR_DATA, that contains a descriptor for the monochrome video buffer (lines 11–15) and a descriptor for each page of the color/graphics

```
 1: ;                       PROGRAM LISTING 13.3
 2: ;
 3: ; V I D E O    D I S P L A Y     B U F F E R
 4: ;
 5: ; D A T A     S E G M E N T     D E F I N I T I O N
 6: ;
 7: SCR_DATA    SEGMENT COMMON
 8: ;
 9: ; DESCRIPTOR FOR MONOCHROME DISPLAY BUFFER
10: ;
11: BUFFER      DW       0B000H               ;SEGMENT ADDRESS
12:             DW       0                    ;OFFSET  ADDRESS
13:             DB       2                    ;TYPE = WORD
14:             DB       25                   ;ROWS = 25
15:             DB       80                   ;COLS = 80
16: ;
17: ; DESCRIPTOR FOR COLOR DISPLAY BUFFER
18: ;
19: PAGE0       DW       0B800H               ;SEGMENT ADDRESS - ORIGIN
20:             DW       0                    ;OFFSET  ADDRESS - PAGE 0
21:             DB       2                    ;TYPE = WORD
22:             DB       25                   ;ROWS = 25
23:             DB       80                   ;COLS = 80
24: PAGE1       DW       0B800H               ;SEGMENT ADDRESS - ORIGIN
25:             DW       4096                 ;OFFSET  ADDRESS - PAGE 1
26:             DB       2                    ;TYPE = WORD
27:             DB       25                   ;ROWS = 25
28:             DB       80                   ;COLS = 80
29: PAGE2       DW       0B800H               ;SEGMENT ADDRESS - ORIGIN
30:             DW       8192                 ;OFFSET  ADDRESS - PAGE 2
31:             DB       2                    ;TYPE = WORD
32:             DB       25                   ;ROWS = 25
33:             DB       80                   ;COLS = 80
34: PAGE3       DW       0B800H               ;SEGMENT ADDRESS - ORIGIN
35:             DW       12288                ;OFFSET  ADDRESS - PAGE 3
36:             DB       2                    ;TYPE = WORD
37:             DB       25                   ;ROWS = 25
38:             DB       80                   ;COLS = 80
39:*SCR_DATA    ENDS
```
*

video buffer (lines 19–38). It is not an assembly module; instead, it is the listing of a source file that is designed to be incorporated into an assembly module through use of the INCLUDE pseudo-operation. To be a separate assembly module it would have to close with an END pseudo-operation.

BIOS Interrupts Revisited

Section 9.3 discusses the BIOS service procedures available through software interrupts 10 hex–1F hex. Interrupt 10 hex provides video I/O services, of which several options are useful in accessing the video buffers. Interrupt 11 hex provides the capability for determining the equipment that is attached to the PC, and it can be used to determine which video adapter is attached to the PC.

The BIOS procedure that services interrupt 10 hex uses the value in the AH-register as a function code (Table 9.3). A function code of 5 selects the active display page for the color/graphics monitor. The page number of the page being selected is passed to the interrupt 10 hex service procedure via the AL-register. The legal page numbers are 0, 1, 2, and 3. For example, to select page 2 (the third page) as the active page, the following instruction sequence can be used:

```
MOV AH,5
MOV AL,2
INT 10H
```

A function code of 15 reads the active display page number for the color/graphics monitor. For instance, the instruction sequence

```
MOV AH,15
INT 10H
```

causes the active display page number to be loaded into the BH-register. A number of the interrupt 10 hex functions require the page number as an input (Table 9.3). To communicate with the active page, it is necessary first to determine which is the active page.

The BIOS procedure that services interrupt 11 hex returns a value in the AX-register that summarizes the equipment that is attached to the PC. Bits 5 and 4 can be used to determine which of the two standard adapters is attached to the PC. If both bits are set, then the monochrome adapter is attached; otherwise, it can be assumed that the color/graphics adapter is attached. With the instruction sequence

```
INT 11H
AND AX,30H
CMP AX,30H
JNE ELSE
```

the jump to ELSE is taken, if the monochrome adapter is *not* attached. The jump is *not* taken, if the monochrome adapter is attached.

Program Listing 13.4 shows the definition of a macro that sets the DS:SI register pair to address the descriptor for the video buffer. The INCLUDE pseudo-operation in line 5 causes the data segment definition in Program Listing 13.3 to be incorporated into the text in Program Listing 13.4 at assembly time. Again, note that Program Listing 13.4 is not an assembly module; it is the listing of a source file that is designed to be incorporated into an assembly module through use of the INCLUDE pseudo-operation. Inclusion of the source file in Program Listing 13.4 into the text of an assembly module indirectly includes the source file in Program Listing 13.3 via the INCLUDE pseudo-operation in line 5.

The definition of the macro appears in lines 15–33 in Program Listing 13.4. The name of the macro is getdscr, and the macro body includes two local labels identified by the LOCAL pseudo-operation in line 16. The macro body begins by setting the DS-register to address the data segment that contains the video buffer descriptors (lines 17–18). The ASSUME pseudo-operation in line 14 instructs the assembler to assume that the DS-register will be set at execution time to address this data segment.

```
 1: ;                      PROGRAM LISTING 13.4
 2: ;
 3: ; V I D E O     B U F F E R    D E S C R I P T O R    D A T A    S E G .
 4: ;
 5:               INCLUDE  B:SCR_DATA.ASM         ;DISPLAY BUFFER DESCRIPTORS
 6: ;
 7: ; MACRO TO SET DS:SI REGISTER PAIR TO ADDRESS DESCRIPTOR FOR
 8: ; VIDEO DISPLAY BUFFER. COMPATIBLE WITH BOTH MONOCHROME  AND
 9: ; COLOR GRAPHICS MONITORS. FOR COLOR GRAPHICS MONITOR, DS:SI
10: ; IS SET TO ADDRESS DESCRIPTOR FOR ACTIVE DISPLAY PAGE.
11: ;
12: ;                            USES AX AND BX REGISTERS.
13: ;
14:               ASSUME   DS:SCR_DATA
15: getdscr       MACRO
16:               LOCAL    ELSE,ENDIF
17:               MOV      AX,SEG SCR_DATA     ;SET DS-REGISTER TO ADDRESS
18:               MOV      DS,AX               ;VIDEO DESCRIPTOR DATA SEGMENT
19:               INT      11H                 ;IF   DISPLAY IS MONOCHROME
20:               AND      AX,30H
21:               CMP      AX,30H
22:               JNE      ELSE
23:               LEA      SI,BUFFER           ;THEN DESCR = ADDRESS OF
24:               JMP      ENDIF               ;         MONOCHROME DESCRIPTOR
25: ELSE:                                      ;ELSE
26:               MOV      AH,15               ;     GET PAGE_#
27:               INT      10H
28:               LEA      SI,PAGE0            ;     DESCR = ADDRESS OF PAGE 0
29:               MOV      AL,7                ;          DESCRIPTOR + PAGE_# * 7
30:               MUL      BH
31:               ADD      SI,AX
32: ENDIF:                                     ;ENDIF
33:*              ENDM
*
```

The macro body contains a double-alternative decision structure that determines which of the two standard adapters is attached to the PC and sets the SI-register to the offset of the appropriate video buffer descriptor. The instructions in lines 19–21 use the equipment check interrupt (interrupt 11 hex) to determine if the monochrome adapter is attached to the PC: If it is, then the instructions in lines 23 and 24 are executed; if it is not, then it is assumed that the color/graphics adapter is attached, and the instructions in lines 26–31 are executed.

The True alternative of the double-alternative decision structure sets the SI-register to the offset of the descriptor for the monochrome display buffer (line 23). The DS:SI register pair now addresses this descriptor. The JMP instruction in line 24 causes the False alternative to be skipped.

The False alternative of the double-alternative decision structure sets the SI-register to the offset of the color/graphics viaeo buffer for the active display page. The instructions in lines 26 and 27 read the active display page number into the BH-register. The LEA instruction in line 28 loads the SI-register with the offset of the page 0 descriptor. The instructions in lines 29 and 30 multiply the page number in the BH-register by 7 (the size of a descriptor), and the ADD instruction in line 31 adds the product to the offset in the SI-register. This sequence produces the offset of the descriptor for the active page's video buffer. The DS:SI register pair now addresses this descriptor.

The macro in Program Listing 13.4 leaves the DS:SI register pair addressing the descriptor for the appropriate video buffer and leaves the AX and BX registers undefined. This macro can be referenced prior to a call to the ADDR procedure (Section 13.2) to set up the descriptor input for that procedure, and it is used in this way in Program Listing 13.5 in the next section.

13.4 Programming Examples

Program Listing 13.6 uses the two-dimensional array components developed in Program Listings 13.2, 13.3, and 13.4 and one additional component to display and move a face around on a video screen. The additional component, shown in Program Listing 3.5, is a procedure to display a predefined figure (shape) on the screen.

Procedure to Display a Predefined Shape

The procedure in Program Listing 13.5 moves a predefined shape into a specified position of the video buffer. The shape must be stored in a data structure of the form shown in Figure 13.7. The first word of the structure specifies the size of the shape. The first byte of this word contains the number of rows (m) and the second byte contains the number of columns (n) required to display the shape. The remainder of the structure is an $m \times n$ two-dimensional word array stored in row-major order that contains the character : attribute pairs that define the shape.

EXAMPLE

The face in Figure 13.8 is a textual shape that requires 7 rows and 11 columns. Figure 13.9 shows the data structure used to represent this shape in memory. The row offsets and the contents of this data structure are shown in hexadecimal. The first word of the structure (the word at offset 0000) contains the size of the shape (7×11). The remainder of the structure is a 7×11 two-dimensional array that contains the character : attribute pairs that describe the shape.

Consider row 3 of the shape (the row that contains the eyes). This row begins at offset 002E relative to the beginning of the data structure. The first and last columns of this row contain the value 2A07 hex. The byte value 2A hex is the ASCII code for an asterisk (*). The byte value 07 is the attribute for normal video with the monochrome adapter, or white on black with the color/graphics adapter. The fourth and eighth columns of this row contain the value 2B07 hex. The byte value 2B hex is the ASCII code for a plus sign (+). Again, the attribute is normal video (white on black). The remaining columns of this row contain the value 2007 hex. The byte value 20 hex is the ASCII code for a space (blank). Again, the attribute is normal video (white on black).

FIGURE 13.7
Word array to store a shape

Offset

Offset		
0000	Number of rows (m)	Number of columns (n)
0002	Character for row 1 column 1	Attribute for row 1 column 1
0004	Character for row 1 column 2	Attribute for row 1 column 2
0006	Character for row 1 column 3	Attribute for row 1 column 3
⋮	⋮	⋮
(2n)	Character for row 1 column n	Attribute for row 1 column n
(2n + 2)	Character for row 2 column 1	Attribute for row 2 column 1
(2n + 4)	Character for row 2 column 2	Attribute for row 2 column 2
(2n + 6)	Character for row 2 column 3	Attribute for row 2 column 3
⋮	⋮	⋮
(4n)	Character for row 2 column n	Attribute for row 2 column n
⋮	⋮	⋮
2(m − 1)n + 2	Character for row m column 1	Attribute for row m column 1
2(m − 1)n + 4	Character for row m column 2	Attribute for row m column 2
2(m − 1)n + 6	Character for row m column 3	Attribute for row m column 3
⋮	⋮	⋮
(2mn)	Character for row m column n	Attribute for row m column n

FIGURE 13.8
Face described by
Figure 13.9

FIGURE 13.9

Two-dimensional array describing face in Figure 13.8

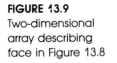

Offset

0000	070B										
0002	2007	2007	2A07	2A07	2A07	2A07	2A07	2A07	2A07	2007	2007
0018	2007	2A07	2007	2007	2007	2007	2007	2007	2007	2A07	2007
002E	2A07	2007	2007	2B07	2007	2007	2007	2B07	2007	2007	2A07
0044	2A07	2007	2007	2007	2007	5E07	2007	2007	2007	2007	2A07
005A	2A07	2007	2007	5C07	5F07	5F07	5F07	2F07	2007	2007	2A07
0070	2007	2A07	2007	2007	2007	2007	2007	2007	2007	2A07	2007
0086	2007	2007	2A07	2A07	2A07	2A07	2A07	2A07	2A07	2007	2007

The procedure in Program Listing 13.5 displays a textual shape at a specified position on the video screen. The prologue in lines 1–14 explains the function of the procedure and describes its interface requirements. On entry to the procedure, the DS:SI register pair must address the data structure that contains the shape, and the DH and DL registers must contain the row and column, respectively, at which the shape is to begin on the screen. The PUT-SHAPE procedure simply copies the shape into the appropriate position of the video buffer.

The assembly module in Program Listing 13.5 includes the definition of three macros that appear in separate macro files. The INCLUDE pseudo-operations in lines 19 and 20 specify the files that contain these macro definitions. The file PUSHPOP.MAC contains the definitions of two macros: pushreg and popreg. A detailed walkthrough of these macro definitions is beyond the scope of this discussion. These macros allow a variable number of operands. The macro pushreg generates a PUSH instruction for each of its operands and a PUSHF instruction. The order of the PUSH instructions is the same as the order of its operands. The macro reference to pushreg in line 27 generates the following sequence of instructions:

```
PUSH   AX
PUSH   BX
PUSH   CX
PUSH   DX
PUSH   DI
PUSH   SI
PUSH   BP
PUSH   ES
PUSHF
```

The macro popreg generates a POPF instruction and a POP instruction for each of its operands. The order of the POP instructions is the same as the order of the operands. The macro reference to popreg in line 57 generates the following

```
 1: ;                      PROGRAM LISTING 13.5
 2: ;
 3: ; PROCEDURE TO DISPLAY A TEXTUAL SHAPE AT THE SPECIFIED POSITION
 4: ; ON THE VIDEO DISPLAY SCREEN (MONOCHROME OR COLOR).
 5: ;
 6: ; INPUTS:   DS:SI   REGISTER PAIR ADDRESSES ARRAY CONTAINING SHAPE.
 7: ;                   FIRST TWO BYTES OF ARRAY CONTAIN SIZE OF SHAPE
 8: ;                   (NUMBER OF ROWS AND NUMBER OF COLUMNS).   EACH
 9: ;                   SUBSEQUENT PAIR OF BYTES IS A <CHAR:ATTR> PAIR
10: ;                   TO BE STORED IN THE VIDEO DISPLAY BUFFER.
11: ;           DH-REG CONTAINS ROW OF STARTING DISPLAY POSITION
12: ;           DL-REG CONTAINS COL OF STARTING DISPLAY POSITION
13: ; OUTPUT:  SHAPE DISPLAYED AT SPECIFIED POSITION ON VIDEO SCREEN
14: ;
15:                                         ;PROCEDURE TO
16:             EXTRN    ADDR:FAR           ;COMPUTE ADDR OF 2D ARRAY ELEMENT
17: ;------------------------------------------------------------------
18: ; M A C R O   D E F I N I T I O N S
19:             INCLUDE B:PUSHPOP.MAC       ;pushreg AND popreg MACROS
20:             INCLUDE B:GETDSCR.MAC       ;GET ADDR OF BUFFER DESCRIPTOR
21: ;------------------------------------------------------------------
22: ; C O D E   S E G M E N T   D E F I N I T I O N
23: CODE        SEGMENT
24:             ASSUME  CS:CODE
25:             PUBLIC  PUTSHAPE
26: PUTSHAPE    PROC    FAR            ;PROCEDURE PUTSHAPE(SPTR,ROW,COL)
27:             pushreg AX,BX,CX,DX,DI,SI,BP,ES ;SAVE REGISTERS AND FLAGS
28:             PUSH    DS                 ;SAVE SPTR
29:             PUSH    SI
30:             getdscr                    ;DESCR = ADDRESS OF VIDEO
31:                                        ;         BUFFER DESCRIPTOR
32:             CALL    ADDR               ;CALL ADDR(DESCR,ROW,COL,
33:                                        ;          RPTR,COFF,RINC)
34:             POP     SI                 ;RESTORE SPTR
35:             POP     DS
36:             CLD                        ;SET DF FOR INCREMENTING
37:             LODSB                      ;#_ROWS = SPTR->BYTE
38:             MOV     AH,0               ;SPTR = SPTR + 1
39:             MOV     CX,AX
40:             LODSB                      ;#_COLS = SPTR->BYTE
41:             MOV     BX,AX              ;SPTR = SPTR + 1
42: REPEAT:                               ;REPEAT
43:             PUSH    BX                 ;   SAVE #_COLS
44:             PUSH    BP                 ;   SAVE COFF
45: _REPEAT:                              ;   REPEAT
46:             LODSW                      ;      (RPTR+COFF)->WORD =
47:             MOV     ES:[DI][BP],AX     ;                  SPTR->WORD
48:                                        ;      SPTR = SPTR + 2
49:             ADD     BP,2               ;      COFF = COFF + 2
50:             DEC     BX                 ;      #_COLS = #_COLS - 1
51:             JNE     _REPEAT            ;   UNTIL #_COLS = 0
52:             POP     BP                 ;   RESTORE COFF
53:             POP     BX                 ;   RESTORE #_COLS
54:             ADD     DI,DX              ;   RPTR = RPTR + RINC
55:             LOOP    REPEAT             ;   #_ROWS = #_ROWS - 1
56:                                        ;UNTIL #_ROWS = 0
57:             popreg  ES,BP,SI,DI,DX,CX,BX,AX ;RESTORE REGISTERS AND FLAGS
58:             RET                        ;RETURN
59: PUTSHAPE    ENDP                     ;END PUTSHAPE
60: CODE        ENDS
61:*           END
```

sequence of instructions:

```
POPF
POP   ES
POP   BP
POP   SI
POP   DI
POP   DX
POP   CX
POP   BX
POP   AX
```

The other INCLUDE file (line 20) is GETDSCR.MAC. This file contains the definition of the macro getdscr from Program Listing 13.4 (line 15). Recall that the text in Program Listing 13.4 contains an INCLUDE pseudo-operation that specifies the file SCR_DATA.ASM, the file that contains the video descriptor data segment definition from Program Listing 13.3. Therefore, the assembly module in Program Listing 13.5 includes this data segment definition.

The PUTSHAPE procedure references one external procedure as indicated by the EXTRN pseudo-operation in line 16. This external procedure is the procedure ADDR from Program Listing 13.2, and it is used to compute the address of the element in a specified row and column of the video buffer. PUTSHAPE begins with the reference to the pushreg macro discussed previously, which saves registers for the caller. Recall that the flags register is included in the registers saved. The instructions in lines 28–35 set the ES:DI:BP register group to address the element in the video buffer specified by the row and column values input to PUTSHAPE via the DH and DL registers. The PUSH instructions in lines 28 and 29 save the pointer to the data structure containing the shape, so that the DS:SI register pair can be used to address the descriptor for the video buffer. The expansion instructions for the reference to the getdscr macro in line 30 set the DS:SI register pair to address the descriptor for the video buffer. The CALL instruction in line 32 invokes the ADDR procedure with the DS:SI register pair addressing the descriptor for the video buffer, the DH-register containing the row number, and the DL-register containing the column number. ADDR returns with the ES:DI register pair addressing the beginning of the desired row in the video buffer, the BP-register containing the offset within that row of the desired column, and the DX-register containing the offset increment needed to move one row within the video buffer. The POP instructions in lines 34 and 35 restore the DS:SI register pair to readdress the data structure that contains the shape to be displayed. The descriptor for the video buffer is no longer needed.

To display the shape beginning at row r, column c on the video screen, a copy of the $m \times n$ two-dimensional array that describes the shape must be stored in the video buffer as follows:

1. Row 1 of the shape array must be copied into row r of the video buffer in column positions c through $(c + n - 1)$.
2. Row 2 of the shape array must be copied into row $r + 1$ of the video buffer in column positions c through $(c + n - 1)$.

3. Row 3 of the shape array must be copied into row $r + 2$ of the video buffer in column positions c through $(c + n - 1)$.

.

.

.

m. Row m of the shape array must be copied into row $r + m - 1$ of the video buffer in column positions c through $(c + n - 1)$.

The nested REPEAT-UNTIL loops in lines 42–56 perform this copy operation. The body of the outer loop is executed once for each row in the shape array, and the body of the inner loop is executed once for each column in the shape array. The instructions in lines 36–41 perform the initialization for this nested loop structure. The CLD instruction in line 36 sets the DF bit of the flags register for incrementing through the shape array. The LODSB instruction in line 37 loads the AL-register with the number of rows in the shape array, and the MOV instructions in lines 38 and 39 expand this value to 16 bits and move it to the CX-register. The CX-register is used as the loop counter for the outer REPEAT-UNTIL loop. The LODSB instruction in line 40 loads the AL-register with the number of columns in the shape array, and the MOV instructions in lines 38 and 41 expand this value to 16 bits and move it to the BX-register. The BX-register is used as the loop counter for the inner REPEAT-UNTIL loop.

The outer REPEAT-UNTIL loop is implemented by the instructions in lines 42–56. The body of the outer loop begins by saving the data needed for performing reinitialization for the inner loop. The PUSH instruction in line 43 saves the number of columns in the shape array, the loop counter for the inner loop. The PUSH instruction in line 44 saves the offset from the beginning of a row to the column at which the display of the shape is to begin. Next, the inner REPEAT-UNTIL loop copies one row of the shape array to the video buffer.

The inner REPEAT-UNTIL loop is implemented by the instructions in lines 45–51. The body of the inner loop executes once for each column in the shape array. The LODSW instruction in line 46 loads the AX-register with a word (character : attribute pair) from the shape array (the array addressed by the DS:SI register pair) and then increments the SI-register by 2, so that the DS:SI register pair addresses the next word of the shape array. The MOV instruction in line 47 copies this character : attribute pair from the AX-register to the element of the video buffer that is addressed by the ES:DI:BP register group. The ADD instruction in line 49 increments the BP-register by 2, so that the ES:DI:BP register group addresses the next element of the video buffer. The operand ES:[DI][BP] is an example of base indexed addressing (Section 8.4). The segment portion of the address is specified by the contents of the ES-register. The offset portion of the address is the sum of the contents of the DI-register and the contents of the BP-register. The ES:DI register pair addresses the element at the beginning of a row, and the BP-register contains the offset from the beginning of the row to the element of interest. The DEC instruction in line 50 decrements the inner loop counter by 1, and the JNE instruction in line 51 transfers control back to the top of the inner loop (line 45), if this loop counter is nonzero.

Suppose the shape is described by an $m \times n$ two-dimensional array and that the shape is to be displayed beginning at row r, column c on the video screen. On the kth iteration of the outer loop ($k \leqslant m$), the inner loop copies the kth row of the shape into row $(r + k - 1)$ of the video buffer in column positions c through $(c + n - 1)$. On entering the inner loop, the DS:SI register pair addresses the first element of the kth row of the shape, the ES:DI register pair addresses the first element of row $(r + k - 1)$ of the video buffer, and the BP-register contains the offset from the beginning of the row to the element in the cth column. The inner loop moves the kth row of the shape array to the video buffer as follows:

1. The first iteration of the inner loop copies the first element of the kth row of the shape array to row $(r + k - 1)$, column c of the video buffer.
2. The second iteration of the inner loop copies the second element of the kth row of the shape array to row $(r + k - 1)$, column $(c + 1)$ of the video buffer.
3. The third iteration of the inner loop copies the third element of the kth row of the shape array to row $(r + k - 1)$, column $(c + 2)$ of the video buffer.

   .
   .
   .

n. The nth iteration of the inner loop copies the nth element of the kth row of the shape array to row $(r + k - 1)$, column $(c + n - 1)$ of the video buffer.

The LODSW instruction in line 46 increments the SI-register, so that the DS:SI register pair increments through the kth row of the shape array. The ADD instruction in line 49 increments the BP-register, so that the ES:DI:BP register group increments through row $(r + k - 1)$ of the video buffer from column c through column $(c + n - 1)$. On exit from the kth execution of the inner loop, the DS:SI register pair addresses the first element of row $(k + 1)$ of the shape array.

Following execution of the inner loop, the outer loop body continues by performing inner loop initialization in preparation for the next iteration of the outer loop body. The POP instruction in line 52 restores the column offset to the offset from the beginning of a row to the column at which the shape's display is to begin (saved in line 44). The POP instruction in line 53 restores the inner loop counter to the number of columns in the shape array. The ADD instruction in line 54 increments the DI-register by the number of bytes in one row of the video buffer (returned by the ADDR procedure in line 32). The ES:DI register pair now addresses the first element in the next row of the video buffer, and the ES:DI:BP register group now addresses the element in the cth column of the next row (in which c is the value input to PUTSHAPE in the DL-register). The LOOP instruction in line 55 decrements the outer loop counter by 1 and transfers control back to the top of the outer loop (line 42), if this loop counter is nonzero.

Suppose again that the shape is described by an $m \times n$ two-dimensional array and that the shape is to be displayed beginning at row r, column c on the video screen. On entering the outer loop, the DS:SI register pair addresses the first element of the first row of the shape, the ES:DI register pair addresses the first element of the rth row of the video buffer, and the BP-register contains the offset from the beginning of the row to the element in the cth column. The outer loop copies the shape array to the video buffer as follows:

1. The first iteration of the outer loop copies row 1 of the shape array to row r of the video buffer in column positions c through $(c + n - 1)$.

2. The second iteration of the outer loop copies row 2 of the shape array to row $(r + 1)$ of the video buffer in column positions c through $(c + n - 1)$.

3. The third iteration of the outer loop copies row 3 of the shape array to row $(r + 2)$ of the video buffer in column positions c through $(c + n - 1)$.

   .

   .

   .

m. The mth iteration of the outer loop copies row m of the shape array to row $(r + m - 1)$ of the video buffer in column positions c through $(c + n - 1)$.

The inner loop body increments the SI-register through a complete row of the shape array (one element per iteration). Therefore, the DS:SI register pair addresses the first element of a different row of the shape array at the beginning of each iteration of the outer loop. At the beginning of the kth iteration of the outer loop, the ES:DI register pair addresses the first element of row $(r + k - 1)$ of the video buffer, and the BP-register contains the offset from the beginning of that row to the element in the cth column of the row. The inner loop body increments the BP-register through n elements of that row of the video buffer (one element per iteration). The POP instruction in line 52 sets the BP-register to the offset from the beginning of the row to the element in the cth column. The ADD instruction in line 54 increments the DI-register, so that the ES:DI register pair addresses the first element of row $(r + k)$ of the video buffer on the next iteration (iteration $k + 1$) of the outer loop.

On exit from the outer loop, the registers are restored for the caller (line 57), and control is returned to the calling procedure (line 58).

Program to Move a Face Around the Video Screen by Moving the Face in the Video Buffer

The main procedure presented in Program Listing 13.6 uses the PUTSHAPE procedure, developed in the previous section, to display a face on the video screen. By repeatedly clearing the video screen and displaying the face in a slightly different position, the procedure causes the face to move across the screen. The assembly module in Program Listing 13.6 contains the definition of

```
 1: ;                        PROGRAM LISTING 13.6
 2: ;
 3: ; PROGRAM TO MOVE A FACE AROUND THE SCREEN
 4: ;
 5:                                          ;PROCEDURES TO
 6:            EXTRN    CLEAR:FAR            ;CLEAR VIDEO SCREEN
 7:            EXTRN    DELAY:FAR            ;DELAY n SECONDS
 8:            EXTRN    PUTSHAPE:FAR         ;DISPLAY A TEXTUAL SHAPE
 9: ;
10: ; S T A C K   S E G M E N T   D E F I N I T I O N
11: ;
12: STACK      SEGMENT STACK
13:            DB       256 DUP(?)
14: STACK      ENDS
15: ;
16: ; D A T A   S E G M E N T   D E F I N I T I O N
17: ;
18: DATA       SEGMENT
19: ;
20: FACE       DB       07,11
21:            DB       20H,07H,20H,07H,2AH,07H,2AH,07H,2AH,07H,2AH,07H
22:            DB                 2AH,07H,2AH,07H,2AH,07H,20H,07H,20H,07H
23:            DB       20H,07H,2AH,07H,20H,07H,20H,07H,20H,07H,20H,07H
24:            DB                 20H,07H,20H,07H,20H,07H,2AH,07H,20H,07H
25:            DB       2AH,07H,20H,07H,20H,07H,2BH,07H,20H,07H,20H,07H
26:            DB                 20H,07H,2BH,07H,20H,07H,20H,07H,2AH,07H
27:            DB       2AH,07H,20H,07H,20H,07H,20H,07H,20H,07H,5EH,07H
28:            DB                 20H,07H,20H,07H,20H,07H,20H,07H,2AH,07H
29:            DB       2AH,07H,20H,07H,20H,07H,5CH,07H,5FH,07H,5FH,07H
30:            DB                 5FH,07H,2FH,07H,20H,07H,20H,07H,2AH,07H
31:            DB       20H,07H,2AH,07H,20H,07H,20H,07H,20H,07H,20H,07H
32:            DB                 20H,07H,20H,07H,20H,07H,2AH,07H,20H,07H
33:            DB       20H,07H,20H,07H,2AH,07H,2AH,07H,2AH,07H,2AH,07H
34:            DB                 2AH,07H,2AH,07H,2AH,07H,20H,07H,20H,07H
35: SAD_MOUTH  DB       02,11
36:            DB       2AH,07H,20H,07H,20H,07H,20H,07H,5FH,07H,5FH,07H
37:            DB                 5FH,07H,20H,07H,20H,07H,20H,07H,2AH,07H
38:            DB       20H,07H,2AH,07H,20H,07H,2FH,07H,20H,07H,20H,07H
39:            DB                 20H,07H,5CH,07H,20H,07H,2AH,07H,20H,07H
40: WINK       DB       1,1,2BH,87H
41: DATA       ENDS
42:*;
```

```
43: ;
44: ; C O D E   S E G M E N T   D E F I N I T I O N
45: ;
46: CODE       SEGMENT
47:            ASSUME   CS:CODE,SS:STACK,DS:DATA
48: PUTFACE    PROC     FAR
49:            PUSH     DS                   ;PUSH RETURN SEG ADDR ON STACK
50:            SUB      AX,AX                ;PUSH RETURN OFFSET OF ZERO
51:            PUSH     AX                   ;ON STACK
52:            MOV      AX,SEG DATA          ;SET DS-REGISTER TO ADDRESS
53:            MOV      DS,AX                ;            DATA SEGMENT
54:            LEA      SI,FACE
55:            MOV      DH,3                 ;I = 3
56:            MOV      DL,18                ;J = 18
57:            MOV      AL,1
58:            MOV      CX,12                ;LOOP_COUNT = 12
```

```
59: REPEAT:                              ;REPEAT
60:            CALL    CLEAR              ;   CLEAR SCREEN
61:            INC     DH                 ;   I = I + 1
62:            INC     DL                 ;   J = J + 1
63:            CALL    PUTSHAPE           ;   DISPLAY FACE @ ROW I COL J
64:            CALL    DELAY              ;   DELAY 1 SECOND
65:            LOOP    REPEAT             ;   LOOP_COUNT = LOOP_COUNT - 1
66:                                       ;UNTIL LOOP_COUNT = 0
67:            ADD     DH,4               ;I = I + 4
68:            LEA     SI,SAD_MOUTH       ;DISPLAY SAD MOUTH @ ROW I COL J
69:            CALL    PUTSHAPE
70:            MOV     AL,5               ;DELAY 5 SECONDS
71:            CALL    DELAY
72:            LEA     SI,WINK            ;WINK LEFT EYE
73:            SUB     DH,2
74:            ADD     DL,7
75:            CALL    PUTSHAPE
76:            CALL    DELAY              ;DELAY 5 SECONDS
77:            RET                        ;RETURN
78: PUTFACE    ENDP
79: CODE       ENDS
80:*           END     PUTFACE
*
```

this main procedure along with the definition of a data segment. The data segment contains the data structure for the face.

The assembly module references three external subprocedures identified by the EXTRN pseudo-operations in lines 6–8. The CLEAR procedure sets every character in the appropriate video buffer to blank, which, in effect, clears the video screen. CLEAR also homes the cursor (i.e., moves it to the upper left-hand corner of the video screen). The CLEAR procedure has no inputs, and it is available in the I/O subprocedure library (I/O.LIB). The DELAY procedure cycles (doing nothing) for approximately n seconds, in which n is the unsigned integer value in the AL-register. DELAY is similar to a solution to Programming Exercise 9.11. This version of DELAY must perform a conversion from seconds to a count of timer interrupts, and it is *not* available in the I/O subprocedure library. The PUTSHAPE procedure is, of course, the procedure from Program Listing 13.5.

The data segment definition in lines 15–41 contains the definitions of the data structures for three shapes. The data structure FACE, defined in lines 20–34, is the data structure from Figure 13.9 that describes the face from Figure 13.8. The data structure SAD_MOUTH, defined in lines 35–39, describes a 2×11 shape that transforms the smiling face in Figure 13.8 into the frowning face in Figure 13.10. By replacing rows 5 and 6 of the shape described by data structure FACE with the 2 rows of the shape described by data structure SAD_MOUTH, the transformation is accomplished. The data structure WINK, defined in line 40, describes a 1×1 shape that is a plus sign ($+$) with an attribute of normal video with the blink bit set. By replacing one of the eyes of the face with this shape, the face is made to wink.

The code segment defined in lines 46–79 contains the definition of one procedure, the main procedure PUTFACE. PUTFACE begins by saving the

FIGURE 13.10

Shape described by data structure FACE with changes described by data structure SAD_MOUTH

return address for DOS (lines 49–51) and setting the DS-register to address the data segment (lines 52–53).

The instructions in lines 54–58 perform the initialization for the REPEAT-UNTIL loop implemented in lines 59–66. The LEA instruction in line 54 loads the SI-register with the offset of data structure FACE. That is, after execution of the LEA instruction, the DS:SI register pair addresses the first byte of data structure FACE. The MOV instruction in line 55 sets the row number in the DH-register to 3, and the MOV instruction in line 56 sets the column number in the DL-register to 18. The DH and DL registers specify a row and column within the video buffer and are inputs for the PUTSHAPE procedure. The MOV instruction in line 57 loads the AL-register with the input for the DELAY procedure. The MOV instruction in line 58 sets the loop counter for the REPEAT-UNTIL loop to 12.

The REPEAT-UNTIL loop is implemented by the instructions in lines 59–66. The loop body is executed 12 times. On each iteration of the loop body, the video screen is cleared (line 60), the row and column positions in the DH and DL register are both incremented by 1 (lines 61 and 62), the face is displayed at the specified row and column (line 63), and a 1-second delay is performed (line 64). The LOOP instruction in line 65 decrements the loop counter and transfers control back to the top of the loop (line 59), if this loop counter is nonzero. On the first iteration of the loop body, the face is displayed beginning at row 4, column 19 on the video screen. On the second iteration, it is displayed beginning at row 5, column 20. On the nth iteration ($1 \leqslant n \leqslant 12$), it is displayed beginning at row $(3 + n)$, column $(18 + n)$. The face is left in each display position for approximately 1 second. Since the screen is cleared between display positions, the face moves down the screen diagonally.

On loop exit, the face is displayed beginning at row 15, column 30 on the video screen. Rows 5 and 6 of the face are on rows 19 and 20 of the video screen, beginning at column 30. The ADD instruction in line 67 increments the DH-register value from 15 to 19, so that the DH and DL registers specify row 19, column 30. The LEA instruction in line 68 sets the DS:SI register pair to address the data structure for the shape SAD_MOUTH. The call to the PUTSHAPE procedure in line 69 transforms the happy mouth into a sad mouth (i.e., transforms the face in Figure 13.8 into the face in Figure 13.10). The instructions in lines 70 and 71 perform a delay of approximately 5 seconds.

With the face displayed beginning at row 15, column 30 of the video screen, the face's left eye is at row 17, column 37. The DH and DL register values currently specify row 19, column 30. The LEA instruction in line 72 sets the DS:SI register pair to address the data structure for the shape WINK, and the instructions in lines 73 and 74 adjust the DH and DL registers to specify row 17, column 37. The call to the PUTSHAPE procedure in line 75 transforms the frowning face to a frowning face with its left eye winking. The call to the DELAY procedure in line 76 produces a delay of approximately 5 seconds before control is returned to DOS (line 77).

13.5   Changing Position of Video Buffer

Section 9.3 provides a brief introduction to direct input/output in the IBM PC Assembly language. That discussion includes a description of the IN and OUT instructions. In this section, the OUT instruction is used to communicate with the video controller on the display adapter.

This video controller has a set of 18 byte registers. The function of many of these registers is beyond the scope of this book, although the function of two of these registers is discussed here and is illustrated in Program Listing 13.7. Register numbers 12 and 13 contain the high- and low-order halves, respectively, of the offset from the beginning of the video memory to the beginning of the video buffer. It should be noted that this offset is a word offset, not a byte offset; that is, a change of 1 in this offset moves the beginning of the video buffer one complete character : attribute pair (2 bytes). This offset is initialized to zero for the monochrome adapter and is initialized to the product of the active page number and 2048 for the color/graphics adapter.

Two IBM PC I/O ports are used to read and/or load the video controller registers on the display adapter: ports 3B4 hex and 3B5 hex for the monochrome adapter and ports 3D4 hex and 3D5 hex for the color/graphics adapter. The first of the two consecutive ports addresses one of the 18 registers, and the second is used for the data that are loaded into or copied from the addressed register.

EXAMPLE

Suppose the PC has a color graphics adapter. The sequence of instructions

```
MOV DX,3D4H
MOV AL,12
OUT DX,AL
```

could be used to select register 12 in the video controller (the register that contains the high-order half of the video buffer offset). Then, the instruction sequence

```
MOV DX,3D5H
MOV AL,08H
OUT DX,AL
```

could be used to load the selected register (number 12) with the value 08 hex.

```
 1: ;                          PROGRAM LISTING 13.7
 2: ;
 3: ; PROGRAM TO MOVE A FACE AROUND THE SCREEN
 4: ;
 5:                                           ;PROCEDURES TO
 6:              EXTRN    CLEAR:FAR            ;CLEAR VIDEO SCREEN
 7:              EXTRN    DELAY:FAR            ;DELAY n SECONDS
 8:              EXTRN    PUTSHAPE:FAR         ;DISPLAY A TEXTUAL SHAPE
 9: ;-----------------------------------------------------------------
10: ; S T A C K    S E G M E N T    D E F I N I T I O N
11: ;
12: STACK        SEGMENT STACK
13:              DB      256 DUP(?)
14: STACK        ENDS
15: ;-----------------------------------------------------------------
16: ; D A T A    S E G M E N T    D E F I N I T I O N
17: ;
18: DATA         SEGMENT
19: ;
20: FACE         DB      07,11
21:              DB      20H,07H,20H,07H,2AH,07H,2AH,07H,2AH,07H,2AH,07H
22:              DB                2AH,07H,2AH,07H,2AH,07H,20H,07H,20H,07H
23:              DB      20H,07H,20H,07H,20H,07H,20H,07H,20H,07H,20H,07H
24:              DB                20H,07H,20H,07H,20H,07H,2AH,07H,20H,07H
25:              DB      2AH,07H,20H,07H,20H,07H,2BH,07H,20H,07H,20H,07H
26:              DB                20H,07H,2BH,07H,20H,07H,20H,07H,2AH,07H
27:              DB      2AH,07H,20H,07H,20H,07H,20H,07H,20H,07H,5EH,07H
28:              DB                20H,07H,20H,07H,20H,07H,20H,07H,2AH,07H
29:              DB      2AH,07H,20H,07H,20H,07H,5CH,07H,5FH,07H,5FH,07H
30:              DB                5FH,07H,2FH,07H,20H,07H,20H,07H,2AH,07H
31:              DB      20H,07H,20H,07H,20H,07H,20H,07H,20H,07H,20H,07H
32:              DB                20H,07H,20H,07H,20H,07H,2AH,07H,20H,07H
33:              DB      20H,07H,20H,07H,2AH,07H,2AH,07H,2AH,07H,2AH,07H
34:              DB                2AH,07H,2AH,07H,2AH,07H,20H,07H,20H,07H
35: DATA         ENDS
36: ;-----------------------------------------------------------------
37: ; M A C R O    D E F I N I T I O N
38: ;
39: ; MACRO TO SET THE BASE ADDRESS OF THE VIDEO BUFFER
40: ;             port AND offset CAN BE WORD REGISTER
41: ;                          WORD MEMORY OR IMMEDIATE
42: ;             USES AL, BX, AND DX REGISTERS
43: ;
44: setbase      MACRO    port,offset
45:              MOV      BX,offset
46:              MOV      DX,port
47:              MOV      AL,12
48:              OUT      DX,AL
49:              INC      DX
50:              MOV      AL,BH
51:              OUT      DX,AL
52:              DEC      DX
53:              MOV      AL,13
54:              OUT      DX,AL
55:              INC      DX
56:              MOV      AL,BL
57:              OUT      DX,AL
58:*             ENDM
```

```
59: ;
60: ;-------------------------------------------------------------
61: ; C O D E   S E G M E N T   D E F I N I T I O N
62: ;
63: CODE        SEGMENT
64:             ASSUME    CS:CODE,SS:STACK,DS:DATA
65: MOVFACE     PROC      FAR
66:             PUSH      DS                    ;PUSH RETURN SEG ADDR ON STACK
67:             SUB       AX,AX                 ;PUSH RETURN OFFSET OF ZERO
68:             PUSH      AX                    ;ON STACK
69:             MOV       AX,SEG DATA           ;SET DS-REGISTER TO ADDRESS
70:             MOV       DS,AX                 ;              DATA SEGMENT
71:             CALL      CLEAR                 ;CLEAR SCREEN
72:             LEA       SI,FACE
73:             MOV       DH,19                 ;I = 19
74:             MOV       DL,70                 ;J = 70
75:             CALL      PUTSHAPE              ;DISPLAY FACE @ ROW I COL J
76:             MOV       AL,1
77:             CALL      DELAY                 ;DELAY 1 SECOND
78:             INT       11H                   ;IF   DISPLAY IS MONOCHROME
79:             AND       AX,30H
80:             CMP       AX,30H
81:             JNE       ELSE
82:             MOV       BP,03B4H              ;THEN PORT = 3B4H
83:             MOV       BX,0                  ;    ST_OFFSET = 0
84:             JMP       ENDIF
85: ELSE:                                      ;ELSE
86:             MOV       BP,03D4H              ;     PORT = 3D4H
87:             MOV       AH,15                 ;     GET PAGE_#
88:             INT       10H
89:             MOV       BL,BH                 ;     ST_OFFSET = PAGE_# * 2048
90:             MOV       BH,0
91:             MOV       AX,2048
92:             MUL       BX
93:             MOV       BX,AX
94: ENDIF:                                      ;ENDIF
95:             PUSH      BX                    ;SAVE ST_OFFSET
96:             MOV       CX,100                ;LOOP_COUNT = 100
97: LOOP_TOP:                                   ;REPEAT
98:             setbase   BP,BX                 ;   SET VIDEO BUFFER TO BEGIN
99:                                             ;        AT ST_OFFSET
100:            MOV       AL,1
101:            CALL      DELAY                 ;   DELAY 1 SECOND
102:            ADD       BX,2                  ;   ST_OFFSET = ST_OFFSET + 2
103:            LOOP      LOOP_TOP              ;   LOOP_COUNT = LOOP_COUNT - 1
104:                                            ;UNTIL LOOP_COUNT = 0
105:            POP       BX                    ;RESTORE ST_OFFSET
106:            setbase   BP,BX                 ;SET VIDEO BUFFER TO BEGIN
107:                                            ;    AT OFFSET ST_OFFSET
108:            CALL      CLEAR                 ;CLEAR SCREEN
109:            RET                             ;RETURN
110: MOVFACE    ENDP
111: CODE       ENDS
112:*           END       MOVFACE
*
```

Similarly, the instruction sequence

```
MOV DX,3D4H
MOV AL,13
OUT DX,AL
```

could be used to select register 13 (the register that contains the low-order half of the video buffer offset). Then, the instruction sequence

```
MOV DX,3D5H
MOV AL,0
OUT DX,AL
```

could be used to load the selected register (number 13) with the value zero.

The preceding four instruction sequences, when executed in the sequence shown, would set the offset for the beginning of the video buffer to the value 0800 hex (2048 decimal), which in effect, selects page 1 of the color/graphics video memory. It has the same effect as the following BIOS interrupt reference:

```
MOV AH,5
MOV AL,1
INT 10H
```

Program to Move a Face Around the Video Screen

The assembly module in Program Listing 13.7 contains the data segment and main procedure of a program that displays a face on the screen and then causes that face to move around the screen by changing the position of the video buffer within the video memory. By incrementing the video buffer offset by 2, each character in the video buffer moves up two positions relative to the beginning of the video buffer, which causes each character being displayed on the screen to move left two character positions along its row. Any character that moves off the left edge of the screen moves back in on the right edge, one row higher. Repeatedly incrementing the video buffer offset by 2, with a 1-second delay between increases, causes the shape to move from right to left on the screen. As it moves off the left edge of the screen, it moves back in on the right, one row higher. Thus, the shape gradually moves from the bottom to the top of the screen.

The assembly module in Program Listing 13.7 contains references to three external subprocedures identified by the EXTRN pseudo-operations in lines 6–8, which are the same three procedures referenced by the PUTFACE procedure in Program Listing 13.6. These procedures are used by the MOVFACE procedure in much the same way that they were used by the PUTFACE procedure.

The data segment definition in lines 15–35 contains the definition of one data structure describing a shape. The data structure FACE, defined in lines

20–34 is again the data structure from Figure 13.9 that describes the face in Figure 13.8.

The assembly module contains the definition of one macro, whose prologue (lines 36–43) explains its function, the operands it requires, and its register usage. The macro sets the base address (i.e., beginning offset) of the video buffer in registers 12 and 13 of the video controller. The macro definition appears in lines 44–58. The name of the macro is setbase, and it has two operands, port and offset. The first operand, port, specifies the first of the two consecutive ports used to communicate with the registers of the video controller (3B4 hex for the monochrome adapter and 3D4 hex for the color/graphics adapter). The second operand, offset, specifies the offset to be loaded into registers 12 and 13 of the video controller.

The macro body appears in lines 45–57. The MOV instruction in line 45 loads the BX-register with the offset, which makes it easy to divide the offset into its high-order and low-order bytes. The MOV instruction in line 46 loads the DX-register with the port number. The OUT instruction in line 48 requires the port number to be in the DX-register. The instructions in lines 47 and 48 select register 12 of the video controller. The INC instruction in line 49 increments the port number to the next consecutive port, so that data can be loaded into that register. The instructions in lines 50 and 51 load register 12 of the video controller with the high-order half of the offset (BH-register value). The DEC instruction in line 52 decrements the port number to the previous port, so that another video controller register can be selected. The instructions in lines 53 and 54 select register 13 of the video controller, and the instructions in lines 55–57 load that register with the low-order half of the offset (BL-register value).

The code segment defined in lines 63–111 contains the definition of one procedure, the main procedure MOVFACE. MOVFACE begins by saving the return address for DOS (lines 66–68) and setting the DS-register to address the data segment (lines 69–70).

The instructions in lines 71–77 initialize the video buffer. The call to the CLEAR procedure in line 71 sets each character in the video buffer to blank. The instructions in lines 72–75 cause the video buffer to be initialized, so that the face is displayed beginning at row 19, column 70 on the video screen, which displays the face in the lower right-hand corner of the screen. The instructions in lines 76 and 77 perform a 1-second delay.

The double-alternative decision structure implemented in lines 78–94 determines the display adapter that is attached to the system. If the monochrome adapter is attached, then the port number (BP-register value) is set to 3B4 hex (line 82), and the video buffer offset (BX-register value) is initialized to zero (line 83). If the monochrome adapter is *not* attached, then the port number (BP-register value) is set to 3D4 hex (line 86), and the video buffer offset (BX-register value) is initialized to the product of the active page number and 2048 (lines 87–93). The PUSH instruction in line 95 saves the initial offset, so that the video buffer position can be restored at the end of the program.

The instructions in lines 96–104 implement the REPEAT-UNTIL loop that causes the face to move on the screen. The MOV instruction in line 96 sets the loop count to 100, so that the loop body executes 100 times. The loop body begins by setting the video buffer offset in registers 12 and 13 of the video controller to the value in the BX-register. This sequence is accomplished by the expansion instructions for the macro reference in line 98. The instructions in lines 100 and 101 perform a 1-second delay. The ADD instruction in line 102 increments the offset in the BX-register by 2 in preparation for the next iteration of the loop body. The loop instruction in line 103 decrements the loop counter by 1 and transfers control to the top of the loop (line 97), if this loop counter is nonzero.

On loop exit, the position of the video buffer is restored. The POP instruction in line 105 restores the video buffer offset in the BX-register to its original value (saved by the PUSH instruction in line 95). The expansion instructions for the macro reference in line 106 load registers 12 and 13 in the video controller with this initial offset. The call to the CLEAR procedure in line 108 clears the video screen before control is returned to DOS (line 109).

A loop count of 100 causes the face to move across the screen $2\frac{1}{2}$ times. A loop count of 754 moves the face from the lower right-hand corner all the way to the upper left-hand corner, which takes about $12\frac{1}{2}$ minutes on a standard PC.

PROGRAMMING EXERCISES

13.1 Write an external FAR procedure to display an 8- or 16-bit integer in hexadecimal form beginning at the current cursor position on the video screen. Your inputs should be one of the following: (a) the AL-register contains an 8-bit value to be displayed, and the BL-register contains 0, the code for the 8-bit display; or (b) the AX-register contains a 16-bit value to be displayed, and the BL-register contains a nonzero value, the code for the 16-bit display. Your procedure should use the array HEX_ASCII from Figure 13.1 and the XLAT instruction to perform the translation.

13.2 The ADDR procedure in Program Listing 13.2 does not completely test for out-of-range subscripts—it does not test for a subscript of zero. In addition, ADDR always calculates the address, even for out-of-range subscripts. Modify ADDR so that it tests for zero subscripts and so that the address is calculated only for valid subscripts.

13.3 The ADDR procedure in Program Listing 13.2 applies to two-dimensional arrays stored in row-major order. Write a similar procedure called ADDR$ that applies to two-dimensional arrays stored in column-major order. Your inputs should be the same as those for the ADDR procedure. Your outputs should be as follow:

The ES:DI register pair addresses the first element in the specified column of the array.
The BP-register contains the offset within the column of the specified row.
The DX-register contains the DI-register offset needed to move 1 column in the array (i.e., the number of bytes per column).
The OF bit of the flags register is set to 1 for an out-of-range subscript.

13.4 Design an algorithm to display a two-dimensional array of signed integers that is stored in row-major order. The array is to be displayed in two-dimensional form with the number of rows and columns specified by a descriptor of the form described in Table 13.2. Implement your algorithm with an IBM PC Assembly language external FAR procedure called PUT2DRM. Your input should be the address of the array descriptor in the DS:SI register pair. Your output should be the elements of the two-dimensional array displayed in rows and columns beginning at the current cursor position. Your procedure should be able to handle both byte and word arrays.

13.5 Design an algorithm to display a two-dimensional array of signed integers that is stored in column-major order. The array is to be displayed in two-dimensional form with the number of rows and columns specified by a descriptor of the form described in Table 13.2. Implement your algorithm with an IBM PC Assembly language external FAR procedure called PUT2DCM. Your input should be the address of the array descriptor in the DS:SI register pair. Your output should be the elements of the two-dimensional array in rows and columns beginning at the current cursor position. Your procedure should be able to handle both byte and word arrays.

13.6 Rework Programming Exercises 13.4 and 13.5 for unsigned integer arrays. Name the new procedures PUT2DRM$ and PUT2DCM$, respectively.

13.7 Define a two-dimensional array as follows:

```
ARRAY DW -501,-502,-503,-504
      DW -505,-506,-507,-508
      DW -509,-510,-511,-512
```

Write a program that uses the ADDR procedure and the procedures developed in Programming Exercises 13.3, 13.4, and 13.5 to perform the following sequence of operations:

a. Interpret the array as a 3 × 4 array stored in row-major order and display it on the screen.

b. Interpret the array as a 3 × 4 array stored in column-major order and display it on the screen.

c. Interpret the array as a 4 × 3 array stored in row-major order and display it on the screen.

d. Interpret the array as a 4 × 3 array stored in column-major order and display it on the screen.

e. Interpret the array as a 2 × 6 array stored in column-major order and display it on the screen.

13.8 Design an algorithm to clear a specified window on the video screen given the row and column of the upper left-hand and lower right-hand corners of the window. Implement your algorithm with an IBM PC Assembly language external FAR procedure named CLEAR_W. Your inputs should be as follow:

The DH-register contains the row at the upper left-hand corner of the window.
The DL-register contains the column at the upper left-hand corner of the window.
The BH-register contains the row at the lower right-hand corner of the window.
The BL-register contains the column at the lower right-hand corner of the window.

Your procedure should clear the specified window of the video screen and should work for both the monochrome and color/graphics monitors. For the color/graphics monitor, your procedure should be page sensitive.

13.9 Design an algorithm to fill the video screen with a specified character : attribute pair. Implement your algorithm with an IBM PC Assembly language external FAR procedure named FILL_SCR. Your inputs should be as follow:

The AH-register contains the character to be displayed in every position on the video screen.
The AL-register contains the attribute to be used in each position.

Your procedure should fill the appropriate video buffer with the specified character : attribute pair and should work for both the monochrome and color/graphics monitors. For the color/graphics monitor, your procedure should be page sensitive.

13.10 Write a main procedure that uses the procedures in Programming Exercises 13.8 and 13.9 to perform the following sequence of operations:

a. Fill the screen with the character DB hex using the attribute 07 hex.

b. Clear a window from row 1, column 1 to row 5, column 16.

c. Clear a window from row 6, column 17 to row 10, column 32.

d. Clear a window from row 11, column 33 to row 15, column 48.

e. Clear a window from row 16, column 49 to row 20, column 64.

f. Clear a window from row 21, column 65 to row 25, column 80.

Note: Your presentation of this program will be better with a delay between each step.

APPENDIXES

INSTRUCTION SUMMARY

The following diagram shows the general format used in this appendix to describe the individual instructions that make up the instruction set of the Intel 8088 microprocessor.

Operation Code

```
┌─────────────────────────────────────────────────────────────────┐
│ Description of operation performed                                │
│                                                                   │
│                                                                   │
├───────────────────────────────────────────────────────────────────┤
│ General form of instruction                                       │
│                                                                   │
│    Notation:                                                      │
│             Items in capital letters must be coded exactly as     │
│             shown.                                                │
│                                                                   │
│             <>    encloses items supplied by the programmer       │
│                                                                   │
│             []    encloses optional items                         │
│                                                                   │
│             The optional label field, denoted by [<label>] in     │
│             the  general  form  of  each  instruction,  is  the   │
│             symbolic  name  to be associated  with the memory     │
│             location at which the instruction is to begin.        │
├───────────────────────────────────────────────────────────────────┤
│ Explanation of operands                                           │
│                                                                   │
│                                                                   │
│                                                                   │
│                                                                   │
│                                                                   │
├─────────────┬────┬────┬────┬────┬────┬────┬────┬────┬────┬────────┤
│             │ OF │ DF │ IF │ TF │ SF │ ZF │ AF │ PF │ CF │        │
│             ├────┼────┼────┼────┼────┼────┼────┼────┼────┤        │
│             │ \  │    │    │    │    │    │    │    │    │        │
└─────────────┴────┴────┴────┴────┴────┴────┴────┴────┴────┴────────┘
                   \
                    \
                     \
                      \
                       U  -> unchanged
                       UD -> undefined
                       R  -> reflects result of operation
                       S  -> set to 1
                       C  -> cleared to 0
                       T  -> toggled (i.e., set to the opposite state)
                       LB -> last bit shifted out
                       SC -> reflects sign bit change on last bit
                             shifted
                       SV -> saved value popped from top of stack
```

AAA
ASCII Adjust for Addition

Adjusts the result of a previous addition of two unpacked BCD
digits. Adjusts the AL-register to contain a valid, unpacked
BCD digit. The upper nibble of the AL-register is cleared.
The carry from this digit is added to the AH-register. AAA
causes the following steps to be performed:
    IF   ((AL-REG and OF hex) > 9) or (AF = 1)
    THEN
         AL-REG is incremented by 6
         AH-REG is incremented by 1
         AF is set to 1
    ENDIF
    AF is copied into CF
    Upper nibble of AL-REG is cleared

[<label>]   AAA   [<comment>]

The operand is implied by the instruction. It is always the
contents of the AL-register.

	OF	DF	IF	TF	SF	ZF	AF	PF	CF	
	UD	U	U	U	UD	UD	R	UD	R	

AAD
ASCII Adjust for Division

Adjusts the dividend prior to division of a two-digit,
unpacked BCD number by an unpacked BCD digit. The dividend to
be adjusted is the two-digit, unpacked BCD number in the AX-
register. The most-significant BCD digit (AH-register) is
multiplied by 10,   and the least-significant BCD digit
(AL-register) is added to this product. The resulting binary
integer is placed in the AL-register, and the AH-register is
cleared.

[<label>]   AAD   [<comment>]

The operand is implied by the instruction. It is always the
contents of the AX-register.

	OF	DF	IF	TF	SF	ZF	AF	PF	CF	
	UD	U	U	U	R	R	UD	R	UD	

AAM
ASCII Adjust for Multiply

Adjusts the result of a previous multiplication of two
unpacked BCD digits, producing two unpacked BCD digits. The
result of the multiplication (AX-register value) is divided
by 10. The quotient (the high-order, unpacked BCD digit) is
placed in the AH-register. The remainder (the low-order,
unpacked BCD digit) is placed in the AL-register.

[<label>]   AAM   [<comment>]

The operand is implied by the instruction. It is always the
contents of the AX-register.

OF	DF	IF	TF	SF	ZF	AF	PF	CF
UD	U	U	U	R	R	UD	R	UD

AAS
ASCII Adjust for Subtraction

Adjusts the result of a previous subtraction of two unpacked
BCD digits. Adjusts the AL-register to contain a valid,
unpacked BCD digit. The upper nibble of the AL-register is
cleared. The borrow into this digit is subtracted from the
AH-register. AAS causes the following steps to be performed:
    IF   ((AL-REG and OF hex) > 9) or (AF = 1)
    THEN
         AL-REG is decremented by 6
         AH-REG is decremented by 1
         AF is set to 1
    ENDIF
    AF is copied into CF
    Upper nibble of AL-REG is cleared

[<label>]   AAS   [<comment>]

The operand is implied by the instruction. It is always the
contents of the AL-register.

OF	DF	IF	TF	SF	ZF	AF	PF	CF
UD	U	U	U	UD	UD	R	UD	R

ADC
Add with Carry

Adds the source operand, the destination operand, and the
carry flag, replacing the destination operand with the sum.

[<label>]   ADC   <destination>,<source>   [<comment>]

<source>   identifies the location of the addend, and
<destination> identifies the location of the augend that
will be replaced by the sum.

The types of the two operands must match (i.e., both must
be byte or both must be word).

<destination>	<source>
General register	General register Memory location Immediate
Memory location	General register Immediate

OF	DF	IF	TF	SF	ZF	AF	PF	CF
R	U	U	U	R	R	R	R	R

```
                              ADD
                            Addition
```

Adds the source operand to the destination operand, replacing the destination operand with the sum.

```
[<label>]      ADD      <destination>,<source>      [<comment>]

   <source>        identifies the location of the addend,  and
   <destination> identifies the location of the augend  that
                  will be replaced by the sum.

   The types of the two operands must match (i.e., both must
   be byte or both must be word).
```

<destination>	<source>
General register	General register Memory location Immediate
Memory location	General register Immediate

	OF	DF	IF	TF	SF	ZF	AF	PF	CF	
	R	U	U	U	R	R	R	R	R	

AND
Logical AND

ANDS each bit of the destination operand with the
corresponding bit of the source operand, replacing the bit
in the destination operand with the result.

[<label>]   AND   <destination>,<source>   [<comment>]

   <destination> identifies the location of the operand that
                 is to be replaced with the result, and
   <source>   identifies the location of the operand that
                 is not to be modified.

The types of the two operands must match (i.e., both must
be byte or both must be word).

<destination>	<source>
General register	General register Memory location Immediate
Memory location	General register Immediate

	OF	DF	IF	TF	SF	ZF	AF	PF	CF	
	C	U	U	U	R	R	UD	R	C	

CALL

The procedure that begins at the memory location specified
by the operand is invoked. The return address is pushed onto
the stack.

[<label>]   CALL   <target>   [<comment>]

   <target>   is the name of the procedure that is being
                      invoked (direct call), or an address
                      expression that specifies the memory
                      location that contains the address of the
                      procedure being invoked (indirect call).

<target>	Description
Procedure name with attribute NEAR	The machine language operand is the difference between the offset of the memory location specified by the target and the offset of the memory location immediately following the CALL instruction. At execution, this difference is added to the IP-reg.
Procedure name with attribute FAR	The machine language operand is the segment and offset of the specified target. At execution, this segment and offset replace the value in the CS:IP register pair.
Address expression of variable with attribute WORD	The machine language operand is the segment register number and offset of the variable. At execution, the contents of the memory location specified by this segment and offset replace the value in the IP-register.
Address expression of variable with attribute DBL WORD	The machine language operand is the segment register number and offset of the variable. At execution, the contents of the memory location specified by this segment and offset replace the value of the CS:IP register pair.
General register (16-bit register)	The contents of the general register replaces the value in the IP-reg.

OF	DF	IF	TF	SF	ZF	AF	PF	CF
U	U	U	U	U	U	U	U	U

CBW
Convert Byte to Word

Expands the signed, 8-bit integer in the AL-register to a signed, 16-bit integer in the AX-register. Extends the sign bit (bit 7 of the AL-register) into bits 0 through 7 of the AH-Register.

[<label>]   CBW   [<comment>]

OF	DF	IF	TF	SF	ZF	AF	PF	CF
U	U	U	U	U	U	U	U	U

CLC
Clear Carry Flag

Resets the carry flag to zero.

[<label>]   CLC   [<comment>]

OF	DF	IF	TF	SF	ZF	AF	PF	CF
U	U	U	U	U	U	U	U	C

CLD
Clear Direction Flag

Resets the direction flag to zero, which causes the automatic update of the DI and/or SI registers following execution of a string instruction to be an increment.

[<label>]   CLD   [<comment>]

OF	DF	IF	TF	SF	ZF	AF	PF	CF
U	C	U	U	U	U	U	U	U

CLI
Clear Interrupt Flag

Reset the interrupt flag to zero, which disables external interrupts. That is, it causes the processor to ignore external interrupts.

[<label>]   CLI   [<comment>]

OF	DF	IF	TF	SF	ZF	AF	PF	CF
U	U	C	U	U	U	U	U	U

CMC
Complement Carry Flag

Changes the state of (i.e., toggles) the CF bit of the flags register.

[<label>]   CMC   [<comment>]

OF	DF	IF	TF	SF	ZF	AF	PF	CF
U	U	U	U	U	U	U	U	T

CMP
Compare

Compares the first operand to the second operand, and sets the flags accordingly. The source operand is subtracted from the destination operand, and the flags are set to reflect the difference. Neither the source nor the destination operand is modified.

[<label>]   CMP   <destination>,<source>   [<comment>]

<destination> identifies the location of the left-hand operand of the comparison, and

<source> identifies the location of the right-hand operand of the comparison.

The types of the two operands must match (i.e., both must be byte or both must be word).

<destination>	<source>
General register	General register
	Memory location
	Immediate
Memory location	General register
	Immediate

OF	DF	IF	TF	SF	ZF	AF	PF	CF
R	U	U	U	R	R	R	R	R

CMPS/CMPSB
Compare String Byte

Compares the byte identified by the DS:SI register pair to
the byte identified by the ES:DI register pair, and sets the
flags accordingly. The byte identified by the ES:DI register
pair is subtracted from the byte identified by the DS:SI
register pair, and the flags are set to reflect the
difference. Neither byte is modified. If the direction flag
(DF) is 0, both the SI and DI registers are incremented by
1; if DF is 1, both the SI and DI registers are decremented
by 1.

[<label>]   CMPS   <source>,<destination>   [<comment>]

[<label>]   CMPSB   [<comment>]

   <source>   identifies the byte array addressed by the
                  DS:SI register pair, and
   <destination> identifies the byte array addressed by the
                  ES:DI register pair.

	OF	DF	IF	TF	SF	ZF	AF	PF	CF	
	R	U	U	U	R	R	R	R	R	

CMPS/CMPSW
Compare String Word

Compares the word identified by the DS:SI register pair to
the word identified by the ES:DI register pair, and sets the
flags accordingly. The word identified by the ES:DI register
pair is subtracted from the word identified by the DS:SI
register pair, and the flags are set to reflect the
difference. Neither word is modified. If the direction flag
(DF) is 0, both the SI and DI registers are incremented by
2; if DF is 1, both the SI and DI registers are decremented
by 2.

[<label>]   CMPS   <source>,<destination>   [<comment>]

[<label>]   CMPSW   [<comment>]

   <source>   identifies the word array addressed by the
                  DS:SI register pair, and
   <destination> identifies the word array addressed by the
                  ES:DI register pair.

	OF	DF	IF	TF	SF	ZF	AF	PF	CF	
	R	U	U	U	R	R	R	R	R	

CWD
Convert Word to Double Word

Expands the signed, 16-bit integer in the AX-Register to a signed, 32-bit integer in the DX:AX register pair. Extends the sign bit (bit 15 of the AX-register) into bits 0-15 of the DX-register.

[<label>]   CWD   [<comment>]

OF	DF	IF	TF	SF	ZF	AF	PF	CF
U	U	U	U	U	U	U	U	U

DAA
Decimal Adjust for Addition

Adjusts the result of a previous addition of two packed BCD digit pairs. Adjusts the AL-register to contain a valid pair of packed BCD digits. The carry from this digit pair is recorded in the CF bit of the flags register. DAA causes the following steps to be performed:

```
    IF    (lower nibble of AL-REG > 9) or (AF = 1)
    THEN
          AL-REG is incremented by 6
          AF is set to 1
    ENDIF
    IF    (upper nibble of AL-REG > 9) or (CF = 1)
    THEN
          AL-REG is incremented by 60 hex
          CF is set to 1
    ENDIF
```

[<label>]   DAA   [<comment>]

The operand is implied by the instruction. It is always the contents of the AL-register.

OF	DF	IF	TF	SF	ZF	AF	PF	CF
UD	U	U	U	R	R	R	R	R

DAS
Decimal Adjust for Subtraction

```
Adjusts the result of a previous subtraction   of   two   packed
BCD digit pairs.   Adjusts the AL-register to contain   a valid
pair of packed BCD digits. The borrow into this digit pair is
recorded in the CF bit of the flags register.   DAS causes the
following steps to be performed:
    IF    (lower nibble of AL-REG > 9) or (AF = 1)
    THEN
        AL-REG is decremented by 6
        AF is set to 1
    ENDIF
    IF    (upper nibble of AL-REG > 9) or (CF = 1)
    THEN
        AL-REG is decremented by 60 hex
        CF is set to 1
    ENDIF
```

```
[<label>]       DAS                                    [<comment>]
```

```
The operand is implied by the instruction.   It is   always the
contents of the AL-register.
```

OF	DF	IF	TF	SF	ZF	AF	PF	CF
UD	U	U	U	R	R	R	R	R

DEC
Decrement

```
Decrements the value   in the specified   register   or   memory
location by 1.
```

```
[<label>]       DEC     <destination>                  [<comment>]
```

```
    <destination> identifies the location of the value   to be
                  decremented.
```

<destination>

| General register |
| Memory location |

OF	DF	IF	TF	SF	ZF	AF	PF	CF
R	U	U	U	R	R	R	R	U

DIV
Divide

For a byte operand, divides the 16-bit, unsigned integer value in the AX-register by the 8-bit, unsigned integer value of the operand, and leaves the quotient in the AL-register and the remainder in the AH-register.

For a word operand, divides the 32-bit, unsigned integer value in the DX:AX register pair by the 16-bit, unsigned integer value of the operand, and leaves the quotient in the AX-register and the remainder in the DX-register.

[<label>]   DIV   <source>   [<comment>]

   <source>   identifies the location of the divisor.

<source>

| General register |
| Memory   location |

OF	DF	IF	TF	SF	ZF	AF	PF	CF
UD	U	U	U	UD	UD	UD	UD	UD

HLT
Halt

Stops the instruction execution cycle of the microprocessor. The microprocessor waits for an interrupt before continuing.

[<label>]   HLT   [<comment>]

OF	DF	IF	TF	SF	ZF	AF	PF	CF
U	U	U	U	U	U	U	U	U

IDIV
Integer Divide

For a byte operand, divides the 16-bit, signed integer value in the AX-register by the 8-bit, signed integer value of the operand, and leaves the quotient in the AL-register and the remainder in the AH-register. For a word operand, divides the 32-bit, signed integer value in the DX:AX register pair by the 16-bit, signed integer value of the operand, and leaves the quotient in the AX-register and the remainder in the DX-register.

[<label>]   IDIV   <source>   [<comment>]

    <source>   identifies the location of the divisor.

<source>

    General register

    Memory   location

OF	DF	IF	TF	SF	ZF	AF	PF	CF
UD	U	U	U	UD	UD	UD	UD	UD

IMUL
Integer Multiply

For a byte operand, multiplies the signed integer value in the AL-register by the 8-bit, signed integer value specified by the operand, and leaves the 16-bit product in the AX-register. For a word operand, multiplies the signed integer value in the AX-register by the 16-bit, signed integer value specified by the operand, and leaves the 32-bit product in the DX:AX register pair.

[<label>]   IMUL   <source>   [<comment>]

    <source>   identifies the location of the multiplier.

<source>

    General register

    Memory   location

OF	DF	IF	TF	SF	ZF	AF	PF	CF
R	U	U	U	UD	UD	UD	UD	R

IN
Input Byte or Word from Port

Transfers a byte from the specified port to the AL-register,
or transfers a word from the specified port pair to the
AX-register.

| [<label>] | IN | AL,<port> | [<comment>] |

| [<label>] | IN | AX,<port> | [<comment>] |

   <port>   specifies   the   port   number   for   a byte
transfer or the first of two consecutive
ports for a word transfer.

The <port> operand can be an immediate value in the range
0-255 or the register designator DX.

	OF	DF	IF	TF	SF	ZF	AF	PF	CF	
	U	U	U	U	U	U	U	U	U	

INC
Increment

Increments the value in the specified register or memory
location by 1.

| [<label>] | INC | <destination> | [<comment>] |

   <destination> identifies the location of the value to be
incremented.

<destination>

General register
Memory location

	OF	DF	IF	TF	SF	ZF	AF	PF	CF	
	R	U	U	U	R	R	R	R	U	

INS/INSB
Input String Byte (PC-AT Only)

Transfers the byte value at the port addressed by the value
of the DX-register to the memory byte addressed by the ES:DI
register pair.   If the direction flag (DF) is 0, the
DI-register is incremented by 1; if DF is 1, the DI-register
is decremented by 1.

[<label>]   INS   <destination>,DX   [<comment>]

[<label>]   INSB   [<comment>]

    <destination> is the symbolic name that identifies the
                  byte array addressed by the ES:DI register
                  pair.

OF	DF	IF	TF	SF	ZF	AF	PF	CF
U	U	U	U	U	U	U	U	U

INS/INSW
Input String Word (PC-AT Only)

Transfers the word value at the port-pair addressed by the
value of the DX-register to the memory word addressed by the
ES:DI register pair. If the direction flag (DF) is 0,
the DI-register is incremented by 2; if DF is 1, the
DI-register is decremented by 2.

[<label>]   INS   <destination>,DX   [<comment>]

[<label>]   INSW   [<comment>]

    <destination> is the symbolic name that identifies the
                  word array addressed by the ES:DI register
                  pair.

OF	DF	IF	TF	SF	ZF	AF	PF	CF
U	U	U	U	U	U	U	U	U

INT
Interrupt

Pushes the flags register value onto the stack, clears the
trap flag and the interrupt flag, pushes the CS-register
value onto the stack, multiplies the interrupt type by 4 to
compute the address of the interrupt vector, loads the
second word of the interrupt vector into the CS-register,
pushes the IP-register value onto the stack, and loads the
first word of the interrupt vector into the IP-register.

[<label>]   INT   <int-type>   [<comment>]

   <int-type>   is an integer in the range 0 - 255 that
                     identifies the interrupt.

The interrupt type identifies an interrupt vector that
contains the segment and offset of the service procedure for
the specified type of interrupt.

OF	DF	IF	TF	SF	ZF	AF	PF	CF
U	U	C	C	U	U	U	U	U

INTO
Interrupt on Overflow

If the overflow flag (OF) is set, then the INTO instruction
causes the processor to perform the following steps:
Pushes the flags register value onto the stack, clears the
trap flag and the interrupt flag, pushes the CS-register
value onto the stack, loads the second word of the Type 4
interrupt vector into the CS-register, pushes the
IP-register value onto the stack, and loads the first word
of the Type 4 interrupt vector into the IP-register. If OF
is not set, then no operation is performed for INTO.

[<label>]   INTO   [<comment>]

OF	DF	IF	TF	SF	ZF	AF	PF	CF
U	U	C/U	C/U	U	U	U	U	U

IRET
Interrupt Return

Pops the top-of-stack item into the IP-register, pops the
new top-of-stack item into the CS-register, and pops the new
top-of-stack item into the flags register.

[<label>]   IRET   [<comment>]

	OF	DF	IF	TF	SF	ZF	AF	PF	CF	
	SV	SV	SV	SV	SV	SV	SV	SV	SV	

Jxxx
Conditional JUMP
(Unsigned Integer)

This group of conditional JUMP instructions provides the
capability to make decisions based on the results of
computations involving unsigned numbers.

[<label>]   Jxxx   <short label>   [<comment>]

    <short label> is the label of an instruction whose memory
                  location is within -128 to 127 bytes from
                  the memory location immediately following
                  the conditional JUMP instruction.

	OF	DF	IF	TF	SF	ZF	AF	PF	CF	
	U	U	U	U	U	U	U	U	U	

Operation
Code	Description	Will Jump If
JA/JNBE	Jump if Above Jump if Not Below nor Equal	CF = 0 and ZF = 0
JAE/JNB	Jump if Above or Equal Jump if Not Below	CF = 0
JB/JNAE	Jump if Below Jump if Not Above nor Equal	CF = 1
JBE/JNA	Jump if Below or Equal Jump if Not Above	CF = 1 or ZF = 1
JE/JZ	Jump if Equal to Zero	ZF = 1
JNE/JNZ	Jump if Not Equal to Zero	ZF = 0

```
                              Jxxx
                        Conditional JUMP
                        (Signed Integer)
```

This group of conditional JUMP instructions provides the capability to make decisions based on the results of computations involving signed numbers.

[<label>]   Jxxx   <short label>   [<comment>]

    <short label> is the label of an instruction whose memory
                location is within -128 to 127 bytes from
                the memory location immediately following
                the conditional JUMP instruction.

OF	DF	IF	TF	SF	ZF	AF	PF	CF
U	U	U	U	U	U	U	U	U

Operation Code	Description	Will Jump If
JG/JNLE	Jump if Greater than Jump if Not Less nor Equal	ZF = 0 and SF = OF
JGE/JNL	Jump if Greater than or Equal Jump if Not Less than	(SF xor OF) = 0 (i.e., SF = OF)
JL/JNGE	Jump if Less than Jump if Not Greater nor Equal	(SF xor OF) = 1 (i.e., SF <> OF)
JLE/JNG	Jump if Less than or Equal Jump if Not Greater than	ZF = 1 or SF <> OF
JE/JZ	Jump if Equal to Zero	ZF = 1
JNE/JNZ	Jump if Not Equal to Zero	ZF = 0

```
                              Jxx
                        Conditional JUMP
                        (Specific Flag)
```

This group of conditional JUMP instructions provides the capability to make decisions based on the current state of a specific flag in the flags register.

```
[<label>]        Jxx      <short label>                    [<comment>]

     <short label> is the label of an instruction whose memory
                   location is within -128 to 127 bytes from
                   the memory location immediately following
                   the conditional JUMP instruction.
```

	OF	DF	IF	TF	SF	ZF	AF	PF	CF
	U	U	U	U	U	U	U	U	U

Operation

Code	Description	Will Jump If
JC	Jump if Carry	CF = 1
JNC	Jump if No Carry	CF = 0
JO	Jump if Overflow	OF = 1
JNO	Jump if No Overflow	OF = 0
JS	Jump if negative Sign	SF = 1
JNS	Jump if Nonnegative Sign	SF = 0
JZ	Jump if Zero	ZF = 1
JNZ	Jump if Not Zero	ZF = 0
JP/JPE	Jump if Parity Even	PF = 1
JNP/JPO	Jump if Parity Odd	PF = 0

JCXZ
Jump if CX-Register Zero

If the value in the CX-register is zero, then control is transferred to the instruction that begins at the memory location specified by the operand.

```
[<label>]      JCXZ    <short label>              [<comment>]

   <short label> is the label of an instruction whose memory
                 location is within -128 to 127 bytes from
                 the memory location immediately following
                 the JCXZ instruction.
```

OF	DF	IF	TF	SF	ZF	AF	PF	CF
U	U	U	U	U	U	U	U	U

JMP

Control is unconditionally transferred to the instruction
that begins at the memory location specified by the operand.

[<label>]   JMP   <target>   [<comment>]

    <target>   is the label of the instruction to which
                        control is being transferred (direct jump)
                        or an address expression that specifies the
                        memory location that contains the address
                        of the instruction to which control is
                        being transferred (indirect jump).

<target>	Description
Label with type attribute NEAR	The machine language operand is the difference between the offset of the memory location specified by target and the offset of the memory location immediately following the JMP instruction. At execution this difference is added to the IP-reg.
Label with type attribute FAR	The machine language operand is the segment and offset of the specified target. At execution, this segment and offset replace the value in the CS:IP register pair.
Address expression of variable with attribute WORD	The machine language operand is the segment register number and offset of the variable. At execution, the contents of the memory location specified by this segment and offset replace the value in the IP-register.
Address expression of variable with attribute DBL WORD	The machine language operand is the segment register number and offset of the variable. At execution, the contents of the memory location specified by this segment and offset replaces the value of the CS:IP pair.
General register (16-bit register)	The contents of the general register replaces value in the IP-register.

OF	DF	IF	TF	SF	ZF	AF	PF	CF
U	U	U	U	U	U	U	U	U

LAHF
Load AH-Register from Flags

Loads the AH-register with a copy of the value in the low-order half of the flags register.

[<label>]   LAHF   [<comment>]

OF	DF	IF	TF	SF	ZF	AF	PF	CF
U	U	U	U	U	U	U	U	U

LDS
Load Pointer Using Data Segment Register

Load the 16-bit general register specified by the destination operand with a copy of the lower 16 bits of the doubleword in memory addressed by the source operand. Loads the DS-register with a copy of the upper 16 bits of the doubleword in memory addressed by the source operand.

[<label>]   LDS   <destination>,<source>   [<comment>]

   <destination> is the designator of the 16-bit general
                  register that is to receive the offset
                  portion of the value of the pointer, and
   <source>   is an address expression that identifies a
                  doubleword memory operand that contains the
                  pointer (segment and offset of a physical
                  memory location).

OF	DF	IF	TF	SF	ZF	AF	PF	CF
U	U	U	U	U	U	U	U	U

LEA
Load Effective Address

Computes the offset of the memory location specified by the source operand. Loads this offset into the 16-bit register specified as the destination operand.

[<label>]   LEA   <destination>,<source>   [<comment>]

   <destination> is the designator of the 16-bit register whose value is to be replaced by the offset, and

   <source>   is the address expression from which the offset is to be computed.

OF	DF	IF	TF	SF	ZF	AF	PF	CF
U	U	U	U	U	U	U	U	U

LES
Load Pointer Using Extra Segment Register

Load the 16-bit general register specified by the destination operand with a copy of the lower 16 bits of the doubleword in memory addressed by the source operand. Loads the ES-register with a copy of the upper 16 bits of the doubleword in memory addressed by the source operand.

[<label>]   LES   <destination>,<source>   [<comment>]

   <destination> is the designator of the 16-bit general register that is to receive the offset portion of the value of the pointer, and

   <source>   is an address expression that identifies a doubleword memory operand that contains the pointer (segment and offset of a physical memory location).

OF	DF	IF	TF	SF	ZF	AF	PF	CF
U	U	U	U	U	U	U	U	U

LODS/LODSB
Load String Byte

Loads the AL-register with the byte addressed by the DS:SI register pair. If the direction flag (DF) is 0, the SI-register is incremented by 1; if DF is 1, the SI-register is decremented by 1.

[<label>]   LODS   <source>   [<comment>]

[<label>]   LODSB   [<comment>]

    <source>   identifies the byte array addressed by the
                   DS:SI register pair.

OF	DF	IF	TF	SF	ZF	AF	PF	CF
U	U	U	U	U	U	U	U	U

LODS/LODSW
Load String Word

Loads the AX-register with the word addressed by the DS:SI register pair. If the direction flag (DF) is 0, the SI-Register is incremented by 2; if DF is 1, the SI-Register is decremented by 2.

[<label>]   LODS   <source>   [<comment>]

[<label>]   LODSW   [<comment>]

    <source>   identifies the word array addressed by the
                   DS:SI register pair.

OF	DF	IF	TF	SF	ZF	AF	PF	CF
U	U	U	U	U	U	U	U	U

LOOP

The value in the CX-register is decremented by 1. If the
resulting value in the CX-register is nonzero, then control
is transferred to the instruction that begins at the memory
location specified by the operand.

[<label>]   LOOP   <short label>   [<comment>]

   <short label> is the label of an instruction whose memory
                 location is within -128 to 127 bytes from
                 the memory location immediately following
                 the LOOP instruction.

OF	DF	IF	TF	SF	ZF	AF	PF	CF
U	U	U	U	U	U	U	U	U

LOOPE/LOOPZ
Loop on Equal/Loop on Zero

The value in the CX-register is decremented by 1. If the
resulting value in the CX-register is nonzero and ZF = 1,
then control is transferred to the instruction that begins
at the memory location specified by the operand.

[<label>]   LOOPE   <short label>   [<comment>]

[<label>]   LOOPZ   <short label>   [<comment>]

   <short label> is the label of an instruction whose memory
                 location is within -128 to 127 bytes from
                 the memory location immediately following
                 the LOOPE (LOOPZ) instruction.

OF	DF	IF	TF	SF	ZF	AF	PF	CF
U	U	U	U	U	U	U	U	U

```
                              LOOPNE/LOOPNZ
                    Loop on Not Equal/Loop on Not Zero
```

The value in the CX-register is decremented by 1. If the resulting value in the CX-register is nonzero and ZF = O, then control is transferred to the instruction that begins at the memory location specified by the operand.

```
[<label>]        LOOPNE   <short label>                    [<comment>]

[<label>]        LOOPNZ   <short label>                    [<comment>]

    <short label> is the label of an instruction whose memory
                  location is within -128 to 127 bytes from
                  the memory location immediately following
                  the LOOPNE (LOOPNZ) instruction.
```

	OF	DF	IF	TF	SF	ZF	AF	PF	CF	
	U	U	U	U	U	U	U	U	U	

MOV
Move Byte or Word

Replaces the value of the destination operand with a copy of
the value of the source operand.

[<label>]   MOV   <destination>,<source>   [<comment>]

    <source>   identifies the location of the value that
                    is to be copied, and
    <destination> identifies where the value is to be moved.

    The types of the two operands must match (i.e., both must
    be byte or both must be word).

<destination>	<source>
General register	General register Segment register Memory location Immediate
Segment register	General register Memory location
Memory location	General register Segment register Immediate

OF	DF	IF	TF	SF	ZF	AF	PF	CF
U	U	U	U	U	U	U	U	U

MOVS/MOVSB
Move String Byte

Replaces the byte addressed by the ES:DI register pair with
a copy of the byte addressed by the DS:SI register pair.   If
the direction flag (DF) is 0, both the SI and DI registers
are incremented by 1; if DF is 1, both the SI and DI are
decremented by 1.

[<label>]   MOVS   <destination>,<source>   [<comment>]

[<label>]   MOVSB   [<comment>]

    <destination> identifies the byte array addressed by the
               ES:DI register pair, and
    <source>   identifies the byte array addressed by the
               DS:SI register pair.

OF	DF	IF	TF	SF	ZF	AF	PF	CF
U	U	U	U	U	U	U	U	U

MOVS/MOVSW
Move String Word

Replaces the word addressed by the ES:DI register pair with
a copy of the word addressed by the DS:SI register pair.   If
the direction flag (DF) is 0, both the SI and DI registers
are incremented by 2; if DF is 1, both the SI and DI are
decremented by 2.

[<label>]   MOVS   <destination>,<source>   [<comment>]

[<label>]   MOVSW   [<comment>]

    <destination> identifies the word array addressed by the
               ES:DI register pair, and
    <source>   identifies the word array addressed by the
               DS:SI register pair.

OF	DF	IF	TF	SF	ZF	AF	PF	CF
U	U	U	U	U	U	U	U	U

MUL
Multiply

For a byte operand, multiplies the unsigned integer value in
the AL-register by the 8-bit, unsigned integer value specified by the operand, and leaves the 16-bit product in the
AX-register. For a word operand, multiplies the unsigned
integer value in the AX-register by the 16-bit, unsigned
integer value specified by the operand, and leaves the
32-bit product in the DX:AX register pair.

[<label>]   MUL   <source>   [<comment>]

   <source>   identifies the location of the multiplier.

<source>

General register
Memory location

OF	DF	IF	TF	SF	ZF	AF	PF	CF
R	U	U	U	UD	UD	UD	UD	R

NEG
Negate

Performs the two's complement of the value in the specified
register or memory location, leaving the result in the
specified register or memory location.

[<label>]   NEG   <destination>   [<comment>]

   <destination> identifies the location of the value to be
                 negated.

<destination>

General register
Memory location

OF	DF	IF	TF	SF	ZF	AF	PF	CF
R	U	U	U	R	R	R	R	R

```
                              NOP
                          No Operation
_____
 Causes  the  microprocessor  to do nothing (i.e.,  to perform   no
 operation).   In effect,   the instruction causes   a delay of 3
 clock cycles.   Produces the same machine code as   XCHG AX,AX.
 ..................................................................
 [<label>]       NOP                                  [<comment>]


 _____
       : OF : DF : IF : TF : SF : ZF : AF : PF : CF :
       :____:____:____:____:____:____:____:____:____:
       : U  : U  : U  : U  : U  : U  : U  : U  : U  :
 _____:____:____:____:____:____:____:____:____:____:_____
```

```
                              NOT
                          Logical NOT
_____
 Performs the one's complement of the value in the    specified
 register or   memory   location,   leaving   the result   in  the
 specified register or memory location.
 ..................................................................
 [<label>]       NOT      <destination>               [<comment>]

     <destination> identifies the location of the value   to be
                   logically inverted.


 _____

                         <destination>
                      _____
                      : General register :
                      :_____:
                      : Memory   location :
                      :_____:


 _____
       : OF : DF : IF : TF : SF : ZF : AF : PF : CF :
       :____:____:____:____:____:____:____:____:____:
       : U  : U  : U  : U  : U  : U  : U  : U  : U  :
 _____:____:____:____:____:____:____:____:____:____:_____
```

OR
Logical OR

Inclusive ORS each bit of the destination operand with the corresponding bit of the source operand, replacing the bit in the destination operand with the result.

[<label>]   OR   <destination>,<source>   [<comment>]

   <destination> identifies the location of the operand that is to be replaced with the result, and
   <source>   identifies the location of the operand that is not to be modified.

   The types of the two operands must match (i.e., both must be byte or both must be word).

<destination>	<source>
General register	General register Memory location Immediate
Memory location	General register Immediate

OF	DF	IF	TF	SF	ZF	AF	PF	CF
C	U	U	U	R	R	UD	R	C

OUT
Output Byte or Word to Port

Transfers a byte from the AL-register to the specified port, or transfers a word from the AX-register to the specified port pair.

[<label>]   OUT   <port>,AL   [<comment>]

[<label>]   OUT   <port>,AX   [<comment>]

   <port>   specifies the port number for a byte transfer or the first of two consecutive ports for a word transfer.

The <port> operand can be an immediate value in the range 0 to 255, or the register designator DX.

OF	DF	IF	TF	SF	ZF	AF	PF	CF
U	U	U	U	U	U	U	U	U

OUTS/OUTSB
Output String Byte (PC-AT Only)

Transfers the byte addressed by the DS:SI register pair to the port addressed by the value of the DX-Register. If the the direction flag (DF) is 0, the SI-Register is incremented by 1; if the DF is 1, the SI-Register is decremented by 1.

| [<label>] | OUTS | DX,<source> | [<comment>] |
| [<label>] | OUTSB | | [<comment>] |

    <source>   is the symbolic name that identifies the byte array addressed by the DS:SI register pair.

OF	DF	IF	TF	SF	ZF	AF	PF	CF
U	U	U	U	U	U	U	U	U

OUTS/OUTSW
Output String Word (PC-AT Only)

Transfers the word addressed by the DS:SI register pair to the port-pair addressed by the value of the DX-Register. If the direction flag (DF) is 0, the SI-Register is incremented by 2; if DF is 1, the SI-Register is decremented by 2.

| [<label>] | OUTS | DX,<source> | [<comment>] |
| [<label>] | OUTSW | | [<comment>] |

    <source>   is the symbolic name that identifies the word array addressed by the DS:SI register pair.

OF	DF	IF	TF	SF	ZF	AF	PF	CF
U	U	U	U	U	U	U	U	U

POP

```
Replaces the value of the destination operand with a copy   of
the 16-bit value at the top of the stack, and   increments the
SP-register by 2.
```

```
[<label>]        POP        <destination>                    [<comment>]

    <destination> identifies where the value popped from   the
                  top of the stack is to be placed.
```

	<destination>	
	General register	
	Segment register	
	Memory location	

OF	DF	IF	TF	SF	ZF	AF	PF	CF
U	U	U	U	U	U	U	U	U

POPA
Pop All General Registers (PC-AT Only)

```
Copies   the   top-of-stack   value   into   the   DI-register, and
increments the SP-register by 2.
Copies the new top-of-stack  value into the  SI-register, and
increments the SP-register by 2.
Copies the new top-of-stack  value into the  BP-register, and
increments the SP-register by 4 (discards SP-register value).
Copies the new top-of-stack  value into the  BX-register, and
increments the SP-register by 2.
Copies the new top-of-stack  value into the  DX-register, and
increments the SP-register by 2.
Copies the new top-of-stack  value into the  CX-register, and
increments the SP-register by 2.
Copies the new top-of-stack  value into the  AX-register, and
increments the SP-register by 2.
```

```
[<label>]        POPA                                         [<comment>]
```

OF	DF	IF	TF	SF	ZF	AF	PF	CF
U	U	U	U	U	U	U	U	U

POPF
Pop Flags

Copies the top-of-stack value into the flags register, and increments the SP-register by 2.

[<label>]   POPF   [<comment>]

	OF	DF	IF	TF	SF	ZF	AF	PF	CF	
	SV	SV	SV	SV	SV	SV	SV	SV	SV	

PUSH

Decrements the SP-register by 2, and stores a copy of the value of the 16-bit operand as the new top-of-stack value.

[<label>]   PUSH   <source>   [<comment>]

   <source>   identifies the location of the data to be pushed onto the stack.

<source>

General register

Segment register

Memory location

Immediate value (PC-AT only)

	OF	DF	IF	TF	SF	ZF	AF	PF	CF	
	U	U	U	U	U	U	U	U	U	

PUSHA
Push All General Registers (PC-AT Only)

| Pushes the eight general registers onto the stack as follows: Decrements the SP-register by 2, and stores a copy of the AX-register value as the new top-of-stack value. Decrements the SP-register by 2, and stores a copy of the CX-register value as the new top-of-stack value. Decrements the SP-register by 2, and stores a copy of the DX-register value as the new top-of-stack value. Decrements the SP-register by 2, and stores a copy of the BX-register value as the new top-of-stack value. Decrements the SP-register by 2, and stores a copy of the SP-register value as the new top-of-stack value. Decrements the SP-register by 2, and stores a copy of the BP-register value as the new top-of-stack value. Decrements the SP-register by 2, and stores a copy of the SI-register value as the new top-of-stack value. Decrements the SP-register by 2, and stores a copy of the DI-register value as the new top-of-stack value. The value that is pushed for the SP-register is the value of the SP-register prior to the push of the AX-register value. |

[<label>]   PUSHA   [<comment>]

OF	DF	IF	TF	SF	ZF	AF	PF	CF
U	U	U	U	U	U	U	U	U

PUSHF
Push Flags

| Decrements the SP-register by 2, and stores a copy of the flags register value as the new top-of-stack value. |

[<label>]   PUSHF   [<comment>]

OF	DF	IF	TF	SF	ZF	AF	PF	CF
U	U	U	U	U	U	U	U	U

                              RCL
                   Rotate Through Carry Left

```
┌──────────────────────────────────────────────────────────────┐
│ Rotates the contents  of the  specified register  or  memory  │
│ location left  the number of bit positions specified by  the  │
│ shift count (1 or the value in  the CL-register).   The  last  │
│ bit shifted out on the left  is recorded in the carry  flag.   │
│ Bits shifted from the carry flag are shifted in on the right.  │
├──────────────────────────────────────────────────────────────┤
│ [<label>]      RCL      <destination>,1              [<comment>] │
│                                                                │
│ [<label>]      RCL      <destination>,CL             [<comment>] │
│                                                                │
│    <destination> specifies  the general register  or  memory  │
│                  location   that  contains  the  value  to be  │
│                  shifted.                                      │
├──────────────────────────────────────────────────────────────┤
```

Word operand

Byte operand

	OF	DF	IF	TF	SF	ZF	AF	PF	CF
	SC	U	U	U	U	U	U	U	LB

RCR
Rotate Through Carry Right

Rotates the contents of the specified register or memory location right the number of bit positions specified by the shift count (1 or the value in the CL-register). The last bit shifted out on the right is recorded in the carry flag. Bits shifted from the carry flag are shifted in on the left.

[<label>]   RCR   <destination>,1   [<comment>]

[<label>]   RCR   <destination>,CL   [<comment>]

   <destination> specifies the general register or memory
                location that contains the value to be
                shifted.

```
   15 14 13 12 11 10  9  8  7  6  5  4  3  2  1  0        CF
      _____        __
+-+->| |  |  |  |  |  |  |  |  |  |  |  |  |  |  | -+----+->|
|  |  |  |  |  |  |  |  |  |  |  |  |  |  |  |  |_|   | _|
|  |_____|   |_|
|_____|
                   Word operand
```

```
                     7  6  5  4  3  2  1  0        CF
                     _____      __
               +-+->| |  |  |  |  |  |  | -+----+->|
               |  |  |  |  |  |  |  |  |_|   | _|
               |  |_____|   |_|
               |_____|
                          Byte operand
```

OF	DF	IF	TF	SF	ZF	AF	PF	CF
SC	U	U	U	U	U	U	U	LB

REP
Repeat

This repeat prefix can be placed before the operation code
of a string instruction, and it produces the following loop:
REPEAT
    Execute following string instruction
    Decrement CX-register by 1
UNTIL CX-register is 0

[<label>]   REP <strng-op>   <operands>   [<comment>]

    <strng-op>   is the operation code of one of the string
                   instructions, and
    <operands>   is the operand list (if any) for the string
                   instruction.

The prefix REP should be used only with the MOVE, LOAD, and
STORE string instructions. If REP is used with the COMPARE
or SCAN string instructions, it behaves exactly like the
REPE/REPZ prefix.

	OF	DF	IF	TF	SF	ZF	AF	PF	CF	
	U	U	U	U	U	U	U	U	U	

REPE/REPZ
Repeat on Equal/Repeat on Zero

This repeat prefix can be placed before the operation code
of a string instruction, and it produces the following loop:
REPEAT
    Execute following string instruction
    Decrement CX-register by 1
UNTIL CX-register is 0 OR ZF is 0

[<label>]   REPE <strng-op>   <operands>   [<comment>]

[<label>]   REPZ <strng-op>   <operands>   [<comment>]

    <strng-op>   is the operation code of one of the string
                   instructions, and
    <operands>   is the operand list (if any) for the string
                   instruction.

The prefix REPE/REPZ should be used only with the COMPARE
and SCAN string instructions. If REPE/REPZ is used with the
MOVE, LOAD, or STORE string instructions, it behaves exactly
like the REP prefix.

	OF	DF	IF	TF	SF	ZF	AF	PF	CF	
	U	U	U	U	U	U	U	U	U	

REPNE/REPNZ
Repeat on Not Equal/Repeat on Not Zero

This repeat prefix can be placed before the operation code of a string instruction, and it produces the following loop:
```
REPEAT
    Execute following string instruction
    Decrement CX-register by 1
UNTIL CX-register is 0  OR  ZF is 1
```

[<label>]   REPNE <strng-op>   <operands>   [<comment>]

[<label>]   REPNZ <strng-op>   <operands>   [<comment>]

    <strng-op>   is the operation code of one of the string instructions, and

    <operands>   is the operand list (if any) for the string instruction.

The prefix REPNE/REPNZ should be used only with the COMPARE and SCAN string instructions. If REPNE/REPNZ is used with the MOVE, LOAD, or STORE string instructions, it behaves exactly like the REP prefix.

OF	DF	IF	TF	SF	ZF	AF	PF	CF
U	U	U	U	U	U	U	U	U

RET
Return

Pops the return address from the top of the stack and transfers control to the instruction at that address. Adds the value of the immediate operand to the SP-register (i.e., pops the arguments from the stack).

[<label>]   RET   [<pop-value>]   [<comment>]

   <pop-value>   is an immediate value that specifies the number of argument bytes to be popped from the stack and discarded.

Procedure Type	Operation of RET Instruction
NEAR	Pops the top-of-stack value into the IP-register, and then adds the optional operand value to the SP-register.
FAR	Pops the top-of-stack value into the IP-Register, pops the new top-of-stack value into the CS-register, and then adds the optional operand value to the SP-register.

	OF	DF	IF	TF	SF	ZF	AF	PF	CF	
	U	U	U	U	U	U	U	U	U	

ROL
Rotate Left

Rotates the contents of the specified register or memory
location left the number of bit positions specified by the
shift count (1 or the value in the CL-register). The last
bit shifted out on the left is recorded in the carry flag.
Bits shifted out on the left are shifted in on the right.

[<label>]   ROL   <destination>,1   [<comment>]

[<label>]   ROL   <destination>,CL   [<comment>]

    <destination> specifies the general register or memory
                  location that contains the value to be
                  shifted.

```
 CF        15 14 13 12 11 10  9  8  7  6  5  4  3  2  1  0

 __
|<-+--+-+- |  |  |  |  |  |  |  |  |  |  |  |  |  |  |<-+--+
|__|  |  | |__|__|__|__|__|__|__|__|__|__|__|__|__|__| |__|
   |  |  |
   |  |_____
   |
   |_____
                        Word operand


           CF         7  6  5  4  3  2  1  0

           __
          |<-+--+-+- |  |  |  |  |  |  |<-+--+
          |__|  |  | |__|__|__|__|__|__| |__|
             |  |
             |  |_____
             |
             |_____
                        Byte operand
```

OF	DF	IF	TF	SF	ZF	AF	PF	CF
SC	U	U	U	U	U	U	U	LB

ROR
Rotate Right

Rotates the contents of the specified register or memory
location right the number of bit positions specified by the
shift count (1 or the value in the CL-register).   The last
bit shifted out on the right is recorded in the carry flag.
Bits shifted out on the right are shifted in on the left.

[<label>]   ROR   <destination>,1   [<comment>]

[<label>]   ROR   <destination>,CL   [<comment>]

    <destination> specifies the general register or memory
                  location that contains the value to be
                  shifted.

| 15 14 13 12 11 10 9 8 7 6 5 4 3 2 1 0 | CF |

Word operand

| 7 6 5 4 3 2 1 0 | CF |

Byte operand

OF	DF	IF	TF	SF	ZF	AF	PF	CF
SC	U	U	U	U	U	U	U	LB

SAHF
Store AH-Register into Flags

Stores a copy of the AH-Register value in the low-order half
of the flags register.

[<label>]   SAHF   [<comment>]

OF	DF	IF	TF	SF	ZF	AF	PF	CF
U	U	U	U	R	R	R	R	R

SAL
Shift Arithmetic Left

Shifts the contents of the specified register or memory
location left the number of bit positions specified by the
shift count (1 or the value in the CL-register). The last
bit shifted out on the left is recorded in the carry flag.
Zero bits are shifted in on the right.

[<label>]   SAL   <destination>,1   [<comment>]

[<label>]   SAL   <destination>,CL   [<comment>]

   <destination> specifies the general register or memory
                 location   that   contains   the   value   to be
                 shifted.

```
   CF        15 14 13 12 11 10  9  8  7  6  5  4  3  2  1  0

 |<-+----+- | |  |  |  |  |  |  |  |  |  |  |  |  | |<-+--0 |
 |__|      | |  |  |  |  |  |  |  |  |  |  |  |  | |
                         Word operand


                     CF        7  6  5  4  3  2  1  0

                   |<-+----+- | |  |  |  |  |  | |<-+--0 |
                   |__|      | |  |  |  |  |  | |
                                  Byte operand
```

OF	DF	IF	TF	SF	ZF	AF	PF	CF
SC	U	U	U	R	R	UD	R	LB

SAR
Shift Arithmetic Right

Shifts the contents of the specified register or memory
location right the number of bit positions specified by the
shift count (1 or the value in the CL-register). The last
bit shifted out on the right is recorded in the carry flag.
A copy of the sign bit is shifted in on the left.

[<label>]   SAR   <destination>,1   [<comment>]

[<label>]   SAR   <destination>,CL   [<comment>]

    <destination> specifies the general register or memory
                  location that contains the value to be
                  shifted.

```
      15 14 13 12 11 10  9  8  7  6  5  4  3  2  1  0      CF
                                                            __
  +-+->!  !  !  !  !  !  !  !  !  !  !  !  !  !  !  ! -+----+->!
  ! !  !__!__!__!__!__!__!__!__!__!__!__!__!__!__!__!    !__!
  ! !            Word operand
  !_!


                              7  6  5  4  3  2  1  0      CF
                                                          __
                          +-+->!  !  !  !  !  !  !  ! -+----+->!
                          ! !  !__!__!__!__!__!__!__!    !__!
                          ! !        Byte operand
                          !_!
```

	OF	DF	IF	TF	SF	ZF	AF	PF	CF
	C	U	U	U	R	R	UD	R	LB

SBB
Subtract With Borrow

Subtracts the source operand and the borrow flag from the destination operand, replacing the destination operand with the difference.

[<label>]   SBB   <destination>,<source>   [<comment>]

    <source>   identifies the location of the subtrahend, and

    <destination> identifies the location of the minuend that will be replaced by the difference.

The types of the two operands must match (i.e., both must be byte or both must be word).

<destination>	<source>
General register	General register Memory location Immediate
Memory location	General register Immediate

OF	DF	IF	TF	SF	ZF	AF	PF	CF
R	U	U	U	R	R	R	R	R

SCAS/SCASB
Scan Byte String

Compares the byte in the AL-register to the byte addressed
by the ES:DI register pair, and sets the flags accordingly.
The byte addressed by the ES:DI register pair is subtracted
from the byte in the AL-register, and the flags are set to
reflect the difference. Neither byte is modified. If the
direction flag (DF) is 0, the DI-register is incremented by
1; if DF is 1, the DI-register is decremented by 1.

[<label>]   SCAS   <destination>   [<comment>]

[<label>]   SCASB   [<comment>]

   <destination> identifies the byte array addressed by the
                 ES:DI register pair.

	OF	DF	IF	TF	SF	ZF	AF	PF	CF
	R	U	U	U	R	R	R	R	R

SCAS/SCASW
Scan Word String

Compares the word in the AX-register to the word addressed
by the ES:DI register pair, and sets the flags accordingly.
The word addressed by the ES:DI register pair is subtracted
from the word in the AX-register, and the flags are set to
reflect the difference. Neither word is modified. If the
direction flag (DF) is 0, the DI-register is incremented by
2; if DF is 1, the DI-register is decremented by 2.

[<label>]   SCAS   <destination>   [<comment>]

[<label>]   SCASW   [<comment>]

   <destination> identifies the word array addressed by the
                 ES:DI register pair.

	OF	DF	IF	TF	SF	ZF	AF	PF	CF
	R	U	U	U	R	R	R	R	R

SHL
Shift Logical Left

Shifts the contents of the specified register or memory
location left the number of bit positions specified by the
shift count (1 or the value in the CL-register). The last
bit shifted out on the left is recorded in the carry flag.
Zero bits are shifted in on the right.

[<label>]   SHL   <destination>,1   [<comment>]

[<label>]   SHL   <destination>,CL   [<comment>]

   <destination> specifies the general register or memory
                 location that contains the value to be
                 shifted.

```
    CF        15 14 13 12 11 10  9  8  7  6  5  4  3  2  1  0

        ___    _____
     |<-+----+- |  |  |  |  |  |  |  |  |  |  |  |  |  |  |<-+--0
     |__|       |__|__|__|__|__|__|__|__|__|__|__|__|__|__|  |
                                Word operand

                     CF        7  6  5  4  3  2  1  0

                         ___    _____
                      |<-+----+- |  |  |  |  |  |  |<-+--0
                      |__|       |__|__|__|__|__|__|  |
                                     Byte operand
```

OF	DF	IF	TF	SF	ZF	AF	PF	CF
SC	U	U	U	R	R	UD	R	LB

SHR
Shift Logical Right

Shifts the contents of the specified register or memory
location right the number of bit positions specified by the
shift count (1 or the value in the CL-register). The last
bit shifted out on the right is recorded in the carry flag.
Zero bits are shifted in on the left.

[<label>]   SHR   <destination>,1   [<comment>]

[<label>]   SHR   <destination>,CL   [<comment>]

    <destination> specifies the general register or memory
                  location that contains the value to be
                  shifted.

```
    15 14 13 12 11 10  9  8  7  6  5  4  3  2  1  0        CF
   _____      __
 0--+->|  |  |  |  |  |  |  |  |  |  |  |  | -+----+->|
       |  |  |  |  |  |  |  |  |  |  |  |  |  |        |__|
       ‾‾‾‾‾‾‾‾‾‾‾‾‾‾‾‾‾‾‾‾‾‾‾‾‾‾‾‾‾‾‾‾‾‾‾‾‾‾‾‾
                    Word operand


                            7  6  5  4  3  2  1  0        CF
                           _____         __
                   0--+->|  |  |  |  |  |  | -+----+->|
                         |  |  |  |  |  |  |  |        |__|
                         ‾‾‾‾‾‾‾‾‾‾‾‾‾‾‾‾‾‾‾‾‾
                              Byte operand
```

OF	DF	IF	TF	SF	ZF	AF	PF	CF
SC	U	U	U	R	R	UD	R	LB

STC
Set Carry/Borrow Flag

Sets the carry flag to 1.

[<label>]   STC   [<comment>]

OF	DF	IF	TF	SF	ZF	AF	PF	CF
U	U	U	U	U	U	U	U	S

STD
Set Direction Flag

```
Sets  the  direction  flag  to 1,  which causes  the automatic
update of  the DI and/or SI registers  following execution of
a string instruction to be a decrement.
```

[<label>]   STD   [<comment>]

OF	DF	IF	TF	SF	ZF	AF	PF	CF
U	S	U	U	U	U	U	U	U

STI
Set Interrupt Flag

```
Sets  the  interrupt  flag  to  1,  which  enables  external
interrupts.  That is,  it causes  the  processor  to  accept
external interrupts.
```

[<label>]   STI   [<comment>]

OF	DF	IF	TF	SF	ZF	AF	PF	CF
U	U	S	U	U	U	U	U	U

STOS/STOSB
Store String Byte

```
Stores a copy of the byte from the AL-register into the byte
addressed by the ES:DI register pair.  If the direction flag
(DF)  is  O,  the DI-register is incremented by 1; if DF is 1,
the DI-register is decremented by 1.
```

[<label>]   STOS   <destination>   [<comment>]

[<label>]   STOSB   [<comment>]

```
   destination>   identifies the byte array addressed  by the
                  ES:DI register pair.
```

OF	DF	IF	TF	SF	ZF	AF	PF	CF
U	U	U	U	U	U	U	U	U

STOS/STOSW
Store String Word

Stores a copy of the word from the AX-register into the word addressed by the ES:DI register pair. If the direction flag (DF) is 0, the DI-register is incremented by 2; if DF is 1, the DI-register is decremented by 2.

| [<label>] | STOS | <destination> | [<comment>] |

| [<label>] | STOSW | | [<comment>] |

destination> identifies the word array addressed by the ES:DI register pair.

	OF	DF	IF	TF	SF	ZF	AF	PF	CF	
	U	U	U	U	U	U	U	U	U	

SUB
Subtract

Subtracts the source operand from the destination operand, replacing the destination operand with the difference.

| [<label>] | SUB | <destination>,<source> | [<comment>] |

<source>   identifies the location of the subtrahend, and
<destination> identifies the location of the minuend that will be replaced by the difference.

The types of the two operands must match (i.e., both must be byte or both must be word).

<destination>	<source>
General register	General register Memory location Immediate
Memory location	General register Immediate

	OF	DF	IF	TF	SF	ZF	AF	PF	CF	
	R	U	U	U	R	R	R	R	R	

TEST

ANDS each bit of the destination operand with the corresponding bit of the source operand, and sets the flags according to the result. Neither the source operand nor the destination operand is modified.

[<label>]   TEST   <destination>,<source>   [<comment>]

    <destination> identifies the location of one operand, and
    <source>   identifies the location of the other
                operand.

    The types of the two operands must match (i.e., both must
    be byte or both must be word).

<destination>	<source>
General register	General register Memory location Immediate
Memory location	General register Immediate

OF	DF	IF	TF	SF	ZF	AF	PF	CF
C	U	U	U	R	R	UD	R	C

XCHG
Exchange

Exchanges the values of the two operands.

[<label>]   XCHG   <destination>,<source>   [<comment>]

   <source>   identifies the location of one of the two
                 values to be exchanged, and
   <destination> identifies the location of the other value
                 to be exchanged.

   The types of the two operands must match (i.e., both must
   be byte or both must be word).

<destination>	<source>
General register	General register
	Memory location
Memory location	General register

	OF	DF	IF	TF	SF	ZF	AF	PF	CF	
	U	U	U	U	U	U	U	U	U	

XLAT
Translate

Replaces the AL-register value with a copy of the byte addressed by the DS:BX+AL register group.

[<label>]   XLAT   [<source>]   [<comment>]

   <source>   is the symbolic name of the byte array
                 addressed by the DS:BX register pair.

	OF	DF	IF	TF	SF	ZF	AF	PF	CF	
	U	U	U	U	U	U	U	U	U	

```
                                     XOR
                               Exclusive OR
```

Exclusive ORS each bit of the destination operand with the
corresponding bit of the source operand, replacing the bit
in the destination operand with the result.

[<label>]   XOR   <destination>,<source>   [<comment>]

    <destination> identifies the location of the operand that
                  is to be replaced with the result, and
    <source>   identifies the location of the operand that
                  is not to be modified.

    The types of the two operands must match (i.e., both must
    be byte or both must be word).

<destination>	<source>
General register	General register Memory location Immediate
Memory location	General register Immediate

OF	DF	IF	TF	SF	ZF	AF	PF	CF
C	U	U	U	R	R	UD	R	C

APPENDIX B

PSEUDO-OPERATIONS

The following diagram shows the general format used in this appendix to describe the individual pseudo-operations recognized by the macro assembler.

Pseudo-Operation Code

Description of operation to be performed by the assembler

General form of pseudo-operation
 	
   Notation:
               <> encloses items supplied by programmer
               [] encloses optional items

Additional information

ASSUME

Instructs the assembler as to how the segment registers will
be associated with the assembly module segments at execution
time.

ASSUME   <seg-reg-assign-list>   [<comment>]

   <seg-reg-assign-list>   is a list of segment register
                        assignments of the form

                                <seg-reg>:<seg-name>
                                     or
                               <seg-reg>:NOTHING

   <seg-reg>   is one of the segment register
                        designators CS, SS, DS, or ES, and
   <seg-name>   is the symbolic name of a segment
                        defined   by a SEGMENT pseudo-
                        operation.

NOTHING states that the specified segment register is not
being used.

COMMENT

Provides a method for entering a sequence of comment lines
without the requirement of a semicolon (;) at the beginning
of each line.

COMMENT <delimiter> <text>
                 <text>
                 <text>
                    .
                    .
                    .
                 <text> <delimiter>

The first nonblank character following the COMMENT keyword is
taken as the <delimiter>. All subsequent characters are
taken as part of the comment, <text>, until another
occurrence of the <delimiter> is detected.

DB
Define Byte

Allocates one or more consecutive data bytes of storage, and
initializes their values.

[<var-name>] DB   <constant-list>   [<comment>]

    <var-name>   is the symbolic name to be associated
                        with the   memory location at which the
                        sequence of data bytes is to begin,   and
    <constant-list> is a   list of   constant   expressions
                        separated by commas.

<constant>	<form>
Binary	A string of binary digits followed by the letter B
Octal	A string of octal digits followed by the letter O or the letter Q
Decimal	A string of decimal digits optionally followed by the letter D
Hexadecimal	A string of hex digits followed by the letter H. The first character must be a digit 0-9.
String	A string of characters enclosed in apostrophes (') or quotation marks (")
Null	? - means that no initial value is specified for the allocated byte.
Duplicate clause	<repeat-count> DUP(<constant-list>)

DD
Define Double Word

Allocates one or more consecutive double words of storage,
and initializes their values.

[<var-name>]   DD   <constant-list>   [<comment>]

<var-name>   is the symbolic   name   to   be   associated
                    with   the   memory   location at which the
                    sequence of double words is to begin, and
<constant-list>   is a   list   of   constant   expressions
                    separated by commas.

<constant>	<form>
Binary	A string of binary digits followed by the letter B
Octal	A string of octal digits followed by the letter O or the letter Q
Decimal	A string of decimal digits optionally followed by the letter D
Hexadecimal	A string of hex digits followed by the letter H. The first character must be a digit 0-9.
Null	? - means that no initial value is specified for the allocated double word.
Duplicate clause	<repeat-count> DUP(<constant-list>)

DQ
Define Quad Word

Allocates one or more consecutive quad words (64 bits) of
storage, and initializes their values.

[<var-name>]   DQ   <constant-list>   [<comment>]

<var-name>   is the symbolic name to be associated
                   with   the   memory location at which   the
                   sequence   of   quad words is to begin, and
<constant-list>   is a   list   of   constant   expressions
                   separated by commas.

<constant>	<form>
Binary	A string of binary digits followed by the letter B
Octal	A string of octal digits followed by the letter O or the letter Q
Decimal	A string of decimal digits optionally followed by the letter D
Hexadecimal	A string of hex digits followed by the letter H. The first character must be a digit 0-9.
Null	? - means that no initial value is specified for the allocated quad word.
Duplicate clause	<repeat-count> DUP(<constant-list>)

```
                                    DT
                            Define Ten Bytes
```

Allocates one or more ten-byte data blocks of storage, and
initializes their values. Is used to define BCD variables.

[<var-name>]   DT   <dec-const-list>   [<comment>]

   <var-name>   is the symbolic name to be associated
                             with the memory location at which   the
                             sequence of data bytes is to begin, and
   <dec-const-list> is a list of decimal constants separated
                             by commas.

<dec-const>	<form>
BCD	A signed or unsigned string of up to 18 significant decimal digits
NULL	? - means that 10 bytes of storage are to be allocated but that an initial value is not specified

DW
Define Word

Allocates one or more consecutive data words of storage, and initializes their values.

[<var-name>] DW   <constant-list>   [<comment>]

   <var-name>   is the symbolic name to be associated with the memory location at which the sequence of data words is to begin, and

   <constant-list> is a list of constant expressions separated by commas.

<constant>	<form>
Binary	A string of binary digits followed by the letter B
Octal	A string of octal digits followed by the letter O or the letter Q
Decimal	A string of decimal digits optionally followed by the letter D
Hexadecimal	A string of hex digits followed by the letter H. The first character must be a digit 0-9.
Address	A label that represents an offset within a segment
Null	? - means that no initial value is specified for the allocated word
Duplicate clause	<repeat-count> DUP(<constant-list>)

END
End of Assembly Module

Defines the physical end of an Assembly module. It must be the last line of every Assembly language source module.

        END   [<label>]   [<comment>]

   <label>   is the symbolic name that specifies the entry point for the executable program.

ENDM
End of Macro Definition

Defines the physical end of a macro definition.	
ENDM	[<comment>]

ENDP
End of Procedure Definition

Defines the physical end of a procedure definition.	
<proc-name> ENDP	[<comment>]
<proc-name> is the symbolic name of the procedure and must match the <proc-name> on the PROC pseudo-operation at the beginning of the procedure.	

ENDS
End of Segment Definition

Defines the physical end of a segment definition.	
<seg-name> ENDS	[<comment>]
<seg-name> is the symbolic name to be associated with the segment and must match the <seg-name> used on the SEGMENT pseudo-operation at the beginning of the segment.	

EQU
Equate

Assigns a symbolic name to the value of a constant expression.	
<name> EQU <constant-expr>	[<comment>]
<name> is the symbolic name to be associated with the value of the <constant-expr>, and	
<constant-expr> is an expression that consists of constants and operators.	
The symbolic name will have the value of the constant expression throughout the entire assembly module.	

=
Equate

Assigns a symbolic name to the value of a constant expression.

<name>	=	<constant-expr>	[<comment>]

<name> is the symbolic name to be associated with the value of the <constant-expr>, and
<constant-expr> is an expression that consists of constants and operators.

From this point until it is reassigned by another = pseudo-operation, the symbolic name will have the value of the constant expression.

EVEN

Instructs the Assembler to advance the location counter to the next even address, so that the next item assembled begins on a word boundary.

EVEN	[<comment>]

The assembler inserts a NOP instruction, if necessary, to to reach a word boundary.

EXITM
Exit Macro

Is used in conjunction with a conditional assembly pseudo-operation to terminate a macro expansion under a specified condition.

EXITM	[<comment>]

EXTRN
External Declaration

Identifies symbolic names used in this assembly module whose attributes are defined in a separate assembly module.

EXTRN	<ext-name-list>	[<comment>]

<ext-name-list> is a list of external name specifications of the form <name>:<type>, and
<type> is one of the following type attributes: WORD, BYTE, DWORD, NEAR, FAR, or ABS.

May be placed anywhere in an assembly module as long as it appears before the first reference to the names that it defines.

```
                              IFxxxx
                        Conditional Assembly
```

Identifies a sequence of instructions and pseudo-operations that are to be included in or omitted from the assembly depending on a condition that can be evaluated at assembly time.

```
              IFxxxx   <argument>                    [<comment>]
                       <block>
              [ELSE                                  [<comment>]
                       <block>]
              ENDIF                                  [<comment>]
```

IFxxxx   is one of the conditional pseudo-operations from the following list,

<argument> is a constant expression, symbolic name, or macro argument used for the condition, and

<block>   is a sequence of instructions and pseudo-operations to be included in or omitted from the assembly.

Pseudo-Operation		Explanation
IF	<expr>	True if the constant expression, <expr>, evaluates to a nonzero value.
IFE	<expr>	True if the constant expression, <expr>, evaluates to zero.
IFDEF	<symbol>	True if the symbolic name, <symbol>, is defined or has been declared with EXTRN.
IFNDEF	<symbol>	True if the symbolic name, <symbol>, is not defined and has not been declared with EXTRN.
IFB	<<arg>>	The pointed brackets around <arg> are required. IFB can be used in a macro definition. True in a specific macro expansion if the operand corresponding to the dummy argument, <arg>, is blank or <>.
IFNB	<<arg>>	The pointed brackets around <arg> are required. IFNB can be used in a macro definition. True in a particular macro expansion if the operand corresponding to the dummy argument, <arg>, is not blank and not <>.

INCLUDE

Provides the capability to embed text from one source code file into the text from another source code file during the assembly process.

INCLUDE <file-spec>   [<comment>]

<file-spec> is an explicit file specification that identifies the disk drive and the file name.

The assembler replaces the INCLUDE pseudo-operation with the text from the file specified by the <file-spec> operand.

LABEL

Assigns a symbolic name to a memory location.

<name>   LABEL   <type>   [<comment>]

<type> is one of the following type attributes:
        WORD, BYTE, DWORD, NEAR, or FAR.

EXAMPLES
        ELSE   LABEL   NEAR
                  MOV   AX,1

        is equivalent to

        ELSE:
                  MOV   AX,1

        BTABLE   LABEL   BYTE
        WTABLE   DW   100 DUP(?)

        allows the array to be accessed by byte or by word.

LOCAL

Identifies dummy labels used in a macro body.   The assembler
generates a unique label for each occurrence of a dummy label
as part of macro expansion.

        LOCAL   <dummy-label-list>   [<comment>]

   <dummy-label-list> is a list of dummy labels separated by
                      commas.

The LOCAL pseudo-operation cannot be used   outside a macro
definition: It must appear between the MACRO pseudo-operation
that marks the beginning of the macro definition and the
first instruction of the macro body. The labels generated by
the assembler are the labels in the range ??0000 - ??FFFF.

MACRO

Defines the beginning of a macro definition,   and   identifies
the macro arguments.

<mac-name>   MACRO   <arg-list>   [<comment>]

   <mac-name> is the   symbolic   name of   the macro (the user-
              defined operation code), and
   <arg-list> is a list of dummy arguments separated by
              commas.

The dummy arguments in the <arg-list> are symbolic names that
are used as operation codes or operands in the instructions
of the macro body. These dummy arguments are replaced by
actual arguments whenever macro expansion occurs.

PAGE

Defines the page size for the assembler-generated listing.

        PAGE   <lines/page>,<char/line>   [<comment>]

   <lines/page> is an integer constant in the range   10 - 255
                that   specifies   the maximum number   of lines
                per page for the listing, and
   <char/line> is an integer constant in the range   60 - 132
                that   specifies   the   maximum   number   of
                characters per line for the listing.

```
                              PROC
                     Procedure Definition
```

Defines the beginning of a procedure definition and indicates the type of the procedure.

```
<proc-name>    PROC     <type-attr>                    [<comment>]

   <proc-name>   is the symbolic name by which the procedure
                 is invoked.
```

<type-attr>	meaning
NEAR (DEFAULT)	The procedure is local to this code segment and can only be invoked by the procedures in this code segment.
FAR	The procedure can be made available to be invoked by procedures in any code segment in the program.

```
                             PUBLIC
```

Identifies symbolic names defined in the assembly module that are to be made available for use in other assembly modules.

```
              PUBLIC   <name-list>                    [<comment>]

   <name-list> is a  list  of  symbolic  names  separated  by
               commas.
```

May be placed anywhere in an assembly module.

PURGE

Deletes the named macro definitions from the assembler's macro table.

          PURGE   <macro-name-list>   [<comment>]

   <macro-name-list> is a list of macro names separated by
                    commas.

Any name in the <macro-name-list> that corresponds to an   IBM
PC instruction mnemonic or assembler pseudo-operation that
was redefined by a macro definition reverts to its original
function.

.RADIX

Allows the programmer to change the default radix from
decimal to any base within the range 2 - 16.

          .RADIX   <constant-expr>   [<comment>]

   <constant-expr> is a constant expression that evaluates to
                    an integer in the range 2 - 16.

The <constant-expr> always uses a radix of 10 (decimal),
regardless of the current default radix. The .RADIX pseudo-
operation does not affect the DD, DQ, or DT pseudo-operations.

SEGMENT
Segment Definition

Defines the beginning of a segment definition and defines the relationships of this segment to other segments in the executable program.

<seg-name>   SEGMENT [<align>] [<combine>] [<class>]

<seg-name>	is the symbolic name to be associated with the memory location at which the segment is to begin,
<align>	identifies the type of boundary for the beginning of the segment,
<combine>	indicates the way in which this segment is to be combined with other segments by the linker program (LINK), and
<class>	is a symbolic name used to group segments at link time. All segments with the same class name are placed contiguous in memory.

<align>	Beginning Address
PAGE	XXX00
PARA	XXXX0 (DEFAULT)
WORD	XXXXE
BYTE	XXXXX

in which X is any hexadecimal digit,
          E is any even hexadecimal digit, and
          0 is the hexadecimal digit 0.

<combine>	Meaning
Blank	Indicates the segment is to be logically separate from other segments, regardless of its placement relative to other segments.
PUBLIC	Indicates that this segment is to be combined with other segments having the same <seg-name> and <class,> producing a single, physical segment.
COMMON	Indicates that this segment is to be overlayed with other segments having the same <seg-name> and <class>. Each of the overlayed segments begins at the same address.
STACK	Indicates that the segment is to be part of the run-time stack segment for the program.
AT <expr>	Indicates that the segment is to begin at the paragraph specified by the value of <expr>.

TITLE

Specifies a title for the assembler-generated listing.

            TITLE   <text>

    <text> is the title to be placed on the   second   line of
            every page of the assembler-generated listing.

PSEUDOCODE

The comments used in the Assembly language procedures presented in this book provide a pseudocode description of the algorithm that is implemented by the procedure. The control structures used in the pseudocode are described in this appendix.

A program is a sequence of control structures. A subprogram is either a function or a procedure. The pseudocode for a function subprogram is as follows:

```
FUNCTION <f-name> (<arg-list>)
    <sequence of control structures>
    RETURN (<value>)
END <f-name>
```

in which

<f-name>	is the symbolic name of the function,
<arg-list>	is the list of symbolic names that is used for the arguments of the function,
<sequence of control structures>	describes the algorithm implemented by the function, and
<value>	is an expression that specifies the value being returned by the function.

The pseudocode for a procedure subprogram is as follows:

```
PROCEDURE <p-name> (<arg-list>)
    <sequence of control structures>
    RETURN
END <p-name>
```

in which

<p-name>	is the symbolic name of the procedure,
<arg-list>	is the list of symbolic names that is used for the arguments of the procedure, and
<sequence of control structures>	describes the algorithm implemented by the procedure.

A <control structure> is either a simple sequence, a decision structure, or a loop structure. The pseudocode statements to be used for each of these control structures are described in the following pages.

Simple Sequence
A simple sequence is a set of instructions that contains no
transfer of control instructions. The instructions are
executed strictly in the sequence that they appear. The
comment on an instruction or group of instructions in a
simple sequence describes the logical steps of the algorithm
that   are performed by that instruction or group   of
instructions.   The pseudocode statements for sequential
instructions include the following:

Statement	Meaning
GET <symbol>	Inputs a value into the memory location specified by <symbol>.
DISPLAY <symbol>	Displays, on the screen, the value in the memory location specified by <symbol>.
DISPLAY <string>	Displays, on the screen, the character string specified by <string>.
PRINT <symbol>	Prints, at the printer, the value in the memory location specified by <symbol>.
PRINT <string>	Prints, at the printer, the character string specified by <string>.
<symbol> = <expression>	The <expression> is evaluated and the resulting value is assigned as the value of the memory location specified by <symbol>.
CALL <p-name> (<arg-list>)	Invokes the <p-name> procedure, and passes to it the data items specified in <arg-list>.

In an <expression>, an operand can be a variable, <symbol>,
or a function reference of the form <f-name> (<arg-list>).
The value of a function reference is the value returned by
the function when invoked with the arguments of <arg-list>.

In an <expression>, +, -, and * are used for addition,
subtraction, and multiplication. Integer division is shown
with the operator /, real division is shown with the
operator //, and the remainder of an integer division is
shown with the operator mod.

EXAMPLES
        COUNT = NUMBER / 2
                means that variable COUNT is assigned
                the quotient of the division of variable
                NUMBER divided by 2.
        COUNT = NUMBER mod 2
                means that variable COUNT is assigned
                the   remainder of the division of
                variable NUMBER divided by 2.

Decision Structures
There are two simple decision structures that are used in the pseudocode.

Single-Alternative Decision

A single-alternative decision structure either performs a sequence of control structures or skips that sequence of control structures depending on the value of a condition. If the condition evaluates to True, then the sequence of control structures is performed. If the condition evaluates to False, then the sequence of control structures is not performed. The pseudocode for a single-alternative decision structure is as follows:

```
IF   <condition>
THEN
        <sequence of control structures>
ENDIF
```

in which
    <condition> is a logical expression that
        evaluates to either True or False and
    <sequence of control structures>
        describes the set of steps to be
        performed if the <condition> evaluates
        to True.

Double-Alternative Decision

A double-alternative decision structure selects one of two sequences of control structures depending on the value of a condition. If the condition evaluates to True, then the first sequence of control structures is selected. If the condition evaluates to False, then the second sequence of control structures is selected. The pseudocode for a double-alternative decision structure is as follows:

```
IF   <condition>
THEN
        <first sequence of control structures>
ELSE
        <second sequence of control structures>
ENDIF
```

in which
    <condition> is a logical expression,
    <first sequence of control structures>
        describes the set of steps to
        perform if the <condition> evaluates
        to True, and
    <second sequence of control structures>
        describes the set of steps to
        perform if the <condition> evaluates
        to False.

Loop Structures

Loop structures provide a mechanism for repeating a sequence of control structures based on the value of a condition. A loop consists of two parts: the loop test and the loop body. The loop body is the sequence of control structures to be repeated. The loop test is the evaluation of the condition on which the decision to execute the loop body is based. There are two loop structures used in the pseudocode appearing in this book.

WHILE Loop

With a WHILE loop, the loop test is at the top of the loop. While the condition evaluates to True, the loop body is executed. When the condition evaluates to False, the loop is terminated. Since the test is at the top of the loop, it is possible that the loop body will not be executed at all. The pseudocode for a WHILE loop is as follows:

```
WHILE <condition>
      <sequence of control structures>
ENDWHILE
```

in which
      <condition> is a logical expression and
      <sequence of control structures>
            describes the set of steps to be
            repeated while the <condition>
            evaluates to True.

REPEAT-UNTIL Loop

With a REPEAT-UNTIL loop, the loop test is at the bottom of the loop. The loop body is executed, and as long as the condition evaluates to False, the loop body is repeated. When the condition evaluates to True, the loop is terminated. Since the test is at the bottom of the loop, the loop body is always executed at least once. The pseudocode for the REPEAT-UNTIL loop is as follows:

```
REPEAT
      <sequence of control structures>
UNTIL <condition>
```

in which
      <condition> is a logical expression and
      <sequence of control structures>
            describes the set of steps to be
            repeated until the <condition> becomes
            True.

Nesting of control structures is allowed as long as one control structure is completely contained within another. That is, a nested control structure must be completely contained within the loop body of a loop structure or within one of the

alternatives of a decision structure. No overlapping of control
structures is allowed. Loop bodies and decision alternatives are
always indented at least three spaces.

EXAMPLE
The following is the pseudocode description of an algorithm to
classify each of the positive integers in the range 2 - 100 as
deficient, abundant, or perfect.

```
LOOP_COUNT = 99
NUMBER = 2
REPEAT
   DIVISOR_SUM = 1
   DIVISOR = 2
   UPPER_LIMIT = NUMBER / 2
   WHILE DIVISOR <= UPPER_LIMIT
      QUOTIENT = NUMBER / DIVISOR
      REMAINDER = NUMBER mod DIVISOR
      IF   REMAINDER = 0
      THEN
            DIVISOR_SUM = DIVISOR_SUM + DIVISOR
            IF   DIVISOR <> QUOTIENT
            THEN
                  DIVISOR_SUM = DIVISOR_SUM + QUOTIENT
            ENDIF
            UPPER_LIMIT = QUOTIENT - 1
      ENDIF
      DIVISOR = DIVISOR + 1
   ENDWHILE
   IF   DIVISOR_SUM = NUMBER
   THEN
         DISPLAY 'PERFECT'
   ELSE
         IF   DIVISOR_SUM < NUMBER
         THEN
               DISPLAY 'DEFICIENT'
         ELSE
               DISPLAY 'ABUNDANT'
         ENDIF
   ENDIF
   DISPLAY NUMBER
   NUMBER = NUMBER + 1
   LOOP_COUNT = LOOP_COUNT - 1
UNTIL LOOP_COUNT = 0
```

APPENDIX D

INPUT/OUTPUT PROCEDURES

This appendix describes the input/output procedures referenced in
the example programs used in the book. The object code for these
procedures is available on diskette.

BLANKS
    This procedure displays a specified number of blanks on the
    screen beginning at the current cursor position.

    Inputs:
        BH-register contains the active display page number.
        DX-register contains the number of blanks to be
            displayed.
    Outputs:
        The specified number of blanks is displayed on the
        screen beginning at the current cursor position.

CLEAR
    This procedure clears the display screen.

    Inputs:
        None.
    Outputs:
        The display screen is cleared.

DIV32
    This procedure performs a 32-bit, unsigned integer divide
    using the restoring method.

    Inputs:
        DX:AX register pair contains the dividend.
        CX:BX register pair contains the divisor.
    Outputs:
        DX:AX register pair contains the quotient.
        CX:BX register pair contains the remainder.

GETDEC
    This procedure accepts a 16-bit integer in signed decimal
    form from the keyboard and returns it to the caller. The
    range of integers allowed is -32,768 to + 32,767. This
    procedure does not prompt for the input; that responsibility
    belongs to the caller. Error messages are output in response
    to input errors, and then another input is accepted.

    Inputs:
        An integer in signed decimal form from the keyboard.
        No input from the caller.
    Outputs:
        AX-register contains the 16-bit, signed integer value
            received from the keyboard.

GETDEC$

This procedure accepts a 16-bit integer in unsigned decimal form from the keyboard and returns it to the caller. The range of integers allowed is 0 to 65,535. This procedure does not prompt for the input; that responsibility belongs to the caller. Error messages are output in response to input errors, and then another input is accepted.

Inputs:
        An integer in unsigned decimal form from the keyboard.
        No input from the caller.
Outputs:
        AX-register contains the 16-bit, unsigned integer value
            received from the keyboard.

GETDEC32

This procedure accepts a 32-bit integer in signed decimal form from the keyboard and returns it to the caller. The range of integers allowed is -2,147,483,648 to +2,147,483,647. This procedure does not prompt for the input; that responsibility belongs to the caller. Error messages are output in response to input errors, and then another input is accepted.

Inputs:
        An integer in signed decimal form from the keyboard.
        No input from the caller.
Outputs:
        DX:AX register pair contains the 32-bit, signed integer
            value received from the keyboard.

GETDC32$

This procedure accepts a 32-bit integer in unsigned decimal form from the keyboard and returns it to the caller. The range of integers allowed is 0 to 4,294,967,295. This procedure does not prompt for the input; that responsibility belongs to the caller. Error messages are output in response to input errors, and then another input is accepted.

Inputs:
        An integer in unsigned decimal form from the keyboard.
        No input from the caller.
Outputs:
        DX:AX register pair contains the 32-bit, unsigned
            integer value received from the keyboard.

GETSTRNG
This procedure accepts a character string from the keyboard
and returns it to the caller. Characters are accepted until
either the user presses RETURN or a total of n characters
has been entered, in which n is supplied by the caller.

Inputs:
ES:DI register pair addresses the buffer that is to
receive the input string.
CX-register contains the length of the input buffer.
Outputs:
CX-register contains the actual length of the input
string.
The specified buffer contains the character string that
was entered.

IDIV32
This procedure performs a 32-bit, signed integer divide
using the restoring method.

Inputs:
DX:AX register pair contains the dividend.
CX:BX register pair contains the divisor.
Outputs:
DX:AX register pair contains the quotient.
CX:BX register pair contains the remainder.

NEWLINE
This procedure displays a RETURN and LINE FEED to the
display.

Inputs:
None
Outputs:
A RETURN and LINE FEED are displayed on the screen at
the current cursor position.

PAUSE
This procedure displays a character string on the screen
beginning at the current cursor position, clears the BIOS
keyboard input buffer, and then waits for a keystroke before
returning to its caller.

Inputs:
ES:DI register pair addresses the first character of
the string.
CX-register contains the length of the character
string.
Outputs:
The input string is displayed on the screen beginning
at the current cursor position.

PUTBIN

This procedure displays an 8- or 16-bit integer in binary form beginning at the current cursor position.

Inputs:
> AL-register contains the 8-bit value to be displayed.
> BL-register contains 0, the code for the 8-bit display.
> or
> AX-register contains the 16-bit value to be displayed.
> BL-register contains a nonzero value, the code for the 16-bit display.

Outputs:
> The input value is displayed in binary form on the screen beginning at the current cursor position.

PUTDEC

This procedure displays a 16-bit integer in signed decimal form beginning at the current cursor position.

Inputs:
> AX-register contains the signed integer value to be displayed.
> BH-register contains the display code:
>> BH < 0 => left-justify in a 6-character field.
>> BH = 0 => display with no blanks.
>> BH > 0 => right-justify in a 6-character field.

Outputs:
> The input value is displayed in signed decimal form on the screen beginning at the current cursor position.

PUTDEC$

This procedure displays a 16-bit integer in unsigned decimal form beginning at the current cursor position.

Inputs:
> AX-register contains the unsigned integer value to be displayed.
> BH-register contains the display code:
>> BH < 0 => left-justify in a 6-character field.
>> BH = 0 => display with no blanks.
>> BH > 0 => right-justify in a 6-character field.

Outputs:
> The input value is displayed in unsigned decimal form on the screen beginning at the current cursor position.

PUTDEC32
> This   procedure displays a 32-bit integer in signed   decimal
> form beginning at the current cursor position.
>
> Inputs:
>> DX-AX   register pair contains the signed integer value
>>   to be displayed.
>> BH-register contains the display code:
>>> BH < 0 => left-justify in an 11-character field.
>>> BH = 0 => display with no blanks.
>>> BH > 0 => right-justify in an 11-character field.
>
> Outputs:
>> The input value is displayed in signed decimal form on
>> the screen beginning at the current cursor position.

PUTDC32$
> This procedure displays a 32-bit integer in unsigned decimal
> form beginning at the current cursor position.
>
> Inputs:
>> DX-AX register pair contains the unsigned integer value
>>   to be displayed.
>> BH-REG contains the display code:
>>> BH < 0 => left-justify in an 11-character field.
>>> BH = 0 => display with no blanks.
>>> BH > 0 => right-justify in an 11-character field.
>
> Outputs:
>> The input value is displayed in unsigned decimal form
>> on the screen beginning at the current cursor position.

PUTHEX
> This   procedure   displays   an   8- or 16-bit integer   in
> hexadecimal form beginning at the current cursor position.
>
> Inputs:
>> AL-register contains the 8-bit value to be displayed.
>> BL-register contains 0, the code for the 8-bit display.
> or
>> AX-register contains the 16-bit value to be displayed.
>> BL-register contains a nonzero value, the code for the
>>   16-bit display.
>
> Outputs:
>> The input value is displayed in hexadecimal form on the
>> screen beginning at the current cursor position.

PUTOCT

This procedure displays an 8- or 16-bit integer in octal form beginning at the current cursor position.

Inputs:
     AL-register contains the 8-bit value to be displayed.
     BL-register contains 0, the code for the 8-bit display.
   or
     AX-register contains the 16-bit value to be displayed.
     BL-register contains a nonzero value, the code for the
               16-bit display.
Outputs:
     The input value is displayed in octal form on the screen beginning at the current cursor position.

PUTSTRNG

This procedure displays a character string on the screen beginning at the current cursor position.

Inputs:
     ES:DI register pair addresses the first character of
               the string.
     CX-register   contains the length of the character
               string.
Outputs:
     The input string is displayed on the screen beginning at the current cursor position.

APPENDIX E

ASCII CHARACTER SET

Video Display Character Set

The following table, reprinted by permission from IBM PC Technical Reference (1502234) (c) 1981, 1982, 1983 by International Business Machines Corporation, lists the characters of the IBM PC Extended ASCII character set. These characters can be generated by both the IBM Monochrome Display and Printer Adapter and the IBM Color/Graphics Adapter.

DECIMAL VALUE →	0	16	32	48	64	80	96	112
↓ HEXADECIMAL VALUE	0	1	2	3	4	5	6	7
0 / 0	BLANK (NULL)	►	BLANK (SPACE)	0	@	P	`	p
1 / 1	☺	◄	!	1	A	Q	a	q
2 / 2	☻	↕	"	2	B	R	b	r
3 / 3	♥	‼	#	3	C	S	c	s
4 / 4	♦	¶	$	4	D	T	d	t
5 / 5	♣	§	%	5	E	U	e	u
6 / 6	♠	▬	&	6	F	V	f	v
7 / 7	•	↨	'	7	G	W	g	w
8 / 8	◘	↑	(	8	H	X	h	x
9 / 9	○	↓	)	9	I	Y	i	y
10 / A	◎	→	*	:	J	Z	j	z
11 / B	♂	←	+	;	K	[	k	{
12 / C	♀	∟	,	<	L	\	l	¦
13 / D	♪	↔	—	=	M	]	m	}
14 / E	♫	▲	.	>	N	^	n	~
15 / F	☼	▼	/	?	O	_	o	△

DECIMAL VALUE →	128	144	160	176	192	208	224	240
↓ HEXADECIMAL VALUE	8	9	A	B	C	D	E	F
0 / 0	Ç	É	á	▒	└	╨	∝	≡
1 / 1	ü	æ	í	░	┴	╤	β	±
2 / 2	é	Æ	ó	▒	┬	╥	Γ	≥
3 / 3	â	ô	ú	│	├	╙	π	≤
4 / 4	ä	ö	ñ	─	─	╘	Σ	⌠
5 / 5	à	ò	Ñ	╡	┼	╒	σ	⌡
6 / 6	å	û	ª	╢	╞	╓	μ	÷
7 / 7	ç	ù	º	╖	╟	╫	τ	≈
8 / 8	ê	ÿ	¿	╕	╚	╪	Φ	°
9 / 9	ë	Ö	⌐	╣	╔	┘	Θ	•
10 / A	è	Ü	¬	║	╩	┌	Ω	·
11 / B	ï	¢	½	╗	╦	█	δ	√
12 / C	î	£	¼	╝	╠	▄	∞	ⁿ
13 / D	ì	¥	¡	╜	═	▌	φ	²
14 / E	Ä	₧	«	╛	╬	▐	∈	■
15 / F	Å	ƒ	»	┐	╧	▀	∩	BLANK FF

IBM PC Graphics Printer Character Set

The following table summarizes the more useful control characters recognized by the IBM PC graphics printer.

ASCII Code   Interpretation

ASCII Code	Interpretation
07 hex	Sounds a beep at the printer
09 hex	Horizontal TAB; TAB stops initialized to every eight columns on the IBM PC graphics printer
0A hex	LINE FEED (advance to the next line)
0B hex	Vertical TAB; acts like LINE FEED on the IBM PC graphics printer
0C hex	FORM FEED (advance to the top of the next page)
0D hex	RETURN (return to the left margin)
0E hex	Turns on the double width print mode (40 characters per line)
0F hex	Turns on the compressed print mode (132 characters per line)
12 hex	Turns off the compressed print mode
14 hex	Turns off the double width print mode
18 hex	Clears printer buffer

The tables on the following pages list the printable characters for the IBM PC graphics printer. The ASCII codes for these characters are given in decimal, binary, and hexadecimal.

Decimal	Binary	Hex	ASCII	Decimal	Binary	Hex	ASCII
32	00100000	20		160	10100000	A0	á
33	00100001	21	!	161	10100001	A1	í
34	00100010	22	"	162	10100010	A2	ó
35	00100011	23	#	163	10100011	A3	ú
36	00100100	24	$	164	10100100	A4	ñ
37	00100101	25	%	165	10100101	A5	ñ
38	00100110	26	&	166	10100110	A6	ª
39	00100111	27	'	167	10100111	A7	º
40	00101000	28	(	168	10101000	A8	¿
41	00101001	29	)	169	10101001	A9	⌐
42	00101010	2A	*	170	10101010	AA	¬
43	00101011	2B	+	171	10101011	AB	½
44	00101100	2C	,	172	10101100	AC	¼
45	00101101	2D	-	173	10101101	AD	¡
46	00101110	2E	.	174	10101110	AE	«
47	00101111	2F	/	175	10101111	AF	»
48	00110000	30	0	176	10110000	B0	▒
49	00110001	31	1	177	10110001	B1	▓
50	00110010	32	2	178	10110010	B2	█
51	00110011	33	3	179	10110011	B3	│
52	00110100	34	4	180	10110100	B4	┤
53	00110101	35	5	181	10110101	B5	╡
54	00110110	36	6	182	10110110	B6	╢
55	00110111	37	7	183	10110111	B7	╖
56	00111000	38	8	184	10111000	B8	╕
57	00111001	39	9	185	10111001	B9	╣
58	00111010	3A	:	186	10111010	BA	║
59	00111011	3B	;	187	10111011	BB	╗
60	00111100	3C	<	188	10111100	BC	╝
61	00111101	3D	=	189	10111101	BD	╜
62	00111110	3E	>	190	10111110	BE	╛
63	00111111	3F	?	191	10111111	BF	┐

Decimal	Binary	Hex	ASCII	Decimal	Binary	Hex	ASCII
64	01000000	40	@	192	11000000	C0	∟
65	01000001	41	A	193	11000001	C1	⊥
66	01000010	42	B	194	11000010	C2	T
67	01000011	43	C	195	11000011	C3	⊢
68	01000100	44	D	196	11000100	C4	—
69	01000101	45	E	197	11000101	C5	┼
70	01000110	46	F	198	11000110	C6	⊨
71	01000111	47	G	199	11000111	C7	‖
72	01001000	48	H	200	11001000	C8	⌐
73	01001001	49	I	201	11001001	C9	╔
74	01001010	4A	J	202	11001010	CA	⩘
75	01001011	4B	K	203	11001011	CB	╦
76	01001100	4C	L	204	11001100	CC	╟
77	01001101	4D	M	205	11001101	CD	=
78	01001110	4E	N	206	11001110	CE	╬
79	01001111	4F	O	207	11001111	CF	⊥
80	01010000	50	P	208	11010000	D0	╨
81	01010001	51	Q	209	11010001	D1	╤
82	01010010	52	R	210	11010010	D2	╥
83	01010011	53	S	211	11010011	D3	╙
84	01010100	54	T	212	11010100	D4	╘
85	01010101	55	U	213	11010101	D5	╒
86	01010110	56	V	214	11010110	D6	╓
87	01010111	57	W	215	11010111	D7	╫
88	01011000	58	X	216	11011000	D8	╪
89	01011001	59	Y	217	11011001	D9	┘
90	01011010	5A	Z	218	11011010	DA	┌
91	01011011	5B	[	219	11011011	DB	█
92	01011100	5C	\	220	11011100	DC	▄
93	01011101	5D	]	221	11011101	DD	▌
94	01011110	5E	^	222	11011110	DE	▐
95	01011111	5F	_	223	11011111	DF	▀

Decimal	Binary	Hex	ASCII	Decimal	Binary	Hex	ASCII
96	01100000	60	`	224	11100000	E0	α
97	01100001	61	a	225	11100001	E1	β
98	01100010	62	b	226	11100010	E2	Γ
99	01100011	63	c	227	11100011	E3	π
100	01100100	64	d	228	11100100	E4	Σ
101	01100101	65	e	229	11100101	E5	σ
102	01100110	66	f	230	11100110	E6	μ
103	01100111	67	g	231	11100111	E7	τ
104	01101000	68	h	232	11101000	E8	Φ
105	01101001	69	i	233	11101001	E9	θ
106	01101010	6A	j	234	11101010	EA	Ω
107	01101011	6B	k	235	11101011	EB	ε
108	01101100	6C	l	236	11101100	EC	∞
109	01101101	6D	m	237	11101101	ED	∅
110	01101110	6E	n	238	11101110	EE	∈
111	01101111	6F	o	239	11101111	EF	∩
112	01110000	70	p	240	11110000	F0	≡
113	01110001	71	q	241	11110001	F1	±
114	01110010	72	r	242	11110010	F2	≥
115	01110011	73	s	243	11110011	F3	≤
116	01110100	74	t	244	11110100	F4	⌠
117	01110101	75	u	245	11110101	F5	⌡
118	01110110	76	v	246	11110110	F6	÷
119	01110111	77	w	247	11110111	F7	≈
120	01111000	78	x	248	11111000	F8	°
121	01111001	79	y	249	11111001	F9	·
122	01111010	7A	z	250	11111010	FA	·
123	01111011	7B	{	251	11111011	FB	√
124	01111100	7C	¦	252	11111100	FC	ⁿ
125	01111101	7D	}	253	11111101	FD	²
126	01111110	7E	~	254	11111110	FE	■
127	01111111	7F		255	11111111	FF	

APPENDIX F

SUPPORT SOFTWARE

Notation:
          <>   encloses items to be supplied by the user.
          []   encloses optional items.

Definitions:

1.   Filename <filename> - from 1 to 8 characters optionally
      followed by a file name extension.

2.   Filename extension - a period (.) followed by from 1 to 3
      characters.

3.   Disk drive identifier <drive-id> - the letter designator for
      the disk drive (e.g., A or B) followed by a colon (:)

4.   Explicit file specification - a disk drive identifier
      followed by a filename. If the disk drive identifier is
      omitted, then the default disk drive identifier, specified
      in the DOS prompt, is assumed.

The following characters are allowed in filenames (including the
filename extension):

   A - Z, 0 - 9, and $, &, #, @, !, %, `, ', (,), -, {, }, and _.

Disk Operating System (DOS)

```
To load and initialize DOS:
   a. Insert the DOS diskette into drive A and close the disk
      drive door.
   b. If the power is off,  then move the power switch to the
      "on" position.
      If the power is on,  then press Del  while holding down
      Ctrl and Alt.
   c. At the  DOS prompt,  enter  the  current  date  in  the
      numeric form  mm-dd-yy,  and press RETURN.
   d. At the DOS prompt,  enter the current time  in the form
      hh:mm,  and press RETURN.
```

DOS Commands

C
H
K
D
S
K
	Function: Checks the disk on the specified drive, and
	          produces a status report on the disk and on the
	          size of the memory, used and available.
	
	Command line:
	          CHKDSK [<drive-id>]

C L S	Function: Clears the video screen. Command line: CLS

C
O
M
P
	Function: Compares two disk files. The asterisk (*) may be
	          used as a universal qualifier in a filename. IF
	          the optional filename is omitted, then it is
	          assumed to be the same as the required filename,
	          and the disk drives must be different.
	Command line:
	          COMP [<drive-id>]<filename> [<drive-id>][<filename>]
	Examples:
	          COMP SORT1.ASM B:
	             Compares the file named SORT1.ASM on the disk in
	             the default drive to the file named SORT1.ASM on
	             the disk in drive B.
	
	          COMP A:*.ASM B:
	             Compares each file on the disk in drive A that
	             has a filename extension of .ASM to the file on
	             the disk in drive B that has the same filename.

```
    ┊ Function: Copies file(s) from the source disk (identified by ┊
  C ┊           the  first  operand)  to  the  destination  disk  ┊
  O ┊           (identified  by the second operand).  The asterisk ┊
  P ┊           (*)  may be used  in a <filename>  as  a universal ┊
  Y ┊           qualifier. If the destination filename is omitted, ┊
    ┊           then  the  source filename  is used  and  the disk ┊
    ┊           drives must be different.                          ┊
    ┊ Command line:                                                ┊
    ┊     COPY [<drive-id>]<filename> [<drive-id>][<filename>][/V] ┊
    ┊ Options:                                                     ┊
    ┊     /V  Specifies  that  each  sector  transferred  to  the  ┊
    ┊         destination disk is to be verified by reading  that  ┊
    ┊         sector back into memory and comparing the data read  ┊
    ┊         with the data written.                               ┊
    ┊ Examples:                                                    ┊
    ┊         COPY B:PROG.ASM PROG1.ASM                            ┊
    ┊             Copies the file named PROG.ASM  from the disk in ┊
    ┊             drive B  to the disk  in the default drive using ┊
    ┊             the filename PROG1.ASM.                          ┊
    ┊                                                              ┊
    ┊         COPY B:PROG.EXE                                      ┊
    ┊             Copies the file named PROG.EXE  from the disk in ┊
    ┊             drive B  to the disk  in the default drive using ┊
    ┊             the same filename (PROG.EXE).                    ┊
    ┊                                                              ┊
    ┊         COPY *.ASM B:                                        ┊
    ┊             Copies  any file  with a filename  extension  of ┊
    ┊             .ASM from  the disk in the default drive  to the ┊
    ┊             disk in drive B using the same filename  in each ┊
    ┊             case.                                            ┊
    ┊ Function: Sets  and/or  displays  the  date  stored  in  the ┊
  D ┊           computer's memory.                                 ┊
  A ┊ Command line:                                                ┊
  T ┊             DATE [mm-dd-yy]                                  ┊
  E ┊ Examples:                                                    ┊
    ┊         DATE 1-17-83                                         ┊
    ┊             Sets the date to January 17, 1983               ┊
    ┊                                                              ┊
    ┊         DATE                                                 ┊
    ┊             Displays the  date  stored  in  the computer's   ┊
    ┊             memory,  and waits for a user response. To keep  ┊
    ┊             the  date  as  displayed,   the  user  presses   ┊
    ┊             RETURN.  To change the date,  the  user enters   ┊
    ┊             the date  in the  numeric form  mm-dd-yy,  and   ┊
    ┊             presses RETURN.                                  ┊
```

```
:  Function: Deletes  one or more filenames  from the directory :
D :            on a disk.  This command behaves   exactly like the :
E :            ERASE command.   The asterisk (*)  may be used as a :
L :            universal qualifier in a filename.                  :
:  Command line:                                                   :
:              DEL [<drive-id>]<filename>                          :
:  Examples:                                                       :
:              DEL EX1.ASM                                         :
:                 Deletes the file named EX1.ASM  on the   disk in :
:                 the default drive.                               :
:                                                                  :
:              DEL B:*.OBJ                                         :
:                 Deletes all files  on the disk in drive B  that  :
:                 have a filename extension of .OBJ.               :
```

```
:  Function: Displays a list with an entry for each file stored :
D :            on the specified disk.   A file's entry in the list :
I :            includes the  complete filename,  the size  (in  :
R :            bytes) of the file, and the date and time that the  :
:            file was last updated.  If  the optional filename  :
:            is  specified,   then  only  the  files  with  the  :
:            specified name are listed.                           :
:  Command line:                                                   :
:              DIR [<drive-id>][<filename>][/W][/P]               :
:  Options:                                                        :
:         /W  Specifies that only the filenames are to be listed, :
:             5 per line.                                       :
:         /P  Specifies that a pause is to occur  after each page :
:             of  the  listing.   The  listing  is  continued  by :
:             pressing any key.                                   :
:  Examples:                                                       :
:              DIR                                                 :
:                 Lists  all files  on the disk  in   the  default :
:                 drive.                                           :
:                                                                  :
:              DIR B:/P                                            :
:                 Lists all files on the disk in drive B, pausing :
:                 after each page of the listing.                 :
:                                                                  :
:              DIR B:*.ASM                                         :
:                 Lists  all files  on the disk  in drive B  that  :
:                 have a filename extension of .ASM.              :
```

```
  Function: Compares  two  diskettes,  sector  by  sector,  to
D           determine if they are identical. This operation is
I           used to verify a DISKCOPY operation.  The DISKCOMP
S           command is not part of the memory-resident portion
K           of DOS.  Therefore,  DOS must be available  on the
C           disk in the default  drive  when  the  command  is
O           issued. DOS then prompts the user to place the two
M           diskettes in the appropriate disk drives.
P                  If  the  first  diskette  is  formatted  with  8
            sectors per track (see the FORMAT command) and the
            second diskette  is  formatted  with 9 sectors per
            track,  then each track  of the first diskette  is
            compared to the first 8 sectors of the same  track
            on the second diskette.   If the first diskette is
            formatted with 9 sectors per track  and the second
            diskette is formatted with 8  sectors  per  track,
            then  the /8 option must be used so that  only the
            first  8  sectors  of  each  track  on  the  first
            diskette  are compared  to the same  track  on the
            second diskette.

  Command line:
            DISKCOMP [<drive-id>] [<drive-id>][/1]


            DISKCOMP [<drive-id>] [<drive-id>][/8]
  Options:
        /1  Specifies  that  only  the first  sides  of the two
            diskettes  are  to  be  compared.  This  option  is
            normally  used  when  single-sided  diskettes  are
            involved.
        /8  Specifies  that  only  the first  8 sectors  of each
            track are to be compared.  This option is used when
            one  or both  of the diskettes are formatted with 8
            sectors per track.
```

D
I
S
K
C
O
P
Y
	Function: Copies the contents of a source diskette onto a destination diskette, producing a backup copy of the source diskette. The DISKCOPY command is not part of the memory-resident portion of DOS. Therefore, DOS must be available on the disk in the default drive when the command is issued. DOS then prompts the user to place the source and target diskettes in the appropriate disk drives. If the source diskette is formatted with 8 sectors per track (see the FORMAT command) and the destination diskette is formatted with 9 sectors per track, then each track of the source diskette is copied into the first 8 sectors of the same track on the destination diskette. A diskette that is formatted with 9 sectors per track cannot be copied to a diskette that is formatted with 8 sectors per track. The DISKCOPY operation formats the destination diskette, if it has not already been formatted.
	
	Command line:
	    DISKCOPY [<drive-id>] [<drive-id>][/1]
	
	Options:
	   /1 Specifies that only the first side of the source diskette is to be copied, and is copied to the first side of the destination diskette. This option is normally used when single-sided diskettes are involved.
	
	Examples:
	    DISKCOPY A: B:
	       Copies both sides of the diskette in drive A to the diskette in drive B.
	
	    DISKCOPY B: /1
	       Copies only the first side of the diskette in drive B to the diskette in the default drive.

E
R
A
S
E
	Function: Erases one or more filenames from the directory on a disk. This command behaves exactly like the DEL command. The asterisk (*) may be used as a universal qualifier in a filename.
	
	Command line:
	      ERASE [<drive-id>]<filename>
	
	Examples:
	    See the DEL command.

```
FORMAT
```

Function: Initializea a diskette. The format operation divides each surface of a 5 1/4 inch diskette into 40 concentric circles called tracks. Each track is divided into sectors. DOS 1.0 divides each track into 8 sectors, and DOS 2.0 and DOS 3.0 divide each track into 9 sectors. Each sector holds 512 bytes of data.

The FORMAT operation also places a directory on the diskette for DOS to use in keeping track of the files that are stored on the diskette. The following table summarizes the diskette space reserved for DOS.

The FORMAT command is not part of the memory-resident portion of DOS. Therefore, DOS must be available on the disk in the default drive when the command is issued. DOS then prompts the user to place the disk to be formatted in the specified drive.

Diskette Type and Format	Total Bytes on Disk	Bytes for DOS Usage	Bytes for User Files
Single-sided 8 sectors/track	163,840	3,584	160,256
Double-sided 8 sectors/track	327,680	5,120	322,560
Single-sided 9 sectors/track	184,320	4,608	179,712
Double-sided 9 sectors/track	368,640	6,144	362,496

Command line:
```
FORMAT [<drive-id>][/S][/V][/1][/8]
```
Options:
/S Specifies that the hidden files IBMBIO.COM and IBMDOS.COM are to be copied from the DOS diskette to the diskette being formatted.
/V Specifies that the user desires to place a volume label on the diskette. DOS prompts the user for the label after the FORMAT operation is complete.
/1 Specifies that the diskette is to be formatted for use as a single-sided diskette, whether or not it actually is a single-sided diskette.
/8 Specifies that the diskette is to be formatted with 8 sectors per track. The default for DOS 2.0 and DOS 3.0 is 9 sectors per track.

```
    ¦ Function: Sets the mode of the video display or the printer. ¦
  M ¦                                                              ¦
  O ¦ Command line:                                                ¦
  D ¦      MODE <char/line>                                        ¦
  E ¦                                                              ¦
    ¦              <char/line> is the   number   of   characters  ¦
    ¦                          per line for the video display      ¦
    ¦                          (40 or 80).                         ¦
    ¦                                                              ¦
    ¦      MODE LPT<#>:[<char/line>][,[<lines/inch>][,P]]          ¦
    ¦                                                              ¦
    ¦                          <#> is the  printer number (1, 2,   ¦
    ¦                          or 3),                              ¦
    ¦                  <char/line> is the number   of  characters  ¦
    ¦                          per line for the printer   (80      ¦
    ¦                          or 132),                            ¦
    ¦                 <lines/inch> is the number   of  lines  per  ¦
    ¦                          inch for the printer (6 or 8),       ¦
    ¦                          and                                 ¦
    ¦                          P specifies continuous retry on     ¦
    ¦                          time-out errors on prints.          ¦
    ¦ Examples:                                                    ¦
    ¦      MODE 40                                                 ¦
    ¦          Sets  the video monitor  to display  40 characters  ¦
    ¦          per line.                                           ¦
    ¦                                                              ¦
    ¦      MODE LPT1:132,8                                         ¦
    ¦          Sets printer number 1  to print 132 characters per  ¦
    ¦          line and 8 lines per inch (88 lines per page).      ¦
    ¦ Function: Change the name of a file  or group of files.  The ¦
  R ¦          asterisk (*) may be used  in  a  <filename>  as  a  ¦
  E ¦          universal qualifier.                                ¦
  N ¦ Command line:                                                ¦
  A ¦              RENAME [<drive-id>]<filename> <filename>        ¦
  M ¦ Examples:                                                    ¦
  E ¦      RENAME B:PROG.BAK PROG.OLD                              ¦
    ¦          Changes the name of file PROG.BAK  on the disk  in  ¦
    ¦          drive B to PROG.OLD.                                ¦
    ¦                                                              ¦
    ¦      RENAME SEARCH.* BIN_SRCH.*                              ¦
    ¦          For all files on the disk  in  the  default  drive  ¦
    ¦          that have a filename of SEARCH (regardless of the   ¦
    ¦          filename extension),  the filename  is changed  to  ¦
    ¦          BIN_SRCH,  and the filename extension remains  the  ¦
    ¦          same.                                               ¦
```

```
:  Function: Sets  and/or  displays  the  time  stored  in  the  :
T:            computer's memory.                                 :
I:  Command line:                                                :
M:              TIME [hh:mm[:ss[.hs]]]                           :
E:  Examples:                                                    :
 :         TIME 18:43                                            :
 :              Sets the time to 6:43 PM.                        :
 :                                                               :
 :         TIME                                                  :
 :              Displays  the  time  stored  in  the  computer's :
 :              memory, and waits for a user response. To keep   :
 :              the time as displayed, the user presses RETURN.  :
 :              To change the time,  the user enters  the time   :
 :              in  the  numeric  form  hh:mm[:ss[.hs]],   and   :
 :              presses RETURN.                                  :
```

```
 :  Function: Displays  the  contents  of  a  file  on the video :
T:            screen.  To ensure a readable output, this command :
Y:            should only be used for ASCII text files.          :
P:  Command line:                                                :
E:              TYPE [<drive-id>]<filename>                      :
 :  Example:                                                     :
 :     TYPE SORT.ASM                                             :
 :              Displays  the contents  of the file named SORT.ASM :
 :              from the disk in the default drive.              :
```

```
 :  Function: Determines  the  status  of the VERIFY option,  or :
V:            sets the VERIFY option.  When the VERIFY option is  :
E:            "on",  each  sector  transferred  to  a  disk  is  :
R:            verified by reading  that sector  into memory  and  :
I:            comparing the data read with the data written.     :
F:  Command line:                                                :
Y:                        VERIFY                                 :
 :                                                               :
 :                        VERIFY ON                              :
 :                                                               :
 :                        VERIFY OFF                             :
 :  Examples:                                                    :
 :     VERIFY                                                    :
 :              Displays the status of the VERIFY option.        :
 :                                                               :
 :     VERIFY ON                                                 :
 :              Sets the VERIFY option to "on".                  :
```

LINE EDITOR (EDLIN)

To invoke EDLIN:
  a. Insert the DOS diskette into the default drive and
     close the disk drive door.
  b. Enter the following command line:

     EDLIN [<drive-id>]<filename>

     DOS loads EDLIN from the disk in the default drive, and
     then EDLIN loads the specified file. If the specified
     file does not exist, then EDLIN creates the file on the
     disk in the specified drive using the specified
     <filename>.

Abbreviations and notation:
  <> encloses items to be supplied by the user.
  [] encloses optional items.

  <line#> denotes the line number of a line in the file
          being edited. Allowable entries are as follows:
              1.   A decimal integer in the range 1 to 65,529.
                   If the specified line number does not exist
                   in the file being edited, then the next
                   available line number is used.
              2.   A pound sign (#) specifies the next
                   available line number (i.e., one greater
                   than the line number of the last line in
                   the file).
              3.   A period (.) specifies the current line.

EDLIN Commands

```
┌──────────────────────────────────────────────────────────────────┐
   Function: Copies lines of text in the file being edited.
C
O  Command line:
P       [<line#>][,<line#>],<line#>[,<copy-count>]C
Y
        If either or both  of the optional line numbers  are
        omitted,  then  the current line number  is assumed.
        The first line of the copy becomes the current line.
   Examples:
      5,9,27C
        Inserts  a copy  of lines 5 - 9,  inclusive,  just
        prior  to  line  27,  renumbering line 27  and all
        subsequent  lines.   The new  line 27  becomes  the
        current line.

      5,7,1,10C
        Inserts 10 copies of lines 5 - 7, inclusive,  just
        prior  to  line 1,  renumbering  line 1  and  all
        subsequent  lines.  The  new  line 1  becomes  the
        current line.
├──────────────────────────────────────────────────────────────────┤
   Function: Deletes lines  of text  from the file being edited.
D            The line  immediately following  the deleted block
E            becomes the current line.
L  Command line:
E              [<line#>][,<line#>]D
T
E              If  the beginning  line number  is omitted,
               then  the current line  is assumed.  If the
               ending  line number  is omitted,  then only
               one line is deleted.
   Examples:
           17D
               Deletes line 17, renumbering all  subsequent
               lines. The new line 17 becomes  the current
               line.

           12,23D
               Deletes     lines    12 - 23,    inclusive,
               renumbering all subsequent lines.  The  new
               line 12 becomes the current line.
└──────────────────────────────────────────────────────────────────┘
```

```
 ¦ Function: Displays a line of text for editing.                    ¦
E¦                                                                    ¦
D¦ Command line:                                                      ¦
I¦                   [<line#>]                                        ¦
T¦                                                                    ¦
 ¦                   If  the  line  number  is omitted  (i.e.,  just  ¦
L¦                   RETURN is pressed),  then  the  line  after the  ¦
I¦                   current line is displayed  for editing.  EDLIN   ¦
N¦                   displays  the  requested  line  and  then moves  ¦
E¦                   the  cursor  to the beginning  of the next line  ¦
 ¦                   on the video screen (the replacement line).      ¦
 ¦                                                                    ¦
 ¦                   Typing  a character  in the  replacement  line   ¦
 ¦                   replaces  the corresponding  character  in the   ¦
 ¦                   displayed line.                                  ¦
 ¦                                                                    ¦
 ¦                   Typing  the  function key,  F1,  causes  EDLIN   ¦
 ¦                   to copy one character  from the displayed line   ¦
 ¦                   to the replacement line.                         ¦
 ¦                                                                    ¦
 ¦                   Typing  the  function key,  F2,  followed by a   ¦
 ¦                   character  causes  EDLIN  to  copy  characters   ¦
 ¦                   from  the displayed  line  to  the replacement   ¦
 ¦                   line,  up to  but  not  including  the  next     ¦
 ¦                   occurrence of the specified character.           ¦
 ¦                                                                    ¦
 ¦                   Typing the function key, F3,  causes EDLIN  to   ¦
 ¦                   copy  the remainder  of the displayed line  to   ¦
 ¦                   the replacement line.                            ¦
 ¦                                                                    ¦
 ¦                   Typing  the  function key,  F4,  followed by a   ¦
 ¦                   character  causes  EDLIN  to move  to the next   ¦
 ¦                   occurrence  of the specified character  in the   ¦
 ¦                   displayed  line,  without  copying  characters   ¦
 ¦                   to the replacement line.                         ¦
 ¦                                                                    ¦
 ¦                   Pressing RETURN  causes EDLIN  to replace  the   ¦
 ¦                   displayed line with the replacement line.        ¦
 ¦                                                                    ¦
 ¦ Function: Exits the line editor,  and saves  the edited text       ¦
E¦                   under the filename that was specified  on entry to¦
N¦                   the editor.  If the file  already existed on entry¦
D¦                   to the editor,  then EDLIN changes the filename   ¦
 ¦                   extension  of the unedited version  of the file to¦
E¦                   .BAK and deletes  any previous backup copy of the ¦
D¦                   file before saving the edited copy.              ¦
I¦                                                                    ¦
T¦ Command line:                                                      ¦
 ¦                   E                                                ¦
 ¦                                                                    ¦
```

I	Function: Inserts lines of text in the file being edited,
N	just prior to the specified line. EDLIN prompts
S	for each line of text with the line number.
E	Pressing RETURN terminates the entry of a line of
R	text. The Ctrl - C (or the Ctrl - Break) key
T	combination terminates the INSERT command. The

I
N
S
E
R
T

Function: Inserts lines of text in the file being edited, just prior to the specified line. EDLIN prompts for each line of text with the line number. Pressing RETURN terminates the entry of a line of text. The Ctrl - C (or the Ctrl - Break) key combination terminates the INSERT command. The specified line and all subsequent lines are renumbered beginning with the line number immediately following the line number of the last line entered. The line immediately following the last line entered becomes the current line.

Command lines:

                    [<line#>]I
                    <line of text>
                    <line of text>
                    <line of text>
                          .
                          .
                          .
                    <line of text>
                    ^C

           If the optional line number is omitted, then the new text is inserted just prior to the current line.

L
I
S
T

Function: Displays, on the video screen, selected lines from the file being edited. The current line does not change.

Command line:

                    [<line#>][,<line#>]L

           If the beginning line number is omitted, then the display begins 11 lines prior to the current line. Line 1 is used if there are not 11 lines prior to the current line. If the ending line number is omitted, then a maximum of 23 lines is displayed.

Examples:
    1,10L

           Displays lines 1 - 10, inclusive, on the video screen.

    12L

           Displays 23 consecutive lines beginning with line 12 (i.e., display lines 12 - 34).

    L

           Displays 23 consecutive lines beginning 11 lines prior to the current line (or beginning with line 1, if the line number of the current line is less than 12).

```
   |  Function: Moves lines of text from one place  to another   in |
 M |            the  file  being  edited.  The  first line  of the |
 O |            block  of lines moved becomes the current line. |
 V |  Command line: |
 E |                  [<line#>],[<line#>],<line#>M |
   |  |
   |            If either or both of the optional line numbers are |
   |            omitted, then the  current line number is assumed. |
   |  Examples: |
   |      5,9,48M |
   |            Moves lines 5 - 9,  inclusive,  just prior to line |
   |            48.    Lines   10 - 47   become     lines   5 - 42, |
   |            respectively,   and   lines 5 - 9 become lines 43 - |
   |            47, respectively. Line 43 becomes the current line. |
   |      6,10,1M |
   |            Moves  lines  6 - 10,  inclusive,  just  prior  to |
   |            line 1.   Lines   6 - 10   become   lines  1 - 5, |
   |            respectively, and lines 1 - 5 become lines 6 - 10, |
   |            respectively.  Line 1 becomes the current line. |
   |_____|
   |  Function: Displays, on the video screen, selected lines from |
 P |            the file being edited.  The   last  line  displayed |
 A |            becomes the current line. |
 G |  Command line: |
 E |                  [<line#>][,<line#>]P |
   |  |
   |            If the beginning line number is omitted,  then the |
   |            display begins with the line following the current |
   |            line.  If the ending line number is omitted,  then |
   |            a maximum of 23 lines is displayed. |
   |  Examples: |
   |      1,10P |
   |            Displays  lines  1 - 10,  inclusive,  on the video |
   |            screen. Line 10 becomes the current line. |
   |      12P |
   |            Displays 23 consecutive lines  beginning with line |
   |            12  (i.e.,  display lines 12 - 34). Line 34 becomes |
   |            the current line. |
   |      P |
   |            Displays 23 consecutive lines  beginning with  the |
   |            line following  the current line.  The  last  line |
   |            displayed becomes the current line. |
   |_____|
   |  Function: Quits  the edit session,  and  does not  save  the |
 Q |            edited text  (i.e.,  aborts the edit session).  On |
 U |            return to DOS,  the files on disk are  the same as |
 I |            they were  on entry  to the editor.  EDLIN prompts |
 T |            the user with the following message: |
   |                                      Abort edit (Y/N)?__ |
   |            The user  enters Y to abort  the edit session,  or |
   |            any other character to cancel the Q command. |
   |  Command line: |
   |                  Q |
   |_____|
```

R
E
P
L
A
C
E
```
Function: Replaces each occurrence of a search string with a
          copy of a replacement string in a specified block
          of text from the file being edited.  Pressing
          Ctrl-Z separates the search string from the
          replacement string.  After each substitution, the
          line that was changed is displayed.  The line
          before the last line changed becomes the current
          line.
Command line:
  [<line#>][,<line#>][?]R[<srch-string>][^Z[<repl-string>]]


          Pressing the function key, F6, is equivalent to
          pressing Ctrl-Z.
              The optional parameter, question mark (?), is
          used to request a prompt after each replacement.
          The prompt asks the user to accept or reject the
          replacement.
              If the beginning line number is omitted, then
          the search begins with the line after the current
          line.  If the ending line number is omitted, then
          the search terminates with the last line in the
          file.
              If the search string is omitted, then the last
          search string that was entered on an R or S
          command is used (see the SEARCH command).  If both
          strings are omitted, then the last search string
          that was entered on an R or S command and the last
          replacement string that was entered on an R
          command are used.  If only the replacement string
          is omitted, then the null string is used.


Examples:
   12,19RAX^ZBX
          Replaces each occurrence of the string AX with the
          string BX in lines 12 - 19, inclusive.

   27,39R;^Z;-->
          Replaces each semicolon (;) with the string  ;-->
          in lines 27 - 39, inclusive.

   RLENGTH^ZLNGTH
          Beginning with the line after the current line,
          replaces each occurrence of the word LENGTH with
          the word LNGTH in the remainder of the file.

   1,9R;^Z
          Delete each occurrence of a semicolon (;) in lines
          1 - 9, inclusive.
```

```
  ¦ Function: Searches a specified block  of text  for the first ¦
S ¦           occurrence  of a specified string.  EDLIN displays ¦
E ¦           the first line found  that contains  an occurrence ¦
A ¦           of the search string.  The displayed line  becomes ¦
R ¦           the current line.  If the search terminates before ¦
C ¦           an occurrence of the search string is found,  then ¦
H ¦           the message                                        ¦
  ¦                           Not found                          ¦
  ¦           is displayed.                                      ¦
  ¦ Command line:                                                ¦
  ¦                 [<line#>][,<line#>][?]S[<srch-string>]       ¦
  ¦                                                              ¦
  ¦           If the beginning line number is omitted,  then the ¦
  ¦           search begins with the line after the current line.¦
  ¦           If  the  ending line number  is omitted,  then the ¦
  ¦           search terminates with the last line in the file.  ¦
  ¦                The  optional  parameter,  question  mark (?),¦
  ¦           causes EDLIN to prompt the user  as to  whether or ¦
  ¦           not  to terminate  the search after  a qualifying  ¦
  ¦           line has been found and displayed. A response of Y ¦
  ¦           terminates  the search.  A response of N continues ¦
  ¦           the   search  beginning  with  the  next  line  in ¦
  ¦           sequence.  If  the question mark is omitted,  then ¦
  ¦           the   search   is   terminated   after  the  first ¦
  ¦           qualifying line is found,  or after  the last line ¦
  ¦           in the specified block has been searched.          ¦
  ¦                If  the search string  is omitted,  then  the ¦
  ¦           last search string  that was entered  on an R or S ¦
  ¦           command is used (see the REPLACE command).         ¦
  ¦                                                              ¦
  ¦ Examples:                                                    ¦
  ¦   1SLENGTH                                                   ¦
  ¦           Searches the file for the first line that contains ¦
  ¦           the word LENGTH. The search begins with line 1.    ¦
  ¦                                                              ¦
  ¦   12,27SPUTDEC$                                              ¦
  ¦           Searches  for  the first  line  that contains  the ¦
  ¦           string PUTDEC$ in lines 12 - 27,  inclusive.       ¦
```

```
 ┊ Function: Inserts the text from a specified file  just prior ┊
T┊           to  the specified line  in the file  being edited, ┊
R┊           renumbering the specified line  and all subsequent ┊
A┊           lines. The first line of the inserted text becomes ┊
N┊           the current line.                                  ┊
S┊ Command line:                                                ┊
F┊              [<line#>]T[<drive-id>]<filename>                ┊
E┊                                                              ┊
R┊           If the line number is omitted,  then the text from ┊
 ┊           the specified file is inserted  just prior  to the ┊
 ┊           current line.                                      ┊
 ┊ Example:                                                     ┊
 ┊   15TB:PROG.ASM                                              ┊
 ┊           Inserts the text from file PROG.ASM on the disk in ┊
 ┊           drive B  just prior  to line 15  in the file being ┊
 ┊           edited.   Renumbers  line 15  and  all  subsequent ┊
 ┊           lines. The new line 15 becomes the current line.   ┊
 ┊                                                              ┊
```

DEBUG Program

To invoke DEBUG:
  a. Insert the DOS or macro assembler diskette in the
     default drive and close the door on the disk drive.
  b. Enter the following command line:

     DEBUG [[<drive-id]<filename>]

     DOS loads DEBUG from the disk in the default drive and
     then transfers control to the DEBUG program. If a file-
     name is specified, then the DEBUG program loads the
     requested file into memory. DEBUG prompts the user with
     a hyphan (-). The user can enter commands to display or
     modify the contents of registers or memory locations,
     and to execute instructions contained in memory. DEBUG
     expects all numeric values to be in hexadecimal.

Abbreviations and notation:
           <> encloses items to be supplied by the user.
           [] encloses optional items.

  <address> denotes the segment and offset of a memory
            location. A colon (:) separates the two parts of
            the memory address. The segment portion of the
            address can be specified as follows:

            1. A segment register designator (CS, SS, DS, or
               ES)
            2. A 1 - 4 digit hexadecimal number, that
               specifies the upper 16 bits of the address of
               the origin of the segment (e.g., 0914
               specifies the origin address 09140)
            3. Omitted, specifying that a default segment
               register is to be used.

            The offset portion of the address must be a 1-4
            digit hexadecimal number, that specifies the
            offset relative to the segment origin. If the
            segment portion of the address is omitted, then
            the separating colon must also be omitted.

    <range> denotes a block of memory locations by
            specifying where the block begins and ends in
            memory. A range of memory locations can be
            specified in either of the following two ways:

                <address> [<offset>]

                in which <address> specifies the segment and
                          offset of the memory location at
                          which the block begins and
                          <offset> specifies the offset within
                          the segment of the memory
                          location at which the block ends.

```
<address> [L <length>]

in which <address> specifies the segment  and
             offset of the memory location at
             which the block begins  and
          <length>  specifies  the  number  of
             bytes in the block.

In either case,  if  the  optional  parameter  is
omitted, then a default end of range is used.
```

DEBUG Commands

```
   : Function: Translates IBM PC  Assembly language   instructions
A :            into  machine  language   and  loads  the  machine
S :            language  instructions  into  consecutive  memory
S :            locations  beginning  at  the  specified  address.
E :            DEBUG   prompts   for   each   Assembly   language
M :            instruction  by displaying  the memory address  at
B :            which the machine language representation  of  the
L :            instruction will begin. Pressing RETURN terminates
E :            the  entry  of  an  Assembly language instruction.
  :            Pressing RETURN by itself  terminates the Assemble
  :            command.
  :               All  immediate  operands  must  be  entered  in
  :            hexadecimal,  and  all  memory  operands  must  be
  :            hexadecimal  offsets  enclosed  in square brackets
  :            (e.g., [4A] ).  A segment override mnemonic  (CS:,
  :            SS:, DS:, or ES:)  is  entered  just prior  to the
  :            operation-code.
  :               RETF is used for return  from a FAR  procedure.
  :            RET is used for return from a NEAR procedure.
  :               The generic forms  for the string  instructions
  :            cannot be used,  and a repeat  prefix  is  entered
  :            just prior to the string operation-code.
  :
  : Command lines:
  :               A [<address>]
  :               <Assembly language instruction>
  :               <Assembly language instruction>
  :                            .
  :                            .
  :                            .
  :               <Assembly language instruction>
  :               <Assembly language instruction>
```

```
      ┆ Function: Display    the    contents   of   a   block   of   memory ┆
    D ┆            locations in hexadecimal and as ASCII characters.         ┆
    U ┆ Command line:                                                        ┆
    M ┆                        D [<range>]                                   ┆
    P ┆                                                                      ┆
      ┆            If   only   the   start   address   for   the   range  is ┆
      ┆            specified, then a total of 128 bytes (8 rows of 16        ┆
      ┆            bytes each) is displayed. If the range is omitted,        ┆
      ┆            then   the   dump   begins   at   the   memory   location ┆
      ┆            immediately  following  the  end  location  for  the      ┆
      ┆            previous dump.  The DS-register  contents are used        ┆
      ┆            as  the  default  segment  origin  address  for  the      ┆
      ┆            start address of the range.                               ┆
      ┆                                                                      ┆
      ┆ Examples:                                                            ┆
      ┆    D SS:0 1F                                                         ┆
      ┆            Displays the contents of stack  segment  locations        ┆
      ┆            beginning at offset 0000 and terminating at offset        ┆
      ┆            001F.                                                     ┆
      ┆                                                                      ┆
      ┆    D DS:08 L 30                                                      ┆
      ┆            Displays 48 (30 hex) locations of the data segment        ┆
      ┆            beginning at offset 0008.                                 ┆
```

```
    ┊ Function: Changes   the    contents    of   a   block   of   memory ┊
  E ┊           locations.                                                 ┊
  N ┊ Command line:                                                        ┊
  T ┊                   E <address> [<byte-constant-list>]                 ┊
  E ┊                                                                      ┊
  R ┊                   <byte-constant-list> is a list of hexadecimal      ┊
    ┊                                        byte constants separated      ┊
    ┊                                        by spaces or commas.          ┊
    ┊                                                                      ┊
    ┊                   The   DS-register  contents   are  used  as  the   ┊
    ┊           default segment origin address  for the address in        ┊
    ┊           an E command.                                              ┊
    ┊                   If the  <byte-constant-list>  is omitted,  then    ┊
    ┊           DEBUG  displays  the  contents  of  the  specified         ┊
    ┊           memory location and prompts the user to change the         ┊
    ┊           value. To leave the value as is,  the user presses         ┊
    ┊           RETURN.  To change the value,  the user types  the         ┊
    ┊           the new byte value in hexadecimal and then presses         ┊
    ┊           RETURN.                                                     ┊
    ┊                   If the  <byte-constant-list>  is present,  then    ┊
    ┊           the constants  from the  list   are  entered  into         ┊
    ┊           consecutive  memory  locations  beginning with the         ┊
    ┊           specified  memory  location.   The  constants  are         ┊
    ┊           entered into memory in the order  that they appear         ┊
    ┊           in the list.                                               ┊
    ┊                                                                      ┊
    ┊ Example:                                                             ┊
    ┊   E 9A4:0 1A 2B 3C                                                   ┊
    ┊           Enters the hex value 1A into memory location 09A40,        ┊
    ┊           the hex value 2B  into memory location 09A41,  and         ┊
    ┊           the hex value 3C into memory location 09A42.               ┊
    ┊ Function: Sets one or more breakpoints in a program, so that         ┊
  G ┊           a selected block of instructions  can be executed.         ┊
  O ┊           Execution begins  with the next instruction  to be         ┊
    ┊           executed in the program being debugged (identified         ┊
    ┊           by the saved  CS:IP register  pair)  or  with the          ┊
    ┊           instruction  at  a  specified  address.  Execution         ┊
    ┊           continues until one of the breakpoints is reached.         ┊
    ┊ Command line:                                                        ┊
    ┊                   G [=<address>] [<address-list>]                    ┊
    ┊                                                                      ┊
    ┊                   <address-list> is a  list  of  addresses           ┊
    ┊                                  separated  by  spaces  or           ┊
    ┊                                  commas.                             ┊
    ┊                                                                      ┊
    ┊                   The optional parameter,  =<address>,  specifies    ┊
    ┊           the memory location at which execution is to begin.        ┊
    ┊           If omitted,  then execution begins  with the next          ┊
    ┊           instruction in the program  being debugged.                ┊
    ┊                   The  addresses  in the  <address-list>  specify    ┊
    ┊           breakpoints  for  the  program.  Execution  is             ┊
    ┊           interrupted when  the  instruction  at one of the          ┊
    ┊           breakpoint addresses is  reached.  The instruction         ┊
```

G
O

at the breakpoint is not executed.

Each address specified with the G command must be the address of the first byte of an instruction in the program being debugged. DEBUG replaces the instruction byte at each breakpoint address with the 1-byte INT 3 instruction (CC hex). On detection of a Type 3 interrupt (i.e., on reaching a breakpoint), DEBUG receives control. DEBUG saves the state of the processor for the program being debugged, displays the processor state to the user, restores the instruction byte at each breakpoint address, and waits for another command from the user. Another G or T command causes DEBUG to restore the state of the processor for and return control to the program being debugged.

The CS-register contents are used as the default segment origin address for any address used in the G command.

The G command uses 6 bytes in the user's stack segment.

If no breakpoints are specified, execution continues until the program being debugged terminates normally.

Examples:

G 10A

Begins execution with the instruction that begins in the memory location specified by the saved CS:IP register pair, and stops execution just prior to the instruction at offset 010A in the segment addressed by the CS-register.

G =91A:0 91A:A8 91A:B2

Begins execution with the instruction that begins in memory location 091A0, and stops execution just prior to the instruction that begins in location 09248 (091A:00A8) or just prior to the instruction that begins in location 09252 (091A:00B2).

H
E
X

A
R
I
T
H

Function: Displays the hexadecimal sum and difference of two hexadecimal numbers.

Command line:

H <hex-integer> <hex-integer>

<hex-integer> is a hexadecimal integer in the range 0 - FFFF.

Example:

H 1AC F8

Displays the sum of 1AC hex and F8 hex followed by the difference between 1AC and F8. In this case, the display would be 02A4 00B4.

	Function: Terminates execution of the DEBUG program, and returns control to DOS.
Q	
U	
I	COMMAND LINE:
T	Q

	Function: Displays the contents of the processor registers for the program being debugged.
R	
E	
G	Displays the contents of a selected processor register, and prompts the user for a new value for the selected register. To keep the register value as is, the user presses RETURN. To change the register value, the user types the new value, in hexadecimal, and then presses RETURN.
I	
S	
T	
E	
R	

Command line:
            R[<reg-name>]

                  <reg-name> is one of the following
                  register designators:
                  AX, BX, CX, DX, SP, BP,
                  DI, SI, CS, SS, DS, ES,
                  IP, PC (same as IP), or
                  F (for the flags register).

            The following abbreviations are used for the
            display and modification of the individual bit of
            the flags register:

                              FLAG   0   1

OF	NV	OV
DF	UP	DN
IF	DI	EI
SF	PL	NG
ZF	NZ	ZR
AF	NA	AC
PF	PO	PE
CF	NC	CY

Examples:
    R
        Displays the contents of the processor registers.

    R CX
        Displays the contents of the CX-register, and waits
        for the user to enter a new value.

```
|  Function: Executes one or more instructions, beginning  with |
T|            the next instruction in the program being debugged |
R|            (identified  by  the saved CS:IP register pair)  or |
A|            beginning  with  the  instruction  at  a specified  |
C|            address.  Execution  continues  until  the  next n  |
E|            single-step  interrupts  occur.  The default value  |
 |            for  n is 1.  The T command  uses 6 bytes  in  the  |
 |            user's stack segment.                               |
 |  Command line:                                                 |
 |                T [=<address>] [<n>]                            |
 |                                                                |
 |                <n> is a count  of the number  of single-step   |
 |                    interrupts to service before execution is   |
 |                    suspended to wait for another command.      |
 |                                                                |
 |                The optional parameter,  =<address>,  specifies |
 |            the memory location at which execution is to begin. |
 |            If omitted,   then execution begins  with  the next |
 |            instruction in the program being debugged.          |
 |                On each single-step interrupt,  DEBUG saves the |
 |            state  of  the  processor  for  the  program being  |
 |            debugged  and displays this processor state to the  |
 |            user.  On each  single-step  interrupt  except for  |
 |            the  last,   DEBUG   restores  the  state  of  the  |
 |            processor and returns control  to the program being |
 |            debugged. On the last single-step interrupt, DEBUG  |
 |            waits for another command from the user. Another G  |
 |            or T command causes DEBUG to restore  the state of  |
 |            the  processor  for  and  return  control  to  the  |
 |            program being debugged.                             |
 |  Examples:                                                     |
 |      T                                                         |
 |            Traces  the execution  of the next instruction  in  |
 |            the program being debugged.                         |
 |                                                                |
 |      T 10                                                      |
 |            Traces  the  execution   of  the  next  16 (10 hex) |
 |            instructions in the program being debugged.         |
```

```
|  Function: Interprets  the contents  of memory  locations  as  |
U|             machine  language  instructions,   and  translates |
N|             these instructions to Assembly language.           |
A|                  All immediate operands are displayed in base 16.|
S|             All memory operands  are displayed  as hexadecimal |
S|             offsets enclosed in square brackets.               |
E|                  A  prefix operator  is displayed  on a separate |
M|             line  immediately  preceding  the  instruction  to  |
B|             which it applies.                                  |
L|  Command line:                                                 |
E|                                                                |
 |                  U [<range>]                                   |
 |                                                                |
 |             If  only  the  start  address  for  the  range  is |
 |             specified, then a maximum of 37 bytes (minimum 32) |
 |             is   unassembled.    The   number  of  instructions |
 |             displayed can vary, since instructions are from 1- |
 |             6 bytes in length.                                 |
 |                  If  the  range  is  omitted,  then  the  display |
 |             begins with the instruction immediately  following |
 |             the last instruction displayed  for  the  previous |
 |             U command.                                         |
 |                  The  CS-register  contents  are  used  as  the |
 |             default  segment  origin  address  for  the  start |
 |             address of the range.                              |
 |                                                                |
 |  Example:                                                      |
 |    U 100 11F                                                   |
 |             Interprets the bytes  from offset  0100 - 011F  in |
 |             the segment  whose  origin  is  specified  by  the |
 |             contents  of  the  CS-register  as  a  sequence of |
 |             machine  language  instructions.   The  first |
 |             instruction is the one that begins at offset 0100, |
 |             and  the  last  instruction  is  the last one that |
 |             begins  at  or  before offset  011F. Displays  the |
 |             Assembly   language   interpretations   for   this |
 |             sequence of instructions.                          |
```

Macro Assembler (MASM)

Function:
   Translates an assembly module from Assembly language to
   machine language.

Command line:
   MASM <source>,[<object>],[<listing>],[<cross-ref>]

   A semicolon (;) may terminate the command line after any
   file specification, and in that case, the remaining output
   files (except for <object>) are simply not generated (the
   <object> file specification is treated as if it had been
   left blank).

Explanation of arguments:
   <source>   identifies the input source code file.
   <object>   identifies the output object code file.
   <listing>   identifies the output file for the assembler-
                generated listing.
   <cross-ref> identifies the output file for cross-reference
                data.

Legal entries for arguments:

| <source> | Explicit file specification |
| | Default filename extension: .ASM |

<object>	Explicit file specification
<listing>	Default filename extensions:
<cross-ref>	.OBJ for <object>
	.LST for <listing>
	.CRF for <cross-ref>
	NUL indicates that the specific output file is not to be generated.
	Blank indicates that the specific output file is to be placed on the diskette in the default drive using the <source> filename with the filename extension replaced by the appropriate suffix (.OBJ, .LST, or .CRF).
	Disk drive identifier indicates that the specific output file is to be placed on the diskette in the specified drive using the <source> filename with the filename extension replaced by the appropriate suffix (.OBJ, .LST, or .CRF).

| <listing> | CON indicates that the assembler-generated listing is to be displayed on the video screen. |

Linkage Editor (LINK)

FUNCTION:

Combines separately assembled object code modules into a single executable module.

Command line:

LINK <obj-list>,[<runfile>],[<mapfile>],[<lib-list>]

A semicolon (;) may terminate the command line after any file specification, and in that case, the remaining output files (except for <runfile>) are simply not generated (the <runfile> file specification is treated as if it had been left blank).

Explanation of arguments:

<obj-list> is a list of object code file specifications separated by spaces or plus signs (+).

<runfile> identifies the output file for the executable machine code.

<mapfile> identifies the output file for the load map.

<lib-list> is a list of library specifications separated by spaces or plus signs (+).

Legal entries for arguments:

<obj-list> <lib-list>	List of explicit file specifications
	    Default filename extensions:
	        .OBJ for <obj-list> items
	        .LIB for <lib-list> items

<runfile> <mapfile>	Explicit file specification
	    Default filename extensions:
	        .EXE for <runfile>
	        .MAP for <mapfile>
	NUL indicates that the specific output file is not to be generated.
	Blank indicates that the particular output file is to be placed on the diskette in the default drive using the first object filename with the filename extension replaced by the appropriate suffix (.EXE or .MAP).
	Disk drive identifier indicates that the specific output file is to be placed on the diskette in the specified drive using the first object filename with the filename extension replaced by the appropriate suffix (.EXE, or .MAP).

<mapfile>	CON indicates that the load map listing is to be displayed on the video screen.

Cross Reference (CREF)

Function:
    Produces an alphabetical listing of the symbolic names
    used in an assembly module. The listing contains a list of
    line numbers for each symbolic name, indicating where in
    the assembly module the name is defined (denoted by #) and
    referenced.

Command line:
    CREF <cross-ref>,<cref-listing>

Explanation of arguments:
    <cross-ref>   identifies the input file that contains the
                    cross-reference data.
    <cref-listing> identifies the output file for the cross-
                    reference listing.

Legal entries for arguments:

<cross-ref>	Explicit file specification Default filename extension: .CRF

<cref-listing>	Explicit file specification
	    Default filename extension: .REF
	Blank indicates that the output
	    <cref-listing> file is to be placed
	    on the diskette in the default
	    drive using the <cross-ref> file-
	    name with the filename extension
	    replaced by the suffix .REF.
	Disk drive identifier indicates that
	    the output <cref-listing> file is
	    to be placed on the diskette in
	    the specified drive using the
	    <cross-ref> filename with the file-
	    name extension replaced by the
	    suffix .REF.
	CON indicates that the output listing
	    file is to be displayed on the
	    video screen.

INDEX

A

Absolute value macro, 231
Abundant number, 186
Accumulator, 4, 39
Activation record, 420
Active display page, 550
Addition
    BCD, 451, 468, 475, 478
    binary, 111, 117
    multiple precision binary,
      275
Address, 5, 33, 60, 75
Address calculations
    segment:offset, 37, 75
    two-dimensional array, 541
Addressing modes, 77, 341
Algorithm
    Ackermann's function, 444
    add and shift method, 310
    BCD multiply, 503
    binomial coefficients, 443
    coin toss simulation, 508,
      526
    Easter Sunday, 222
    Euclid's GCD, 193, 244,
      245, 446
    Fahrenheit-to-centigrade,
      130
    insipid integers, 193, 245
    large integer, 362, 372,
      373
    least common multiple
      (LCM), 444

    palindrome detection, 198,
      372
    Pascal's triangle, 443
    perfect, abundant,
      deficient number, 186
    Pythagorean triples, 244,
      245
    random number
      generator, 215, 243, 508
    recursive Fibonacci, 418,
      424
    recursive $2**n$, 417
    restoring method, 311
    Russian Peasant's Method,
      286, 306, 444
    secret message translation,
      350, 537
    shift and add method, 306
    sieve of Eratosthenes, 356,
      521
    step function, 166
    sum of cubes, 134, 163
    sum of first n odd positive
      integers, 177
    Towers of Hanoi, 444
    Ulam's conjecture, 192,
      243, 305
Align type, 506
ALU, 4
Argument list, 220
Arithmetic shift operation,
    248, 282
Array descriptor, 545
Array elements, 313, 540

Arrays
    one-dimensional, 313, 534
    two-dimensional, 540
      ASCII, 68, 549, A-83
ASCII-to-BCD conversion,
    456
Assembler, 2, 53
Assembler-generated listing,
    137
Assembly language, 2, 18
Assembly module, 42, 46,
    196
Attribute decoder, 549

B

Backup file, A-99
Base address, 313, 315
Base addressing, 345
Base-indexed addressing, 347
Base pointer register (BP), 40
Base register, 39
BCD arithmetic, 451, 468
BCD conversions, 460
BCD input/output, 486
BCD number system, 337,
    447, 449
    overflow in, 478
BCD representations, 456
    packed sign-magnitude,
      457
    packed ten's complement,
      458

unpacked sign-magnitude, 456
BCD-to-ASCII conversion, 337, 348, 463
Binary codes, 448
Binary number system, 21, 60
Binary-to-decimal conversion, 22
Binary-to-graycode conversion, 272
Binary-to-hexadecimal conversion, 31
Binary-to-octal conversion, 28
BIOS, 374, 377, 554
Bit, 22, 60
Blink attribute bit, 551, 553
Breakpoint, 380
Bus, 3
Bus interface unit (BIU), 34, 36
Byte, 33, 60

C

Call-by-location, 201
Call-by-value, 201
Caller, 196
Calling a subprocedure, 200
Carry, 42, 113, 275
Ceiling function, 448
Character generator, 549
Character string, 113
Class name, 507
Code segment, 38, 44
Color
   background, 551
   foreground, 551
   monitor, 548
Column major order, 541
Comment, 44, 45
Common data, 507, 518
Complement
   one's, 62, 66

two's, 65
ten's, 450
Computer architecture, 3, 33
Computer
   hypothetical, 7
Conditional assembly, 233
Constant
   BCD, 460
   binary, 69, 70
   character, 69
   decimal, 69, 71
   definition of, 73, 459, 460
   hexadecimal, 69, 71
   octal, 69, 71
Control flags, 41
Control key, 400
Control structure, 149, A-72
Control unit, 4
CPU, 3, 4, 34
CREF, A-115
Cursor, 393, 394

D

Data segment, 38, 44
Data transfer instructions, 78
DEBUG, 56, 95, 137, A-105
DEBUG commands
   Assemble, A-106
   Dump, A-107
   Enter, A-108
   Go, A-108
   Hex Arithmetic, A-109
   Quit, A-110
   Register, A-110
   Trace, A-111
   Unassemble, A-112
Decimal number system, 20
Decimal-to-binary conversion, 24
Decimal-to-hexadecimal conversion, 30
Decimal-to-octal conversion, 27
Decision structures, 156, A-74

Deficient number, 186
Destination operand, 341
Direct addressing, 77, 341, 343
Direct input/output, 408
Direct reference, 421
Directly recursive, 421
Disk drive identifier, 53, A-88
Display (video) adapter, 548
Division
   BCD, 474
   binary, 126
   by power of two, 249, 251, 281
   multiple precision binary,

DOS, 51, A-88
DOS commands
   CHKDSK, A-89
   CLS, A-89
   COMP, A-89
   COPY, A-90
   DATE, A-90
   DEL, A-91
   DIR, A-91
   DISKCOMP, A-92
   DISKCOPY, A-93
   ERASE, A-93
   FORMAT, A-94
   MODE, A-95
   RENAME, A-95
   TIME, A-96
   TYPE, A-96
   VERIFY, A-96
Double alternative decision, 159, A-74
Double word, A-59
Dummy argument, 220
Dummy label, 232
Duplicate clause, 72

E

EDLIN, 52, A-97
EDLIN commands

Copy, A-98
Delete, A-98
Edit line, A-99
End edit, A-99
Insert, A-100
List, A-100
Move, A-101
Page, A-101
Quit, A-101
Replace, A-102
Search, A-103
Transfer, A-104
Effective address
    computation, 37, 75, 342
Encoding, 448
Equipment check interrupt,
    398, 555
Excess 2^{N-1} number system,
    67
Executable code file
    (executable module), 55
Executable program, 55, 195
Execution unit (EU), 34, 35
Explicit file specification, 53,
    A-88
Exponentiation, 243, 305
Extra segment, 39

F

Factorial function, 311, 443
FAR procedure, 50, 208
Fibonacci sequence, 311,
    418, 424
Filename, 53, A-88
Filename extension, 53, A-88
Flag bit operations, 268
Flags register, 40
    auxiliary carry flag (AF),
        42
    carry flag (CF), 42, 248,
        275
    direction flag (DF), 41,
        320
    display of, 98, 272

interrupt flag (IF), 41
overflow flag (OF), 41, 248
parity flag (PF), 42
sign flag (SF), 41
trap flag (TF), 41, 377,
    378, 386
zero flag (ZF), 41
Floor function, 249
Form feed, 406
Function, 198, A-72

G

Graphics, text, 548
Gray code, 272
Gray code-to-binary
    conversion, 272
Greatest common divisor
    (GCD), 193, 244, 245

H

Hexadecimal number system,
    29
Hexadecimal-to-binary
    conversion, 32
Hexadecimal-to-decimal
    conversion, 30

I

IBM PC, 1
IBM PC-AT, 1, 106
IBM PC-XT, 1, 106
Immediate addressing, 77,
    342
Implication operation, 273
Indexed addressing, 345
Indexing, 315
Index register, 4, 40, 316
Indirect reference, 421
Indirectly recursive, 421

Input/output (I/O), 3, 7, 392,
    408, 486
Input/output library, 46, 57,
    116, A-77
Insipid integers, 193, 245
Instruction cycle, 4, 9, 149
Instruction pointer register
    (IP), 39
Instruction register, 4, 8
Instructions
    AAA, 468, A-2
    AAD, 474, A-2
    AAM, 474, A-3
    AAS, 471, A-3
    ADC, 278, A-4
    ADD, 117, A-5
    AND, 259, A-6
    CALL, 200, A-7
    CBW, 129, A-8
    CLC, 268, A-8
    CLD, 268, 320, A-8
    CLI, 268, 376, A-9
    CMC, 268, A-9
    CMP, 160, A-10
    CMPS, 328, A-11
    CMPSB, 325, A-11
    CMPSW, 326, A-11
    CWD, 129, A-12
    DAA, 475, A-12
    DAS, 476, A-13
    DEC, 120, A-13
    DIV, 126, A-14
    HLT, 410, A-14
    IDIV, 127, A-15
    IMUL, 124, A-15
    IN, 409, A-16
    INC, 120, A-16
    INS, 412, A-17
    INSB, 412, A-17
    INSW, 412, A-17
    INT, 377, A-18
    INTO, 380, A-18
    IRET, 376, A-19
    JA/JNBE, 151, A-19
    JAE/JNB, 151, A-19
    JB/JNAE, 151, A-19

JBE/JNA, 151, A-19
JC, 152, A-21
JCXZ, 182, A-22
JE, 151, 152, A-19, A-20
JG/JNLE, 152, A-20
JGE/JNL, 152, A-20
JL/JNGE, 152, A-20
JLE/JNG, 152, A-20
JMP, 154, A-23
JNC, 152, A-21
JNE, 151, 152, A-19, A-20
JNO, 152, A-21
JNP/JPO, 152, A-21
JNS, 152, A-21
JNZ, 151, 152, A-19, A-20, A-21
JO, 152, A-21
JP/JPE, 152, A-21
JS, 152, A-21
JZ, 151, 152, A-19, A-20, A-21
LAHF, 269, A-24
LDS, A-24
LEA, 87, A-25
LES, A-25
LODS, 328, A-26
LODSB, 322, A-26
LODSW, 323, A-26
LOOP, 175, A-27
LOOPE/LOOPZ, 176, A-27
LOOPNE/LOOPNZ, 176, A-28
MOV, 78, A-29
MOVS, 328, A-30
MOVSB, 320, A-30
MOVSW, 320, A-30
MUL, 122, A-31
NEG, 121, A-31
NOP, 93, 102, A-32
NOT, 263, A-32
OR, 260, A-33
OUT, 409, 568, A-33
OUTS, 413, A-34
OUTSB, 412, A-34

OUTSW, 413, A-34
POP, 81, 107, A-35
POPA, 106, 219, A-35
POPF, 82, A-36
PUSH, 81, 106, A-36
PUSHA, 106, 219, A-37
PUSHF, 82, A-37
RCL, 253, A-38
RCR, 253, A-39
REP, 330, A-40
REPE/REPZ, 332, A-40
REPNE/REPNZ, 334, A-41
RET, 95, 106, 200, A-42
ROL, 252, A-43
ROR, 252, A-44
SAHF, 269, A-44
SAL, 249, A-45
SAR, 248, A-46
SBB, 278, A-47
SCAS, 328, A-48
SCASB, 326, A-48
SCASW, 326, A-48
SHL, 251, A-49
SHR, 250, A-50
STC, 268, A-50
STD, 268, 320, A-51
STI, 268, 376, A-51
STOS, 328, A-51, A-52
STOSB, 323, A-51
STOSW, 323, A-52
SUB, 117, A-52
TEST, 264, A-53
XCHG, 80, A-54
XLAT, A-54
XOR, 260, A-55
Integer arithmetic instructions, 115
Intel
80286, 1, 106
8086, 1
8087 numeric coprocessor, 458, 460
8088, 1, 34, 106
8253 Programmable timer, 381

8259 interrupt controller, 376, 381, 410
Interrupt, 374
BIOS, 392
breakpoint, 380
divide overflow, 377, 378, 382
external, 376, 410
internal, 377
keyboard, 376, 381, 398, 410
maskable, 375
nonmaskable, 375, 376, 377, 380
overflow, 380
predefined, 378
single-step, 377, 378, 387
system-defined, 381
time-of-day, 406
timer, 381, 408, 410
type, 375
user-defined, 378, 382
vector, 375, 382, 386
Interrupt request line (INTR), 376

J

JUMP instructions, 149
conditional, 151
unconditional, 151, 154

K

K, 33
Keyboard, 376, 381, 398, 410

L

Label, 171
dummy, 232
macro, 231

Least significant bit (LSB), 247
Line feed, 406
Linear congruential method, 215
Library, 55
LIFO, 43, 206
LINK, 43, 54, 209, 505, A-114
Load map, 55, 508, 511, 514, 529
Local data segment, 214
Logical expression, 156
Logical operations, 258
Logical shift operation, 250, 285
Loop body, 172, 318, A-75
Loop instructions, 175
Loop structures, 172, 318, A-75
Loop test, 172, A-75

M

Machine language, 2, 9
Macro
  definition, 220
  expansion, 220
Macros
  absolute value, 231
  clear flag bit, 274
  greatest common
    divisor (GCD), 245
  mod function, 225
  multiply immediate, 221, 246
  push all and pop all, 230, 246
  set flag bit, 274
  32-bit left rotate, 312
  32-bit right rotate, 312
  32-bit right shift, 312
Main procedure, 195
MASM, 53, A-113
Megabyte, 75
Memory, 3, 5, 33, 60

Memory addressing, 77, 342
Memory address register, 9
Memory data register, 9
Memory size interrupt, 398
Microcomputer, 3
Microprocessor, 2, 34
Mnemonic, 44
Mod function macro, 225
Mod 16 counter, 262
Mode command, 138
Modularity, 197
Modulo 2^N number system, 61
Monochrome display, 548
Most significant bit (MSB), 247
Multiple precision
  arithmetic, 275
Multiple register shift, 281
Multiplication
  BCD, 474
  binary, 122
  by power of two, 249, 251, 281
  multiple precision binary, 294, 306, 310

N

NEAR procedure, 50, 203
Negation
  BCD, 450, 483
  binary, 62, 63, 66, 67
  multiple precision binary, 299
Nested control structures, 185, A-75
Nibble, 338
Nibble array, 338
Nonmaskable interrupt line (NMI), 376
Nonreusable subprocedure, 419

Number systems
  BCD, 337, 447, 449
  binary, 21
  conversions between, 22, 24, 27, 28
  decimal, 20
  excess 2^{N-1}, 67
  hexadecimal, 29
  modulo 2^N, 61
  octal, 26
  one's complement, 62
  positional, 20
  sign-magnitude, 62
  ten's complement, 450
  two's complement, 65

O

Object code file (object module), 43, 53
Octal number system, 26
Octal-to-binary conversion, 28
Octal-to-decimal conversion, 27
Offset, 87
One's complement number system, 62
Operand, 45
Operation code, 9, 45
Operators
  OFFSET, 87
  SEG, 86
Overflow, 115, 164
  detection, 143, 284, 285, 478
  divide, 126, 127
  flag, 41
  interrupt on, 380
Overhead, 242

P

Packed array, 338

Page
  color monitor, 393, 397, 553-557
  printer, 406
Palindrome, 198
Paragraph boundary, 37, 48
Parameter passing, 200, 201, 345, 423
Parity, 42, 272
Perfect number, 186
Pipeline architecture, 37
POPA macro, 230
Pop operation, 43, 81
Ports, 7, 408, 410, 568
Positional number system, 20
Predefined interrupts, 378
Preorder traversal, 440
Printer, 381, 404
Print screen, 381
Procedure, 196, A-72
  FAR, 50, 208
  NEAR, 50, 203
Processor status word, 4
Program counter, 4, 8, 39
Program segment prefix (PSP), 92
Pseudocode, A-72
Pseudo-operations, 20, 43, 45
  ASSUME, 49, 78, A-57
  COMMENT, A-57
  DB, 69, 314, A-58
  DD, A-59
  DQ, A-60
  DT, 460, A-61
  DW, 70, 314, A-62
  END, 50, A-62
  ENDM, 220, A-63
  ENDP, 50, A-63
  ENDS, 49, A-63
  EQU, 74, 91, A-63
  EQUAL (=), A-64
  EVEN, A-64
  EXITM, A-64
  EXTRN, 48, 210, A-64
  IFxxxx, 233, A-65
  INCLUDE, 230, A-66
  LABEL, A-66
  LOCAL, 232, A-67
  MACRO, 220, A-67
  PAGE, 137, A-67
  PROC, 50, 203, A-68
  PUBLIC, 210, A-68
  PURGE, A-69
  .RADIX, A-69
  SEGMENT, 48, 505, A-70
  TITLE, 138, A-71
PUSHA macro, 230
Push operation, 43, 81
Public names, 210, A-68
Pythagorean triples, 194, 244, 245

R

Radix, 20
Radix point, 20
Random access memory (RAM), 33
Random number generator, 215, 243, 508
Read only memory (ROM), 33
Recursion, 416
  depth of, 422, 440
  termination of, 418
Recursive algorithms, 417
Recursive definition, 416
Recursive subprocedure, 421
Reentrant subprocedure, 420
Registers, 4, 37
Register addressing, 77, 341
Register indirect addressing, 344
Relational expression, 156
Repeat prefixes, 330
REPEAT-UNTIL loop structure, 173, 177, A-75
Returning from a subprocedure, 200
Rotate operations, 252
  rotate through carry, 253
straight rotate, 252
Row major order, 541

S

Saving and restoring registers, 201
Scalar, 313, 341
Scan code, 376, 381
Segment
  alignment of, 506
  code, 38
  combining, 506, 507, 526
  common, 507, 518
  data, 38, 214
  definition, 42
  extra, 39
  origin, 37
  overlay, 507, 518
  override prefix, 344, 532
  public, 506
  registers, 37
  stack, 38, 81, 506, 516
Serially reusable subprocedure, 419
Shift instructions, 248
Shift operations, 247
  multiple register, 281
Short label, 153, 171
Sign bit, 62, 63, 65, 67
Sign extension, 129
Sign-magnitude number system, 62
Signed integers, 65
Simple sequence, A-73
Single alternative decision, 157, A-74
Single-step interrupt, 377, 378
Single-step mode, 41, 102, 378, 386
Source code file (assembly module), 52
Source operand, 341

Stack
    parameter passing via, 345,
      423
Stack pointer register (SP),
    40, 81
Stack segment, 38, 43, 81,
    506, 516
State variable, 420
Status flags, 41
Storage cell, 5, 33
String instructions, 319
    generic forms, 328
Subprocedure, 195
    active instance of, 422
    FAR, 208
    interface, 199
    NEAR, 203
    nonreusable, 419
    recursive, 421
    reentrant, 420
    serially reusable, 419
    types of, 198
    uses of, 196
Subroutine, 199
Subscripting, 315
Subtraction
    BCD, 453, 471, 476
    binary, 114, 117
    multiple precision binary,
      277

Support software, 51, A-88
Symbolic names, 45
System-defined interrupts,
    381
    hardware, 381
    software, 381

T

Text graphics, 548
Time-of-day, 406
Timer, 408
Top-of-stack, 43, 81
Transfer of control, 149
Truth table, 259, 260, 261,
    263
Ten's complement number
    system, 450
Two's complement number
    system, 65
Two-dimensional array, 540

U

Ulam's conjecture, 192, 243,
    305

Unsigned integer, 61
    user-defined interrupts,
      378, 382

V

Video adapter, 548
Video buffer, 549, 568
    color/graphics, 550
    monochrome, 550
Video controller, 549
Video monitor
    color/graphics, 548
    input/output with, 393
    monochrome, 548

W

WHILE loop structure, 172,
    182, A-75
Word, 33, 60